The Mind Matters

Consciousness and Choice
in a Quantum World

DAVID HODGSON

CLARENDON PRESS · OXFORD

Oxford University Press, Walton Street, Oxford OX2 6DP
Oxford New York Toronto
Delhi Bombay Calcutta Madras Karachi
Kuala Lumpur Singapore Hong Kong Tokyo
Nairobi Dar es Salaam Cape Town
Melbourne Auckland Madrid
and associated companies in
Berlin Ibadan

Oxford is a trade mark of Oxford University Press

Published in the United States by
Oxford University Press Inc., New York

First published 1991
First issued in paperback 1993

British Library Cataloguing in Publication Data
Data available

Library of Congress Cataloging in Publication Data
Hodgson, David (David H.)
The mind matters: consciousness and choice in a quantum world/David Hodgson.
Includes bibliographical references and indexes.
1. Mind-brain identity theory—Controversial literature.
2. Consciousness. 3. Choice. 4. Quantum theory. 5. Philosophy of mind. I. Title.
B105.M55H63 1991 128'.2—dc20 90-47824
ISBN 0-19-824292-1
ISBN 0-19-824068-6 (pbk.)

3 5 7 9 10 8 6 4 2

Printed in Great Britain
on acid-free paper by
Biddles Ltd, Guildford and King's Lynn

PREFACE

As a child, I was told that our eyes are like cameras, and I wondered how the 'pictures' which these camera-eyes made inside our heads were themselves 'seen': was there another camera in the brain to take pictures of the pictures, and if so, what then? Later, I was troubled by the conflict between the feeling of freedom to choose and act, and the apparent universality of physical causation. Later again, it struck me that much reasoning, including legal reasoning, was of its nature inconclusive; in particular where opposing considerations were not commensurable, and could be resolved only by some poorly defined 'weighing' or 'judgment'.

Over the years, I continued to be intrigued by these questions, although the idea of writing a book about them did not begin to form until about twelve years ago. I read Hofstadter's *Gödel, Escher, Bach*, and was impressed; but I felt it was fundamentally incorrect, and I wanted to pursue the matter. I went to books in its bibliography, and on to other books about the mind, computers, quantum physics, and so on. I accumulated a mound of notes on these books, my reactions to them, and my developing ideas. Eventually, I began to get these into some order, at first for my own satisfaction, and ultimately in the belief that I had something worthwhile to say to others.

Until the last couple of years, this was a solitary endeavour, much of it done on twice-daily forty-minute train journeys to and from my chambers in the city of Sydney. At this stage, my main intellectual debts were to such people as Hofstadter, Dennett, Boden, Putnam, Popper, Nozick, Nagel, Swinburne, Parfit, d'Espagnat, and Davies, through their writings. Also the work and example of Sir John Eccles, promoting the cause of dualism in hostile times, emboldened me in my thinking; although my conclusions turned out to be rather different from his.

Subsequently, I received more direct assistance. Draft chapters for Parts I and II were read by Professor Jonathan Stone, physiologist and commentator on artificial intelligence; for Part III by Professor Don Melrose, theoretical physicist; and for Parts I, II, and IV by Professor John Finnis, philosopher of law and much else. All made penetrating comments and useful suggestions. I also received helpful comments from Philip Hodgson, Sue Hodgson, Paul Crowe, Marcus Young, and advisers and editors at Oxford University Press.

Any errors and infelicities which remain are all my own work.

My greatest debt is to my wife Raewyn: for the major task of entering my handwritten drafts into the word processor; for her understanding of my periods of preoccupation and detachment from family activities; for valuable discussions on many aspects of the project; and for her encouragement and her companionable participation with me in its ups and downs (doubling the joys and halving the disappointments). This book is dedicated to her.

D.H.

CONTENTS

LIST OF FIGURES

INTRODUCTION

SCIENCE has provided insights into many great questions about the natural world: the origins and present constituents of the universe, the structure of space and time, the nature and behaviour of fundamental particles, the forces of nature, the origins and evolution of life, the genetic code and the functioning of living things, and so on. This book is about another great question about the natural world, into which science has provided important and accessible insights: 'the mind–matter question' (sometimes called 'the brain–mind question'), concerning the relationship between mind (or consciousness), on the one hand, and matter (specifically, the brain), on the other. This question can be shortly stated as follows:

> How are *conscious mental events* (such as my hearing a sound or feeling a stab of pain) related to the *physical events* associated with them (presumably involving the firing of many neurons in my brain)?

This is a question which concerns matters central to the life of every human being. I find it particularly intriguing on at least three counts. First, although some claim otherwise, it is an unsolved mystery. Nothing like a satisfactory answer has been given. A solution is not (yet?) within the reach of science, and the question is still a legitimate topic for speculation by philosophers, indeed by anyone so inclined. Secondly, it is a mystery which may be amenable to solution. Much light has been shed on it by various branches of science, and the speculative steps necessary to arrive at an answer may not be large. Thirdly, if a satisfactory answer can be found and justified, it could in turn provide substantial insights into really intractable questions concerning the human condition which are well beyond the scope of science, such as: the freedom of the will; the nature of the human self; the status of morality; the soul; the existence of God; the purpose of life. Thus, I see the mind–matter question not merely as being important in itself, but also as providing a promising line of approach to the great mysteries of human existence.

To expand a little on the two sides of the relationship in question:

1. Light reflected from the surface of my red pen is focused by the lenses of my eyes on to the retinas; and this results in electrical–chemical signals going to my brain, and then in further electrical–chemical processes within my brain: and *I see the red pen*, I am aware of its shape, its colour, its position and orientation in space. How is my subjective conscious experience in

seeing the pen related to the physical events, the objective physical processes, which go on in my brain?

2. I shut my eyes and write these words. My hand performs certain operations, which (I believe) are caused by signals from my brain. These are in turn caused by processes within my brain. I know what it is I am writing (somewhat untidily), but not because I observe it: there is sensory input from my arm and hand—Sherrington called it proprioception (see Sherrington 1951, ch. 11; Sacks 1986, ch. 3)—but my knowledge is not derived from passive observation via this input. I know what I am writing because *I am consciously doing it*. How is this subjective aspect of my action in writing the words (sometimes called 'volition') related to the objective processes in my brain and the signals to and operations of my hand?

These are just two examples. They are taken from the wide range of conscious mental events, which also include such matters as feeling pain, tasting food, feeling fear or desire or elation, deliberating on a problem, making a decision, and self-consciously reflecting on one's own mental processes.

The great question of the relationship of mind and matter in fact involves a collection of related questions, including the following:

1. What is the general nature of the relationship between mental events (in particular, conscious experiences, conscious thoughts, and the subjective conscious aspect of intentional actions) and physical events (in particular, associated brain processes)?

2. Are such mental events caused by, and do they in turn cause, physical events? If so, how?

3. Can all physical events (including those involved in human behaviour) be fully accounted for in terms of physical events and the laws of physics, without any reference to mental events? Or do mental events make some difference to what happens which cannot be explained in terms of physical laws acting upon physical events? If so, what difference, and how do mental events make such a difference?

4. Could a computer in principle perform all the objective functions of the human brain–mind? Could it do so without being conscious? Could it be conscious?

5. By virtue of what properties of the brain, and of certain physical events in the brain, does it come about that such physical events are associated with conscious mental events?

A further example may illustrate some of these questions. I am sitting at my desk. I hear voices, apparently in the next room. After short deliberation, I decide to see what is going on. I get up and move towards the door.

This brief scenario can be considered as a sequence of objective physical events. Sound-waves reach my ears. Events within my ears cause signals to go to my brain. There is neuron activity within my brain associated with my hearing and interpreting the sounds; and with the process of deciding to investigate; and with the initiating of the actions. There are signals from my brain to the appropriate muscles. And there are movements of the appropriate muscles, so that I get up and walk.

However, there appear also to be subjective mental events associated with at least some of those physical events. I *hear* the sounds as voices in the next room. I *deliberate* and *decide* to see what is going on. I *do* (subjectively) the actions of getting up and walking.

In relation to questions (1) and (2) above, it could be suggested that my hearing voices is *caused* by certain neuron activity in my brain, which in turn is caused by signals coming from my ears. Alternatively, it could be suggested that my hearing voices, on the one hand, and the associated neuron activity in my brain, on the other, are *identical*, perhaps being different aspects or manifestations of the same events; somewhat as, for example, the heat of a substance and the random motion of its molecules are identical, being different aspects or manifestations of the same events.

In relation to question (3), one view could be that my deliberation, and decision to go and see what is going on, are associated with a complex series of physical events in my brain, which proceed according to ordinary physical laws: the course of such events, and thus my decision, must be as determined by such laws. Another view could be that my decision is not wholly determined by the physical events and ordinary physical laws; that my deliberation and decision may somehow override or deflect them, or else select between alternatives themselves left open by them.

The former view is compatible with the idea, concerning question (4), that the human brain is merely a complex machine, somewhat like a computer. Just as a computer, operating as a machine and following ordinary physical laws, can receive information, process it, and respond appropriately, so it is with the human brain. According to this theory, there is no reason in principle why all operations of a human brain could not be simulated by a computer; and indeed why computers could not be conscious agents, not significantly different from human agents. This is the mechanistic view of the brain–mind.

I have said that the mind–matter question remains a topic of philosophy. It might be thought that it is accordingly of specialist academic concern only, and is not amenable to any resolution but only to interminable inconclusive argument. However, the five questions which I have posed are, I think, factual questions concerning the natural world, which are to a considerable extent subject to scientific investigation and perhaps (ultimately) resolution. In recent times, various branches of science have made great advances in areas which bear on these questions:

1. psychology: concerning the operation of human perception, feeling, thinking, and behaviour;
2. neurophysiology: concerning the pattern, connections, structure, and functioning of the neurons of the brain, and the relationship of this to various aspects of sensation, perception, emotion, thinking, and action;

3. microbiology: concerning the details of transmission of signals within the brain; and also concerning the genetic code, and its contribution to the development and functioning of human beings;
4. computer science: concerning computer modelling of various aspects of brain function (including perception and the processing of information), and the creation of artificial intelligence; and
5. quantum physics: concerning the nature of matter, the indeterminacy of certain physical events and states, and (possibly) the role of consciousness in the occurrence of physical events.

Nevertheless, there remain areas which bear on these five questions, but which are primarily in the domain of philosophy: for example, the relationship between language and reality; the use of language in dealing with particularly slippery and elusive concepts; and the nature and effect of formal and informal reasoning. The last area, and in particular informal 'plausible' reasoning (and I use the word 'plausible' in this book without any derogatory suggestion), is, I think, of central significance to the mind–matter question, although it does not generally seem to have been regarded as such; and it plays an important part in the arguments of this book. Legal reasoning is one important example of reasoning which is rational and to a considerable extent structured, but in which formal logic plays quite a minor part. Speculation on how legal reasoning could be performed by artificial intelligence was one of the origins of this book.

I am not a scientist or a professional philosopher, although I have had academic training in philosophy and practical experience in informal plausible reasoning, and I have read widely in the other areas. In some ways, my lack of specialist qualifications may be no great disadvantage in relation to the mind–matter question, because the topic requires some appreciation of all relevant areas; and many authors seem to concentrate too much on the insights provided by their own speciality. To my mind, most computer scientists and neurophysiologists pay too little regard to consciousness and subjectivity; and I also believe that few writers outside the field of quantum physics take adequate account of its important and (to me) amazing implications.

I was led to consider quantum physics in some detail by the following considerations. Common-sense reasons (some of which are elaborated in Part II of this book) favour the view that mental events have some impact on what happens, over and above the operation of physical laws upon physical events. On the other hand, it is difficult to see how mental events could override the operation of physical laws upon physical events. The formulation of quantum mechanics in the 1920s, and the discovery that it involved some indeterminacy and some indeterminism, suggested a possible reconciliation of these two approaches: the laws of physics, it seemed, left room for the efficacy of mental events. However, as we shall see in Section 3.4, this view has not found very much support in discussions of the mind–matter question; although the assertions which have been made about this have in general been supported only by rather cursory argument.

I felt that I could not come to any satisfactory conclusion on the mind–matter question without a careful assessment of the relevance to it of quantum mechanics; and that this in turn required some understanding of quantum mechanics itself. This led me to various popular expositions of the subject, including Hoffmann (1963), Zukav (1979), Wolf (1981), Davies (1982*b*), Pagels (1983), Polkinghorne (1984), and Gribbin (1985). Although I found some of these quite informative, I decided that understanding quantum mechanics required some understanding of the actual mathematics involved. So I turned to textbooks: Dirac (1958); Schiff (1968); Merzbacher (1970); Landshoff and Metherell (1979); and Martin (1981). I found them rather heavy going. Ultimately, I believe I reached some understanding of the subject, helped by textbooks containing more explanations: Bohm (1951); Feynman *et al.* (1963); Gillespie (1970; Davies (1984); and Sudbery (1986).

I went also to various books and articles on the interpretation and philosophy of quantum mechanics referred to in the bibliography. These revealed deep disagreements and lively controversy on the interpretation and implications of quantum mechanics, but left me convinced that quantum mechanics was relevant to the mind–matter question; and indeed was relevant not merely in the way which I originally contemplated, but in other ways as well. In particular, quantum mechanics has important implications for the nature of matter, which have to do with what is called the measurement problem of quantum mechanics, and also the non-locality of certain quantum processes; and which need to be taken into account in any consideration of the mind–matter question.

Since there was no generally accepted view of quantum mechanics which I could adopt as my starting-point, I decided to give in this book a substantial account of some of the basic ideas and mathematics involved, and to express my own views on interpretation and implications. The account which I give of the ideas and mathematics is one which I believe I would have found helpful at the outset of my attempt to understand the subject; and it may be that there are people, interested in the mind–matter question, and moderately mathematical but unfamiliar with the mathematics of quantum mechanics, who will find this account helpful. The account also serves as the basis of my discussion of the interpretation and philosophical implications of quantum mechanics.

I suggest answers to the questions (1) to (4) mentioned earlier. I do not suggest they are final resolutions (this is, after all, more a work of philosophy than of science); but I hope that these answers, and my supporting arguments, are a worthwhile contribution towards resolutions which will eventually be achieved by further scientific and philosophical work. My suggested answers can be summarized as follows:

1. Mental events and their associated physical events are different aspects or manifestations of the same (comprehensive) events.

2. Mental events can with some qualifications be considered as causing and being caused by physical events.

3. Mental events do make a difference to what physical events occur, which cannot be fully explained in terms of physical laws acting on physical events: *the mind matters*. In particular, mental events make such a difference by virtue of informal plausible reasoning, which cannot be completely formalized, and which requires consciousness.

4. Accordingly, a computer could perform all the objective functions of a human brain–mind only if it were conscious. And consciousness requires properties beyond those of present-day computers.

I also suggest a tentative answer to question (5), that is, by virtue of what properties of the brain, and of certain physical events in the brain, does it come about that such events are associated with conscious mental events. This answer draws on the discussion of questions (1) to (4), and on considerations suggested by the theory of evolution and the quantum theory.

Answers (3) and (4), in particular, are contrary to what appears to be the current consensus in this area, especially in the various scientific fields, but also to a somewhat lesser extent in philosophy: this consensus would not allow any causative role to mental events, or to consciousness, that could not in principle be fully accounted for in terms of physical events and the laws of physics. This consensus is reflected in a number of important and influential recent books: for example, *Purposive Explanation in Psychology* and *Artificial Intelligence and Natural Man* by psychologist–philosopher Margaret Boden, (1972, 1977), *Brainstorms* by philosopher Daniel Dennett (1978), *Gödel, Escher, Bach* by computer scientist Douglas Hofstadter (1980), and *Neuronal Man* by neurobiologist Jean-Pierre Changeux (1986).

As stated earlier, the mind–matter question bears on other great questions, which are further removed from science, and which may be considered 'merely' philosophical. In my view, this does not make these other questions less worthy of consideration, although it does mean that such consideration is likely to be inconclusive, and that suggested answers must be considered more speculative. These further questions, which I briefly consider in the last part of this book, are the following:

6. Freedom of the will. What could this be? Do we have it? Can an account be given according to which our choices are not predetermined yet not random, without postulating some mysterious faculty which is not brain-dependent?

7. The self. What is this 'I', the apparent 'subject' of mental events, the experience–actor of conscious experiences, thoughts, and actions? What, if anything, constitutes the identity and/or continuity of the human self?

8. The passage of time. Do future events exist (tenselessly) at locations in space-time, so that the passage of time, the phenomenon of 'becoming', is illusory?

9. Morality. What is its status? What, if anything, is its significance in relation to our choices?

10. The soul. Is the self an immortal 'soul', or has it some relation to an immortal soul?

11. God and the purpose of life. How does consideration of the mind–matter problem bear on the questions of the existence and nature of God, and the purpose of life?

The structure of this book is as follows:

Part I is introductory. I summarize some views basic to my general approach. I elaborate on mental events, and the distinctions between them and physical events; and trace possible views on the relationship between the two. And I outline what I see as the current consensus on the question in science and philosophy.

Part II presents my main arguments against the mechanistic view of the brain–mind, which is at the heart of the current consensus.

Part III considers quantum physics, its basic mathematics, its interpretation, and some of its implications for the mind–matter question.

Part IV gives my suggestions for the resolution of the mind–matter question; and, in the light of those suggestions, outlines possible answers to the questions I have identified as (6) to (11) above.

I have long been struck by what appears to be a pervasive climate of opinion in Western (or at least English-speaking) society that science dictates a view of the world as essentially material, mechanistic, and value-free. In saying this, I do not overlook the rise of 'new-age philosophy', many manifestations of which seem eccentric, or worse, but which I take also to include the stimulating ideas found in such books as Pirsig (1974), Bohm (1980), Capra (1983), Sheldrake (1983), Wilber (1983), Weber (1986), Peat (1987), and Bohm and Peat (1989). Such work has made little impression on general public perceptions, and perhaps even less on 'mainstream' science and philosophy: it is considered over-speculative, and its treatment of consciousness does not fully come to grips with the hard scientific and philosophical questions concerning the brain–mind. However, I believe (and in this respect I agree with some new-age thinkers) that the science of this century, properly understood, is consistent with, indeed supports, the view that reality is not essentially material, that consciousness is important and causally relevant, and that values are not merely subjective or illusory. In this book I try to make good this view, in an accessible way, taking account of relevant hard questions, and raising some hard questions of my own concerning such mainstream topics as computers, causation, reasoning, and evolution.

Postscript

The draft of this book was submitted for publication in June 1989. In October 1989, mathematical physicist Roger Penrose published *The Emperor's New Mind* (Penrose 1989), which adopts an approach broadly similar to that of my book, and covers many of the same topics. However, he deals in greater detail with mathematical matters, and particularly with the relationship between mathematics and computation; while our respective accounts of quantum physics are very different. On the other hand, I deal more with traditional philosophical approaches and problems, advance more non-mathematical arguments, and perhaps suggest a more complete account of mind. There are areas where I disagree with Penrose, and I will advert to some of these. In general, I would like to think that the two books are complementary contributions to the non-mechanistic view of the world.

In about January 1990, I became aware of another book published in 1989 linking quantum mechanics and mind: Michael Lockwood's *Mind, Brain and the Quantum*. In the case of this book, however, while I agree of course with the association of mind and quantum mechanics, and agree also with Lockwood's general approach to philosophy and science, and with some of his arguments against some consensus views, I most strongly disagree with his main conclusions. These involve asserting that the universe is deterministic, that time does not pass, and that the relative state (or many worlds) interpretation of quantum mechanics is the preferable one. This last assertion is central to Lockwood's position: I believe that it is demonstrably implausible, and I try to show this in Section 14.6. More generally, my treatment throughout this book of mechanism, and of choice, challenges all three of these assertions.

More recently, yet another book associating quantum mechanics and mind has appeared, also originating in Oxford: Danah Zohar's *The Quantum Self* (1990). This book does not advance detailed arguments against mechanism or give a detailed exposition of quantum mechanics and its interpretation; and sometimes it perhaps subordinates rigour of exposition to communication (for example, as the author herself notes, in its description of Wheeler's delayed choice version of the two-slit experiment). However, apart from the adoption of a kind of panpsychism, the account given of mind and its place in the world is quite compatible with my own; and for me her book is a worthwhile elaboration of the kind of approach which I advocate in this book.

May 1990

I

Preliminaries

IN this part, I undertake three tasks.

First, in Chapter 1, I outline my general approach to the topic of the book, and some assumptions implicit in that approach. Broadly I see science and philosophy not as entirely separate and mutually exclusive pursuits, but rather as overlapping areas on a continuum of human effort towards knowledge and understanding of reality. Since this view appears opposed in various respects to views of some prominent thinkers, it requires some exposition. So the chapter contains comments on the objectives of and relationship between science and philosophy; and on reality and truth. I also briefly consider some aspects of the doctrine of mechanism, and relate it to associated ideas of determinism and reductionism.

Next, in Chapter 2, I embark on the main topic of this book, by considering mental events. I try to make clear what I take mental events, and consciousness, to be; and how I see mental events as differing from physical events. I then briefly outline some of the views which have been advanced on that relationship.

Finally, in Chapter 3, I look in a little more detail at current views on the relationship, particularly at what I see as the broad consensus which exists in science and (to a lesser degree) philosophy. I conclude the chapter by looking briefly at quantum physics, and its impact (or lack of impact) to date on the consensus.

1

General Approach and Assumptions

I APPROACH the subject matter of this book as a person trying to understand the reality of the relationships between physical events and mental events. I believe that these events and these relationships *are* a matter of reality—that they are aspects or parts of the real world—and that what would make assertions concerning them true, or approximately true, is some sort of correspondence between the assertions and reality. I see it as a task of philosophy, as well as of science, to contribute to knowledge and understanding of these aspects of reality. This rules out a sharp division between the roles of philosophy and science in this area; and an understanding of philosophy as concerned only with words and concepts, as distinct from the real world.

This approach is not in accordance with some influential views on reality, truth, science, and philosophy. For example, Medawar (1986) contends for a clear demarcation between philosophy and science, apparently with only the latter giving any sound basis for knowledge of the real world. Even as regards science itself, Kuhn (1970) seems to suggest that there are only rival theories, none of which can be considered true, or approximately true, or even closer to being true than other theories; while Popper (1959) asserts that, whilst scientific theories can be falsified, they can never be established even to be probably true or approximately true. And according to philosophers such as Putnam (1981), truth is no more than justifiable assertability, and is not an absolute matter involving some sort of correspondence to reality.

These are huge topics, and I will not discuss them in depth. However, a brief exposition of my views is appropriate: this will both bring to light some fundamental assumptions underlying my approach in this book, and also introduce matters relevant to some of the arguments.

1.1. Philosophy and Science

This book is written in the belief that an important (perhaps the most important) objective of science and philosophy is to extend our knowledge and understanding of reality, including the universe, this planet, living things, and humanity and its activities. A number of points arise from this:

1.1.1. *Realism*

In Davies and Brown (1986: 124), physicist and author Paul Davies puts forward a view about reality and science which now has considerable support:

> my position . . . is that physics concerns making models, that we make models of the world about us, to help us to relate one type of observation to another. And we either have good models or less good models. And that there is no such thing as a 'real world' in the sense of something which exists 'out there' to which our models are mere approximations.

The 'models' mentioned here are not miniature replicas but, rather, theoretical representations constructed from mathematical and/or natural language. Theoretical physicist and cosmologist Stephen Hawking (1988: 9, 139) expresses a similar view; and a 'models' approach is also developed at some length by philosopher Nancy Cartwright (1983). (I look at her position in Section 1.2.) On the other hand, in Davies and Brown (1986: 50), in response to another expression of Davies's position, theoretical quantum physicist J. S. Bell asserts that he does 'find it helpful, the idea that there is a real world there', which scientists try to 'account for' with their models.

I do accept, as suggested by d'Espagnat (1989: 27–8), that a 'models' or 'instrumentalist' approach is an appropriate methodology for the actual practice of physics, as it avoids talking about things which cannot be tested; but Davies and Hawking appear to go further, and to assert that scientific theories cannot be considered as expressing truths about an external reality. On questions of reality and truth as such, I am firmly on the side of J. S. Bell. I am, explicitly, a realist: which is to say that there must be a reality, which is *at least in part* independent of our experiences of it and our assertions (including our theories and 'models') about it; and that (leaving aside any problems about the *meaning* of our assertions) it is reality and its properties which determine whether our assertions are true or not. I say 'at least in part', because I believe that our experiences and our assertions are themselves part of reality, and influence other parts. I say 'explicitly', because I believe that all writers on science and philosophy are in some sense realists, at least implicitly, even if they deny it: they assert views (as being true) and seek to refute other views (as being false); and if that truth or falsity is not put forward as something depending on reality, then their enterprise seems pointless.

Returning to Davies, one may ask what is the 'world' of which he says 'models' are made, if not the real world; does he consider his own assertion to be true; and, if so, in what does that truth consist, and why does he attribute truth to this assertion, and not to well-supported scientific theories?

I will be expanding later on what I mean by truth: broadly speaking, I accept a 'correspondence' theory of truth, so that an assertion is true if it corresponds (in a way which I will elaborate) with reality. In identifying an objective of extending knowledge and understanding of reality, rather than of discovery of truth, I have two main considerations in mind. First, knowledge involves not merely truth (that is, true belief), but also some appropriate justification of the belief; and certainly the relevant objective of science and philosophy is not merely to discover, or to make, assertions which are true or approximately true, but also to justify them. And secondly, I extend the objective to understanding, which seems to be more than knowledge; although I will not attempt here to consider just what more is involved in understanding, and for the most part I need be concerned only with knowledge.

My thinking on realism and truth has been assisted by the writings of the Harvard philosopher Hilary Putnam; although, as will appear, I do not fully agree with the somewhat relativistic approach to truth taken in his more recent work.

Putnam's writings in the 1960s and early 1970s advocated a straightforward realism. In the introduction to Putnam (1979c), he writes:

The statements of science are in my view either true or false . . . and their truth or falsity does not consist in their being highly derived ways of describing regularities in human experience. Reality is not a part of the human mind; rather the human mind is a part—and a small part at that—of reality. (p. vii)

Apart from the quantitative assessment of the human mind—I would rather say that the human mind is an important part of reality—I concur with this.

Later in the book, Putnam notes two categories of arguments for realism with respect to the empirical sciences. First, negative arguments to the effect that 'various attempts to reinterpret scientific statements as highly derived statements about sense-data or measurement operations or whatever are unsuccessful'. Secondly, positive arguments to the effect that realism 'is the only philosophy which doesn't make the success of science a miracle' (Putnam 1979c: 72–3).

I believe that such arguments are compelling; and I suggest also that realism is supported by the argument advanced by Putnam that the relativistic views of Thomas Kuhn and others are self-refuting. If one asserts that there are only rival scientific theories, which cannot be compared and evaluated with respect to each other because they are 'incommensurable', then what is the status of this assertion itself? Why should it have any superior status to that of scientific theories, or of any rival assertion about scientific theories?

In Putnam's more recent writings, another theme becomes important: the rejection of what he calls metaphysical realism, the belief that there is a 'ready-made world', with a structure entirely independent of our descriptions of it, so that it can be described by One True Theory. In his book *Reason, Truth and History* he calls this the 'externalist' perspective, which he expresses as follows:

the world consists of some fixed totality of mind-independent objects. There is exactly one true and complete description of 'the way the world is'. Truth involves some sort of correspondence relation between words or thought-signs and external things and sets of things. (Putnam 1981: 49)

He goes on to argue in favour of an 'internalist' perspective, according to which '*what objects does the world consist of?* is a question that it only makes sense to ask *within* a theory or description'. As he puts it:

'Objects' do not exist independently of conceptual schemes. *We* cut up the world into objects when we introduce one or another scheme of description. Since the objects *and* the signs are alike *internal* to the scheme of description, it is possible to say what matches what. . . . If, as I maintain, 'objects' themselves are as much made as discovered, as much products of our conceptual invention as of the 'objective' factor in experience, . . . then of course objects intrinsically belong under certain labels; because those labels are the tools we used to construct a version of the world with such objects in the first place. (Putnam 1981: 52, 54)

In this approach, Putnam adopts views put forward by philosopher Nelson Goodman, especially in *Ways of Worldmaking* (Goodman 1978), to the effect that reality is conceptualized by humans in various ways, resulting in many 'versions' of the world, none of which can be considered the single absolute true version. In Putnam (1983*b*: 162), he writes:

In his writings, Goodman has consistently reminded us that there is no such thing as *comparing* any version with 'unconceptualized reality'. We do check scientific theories against experiential data; but experiential data, as Goodman points out . . . are themselves doubly the result of construction and interpretation: construction by the brain itself, and construal through the need of the subject to use language and public concepts to report and even grasp what he 'sees'. Comparison of theory with experience is *not* comparison with unconceptualized reality . . . It is comparison of one or another version with the version we take to be 'experience' in the given context.

However, Putnam contends that this does not lead to a subjective view of truth: rather, truth is some sort of idealized rational acceptability, or idealization of justification.

I agree with much of this, and I think that it reveals the element of truth in Paul Davies's position; but I think it goes a little too far towards a relativistic view of truth and reality.

In the first place, it does seem clear that we have no access to unconceptualized reality, against which to check the truth of our assertions; and this for the two reasons asserted by Goodman, which I would express as follows:

1. Our experience is the result of construction by the brain of models (here, in the general sense of representations) of the external world: to put it at its lowest, my perceptual experience in seeing my pen is far more closely associated (causally and temporally) with events in my brain than with events at the surface of the pen itself.

2. These models or representations, and our understanding of them, are based on our conceptual systems and theories as well as on 'raw' sensory

data: I see my pen as a pen because I already have a conceptual scheme in which pens have a place. To paraphrase an argument in Churchland (1984: 79–80): in seeing my pen, I make a perceptual judgement involving the application of the concept 'pen'; this concept is a node in a network of concepts, with its meaning at least influenced by its place in that network; the network of concepts involves a theory, at least of categories into which the world is or can be divided, and the relations holding between those categories; and so seeing my pen presupposes a theory.

The latter point is the one stressed by Putnam: our perception and knowledge of, and so our access to, reality are to a large extent shaped by our concepts and our language. This is particularly so in relation to abstract and social concepts such as 'truth', 'democracy', and 'money'. In relation to these, as pointed out in Taylor (1985: 270–5), our concepts and language are at least partially *constitutive* of the reality in question. Even in relation to ordinary middle-sized objects which are the most familiar constituents of our world, classification in many cases depends at least in part on human intentions and purposes, which are in turn partially constituted by concepts and language. This is the case not only with artefacts, such as those we call 'pens' or 'chairs'; but also with many natural objects, such as those we call 'vegetables' or 'minerals'. In relation to other natural objects, such as those we call 'mountains' (as distinct from 'hills') and 'trees' (as distinct from 'bushes'), the classification and the concepts could have been different, perhaps with equal justification: so we see trees as trees partly because we happen to divide plants into classes in a particular way which includes the concept 'tree'. We tend to believe that our conceptual schemes 'carve Nature at her joints' (to use a phrase from Churchland 1986: 321), but in this we may be deceived: other schemes may be equally, or even more, appropriate.

One may accept that in the natural world there are what may be called natural kinds, objects existing in natural categories, quite independently of the conceptual and linguistic activities of human beings: for example, elements such as hydrogen and gold; modes of their existence, such as solid and liquid; species of living things, such as dogs and human beings. But even in relation to natural kinds there is often some conceptual flexibility, so that different conceptual schemes may be equally appropriate. For example, does one classify isotopes of an element (having varying numbers of neutrons in the nucleus, but generally similar chemical properties) as cases of the element, or not? In any event, natural kinds are only a part of our overall conceptual system, and the way we see and think about (for example) a dog will generally involve our applying concepts which are not (or may not be) natural kinds, such as brown, pet, leg, head, tail, dachshund, and so on.

However, I do not think that these considerations require abandonment of a correspondence theory of truth, or adoption of a relativistic theory of reality and truth. They do mean that, as regards reality 'untainted' by conceptualization, the truth or falsity of an assertion may be considered as dependent both on the relation of that assertion to reality as conceptualized within the language of the assertion, and on the satisfactoriness or otherwise of this conceptualization.

In those cases where the meaning of an assertion is clear, and there is no question about the satisfactoriness of the conceptualization, I do not see why truth is not an absolute matter, involving correspondence with reality as conceptualized.

In those cases where the meaning of an assertion is not clear, and especially where there is a problem with the adequacy of the concepts and the language, then I think the Putnam approach is appropriate, so that truth becomes (at least in part) a matter of rational acceptability or idealized justification. Even in ordinary discourse, where an assertion contains a word whose meaning or application is uncertain, its truth or otherwise is not a simple matter of correspondence or non-correspondence with reality: it also involves resolution of the meaning or application of the problematic word, and that resolution can often be put on no stronger basis than rational acceptability.

More general problems of the satisfactoriness of the language and its concepts rarely arise in ordinary discourse: the conceptualization of the world is for the most part a communal and historical activity, bound up with the development of language, and it is generally not subject to challenge in any particular assertion or group of assertions. However, individuals can tinker round the edges, and scientific advances may demonstrate the inadequacy of existing concepts and bring about changes. When I come to discuss the quantum theory, for example, it will appear that what is called the Copenhagen interpretation of that theory was adopted partly as the result of a perceived powerlessness to escape from existing conceptual schemes, while at the same time the theory was in fact radically changing (in the scientific world at least) concepts such as 'wave' and 'particle'.

It has been said that one of Ludwig Wittgenstein's main contributions to modern thought was his insistence that it is impossible to deal with a reality beyond the bounds of language. I think that such insistence tends to obscure that there is a huge grey area not entirely within such boundaries and not entirely beyond them: in this area one must proceed cautiously, accepting that there are inadequacies in conceptualization; and one may hope that thereby the boundaries of language may ultimately be extended.

Returning to the first of the two points mentioned earlier, the fact that our only experience of external reality is via models or representations constructed by our brains, this similarly does not require one to abandon realism. I will be considering this matter in Sections 2.4 and 8.1, so I will be brief here. We take the world, and the objects in it which we perceive, to have the properties of our (best) perceptual models or representations of them, as present in consciousness and as recollected in memory: shapes, colours, textures, solidity or softness or fluidity, taste, sound, hotness or coldness, etc.

And we have good justification for doing so. These sensible properties may be considered as those of things-for-us, to use Kant's terminology, and not of things-in-themselves; but I do not think this makes them any the less real properties. Other properties we can come to know through inference, notably through the construction and testing of scientific theories.

1.1.2. *Knowledge and Language*

Although human knowledge is to a considerable extent dependent on concepts and language in ways outlined above, it is clear that not all human knowledge is expressed, or even fully expressible, in language. This is so, even if 'language' is taken in a wide sense, as including not merely natural languages using words, but also 'languages' which use symbols (as in mathematics) or pictures (such as plans and diagrams). Many things we know to be true, without ever having (or even being able) to express them in words (or symbols, or pictures): this point is elaborated in Polanyi (1973, ch. 5).

For example, we have and remember visual perceptions which we do not, and often cannot fully, put into words: they can be used to base verbal reports, but usually they are not exhausted by such reports. When I watch a football match, I know that certain events which I see are indeed occurring, even though I do not attempt to put them into words. Many of the events I may remember, still without putting them into words. I may put such an event into words, for example by describing to another person what happened when a try was scored: but I do not need to do this in order for me to know (in substance) what happened when the try was scored. I know this before I describe it to anyone (including myself); and it is unlikely that any description I do give will exhaust my non-verbal knowledge of the event.

In saying this, I am not asserting that such knowledge is not encoded in some 'language of the brain'. It would seem that all knowledge which a person has is somehow encoded in his or her brain, in ways which may or may not have affinities with language; although the relevant code has not yet been 'cracked', and I will be questioning whether the code for certain types of knowledge is as good as the knowledge itself.

Quite apart from this qualification, while human knowledge is not limited to or fully encapsulated in language, knowledge is most usefully organized, preserved, expressed, and communicated by language. Furthermore, science and most Western philosophy (at least) are directed towards knowledge which is expressed explicitly and directly in language. From the standpoint of science and Western philosophy, knowledge which is not so expressed is of limited use.

Such a standpoint is not, however, common to all disciplines and approaches. For example:

1. Mysticism. As I understand it, the knowledge which is sought and perhaps achieved through mystic philosophies and religions is not fully or directly expressible in language.

2. Artistic endeavour. Knowledge of the world, and of humanity in particular, may be sought, gained, and expressed through artistic endeavour, perhaps especially through literature. Such knowledge, however, will often be expressed obliquely rather than explicitly and directly.

3. Knowing how. Knowledge may also be indicated by the ability to act effectively and successfully in such matters as personal relationships, business affairs, and politics. Indeed, even scientific knowledge may be indicated by the ability to experiment successfully, and otherwise to achieve desired results in practice. Such 'knowing how' (as opposed to 'knowing that') depends considerably on aspects of human ability which are very important, but, like such things as artistic or musical ability, they are not central to the knowledge sought by science and philosophy.

1.1.3. *The Role of Philosophy*

I have said that science and most Western philosophy are both directed towards the extension of knowledge of reality expressed directly in language. This is none the less true of science because science may also be directed towards manipulation of the world as well as knowledge of it. The great distinction between science and philosophy is the experimental character of the former: the assertions of science are characteristically testable. Expressions of this distinction are often coupled with unfavourable comments about philosophy, to the effect that if an assertion is not testable it is virtually meaningless.

For example, the distinguished immunologist and science essayist Sir Peter Medawar contended that questions about the origin, destiny, and purpose of man are unanswerable, or at least that there is no point in asking whether proposed answers are true or not, 'at all events if we use truth in the conventional sense of correspondence with reality, because we have already agreed that answers of that kind will not do' (Medawar 1986: 92). I disagree with that approach, on two counts:

1. It overlooks that scientific theories are generalizations depending upon informal plausible reasoning of the same type as is used (and evaluated) in philosophy, as well as upon experiment. Medawar himself notes that 'No inductive generalization can contain more information than the sum of its known instances', and concludes that 'An inductive law is a hypothesis that has no claim whatsoever to certainty' (1986: 80). Popper (1959) goes further, and asserts that induction and similar procedures cannot establish even probable, approximate, truth. Along with most scientists and philosophers of science, I disagree with this view of Popper's; but his arguments can be

avoided only by accepting that informal plausible reasoning (of the type available to philosophers) can show a probability of approximate truth. (This argument can be taken further, by pointing to the dependence even of experimental data on perception, and therefore on interpretation and theory, but this is unnecessary here.)

2. The approach is self-refuting, in the same way as a related approach, logical positivism. Logical positivism asserted: 'A statement must be analytic, empirically testable, or nonsense.' Well, *that* statement is certainly neither analytic nor empirically testable, so presumably it is nonsense (see Putnam 1983*b*: 184). There are many aspects of reality, perhaps the most important aspects, in which we are interested but which are not (or are not yet) amenable to experiment, including some of the central topics of this book. Even though areas amenable to experiment are continually expanding, there will always be questions asked which science cannot answer. To suggest that such questions are meaningless or unanswerable is to make a philosophical assertion which must either be purely dogmatic or itself be supported by the very type of philosophical reasoning which it denigrates.

My contention is that just as science depends ultimately on plausible human reasoning as well as experiment, so plausible human reasoning can be applied to philosophical questions to decide whether or not they are meaningless or unanswerable, and (if not) to suggest and justify answers.

1.2. Truth and Language

I need to say a little more about truth as correspondence with reality, in order both to complete the discussion of the previous section, and to prepare for some of the arguments of Part II.

1.2.1. *The Meaning of Truth*

'Truth' is, I take it, simply 'the quality of being true'. 'True' is sometimes said to mean 'corresponding to fact or reality' or 'in accordance with fact or reality'; and in general terms I accept this.

One important application of the concept 'true' is to statements or assertions, and in relation to this application I take the correspondence in question to be one of assertion and meaning. That is, in relation to statements I take 'corresponding to fact or reality' as meaning substantially the same as 'asserting actual event(s) and/or state(s) of affairs'. (This is, I think, rather like Tarski's 'disquotation' theory of truth, according to which 'ravens are black' is true if and only if ravens are black.) In this sense, the concept can be applied to those sentences of natural languages which are assertions; and also to assertions made otherwise than by a sentence in a natural language, for example to assertions made wholly or in part by signs, diagrams, or conduct.

The concept 'true' is also applied to beliefs; and where a belief can be taken to be in substance an assertion (in that the belief can be expressed in words as an assertion), one can adopt the same analysis of truth as correspondence to reality, with the correspondence being one of assertion or meaning.

However, as contended in the previous section, it is not necessary that a belief be expressed, or even expressible, in words, in order that it can be said to be true: we can know that events which we observe are occurring, without our putting them into words; and we can later know that they occurred, without our putting our memories of them into words. Such knowledge, like any knowledge, surely involves true beliefs; so an account of truth should apply to beliefs of this kind, even though they are not put into words.

Similarly, the concept 'true' can be applied to perceptions, at least in so far as perceptions comprise beliefs. It is difficult, perhaps impossible, to distinguish (for example) my perception of the events of a football match I am watching from my associated belief that the events which I perceive are in fact occurring. I see a try being scored, and I believe (without putting this into words) that this event which I see is occurring: the content of the belief and the content of the perception seem to be essentially the same.

In relation to beliefs not expressed, or perhaps even expressible, in words, and in relation to perceptions, it may be questioned whether the analysis of truth as correspondence to reality, with the correspondence being one of meaning or assertion, is appropriate. One could say that, even in such cases, an assertion is involved, namely the assertion that the content of the belief or perception accurately represents actual events and/or states of affairs. I think this is correct: a perception involves both a model or representation of events and/or states of affairs and an assertion that this model or representation accurately represents actual events and/or states of affairs. However, to some extent this begs the question: accurate representation involves some kind of correspondence between the content of the belief or perception and the relevant reality; and if this content is not expressed or expressible in words, it would seem that the correspondence cannot be one of assertion or meaning.

My answer is as suggested in outline in the previous section, to be taken up in Sections 2.4 and 8.1, namely: although perceptions involve models or representations of the external world constructed by the brain, the properties of such models or representations are (when the perception is accurate) properties of the real objects, events, and/or states of affairs which are perceived. In the case of present perception, then, the relevant correspondence could be *identity of perceived properties with properties of reality*; while in the case of other non-linguistic beliefs, it could be the identity of recollected properties with properties of reality.

Subject to that qualification, then, I contend that an assertion, such as a statement or an assertion of the content of a belief, is true if it asserts an actual event and/or state of affairs. The required correspondence to fact or reality is assertion of (part of) reality, that is, a correspondence by way of meaning. Now, meaning is itself sometimes defined by reference to truth, or truth-conditions; so that knowing the meaning of a statement is defined as knowing what would be the conditions or circumstances in which the statement could be truthfully asserted. In relation to such definitions of meaning, my approach to truth would involve some circularity.

This does not greatly trouble me. I am not convinced that definitions or explanations of meaning in terms of truth or truth-conditions are entirely satisfactory. For example, as pointed out in Taylor (1985: 274–5), since the object of the truth-conditional approach is to provide understanding of the language in question, a truth-conditional theory of meaning requires understanding of the circumstances in which statements are true (the 'truth-conditions') prior to and independently of understanding that language. However, in the case of many aspects of reality, such as social practices (such as the practice of democracy), the relevant circumstances are partially *constituted* by the language, and so the circumstances cannot be understood unless the language is already understood. I would suggest also, more generally, that, having regard to the conceptualization of reality by language considered in Section 1.1, some understanding of language is often required before truth-conditions can be understood.

1.2.2. *A General Problem*

One general problem of a 'correspondence' theory of truth, perhaps any theory of truth, arises from the interrelationships of language and reality. I have noted that reality as we know it is conceptualized by our language, and also that our language and our concepts are themselves part of reality. In various ways human beings construct systems—scientific theories, mathematical systems, linguistic and conceptual systems—which may model aspects of reality, and at the same time may themselves be aspects of reality. When assertions are made in the language of such systems, it may be unclear whether the assertion is merely within the system (in which case meaning and truth may be irrelevant) or about the system (in which case the relevant reality is the system itself), or about the world outside the system.

The philosopher Sir Karl Popper has distinguished three 'worlds' which make up the reality which we experience:

World 1: the objective world of events and things, considered quite apart from human consciousness.

World 2: the subjective world of human consciousness.

World 3: creations of human consciousness and intellect.

Now these three 'worlds' are not sharply distinct from each other. For example, as Popper recognizes, World 3 objects, such as symphonies and novels, may be embodied in World 1 objects, such as musical scores and books. In addition, there is the more fundamental intrusion of World 3 into

World 1 by reason of the already noted conceptualization of reality (including World 1) which is effected by natural languages (which are part of World 3). Notwithstanding this, I think that the classification is a useful one, and I will from time to time use it in this book.

In the terms of this classification, World 3 includes natural languages, scientific theories, and mathematics: it therefore includes assertions of scientific theories (such as $E = mc^2$) and of mathematics (such as $d(x^2)/dx = 2x$). It may be possible to consider an assertion such as $E = mc^2$ as part of reality (being part of World 3) and also as an assertion about World 1: however, it can make sense in the latter way only if considered in the context of other (World 3) assertions of the scientific theory of which it is part. It may be doubted whether a statement such as $d(x^2)/dx = 2x$ can be considered as a direct assertion about World 1 at all: although many true assertions about World 1 can be made on the basis of the mathematical system of which this statement is part, it may be that the only possible reality or state of affairs asserted by the statement itself is a World 3 reality, part of which is the statement. Thus in both cases problems arise for a correspondence theory of truth.

In relation to scientific theories, this sort of problem is illustrated in the work of philosopher Nancy Cartwright, who asserts that fundamental equations of physics 'do not govern objects in reality; they govern only objects in models' (Cartwright 1983: 129). She regards a model constructed by a scientific theory as 'a work of fiction' (p. 153), which is realistic to the extent that 'it presents an accurate picture of the situation modelled: it describes the real constituents of the system—the substances and fields that make it up—and ascribes to them characteristics and relations that actually obtain' (p. 149). Consistently with this, she argues that general laws of physics do not state facts. For example, Newton's law of gravitation does not do so, because it deals with a force said to be due to gravity alone; whereas in fact there is no such force: 'In interaction a single force occurs—the force we call the "resultant"—and this force is neither the force due to gravity nor the electric force' (p. 60). Rather, she says, it is the force represented in scientific models by the vector sum of *all* operating forces.

Now, in many situations, scientists do construct 'models' which are representations of aspects of reality which are simplified either deliberately or as a matter of necessity; and Cartwright's remarks (at pp. 149–53) are appropriate for such models. However, many scientific theories do not purport to be simplified models of aspects of reality: rather, they shade into (and sometimes modify) the conceptualization of reality which, as we have seen, is involved in all natural language. If Cartwright's approach is applied to those scientific theories which are *not* simplified models, then her approach seems self-refuting in the way previously outlined: how can her assertions have a better claim to truth than the assertions of such scientific theories, which contain some of our best-supported assertions about reality?

In relation to scientific theories in this category, I contend that questions of truth and falsity can be approached in the same way as in the case of assertions in ordinary language; so that these questions depend both on the adequacy of the conceptualization of reality proposed by the theory (and the language in which it is expressed), and on the correspondence of assertions with reality as so conceptualized. The former aspect is in substance a matter of rational acceptability; and only when the former aspect is unproblematic does truth become an absolute matter of correspondence with reality.

On this approach, to return to Cartwright's example of Newton's law of gravity, I see no reason why a gravitational force, being a component of or contribution to a resultant force, cannot be regarded as something that really exists, being carved out of reality by the conceptual system presupposed in Newton's law; in the same way as pens and legs and mountains are carved out of reality by the conceptual systems of ordinary language. If that is correct, then I see no reason why one cannot regard fundamental equations of physics as making assertions about World 1 reality *as conceptualized*, as well as being parts of systems or models which are part of World 3; and therefore as being true or approximately true.

This approach incidentally suggests an area of operation for Kuhn's views to the effect that different scientific theories cannot be compared because they are incommensurable. In so far as scientific theories conceptualize the world, their truth or otherwise is a matter of rational acceptability; and in so far as different theories conceptualize the world in different ways, there may indeed be no 'common scale' on which their relative merits can be assessed. I would, however, suggest that there can still be comparative assessment of the rational acceptability of the different theories; but this comparison will itself be in terms only of rational acceptability, rather than any straightforward correspondence with reality.

Finally, to return to the case of mathematics: although I have doubted that a statement such as $d(x^2)/dx = 2x$ is a direct assertion about World 1, I do consider that *some* mathematical statements can be regarded as such assertions. For example, numbers are properties of groups of objects occurring in World 1, and the results in World 1 of arranging such groups in various ways to make other groups (which similarly have numbers as properties) accords with the results of mathematical operations with the relevant numbers. Thus, if you have one group of three apples and another of two apples, and combine them, you start with two groups respectively having the property three (or 'threeness') and two (or 'twoness'), and end up with one group having the property five (or 'fiveness'): in that way, $3 + 2 = 5$ may be considered to be about World 1. Similar remarks can be made about quantities, geometrical shapes, etc. However, in more complicated mathematics there is an element of invention, which can lead to the connections with World 1 becoming more indirect and perhaps tenuous. It can accordingly become difficult to ascertain if a mathematical assertion is about World 1, or World 3, or both.

1.3. Truth and Necessity

My views on reality, truth, and language lead me to be somewhat sceptical about so-called necessary truths. I suspect that at least some of such truths would on full examination turn out to be no more than axioms or rules of inference of formal systems (especially of logic and mathematics) which we use (and cannot help using) to reason about the world.

As we will see when I consider formal systems, the elements of such systems (such as well-formed sentences, axioms, rules of inference, and theorems) do not as such have meaning, or application to the world outside the system; but if the axioms and theorems of a particular system can be considered as assertions having meaning and application, then (it is said) the system may encapsulate many truths about the world. However, it seems to me that when one does consider the elements of a formal system as having meaning and application in this way, then the 'necessity' of the truth of at least some axioms and rules of inference becomes suspect; so that even some laws of logic are not necessarily true when applied to statements considered as having meaning, as making assertions about the world. This view is akin to the view that pure mathematics deals in analytic necessary truths, while applied mathematics deals in synthetic contingent truths; but I am expressing a more general view, and I do not think that the dichotomy is quite so simple.

I will not attempt a full consideration of these matters, but some discussion is necessary. My scepticism about necessary truths is associated with the importance accorded in this book to informal plausible reasoning; and also with some tolerance towards the existence in scientific and philosophical theories of apparent contradictions, particularly in areas where our conceptualization of reality is inadequate. (I will give as an example of this Bohr's principle of complementarity.) Furthermore, it is helpful to have some knowledge of formal systems in order to consider such things as computing machines and information processing. So I will look briefly in turn at necessary truths and formal systems.

1.3.1. *Necessary Truths*

A distinction has been drawn in philosophy between two classes of true statements, namely statements which are necessarily true, and those which are only contingently true, in the sense that they could have been false. There are associated distinctions between logical truths and empirical truths; and analytic statements and synthetic statements. The former in each case are said to be statements which must be true, and which require no observation or other empirical verification to establish them as true: the latter in each case are statements which can be known to be true only by observation or other empirical means, so that, had the results of observation etc. been different (as they could have been), the statements would not have been true. I do not attach great importance to these distinctions, and am sceptical of claims that anything is a necessary truth and cannot be questioned. I will look at some classes of so-called necessary truths, and explain why I question their necessity.

1. Tautologies. One class of statements said to be necessary truths are tautologies. These may be explicit:

All male persons are male persons.

They may be implicit:

All fathers are male.

However, if one is dealing with sentences considered as having meaning, as asserting something about the world, then even an explicit tautology is necessarily true only if words used as both subject and predicate in the same sentence have exactly the same meaning each time. If there is a question about this, an answer to that question will generally involve (at least) a consideration of meaning based on actual usage and thus be (at best) a contingent empirical truth. And if the subject and predicate do not have exactly the same meaning, then again the apparent explicit tautology is not a necessary truth. For example, consider the statement made by a businessman to excuse some sharp dealing he has engaged in:

Business is business.

One would usually not understand the word 'business' as being used with the same meaning in both places, and one would therefore understand the statement in such a way that it is not necessarily true.

Similarly, an implicit tautology is necessarily true only if a definition comprising or including the predicate can be substituted for the subject without any change of meaning of the statement. For example, consider the proposed definition:

A true statement is one which corresponds to reality.

One would usually not understand this statement in such a way that the subject simply *means* the predicate, so as to make the statement a tautology. Rather, one would take the subject as a word or concept, the meaning of which is not supplied by the word itself as used in the statement, but which, rather, is supplied by the predicate; so that the truth or otherwise of the statement is subject to enquiry, for example by considering how 'true statement' is used in ordinary language.

2. Principles of logic. Another class of necessary truths are the principles of logic, such as:

If all X are Y, and A is X, then A is Y.

Nothing can be both A and not-A.

Everything is either A or not-A.

Closely related to these are the following statements concerning statements (where p and q are any statements):

If p, and p implies q, then q.

Not both p and not-p.

Either p or not-p.

If p and (q_1 or q_2), then (p and q_1) or (p and q_2).

Principles of logic can, I think, be regarded as axioms or rules of inference of a formal system which is (at least roughly) instantiated in aspects of natural languages, and which involves *inter alia* rules for using such 'strings of symbols' as 'if', 'then', 'implies', 'either', 'or', 'not-', 'both', and 'and'. The reason why we regard them as necessarily true seems to be that we cannot help using such a formal system in reasoning about the world; and this in turn probably has something to do with the structure of the world, including our brains–minds.

Nevertheless, I do suggest that some principles of logic are not necessarily true when applied to meaningful words and statements, particularly in cases where there are problems about the conceptualization of reality presupposed by those words and statements. Quantum physics provides a number of examples, as we will see. Thus, prior to about 1900, scientists would confidently have asserted:

All waves are periodic processes extended in space.
No particles are periodic processes extended in space.
Therefore nothing can be both a wave and a particle.

However, by 1930 scientists were confidently asserting that photons and electrons were both waves and particles, and Bohr had devised his principle of complementarity to deal with this seeming contradiction. I will elaborate on this later. Further, if p is the proposition that a certain particle is within a particular range of momenta, and q_1 and q_2 are statements that the same particle is within a particular range of positions (different in each case), then according to quantum mechanics 'p and (q_1 or q_2)' does not imply '(p and q_1) or (p and q_2)'.

3. The liar's paradox. A simple example, unconnected with quantum mechanics, of a principle of logic which is not necessarily true is provided by the statement 'Either p or not-p'. This is shown not to be necessarily true by the 'liar's paradox':

This sentence is not true.

The paradox is this: if the sentence is true, then it is not true; but if the sentence is not true, then it is true. Accordingly, the seemingly necessary truth 'p or not-p' apparently does not hold. It might be said that the problem arises because of self-reference. However, each of the following sentences refers to itself, but can be seen to be unambiguously true:

This sentence is six words long.

This sentence refers to itself.

Further, similar paradoxes can be created without self-reference, for example by the two sentences:

The next sentence is not true.

The previous sentence is true.

Bertrand Russell suggested a solution to the paradox by postulating a distinction between ordinary languages (which are about non-linguistic reality) and what he called metalanguages (which are about other languages); and by suggesting that a distinction should be drawn, in the case of statements involving the liar's paradox, between the function of such statements as part of an ordinary language, and their function as part of a metalanguage. According to Russell, in each of its functions the statement expresses a different proposition; and the paradox arises because of conflation of these two functions. However, consistently with what I have said about the conceptualization of reality by language, and the associated interdependence of Popper's World 1 and World 3, I would contend that no language is about strictly non-linguistic reality, and that the interpenetration of language and reality is too great and too complex for Russell's distinction to be a satisfactory one.

I suggest that there is a simpler solution to the liar's paradox. The reality or state of affairs, in relation to which the truth or otherwise of the statement 'This sentence is not true' is determined, is itself inversely dependent on the truth of the statement: this dependence is such that, if the statement were true, this would mean that the relevant reality was otherwise than as the statement asserted; while, if the statement were not true, the relevant reality would be as asserted by the statement. In either case, there is a contradiction. Thus, because of the particular form of the proposition p, the so-called necessary truth 'p or not-p' does not hold. In the case of 'This sentence is not true', each of p and not-p involves self-contradiction, so that neither can be true.

In my view, this should neither surprise nor trouble us. It arises only because of the content of the particular statement: this content makes the reality, against which its truth must be determined, itself inversely dependent on its truth. The matter would be more significant if the state of affairs or reality against which the truth of the statement must be determined did *not* depend on its truth. This is the importance of Gödel's theorem, which I will consider in Section 5.7. It asserts that, within certain powerful formal systems, a sentence which is similar to the liar's paradox can be expressed as a mathematical statement (that a certain equation does not have a solution); and the state of affairs against which the truth of that mathematical statement is determined is not itself dependent on the truth of that statement.

4. Mathematical statements. The last class of necessary truths which I look at here are mathematical statements, such as:

$$3 + 2 = 5,$$
$$\mathrm{d}(x^2) \,/\, \mathrm{d}x = 2x,$$

and

> The square on the hypotenuse is equal to the sum of the squares on the other two sides.

I have noted the suggestion that, whereas applied mathematics deals in synthetic contingent truths, pure mathematics deals in analytic necessary truths. The truths of pure mathematics may be regarded as axioms, rules of inference, and theorems of formal systems. I deal briefly in the next section with formal systems, and I say there that such a system does not deal directly with truth, but rather with theorems that can be derived from the axioms of the system, using the system's rules of inference. If the axioms are themselves true, and the rules of inference are valid, then the theorems of the system will also be true: however, this is not necessarily the case with formal systems. It is said on the one hand that pure mathematics consists of formal systems which deal only in axioms, rules, and theorems rather than truth; and that truth comes into the picture only when one considers the application of these systems. It is said on the other hand that mathematics reflects order that exists in the world (that is why it is readily applied), so its statements are true. The former view treats pure mathematics as a free creation of the human mind, the latter as something largely discovered, rather than invented, by the human mind.

My view is that there are some aspects of mathematics which are not as such true, and are best regarded as invented formal systems which may or may not turn out to have application: for example, Euclidean geometry, in so far as it includes and depends upon the parallel postulate (to the effect that parallel lines, however far extended, never meet). However, there are other aspects of mathematics which seem not only to be true, but also to be so deeply and closely bound up with the way the world is that they cannot readily be regarded as other than true: for example, if the basic axioms, rules, and theorems concerning natural whole numbers were not true and accepted by us as true, we could not count or deal with numbers at all. However, I am not sure that this makes them necessarily true in the full sense: just as Euclid's parallel postulate came to be questioned, and ultimately rejected as a truth rather than merely an axiom, so might other mathematical truths which we accept today.

1.3.2. *Formal Systems*

The notion of a formal system is important in relation to truth, logic, and mathematics. It will also have some importance in this book, in relation to considering the mind as a machine or mechanism. Formal systems are dealt with in some detail in Hofstadter (1980): I will merely outline their main features.

A formal system comprises the following elements:

1. Symbols. A formal system uses a definite collection of symbols: they may be numbers, and/or letters, and/or any other symbols. Usually, they include a symbol for negation.

2. Syntactical rules. A formal system has rules which determine which groups or strings of symbols count as well-formed sentences for the system. These rules may be likened to rules of spelling and grammar in ordinary languages. Strings which do not comply with these rules may (loosely) be thought of as meaningless: however, the rules are syntactical only, and even well-formed sentences, considered in relation to the formal system, strictly do not have any meaning outside the system.

3. Axioms. A formal system specifies certain well-formed sentences as axioms, the basic well-formed sentences of the system. They may (loosely) be thought of as assumptions, or as the basic true statements of the system: however, since, in relation to the formal system, the axioms have no meaning outside the system, strictly they cannot (on my approach to truth) be true. Axioms are the starting-point for the process of derivation or selection or proof of other well-formed sentences, called theorems, which may, like the axioms, (loosely) be thought of as true statements of the system.

4. Rules of inference. A formal system has rules, which enable the derivation or selection or proof of other well-formed sentences, the theorems, from the axioms, and also from other theorems of the system. These may be rules of logic and/or rules of mathematics, though they need not necessarily be such rules.

5. Theorems. The theorems, or conclusions which can be proved from the axioms by means of the rules of inference, may or may not be considered as part of the formal system itself. The formal systems generally discussed are those which are finitely describable, in the sense that elements (1) to (4) are so describable. However, such finite systems may enable the derivation of infinitely many theorems. Perhaps it is best to regard elements (1) to (4), plus the theorems which at any time have been proved, as making up the formal system; with theorems yet to be proved being considered as being potential elements of the system.

Although well-formed sentences of a formal system, considered in relation to the system, do not have any meaning outside the system, such sentences may also be sentences of some language in which they *do* have meaning. In that event, the formal system may express truths: it may indeed be a convenient means of encapsulating in a compact way a considerable body of truths. If the axioms of the system, considered as sentences of a language, are true, and if the rules of inference of the system are valid rules of inference for that language, then (at least if there are no problems about meaning and/or conceptualization) the theorems of the system will also be true: a finite system may then summarize an infinity of truths. I will not here consider what is required for the rules of inference to be valid: however, one important requirement is that they must be such that they cannot give rise to inconsistency, that is, cannot show that both a sentence and its negation are theorems.

Geometry and arithmetic, as taught in schools, have similarities to formal systems. Euclidean geometry in particular has a small number of axioms and rules of inference, from which can be derived an infinity of theorems. However, as taught in schools, the axioms and rules are to a large extent expressed in ordinary language, and are understood as having meanings in that language; and proofs of theorems generally involve using those meanings, in ways that allow the proofs to be more briefly stated than strict proofs within a strict formal system could be. Arithmetic, as taught in schools, is perhaps less like a formal system, since it is generally not presented in terms of axioms, rules of inference, and theorems. However, it can be presented as a formal system; and it has in fact been formalized in various ways, initially by Giuseppe Peano in the late nineteenth century.

Truth can be related to formal systems in two ways, which can be illustrated in relation to Euclidean geometry (although, as I have said, this is not a formal system in the full sense, by reason of its partial dependence on the meanings of the words used in its axioms, rules of inference, and theorems). First, Euclidean geometry is itself part of World 3, and true statements can be made about it as part of World 3; and secondly, the axioms of the system (apart from the parallel postulate) may be considered to be true in relation to aspects of World 1, its rules of inference are valid, and so its theorems (except in so far as they are derived from the parallel postulate) may similarly be considered to be true in relation to aspects of World 1.

It is important to note that for a system to be a formal system, strictly so called, its rules must be precise and unambiguous, so that their application is purely mechanical, and always gives an unambiguous result. In relation to any finite string of symbols, a purely mechanical application of the syntactical rules will, in a number of discrete steps, determine whether that string is a well-formed sentence. In relation to any well-formed sentence, a purely mechanical application of the rules of inference will, in a number of discrete steps, determine whether that sentence can be derived in one step, by the rules of inference, from any one or more of a finite group of other well-formed sentences (which may be axioms and/or theorems of the system).

Accordingly, any finite formal system can be represented by a computing machine. As discussed in Rucker (1984: 173–4), such a machine could be programmed to perform the following operations:

1. Generate a new string of symbols. (It could generate strings in sequence, for example by producing in order all one-symbol strings, then all two-symbol strings, and so on.)

2. Check this string against the syntactical rules to determine if it is a well-formed sentence. If so, add it to a store (called *W*) of such sentences, and proceed to (3). If not, return to (1).

3. Check whether this string is an axiom. If so, add it to a store (called *T*) of axioms and theorems.

4. Check in turn all well-formed sentences stored in *W*, which are not already in *T*, for derivability in one step by the rules of inference from any one or more of the axioms and theorems stored in *T*. Add each sentence for which the answer is yes to *T*, and print it out.

5. Return to (1).

This machine will then progressively print out the theorems of the formal system: the formal system can thus be considered as in a sense equivalent to such a theorem-producing machine.

Rucker contends that the converse is also true: that any machine can be represented by a formal system, even a machine which interacts with its environment (1984: 173–4). He develops this contention by reference to digital computers, and (more generally) machines which pass through successive states in accordance with programmed rules. It seems clear, therefore, that his contention should be considered as limited to what are called digital or discrete-state machines, whose states can be considered as changing by discrete steps; and not as extending to analogue machines, whose states vary continuously.

So considered, and leaving aside any question of interaction of the machine with its environment, Rucker's contention seems correct. The state of the machine at any time can be encoded as an axiom or axioms of a system, and the programmed rules and/or laws of nature which determine each transition into a new state can be encoded in rules of inference of the system. These rules may be such as permit only one transition at each stage (in the case of a deterministic machine) or more than one (in the case of an indeterministic machine, for example one using a Geiger counter to determine which transition to make). In either case, successive states of the machine (including any output of any such state) would be represented by, and encoded in, theorems of the system. For a machine which is finite, one would expect that the axioms and rules of inference would similarly be finite.

However, if the machine interacts with its environment, the transition to be made at each stage will depend on both the state of the machine at that stage and the input from the environment at that stage. If that input can itself be expressed as a theorem of a finite formal system, then the next state to which the machine is transformed could presumably be expressed as a theorem of a system; or, at least, as part of a theorem of a finite system comprising both the machine and its environment. However, if the input cannot be so expressed, because the environment itself cannot be represented by a finite formal system, then I do not see how a finite formal system could represent the machine interacting with its environment.

With those qualifications, Rucker's contention seems sound, so that there is a two-way correspondence between formal systems and digital or discrete-state machines.

1.4. Mechanism

As I have said, a major theme of this book is criticism of mechanism, in particular the mechanistic view of the brain–mind. Before proceeding, I should try to make clear what I understand by mechanism, and how I think it relates to associated ideas, such as determinism and reductionism.

1.4.1. *Laplacean Determinism*

The most thoroughgoing expression of both mechanism and determinism is the view put forward by the eighteenth-century mathematician Pierre Laplace. He supposed that the entire universe (including human brains and their constituents) consists of a few kinds of basic objects moving through space in accordance with Newton's laws of motion. As we will see when I come to discuss classical physics, those laws are such that, if one knows the position and motion of an object at any instant of time (the initial conditions), and knows the magnitude and direction at all times of all the forces acting on it between that time and any earlier or later time, one can calculate its position and motion at that earlier or later time. The position and motion of objects, and the magnitude and direction of forces, can be represented as quantities (numbers of various units of distance, rotation, velocity, mass, acceleration, etc.), to which purely quantitative mathematical laws can be applied to give precise results representing other positions and/or motions of objects. A further law devised by Newton, his law of gravitation, enabled calculation of the forces of gravity operating among any two or more particles, given their mass and position; and Laplace assumed that any *other* forces must similarly be in accordance with some finite number of quantitative physical laws, enabling them to be calculated under any given circumstances.

From all this, Laplace concluded that, given knowledge of the relevant laws, and of the state of the universe at any one time, the state of the universe at any other time could (in principle) be calculated. Such knowledge and such calculations would be beyond any human being, but that did not affect the principle. This view does not deny the possibility of other, perhaps non-quantitative, descriptions of objects and their development over time. However, it asserts that unless these representations or descriptions, and any laws or principles governing their time development, can in principle be systematically reduced to or correlated with the fundamental mechanistic representations and laws, then they will at best be mere approximations, with a degree of accuracy dependent on the degree to which such reduction or correlation is possible.

This view is deterministic: the state of any part of the universe at any time is wholly and unequivocally determined by the state of the universe at some earlier time, plus some finite number of laws of nature. It is also mechanistic: the whole universe is conceived of as a machine, whose great diversity of parts and their operation can (to adopt the words of physicist David Bohm) 'be reduced completely and perfectly to nothing more than consequences of the operation of an absolute and final set of purely quantitative laws determining the behaviour of a few kinds of basic entities or variables' (Bohm 1984: 37).

So far as human brains and human minds are concerned, this view has no place for any non-physical causes. The physical world is closed: what happens is wholly determined by physical forces operating on physical objects in accordance with quantitative physical laws, and the physical forces are in turn wholly determined by quantitative physical laws applying to physical objects. Even today one occasionally finds this sort of view put forward as something obviously true: if something non-physical, like a mind or a mental event, could cause a molecule to swerve in its path, laws of physics (such as laws requiring conservation of energy and also conservation of momentum) would be violated (see Levin 1979: 84–6; Searle 1984: 92).

1.4.2. *Indeterministic Mechanism*

Laplacean determinism, and the apparent exclusion of non-physical causes by conservation laws, have been challenged in two main ways in this century: by quantum mechanics, and by a number of ideas which may now be grouped under the fashionable name 'chaos theory'. However, while both of these, and perhaps especially their combination, severely damage absolute determinism, they do not require rejection of mechanism.

1. Quantum mechanics. As we will see, according to the standard interpretation of quantum mechanics, individual events in the micro world of atoms and their constituents cannot (as a matter of principle) be predicted: all that can be predicted are probabilities for the occurrence of such events, and the statistics for their occurrence in large numbers of cases. Further, this is not a matter of deficiency of knowledge, but is just how the world is. This does not involve general unpredictability on the macro scale of the objects of our everyday experience, because their behaviour depends principally on the statistics of huge numbers of micro events, in relation to which there is practical certainty. However, as we will see, in various ways unpredictability of the outcome of individual micro events can infect the macro world, and so the standard interpretation of quantum mechanics is inconsistent with full Laplacean determinism.

Further, since according to quantum mechanics different outcomes are generally possible at the micro level, and at least sometimes possible at the macro level, the argument against non-physical causes based on conservation principles can be circumvented: if the non-physical causes merely selected between outcomes, all of which are possible according to quantum mechanics, then no physical law would be violated.

However, according to the standard interpretation of quantum mechanics, the possible outcomes occur purely at random within the probability parameters, and nothing other than mechanistic and pure-chance processes are suggested. The development over time of states of affairs involves two processes, one completely deterministic (in accordance with the equation devised by Erwin Schrödinger, which is just as deterministic and mechanistic as Newton's laws of motion), and the other purely random (within the probabilities determined by that equation). The standard interpretation of quantum mechanics can thus be regarded as mechanistic, albeit partially indeterministic. It is consistent with the existence of quantitative physical laws operating at all levels of description, generally unaffected by the element of randomness at the microscopic level: the randomness itself necessitates no departure from mechanism, and (arguably) only a minor departure from Laplacean determinism.

Incidentally, it will be noted that I am using 'determinism' in a sense stronger than 'mechanism', as indicating in effect the Laplacean view. However, sometimes 'determinism' is used in what may be a much weaker sense, as involving no more than the ubiquity of causation, the notion that every event is caused by some other events. If causation is here taken to mean causation in strict accordance with unequivocal, purely quantitative laws, like Newton's laws of motion, then this sense of determinism is similar to the one I am using. If, however, causation is taken merely as involving tendencies to bring about certain effects, then this sense of determinism is far weaker, and really not very controversial: I do not think anyone would be concerned to deny it.

2. Chaos theory. The other area of challenge to Laplacean determinism arose with the realization that infinite knowledge is in principle unobtainable, and that uncertainty to any degree, however small, concerning the position or motion of an object at one time can lead to great uncertainty in the predictions made for another time, even on the basis of deterministic laws. It is said that the difference made at one place and time by a beat of a butterfly wing can cause a cyclone to occur at another place and time. To ascertain the position and motion of an object, measurement is required, and measurement can never be 100 per cent precise: exact or infinite precision is not possible, so one can never precisely know the initial conditions. Therefore, deterministic physical laws governing the motion of objects at best enable predictions of the range over which future outcomes can occur, and probabilities within that range. Classical statistical mechanics dealt with such predictions generally in

relation to stable and/or linear systems, where the range of possible outcomes tends to be quite narrow; whereas the more recent chaos theory does so in relation to unstable and/or non-linear systems, where the range of outcomes may be extensive (see generally Prigogine and Stengers 1984; Davies 1987; Gleick 1988).

The circumstance that we cannot know initial conditions (and thus cannot know outcomes) precisely does not necessarily mean that such conditions and outcomes do not actually have precision; although the instrumentalist methodology may suggest that one should not consider what in fact exists to be more determinate than measurement can show it to be. This point is reinforced by a principle of quantum mechanics which I will discuss later, namely the Heisenberg uncertainty principle, according to which uncertainty concerning position and uncertainty concerning motion cannot *together* be reduced below a certain finite limit. Even uncertainty at this limit can in some situations rapidly produce great uncertainties in the results predicted on the basis of wholly deterministic physical laws. Barrow and Silk give a telling illustration from a favoured arena of classical physics, the billiard table:

Suppose we forget about the effects of air resistance and friction that stop the ball moving on a real table. If we could hit the ball with absolute precision, we could, using Newton's laws of motion, predict the subsequent position and speed of all the balls exactly. . . . Suppose we could know the starting state even as well as quantum theory allows. This would then enable us to reduce our uncertainty about the cue ball's position to an accuracy billions of times smaller than the size of an atomic nucleus. Yet after only about fifteen collisions with other balls, this infinitesimal uncertainty expands to the dimension of the entire table. (Barrow and Silk 1984: 184)

This second area of challenge is somewhat damaging to determinism, although by itself it does not suggest that the physical world is not closed, or that any development over time is otherwise than mechanistic; and even in combination with quantum mechanics it does not exclude indeterministic mechanism.

We will see that the current consensus on the mind–matter question favours mechanism, *inter alia* on the ground that this gives the best explanation of the operation of the mind. Certainly, quantum mechanics and chaos theory do not require its rejection. Rather, they make possible a rejection of mechanism, by allowing 'room' for the operation of some causation which is not completely determined by quantitative physical laws—what may be called 'agent causation', a term discussed in Flew and Vesey (1987: 9–12). However, this would need to be supported by *other* arguments; and in this book I present other arguments for a rejection of mechanism.

1.4.3. *Reductionism*

The mechanistic view is closely associated with what is called reductionism: in general terms, this is the view that the properties and the operation of any entity are the consequences of, and are fully explicable in terms of, the properties and operation of its component parts. Contrasted with this is what is called holism, the view that wholes may be greater than the sum of their parts, and have properties (sometimes called emergent properties) which are not mere consequences of, and are not explicable in terms of, the properties and operation of their component parts.

The mechanistic view that the operation of the whole universe is explicable in terms of a finite number of quantitative laws applying to, and determining the operation of, a finite number of basic quantitative entities or variables is highly reductionist. Another expression of reductionism is the assertion that all sciences ultimately reduce to physics: sociology is reducible to psychology, psychology to biology, biology to chemistry, and chemistry to physics. In one sense, reductionism does not require complete denial of emergent properties: all that physics can tell us concerns the when, where, and how much of various measurable quantities; and many properties with which we are acquainted are just not measurable (in particular, properties of our subjective experiences). However, according to the reductionist view, such non-measurable properties have no effect on what happens, except in so far as they reduce to or can be correlated with the measurable quantities with which physics is concerned.

Reductionism is to a degree presupposed in much practical scientific work. For example, when an engineer designs a bridge, he or she is not troubled by the circumstance that its overall shape and dimensions are different from those of any previous structure. He or she assumes that the properties and behaviour of the whole structure can be calculated by the use of a limited number of purely quantitative laws, applied to its parts, its component materials, its dimensions, and its constituent geometric shapes. He or she disregards any possibility that some novel feature of its shape or its dimensions would involve some property or behaviour of the whole which could not be so calculated.

Nineteenth and twentieth-century science has had considerable success in reducing biology to chemistry, and in reducing chemistry to physics. Quantum physics has played an important role in both these areas, although, as we will see, there are aspects of quantum physics which are anti-reductionist. The reduction of psychology to biology, however, is far from being achieved, and it is the contention of this book that it cannot be achieved.

1.4.4. *The Bogy of Mechanism*

I will conclude this outline of mechanism by looking briefly at how the problem posed by mechanism for human freedom and responsibility was dispatched by the Oxford philosopher Gilbert Ryle in his influential book *The Concept of Mind*. Ryle suggested that we should not be concerned about what he called 'the bogy of mechanism'. He compared the laws of nature to the rules of the game of chess, and pointed to how scope is left in that game for the exercise of intelligence and choice (Ryle 1949: 77). He went on to suggest that quantum physics had nothing to do with human freedom and responsibility:

The modern interpretation of natural laws as statements not of necessities but of very, very long odds is sometimes acclaimed as providing a desiderated element of non-rigorousness in Nature. Now at last, it is sometimes felt, we can be scientific while reserving just a very few occasions in which appraisal-concepts can be properly applied. This silly view assumes that an action could not merit favourable or unfavourable criticism, unless it were an exception to scientific generalisations. (p. 80)

I think this is misconceived. The rules of chess generally leave open alternatives concerning the piece to be moved and the square to which it is to be moved; and it is precisely this which leaves room for the exercise of intelligence and choice. However, the mechanistic laws of pre-quantum physics leave open no such alternatives: given all relevant initial conditions and the relevant laws, only one result is possible at any particular later time. It is only in quantum physics that quantitative physical laws of nature leave open true alternatives, given all relevant initial conditions. And it is a real question, considered in this book, whether this leaves room for the operation of some non-mechanistic intelligence and choice, or whether (rather) intelligence and choice is itself entirely mechanistic. In any event the only way in which the bogy of mechanism can be overcome along the lines of Ryle's chess example is by way of something like what he describes as a 'silly view'. This book advocates such a silly view.

2

Mental Events

I HAVE stated the mind–matter question in terms of the relation between mental events and physical events. It is therefore necessary to consider with some care what are mental events and what are physical events. In drawing a distinction between the two categories, I do not assume either that mental events are *not* identical with certain physical events, or that they are identical: I am saying only that the two categories can be described differently, and that these different descriptions may or may not be of entirely distinct events.

I start with what I take to be the central case of mental events, namely the fully conscious experiences, thoughts, and actions of normal human beings (considered subjectively). Then I proceed to deal with other cases, to consider the related concepts of 'consciousness' and 'mind', and to make some more detailed comments on one class of mental events, namely perception, and its relation to the world. Next I set out some important distinctions between mental events and physical events. And finally I outline some possible accounts of the general nature of the relationship between physical events and mental events.

2.1. The Central Case

So, I take the central case of mental events to be the subjective aspect of fully conscious experiences, and fully conscious thoughts and actions, of normal human beings; that is, to be such experiences, thoughts, and actions as they appear to, or are felt by, or are known to the person having the experiences, thinking the thoughts, or doing the actions.

2.1.1. *Actions*

It may seem paradoxical to cite actions as examples of mental events, although the idea that there is a mental element to intentional actions is very familiar. For example, in Anglo-American criminal law, generally a person cannot be found guilty of a criminal offence unless he did the prohibited act with *mens rea*, a guilty mind.

An intentional action—say, when one man strikes another—can be regarded as an overall physical–mental process performed by a person, a physical–mental being. However, there appear to be distinguishable aspects to this process: physical events or processes (processes of the physical brain and the body) and mental events or processes (the conscious subjective 'doing' of the action).

The 'physical events' aspect is describable in terms of objective impersonal events, having no reference to any person or conscious subject. Such a description is independent of any particular point of view: if one leaves aside any regard to the subjective aspect of the action, then the physical events (including brain processes) have a broadly similar character for everybody, including the person doing the action. The physical aspect can be given different levels of description—processes of macro objects such as brains and arms (or neurons, nerves, and muscles) or of micro objects such as atoms and molecules—but all of them appear to reduce ultimately to physics: the time development of measurable physical quantities such as position, velocity, mass, electric charge, etc.

The 'mental events' aspect cannot be described without reference to the person doing the action, the conscious subject, and to his point of view. This aspect has a character for the person doing the action which is unique to that person (he sees it 'from the inside', as his doing), and very different from its character for all other persons (who see it only 'from the outside'). In saying this, I do not at this stage make any assumption about the nature of the conscious subject (for example, whether 'it' exists only in a World 2 of mental events, or is just the whole physical–mental being, considered subjectively): I look at this in Chapter 17.

Our ordinary descriptions of intentional actions generally embrace both aspects; and even when we do notionally separate out a mental element, we may not be drawing precisely the distinction I have drawn. Thus the criminal law on *mens rea* is sometimes expressed in terms of an 'act of the will' to do the bodily movement concerned; and this may suggest an act of the will or volition which itself consists both of physical brain processes and of subjective mental processes. A similar approach is implied in Searle (1984), where he discusses carving off each of two components of an action (pp. 63–4). He cites an experiment of the physiologist Wilder Penfield, where electrical stimulation of part of the cortex causes movement of the patient's limbs: the physical component without the mental. And he cites experiments by the nineteenth-century American psychologist William James, in which a patient's arm is anaesthetized and held at his side in a dark room, and he is ordered to raise it; after he complies with the instruction, he is surprised to be told that his arm did not go up: the mental component without the physical.

In so far as the distinction referred to in the previous paragraph appears to include some physical events (brain processes associated with volition) in the mental aspect of intentional action, it seems less fundamental than the one which I have drawn. Further, it tends towards falling foul of an infinite regress discussed in Ryle (1949: 67). If what makes a physical action intentional is some distinct act of will, it seems reasonable to say that this can only be so if the act of will is itself intentional. Then, presumably, to make the act of will intentional, there would need to be a further distinct act of will; and so on *ad infinitum*. This regress is avoided if one says that what makes a physical action intentional is not some distinct act of will, but a particular character of the internal mental aspect of the action; namely that a person or conscious subject is consciously doing the action.

I think that the internal 'mental events' aspect of intentional action is well brought out by the example of writing with one's eyes shut (see Anscombe 1957: 53). One does not passively observe what one is writing, but one does know what one is writing, just because one is doing it. The mental events involved in this doing and knowing can be distinguished from any physical events, including processes of the neurons of the brain as well as of nerves, muscles, and hand.

The subjective conscious aspect of deliberate actions is sometimes called 'volition' or 'willing'. By using the expression 'volition', I do not mean to suggest that conscious actions necessarily involve quick, highly active, mental episodes: I accept, as suggested in Swinburne (1986: 94), that intentional actions often are more a matter of an agent allowing them than actively 'willing' them, and also that they often persist for a long time, so that taking a long walk can be regarded as an intentional action. Swinburne uses the term 'purposing', rather than 'willing' or 'volition', because of what he considers to be misleading implications of the latter terminology: I prefer to use the traditional terminology, while recognizing (and, I hope, avoiding) the possibility of thereby misleading or being misled.

2.1.2. *Other Examples*

Mental events also include the events in the following categories (always, as appearing to, or felt by, or known to the person in question). There is no suggestion that these categories are exhaustive, or that they are mutually exclusive. Clearly, an experience and/or action may fall under two or more of the categories:

1. Pain. One can readily distinguish the actual subjective feeling of pain from the physical processes in the brain which must be associated with that feeling, and from the pain reactions (withdrawal, grimacing, rubbing, crying, etc.) which may accompany feelings of pain and may be observed by others. The distinction between conscious mental events and physical events is probably clearer in the case of pain than most other examples, even perception of colour: this would seem to be the basis of the view (with which I agree) expressed by psychologist Jeffrey Gray that the central problem of consciousness concerns such matters as pain, rather than such matters as intentions (Gray 1987: 465).

I do not suggest that the criteria for using the concept 'pain' are purely internal: there are also outward behavioural criteria for use of this concept, as for the use of other mental concepts; and the internal and external criteria may be considered as 'inextricably bound together in a single public concept' (see Nagel 1986: 22, commenting on the views of philosopher Ludwig Wittgenstein). However, I do say that, at the least, one can distinguish the internal criteria (of subjective feeling), and the outward criteria (of behaviour); and I point to the former as involving subjective conscious mental events. I would also say, although this is not necessary for my arguments, that it is the internal criteria which are the more important, not only in relation to one's own pains, but also in relation to the pains of others: our concern for the suffering of pain by other persons relates essentially to what we believe they are *feeling*, not to their outward bodily movements.

2. Emotions. The point that there are external as well as internal criteria for the application of mental concepts applies also (and perhaps more so) in relation to emotions. Emotions such as fear, desire, anger, and elation are probably best regarded as mental states, which are manifested both in characteristic behaviour and in characteristic subjective mental episodes or events. These characteristic mental events may perhaps be analysed into more basic categories of mental events, such as thoughts, feelings, and/or some kind of 'colouring' of experiences generally. However that may be, we know what it is like (subjectively) to be afraid, to desire something, to be angry, or to be elated. The thoughts, feelings, etc. related to such emotions which each of us subjectively experience are also mental events.

3. Perception. Mental events include also the subjective aspect of various kinds of perception. Perception is generally regarded as involving both sensation (experiences normally brought about by the senses) and cognition (coming to know or believe something). It is not generally possible in perception clearly to separate out 'pure' sensations, that is, sensations uninfluenced by the accompanying process of cognition. However, even though perception is not just sensation, it has a subjective aspect, of which sensation is an important part.

The subjective aspect of perception by taste, smell, and touch involves mental events: the actual tasting (taste-experience, not just discrimination or choice by tasting) of food; the actual smelling (smell-experience, not just detection by smell) of such things as coffee or motor vehicle exhaust fumes; and the actual feel (again, not just detection, but subjective feel) of the surface texture of, and/or heat or coldness of, objects.

Hearing can be considered objectively as the means whereby we detect objects or events by sound, discriminate by sound between different objects or events, and receive information by means of spoken words: but the subjective hearing of the sounds, as experienced by the person doing the hearing, involves mental events. And similar comments can be made about seeing.

4. Thinking. Thinking may be taken to include unconscious or subconscious mental activity. For example, from time to time ideas come unbidden into our conscious thoughts, and this is presumably the result of some brain–mind processes: such processes could be called mental events. However, in my central case I include only fully conscious thinking, which one may engage in, for example, when deliberating with full attention on a problem to be solved.

5. Choosing. In one sense, choosing or deciding is a particular subclass of the previous category: it is part of the process of deliberating on a problem, namely that part by which the solution is arrived at. In another sense, choosing or deciding is involved in performing conscious actions, discussed earlier. Although most conscious actions are not the outcome of a process of conscious deliberation, they do appear to be choices, in the sense of being things we could either do or not do, as we choose. In any event, when I talk of choosing or deciding as a mental event, I mean the subjective choosing or deciding, that is, the choosing or deciding as experienced at the time by the person consciously choosing or deciding.

6. Self-consciousness. When a human being reflects self-consciously on his own mental processes, this is perhaps just a particular case of thinking (category (4) above). However, I mention it separately, for a number of reasons. First, self-consciousness or self-awareness is sometimes considered a peculiarly human capacity, which (it is said) animals do not have. Secondly, some discussions of consciousness and mind have substantially identified consciousness with self-consciousness, and have in effect suggested that this is the distinctive property of minds. I do not take this approach: I do not think it accords with ordinary usage of the word 'consciousness', and I think it obscures the basic question concerning the mind–matter distinction, namely the relationship between conscious mental events (in the wide sense I adopt) and objective physical events. I use 'consciousness' as generally synonymous with 'awareness', so that feeling pain is an example of consciousness; and so that 'self-consciousness' is a subclass of consciousness, itself requiring basic consciousness. Thirdly (and this is related to the second point), it has been suggested by computer scientists that consciousness is a 'system's knowledge of itself'. This seems to be reaching for some idea of self-consciousness *without the consciousness*; and while such an idea may be useful in considering parallels between the human brain–mind and the computer, it directs attention away from the central problems of the mind–matter distinction.

2.1.3. *Experiencing and Doing*

The examples given in the preceding sections illustrate a basic distinction between two broad classes of mental events, or perhaps of aspects of mental events (because events of both classes may be combined in what is best treated as a single mental event). This distinction is between experiencing (or experiences) and doing (or actions), between being a passive spectator (as it were) in a mental event and being an active participant in it.

Perhaps the clearest case of experiencing is that of category (1), feeling pain. In relation to the mental event involved, the person subjectively feeling the pain is substantially a 'spectator': the pain happens to and is experienced by him, and there is little if any element of action by him in this event. He may take action as a result of the pain, and the pain itself may be greater or less by reason of his mental attitude towards it (which could involve some element of action or doing by him), but the actual experience of the pain is substantially passive.

The clearest cases of doing are category (5) and Section 2.1.1, the fully conscious choices and actions of human beings. Such mental events, and the latter in particular, may be monitored by observations made by the person doing the action, and such observations will involve a significant element of relatively passive experiencing; but the subjective conscious aspect of the action itself, the volition, is substantially action or 'doing'.

Categories (4) and (6), concerning thinking and self-consciousness, appear to be cases where the 'doing' aspect often predominates, but perhaps not to the same extent as in the cases of choice and action. We know little of how our subconscious mental processes work but, just as we learn to control our bodily movements, we do learn to a considerable extent to control our thinking; so that when we are deliberating on a problem we have considerable control over how our thinking goes forward. However, we do not have complete control. Thoughts *just occur to us* from time to time. Further, particularly under the influence of our emotions, our thinking can proceed in ways which we do not want and in respect of which we have little control. So to some extent we experience our thinking rather than do it.

Finally, as regards category (3), the various cases of perception through the senses, the experiencing aspect would seem generally to predominate, although the doing aspect may be significant. Sometimes the person concerned is actively looking or listening for something, and his actions and intentions in so doing will not only affect what he sees or hears, but probably be an inseparable part of the mental events involved. Even when a person is not actively looking or listening for something, there may still be some measure of doing in his looking or listening, which coupled with his thoughts at the time (including his beliefs and expectations) will generally affect what he sees or hears; and in these ways also, some element of doing may be involved.

Although the two classes of mental events which I distinguish are often combined in mental events of the types I have considered, the distinction between them is, I contend, an important one of which we are all aware. I do not see how anyone could say that he or she was completely unaware of any difference, in his or her own mental life, between experiencing and doing. The distinction is, I think, fundamental; and it is one which should be accounted for by any satisfactory theory of mind.

2.2. Other Cases

In Section 2.1, I dealt with what I consider to be the central case of mental events, namely the fully conscious experiences, thoughts, and actions of human beings: in the light of the discussion in Section 2.1.3, I will often just refer to experiences and actions, because in my view thoughts can be considered as some combination of experiences and actions, as outlined above.

I turn now to deal with what are, or might be considered to be, other but less central cases of mental events.

2.2.1. *Less than Fully Conscious Human Experiences and Actions*

In addition to fully conscious acts and experiences as discussed above, there are acts and experiences which appear to involve some consciousness, but of a lesser degree. For example:

1. Lack of attention, distraction. When concentrating on some particular aspect of one's environment, perhaps listening to what someone is saying, one may see or hear things and do things without being fully conscious of them. In such a situation, if the occasion arises to recall what one saw, heard, or did while thus distracted, one can sometimes do this. For example, a person walking down a city street engrossed in conversation with another person may see what traffic near him is doing without taking any notice of it; but if an accident occurs so as to attract his full attention, he may then be able to describe the accident, and even to describe what the vehicles involved were doing just prior to the accident. In such a case, in one way we would like to say that he was not conscious of what the vehicles were doing, because he was totally engrossed in the conversation, and but for the accident he would never have remembered it; in another way, we would like to say that he must have been conscious of what the vehicles were doing, albeit at some low level, because he was able to recall and report it.

2. Dreaming. Dreams would seem to be some sort of conscious experiences, but again at some low level of consciousness: they occur generally when the person concerned is asleep, and therefore (in broad terms) unconscious; and they are remembered generally only if the person wakes up during or immediately after the dream.

3. Hypnosis. When a person acts under hypnosis, he would appear to be aware of his surroundings and (subject to the suggestions of the hypnotist) to have some control over his actions. However, he would not seem to be conscious in the full sense, and generally (as I understand it) does not later remember what occurred. I would be inclined to class such cases as involving mental events, and as involving some consciousness.

2.2.2. *Subconscious Human Experiences and Actions*

Psychologist Carl Jung asserts that 'consciousness can . . . be equated with the relation between the ego and the psychic contents'; but that the whole psyche includes not only consciousness, but also 'the illimitable field of unconscious occurrences as well' (Jung 1983: 212–14). And he goes on to suggest that included in such unconscious occurrences are contents which fall below the threshold of consciousness, and disagreeable contents which are repressed. A question arises as to whether these 'contents' involve some kind of consciousness which is not integrated into the consciousness of the 'ego'; or whether they involve no kind of consciousness whatsoever. In any case, they involve events which might be called mental events. The following are some examples:

1. Subconscious thoughts. I have already referred to the example of processes whereby thoughts come unbidden into one's consciousness. In such a case, some subconscious brain or mental processes must be involved; and these processes might be called mental events, even though they are not conscious. More generally, there are vast numbers of brain processes continually occurring of which we are not conscious but which in various ways underlie our conscious mental processes, particularly the preconscious processes which occur in such activities as seeing, hearing, and understanding language. Some at least of these might be called mental events.

2. Blindsight. This is a phenomenon which has been shown to occur in some cases where damage to part of the brain has resulted in a person being unable to see (in the normal sense) events or objects in parts of his visual field. However, when an event occurs or an object is placed in such a part of his visual field, the person is sometimes able quite accurately to report this, but unable to give any account of how he is able to do so: he cannot (he says) see anything there.

3. Split brains. There have been cases where, in order to treat seriously disabling epilepsy, the corpus callosum (the massive bundle of nerve fibres joining the two hemispheres of the brain) has been severed. The patient has then at least superficially been able to live a normal life. However, the dominant hemisphere (generally the left) does not have immediate access to information received by the other hemisphere (in particular, that contained in the left portion of the visual field), and does not fully control the left side of the body. The patient talks normally, using the dominant hemisphere. Controlled tests show that the other hemisphere is receiving and processing information from its side of the visual field, and is directing some actions of its side of the body. The question arises whether this hemisphere is or is not conscious; that is, whether it has some consciousness of its own, distinct from the consciousness of the verbally communicating dominant hemisphere.

I leave open for the moment whether these cases do or do not involve a kind of consciousness which is not integrated into the full consciousness of the person: it does not really matter for most of my discussion. However, my views on animals (discussed next) would make it difficult to deny consciousness (for example) in relation to the right hemisphere of a split brain.

2.2.3. *Animals*

By reason of the similarities of the brains of mammals to those of man, and of the similarities in observed behaviour, I believe that mammals are conscious, and that (adopting the categories of mental events referred to earlier) pain, perception, and conscious action can be attributed to them; similarly, thinking and choosing probably can, at varying levels; though self-consciousness probably cannot. In particular, it is, I think, very difficult to deny that apes on the one hand, and domestic animals such as dogs and cats, on the other, are conscious. See Rollin (1989).

As one moves through the 'tree' of evolution away from *Homo sapiens*, the attribution of consciousness becomes progressively more doubtful, and the similarity of any associated mental events to those of human beings similarly becomes more doubtful. However, I am inclined to believe that there is some sort of consciousness in quite primitive animals: I would think, for example, that the possession of eyes (suggesting an associated elaborate central nervous system) is some evidence of consciousness in a species. On the other hand, I think there is little reason to believe that plants are conscious in any reasonable sense of the word.

To some extent, these must be matters of speculation. However, they link up with what I say later, particularly in Chapter 6, about evolution and consciousness.

2.2.4. *Computers*

For reasons which will become clearer as this book progresses, I do not believe that computers are conscious or that mental events (in the sense discussed above) can be attributed to them. For the moment it suffices to say that everything that computers do can be understood in terms of the operations of electrical circuits, and/or in terms of objective performance in accordance with instructions: there is no need to postulate consciousness to explain any aspect of their performance; and there is no mechanism or function of computers which can be pointed to as causing or explaining consciousness in the computer. Until it can be shown what it is that causes or explains consciousness in humans and animals, and also that this feature occurs in computers, the attribution of consciousness to computers seems to me to be superstition.

2.3. Mind and Consciousness

It will be apparent from my discussion in Sections 2.1 and 2.2 that I closely associate mental events and consciousness: the mental events with which I am mainly concerned are events involving (and indeed constituting) consciousness. There are other events which might be called mental events (see example (1) in Section 2.2.2), but I am less directly concerned with them. When I talk of mental events in this book, I am generally referring to conscious experiences–actions.

It will also be seen that I have discussed mental *events* rather than mental *states*. Sometimes the expression 'mental states' is used in relation to prolonged mental events: for example, a feeling of elation extending over a period of time might be called a mental state rather than a mental event. In this book, I use the expression 'mental event' even for such prolonged experiences: I do not suggest any rules for determining what are the limits (in time or otherwise) of single mental events. I will generally reserve the expression 'mental states' to refer to matters of disposition rather than of experience. The distinction is not always a clear one. To be affected by an emotion such as elation is dispositional, involving tendencies to characteristic behaviour and feelings, and so (in the terminology I use) such an emotion is a mental state; while actual feelings of elation associated with this mental state are mental events.

Mental states generally affect and colour mental events. For example, knowledge (both 'knowledge how' and 'knowledge that') I take to be a mental state. 'Knowledge how' is a necessary precondition for any action, whether physical or mental: that is, for any volition. In order to do it, you have to know how to do it. 'Knowledge that' affects mental events in various ways, for example how we perceive things. Further, items of such knowledge can be summoned into our conscious thoughts (involving an exercise of 'knowledge how' in relation to one's memory), and then used in our conscious deliberations.

Certain mental states may be considered to be basic and irreducible components of mental life: for example, Swinburne identifies five basic components of mental life, two of which (desires and beliefs) are continuing mental states, while the other three (sensations, thoughts, and purposings) are conscious episodes (or mental events) (Swinburne 1986: 18). However, I concentrate more on mental events than on mental states in this book, because I think that the mind–matter distinction is best considered in relation to consciousness. Mental states are relevant to consciousness, but (in general) only by way of being manifested in mental events (such as awareness of, or thoughts about, one's desires and beliefs), or colouring mental events.

What then of 'mind'? The word is relevantly defined in the *Concise Oxford Dictionary* as the 'seat of consciousness, thought, volition, and feeling'. In general terms, I adopt that definition: the word can be considered as an abstract noun referring collectively to each person's mental events, or alternatively as referring to the subject of such mental events, the subjective experiencer–actor who experiences and acts in those mental events. However, although I accept that approach, I recognize that it could be suggested that it reifies what is not a thing, and postulates a mental 'ghost' in the machine of the body: to deflect such a suggestion, I will for the most part discuss mental events rather than mind.

I do say, however, that although it has been confidently said that, just as science has laid all sorts of 'ghosts' in the past, such as gods, witches, the life-force, etc., it will surely lay 'the ghost in the machine', there seems to me to be an important difference: mental events, as I have discussed them, surely occur. I do not see how this could honestly be denied. Even if 'the ghost in the machine' is no more than each person's mental events, considered collectively, it is there to be understood and explained if possible, not to be laid or exorcized.

2.4. Perception

The relationship between mental events and the external world is especially close and complex in the case of human perception, and in particular visual perception or seeing.

2.4.1. *A Description of Seeing*

I see my red pen. How does this happen? As I understand it, something like this.

Light which falls on the pen is partially reflected by the surface of the pen. Some of this reflected light enters my eyes, and is focused on to the retina of each eye. This causes a response of the cells of the retina, which in turn gives rise to a pattern of nerve impulses going to my brain. There results some pattern of activity of some of the estimated 3×10^9 neurons (and perhaps 10^{14} or 10^{15} connections between neurons) which are in my brain (see Changeux 1986: 51–2). And *I see the red pen*.

My seeing the pen (here meaning the subjective mental event, the last aspect of the process I have described, not the whole process) is associated in some close way with the pattern of activity of the neurons and connections (which activity is an objective physical event or pattern of events). The nature of that association is little understood. The objective physical event (the pattern of activity of neurons and connections) may or may not be identical with the subjective mental event (my seeing the pen, considered subjectively); and if the physical event and the mental event are identical, that is, are somehow the same event, then they would seem to be distinguishable aspects of that event.

Some things can be said in general terms about the organization of the neuronal events. I have already said, in Section 1.1, that our experience of reality is via models or representations constructed by our brains, an approach which was proposed by psychologist Kenneth Craik (1943), and which has been developed in relation to visual perception particularly by psychologist David Marr (see Marr 1982; Frisby 1979). This work takes an information-processing approach to perception, seeking to describe it in ways capable of computer simulation: it is thus part of what is called cognitive psychology. According to this approach, the model or representation of part of the world which constitutes a perception is a conjectural construct that accounts for the stimuli our senses actually receive (see Barlow 1985: 17). It is conjectural, because like the generalizations of science it goes beyond the raw data. This construct can be considered as being generated in three stages (see Gregory 1984: 396–8): first, the sense organs act as transducers converting patterns of received energy into signals; secondly, these signals are accepted by the brain as representing variables in the world according to a conventional code used by the brain, which (together with contextual information) enables the signals to be appreciated as data; and thirdly, a perceptual hypothesis is constructed from the data, this being the conjectural model referred to earlier.

The processes which take place in these stages are unconscious or preconscious. One aspect of these processes, noted in Delbrück (1986: 109–113), is that information is abstracted from the sensory input, so that our consciousness has no access to the raw data, but only to a highly processed portion of the sensory input, whereby in the result we perceive objective properties of objects. As examples, Delbrück notes the constancy with which we perceive (1) the colour of objects in a multicoloured scene, regardless of the colour of the light illuminating the scene; (2) the position of objects in a stationary scene while one is voluntarily moving head or eyes; and (3) the size of objects as they approach or recede.

This can be compared with what occurs when we see coins otherwise than with their face perpendicular to the line of vision, and take their oval appearance as a sign that they are round. Generally this also occurs preconsciously, and can be taken as another case of looking *through* data to objective properties of objects (see Putnam 1983: 156).

There has been much progress in psychological and physiological work on seeing, and in computational simulation of preconscious processes of the kind outlined above. But as to how all this produces and/or is associated with conscious visual experiences, there is still mystery. Indeed, as regards the relevant patterns of neural firings in the visual cortex, there is not even any explanation of what it is about these patterns themselves (as distinct from their causal antecedents associated with the eyes) which associates them with visual experiences, whereas very similar patterns in a different part of the cortex are associated with auditory experiences.

It *may* ultimately be possible to observe and describe in minute detail and completeness the patterns of activity of neurons and connections in the human brain, and to understand such patterns and their functions so well that, for example, an observer could say, on the basis solely of his or her observation of such activity in my brain, that I am seeing a red pen. However, in making this observation of the activity in my brain he or she would not observe anything that looks like a red pen, but, rather, a pattern which he or she would recognize as some sort of code for my seeing the pen.

To take an imperfect analogy. There may be some similarity between nerve impulses passing to my brain from the retinas of my eyes, and the signals (say, representing the appearance of a red pen) received by a television set. The nerve impulses are processed in my brain, and the signals are processed by the television receiver. But there is in my brain nothing remotely similar to a television screen on which a picture of the red pen is displayed: if there were, I would presumably need to *see it*, and the whole process would have to begin again.

The processing by my brain of the nerve impulses from the retinas is of quite a different kind from the processing of signals received by a television set. However, both the impulses and the signals can be regarded as involving codes for the appearance of the red pen. When I see the red pen, that can be regarded as being, in a sense, the decoded message. Other persons can see the red pen if they look at it; but if they observe only my brain, they will at most observe events in which my seeing the red pen is encoded. One could conceive of a machine which could observe my brain activity, and decode it, and perhaps display on a screen or as a hologram the red pen which I see; but the presentation of this image would obviously be a different event from my seeing the pen.

2.4.2. *Sensation and Cognition*

There is a distinction drawn, in relation to perception, between sensation and cognition. Sensation is that which is presented in consciousness by the senses, considered (so far as possible) apart from any question of cognition, or acquisition of knowledge or belief, in relation to what is so presented. Most if not all cases of perception involve cognition as well as sensation.

Considering the examples of mental events given earlier, one can most readily think of pure sensation in relation to feeling pain. Even here, however, belief and recognition are generally involved, as one identifies the type of pain concerned, the part of the body affected, etc. These cognitive aspects will to some extent affect the experience, the mental event, generally clarifying what is experienced. In relation to perception in general, and seeing and hearing in particular, belief and recognition play an important role. When a person sees an object, he generally sees it *as* that object, recognizes it, and believes that it is the object. If he does not do so, perhaps because he is not fully conscious or is disorientated, he may just see shapes and colours: something like pure sensation. In such a case, however, the person concerned will generally try to interpret what he sees; and if he is successful, he will then recognize and see the object, in which event more than sensation will be involved.

Even if it were possible to isolate the sensation component of seeing, and to be aware only of what have been called sense-data, this would generally be a difficult exercise, and not something likely to reduce error or uncertainty in one's knowledge or beliefs. Even if one could somehow isolate sense-data which were certain, without cognition one would be unable to understand, assimilate, describe, or use them in any helpful way, so these sense-data could hardly be considered as knowledge. It is by recognition of what one sees that one can arrive at the clearest and fullest knowledge of the content of one's visual experience.

A clear example is the hearing of human voices. When one tries to hear the sounds of voices accurately, one does not concentrate on any sense-data, or on patterns of tones presented to consciousness. Rather, one tries to hear and understand the *words* which are spoken, and if one is successful one seems to have a fuller and clearer knowledge of what is heard than one could otherwise arrive at: to concentrate on the patterns of tones rather than the words would hinder this process. The difference is similar to that between hearing words spoken in one's own language, and hearing words spoken in a language of which one has no understanding: in the latter case, there is merely a jumble of sound which conveys little information.

2.4.3. *Do We See Things or Images?*

Our perception of objects can be looked at in two ways:

1. As a mental event. This is the subjective conscious experience (as of seeing a red pen), which is associated with the pattern of activity in my brain, which in turn is caused by earlier events, some of which occur at the surface of the pen. This event comprises the association of a conscious subject ('me') and the appearance to me of the object, combined with belief or knowledge about the object. This belief or knowledge involves *inter alia* objectifying my experience: I do not consider the experience as my being aware of an appearance or image of the object, but rather as seeing the object itself.

2. As a whole process. Instead of abstracting the subjective mental event, one can look at perception as including the subjective mental event but as also extending to the whole physical–mental process in which the person (a physical being as well as a conscious subject) sees the object itself. I believe that in ordinary language, when we talk of a person seeing something, we are generally referring to this whole physical–mental process rather than to just the subjective mental event.

So, when we talk of a person seeing a pen, we mean that he sees the pen, not an image of it. This ordinary usage is soundly based: the appearance of the pen, as visually presented, is objective in the sense that it will be much the same to anyone with normal eyesight who sees the pen in similar conditions; and the associated cognition involves a well-founded belief that what is seen is the pen itself, not merely an image of it.

However, if one does concentrate on the subjective mental event, it is inescapable that the immediate conscious experience by the conscious subject must be of an image or model of the object. The experience is associated with, and is a decoding of and a construct from, physical processes in the brain; and the experience is far more closely associated with these processes in the brain than with processes in or on the object seen. This is obvious when one considers the causal account of seeing an object, and in particular the associated time lapse: the visual experience is based on events which occurred at the surface of the object, not at the time of the conscious experience, but rather some time earlier, when the relevant light left its surface. Thus, when one sees the sun just setting at the horizon, the sun is in fact already below the horizon: the visually presented orange disc is an image built from light which left the sun about eight minutes earlier. This image is located in space by one's brain–mind at the place from which the light apparently came, and this is not necessarily the place where the object then is.

As suggested earlier, however, one takes the visually presented appearance of an object, and the properties displayed thereby (shapes, colours, textures, etc.) to be properties of the object itself. I do not think that so-called illusions (such as the apparent oval shape of a coin whose face is not perpendicular to the line of sight) count against the view: it is an objective property of a disc that it presents an oval appearance from such an angle, and in any event we generally look through this appearance to perceive the coin's roundness. So, the conjectural construct, which in perception represents what is perceived, has properties of what is perceived, and also involves an assertion or belief that these *are* properties of what is perceived. In saying this, I do not intend to deny that there is any distinction between so-called secondary qualities (properties which things have only in virtue of the way they appear to us, such as colour, taste, and smell) and primary qualities (properties which things seem to have independently of how they appear to us, such as shape, size, location, and mass). One can regard being red as a real property of a real object, while at the same time recognizing that this property may be just that of appearing red to normal human beings in appropriate lighting conditions, and may be explained by more basic properties of the object, which are independent (or at least *more* independent) of how the object appears to us.

Thus it is things, not images, that we see, when that word is used in the ordinary way and when attention is not confined to the subjective 'mental event' aspect of seeing. However, when attention is so confined, it must be that what is visually present in consciousness is an image or model or representation, but (in cases of accurate perception) one which has properties of the thing seen, combined with a well-founded belief that the thing seen has these properties.

2.5. Differences between Mental Events and Physical Events

The distinction between mental events and physical events may be further developed by discussing a number of differences between the two classes of events.

2.5.1. *The Two Elements of Mental Events*

Mental events generally involve an association of two elements, a subject, a subjective experiencer–doer, and the content of consciousness, the experience or volition, with the former being conscious of the latter. I do not think that any notion of 'free-floating' experiences or volitions makes sense: we can conceive of experiences or volitions only in association with a subject, a subjective conscious entity which experiences or acts. As described by philosopher Ted Honderich, what is fundamental to consciousness is '*the interdependent existence of subject and object*' (Honderich 1987: 445). A similar idea is expressed as follows in Barrett (1987):

Wherever there is consciousness, there is a point of view from which things are seen, and hence subjectivity of one kind or another. We cannot imagine a consciousness that is just consciousness but not the consciousness of some being or other, whether bird, bat, fish, or human. Consciousness and subjectivity are thus coextensive. (p. 124)

Thus, as discussed in relation to actions as mental events, mental events are describable only with reference to the point of view of a conscious subject, and they have a character for that subject which is different from their character for all other persons; whereas physical events are describable objectively and have a broadly similar character for everyone.

This idea can also be expressed in terms of the experience being an attribute, property, or activity of the subject, rather than a second 'substance' to which the subject has some relation (see Swinburne 1986: 23; Lycan 1987: 16, 79–88). So, it can be asserted that pain is not an immaterial 'thing' which a person or conscious subject encounters, but rather is an activity, or adverbial qualification of an activity, of the person or subject: he or she does not encounter a thing called a pain, but rather he or she 'pains', or exists painfully. However, this way of thinking seems to bear within it an assumption that the conscious subject is some sort of thing or substance, which is an assumption I do not make. And one can also assert, as Hume in effect did (see Section 17.2 below), that an experience such as a pain is an immaterial thing or substance; and that it is no more than an attribute of such an experience that it is the experience of some subject or other.

Indeed, this illustrates the interdependence of subject and experience, which is part of the peculiar dual nature of mental events. It would seem that the subject can be considered the 'substance' of which the experience is an attribute or activity; and that also, with as much or as little validity, the experience can be considered the 'substance' of which the subject is an attribute: whereas, in the objective world, there is generally little question about what is substance and what is attribute or activity.

I am not at this stage advancing any particular view of the subject, for example that it is some continuing or stable self, or that it has an existence independent of the mental events: all I am saying is that mental events have these two elements. In the case of *my* mental events, these elements appear to be *me* (considered as a subjective conscious entity) and the content of my conscious experiences and volitions. The content of my conscious experiences and volitions only exists or occurs in association with 'me': whether this is always the *same* me, however, is another matter, which will be looked at in Chapter 17. At its lowest, this 'me' can be considered as like a canvas, or succession of canvases, on which experiences (here including volitions) are painted (see Schrödinger 1967: 96). So, I am adopting the Cartesian premiss 'I think', in that my thinking is done by me; but not necessarily Descartes's conclusion 'I am', which can be taken as implying both some permanence or stability in the 'I', and some existence of the 'I' independent of the thinking.

On the other hand, physical events, and in particular the brain processes which I take to be associated with mental events, do not involve a combination of two elements in this way. The mental event involved in my seeing the pen brings together the subjective 'me' and the appearance of the pen, coupled with beliefs about the pen. The corresponding physical events in the brain are caused by the pen, but (except to the extent that they may be associated with the mental event) they do not comprise or otherwise involve either me or the pen's appearance. The physical events can perhaps be regarded as comprising two elements, namely the relevant neurons of my brain and the pattern of their activity: but, so far as we know, the former are not conscious of the latter, except in so far as they involve the mental event of me being conscious of the pen's appearance.

2.5.2. *Privacy of Mental Events*

Closely connected with this association of two elements is the point that mental events are private to the subject involved, whereas physical events are public in that they may in principle be observed by anyone. I do not say that other persons can have no knowledge of the mental events of a subject: just as there must be public criteria for the application of concepts such as 'pain', so also one can know that another person is in pain. However, the subject's knowledge of his own pain is very different from the knowledge which other persons may have of it: he alone *feels* it.

The conceivability (not necessarily possibility) adverted to earlier, of constructing a machine capable of 'decoding' patterns of a person's brain activity so as to display to others something of what the person is seeing or thinking, does not contradict this privacy postulate: the display, not the person's conscious experience, would be a public physical event; and another person's observation of that display would involve a private conscious experience in that other person, albeit one which may be very similar to the original. Even in the unlikely (perhaps impossible) event that such a machine could directly induce in another person an experience identical to the original, still all one would have would be two private conscious experiences, which would be identical, except as regards the subject having each experience.

2.5.3. *Preferred Descriptions of Mental Events*

Physical events may be described with reference to any convenient physical framework and at any convenient level of description: no description has any intrinsic superiority or pre-eminence. However, in the case of mental events, there is generally a preferred or pre-eminent description, namely that which is in accordance with the conscious subject's understanding of the mental event.

For example, when I see my pen, the physical events involved can be described in terms which identify the pen by its molecular configuration, or by its grosser material make-up, or indeed in any convenient way, and in any case giving its position with reference to any points in the room, or house, or universe. However, the mental event can be fairly described only in terms which identify the pen by features which I understand the pen to have. Unless I know and have in mind the pen's molecular configuration, it would be misleading to describe the mental event involved as comprising awareness of an object having such-and-such molecular configuration.

The point is very clear in relation to voluntary actions. When I write these words, a fair description of the mental aspect of my action must be in terms of what I am intending to do, namely write the words. A description in terms of the geometrical motions of my hand may be appropriate for the physical movements involved, but could not be a fair or appropriate description of the mental element of the action, the volition (cf. Searle 1984: 57–9).

This feature is related to the two points previously mentioned. An essential feature of a mental event is what it is *like* for the conscious subject to have the experience and/or do the action in question (see Nagel 1974). Accordingly, to describe a mental event in terms foreign to what it is like for the subject, to the subject's understanding of it, would be inappropriate and misleading.

This point and the previous one are related to another alleged characteristic of mental events, namely that they are *infallibly* known to the subject. I am sceptical about infallibility of any kind. It seems to me that mental events often involve interpretation, understanding, application of language, etc., in relation to which mistakes are possible. It may be that there is infallibility concerning some aspects of some mental events, but if so I do not know how to identify them.

2.5.4. *The Holistic Nature of Mental Events*

I suggested in Section 1.4 that, when an engineer designs a bridge, he or she may be confident that it will not fall down, even though the span, the configuration, and the materials are different from those of any bridge previously built. The behaviour of the whole bridge may be calculated from the behaviour of its constituent parts, which will be well known from theory based on previous experience: it does not matter that the whole bridge is different from anything previously constructed.

This is because of the generally reductionist character of physical events and objects: at least in principle, the workings of an aggregate of such events (or of a composite object) can notionally be reduced to, in the sense that they are explained and determined by, the workings of the component events (or of the parts of the object). This in turn is related to the point that physical events and objects can be expressed in terms of measurable properties developing in accordance with quantitative physical laws. Differences between physical events and objects can be expressed quantitatively, and the effects of such differences calculated; and the components of physical events and objects can be expressed quantitatively, and their contributions to a composite event or object can be calculated. The development of the whole is thus systematically related to the development of component parts.

Mental events, on the other hand, appear to have an holistic character: they cannot be notionally divided into components, the operations of which are systematically related to the operation of the whole. Mental events cannot in general be represented in terms of quantitative properties developing in accordance with quantitative laws, *inter alia* because mental events, as such, just do not have quantitative measurable properties. A person may be asked to rank intensities of pains on a scale of one to ten, and may appear to perform quite consistently in doing so. But this is not precise measurement, it cannot be checked, and interpersonal comparisons are problematic. Further, with more complicated mental events scaling is progressively less feasible; and, even in relation to pain, one cannot devise quantitative laws which determine its effects in particular cases—at best, one can suggest tendencies. Thus when a mental event differs from an earlier mental event, it will generally not be possible to predict precisely what (if any) effect or operation this difference will have, because one cannot quantify the difference, or say what operation various components or aspects of mental events have.

It might be contended that this is only a matter of a present lack of knowledge. Previously, it was not known how a global property of an object, such as solidity, was caused or explained by the properties of the constituent parts of that object, and it might have been argued that such a global property had an holistic character. Just as we now understand how such global properties are caused or explained by properties of constituent parts, we might in the future understand how the properties and operation of mental events are caused or explained by the properties of their constituent parts or components. However, objective global properties are unlike mental events in that they are objective and measurable. Further, it may be questioned whether mental events even have constituent parts or components in the sense in which physical objects or physical events have constituent parts. Into what components can my seeing a red pen be divided, other than the two interdependent elements of 'me' and the content of the experience?

It is conceivable that one could come to know what characteristics of mental events are associated with what physical events; and it could then be suggested that mental events can be analysed into parts by means of analysis of the associated physical events. However, even if this were possible, it does not really contradict the holistic character of the mental events, considered as such. In fact, the possibility of such a procedure is challenged in this book: I argue that mental events are irreducibly holistic, and can have effects not fully explicable by reference to the associated physical events.

2.5.5. *Mental Events not Simply Located in Space*

Physical events are located and extended in both time and space, or a combination of the two ('space-time': see Section 9.2). Mental events seem to be located and extended in time much as are physical events; but do not seem in general to be located or extended in space in the same way as are physical events. One can say that the physical events associated with my deliberating on a problem are located in a particular area of my brain, but one does not readily say that my thoughts themselves are located there: to them, location seems irrelevant.

It is when one considers the location in space of experiences associated with seeing that the point perhaps becomes clearest. I have previously suggested that the representation of a seen object is placed by the brain–mind in space where the light came from: this representation is part of the conscious experience, but so also is the experiencer, the subject, who (or which?) is located (if anywhere) in the brain (perhaps a couple of inches behind the eyes!); and so also are the beliefs associated with the experience. Is it reasonable to consider the total experience as being located in two or more widely separated places? I do not think so. I would suggest rather that location in space is a concept inapplicable to the experience.

On this approach, what I have called the placing of the representation in space does not concern the location of the conscious experience, but, rather, is a property of the representation, which in turn is one basis for our conception of the space in which we consider physical objects and events to be located.

2.5.6. *Intentionality*

It is said to be a characteristic of mental events, and not of physical events, that they have what is called 'intentionality'; which means that they are about something. I am not certain how helpful this is as a general distinction between mental events and physical events. A felt sensation of pain is a mental event, but it is not about something else. On the other hand, a book may be about something; but it is a physical object, and may be considered as a collection and succession of physical events; although it can be contended that a book is about something only because it can be so understood by a person reading it, that is, by means of mental events. I think that the capacity of some mental events to refer to objects and events in the external world is of some significance, and I will consider it further in Chapter 8.

2.6. Possible Relationships between Mental Events and Physical Events

There can be no doubt that mental events have a close association with physical brain events. What is the general nature of this association?

2.6.1. *Terminology*

Many different views have been suggested over the centuries during which this sort of question has been considered; that is, since at least about 500 BC. However, the mind–matter question has not always been approached (as I approach it) in terms of the relationship between mental events and physical events: sometimes it has been in terms of the relationship between mental states and physical states, and sometimes in terms of the relationship between two different kinds of substance, mind and matter. This variety of approach does contribute to some problems of terminology, in particular in relation to words such as 'dualism', 'monism', 'materialism' or 'physicalism', and 'idealism'.

The word 'dualism' was originally used in relation to theories according to which mind and matter were different kinds of substance. Similarly, the word 'monism' was used in relation to theories according to which there was only one kind of substance: such a theory was called 'materialism' or 'physicalism' if the substance in question was said to be material or physical; and 'idealism' if the substance was said to be mental.

Most discussions today are in terms of mental and physical events or processes, rather than in terms of different types of substance. The same terminology is used for the analogous cases, but with some variability.

2.6.2. *Some Alternatives*

What then are the possible relationships between mental events and physical events?

One type of theory has it that mental events and their associated physical events are two different aspects or manifestations of the same events, two sides as it were of the same coin: this is called the dual aspect theory. It is generally regarded as one type of monism or identity theory; but whether it is best regarded as such, or as a type of dualism, depends, I think, on the details of the theory. I believe that the dual aspect theory is the most plausible approach, and I will return to it.

A second possibility is that physical events and mental events are quite separate: theories which assert this are unequivocally dualistic. Three main versions can be distinguished. In two of them, it is held that physical events *cause* mental events: this can then be combined either with the view that the mental events also cause physical events, or with the view that they do not. The former combination is generally called interactive dualism; while the latter is generally called epiphenomenalism, because mental events are treated as 'epiphenomena', mere by-products of physical events. The third dualistic theory is called psychophysical parallelism, and it holds that physical events and mental events proceed in parallel without either having a causal influence on the other.

Some versions of psychophysical parallelism have considerable similarity to the dual aspect theory: although the former theory is dualist and the latter might be considered monist, there seems little difference between (on the one hand) a theory which says that mental events and physical events are associated by non-causal correlations, and (on the other) a theory which says that they are two aspects or manifestations of the same event.

Finally, there are wholly monistic theories which assert that there only *appear* to be two types of events, and that there really is only one type of event. Physicalism or materialism asserts that there are only physical events; idealism asserts that there are only mental events; while neutral monism asserts in effect that the one type of event is neither exactly physical nor exactly mental.

A strict physicalism of events asserts that there are only physical events and states, and there are not any mental events and states at all: if this is taken literally, it is in my view indefensible, as I think nothing is more certain than that mental events occur. However, generally those who profess physicalism are really advocating only a physicalism of substances, with something like a dual aspect view of events, and that clearly is plausible.

Idealism asserts that there are only mental events and states, and that physical events and states are merely constructs from them. This view has a respectable pedigree, and may even be correct. However, it does not solve the problem: even regarding physical events and states as constructs from mental events and states, it is clear that mental events and states are closely associated with particular classes of such constructs, namely neural activity in brains. One can then ask: what is the relationship between mental events and states, and those particular constructs? The problem seems to be much the same as that of the relationship between mental events and states, and physical events and states, with similar possible answers.

Neutral monism may be taken as asserting that there are events which are neutral (neither physical nor mental) and which are manifested by physical events and by mental events, in which case this view seems indistinguishable from the dual aspect theory. If it is taken as asserting merely that there are neutral events, without any reference to manifestation by physical events and mental events, then I find it obscure.

2.6.3. *Examples*

These theories can be illustrated by reference to two types of mental event:

1. Pain. Pain generally occurs when the excitation of one or more appropriate nerves causes certain neuronal activity in the brain, which one feels as pain. According to the dual aspect theory, the sensation of pain and the neuronal activity are two aspects of the same event, rather as heat in an object and the random motion of its molecules are two aspects of one event. Thoroughgoing dualistic theories would assert that the subjective sensation of pain and the neuronal activity are different events or groups of events. Both interactive dualism and epiphenomenalism would assert that the latter is caused by the former; whilst psychophysical parallelism would assert that the two simply happen together.

2. Action. The mental doing of the action, the volition, is associated in some way with neuronal events in the brain, which cause a signal to go to the relevant muscles of the body, so that the muscles contract and the action takes place. The association between the volition and the neuronal activity would be as for pain in relation to the dual aspect theory and psychophysical parallelism. In relation to the other dualist theories, however, there would be differences. According to interactive dualism, the volition causes neuronal activity, and is itself not entirely predetermined by prior neuronal activity. According to epiphenomenalism, there is merely a feeling of volition which is itself an experience caused by neuronal activity.

It will be seen that interactive dualism could involve some discontinuity in objective physical processes, and explicitly leaves open the possibility of freedom of the will. Epiphenomenalism involves no discontinuity, and would appear to exclude any possibility of freedom of the will. The dual aspect theory could be consistent with freedom of the will, in either of two ways: first, if such freedom is compatible with determinism; and secondly, if, by reason of the mental aspect of the single events, events occur which are not wholly determined by the physical aspect. The former possibility ('compatibilism') involves difficult and somewhat technical arguments (see, for example, Watson 1982: 2–4, and the articles there referred to, and Honderich 1988). The view that determinism (in the strong sense I am considering) is compatible with free will is, I believe, implausible (see Searle 1984: 89) and I do not pursue it. The latter possibility, on the other hand, is central to the argument of this book. In any event, on the dual aspect theory, it seems generally correct to regard mental events as both caused by and causing physical events; that is, to the same extent as one so regards their identical physical brain events.

2.6.4. *The Dual Aspect Theory*

As suggested earlier, I think that the most plausible approach accepts that mental events (the subjective mental processes involved in conscious experience and action) and physical events (the associated objective brain processes) are both aspects or manifestations of processes which comprehend the mental and the physical.

This approach asserts at least a token–token identity between the mental and the physical: that each particular (or 'token') mental event is as a matter of fact the same as some particular (or 'token') physical event or events. The mental event just *is* the physical event 'seen from the inside'. If no more than this is asserted, and in particular if there is no suggestion of any knowable correlation between types of mental events and types of physical events, then it is hard to see how this sameness could be evidenced, or even understood: the nature of the sameness, and of any correlation between mental events and physical events, is left a mystery.

Most advocates of a dual aspect theory assert a type–type identity between the mental and the physical: that the identity of mental events and physical events is associated with systematic correlations between types of mental events and types of physical events. These correlations need not be direct or simple: in one important version, functionalism, the correlations are in terms of functional or causal relationships. On this view, there are discoverable correlations which would enable one to derive, from sufficient information about physical events in the brain, information about the corresponding mental events.

Many persons adopting this view contend that, in principle, *all* properties of mental events could be derived from discoverable correlations and from sufficient information about the relevant physical events. That is, they contend that there are discoverable psychophysical laws (sometimes called 'bridge rules', because they provide a bridge from the physical to the mental) which determine precisely what mental events are associated with what physical events. This is associated with what is called the principle of the supervenience of the mental on the physical; which is to the effect that, given two entities or events with the same physical properties, one of which has certain mental properties, then the other must have the same mental properties (see McGinn 1987: 281).

However, I do not think this is a necessary feature of this general approach: it can be contended that the correlations can only enable derivation of *some* properties of mental events. It is particularly in relation to this sort of view, which may leave some autonomy to the mental, that I think that the label 'dualism' could be appropriate to a dual aspect theory.

What I take to be the contemporary consensus (discussed in the next chapter) combines a dual aspect approach with reductionist and mechanistic views; although some consensus writers would reject the 'dual aspect' label, on the grounds that brain–mind events have many (not just two) 'aspects', and that there are many different kinds of consciousness and mental events, which it would be misleading to group together as just one of two aspects of brain–mind events. On this consensus approach, although the relevant processes have both physical and mental properties, the development over time of such processes is determined by quantitative physical properties changing in accordance with quantitative physical laws.

The view which I advocate in this book combines a dual aspect approach with holistic and non-mechanistic views. On my approach, the development over time of physical–mental processes is affected by mental properties and mental events in ways not completely explicable by physical properties and physical laws, and correlations between the physical and the mental do not account for all mental properties.

Finally, for completeness I should note one particular view which can be regarded as a kind of dual aspect theory: panpsychism. This is the view that there is a psychic or mental aspect to *every* physical state or event. It has some importance historically, but is not prominent today: it seems generally accepted now that physical states and/or events do not have associated mental states and/or events unless the former are of some complexity and organization.

3

The Consensus

In 1949, in *The Concept of Mind*, Ryle identified what he called 'the official view' of the relationship of the mind and the material world: Descartes's dualism with regard to substances, which Ryle called the doctrine of 'the ghost in the machine'. Whether or not that doctrine really had much support at the time among philosophers and scientists, it certainly has little now. In so far as there is a consensus now in the disciplines concerned with the problem, it most closely approximates to the dual aspect theory which I referred to in the previous chapter, in a reductionist and mechanistic version. This is particularly so in the area of computer science and artificial intelligence, and generally, but not universally, so in the areas of neurophysiology and psychology. It is in philosophy that there is perhaps the greatest divergence of views and the strongest representation against this consensus; though even here the consensus predominates.

In this chapter, I outline the consensus, first in philosophy, and then in science in various relevant branches. My purpose here is not to provide a comprehensive review or criticism of the views which I mention: it is rather to give an outline or map of important current approaches, in order to support my assertion that there *is* a broad mechanist consensus, and to provide a background for my own approach. Such criticism as there is merely points to connections with my arguments in Part II, and makes the negative point that dissenters from the consensus have not given a substantive account of how a non-mechanistic mind could work in association with a physical brain.

I note the appeal of the consensus as being a 'scientific' and prima facie a plausible view. However, I will be suggesting that its appeal as a scientific view is overrated, being to some extent a hangover from the science of classical physics, what might be called the 'billiard ball' view of the world. As an introduction to this suggestion, I refer to what appears on the face of it to be a contrary trend in science, namely the new physics, particularly the quantum theory. I indicate briefly the respects in which that theory could perhaps weigh against the mechanist position, and go on to state briefly why in my opinion it has as yet had little impact.

3.1. In Philosophy

Ryle (1949) countered what he called 'the official view' with an analysis of mind in terms of dispositions to act in various ways, and of adverbial descriptions of various sorts of action. Voluntary actions were not actions preceded by some performance by an immaterial mind, but were just actions performed in a particular way, i.e. intentionally. Perception was not the registration of what was perceived on some immaterial inner screen, but, rather, the ability to report and describe what was seen, and tendencies to act in ways appropriate to what was seen. Such ability and such tendencies were dispositional properties, that is, properties indicating dispositions to act in particular ways in particular circumstances. Similarly, emotions such as anger comprised dispositions to act in particular ways in particular circumstances, such as to shout, to tremble, to act aggressively, etc., particularly in the presence of the object of the anger.

Such an approach had affinities with the behaviourist psychology of Watson and Skinner. In psychology, that approach has generally given way to the view that study of human behaviour is incomplete and unsatisfactory without reference to reasons, intentions, desires, beliefs, purposes, etc.; that is, the very sort of considerations eliminated by the behaviourist approach. Furthermore, in so far as the behaviourist approach ignored or treated as irrelevant the subjective aspects of experience and action, it failed to do justice to important features of human existence.

In philosophy, too, there is now little support for behaviourism, in the narrow sense advocated by Watson and Skinner, and perhaps Ryle. The consensus recognizes the validity and importance of explanations of human behaviour in terms of reasons, intentions, desires, beliefs, purposes, etc.; and in general does not deny the existence and importance of conscious mental events. However, it is like behaviourism in denying the existence of an immaterial mind, and in denying that mental events can have any independent causal effect.

3.1.1. *An Outline of the Predominant View*

Stated broadly, the predominant position in philosophy represents 'mind' as a global property of the brain; and mental events as an aspect or property of brain processes. This position does not deny causal efficacy to mental events, but asserts that such causal efficacy (1) is not independent of the causal efficacy of the brain events, which themselves provide maximal explanations of what physical processes take place; but rather (2) is associated with an alternative ('different level') account and explanation of the same events.

Thus on this view the physical world is closed: an explanation (which is as complete as possible) of the physical events involved in human behaviour could in principle be provided with reference to no more than physical events and physical laws. On the other hand, useful (and indeed the only comprehensible) explanations of human behaviour are those given in terms of reasons, intentions, desires, beliefs, etc.; and indeed human behaviour as such can only be meaningfully described with reference to such mental concepts. In particular, such behaviour cannot be described by reference only to physical events and physical laws; though there is nothing in the physical events involved in human behaviour which cannot be given as full as possible an explanation in terms of physical events and physical laws.

A number of analogies have been suggested. A mental event such as a sensation of pain could bear the same sort of relationship to the associated physical events as heat does to the motion of molecules; or alternatively mind could bear the same sort of relationship to the brain as a global property such as solidity or liquidity bears to the interrelationship of the constituent molecules of the material in question.

Again, the operation of an internal combustion engine can be described in terms of the movement of parts such as pistons and the crankshaft: it can in theory at least also be described in terms of the motion of the atoms of which the engine is constituted. The latter would give a complete explanation of the movements of the engine. However, it would not give any indication of what pistons or crankshafts were, or of the role of pistons and the crankshaft in the workings of the engine: this requires a different level of description. Similarly, an account of human action in terms of the physical events of the brain, the pattern of neuronal activity, gives a complete explanation of the movements involved. It gives no indication of what desires or beliefs are, or of the role of desires and beliefs in human action, this requiring a different level of description.

It is sometimes said that on this approach no pre-eminence is given to the physical over the mental, or vice versa: both operate consistently at their respective levels of description; and it is no more true to say that neurons 'push' thoughts than to say that thoughts 'push' neurons (see Hofstadter 1980: 170, 1986: 604–50). However, since physical events are considered as governed by precise and ascertainable quantitative laws, whereas apparently no such laws can apply to mental events, it seems to me that some pre-eminence is in substance given to the physical explanations. As described by Searle (1984: 93–4), physics works 'from the bottom up'—high-level phenomena are grounded in low-level phenomena obeying physical laws; 'top-down' causation—such as causation by intentional acts—only works because the top level (the intentional acts) is already grounded in (and determined by) the bottom level.

3.1.2. *Physicalism*

I suggested earlier that an extreme physicalism of events would involve denying that there are such things as mental states and mental events at all; but that for the most part those who profess physicalism (or materialism) are advocating a physicalism of substance, combined with something like a dual aspect theory of events. They assert that mental events are identical with physical events within an organism's central nervous system or brain. The theory is sometimes called central state materialism.

Most advocates of this approach, however, do not now assert a straightforward type–type identity between mental events and physical events (see, for example, Armstrong 1968: 82). They consider that organisms quite unlike human beings could have mental events; and further consider it unlikely that there will be the same patterns of neuron firings whenever, for example, one person or another 'thinks of next summer's vacation'. They suggest that what picks out particular types of mental events and mental states are the functional or causal relations between them and other (mental and physical) events and states: and it is from these relationships that one can identify those mental events and states which correspond to particular physical events and states.

3.1.3. *Functionalism*

It is sometimes asserted that the view generally called functionalism denies a type–type identity between mental states and events and physical states and events (see Putnam 1975a: 293). However, as suggested by Dennett (1978: xiv–xix), the types of physical event may be identified not by having something physical in common, but in some other way having to do with causal or functional roles.

I will look at some views of three philosophers who have taken this approach.

1. Putnam. One of the early advocates of this approach was Hilary Putnam. As with other exponents of the approach, Putnam adopted the analogy of the computing machine. In the introduction of Putnam (1975a), he notes:

According to functionalism, the behaviour of, say, a computing machine is not explained by the physics and chemistry of the computing machine. It is explained by the machine's *program*. Of course, that program is realized in a particular physics and chemistry, and could, perhaps, be deduced from that physics and chemistry. But that does not make the program a physical or chemical property of the machine; it is an abstract property of the machine. Similarly, I believe that the psychological properties of human beings are not physical and chemical properties of human beings, although they may be realized by physical and chemical properties of human beings. (p. xiii)

One significant exposition of Putnam's views is in his article 'Philosophy and Our Mental Life' (Putnam 1975a: 291–303). In it, he introduces the idea of functional isomorphism:

Two systems are functionally isomorphic if *there is a correspondence between states of one and states of the other that preserves functional relations*. [Accordingly] if *T* is a correct theory of the functioning of system 1, at the functional or psychological level, then an isomorphism between system 1 and system 2 must map each property and relation defined in system 2 in such a way that *T* comes out true when all references to system 1 are replaced by references to system 2, and all property and relation symbols in T are reinterpreted according to the mapping. [Thus] two systems can have quite different constitutions and be functionally isomorphic. For example, a computer made of electrical components can be isomorphic to one made of cogs and wheels. (pp. 291–2)

And accordingly, assuming that human beings 'are, as wholes, just material systems obeying physical laws', then:

mental states, e.g. *thinking about next summer's vacation*, cannot be *identical* with any physical or chemical states; [because] to identify the state in question with its physical or chemical realization would be quite absurd, given that that realization is in a sense quite accidental . . . (p. 293)

Pausing there, the denial of identity here would appear to be a denial of a type–type identity, where the physical type is classified according to the physical properties of the actual physical realization: there is surely no denial of token–token identity (indeed, that is assumed); nor of type–type identity, where the physical type is classified according to its causal or functional role. Assuming that the mental state in question is 'thinking about next summer's vacation', then on Putnam's approach any particular case of such a state must have a token–token identity with some physical states and/or events of the brain of the relevant person; and those physical states and/or events will be identified by their causal or functional role.

Putnam's point, as I understand it, is that the brain of such a person, and a quite different system (say, an electronic computer), could be functionally isomorphic: in which case certain physical states and/or events of that different system could similarly constitute 'thinking about next summer's vacation', even though the physical make-up of the two systems is different. Even as between different human brains, 'thinking about next summer's vacation' could be realized in quite different patterns of neuronal activity: however, these different physical states and/or events must then have some relevantly similar causal or functional roles in the respective brains, so that they could be classified together as the relevant 'type' because of their relevantly similar functional roles.

Putnam then argues (pp. 295–7) that explanations of human behaviour in terms of mental states such as beliefs and desires do not reduce to explanations in terms of physical states and events, and indeed that a causal explanation in terms of physical states and events may be no explanation at all; yet, all this is consistent with our being (as wholes) no more than material systems obeying physical laws.

To illustrate this, he considers alternative explanations of why a square peg passes through a certain square hole, but not through a certain round hole: one, in terms of the microstructure of the relevant objects and quantum mechanics; and the other, in terms of the rigidity of the objects and their relevant geometrical relationships. The latter, high-level, explanation brings out the relevant features of the situation, and will apply (independently of the particular microstructures involved) wherever those high-level features are present: it is in that sense autonomous, and it does not reduce to the former explanation. The former conceals (or at least does not disclose) those relevant features, and in substance fails as an explanation. Yet, of course, the objects *are* no more than systems with a certain microstructure obeying the laws of quantum mechanics.

Similarly, explanations of human behaviour in terms of beliefs and desires disclose relevant features, are autonomous (in that they apply independently of the physical realization of such states), and do not reduce to explanations in terms of physical states and events. Yet, as with the square peg and the round hole, none of this is inconsistent with each person being a physical system operating in accordance with physical laws.

As we will see, some of Putnam's later writing does not sit altogether comfortably with his functionalism, but I do not believe he has expressly abandoned it.

2. Dennett. Another prominent exponent of functionalism is Daniel Dennett. His views are expounded notably in a series of articles collected in his book *Brainstorms*, in which he considers three brands of physicalism (Dennett 1978: xiv–xix).

The first he calls the type identity theory. According to this theory, every mental event is (identical with) a physical event in the brain; and in each case where two persons have something mental in common (e.g. believing that snow is white), it is in virtue of having something physical in common. He notes that this theory is too strong, because (in accordance with views noted earlier) the physical realization of a mental event is in a sense accidental; and he suggests that this objection gave rise to a second version, which he calls Turing machine functionalism. (I will describe the notion of a Turing machine in Section 3.2, when looking at artificial intelligence: this notion was used by Putnam particularly in his early articles on functionalism.) According to this version, when two persons have something mental in common, they 'need not be physically similar in any specifiable way, but they must both be in a "functional" condition or state specifiable in the most general functional language'.

Dennett contends that this version also is too strong, leading him to suggest a third version, his preferred version, which he calls type intentionalism. On this version, 'every mental event is some functional, physical event or other, and the types are captured not by any reductionist language but by a regimentation of the very terms we *ordinarily* use'. This regimentation is required in so far as 'our familiar mentalistic idioms (thoughts, desires, beliefs, pains, sensations, dreams, experiences) fail to perform' the task of 'referring to members in good standing of usefully distinct items in the world' 'because they embody conceptual infelicities and incoherencies of various sorts'.

Dennett enlarges on this version (pp. 3–6) by discussing what he calls intentional systems, which he defines as systems 'whose behaviour can be—

at least sometimes—explained and predicted by relying on ascriptions to the system of beliefs and desires'. In order to illustrate his approach, he considers the case of a chess-playing computer, and the different strategies or stances one might adopt as its opponent in seeking to predict its moves: first, a design stance, on the basis of the system's functional design, irrespective of its physical constitution; secondly, a physical stance, on the basis of the physical state of the object, applying physical laws; and thirdly, an intentional stance, 'ascribing to the system *the possession of certain information* and supposing it to be *directed by certain goals,* and then . . . working out the most reasonable or appropriate action on the basis of these ascriptions and suppositions'. In fact, a person playing chess against a computer would generally adopt something like the third stance, although (I would suggest) taking into account the system's apparent abilities and idiosyncrasies, and working out the most likely move having regard to these.

On Dennett's approach, it would seem that types of mental event and mental state are identified in accordance with something like the intentional stance. They are not identified by reference to the physical state and operation of the physical organism: as argued by Putnam and others, this is accidental. They are not identified by reference to any low-level functional structure of the organism. This too may be considered accidental: in the same way that a single computer program in a high-level computer language such as BASIC or FORTRAN can be realized in different programs in a computer's own internal binary code, so also a mental state and/or event could perhaps be realized in different functional states and events of whatever is the basic code used by the brain.

As I understand him, Dennett does not contend that a chess-playing computer necessarily *has* mental states and/or events, but, rather, he is seeking to elucidate the kind of criteria on the basis of which types of mental states and/or events can be identified or 'captured' in terms of types of physical events.

3. Shoemaker. A possible difficulty of the general approach of functionalism is that, while it may appear to give a satisfactory account of mental states such as beliefs and desires, it may seem inadequate in relation to what are often called qualitative mental states or qualia (and which I would call mental events with a significant sensory content), such as sensations of pain and visual sensations of colour. It seems that each of us is aware of types of qualia in a way which does not involve any knowledge of their causal or functional roles, and indeed leaves it contingent whether qualia of the same type have the same causal or functional roles. This matter has been considered by Sidney Shoemaker in a number of articles (Shoemaker 1984).

Shoemaker refers to two particular problems, the inverted spectrum and absent qualia.

As regards the former, it is quite conceivable (and impossible conclusively to refute) that the subjective sensations of colour of different persons are quite different; for example, that things that appear (subjectively) blue to one person, appear (subjectively) red to another, and vice versa. If one such thing happens to be the cloudless daytime sky, then of course both of those persons will call it 'blue', even though one of them sees it as having the colour which the other attributes to human blood; and nothing in the behaviour of either would (conclusively) demonstrate the subjective difference. (If one has difficulty with the notion of such an intersubjective difference, one can approach the problem by first considering the possibility that a person might wake up one day to find his own subjective spectrum inverted, so that he now sees the sky as having the colour which he previously attributed to blood, and vice versa; and then proceeding to speculate that this very difference might exist, undetected, between two different persons at the same time.)

As regards the latter, it seems conceivable that two mental states could be functionally identical, even though in one case the organism (person?) in question is in pain, and in the other feels nothing at all. The inputs (perhaps injury, resulting in appropriate nerve signals), outputs (nerve signals producing grimacing, flinching, etc.), and successor states (avoidance behaviour, etc.) could be identical, even though in one case the quale (pain) is present, and in the other case it is absent.

If functionalism requires us to say that the subjective differences in these cases do not involve *any* difference in the mental states involved (so that, for example, the organism which feels nothing must be said to be in pain, because of the *functional* similarity of its state to that of the organism which actually *feels* pain), then functionalism could seem an unsatisfactory account of mental states (and mental events).

Shoemaker deals with this problem *inter alia* in two articles (1984: 184–205, 308–26). His main argument assumes a causal theory of knowledge which would 'imply that states or features that are independent of the causal powers of the things they characterize would be in principle unknowable'. Then,

if ... we take qualitative character to be known in the ways we take human feelings to be knowable (at a minimum, if it can be known introspectively), then it is not possible, not even logically possible, for a state which lacks qualitative character to be functionally identical to a state that has it. (p. 191)

In a nutshell, if states involving subjective feelings of pain could be functionally identical with states not involving such feelings, then we could never *know* whether or not we actually have feelings of pain—which is absurd.

This argument illustrates a dilemma of physicalism and functionalism. Its advocates want to say (*a*) that mental states and events are nothing but physical states and events, viewed differently (i.e. from the 'inside'); (*b*) that everything that happens can be considered as the result of physical laws operating on physical states and events; and (*c*) that mental states and events can be identified by their functional or causal role. If one combines (*b*) and (*c*), it would seem that the functional or causal role of mental states and events will be entirely determined by their associated (indeed, identical) physical states and events: the physical states and events do not 'need' their associated mental states and events to have the effects which they do have. Thus one has the possibility of inverted spectra or absent qualia, unless one takes the Shoemaker line: yet this line strongly threatens (*b*). I will consider this further in Chapter 7.

3.1.4. *Apparent Dissenters*

Not all philosophers adopt the physicalist–functionalist approach. However, of those who do not, there are some whose views are not really a substantial departure from the consensus.

1. Davidson's anomalous monism. One approach sometimes regarded as dissenting, but which in my view does not radically differ from the foregoing, is that of Donald Davidson in such articles as 'Mental Events' and 'Psychology as Philosophy' (Davidson 1979, 1976).

Davidson emphasizes the point that mental events cannot be brought under and explained by quantitative causal laws of the type which explain physical events. This is for at least two reasons: (*a*) the descriptions of mental events do not have, and cannot have, the quantitative precision which would be necessary for this; and (*b*) in ascribing mental events and mental states to others, or even to ourselves, we must be sensitive to considerations of rationality which themselves cannot be reduced to a closed formal system.

These considerations are capable of being used to argue against the predominant view: they are indeed not unlike some of my points in Part II. However, Davidson accepts that the physical world is closed, and argues to a different conclusion. He accepts (*a*) that causation involves laws; (*b*) that mental events cause, and are caused by, physical events; and (*c*) that there cannot be laws governing mental events. His conclusion is that mental events must be (that is, I interpolate, be identical with, but a different aspect of) physical events; for, otherwise, (*a*) and (*c*) would involve denying (*b*).

So, we have an identity theory, and Davidson himself regards it as a form of monism. However, the identity falls short of a complete type–type identity: Davidson's argument is against any complete systematic correlation of types of physical event with types of mental event, that is, against the existence of strict psychophysical laws (and, consistently, against the existence of strict psychological laws). Hence the label 'anomalous monism'.

The absence of systematic correlation of types might appear to allow for some autonomy of mental events. However, as stated above, Davidson accepts that the physical world is closed; so that everything which happens, that is, every physical event, must be determined (so far as it can be determined) by physical laws operating on physical events. One thing mental events cannot do, then, is to make some difference to what happens physically, from what is determined according to physical laws and physical events (see Searle 1984: 93–4; Kim 1985: 383–4). It is for this reason that I suggest that Davidson's position is not a significant dissent from the consensus: his acceptance of the identity of mental and physical events (even if only a token–token identity), and of the closedness of the physical world, aligns him with the consensus; and only his denial or questioning of systematic correlations between physical and mental types separates him from it.

2. Searle. John Searle is often presented as a dissenter from the predominant view, in particular because of his rejection of the likening of the mind to a digital computer. This rejection is based on his assertion that the program of a digital computer involves only syntax (rules for arranging and manipulating symbols), not semantics (meaning).

He illustrates this with his famous Chinese room thought experiment (Searle 1980) by asking us to compare a computer to a person in a room with sets of rules for dealing with sequences of symbols, passed into the room, so as to produce other sequences of symbols, which are then passed out of the room. The sequences of symbols handed in are in fact questions in Chinese: if the rules are followed correctly, then the sequences of symbols handed out will be sentences in Chinese, which give satisfactory answers to the Chinese questions. The person does not in fact understand Chinese. That, Searle says, is all that a computer can do, viz. transform inputs of some sort into outputs of some sort, without having any understanding, any knowledge of the meaning of those symbols.

Searle also denies (Searle 1984: 80–2) that it is possible to relate all mental events to physical events in any systematic way. This is principally because social phenomena (such as money) are not grounded systematically in physical processes: for something to be money, all that is necessary is that people *believe* that it is money, and there are no limits to what may physically constitute money. Accordingly, there cannot be systematic correlation between the mental state of believing something to be money, and any physical states and/or events.

It is not clear to me whether Searle is here merely denying the physical type–type identity approach, or whether he is seeking also to deny the functionalist approach of (say) Dennett. If the latter, then his views do seem at odds with the consensus. Yet he also asserts (1984: 18–22) that mental states and mental events are 'caused by' brain states and brain events, in the same way as the solidity of a material is 'caused by' the lattice structure of the molecules of that material; and he accepts that the physical world is closed in the sense that I have discussed earlier.

In other words, Searle's difference from the consensus is essentially that there is no thoroughgoing systematic correlation between mental events and physical events, so that his position seems very close to Davidson's. It seems to me that this aspect of his views does not sit well with his likening of the mind to global properties of matter, because in relation to global properties of matter there is clearly a systematic discoverable correlation between the properties of the constituent systems and the global properties; whereas Searle apparently denies such a correlation in relation to the mind. However that may be, I suggest that Searle cannot be regarded as a significant dissentient from the consensus.

3.1.5. *Dissenters*

There are a number of prominent philosophers who either strongly express scepticism concerning the matter or else dissent from the consensus. Examples of the former are Robert Nozick and Thomas Nagel; and of the latter are Charles Taylor, Richard Swinburne, and Karl Popper.

1. Nozick. Nozick's *Philosophical Explanations* (1981) is a wide-ranging and stimulating book. Its general approach is to explore, rather than to seek to justify a point of view; and this is true of the approach to the mind–matter question in the chapter entitled 'Free Will'. He sketches a view of free choice by non-random weighting of reasons (pp. 294–307), and goes on to relate this in various ways to the question of freedom of the will and the mind–matter question generally. The discussion anticipates some of the ideas in Chapters 5 and 6 of this book. However, no conclusions are reached, and the book does not advance a theory to challenge the consensus.

2. Nagel. In his celebrated article 'What Is it Like to Be a Bat?' (1974), Nagel forcefully makes the point that the subjective character of experience, what it is *like* for an organism to have the experience, 'is not captured by any of the familiar, recently devised reductive analyses of the mental, for all of them are logically compatible with its absence'. (This is essentially the line of argument which Shoemaker sought to deal with, in the way outlined above.) However, Nagel does not develop a theory of the relationship between mind and matter, or of the relationship between mental events and physical events, which could be set against the consensus; nor is any contention raised against the view that the physical world is closed, and physical explanations complete.

In *The View from Nowhere* (1986) Nagel approaches this and other problems by considering two standpoints from which we can view the world: an objective standpoint, transcending our own experience, a view from nowhere in particular; and a subjective standpoint, an individual's particular personal view of the world. He suggests that 'the attempt to give a complete account of the world in objective terms detached from these [subjective, individual, human] perspectives inevitably leads to false reductions or to outright denial that certain patently real phenomena exist at all' (p. 7). He does not in fact integrate the two standpoints, leaving an unresolved perplexity which he would no doubt consider embodies 'more insight than any of the proposed solutions' (p. 4).

To me, this approach echoes those of quantum physicist Erwin Schrödinger and microbiologist Max Delbrück, who consider the problems of the mind–matter distinction a result of the cut between the observer and the observed, itself necessary for the existence of objective science, but necessarily introducing distortions (see Schrödinger 1967; Delbrück 1978, 1986). It also, perhaps even more closely, echoes views of quantum physicist and philosopher Niels Bohr, to the effect that in some circumstances, because of the inadequacy of our language or viewpoint, reality can best be represented by two accounts which are apparently inconsistent (yet not repugnant, because not applying in the same situations) but complementary (in that only with both is there an adequate representation of the world) (see Bohr 1958).

Still, again there is no theory significantly to challenge the consensus.

3. Taylor and Swinburne. A number of philosophers give accounts in support of freedom of the will, which picture human beings as acting for reasons, and at least implying that the physical movement of their bodies (and physical events in the brain) do not have a complete explanation in terms of physical causes.

For example, Taylor (1982) gives an account of free will as involving choice between different kinds of reasons. He also seeks to accommodate freedom of the will to physics and chemistry. In a 1971 article 'How is Mechanism Conceivable?' (Taylor 1985: 164–86), he discusses possible relationships between explanations of behaviour in terms of psychology, and in terms of physics and chemistry; and suggests that reduction of psychology to physics and chemistry can be avoided:

the present principles of neurophysiology, and *a fortiori* those of physics and chemistry, would be supplemented by concepts of quite a different kind, in which, for instance, relations of meaning might become relevant to neurophysiological process. (p. 185)

However, he does not show what those principles might be.

Similarly, Swinburne (1986) gives an account of human free will as operating in cases where there is a conflict between the person's belief that one action would be good or right, and his desire to do a different action. Also, he argues against thoroughgoing reductionism:

physics and chemistry could not possibly explain why the brain-events to which impinging light gives rise, in turn give rise to sensations of blueness (as opposed to redness) . . . because mental properties fall outside the subject matter of physics and chemistry. (p. 186)

This last point is accepted by many consensus thinkers (e.g. Shoemaker (see above) and Boden (see below)), giving rise to the dilemma discussed in relation to Shoemaker. The point about free will cannot be accepted by consensus thinkers, and raises the problem of reconciling free will to physics and chemistry: Swinburne seeks to do this by reference to quantum theory (1986: 238–47), a matter which is a major theme of this book.

I think it is fair to say not only that views such as these are in a minority in philosophy, but also that they have little influence in the scientific areas dealing with the brain.

4. Popper. *The Self and its Brain* by Popper and Eccles (1977) directly attacks the consensus. So far as Popper's contribution is concerned, it presents a number of persuasive arguments against non-interactionist views, making points similar to some of mine in Part II. However, like other dissentients, he gives no positive theory of how mental events and physical events interact, or of how mental events occur. Co-author neurophysiologist John Eccles, for his part, offers an account of the interaction of mental and physical events, but this account involves postulating a mysterious immaterial mind, with no account either of how it could work or why (given its assumed capabilities) it needs a complicated physical brain to assist it at all.

Again, it seems that this work has had little impact on the consensus.

3.2. In Computer Science

The consensus is reflected even more strongly in the various branches of science concerned with the problem. The general approach adopted by most scientists is well expressed by physicist and science writer Paul Davies in the chapters on mind, soul, and self in his book *God and the New Physics* (1983), substantially adopting the approach of the functionalist philosophy of mind.

Dealing with the analogy of the computer, he writes:

At the neural (brain cell) level, the human brain is equally mechanical and subject to rational principles, yet this does not prevent us from experiencing feelings of indecision, confusion, happiness, boredom and irrationality. (p. 78)

On dualist approaches, he ventures the opinion that:

the dualist theory falls into the trap of seeking a substance (the mind) to explain what is really an abstract concept, not an object . . . Mind and body are not two components of a duality, but two entirely different concepts drawn from different levels in a hierarchy of description . . . abstract, high-level concepts can be equally as real as the low-level structures which support them, without any mysterious extra substances or ingredients. (pp. 82–3)

And he notes:

There seems to be no scientific evidence for any special divine quality in man, and no fundamental reason is apparent why an advanced electronic machine should not, in principle, enjoy similar feelings of consciousness as ourselves. (p. 96)

It is in the field of computer science that one finds perhaps the strongest expression of the mechanistic and reductionist approach of the consensus. It seems almost universally assumed and accepted by workers in the field that human intelligence (and other workings of the human brain–mind) is based on the mechanistic operation of a physical system which could in principle be fully simulated, and indeed duplicated, by a computer.

3.2.1. *Some Background*

This assumption and acceptance has its origin in what is called the Church–Turing thesis: this thesis, attributed to both logician Alonzo Church and to mathematician Alan Turing, was formulated independently by each of them, in different contexts. It concerns the realization or carrying out of effective procedures or algorithms, that is, of procedures involving discrete steps each one of which is unequivocally determined by unambiguous rules or directions. As formulated by Turing, the thesis asserts that a machine could be devised for the realization of any such procedure. Turing envisaged a single universal Turing machine which could carry out any and all such procedures.

1. The Turing machine. The idea of a Turing machine was introduced in Turing's 1937 article 'On Computable Numbers, with an Application to the *Entscheidungsproblem*'. The last word ('decision problem') refers to a problem posed by mathematician David Hilbert in 1900 (Hilbert's 23rd problem): the devising of an algorithm for determining the truth or falsity of any statement in formal logic, and thereby of any mathematical statement. (In line with my discussion in Chapter 1, I would put the problem in terms of provability or theoremhood of mathematical statements, within formal systems sufficiently powerful to comprehend substantial areas of mathematics; but for this discussion this difference in terminology does not matter.)

Turing showed that there were statements which no algorithm could determine to be true or false in a finite number of steps by postulating a hypothetical machine (a 'Turing machine') with the following features. First, a tape of limitless length, divided into equal segments on which data could be encoded by means of symbols, generally the symbols '0' and '1'. Secondly, a head which could change the data, as follows: it would read the existing symbol on the segment at which it was positioned; either leave that symbol as it was, or change the symbol; then move to one or other of the adjoining segments and repeat the process; and so on. Thirdly, a mechanism to cause the head to operate in accordance with an unchangeable set of instructions: at each step, the determination of the applicable instruction would be on the basis of two conditions, namely the current symbol and the current 'state' of the mechanism (or 'machine state'); and the instruction would then determine three matters, namely the symbol to be left at the current segment (i.e. the existing symbol or a changed symbol), the machine state for the next step, and the direction of travel to the adjoining segment (left or right).

Thus, an instruction could, for example, be symbolized $(0, S_m)(1, S_n, R)$, meaning: 'if the current symbol is 0 and machine state is S_m, change the symbol to 1, change the machine state to S_n, and move one segment to the right'. It is clear that, for substantial algorithms, there might need to be a very large number of different instructions and accordingly a large number of different machine states: if only two symbols 0 and 1 were used, then there would have to be at least one machine state for each two different instructions. For the purposes of Turing's discussion, it was not necessary to identify or describe the various machine states otherwise than by assigning a distinctive symbol (such as S_m, S_n, etc.) and by specifying the various symbols in the various instructions. Any mechanical realization of the various machine states would be satisfactory, provided it was apt to give effect to the symbolized instructions. (In this, one sees an important precursor of functionalism.)

Then, Turing showed that, given any algorithm, one could devise a Turing machine (that is, a set of instructions) which would carry it out, so that the data tape would commence containing the starting-point of the algorithm (in code), progress through the results of its intermediate steps (also in code), and (if the algorithm terminated) end up with its final result (still, of course, in code).

Next, and very importantly, Turing showed that it was possible to devise a universal Turing machine which could, given the right data on its tape, carry out any algorithm which could be carried out by any particular Turing machine; that is, any algorithm at all. This was because the instructions of any particular Turing machine could themselves be encoded on one part of a tape, alongside the encoding of the starting-point of the algorithm on another part of the tape: the universal Turing machine's instructions would be such that it would shuttle back and forth between the two parts of the tape, 'ascertaining' from the encoding of the particular Turing machine what instructions should be followed as regards the symbols on the other part of the tape. In the result, the same operations would (eventually) be performed on the latter as would have been performed by the particular Turing machine.

In relation to Hilbert's problem, Turing argued that if an algorithm could determine the truth or falsity of a logical or mathematical statement in a finite number of steps, then some Turing machine could also do so in a finite (though perhaps larger) number of steps: such statements (or the numbers by which they were encoded) he called computable numbers. He then showed that there existed mathematical statements which could not be 'computed' by any Turing machine in a finite number of steps; and which accordingly could not be shown to be true or false by any algorithm.

However, in the present context, it is the notion of a universal Turing machine which is important, historically and conceptually. The historical importance is as a stage in the development of the computer. A universal Turing machine as such has never been built, and it would be too slow to be a practical computer; but its logical scheme was adapted to form the basis of today's digital computers: modern digital computers are equivalent to universal Turing machines. The conceptual importance, so far as the brain–mind is concerned, is clear: leaving aside questions arising from analogue processes in the brain (i.e. respects in which the brain does not operate by discrete steps), if the human brain is in substance a machine for computing, or processing information, then anything the human brain can do by way of computing, or processing information, can be done by a sufficiently powerful computing machine. The fact that the human brain is composed of living nerve-cells, while the computing machine is composed of lifeless mechanical and/or electronic parts, is irrelevant.

2. Von Neumann computers. About ten years after Turing's article, the mathematician John von Neumann and others applied Turing's scheme to formulate the basic plan of modern digital computers. Very broadly, a 'von Neumann computer' comprises a central processing unit (or CPU), where arithmetical and logical operations are executed (corresponding to the unchangeable instructions mechanism of a universal Turing machine); and a memory unit where data, including changeable instructions, are stored (corresponding to the tape of a universal Turing machine: the changeable instructions, called the program, correspond to the encoding on the tape of the instructions of particular Turing machines). Both the CPU and the memory unit operate electronically: the memory unit stores the data in a binary code, originally using valves and more recently using transistors and silicon chips. The computer operates by transferring data from memory to the CPU, processing it there, and then transferring the processed data back to memory. In modern computers, this cycle may be performed millions of times per second.

Such computers can process data quickly, but still, like a Turing machine, they do so one step at a time: accordingly, they are called serial computers, whereas computers which take a number of steps at the same time are called parallel computers. Serial computers are not limited to processing one 'bit' of information (such as whether a symbol is a '1' or a '0') at a time: generally they transfer and process the information in 'words' which contain 4, 8, 16, or 32 bits. Still, anything such computers do could, in principle, be done in the same order (but in more steps and greater time) by a universal Turing machine.

Computers for general use have other parts as well; in particular, sections for introducing programs and data into the memory section, and sections for giving out the results of computation. Very often programs are introduced by means of magnetic tape or disc, and data by means of a typewriter keyboard. Data can also be recorded on, and can be introduced by means of, magnetic tapes and discs. Output is generally by a screen or printer. At both input and output stages, information has to be transformed, in the former case into the machine's binary code, and in the latter, into some form which the human user can comprehend.

3. Parallel processing and neural nets. Some computers in use have a number of processing units, which can operate at the same time. A scheme sometimes used in supercomputers is to have a series of processing units,

each of which in turn partially processes each piece of data, in such a way that as soon as the first piece of data is passed on to the second processor, the first processor starts on the second piece of data, and so on.

Work is proceeding on computers in which there is more extensive parallel processing, where very many steps in information processing are taken at the same time by different processing units. Such machines depart from the von Neumann plan in that steps are taken simultaneously, not just serially or sequentially; but they follow it in that all computations involve discrete steps between discrete states: that is, they are still digital rather than analogue. They also follow it in that they conform to what is known as the 'top-down' approach to programming: they are provided with quite elaborate predetermined programs to follow. They can modify such programs as they proceed, but that ability is itself part of the original elaborate program.

Work is also proceeding on a quite different conception, using what is called a neural net, and adopting a bottom-up approach to programming. Here, the aim is to construct something akin to a network of neurons in a human brain, provided with relatively simple programs which enable it to learn by experience, as a human being does.

Networks of human neurons are functionally similar to electronic circuits, in that each neuron can fire (discharge an electric current), or not fire; and if it fires the current is received by other neurons through junctions called synapses; these discharges are in discrete pulses, which (for each neuron) do not vary in size, but only in number and frequency. However, an individual neuron is far more complex than an electronic switch: it may receive impulses from 1,000 or more other neurons, and transmit its own impulses to a similar number of neurons. Whether or not a neuron fires, and if so with what frequency and for what time, is a function of the input to the neuron. Some of the inputs are excitory, some are inhibitory, and their effect varies with the 'strength' of the connections at the synapses. Further, the strength of the connections at the synapses can be changed over time: such change is considered to be one important way (if not *the* way) in which things are learnt or memorized by human beings. Accordingly, rather than being like a switch, each neuron of a human brain performs computational functions.

Neural nets, then, comprise substantial numbers of electronic components, capable of computational functions similar to those apparently performed by human neurons. Such nets can be made using random access memory (RAM) silicon chips as the 'neurons': generally, the elements of such nets operate digitally, although they can in principle simulate the operation of continuously varying (analogue) units to arbitrary degrees of accuracy. Considerable success has been achieved with such neural nets in fields such as pattern (and even human face) recognition. However, it seems unlikely that the bottom-up, neural net approach will entirely displace the top-down, pre-programmed approach using machines based on Turing's and von Neumann's ideas. The top-down approach has had spectacular success in areas traditionally believed to be accessible only to persons of high intellect: storage, organization, and retrieval of great quantities of precisely stated information; elaborate mathematical calculation; deriving logical implications from complicated premisses; playing chess. It has had little success in areas traditionally regarded as indicating 'mere' ordinary human abilities and common-sense: dealing with ordinary language; perception; informal, common-sense reasoning; coping in various ways with a complex changing environment. It is in the latter areas that it seems that a learning neural net may have advantages, and it seems reasonable to expect that the best systems will make use of both approaches.

Furthermore, in accordance with the Church–Turing thesis, a universal Turing machine, or a general-purpose von Neumann computer, could carry out any procedure which could be carried out by a digital neural net; although, since it would do so one step at a time in sequential order, it would probably take far longer (see Johnson-Laird 1988: 191). So the notion of a universal Turing machine is still relevant to what it is possible for machines to achieve.

3.2.2. *Views of Computer Scientists*

I turn now to consider views put forward by computer scientists on the relationship between computers and artificial intelligence on the one hand, and the human brain–mind on the other hand.

1. Turing on machine intelligence. A useful starting-point is another important article by Alan Turing, 'Computing Machinery and Intelligence', published in 1950. In this article, Turing poses the question 'Can machines think?', and proceeds to answer it somewhat indirectly, because of uncertainty of the meaning of 'think'.

He first proposes a test of the capabilities of computing machines.

A person is given two computer terminals, and is allowed to put to either or both terminals any questions on any topic, and to follow up by further questions any answers as displayed by the terminals. The answers provided by one terminal are supplied by a human being, those provided by the other are supplied by a computer. The person asking the questions is required to determine which answers are supplied by a human being, and which ones by a computer. Turing suggests that if such a test could not reliably distinguish between the human being and the computer, then there would be no justification for denying that machines could be intelligent and could think. If machines could in relevant respects *behave* indistinguishably from human beings, then there would be no basis for asserting that human beings have abilities of thinking and of intelligence which a machine could not have.

Turing does not suggest that any computer and program devised in his time could have passed such a test; nor, I believe, does any computer scientist now suggest that any computer and program devised to the present time could do so. What is suggested, however, is that there is no reason in principle why a computer and program could not be devised which could pass such a test; and (which comes to the same thing) that there is no strategy of questioning which could be devised which could be assured of discriminating between the human being and the computer. Accordingly, any difference which might be considered to flow from the organic basis of human mental life as against the electronic basis of artificial intelligence does not give rise to any discernible difference in behaviour.

The article goes on to deal with a number of possible objections to the proposition that computing machines could think.

Turing starts with the theological objection (thinking is a function of the soul, which God has given to human beings, but not to machines), and the 'heads in the sand' objection (the consequences of machines thinking would be too dreadful), to both of which he gives short shrift.

Next, he considers the mathematical objection: that a number of results of mathematical logic show that there are limitations to the powers of discrete-state machines (including results produced by Gödel, which I look at later, by Church, and by Turing himself). Turing's short answer, which is generally adopted by consensus thinkers today, is that it has not been shown that such limitations do not also apply to the human intellect. Turing recognizes that this answer is by no means conclusive.

Turing then considers an argument from consciousness: that only a machine conscious of thoughts and feelings could be said to think. He suggests that this is really to argue that the only way to be sure that a machine thinks is to *be* that machine; which implies that the only way to know that another *person* thinks is to be that person. Turing suggests that his test is more satisfactory than this solipsistic approach. (This book contends, among other things, that arguments based on consciousness are far stronger than Turing's account suggests.)

Next come arguments from various disabilities, and Lady Lovelace's objection. (Lady Lovelace was a colleague of Charles Babbage, who in the nineteenth century devised the 'Analytical Engine', a mechanical precursor of the computer.) As to the former, Turing suggests that any alleged *relevant* disabilities of machines could be the subject of his test. The latter refers to a memoir of Lady Lovelace to the effect that the Analytical Engine could not '*originate* anything', but only 'do *whatever we know how to order it* to perform'. Turing contends that this underestimated the abilities of machines. (A further possible reply, which is not given in Turing's article, is that human beings themselves are machines, developed and programmed by evolution and environment; and so are no different in relation to originality from computing machines.)

Turing then considers the argument from continuity of the nervous system. The human nervous system is not a discrete-state machine: although Turing does not put it in these terms, the operation of the brain appears to be (at least partly) analogue rather than wholly digital, in particular in that the duration and frequencies of neural firings appear to vary over a continuous range, and not to be restricted to discrete values. However, Turing contends in effect that a discrete-state machine can simulate the operation of an analogue machine to any necessary degree of approximation. (We now have the familiar example of digital processing of sound-recording, giving very close simulation of the original continuous sound, and at least equalling the best analogue recordings of that sound.)

Next, Turing considers the argument from informality of behaviour: that it is not possible to produce a set of rules purporting to describe what a man would do in every conceivable circumstance. Turing argues that we are not justified in asserting that human conduct is not the result of laws of nature acting on the human body and brain. (This is an argument which, like that from consciousness, I seek to develop in this book.)

Finally, Turing considers the argument from extra-sensory perception: that human beings have a capacity for ESP, which puts into question the applicability of the laws of physics to human beings, and suggests that there might be more to thinking than carrying out algorithms. Somewhat surprisingly, Turing thought this argument 'quite a strong one', because 'the statistical evidence, at least for telepathy, is overwhelming'. There is little support for this view from consensus thinkers; and it is not an argument which I pursue.

2. Other consensus views. Turing's approach, as expressed in his two noted articles (but probably excluding his remarks on ESP) seems to be accepted, virtually without question, by today's workers on artificial intelligence: in particular, the views that universal discrete-state machines can be built (and, now, have been built) which can perform *any* algorithms which can be performed by *any possible* discrete-state machine; that the human brain is a finite physical object, operating in accordance with ordinary physical laws, and is itself therefore a machine, if not a discrete-state machine; that the operation of the brain can in principle be simulated to any desired degree of approximation by a universal discrete-state machine; and that, since the only evidence of internal states (or, as I would say, mental events) in other persons is their behaviour, such states must be attributed to a discrete-state machine whose behaviour sufficiently simulates that of a human brain.

On the question of mental states and events, and consciousness, some workers on artificial intelligence go further. For example, John McCarthy, head of the Artificial Intelligence Laboratory of Stanford University, is said to have asserted that even simple machines can have *beliefs*; for example, that a thermostat has, at different times, the beliefs 'it's too cold' and 'it's not too cold'! I do not know whether or not he was serious about this.

Not untypical of the attitude of such workers towards consciousness is that attributed to MIT's Marvin Minsky that consciousness is overrated, involving no more than a very imperfect summary of what is going on in the brain; that people do not know most of what is going on in their brains, and in particular do not know where their ideas come from; and that, once the mechanism of consciousness is understood, it can be put into machines.

Another quite common assertion by workers in artificial intelligence is that machines will soon (or sooner or later) equal human beings in general intelligence, and thereafter outstrip them: such views sometimes portray these machines as evolutionary successors to mankind. In the early years of artificial intelligence research, it was predicted that machines would achieve the general intelligence of human beings within a few years. Such predictions have not been fulfilled. However, similar predictions continue unabated, although there is generally more caution in saying when.

One interesting idea along these lines is attributed to Irving John Good in answer to a remark made by the British scientist Lord Bowden. As recorded in Evans (1980: 195), Bowden said that 'there seemed to be little point in spending vast sums of money on creating a computer as intelligent as a human when the world was already heavily overpopulated with intelligent beings all of whom could be created quite easily, relatively cheaply and in a far more enjoyable way'. Good's comment was that, with a bit more money and effort, one could make a computer *more* intelligent than a human being; and then, with the help of that computer, make one which was more intelligent still; and so on. At each step, the improvements could be expected to be greater, and the result would be an exponential increase in the capabilities of successive generations of computers. Eventually, it is suggested, there will be machines whose intelligence is so superior to ours that (in the words of science fiction writer Arthur C. Clark) human beings will be lucky if the machines are willing to keep them as house pets.

In somewhat similar vein are statements reported in the Press in 1987 by Hans Moravec, director of the Robotics Institute at Carnegie Mellon University (which is, with MIT, one of the centres of artificial intelligence research). Moravec is reported as saying that, in an astonishingly short time, scientists will be able to transfer the contents of a person's mind into a powerful computer, and in the process make him, 'or at least his living essence', virtually immortal; that the human race is designing its successors, which are carrying on all our abilities, only doing it better. He suggests one scenario for digitizing the contents of the human mind, which will be 'made plausible' in the next fifty to a hundred years: to hook up a super powerful computer to the corpus callosum, the bundle of nerve fibres that connects the two hemispheres of the brain; and to program it to monitor the traffic between the two and, eventually, to teach itself to think like the brain. This view is elaborated in Moravec (1988).

Views like those of Minsky, Good, and Moravec do not follow as a matter of necessity from the consensus approach. Many consensus thinkers on artificial intelligence are sceptical about whether computers will ever attain or exceed the general intelligence of human beings (see, for example, Boden

1977; Hofstadter 1980; Aleksander and Burnett 1987). Further, many would regard Moravec's suggestion of immortality of a person, or of his 'living essence', through a machine, as presupposing philosophical doctrines concerning a person's 'essence', or (presumably) self, which are not themselves part of the consensus. (I touch on this matter in Chapter 17.)

However, these views are consistent with the consensus, and may be considered as one expression of it.

3. *Gödel, Escher, Bach.* One of the best expressions of the consensus by a computer scientist is the Pulitzer Prize-winning book *Gödel, Escher, Bach* by Douglas Hofstadter. The book contains elaborate and careful discussions of formal systems and of Gödel's theorem (on which, see Section 5.7); but, more importantly for present purposes, it contains discussions of meaning, informal reasoning, and consciousness in relation to artificial intelligence, in which the consensus view is put strongly, without ignoring or trivializing the problems involved. The book persuasively suggests how intelligence and purposive behaviour can be exhibited by the interactions of non-intelligent and non-purposive units. I will refer to some of its arguments in Chapters 4 and 5.

3.2.3. *Dissenters*

Of those actually working in computer science and artificial intelligence, one notable person who could be classed as a dissenter is Joseph Weizenbaum, whose *Computer Power and Human Reason* (Weizenbaum 1984) argues a case against entrusting computers with certain types of decision. However, his argument is based less on a rejection of mechanism than on the dangers of placing reliance on computer calculations too complex for human reason to follow and monitor. The book raises questions concerning the possibility of fully mechanizing human reasoning, but does not argue strongly one way or the other: on the fundamental question of mechanism, Weizenbaum appears to be an agnostic. However, in the company of workers on artificial intelligence, this surely counts as dissent.

More recently, in Winograd and Flores (1986), prominent computer scientist Terry Winograd emerges as an outright dissenter. He contends 'that one cannot construct machines that either exhibit or successfully model intelligent behaviour' (p. 11). He uses *inter alia* ideas of the existentialist philosopher Martin Heidegger concerning the interdependence of the objective and the subjective worlds; but he does not suggest what it is about brains as physical objects which makes them so different from computers.

3.2.4. *Views of Philosophers on Artificial Intelligence*

I have already referred to views of philosophers such as Putnam and Dennett, in which the consensus view is supported by reference to work on computers and artificial intelligence. In the next section, I mention the philosopher–

psychologist Margaret Boden, whose book *Artificial Intelligence and Natural Man* (Boden 1977) is a strong expression of the consensus view from a philosophical–psychological standpoint (see also Sloman 1978; Haugeland 1981, 1985).

Perhaps the best-known exponent of the view that computers will never be able to match the performance of the human brain–mind is Berkeley philosopher Hubert Dreyfus. However, his 1972 book *What Computers Can't Do* (Dreyfus 1979) does not appear to be an attack on mechanism, as such: rather, it seems to be, in Turing's terms, an argument from 'various disabilities'. Dreyfus contends that much human knowledge and ability is not expressed or expressible in propositions of the kind dealt with by computers: it is innate, tacit, a matter of knowing how rather than knowing that, acquired by experience of the world gained through the operation of a human body. Dreyfus undoubtedly shows examples of human capabilities which will be extremely difficult to mechanize; and there is force in his association of human capabilities with the human body. However, in the absence of a general argument against mechanism, and a general theory of non-mechanistic causation, his argument for some fundamental limitations on computers seems flawed. Further, the arguments based on the human body seem to be answerable. Computers could (it can be argued) simulate the input of the human body to the brain–mind; and, in any event, just because computers have *different* capabilities because of the absence of a body, this does not necessarily make them *inferior* or (more importantly for this book) incapable of supporting conscious mental events.

3.3. In Brain Sciences

I will complete my outline of the consensus by looking in turn at contemporary views on the mind–matter problem in biology (especially neurophysiology and microbiology) and psychology.

3.3.1. *Biology*

A notable recent exposition of the consensus from the point of view of a neurophysiologist is Jean-Pierre Changeux's best-selling book *Neuronal Man* (Changeux 1986). This book gives a wide-ranging account of the brain, its components, the details of its operation, its functions, its development, its origins.

At the end of an examination of the operation of nerve-cells of the brain (or neurons) in relation to various aspects of behaviour, the author concludes:

The data obtained so far, although fragmentary, are sufficient for us to safely conclude that all behaviour, all sensation, is explicable by an *internal mobilization* of a topographically defined set of nerve cells . . . All these observations and reflections lead not only to an explanation of the internal mechanisms of behavior but to the adoption of a deterministic point of view . . . The anatomical and chemical organization of this machine is fantastically complicated, but the simple fact that it can be broken down into neuronal cogwheels whose movements can be recorded justifies the outspoken theories of the eighteenth-century mechanists [including, presumably, Laplace]. (pp. 124–6)

In the last chapter (pp. 275–7), Changeux again expresses views which accord with the dual aspect, functionalist approach outlined above. There are, however, suggestions in the Preface to the 1986 Oxford edition of the book that Changeux is not completely happy either with any analogy with serial computers, or with functionalist theories, which make mental properties independent of their physical realization:

The traditionally hierarchical and computational (or digital) views about the functioning of computers have been improved upon or, quite simply, replaced by models where the massive parallelism of the input and the analogical character of the representations predominate. In psychology also functionalist theories—whose purpose is to explain the psyche in terms of (if not reduce it to) formal operations which are independent of their neuronal substrata—are tending to break the spell of their platonic seduction, and attempts at synthesis between psychology and the neurosciences are appearing more and more fruitful. (p. xiv)

The views hinted at here may be likened to those of psychologist Philip Johnson-Laird that consciousness is a property of a class of *parallel* computational procedures; and that while the same *results* of computation could also be obtained from *serial* computational procedures, the latter procedures cannot give rise to consciousness (Johnson-Laird 1987: 257, 1988: 366–7).

These matters, however, I see as details within the broad dual aspect, mechanistic approach of the consensus. Consensus views are also expressed by neurophysiologists Steven Rose, Colin Blakemore, and J. Z. Young (see Rose 1976; Blakemore 1977, 1985, 1988; Young 1985, 1987).

There are a minority of opposing views. I have already mentioned Sir John Eccles. Earlier, the pioneering neurophysiologist Sir Charles Sherrington, in his 1937–8 Gifford Lectures, called the interaction between body and mind 'theoretically impossible', but preferred to think that it does happen (Sherrington 1951: 248). The split-brain researcher Roger Sperry has sometimes been cited as an opponent of mechanism, and he does express support for mind–brain interactionist views. However, in expounding his position (for example, in Sperry 1983), he expresses views which are consistent with the consensus:

The mental entities transcend the physiological just as the physiological transcend the molecular, the molecular the atomic and the subatomic, etc. . . . I have used the example of how a wheel rolling downhill carries its atoms and molecules through a course in time and space and to a fate determined by the overall system properties of the wheel as a whole and regardless of the inclination of the individual atoms and molecules. The atoms and molecules are caught up and overpowered by the higher properties of the whole. One can compare the rolling wheel to an ongoing brain process or a progressing train of thought in which the overall properties of the brain process, as a coherent organizational entity, determine the timing and spacing of the firing patterns within its neuronal infrastructure. (pp. 92–4)

This may be compared to Young (1985):

That we have conscious minds seems to me to be indisputable, but mind is an aspect of the functioning of the brain, not something that can exist apart from the brain . . . As very rough analogies we might say that mind is a property of the brain as rotation is a property of a wheel, or calculation of a computer. (p. 2)

Turning to microbiology, although this subject is not so directly concerned with the actual operation of the brain, one finds the consensus view of the mind–matter question reflected in works such as *Chance and Necessity* by Nobel Laureate Jacques Monod (Monod 1977). The consensus approach is also reflected in the view of living things, including human beings, as survival machines for genes, presented by biologist Richard Dawkins in *The Selfish Gene*. As he puts it in a later essay:

Our bodies, then, are machines for propagating the genes that made them; our brains are the on-board computers of our bodies; and our behaviour is the output of our on-board computers. (Rose and Appignanesi 1986: 66)

Again, among microbiologists one can find a minority of somewhat opposing views. One notable microbiologist whom I am inclined to regard as a dissenter is another Nobel Laureate, Max Delbrück, in his book *Mind from Matter?* (Delbrück 1986), based on his contribution to the Thirteenth Nobel Conference. Although he, like Dawkins and Monod, regards mind as 'a product of adaptation in response to selection pressures, as is anything else in biology' (Delbrück 1978: 164), he seems to reject a thoroughgoing reductionist, mechanistic view. In Delbrück (1986) he writes:

To summarize, the Cartesian cut between observer and observed, between inner and external reality, between mind and body, is based on the illusion that the physical world has no subjective component. This illusion arises from the high degree of quantitative reliability of scientific statements about the outer, physical world. Their quantitative reliability makes us forget that these statements are as related to subjective experiences as statements about the inner, mental world. (p. 249)

This could be interpreted as suggesting panpsychism, or idealism. However, in the introduction to Delbrück (1986: 13–16), Gunther Stent suggests, correctly I think, that the author is adopting a view similar to Bohr's principle of complementarity. There is a 'conspiracy of nature' which prevents us observing reality at its deepest level without disturbing it; observer and observed are inseparable; in any observation, the place at which the line is drawn between observer and observed is a subjective choice by the observer; and so *any* single perspective is necessarily incomplete and distorted.

3.3.2. *Psychology*

In the field of psychology, there seems little significant dissent from the consensus. As stated earlier, there is no longer wide acceptance of the outright behaviourist doctrines of Watson and Skinner; but actual psychological work seems to proceed on an assumption of determinism. In so far as attention is paid to mind–matter questions, much stress is placed on the computer analogy.

One of the leading movements in psychology today, cognitive psychology, approaches the mind as an information-processing mechanism. As explained in Churchland (1984), its aim

is to account for the various activities that constitute intelligence—perception, memory, inference, deliberation, learning, language use, motor control, and so on—by postulating a system of internal states governed by a system of computational procedures, or an interactive set of such systems governed by a set of such procedures. (p. 92)

(See generally Gardner 1987.) There is a close connection between cognitive psychology and artificial intelligence, although it is not a necessary aspect of artificial intelligence, as it is of cognitive psychology, that the actual processes used by the human brain are studied or simulated.

The approach of cognitive psychology has been applied with considerable success, for example to preconscious processes in visual perception, by psychologists such as the late David Marr. Towards the end of his book *Vision* (Marr 1982) he notes in relation to information-processing problems that can be solved well, using the approach of cognitive psychology: 'The most fruitful source of such problems is operations that we perform well, fluently, and hence unconsciously, since it is difficult to see how reliability could be achieved if there was no sound underlying method' (p. 347). However, he recognizes that the approach has greater problems in relation to conscious mental processes:

Unfortunately, problem-solving research has for obvious reasons tended to concentrate on problems that we understand well intellectually but perform poorly on, like mental arithmetic . . . or the game of chess . . . I have no doubt that when we are doing mental arithmetic we do something well, but it is not arithmetic, and we seem far from understanding even one component of what that something is. (pp. 347–8)

Despite such reservations, it seems a general view among psychologists that the information-processing model solves the mind–matter problem. Not untypical are the views of Morton Hunt in *The Universe Within*:

The mind–body problem, on the other hand, is one that information-processing theory does answer. What has seemed to philosophers to be mind—a different sort of stuff from the brain—is not a separate stuff at all, but a series of processes of immense complexity, the integration of millions or billions of neural events. We call some of these macroevents 'ideas', but they are actually *sets of physical microevents*—concatenations of impulses, coded and processed and stored in memory. A computer has no soul but only tangible parts, yet by means of its programs, it can simulate certain aspects of human thought. So, too, with our mind: it is not something apart from the brain, but it is the brain's programs, the brain's total set of symbol manipulations . . . Those mental processes we call thoughts or, more broadly, mind, are thus *epiphenomena*—secondary or collective effects of the brain's biological processes, much as a flame is the composite effect of trillions of chemical microevents occurring at the molecular level. (Hunt 1984: 62–3)

The use of the word 'epiphenomena' may be questioned, as Hunt appears to recognize that thoughts have a causal role, at the appropriate level of description; and indeed (perhaps inconsistently) seems to leave open the possibility of a causal role for consciousness and willing (pp. 337–44). But, in general, this seems a typical consensus approach.

To my mind, some of the best and most persuasive expressions of the consensus from a psychologist are to be found in the writings of psychologist–philosopher Margaret Boden, particularly in *Purposive Explanation in Philosophy* (1972) and *Artificial Intelligence and Natural Man* (1977). Her approach can be seen in Boden (1972: 317–21) and also, most illuminatingly, with reference to artificial intelligence, in Boden (1977: 397–432):

one must be 'antireductionist' in allowing that intentionality is an essential feature of psychological reality, one that could *not* be expressed by a theoretical vocabulary lacking the subject–object distinction. For one of the important senses of 'reductionism' in psychology is the (mistaken) view that psychological descriptions and explanations are mere shorthand for complicated sets of nonpsychological statements about the brain, so that psychological statements could be translated into physiological ones without loss of meaning.

The other sense of 'reductionism' that is relevant here is the view that subjective psychological phenomena are totally dependent on cerebral mechanisms, much as the information-processing functions of a program are grounded in the engineering details of the computer on which it is being run. (Boden 1977: 427–8)

Boden advocates reductionism in the latter sense. Her assertion of total dependence of purposive (and, by implication, other mental) phenomena on causal, neurophysiological mechanisms, coupled with an insistence that accounts or explanations of behaviour in terms of purposive mental phenomena cannot be wholly reduced to mechanistic physical terms, has affinities with the functionalist approach of philosophers like Putnam.

Boden goes on to assert that 'the crucial notion in understanding how subjectivity can be grounded in objective causal mechanism is the concept of an internal model or representation'. Boden continues:

It is possible for the categories of subjectivity to be properly attributed to human beings because bodily processes in our brains function as models, or representations, of the world—and of hypothetical worlds—for the individual concerned. . . . To identify or describe the neural processes concerned *as* models is itself to ascribe meaning, or intentionality, to them. They could alternatively be described, at least in principle, at the level of 'objective' physiological events . . . At this level, however, the meaning cannot be expressed and so their (psychological) function in the life of the individual is lost to view . . . (1977: 428–9)

Boden's writing is very persuasive of the inadequacy of behaviourism on the one hand, and of the adequacy of a fundamental mechanistic view on the other; and fits well with much work on artificial intelligence.

3.4. The Impact of Quantum Physics

The view which I have called the consensus is plausible, particularly as expounded by writers such as Dennett, Changeux, Boden, and Hofstadter. It is associated with what is said to be the scientific approach to causation and determinism; with a reductionist viewpoint; with the elimination of mysterious entities (witches, ghosts, now minds); and with an empirical, tough-minded approach. Contrary views are said to be unscientific and tender-minded. However, there is a contrary trend in science itself. The so-called 'new physics', and in particular quantum physics, is associated with ideas opposed to those previously considered scientific, supporting in particular: indeterminism rather than determinism; holism rather than reductionism; the existence of a mysterious underlying reality; and indications that consciousness is important in physical processes.

I will sketch some respects in which quantum physics may tend to undermine what is considered the scientific approach to the brain–mind problem (this is only a brief outline: I consider quantum physics in more detail in Part III); and then I will outline why in my view these considerations have as yet had little impact on the consensus.

3.4.1. *Aspects of Quantum Physics*

1. Indeterminism. It is well known that quantum physics asserts that, on the micro scale of atoms and smaller entities, it is not generally possible to predict individual events with certainty: as regards events on that scale, quantum physics can generally give only probabilities. Of course, this does not involve general inconsistency with accurate predictions of events on the macro scale, since such events generally involve huge numbers of events on the micro scale, combined in such a way that uncertainties cancel out, and probabilities on the micro scale become virtual certainties on the macro scale.

The fact remains, however, that indeterminacy of predictions on the micro scale *can* produce similar indeterminacy on the macro scale. Indeed, when any measurement of an individual micro event is made, this is precisely what happens: the technique of making such a measurement involves producing a macro effect from the individual micro event; so that it is possible, on the macro scale, to distinguish between the occurrence of the individual micro event from its non-occurrence. Accordingly the macro event which represents the result of the measurement (such as the click of a Geiger counter) is unpredictable to the same extent as is the corresponding micro event (such as an individual emission due to radioactive decay). The projection of indeterminacies on the micro scale into the macro scale can occur naturally as well. For example, it has been shown that a cell on the retina of the human eye can respond detectably to a single photon of light (see Schnapf and Baylor 1987).

2. Uncertainty. Quantum physics involves not only indeterminism in relation to predictions of the future, but also uncertainty or indeterminacy in relation to existing states. Heisenberg's celebrated uncertainty principle asserts that a micro entity cannot at the same time have a precise position and a precise motion (or momentum). This principle is sometimes presented as if it followed simply as a practical matter from the process of measurement, from the disturbance necessarily caused to micro entities by the interaction necessary for measurement: however, in fact it follows from a precise mathematical relationship, which in turn follows as a matter of necessity from the mathematics of quantum theory itself. In other words, the mathematics of quantum theory entails the uncertainty principle; while the practical considerations associated with the process of measurement 'protect' the theory, by preventing disproof of it by way of achieving measured results conflicting with the theory's mathematics.

3. Complementarity. Associated with the uncertainty principle is the principle of complementarity attributed to Niels Bohr. At one level, this views micro entities as having dual natures, as being both particles and waves. As particles, they may have precise position, but not precise motion or momentum; as waves, they may have precise momentum, but not precise position. Experimental arrangements for precise measurement of one aspect (say, position) preclude those for precise measurement of the other aspect (momentum), so no incompatibility can arise in practice.

This view of micro entities as having dual natures suggested to Bohr an analogy applicable to the brain–mind, namely that when the brain–mind was observed and tested as a physical object in which physical processes occur, manifestation of its aspect as a conscious mind would be precluded by such observations and tests (see Bohr 1958: 92–3). Thus, the brain–mind may have two apparently contradictory aspects (as a mechanistic physical object and as a freewilling mind) which cannot simultaneously be displayed, so that no incompatibility can arise in practice.

More generally, what is sometimes called Bohr's philosophy of complementarity suggests that, in areas where our concepts are inadequate, it may be necessary to use two modes of description of an entity which are mutually exclusive, yet involve no practical inconsistency in that the conditions under which the entity is manifested under one description preclude the possibility of its manifestation under the other description. This may be applied to the brain–mind in the way outlined; and also in a more general or abstract way in relation to the human self or subject as both actor and observer (along the lines mentioned earlier in relation to Delbrück and Nagel; see Bohr 1961: 96, 119).

4. Holism. As we shall see in greater detail in Part III, quantum theory also implies that the behaviour of composite systems is not always a function of, or calculable from, or caused by, the behaviour of the component parts of that system which can themselves be understood in isolation from the whole system: in at least certain situations, where micro events are measured, the behaviour of component parts of a composite system is rather a function of behaviour of the whole system. This is perhaps most clearly illustrated by the Aspect experiments concerning the Bell inequality, which I deal with in Chapter 15.

5. The role of consciousness. As we shall see, quantum physics assigns an important role to the observer. One particular suggestion that consciousness has a causative role in the physical world arises in this way. Where a measurement of a micro system is made which is appropriate to distinguish between results which are possible but not certain, only one of the possible results will be measured. However, until the measurement is made, all the possible results remain possible: so the question arises, at what stage in a process of measurement can it be said that the measurement is actually made, so that a particular result becomes actual and the other possibilities are eliminated? This question is significant, because the theory as generally understood indicates that the existence of a range of possibilities prior to measurement is not due to incomplete knowledge of the system, but is an objective property of the system itself; and, similarly, after measurement the actuality of one result and the elimination of the others is also an objective property of the system. So it is meaningful and important to ask, when does this change (which is sometimes called 'the collapse of the wave function') occur. One important suggestion (advocated by distinguished physicists such as Eugene Wigner) is that it only occurs when the person making the measurement actually becomes conscious of the result. I will argue in Chapter 14 that this suggestion faces difficulties, at least if taken literally in this form. However, the considerations underlying it are relevant to a rejection of mechanism; and it is significant that distinguished physicists, who are researching directly the very physical matter whose behaviour is supposed to explain mind, have found it necessary to invoke mind to explain the behaviour of that physical matter.

3.4.2. *Quantum Physicists and the Brain–Mind*

I have already referred to two ways in which some physicists have related quantum physics to the mind: Bohr's analogy based on his principle of complementarity, and the Wigner view on the role of consciousness in measurement. In fact, many physicists with an interest in philosophy have considered quantum physics as relevant to mind.

1. Quantum indeterminism and freedom of the will. It was noted by Eddington as early as 1927 that the indeterminism provided by quantum physics left room for the operation of freedom of the will (see Eddington 1929, ch. 14). In more recent writings by physicists and mathematicians such as Richard Schlegel, Henry Margenau, Henry Stapp, and Roger Penrose, the notion of quantum indeterminacy leaving room for the operation of rational choice is revived and advocated (see Schlegel 1980: 262–89; LeShan and Margenau 1982: 240–3; Stapp 1985; Penrose 1987, 1989).

2. Heisenberg and d'Espagnat. Views somewhat similar to those of Bohr have also been expressed by another of the great pioneers of quantum mechanics, Werner Heisenberg. For example, in Heisenberg (1989), he notes that during the nineteenth century, 'some scientists were inclined to think that the psychological phenomena could ultimately be explained on the basis of physics and chemistry of the brain' (p. 94); and goes on to assert: 'From the quantum-theoretical point of view, there is no reason for such an assumption.' He continues:

We would never doubt that the brain acts as a physico-chemical mechanism if treated as such; but for an understanding of psychic phenomena we would start from the fact that the human mind enters as object and subject into the scientific process of psychology.

A more recent expression of a similar view is by the physicist Bernard d'Espagnat. He presents a view of the world of observed macroscopic objects (presumably including brains and brain-cells) as a construct by human minds from regularities in observed phenomena; while the existence of such regularities is explained by a 'far' and 'non-physical' reality, the 'elements' of which can be related 'neither to notions borrowed from everyday life . . . nor to localized mathematical entities' (d'Espagnat 1983: 157–67).

3. Schrödinger's view of mind. Another pioneer of quantum mechanics, Erwin Schrödinger, did not accept that freedom of the will could be explained as operating within the leeways allowed by quantum indeterminism. However, in *Mind and Matter* (Schrödinger 1967) he argued eloquently for a view which gives central importance to the conscious observer. As I understand it, his view of mind involved *inter alia* the following: the meaninglessness and futility of events unless observed by conscious beings; the lack of any pre-existing division between the observer and the observed; the distortions necessarily resulting in the scientific view of the world by reason of its

artificial separation of the observer from the observed; the retention of freedom of the will by considering the observed world as being in substance a creature of the observer. I find this last view difficult to understand or to accept, but Schrödinger's work does illustrate further the variety of philosophical views arising out of quantum physics.

3.4.3. *Influence of Quantum Physics on the Consensus*

Quantum physics has had little impact on the consensus. When it is not ignored by philosophers, or computer or brain scientists, it is generally dismissed by assertions which: (1) assume that its only relevance concerns the indeterminism of predictions of micro events; (2) assert that such indeterminism does not have any relevant effects at the macro scale of cells of the brain, and is therefore irrelevant; and (3) further assert that, if any effects of indeterminism did occur at such level, they would only hinder the rational operation of the brain–mind, being in principle unpredictable and random.

Quantum theory received its initial substantial formulations over sixty years ago. If it *is* relevant to mind, the question arises: why has such relevance had little careful consideration by philosophers of mind, computer scientists, and brain scientists? It seems to me that there may be at least three factors involved: first, it may be that the principles of quantum physics are not widely or well understood by workers in those other disciplines; secondly, there are deep disagreements among physicists themselves as to the implications of quantum physics; and thirdly, there are other aspects of the new physics which may tend against any view of mind or mental events as having independent causal efficacy.

As to the first factor, there is little to say, except to point to the lack of detailed and careful consideration of quantum physics in the relevant work of philosophers of mind, computer scientists, and brain scientists; although, in recent times, philosophers have written in depth on the general philosophy of quantum physics, (see, for example, Krips 1987; Gibbins 1987; Redhead 1987). In Part III, I give an account of quantum theory which I hope is accessible and at the same time sufficient for the purpose of understanding some of its implications for the nature of mind.

As to the second, I will consider in Chapter 14 the disagreements about quantum physics itself and about some of its general implications.

As to the third, I will consider in Chapter 18 what seems to me the most important strand arising from recent physics which tends against the causal efficacy of mind, namely the denial of the passage of time.

In addition, there are some significant arguments concerning quantum physics which have been put by consensus writers. They can be considered under three headings: the scale of brain functions, their statistical character, and the role of randomness.

1. The scale of brain functions. I have already mentioned the contention that since brain-cells are macro objects, and their firings are macro events, quantum indeterminacies are irrelevant to their operation. I have also mentioned a possible answer, to the effect that indeterminism at the micro scale can be magnified so as to create indeterminism at the macro scale. However, it is put with some plausibility by physicist Paul Davies that this would only impair the functioning of the brain:

the idea that mind finds its expression in the world by courtesy of the quantum uncertainty principle is not really taken very seriously, not least because the electrical activity of the brain seems to be more robust than that. After all, if brain cells operate at the quantum level, the entire network is vulnerable to random maverick quantum fluctuations by any one of myriads of electrons. (Davies and Brown 1986: 33)

2. The statistical character of brain functions. It is sometimes contended that, in addition to each brain-cell being a macro object and each neural firing a macro event, human behaviour is a function of even grosser matters, namely the statistics of firings of large numbers of neurons, and, accordingly, that the possibility of quantum indeterminacies being important is all the more remote. One source of this view is von Neumann's monograph *The Computer and the Brain* (1958), in which the author argues (pp. 79–82) that the language or code used by the brain must depend on statistical properties of neural firings, rather than on individual events, giving it less depth and precision but greater reliability than it otherwise would have.

Along similar lines, we find in Boden (1972) the following:

Recent neurophysiological research suggests that the response of individual nerve cells to stimulation is stochastic, or indeterminate, in that it requires statistical analysis in terms of probability of firing. Any meaningful statement of the relation between an individual neural response and a particular stimulus is thus impossible. This indeterminacy rests on spontaneous random activity at the synapses . . . Synaptic activity may or may not involve indeterminacy at the quantal level. Even if it does, the 'unpredictability' of human behaviour . . . would not thereby be vindicated. Indeed . . . a radical indeterminism at the origin of action would be incompatible with human freedom and responsibility, rather than essential to it . . . (p. 333)

Boden here combines the point about the statistical character of brain functions with the point about randomness being inimical to human responsibility. However, what she says about the former point does suggest that it may be damaging to the first argument which I considered, rather than cumulative with it. Indeed Boden asserts that neural firings *are* affected by 'random' activity at the synapses, of such a character that it *could* be affected by quantum indeterminacy. The 'robustness' asserted by Davies is achieved (according to Boden) *not* by any immunity of neurons to affection by quantum fluctuations, but rather by the statistical character of neural activity (which, by implication, substantially cancels out such fluctuations).

3. The role of randomness. Boden and others simply contend that randomness is inimical to human responsibility. Dennett suggests a way in which randomness could play a part, even a useful part, in human decision-making. In Dennett (1978: 286 ff.) he suggests that quantum indeterminacy could in a random manner produce considerations, some of which the agent could reject as irrelevant, and the others of which could then function in a (deterministic) reasoning process. This approach is further considered in Dennett (1984: 77n., 119 ff.) to the effect that although there could be advantages (in an evolutionary sense) in having a mechanism for random generation of considerations, such advantages are no greater for 'genuine' random processes (based, for example, on quantum indeterminacies) than for pseudo-random (mechanistic) processes (which could, for example, be provided by programs of the type available for use in today's computers). Dennett's suggested role for randomness has some affinities with the thesis of Kane (1985), but it is not that usually suggested by those persons who regard quantum indeterminacy as important in relation to human freedom: such persons usually suggest, rather, that what is random from the physical point of view may be chosen from the mental point of view; and this is the approach which I pursue.

So: the consensus view is that, notwithstanding quantum physics, the physical states and events of a brain immediately after a conscious decision is made can in principle be given a correct and maximal explanation in terms of the physical states and events of the brain immediately before such decision, and in terms of the operation of physical laws. This explanation may not be complete, because at the micro level physical laws give only probabilities. However, at the macro level these probabilities produce near-certainties; and, in so far as they do not, what occurs is a matter of pure chance. Certainly, reference to the conscious decision could not complete the explanation, in so far as it is incomplete.

This view would allow that an explanation of the action can be given in terms of the person's decision and his or her reasons for it, and that this may be the most useful explanation; and consensus writers such as Putnam and Boden contend that this explanation is not contained within, and is not reducible to, the physical explanation. However, the consensus view denies that the intentional explanation could ever explain the occurrence of one, rather than any other, of any alternatives which might, because of quantum indeterminacies, be left open by the physical explanation.

II

Against Mechanism

IT is my view that the dominance of the mechanist consensus is unfortunate. Its advocates assert that it does not devalue humankind; that human beings are no less marvellous if all their workings comprise no more than physical events in the body and brain (the complete works of Shakespeare are after all 'only' words); and that the circumstance that mechanistic human beings may be on the verge of making similar machines, which operate just as the human brain–mind does, makes human beings (if anything) all the more marvellous. Furthermore, if the consensus view is true then it must be best to recognize this: to cling to a false myth could only be harmful.

However, my contention is that the consensus view is false. I suggest that the prevalence of a mechanistic view of human beings contributes to an intellectual climate in which materialistic values flourish. I do not contend that such a view has caused the widespread loss of spiritual values in Western countries, and I do not argue in favour of acceptance of any particular religious faith. Rather, I say that the mechanistic view of human beings is inconsistent, or at least sits very uneasily, with both religious faith and respect for moral values; whereas the view of human beings which I advocate (as being capable of choosing in accordance with reasons in ways not causally pre-determined) is more conducive to an intellectual climate in which moral and spiritual values can flourish.

All this is a manifesto rather than an argument: the argument of this book is simply against the truth of the mechanistic view.

So, in this part, I set out arguments against mechanism, and for the view that mental events do have an independent causal role. Many of these arguments overlap and are interdependent, and to some extent might be considered as stating at some length and in various ways one basic argument: the human brain–mind uses rational procedures which go beyond and are not reducible to logic or other formal reasoning; which are consciousness-dependent; and which must (with consciousness) have been selected by evolution. However, although this is the central theme, there are variations, and some arguments with independent force.

4

More and Different Information

IF the brain–mind operates mechanistically, then in principle its operations can be fully expressed as a series of algorithms or effective procedures, and in principle they can be fully carried out or simulated by a computer. It is sometimes asserted that computers with consciousness may be developed, or even that they exist now; but, whether or not this is so, it is clear that existing computers operate by performing series of algorithms. And the carrying out of algorithms does not require consciousness: it is of the essence of algorithms that they can be performed mechanically and without consciousness. So: the operation of computers as presently understood does not require consciousness; consciousness is not 'designed into' any computer; and it seems probable, therefore, that computers are not conscious. Accordingly, one step towards showing that the human brain–mind does not operate mechanistically is to show that it operates differently from a non-conscious computer. And the first respect in which I contend that the human brain–mind operates differently from a non-conscious computer is that it has information or knowledge which such a computer could not have: namely, that information or knowledge which requires consciousness.

I am not at this stage asserting that the human brain–mind uses this information in any relevant sense. Just as consciousness itself (or mental events) may be either causally irrelevant, or else merely another level of description of non-conscious reality (or physical events), it may be similarly with consciousness-dependent information. However, the fact remains that the human brain–mind has this information, whereas a non-conscious computer cannot have it.

4.1. Consciousness-Dependent Information

There is certain information which can only be known by or conveyed to a conscious being or entity: such information can be encoded, and can be transmitted in a coded form; and codes for such information can be conveyed to, processed by, and (in some sense at least) 'known by' non-conscious computers. However, codes for such information are not the same as the information itself: for an entity to have the information itself, there needs to be a 'decoding' by the brain–mind (or some equivalent) of a conscious being.

What is this information? It is just the content of consciousness in its various forms, the experience and/or volition aspect of mental events. I will consider some examples.

4.1.1. *Sense Perception*

Only a conscious being or entity can have the information or knowledge what something actually looks like, what something sounds like, what something tastes or smells like, what pain feels like.

1. Colours. The point is clearly made with reference to colours. No description of the colour blue can convey, to a man blind from birth, the information *what the colour blue looks like*. Such a man could be given any amount of descriptions of the colour blue. He could know any number of true statements about the colour blue; about blue things and their properties; about the wavelengths and energies and properties of blue light; about all words which relate to the colour blue and blue things; about all associations which the colour blue, the word 'blue', and blue things, may call up for human beings; and so on. He could, perhaps by analogy with musical sounds, have considerable theoretical understanding of what it is like to see colour, and of the aesthetic significance and effects of colour. All this knowledge and understanding could be well integrated into his general knowledge and understanding of the world.

There are instruments which can convey to a blind person information about the shapes of objects by means of sensations of touch imparted by means of a grid attached to his back. Such an instrument could no doubt detect blue light by its energy or wavelength, and could provide tactile information concerning the colour of the objects thus 'seen'; so that our blind man could reliably recognize blue things. He could certainly cause a screen to display the colour blue. Conceivably, such a man could pass a Turing test conversation about the colour blue: that is, he could possibly avoid being found out to be blind rather than sighted. He could be considered as 'having the concept' blue, and in a sense as knowing 'all there is to know' about it.

However, I suggest, unless somehow a sensation of blue occurred in his brain–mind, he would not know, or have the information, 'what the colour blue looks like'.

The same can be said about a non-conscious computer; *a fortiori* because such a computer lacks not just visual consciousness, but any consciousness whatever. Such a computer could have, in coded form, any amount of information about the colour blue, blue things, and so on. It could process such information, and relate it to any other information which the computer has. It could 'recognize' blue things. It could display the colour blue on an output screen. But again, unless it had some kind of visual consciousness, it *could not* have the information 'what the colour blue looks like'.

On the other hand, a normally sighted person does have this information, certainly (for example) when actually looking at a cloudless daytime sky. I would suggest that he or she has it at other times as well, through an ability to recall and imagine the appearance of the colour; but this is not necessary for my argument here.

2. Other visual matters. Although the point is most obvious in relation to secondary qualities such as colour, the same point can be made about the appearance of shapes, and about the overall appearance of objects.

A computer can have information which encodes all the features of a square or a circle which are relevant to its appearance: but this is not the same as the computer having the information 'what a square (or circle) looks like'. In relation to shapes, a man blind from birth could to some extent have this information, since he could feel shapes with his hands, and could relate described shapes to how they would feel, and could thereby build some sort of 'picture' of the shapes. No doubt, he could form some such picture with the aid of the instrument referred to earlier, giving tactile information on his back. But a non-conscious computer could not do this, having no conscious sense information at all upon which to base any sort of picture.

The overall appearance of things is largely built up of colours and shapes; and so similar arguments apply as apply to colours and to shapes. Indeed a non-conscious computer would not even have the information what *appearance* is (and, for example, how it differs from sound) except in terms of being associated with light (instead of pressure waves) and in terms of the sort of information it can convey, and in terms of *statements about* appearance: it would not have the immediate information about this that a sighted person has.

3. Sounds, tastes, smells. A non-conscious computer could have in coded form, and could process in various ways, all sorts of information about (say) what a violin sounds like. It could no doubt identify the sound of a violin. However, it could not have the information 'what a violin sounds like': to have that information, it would have to be conscious, and to be able (or have been able) to hear. As with colours, sounds are not the same as codes for sounds. And the same can be said for tastes (such as the taste of strawberries) and smells (such as the aroma of coffee).

4. Pain. Only a conscious being or entity can know, or have the information, 'what pain feels like'. A non-conscious computer could have (in code) every conceivable description of pain, and every conceivable true statement about pain; and could have (in code) instructions for appropriate reactions to events associated with various (coded) descriptions of pain. But it could not know how pain feels. Dennett perhaps suggests the contrary in his article 'Why you can't Make a Computer that Feels Pain' (in Dennett 1978: 190 ff.), but this suggestion has plausibility only in so far as it is assumed that a computer could instantiate what he calls 'a good physiological sub-personal

theory of pain', *and* that such a computer would then actually feel pain, that is, would be conscious.

4.1.2. *Emotions and Volitions*

Similarly, only a conscious being or entity can know, or have the information, what fear, desire, elation, etc. actually feel like; or what it feels like to *do* something. It is not possible to convey this information to a non-conscious computer: it can have any number of descriptions of and true statements about such matters, but not knowledge of how emotions or volitions actually feel.

4.1.3. *Thought*

Only a conscious entity could know what it feels (or is) like to think. And, in so far as thinking involves understanding the meanings of words and senten-ces, this in turn depends upon information of the kind referred to in Sections 4.1.1 and 4.1.2; so that such meanings cannot be understood by a non-conscious computer. Such a computer could have (in code) all conceivable statements of what words can be substituted for a particular word, of how that particular word can be used in statements, and giving answers to all conceiv-able questions about that word. But the meaning of the word 'blue' or the word 'music' is obviously more than this; and I contend that the meaning of the word 'square' is more than this. As I have suggested, a person who has been blind from birth may be given some idea about what colours are, per-haps by analogy with sound; and a person who has been deaf from birth may be given some idea of what music is, by analogy with patterns of colour. However, a computer without any conscious sense experience at all could not have such information.

4.1.4. *The Churchland Contention*

It has been contended (separately) by philosophers Paul Churchland and Patricia Churchland that knowledge of the appearance of colours does not involve any different information from that which a computer could have, but involves only a different form of the same information. Paul Churchland puts it this way:

The difference between a person who knows all about the visual cortex but has never enjoyed the sensation-of-red, and a person who knows no neuroscience but knows well the sensation-of-red, may not reside in *what* is respectively known by each (brain states by the former, nonphysical *qualia* by the latter), but rather in the different *type*, or *medium*, or *level* of representation each has of exactly the same thing: brain states. . . . *the brain uses more modes and media of representation than the mere storage of sentences*. All the identity theorist needs to claim is that those other modes of representation will also yield to neuroscientific explanation. (Churchland 1984: 34)

In similar vein, in Churchland (1986: 323–34), Patricia Churchland deals with a contention of Frank Jackson. In Jackson (1982), an example is given of a neuroscientist ('Mary') who is raised from birth in a wholly white, grey, and black environment, and is *never* exposed to any other colour. Jackson contends that even if Mary through her scientific studies comes to know everything there is to know about the brain and its visual system, there will be something which she does not know: what it is like to see red. Patricia Churchland argues that one can 'know about' things in at least two different ways: by ability to manipulate the relevant concepts, and by pre-linguistic apprehension. She continues: 'if there are two (at least) modes of knowing about the world, then it is entirely possible that what one knows about via one method is identical to what one knows about via a different method' (p. 332).

Churchland also argues against Jackson's contention that Mary could not know what it is like to see red: 'whether or not she can recognize redness is clearly an empirical question, and I do not see how in our ignorance we can confidently insist that she must fail . . . she might even be able to produce red in her imagination if she knows what brain states are relevant' (p. 333). These last points (similar to an observation in Wittgenstein 1974: 104e) do not contradict my argument here. I fully accept that non-conscious computers (and blind human beings) may have equipment which enables them to *recognize* (in the sense of *identify*) redness. And I do not question that conscious beings could induce in themselves, or have induced, sensations which they have not previously experienced: I accept that even blind persons could experience sensations of colour if appropriate brain events somehow occurred.

However, the other point made by both Churchlands *is* relevant, and I dispute it. I contend that 'what red looks like' is, obviously, different information from that constituted by physical brain events, or indeed by any non-sensory code. To suggest that it is only a different 'mode' of knowing something is (to put it at its lowest) to leave open whether differences in modes of knowing are significant. Even if it is 'only' a different mode of knowing, this *is* a difference. Whether or not this difference involves any difference in *function* between brains and computers is another matter, which I take up in later chapters: but the difference itself is undeniable.

Paul Churchland might respond with another argument (one which he uses to oppose the 'argument from introspection' against his identity theory): his argument which suggests that sense information is just an inadequate and perhaps misleading version or summary of much fuller and more accurate information, which itself can be fully encoded. In Churchland (1984), he writes:

the argument is deeply suspect, in that it assumes that our faculty of inner observation or introspection reveals things as they really are in their innermost nature. This

assumption is suspect because we already know that our other forms of observation—
sight, hearing, touch, and so on—do no such thing. The red surface of an apple does
not *look* like a matrix of molecules reflecting photons at certain critical wavelengths,
but that is what it is . . . If one's pains and hopes and beliefs do not *introspectively*
seem like electrochemical states in a neural network, that may only be because our
faculty of introspection, like our other senses, is not sufficiently penetrating to reveal
such hidden details. (p. 15)

This approach, however, cannot justify the reduction of the mental to the
physical, or the reduction of sensations to being mere approximations to more
complete objective information. As pointed out in Swinburne (1986: 191), the
very success of science in 'reducing' colour to critical wavelengths of electromagnetic radiation, and in 'reducing' heat to the random motion of molecules,
was achieved by distinguishing between the underlying causes of phenomena,
and the sensations which they bring about in observers: by 'separating off the
phenomenal from its causes, and only explaining the latter'. Swinburne points
out that reduction by the device of denying that apparent properties, such as
colour, heat, etc., belong to the physical world, cannot be applied to the
sensations themselves. It may be accepted that our sensation of red does not
reveal the hidden details of the matrix of molecules at the surface of an apple;
but then neither do these 'hidden details', considered objectively as structures
and events, reveal the appearance of red.

Thus, while the red surface of an apple may be 'a matrix of molecules
reflecting photons at certain critical wavelengths', that does not mean that the
sensation of red is nothing more than some pale reflection of, or approximation to, such a matrix. The red appearance of the apple is information different from, and not reducible to, statements about any matrix of molecules
and the wavelengths of the light which they reflect, or any other encoding of
information about such matrix and wavelengths (except in so far as the red
appearance itself can be regarded as such an encoding).

4.1.5. *Human Chauvinism?*

It has been suggested to me that my argument is fallaciously human-centred.
Colours look as they do to humans because of their particular equipment for
colour vision, with different kinds of receptors for three colours (humans are
'trichromats'); whereas some animals have a larger or smaller number of
different kinds of colour receptor. Turtles, I am told, have more; and two
examples of what we see as red could appear as different to a turtle as red and
green appear to us. So it is impossible to say what red *really* looks like.
Furthermore, other entities (and even computers) may have a whole range of
experiences unknown to us: a computer might 'feel' a number such as
0111001001000101 in a way incomprehensible to humans.

This does indeed suggest that 'what the colour red looks like' may have to
be related to the perception of normal human beings: as recognized in Nagel

(1974), other animals may indeed have experiences we cannot know about. But this does not touch my point that we do have information which non-conscious entities cannot have. And, while I cannot prove conclusively that computers are not conscious, the considerations set out at the beginning of this chapter suggest that they are not, and this will be reinforced by later arguments.

4.2. Information and Codes

I do not suggest that the information referred to in Section 4.1 cannot be transformed into code. I do accept that it can be encoded; and in this section I consider further what this involves.

4.2.1. *Encoding Consciousness-Dependent Information*

The question of encoding consciousness-dependent information can be approached in at least two ways. First, one can consider how (for example) visual information is encoded at its source, transmitted to the observer, and decoded in the brain–mind of the observer so that the observer has the visual information. Secondly, one can focus on the relationship between mental events and associated physical events in the brain, treating the latter as in some way encoding the former. Whichever viewpoint is adopted, my contention is that at least some information contained in the content of the relevant experience is not contained in any encoding of it.

1. The transmission of visual information. Information about the visual properties of an object (such as shapes, colours, etc., which I have contended to be real properties of the object-for-us) is encoded in the light which leaves the object, enters the eyes, and is focused so as to form an 'image' on the retinas; it is further encoded in the signals which are sent to the brain; and the brain further processes these signals, resulting in further brain events in which the visual information is encoded. The information is apparently decoded by the brain–mind when the person sees the object: the shapes and colours and other visual features of the object are present in the visual experience. The process can be compared to electromagnetic signals containing coded information, which are received and processed by a television set, and decoded in being displayed on a screen.

However, the parallel is not complete, because the information displayed on the screen is not *known* in any significant sense by the television set, and cannot be used or processed by it: for that information to be used or processed, it must be (for example) either encoded in a language which a computer can use, or else seen by a person as originally outlined. Further, a person's seeing an object cannot be explained by suggesting the creation of a television-like image in the brain, because this image would itself need to be 'seen' in order to complete the process.

2. *Mental events encoded in physical events.* More generally, I accept that all mental events, including those involved in sense perception, emotion, acting, and thinking, have associated brain events which in some sense encode them. I have contended that mental events have two interdependent elements, that is, not merely the content of the relevant experiences and/or volitions, but also the subject which is experiencing or acting. However, it may be accepted that the associated brain events can be considered as encoding the content of the relevant experiences and/or volitions. Furthermore, in so far as the content of experiences and/or volitions is encoded in physical brain events, it may be that this encoding can be conveyed to and 'known' by a non-conscious computer. Just as all visual information can be encoded, transmitted, and processed (as it is in the case of television transmission and reception), so perhaps also the contents of all conscious experiences and/or volitions can be encoded (as indeed they are in physical brain events); and, as so encoded, they can in principle be described in a code which a non-conscious computer can accept and operate with.

3. *Limitations on encoding.* What I am suggesting is that at least some of the information contained in the content of an experience (say, a visual experience) is not contained in any physical encoding of it. It might be thought that, if information is encoded, then surely *all* the information is contained in the coded form. I do not accept this, although different views are possible on what it is for 'information' to be 'contained'.

I contend that in the case of a secret code where decoding can be achieved by application of rules, the encoded information is contained in (no less than) the coded form plus the rules for decoding. Similarly, if decoding can only be performed by a particular instrument such as a television set, the coded form alone (the broadcast signals), in the absence of such an instrument, does not contain the same information as would be displayed by the television set. *A fortiori*, if decoding can be effected only in mental events of a being or entity which is conscious, there may be information in the decoded material (the content of experiences and/or volitions) which is not contained in the coded form constituted by the physical brain events. To return to my original example, what a colour looks like is, plainly, different information from any code: it may be transmitted by code, but unless and until appropriately decoded, this information is not received.

My use of the word 'information' here may be thought to be different from the use of the word in computer science, and in information theory: it may be thought that in these areas no difference is recognized, or even allowed, between different encodings of the 'same' information. However, I suggest that my use is in accordance with ordinary usage, and expresses a significant truth. And in fact there are ideas in information theory and computer science which accord well with my approach. My position can be likened to two broad ideas discussed by computer scientist Joseph Weizenbaum.

First, there is the idea exemplified by the thesis of information theory pioneer Claude Shannon, referred to in Weizenbaum (1984: 209), that 'even in abstract information theory, the "information content" of a message is not a function of the message alone but depends crucially on the state of knowledge, on the expectations, of the receiver'. So, I suggest, if a message is in secret code, its information content is partly a function of the receiver's knowledge of the code; and if a message includes consciousness-dependent information, then its information content is partly a function of the receiver's capacity for conscious awareness.

Secondly, there is the idea, referred to in Weizenbaum (1984: 213), that there is information which perhaps cannot 'be represented in the form of computer programs and data structures at all'. I suggest that the consciousness-based information I have been discussing is just such information.

4. One difference between brains and computers. This discussion points to a significant difference between brains and computers. All information processing by a computer is performed in the computer's code (and, for this purpose, different codes may be equally satisfactory); and decoding by the computer takes place for the purpose of output. It may be that all actual information processing by the human brain is in code; but even if this is so, the fact is that the brain–mind does 'decode' at least some information at a stage between input (through the senses) and output (say, conveying information to others, or behaviour generally), in order that the person has conscious experiences. Because of this internal decoding, the brain–mind has information which (I suggest) is not and cannot be contained in code; and maybe it uses it. In a present-day computer, there is no decoding between input and output: no such internal decoding is designed into such computers, and none is contemplated in the functioning of such computers. If such decoding did take place, the computer simply could not use the decoded material. To suppose that somehow such decoding (and therefore consciousness) just happens in a computer would be, I suggest, baseless superstition.

4.2.2. *Hofstadter on Codes and Meaning*

A subtle and carefully argued contention, contrary to my views here, is to be found in Chapter 6, entitled 'The Location of Meaning', of Hofstadter's *Gödel, Escher, Bach*. This chapter contains a discussion of 'how meaning is split among coded message, decoder, and receiver'. Hofstadter asks 'whether meaning can be considered to be inherent in a message, or whether meaning is always manufactured by the interaction of a mind or a mechanism with a message'; and presents 'a case for the universality of at least some messages'.

Hofstadter refers to the idea that a gramophone record 'contains the same information as a piece of music, because of the existence of record-players, which can "read" records and convert the groove-patterns into sounds' (p. 158). He suggests that it is 'natural . . . to think of the record as an *information-bearer*, and the record-player as an *information-revealer*'; and refers to an impression that decoding mechanisms such as record-players 'simply reveal information which is intrinsically inside the structures' (that is, of information-bearers such as records) 'waiting to be "pulled out" '.

Hofstadter speculates about what would count as a 'successful deciphering' of a gramophone record of Bach's music by an alien civilization:

Evidently, the civilization would have to be able to make sense out of the sounds. Mere production of sounds is in itself hardly worthwhile, unless they have the desired triggering effect in the brains (if that is the word) of the alien creatures. And what is that desired effect? It would be to activate structures in their brains which create emotional effects in them which are analogous to the emotional effects which we experience in hearing the piece. In fact, the production of sounds could even be bypassed, provided that they used the record in some other way to get at the appropriate structures in their brains. (p. 163)

He suggests (p. 166) that a rough classification can be made of three levels of information contained in a coded message:

1. the 'frame message', to understand which 'is to recognize the need for a decoding-mechanism';
2. the 'outer message', to understand which 'is to build, or know how to build, the correct decoding-mechanism'; and
3. the 'inner message', to understand which 'is to have extracted the meaning intended by the sender'.

Hofstadter gives the example of decipherment of ancient texts. If one sees lines of Egyptian hieroglyphics, one recognizes that they contain a message, and that a decoding mechanism or method is needed (and so one understands the 'frame message'). Until the discovery of the Rosetta Stone, no one in modern times knew how to construct such a mechanism or method. Now, there is at least partial knowledge of this 'outer message', so that at least part of the 'inner message' can be extracted.

He discusses the 'idea that before you can understand any message, you have to have a message which tells you how to understand that message', and so on *ad infinitum* (p. 170), and points out that we *do* understand messages, because 'our intelligence is instantiated in physical objects: our brains':

Their structure is due to the long process of evolution, and their operations are governed by the laws of physics. Since they are physical entities, *our brains run without being told how to run* . . . brains come equipped with 'hardware' for recognizing that certain things are messages, and for decoding those messages.

Hofstadter likens this brain hardware (in relation to verbal messages) to juke-boxes (in relation to gramophone records), and he goes on to draw his conclusion in relation to the universality of some messages:

[The] uniformity of 'human jukeboxes' establishes a uniform 'language' in which frame messages and outer messages can be communicated. If . . . we believe that human intelligence is just one example of a general phenomenon in nature—the emergence of intelligent beings in widely varying contexts—then presumably the 'language' in which frame messages and outer messages are communicated among humans is a 'dialect' of a *universal* language by which intelligences can communicate with each other . . . This would allow us to shift our description of where meaning is located. We could ascribe the meanings (frame, outer, and inner) of a message to the message itself, because of the fact that deciphering mechanisms are universal—that is, they are fundamental forms of nature which arise in the same way in diverse contexts. (p. 171)

This discussion can be considered as directed against the two broad ideas discussed in Weizenbaum (1984), which I referred to earlier.

First, it will be recalled, there is the idea exemplified by the thesis of Shannon, referred to in Weizenbaum (1984: 209), that 'even in abstract information theory, the "information content" of a message is not a function of the message alone but depends crucially on the state of knowledge, on the expectations, of the receiver'. Hofstadter himself refers to a similar idea in relation to the information contained in the genetic code, that 'in order for DNA to have meaning, *chemical context* is necessary' (p. 162): that is, the information contained in the DNA itself is not sufficient for the creation of a complete organism, without the environment of chemical substances in which the organism develops under the guidance of the genetic material. Hofstadter opposes to this the idea that the DNA 'has such *compelling inner logic* to its structure that its message could be deduced' by an intelligence, even in the absence of the chemical context.

Secondly, there is the idea, referred to in Weizenbaum (1984: 213), that there is information which perhaps cannot 'be represented in the form of computer programs and data structures at all'. Against this, Hofstadter contends that the meaning of a message, and the information it conveys, can be wholly contained in a coded message.

I disagree with Hofstadter on both counts. The 'message' encoded in the light reflected from the surface of my red pen includes the appearance of the colour red: and I repeat that this appearance is plainly different from any code. I have the information, what red looks like, which a person blind from birth or a non-conscious computer cannot have: that information is a function not of the message alone, but depends crucially on its receipt by an organism with colour vision. The information is successfully conveyed by the coded message only when the message is placed in a particular context, that is, when it is received by a particular type of 'receiver': a receiver capable of having conscious visual experiences.

I suggest that Hofstadter gives a *reductio ad absurdum* of his own position in 'A Conversation with Einstein's Brain' (Hofstadter and Dennett 1981: 431–4), where the idea is put forward that one can enjoy a piece of music by looking at the score (or even at a gramophone record!), because all the patterns of the music are contained there just as they are in the sounds when the music is played. No doubt musical people can derive musical enjoyment from reading a musical score; but only, as Hofstadter seems to accept (in Hofstadter 1980: 163), because they can imagine what the music sounds like. The *patterns* of the music are contained in the score, but music is not just patterns: it is patterns of *sound*. The score is a code for these patterns of sound, but the code is not the same as the decoded material, in this case the sounds themselves; and these can be known only to a conscious being or entity.

Quite apart from this, even if one accepts Hofstadter's analysis, his thesis is not made out. There is still, in addition to the message contained in the patterns on the musical score or gramophone record, the enjoyment derived from these patterns, the 'emotional effects' which Hofstadter talks about in relation to the alien civilization. Hofstadter does not suggest that this enjoyment itself is part of the message, or that it can be fully encoded in a message. Even on his view, it would seem, *what it is like to enjoy the music* is known to the person who derives the enjoyment; yet this knowledge is not contained in the coded message.

And, perhaps most damaging of all, his thesis depends on proposing a universal deciphering mechanism, by which 'intelligence' can extract the meaning of the 'universal language' so that the meaning of the message is *still* something *other* than the code in which it is transmitted. And Hofstadter gives no reason to believe that non-conscious computers could be intelligences having such a deciphering mechanism.

4.3. The Integration of Information

There is another important respect in which information available to conscious beings or entities seems different from that available to non-conscious computers: namely that large amounts of information seem to be available *all at once* in conscious experiences, without any necessity to scan. Indeed, on the basis of its Latin derivation, 'consciousness' can be taken as *meaning* 'knowing things together' or 'all at once'.

An extraordinary aspect of seeing, for example, is that so much data is presented all at once, graphically, simply, comprehensively, with every part apparently available for immediate attention. Similarly in relation to hearing. Sound-waves are simple codes for carrying very complex information: all the information involved, for example, in any number of musical instruments playing together, and in any number of voices talking or singing, can be encoded on a single wavy line of a gramophone record. Extraction of this complex information occurs in various stages in the hearing process, but is completed only at the stage when a person actually hears the relevant sounds and voices, and can identify the instruments, the melodies, the words. All this information is then available, not in code and not requiring any scanning, but immediately.

At any time of full consciousness, there is a totality of information of which one is aware, namely what one is seeing, and/or hearing, and/or feeling, and/or thinking, and/or doing. One is aware all at once of this information, although it must be related to millions of neuronal events which are sequential in time and separated in space. To some extent, the all-at-once character of conscious experience could depend on short-term memory; but this does not avoid the necessity of the conscious experience somehow spanning space and possibly also time. It is not plausible to believe that conscious experience arises at some single place in the brain: any such experience must, as I have said, be associated with a pattern of millions of events separated in space.

It might be replied that similar integration takes place without consciousness, for example when thousands of events combine to give a single television picture. However, the information contained in a complete television picture is available all at once for use and processing only in the mind of a person looking at it: such information can be made available to a non-conscious computer only in the code used by such a computer, which would then have to scan the information so encoded in order to extract particular pieces of information required for its use.

On any view, the visual information from seeing, and auditory information from hearing, comprises huge amounts of information presented comprehensively, graphically, and simply. At least a question is raised whether all this is an irrelevance, a superfluity: that is, could the survival of species have been equally well promoted by the non-conscious performance of algorithms on the objective physical structures and events which underly such conscious experiences?

The last remark leads to the thought (which will be pursued in Chapter 6) that there may be evolutionary advantages in being aware of, and able to think with and about, actual appearances, sounds, etc., and not merely codes for them. For example, it may be easier to derive and support analogies from appearances than from mere codes or descriptions. It might be possible to detect similarities between things which are not yet encoded as similar. It might be easier to weigh similarities and differences. A non-conscious entity could presumably detect similarities and differences, and assign point scores to each, and come to some mathematically based conclusion; but a comparison of actual appearances (as now presented and as remembered) could be more advantageous.

4.4. Dretske and Digital Information

It could be argued that the approach I am putting forward confuses sensation on the one hand, with knowledge and belief on the other: that while sensation

(the look, sound, feel of things) involves consciousness-dependent information, nevertheless such information is not carried over into the cognitive
centres of the brain, and cannot be the subject of knowledge and belief. All
that can be the subject of knowledge and belief is information of a type
available to non-conscious computers.

Such a view appears to be the thesis of the book *Knowledge and the Flow of
Information*, by philosopher Fred Dretske, which according to its preface
seeks to show that for purposes of understanding that facet of human mental
life which has to do with cognitive capabilities, it is not necessary to think of
human beings as other than complex physical systems.

Dretske asserts (Dretske 1981: 142) that 'Sensation . . . is informationally
profuse and specific in the way a picture is. Knowledge and belief, on the
other hand, are selective and exclusive in the way a statement is.' He treats
the former as 'analog', the latter as 'digital'.

I accept the first sentence of the quotation. I also accept, as Dretske asserts,
that sensory experience is not 'carried over in toto to the cognitive centers'.
However, in my view there can be carried over to the cognitive centres (so
that the content of belief or knowledge can include) substantial parts of
sensory experience. This is, I think, shown by our ability to remember events
which we have witnessed, in substance by picturing them in our minds, and
then from such recollections to formulate entirely new descriptions of what
we saw: for example, how a try was scored in a football match. I remember
what the colour blue looks like, and can imagine it. I remember what tooth-
ache feels like, and can (with more difficulty) imagine that. If such beliefs or
knowledge concerning the events seen, or the colours or pains experienced,
are 'digital' according to Dretske's distinction, then it is difficult to see what
is not 'digital'.

(I hope I am not here being guilty of something akin to the fallacy, identified by Wittgenstein, of suggesting that we generally recognize things by
comparing them with some kind of sample pictured in our minds. It seems to
me that I do sometimes recall things by 'picturing' them; and even that
sometimes, in doubtful cases, I do use such 'pictures' as an aid to recognition
of people or places, particularly where changes have occurred since I last saw
them.)

Furthermore, it seems to me that Dretske's thesis puts too great a gulf
between sensation and cognition. I would suggest that perception is an amalgam of sensation and cognition, in which the two aspects are inextricably
interwoven. The normal case of perception involves recognition (and, accordingly, cognition—belief or knowledge): I cannot separate the cognition aspect
of seeing my red pen from the visual sensations of colour and shape. These
visual sensations are just as they are partly *because* I recognize what I see as
being a pen.

Consistently with his approach to sensation, and to knowledge and belief,
Dretske asserts (1981: 199) that for an internal state to qualify as a cognitive

structure (that is, as knowledge or belief), two conditions must be satisfied: (1) the internal state must have 'semantic content', which Dretske says (p. 190) is information carried in completely digitalized form; *and* (2) 'it must be this content that defines the structure's causal influence on output'. He asserts (pp. 200–1) that sensory experience does not qualify as a cognitive structure, because although it has semantic content (namely all the information it contains expressed in sentences which put such information in completely digitalized form), this content exercises no control over output.

Again, I would contend that this is wrong, on two grounds.

First, I contest the suggestion that all sensory experience can be expressed in sentences. To take my original example of the appearance of a colour: to what extent can the information 'what blue looks like' (referring to the actual appearance of the colour) be 'digitalized'? I suggest that it cannot be, that no collection of statements about the colour can carry or express such information, except to an entity which already has this information.

Secondly, I suggest that recollection of a sensory experience may control output, at least in the sense that one may use such recollection to imagine, and to describe, and (perhaps) to recognize something. If it is asserted that in so using it, one 'digitalizes' the sensory experience, then as before this seems to rob the word of any meaning. It might be contended that the information itself has no effect on output, that only associated brain processes 'digitalized' from the information can have such effect. To me that contention does not seem correct: I seem to rely on my experiences of the colour blue (i.e. its actual appearance) to imagine the appearance of blue things, and sometimes to recognize other instances of it, which may not be identical to any instance of it which I have previously seen. Whether this apparent reliance is in fact effectual or not is similar to the main question of this book.

5

Plausible Reasoning

IN Chapter 4, I argued that the brain–mind *has* information which is not available to a non-conscious computer, but I did not go on to contend that it *uses* such information in any way not equivalent to a computer's use of a coded version of it. In this chapter, I begin to argue that the brain–mind *does* use such information. The broad proposition of this chapter is that the conscious brain–mind uses rational procedures which have not yet been fully expressed as formal procedures by philosophers or scientists, and which probably cannot be so expressed. The point is that a non-conscious computer (or a mechanistic brain) could not reason, or process information, except in accordance with algorithms, formal procedures expressed by definite rules. If the brain–mind does use rational procedures which cannot be fully expressed as formal procedures, then it is not mechanistic. In short: human reason cannot be formalized; therefore it cannot be mechanized; therefore the brain–mind is not mechanistic.

5.1. Formal and Plausible Reasoning

Some human reasoning proceeds in accordance with algorithms; that is, it follows precise and unambiguous rules. In particular, some human reasoning explicitly follows the extensive and valuable rules of logic and mathematics. These rules have greatly assisted rational human thinking, both extending its range and assisting in the detection of errors. However, formal reasoning in accordance with such rules is only a small part of human reasoning: another part is informal plausible reasoning, which is both ubiquitous and important.

5.1.1. *The Ubiquity of Plausible Reasoning*

Mathematician George Polya, in his book on *Mathematics and Plausible Reasoning*, tells us that 'the inductive evidence of the physicist, the circumstantial evidence of the lawyer, the documentary evidence of the historian, and the statistical evidence of the economist belong to plausible reasoning' (Polya 1954, vol. i, p.v.). Indeed, I would say that most of human reasoning is non-logical plausible reasoning. For example:

1. Scientific and philosophical works. If one examines almost any scientific or philosophical book or article, one will find that (mathematics aside) most arguments which are presented are not valid logical arguments, but are informal plausible arguments. It may be possible to put such arguments, or at least some of them, into a valid logical form; but this will generally only be by supplying major premises which may well be less acceptable than the informal arguments themselves. Generally, at some stage in any such argument one will find some appeal made to terms requiring judgement, weighing, preference, reasonableness, etc.

2. Law. The decisions which are continually made and set out at length by judges presiding over court cases generally involve the weighing of countervailing considerations, which are of different types, and which apparently cannot be expressed as commensurable quantities. Such decisions are reasoned, but cannot be expressed as the application of algorithms to accepted premisses.

3. Practical reasoning. More generally, in many situations, a person has to decide what to do on the basis of non-commensurable considerations. For example, duty may point one way, and expediency may point another way. In each case, assuming that both opposing contentions are accepted as having weight, and in the absence of a single scale on which the opposing considerations could both be measured, a choice between them could not be made, otherwise than randomly, by any algorithm or by any mechanistic process. We make such choices by some process of 'weighing' these incommensurable considerations; and this process is generally considered rational.

I will elaborate on some of these cases later. In them, I have not included certain examples of human rationality which appear even more difficult to formalize, such as literary creativity and humour; this is because I believe my point can be made more clearly and directly by reference to plausible reasoning.

5.1.2. *The Importance of Plausible Reasoning*

Polya also asserts that 'Strictly speaking, all our knowledge outside mathematics and demonstrative logic . . . consists of conjectures' and that 'we support our conjectures by *plausible reasoning*' (p.v).

Certainly, all such knowledge which goes beyond particular observations or perceptions can be supported only by plausible reasoning: formal or logical or deductive reasoning, as Polya reminds us, is 'incapable of yielding . . . new knowledge about the world around us'. And, as mentioned in Chapter 1, even particular observations depend in part upon theories accepted by the observer; and those theories themselves must go beyond particular observations or perceptions, so must also depend on plausible reasoning.

There are respected views put forward that such plausible procedures as induction cannot show even a probability of approximate truth of general statements, notably by Sir Karl Popper in *The Logic of Scientific Discovery* (Popper 1959). However, the mainstream of scientific and philosophical thought is to the contrary: it is generally accepted that, although scientific theories must go beyond what can be established by observation and logic, such theories can be supported by plausible reasoning and thereby shown to have a probability of approximate truth. Otherwise, having regard to the theory-dependent character of observation, there would be no sound basis for believing anything. Indeed, the main arguments used by Popper to support his own position are plausible arguments; so, if he asserts his position as true (as he does), how can he deny that plausible arguments can support the truth of scientific theories?

The whole edifice of human knowledge is based in part on plausible reasoning; and our confidence in human knowledge generally can be no greater than our confidence in plausible reasoning.

5.1.3. *Implications*

There are no hard-and-fast rules for plausible reasoning. As Polya says,

Plausible reasoning is hazardous, controversial, and provisional. . . . The standards of plausible reasoning are fluid, and there is no theory of such reasoning that could be compared to demonstrative logic in clarity or which would command comparable consensus. (p. v)

Efforts have been made to formulate rules for, and thereby formalize, aspects of plausible reasoning: Bayes's probability calculus and Carnap's work on induction are examples. However, as I will seek to show, such efforts do not and cannot capture informal rationality.

So: an important part of rational human thought is plausible reasoning; plausible reasoning does not explicitly follow precise and unambiguous rules; it has not as yet been possible to formulate rules such that to follow them would be equivalent to engaging in plausible reasoning; and it is probable that such rules cannot be formulated.

In this chapter, I develop the idea that there are deep theoretical problems about formalizing plausible reasoning, and that these deep problems are similarly problems for the mechanistic view of the brain–mind. In order to demonstrate these theoretical problems, I will need to look in a little detail at some types and aspects of plausible reasoning.

5.2. Induction

The area of plausible reasoning which has received most attention from philosophers is induction, the process of supporting general statements, such as hypotheses or theories stating laws of nature, on the basis of particular or singular statements, such as reports of observations or experiments. Sometimes, induction is regarded as including the formulation of general statements on the basis of particular statements, but I am not so concerned with this: the plausible reasoning with which I am concerned relates to justification rather than to discovery. Although the processes by which human beings hit upon hypotheses to be tested are an important area of human rationality, they are (like literary creativity and humour) less central to my discussion than the processes of justifying hypotheses and other general or universal statements, and thereby showing their rational acceptability.

So, if one seeks to justify the assertion 'All ravens are black' on the basis that all ravens observed to date have been black, this is a case of induction or inductive inference. Most actual uses of induction are far more complex than this example, but they all involve the same basic process. The experimental or observational evidence for any scientific theory, if expressed as statements, comprises large numbers of particular or singular statements, which are particular instances which follow from the universal statements of the theory. The support which this evidence gives to the theory is accordingly by way of induction.

Thus, prior to the emergence of the theory of relativity, the experimental and observational justification for Newton's laws of motion was that all *observed* motion of bodies was (within the limits of experimental accuracy) in accordance with those laws. There have now been observations of motion *not* in accordance with those laws, and classical mechanics has been displaced by and subsumed in the theory of relativity. The particular experimental observations which supported classical mechanics (within their limits of accuracy) have not been falsified: observable motion *is* substantially in accordance with classical mechanics, except in fairly extreme circumstances involving high speed and/or large mass which had not been dealt with experimentally until towards the end of the last century. So, the particular statements which supported the theory have not been falsified, but they did not conclusively support the theory; the theory is now disproved by experiments and observations made in different circumstances; but it is still considered as approximately true, within certain limits of speed and mass.

5.2.1. *The Problem of Induction*

The question of whether inductive inferences are or may be justified, and if so under what conditions, is called the problem of induction. An early exposition was by eighteenth-century British philosopher David Hume. Hume in fact concentrated on one particular aspect of the problem, the respect in which inductive inferences involve begging the question or (to look at it another way) infinite regress. In *An Enquiry Concerning Human Understanding*, Hume writes:

all inferences from experience suppose, as their foundation, that the future will resemble the past and that similar powers will be conjoined with similar sensible qualities. If there be any suspicion that the course of nature may change, and that the past may be no rule for the future, all experience becomes useless and can give rise to no inference or conclusion. It is impossible, therefore, that any arguments from experience can prove this resemblance of the past to the future; since all these arguments are founded on the supposition of that resemblance. (Hume 1962: 57)

In *The Logic of Scientific Discovery*, Popper restates this argument in terms of an infinite regress: if there is a principle of induction which can, in combination with particular statements, justify universal statements, then this principle must itself be a universal statement, requiring a principle of induction to justify it; and so on *ad infinitum* (Popper 1959: 29).

Hume (and Popper) extend this argument so as to apply it to inferences from particular statements to the *probability* of universal statements. In his *Abstract of a Treatise of Human Nature*, Hume writes:

Nay, I will go further and assert that he could not so much as prove by any *probable* arguments that the future must be conformable to the past. All probable arguments are built on the supposition that there is this conformity betwixt the future and the past, and therefore can never prove it. (Hume 1962: 294)

Popper questions the use of 'probability' in this connection (1959, §80); but he proceeds to show that, even if a satisfactory account of the probability of a hypothesis can be given, the problem of induction is not thereby overcome. A statement that a hypothesis is probable, or probably true, cannot be deduced from particular statements, unless the latter are combined with some principle of induction (in this case, justifying a conclusion that a hypothesis is probable). To be relied on, *that* principle must be accepted as true or probably true. In the former case, the original problem of induction is raised; while in the latter, the present problem is raised. So there is still an infinite regress (1959, §81).

The solution which Hume offered for the problem which he identified in this way was to the effect that inductive inferences are an expression of human habit. Barrett states it thus:

We have made the inference in the past, and it worked; and we continue to do so out of the inertia of human habit. Thus the whole edifice of science . . . becomes merely a highly formal expression of human habit. (Barrett 1987: 45)

On this approach, inductive inferences are not a matter of reason, but merely of habit.

5.2.2. *Restatement of the Problem*

Although Hume's argument is important and influential, it seems to me an incomplete statement of the problem. For one thing, it assumes that particular statements about the past are independent of theories: it takes no account of the extent to which particular observations, and particular statements based on them, are themselves dependent on theories, on universal statements. I briefly adverted to this matter in Section 1.1, and it is not central to my discussion here.

More importantly for present purposes, Hume's discussion runs together two matters, which are best considered separately: (1) the question whether the future will be 'like' the past, in at least some respects; and (2) the question how, in what respects, will the future be like the past.

As regards the first question, so long as changes occur, the future will not be identical with the past: at most, it will be like the past in some respects. An assertion to this effect, without specifying in *what* respects, cannot be more than an assertion that there are regularities in our world: the principle of the uniformity of nature (see Popper 1959: 252–3). At the extreme, this merges with determinism: the assertion that the regularities in our world are such that the future is determined in every respect by the past. However, the bare assertion that there are *some* regularities, so that the future is *in some respects* like the past and determined by the past, seems to be a minimum requirement for any rational view of the world.

It is in relation to the second question that one comes to the *content* of the similarities between the past and the future, of the regularities or laws of nature. As put by Goodman:

our predictions cannot be based upon the bald principle that the future will be like the past. The question is *how* what is predicted is like what has already been found. Along which among countless lines of similarity do our predictions run? (Goodman 1970: 24)

On this second question, Hume's appeal to habit seems prima facie inadequate (whatever its merits in relation to question (1)): habit could explain why we continue to adopt and act upon existing theories, those which are for the time being accepted as stating the regularities in our world; but it does not obviously explain how it is we criticize existing theories and adopt new ones. However, it is conceivable that, at a deeper level, our inductive and other scientific methods *are* merely a matter of habit, in the sense that they are procedures ('habits of thought') selected as useful by evolution because they have worked; and this is a possibility which I consider later.

Habit could explain our adoption of the basic principle of the uniformity of nature, the assertion that there are some regularities, giving no information regarding the content of such regularities. I would contend, however, that our adoption of that principle has ample rational justification: it is presupposed in any rational discussion of the world; it cannot be falsified, in that any attempt to do so would presume its truth; it is, in short, appropriate to be accepted as being a priori true.

Inductive principles concerning the content of the regularities cannot, however, reasonably be accepted as true a priori: the question-begging involved in seeking to establish such principles empirically cannot be overcome in that way. Any principle of induction which could, together with established particular statements, enable the deduction of general statements would be falsified as soon as one general statement so deduced was falsified. It is not conceivable that an infallible principle could be formulated, nor would we be justified in accepting such a principle as true a priori (see Popper 1959: 253–4). As regards inductive principles enabling deduction of the *probability* of general statements, there is not the same problem of their being falsified; but again it is inconceivable that one could formulate an infallible principle, and one would not be justified in accepting such a principle as true a priori.

So the problem of induction remains. A more recent expression of essentially the same matter is the 'law of conservation of information' asserted by Sir Peter Medawar:

No process of logical reasoning—no mere act of mind or computer-programmable operation—can enlarge the information content of the axioms or premises or observation statements from which it proceeds . . . there is *no* process of logical reasoning by which we can proceed from these respective sets of particulars to the general laws that embody them . . . No inductive generalization can contain more information than the sum of its known instances. (Medawar 1986: 79–80)

5.2.3. *Attempts to Formalize Induction*

It seems clear that premisses consisting of particular observations cannot support as a matter of *certainty* general conclusions going beyond the particular premisses. However, it is not so clear that particular premisses cannot support the *probability* or *likelihood* that general conclusions are approximately true. It is conceivable that Hume's and Popper's argument to the contrary is not conclusive: for example, it may be possible to give some meaning to probability which is not vacuous, and yet which is such that the probability of a general statement *is somehow* contained in an assemblage of particular statements. It is also conceivable that such support by particular premisses of the probability or likelihood of a general statement could be formalized; and that such probability or likelihood could be expressed quantitatively. There have been attempts to formalize induction along these lines, typified by those of Bayes and Carnap.

1. Bayes. In the eighteenth century, Thomas Bayes formulated and developed a theorem of probability calculus, known as Bayes's theorem. It asserts, roughly, that the probability of a hypothesis H, given evidence E, is: the probability of the evidence E, given the hypothesis H; multiplied by the prior probability of H; and divided by the prior probability of E:

$$P(H, E) = P(E, H) \times P(H) / P(E).$$

The theorem thus implies that the increase in probability which a hypothesis receives when its consequences are verified by experiment is proportionate to the *unlikelihood* of those consequences.

If (as will often be the case) the evidence (that is, the particular experiment or observation) is a necessary consequence of the hypothesis, there is no difficulty in quantifying $P(E, H)$: it is 1. (For example, if the hypothesis H is that all ravens are black, and the evidence E is that a particular raven is black, then $P(E, H)$—the probability of the evidence E given the hypothesis H—is 1.) The problem with Bayes's theorem lies in the quantification of $P(H)$ and $P(E)$: the *prior* probabilities. If the prior probability of the hypothesis is set at zero (as Hume and Popper might do), then no amount of evidence will make its probability other than zero. If one does not set it at zero, then at what *does* one set the prior probability of the hypothesis; and, similarly, the prior probability of the evidence? Bayes's theorem itself cannot tell us, so it does not solve the problem of deriving probable conclusions from particular premisses.

2. Carnap. In the twentieth century, the German logical-positivist philosopher Rudolf Carnap developed an elaborate logic of induction, based in part on Bayes's theorem. Application of this method is by means of a confirmation-function or c-function, which enables calculation of a numerical value for the confirmation of a hypothesis.

One question in relation to this approach concerns the relationships between degree of confirmation of a hypothesis, the probability of the hypothesis, and the rationality of believing it to be true or approximately true. I mentioned earlier that Popper (1959, §80) questions the use of probability in connection with induction. In particular, he argues that the probability of a hypothesis is quite different from the probability of an event, the latter being connected with a notion of statistical frequency. In sections 81 and 83, he considers corroboration (which he takes as roughly synonymous with, but preferable to, 'confirmation'). He accepts that a theory or hypothesis can be accorded some positive degree of corroboration if it is compatible with all accepted particular statements, and if some accepted particular statements can be derived from it. He contends that in addition one needs a notion of degree of corroboration, which in turn requires consideration of the severity of the tests to which the hypothesis has been subjected.

Popper then argues that the less probable a hypothesis is, the more severe are the tests to which it can be subjected; and accordingly there may be an inverse relationship between the probability of a hypothesis and the degree to which it is corroborated. Later, he contends that 'it is a mistake to think probability may be interpreted as a measure of the rationality of our beliefs'; that degree of corroboration 'must not be interpreted . . . as a degree of the rationality of our belief in the *truth* of' a hypothesis; but that 'it is a measure of the rationality of *accepting*, tentatively, a problematic guess' (pp. 414–15).

I do not propose to go deeply into these problems here. I will be proceeding on the assumption that there is a sense in which the probability of a general statement *is* a measure of the rationality of a belief in the truth, or approximate truth, of that general statement. This is roughly the sense used in courts of law, where decisions are often expressed as being made 'on the balance of probabilities', or on the basis of facts which are found to be true 'more probably than not'. In relation to probability in this sense, I take it that confirmation or corroboration, or degrees of confirmation or corroboration, is relevant; and that in general terms the greater the confirmation or corroboration of a statement, the greater the probability of its approximation to the truth. To adopt the words of Putnam:

the very factors that make it rational to accept a theory 'for scientific purposes' also make it rational to believe it, at least in the sense in which one ever 'believes' a scientific theory—as an approximation to the truth which can probably be bettered, and not as a final truth. (Putnam 1979: 356)

What I do not assume, but will now consider, is whether there are (as suggested by the work of Bayes and Carnap) satisfactory formal ways of assigning numerical values to probability in this sense, or to degrees of confirmation, in connection with inductive inference.

5.2.4. *Against the Formalization of Induction*

I have already referred to the need, in relation to Bayes's theorem, for the assignment of prior probabilities, and I will return to this. I will also consider some other arguments.

1. The severity of the tests. It seems reasonable to accept that the more severe the tests to which a theory has been subjected, the greater the corroboration. Indeed, this is recognized by Bayes's theorem: the greater the prior improbability of the confirming event, the greater the probability accorded to the hypothesis by the occurrence of the confirming event. As Popper says, 'a theory is the better confirmed the more ingenious our unsuccessful attempts at its refutation have been' (1959: 401–2). *But*, as Popper continues, 'one cannot completely formalize the idea of a sincere and ingenious attempt'.

2. Hempel's paradox of confirmation. Associated with this idea is the paradox of confirmation of philosopher Carl Hempel. In Hempel (1965: 11–20) he points out that the statement 'All ravens are black' is formally equivalent to the statement 'All non-black things are non-ravens'; and that therefore anything that confirms the latter statement must also confirm the former statement. My red pen is an instance of something which is non-black and a non-raven, and the statement 'This red thing is my pen' would confirm 'All non-black things are non-ravens', and thus would confirm 'All ravens are black'; which is absurd.

Hempel refers to two possible solutions of this paradox (pp. 19–20): one solution makes the confirmation, or lack of it, depend on what other evidence is available; and the other points to differences in the degree of confirmation, in that the confirmation provided by a red pen is less than that provided by a black raven, because there are many more non-black things than there are ravens. I do not think either solution protects a purely formal theory of confirmation: rather, I think that the paradox strongly suggests that confirmation (and induction) cannot be formalized.

I contend that the fact that my pen is red has absolutely nothing to do with the probability that all ravens are black (apart from not refuting it); whereas the fact that one raven is black has *something* to do with the probability that all ravens are black (quite apart from not refuting it). And this is *not* because there are more non-black things than there are ravens, but because of other facts about ravens and about the way the world works; and the relevance of these other facts cannot be formalized, except by means of further inductive arguments involving the same problems.

A useful discussion of this paradox is that by J. L. Mackie (1968: 165–76); and, although Mackie claims that the paradox is resolved, I contend that his resolution confirms that confirmation cannot be completely formalized: it requires consideration of such matters as 'genuine tests' of hypotheses, which as Popper contends cannot be formalized.

3. Goodman's new riddle of induction. In *Fact, Fiction and Forecast*, philosopher Nelson Goodman formulated what he called 'the new riddle of induction' (Goodman 1965, ch.3), which is as follows. Our past experience that all emeralds we have observed are green supports the hypothesis that all emeralds are green. Suppose that there is a predicate 'grue', where a thing is grue either if it is examined before AD 2000 and is green, or if it is not so examined and is blue. Then, in 1990, the same evidence would equally support the hypothesis 'all emeralds are grue' and the hypothesis 'all emeralds are green'; yet these two hypotheses yield incompatible predictions in relation to examinations of emeralds after the year AD 2000. Why should the predicate 'green' be projected, rather than the predicate 'grue'?

One obvious answer is that the predicate 'green' is 'entrenched', and has been the subject of successful projections: this answer is similar to Hume's reference to habit, and it does not explain why (as we assume to be the case) it is *rational* to project green rather than grue.

It has been contended that 'grue' is a peculiar sort of predicate, containing as it does a time reference; and there is some force in this. However, it has not been possible to identify formal characteristics which distinguish those predicates which are rationally projectable from those which are not. It seems to be accepted by those who have considered the matter that it is not possible to identify, by formal or syntactical means alone, those terms which can reasonably be projected.

4. The need for prior probabilities. For me, some of the best writing on this topic is by Hilary Putnam: I find convincing his assertions to the effect that the various paradoxes, problems, and riddles of induction and confirmation are related to the need for prior probabilities, referred to in connection with Bayes's theorem. He writes:

It is easily shown that all possible inductive logics depend implicitly or explicitly on this: An *a priori* ordering of hypotheses on the basis of 'simplicity', or on the basis of the kinds of predicates they contain, or of the form of the laws they propose, or some other basis. To refuse to make any *a priori decisions* as to which hypotheses are more or less plausible is just to commit oneself to never making any inductive extrapolation from past experience at all; for at any given time infinitely many mutually incompatible hypotheses are each compatible with any finite amount of data . . . (Putnam 1979*c*: 352)

He treats the problem similarly in Putnam (1983*b*: 299, 300). In *Reason, Truth and History* (Putnam 1981: 194), he expressly assimilates this need for prior probabilities with Goodman's new riddle of induction: 'From a Bayesian point of view the need for a decision as to which predicates are projectable and which are not before one can make an induction is just one special case of the need for a prior.' (By 'a prior', Putnam means 'a prior probability function', that is, a spectrum of hypotheses with some given prior probabilities.) He goes on to suggest (p. 195) that the success of science is due to a set of methodological maxims, which 'are not rigorous formal rules' but 'do require informal rationality, i.e. intelligence and common sense, to apply'.

This may be compared with W.H. Newton-Smith's discussion, in *The Rationality of Science* (Newton-Smith 1981: 225–32), of the good-making features of scientific theories, which he considers under the headings observational nesting (preserving the observational success of predecessor theories), fertility, track record, inter-theory support, smoothness, internal consistency, compatibility with well-grounded metaphysical beliefs, and simplicity. Newton-Smith calls these: 'a family of vague, hedged principles which may conflict'; 'not algorithms admitting of mechanical application'; 'fallible indicators of verisimilitude'.

5.2.5. *The Relevance to Mechanism*

It is my contention that these questions are highly relevant to the plausibility of mechanism. This relevance has, to my knowledge, never been stressed in discussions of mechanism, or the mind–matter question. It is, however, hinted at in the writings of Putnam and others.

For example, Putnam (1979*c*: 270–304) contends that the 'project of defining a *quantitative* concept of "degree of confirmation" . . . is misguided'. In support of this contention, he draws what he regards as a counter-intuitive consequence of the contrary view: it would be 'possible in principle to build an electronic computer such that, if it could somehow be given all the observational facts, it would always make the best prediction' so that '*Science could in principle be done by a moron* (or an electronic computer)' (p. 290).

In *Reason, Truth and History*, he puts a similar point in a different way: 'there does not seem to be any good reason to think that there would be a set of rules which could distinguish between reasonable and unreasonable priors and which would be any simpler than a complete description of the total psychology of an ideally rational human being' (Putnam 1981: 192). And finally, in Putnam (1983*b*: 198), he writes:

Today, a host of negative results, including some powerful considerations due to Nelson Goodman, have indicated that there *cannot* be a completely *formal* inductive logic. Some important aspects of inductive logic can be formalized . . . but there is always a need for judgments of 'reasonableness'. . . . Today, virtually no one believes that there is a formalizable scientific method, one that can be completely formalized without formalizing complete human psychology (and possibly not even then).

And in similar vein, Polya writes: 'you can build a machine to draw demonstrative conclusions for you, but I think you can never build a machine that will draw plausible inferences' (Polya 1954: ii. 115).

I do not think that the last assertion is disproved by the existence of computer programs for applying 'heuristics' or rules of thumb: they still draw conclusions which are demonstrative, in the sense that they are required or compelled by the data plus the program; and at best such programs merely approximate in a limited way some human plausible reasoning.

Putnam was probably not, in the passages to which I referred, arguing against mechanism: he was after all a founder of functionalism, one of the key doctrines of the mechanist consensus. Indeed, it could be contended that he was saying (with only an over-cautious qualification at the end) that there *are* mechanistic rules equivalent to a complete description of the psychology of a human being; but that the complexity of these rules prevents us from formalizing induction, and from making machines to carry it out. However, the arguments which he (with others, like Goodman) advances against the possibility of formalizing induction proceed on matters of principle, not on matters of complexity; and they do in fact constitute powerful arguments against mechanism. Particularly is this so when they are combined with arguments concerning the objectivity of reason, which is another theme on which Putnam has written very persuasively.

The debates on induction suggest strongly that there can be no formal or syntactical explanation or justification of the rationality of induction. It would appear to follow that either there is such a thing as informal rationality, which cannot be mechanized; or alternatively our inductive methods are only pseudo-rational procedures which happen to work. Our inductive procedures work; they apparently do not do so because their *formal* properties are such as to base rationality; so either they have non-rational properties selected by evolution, which in fact are suitable to deal with the problems facing human beings, or else they have some non-formal rationality. The former alternative, similar to Hume's appeal to human 'habit', is one mode of 'naturalization' of reason and denial of its objectivity, which Putnam attacks.

To put this another way. A conclusion of a process of formal reasoning can contain no more information than the premises. A statement concerning the probability and/or verisimilitude of a universal statement does not report observations: it contains information which cannot be observed, and which accordingly is not contained in any particular statement or assemblage of particular statements. Such a conclusion, therefore, cannot be derived by formal reasoning from premises comprising particular statements (reports of observations), but can be reached from particular statements only with the aid of *informal* inductive procedures. These procedures either do have objective rationality; or else they do not have it, although generally they *do work*, having been selected by evolution.

5.2.6. *Evolution-Selected Habits*

So, to escape the conclusion that there is an informal rationality, which cannot be mechanized, one has to explain the effectiveness of induction (and our informal rationality generally) on the basis of evolution-tested habits of thought. There are at least two severe problems with this.

One is that our habits of thought seem to have applications far beyond what is helpful to survival and reproduction, and seem to work in all sorts of areas and circumstances remote from those in which they evolved. Nagel writes:

But the capacity to form cosmological and subatomic theories takes us so far from the circumstances in which our ability to think would have had to pass its evolutionary tests that there would be no reason whatever, stemming from the theory of evolution, to rely on it in extension to those subjects. In fact if, *per impossibile*, we came to believe that our capacity for objective theory were the product of natural selection, that would warrant serious skepticism about its results beyond a very limited and familiar range. An evolutionary explanation of our theorizing faculty would provide absolutely no confirmation of its capacity to get at the truth. Something else must be going on if the process is really taking us toward a truer and more detached understanding of the world. (Nagel 1986: 79)

The other great problem of equating informal rationality with evolution-selected habits of thought (and thus denying the objectivity of reason) is that it is self-defeating, along the lines argued powerfully in Putnam (1983*b*: 184–204, 229–47, 287–303). By entering into any discussion of questions of rationality, we thereby accept that such questions can be advanced by rational arguments: yet if informal rationality is no more than evolution-selected habits of thought, there is just no basis for believing in the rational evaluation of competing arguments. I look at this further in Section 5.6.

5.3. Characteristics of Plausible Reasoning

In this section I consider some of the characteristics of plausible reasoning generally, in order further to assess the possibility of such reasoning being reduced to formal steps.

5.3.1. *The Relationship with Language*

Plausible reasoning is related in various ways to language, and to questions concerning language.

1. The application of words. The very application of language often involves plausible reasoning, for example in that it is not possible to specify unambiguous rules for the application of even commonly used words, such as 'tree' or 'chair' or 'table': in borderline cases, the application of such words is a matter of judgement, which cannot be formalized, but *can* be supported or challenged by inconclusive but persuasive plausible reasoning.

This sort of problem occurs in everyday life; but it is particularly well illustrated by a common task of lawyers: the interpretation of legal documents and of statutes. In many court cases, there is a legal document (a contract, a will, etc.) or a statute whose application to the facts of the case is unclear: no algorithms can determine the result, but extensive plausible arguments can be advanced for rival interpretations. The result is a matter of judgement, very often one on which minds can reasonably differ; although very often also there can be a considerable degree of consensus on the 'correct' or 'best' interpretation. Furthermore, the fact that cases like this continually arise, notwithstanding the best efforts of the lawyers who draw contracts and wills, and of statutory draftsmen, points up the difficulty, I would say impossibility, of providing, by means of rules, an unambiguous result for all fact situations which can arise.

Wittgenstein in his *Philosophical Investigations* (Wittgenstein 1974) examined the question how it is possible to determine the correct application of a word. There is an illuminating discussion of the question in Nozick (1981), from which it can be seen how this problem is very similar to the problem of induction, and how Wittgenstein's solution can be likened to Hume's appeal to habit in relation to induction:

> We do have a record of (some) past applications of the word, correct applications and incorrect ones. Does that fix how the word is to be applied in the future? Just as through any finite set of points an infinite number of curves can be drawn, so different hypotheses or rules about applying the term are compatible with all past data-points of application. . . . Adding verbal instructions to past applications does not eliminate all but one way to apply the term, for these instructions themselves need to be applied in one of the many different possible ways . . . In Wittgenstein's view, correctness in the application of a term is constituted by the way we actually go on to apply it. Nothing past fixes, logically determines, an application as correct, but it is just a fact about us that confronted with past teachings and applications we will go on a certain way, and we will all go on the same way. (Nozick 1981: 144–5)

In the note to this, Nozick suggests that 'The most plausible view is that certain underlying processes cause us to apply the term in a certain way in a new instance, given the past applications' (p. 675), these underlying processes being similar in all human beings because of our physical (i.e.

neuro-physiological) similarities (presumably having been selected as useful by evolution). He goes on to hint at, but not really get to grips with, the problems raised by such an attempted 'naturalization' of plausible reasoning, which I touched on at the end of the last section.

Consistently with my view of induction, I contend that such an appeal to habit, or to non-rational processes or structures in human beings, *cannot* explain our application of words to new situations. It is in fact just not true that in all cases we 'all go on the same way': for example, as mentioned earlier, real questions about the meaning of words constantly arise in courts of law, in relation to which minds can and do reasonably differ, and which are resolved by the application of inconclusive, but plausible, informal reasoning.

I am not here saying that a computer could not be given rules which would enable it to use a concept such as 'table': of course it could and, by using such rules, it could probably apply the word correctly in most clear cases, and could perform reasonably in many borderline cases (for example, whether the word 'table' applies in a particular context to a counter top at which people sit to eat meals). I do suggest, however, that we in fact use *informal* reasoning in this area, which a computer could not use; and I do suggest that we thereby do *better* than a computer could do, especially in difficult cases. (Indeed, it appears from Terrace (1984: 270) that pigeons can do better than today's computers in this area!)

2. Indeterminacy of translation. Similar questions are raised by W. V. O. Quine's views on translation. In *Word and Object* (Quine 1960), he argues for the indeterminacy of translation: that we can know everything about the circumstances in which sentences of an unfamiliar language are assented to by users of that language, yet still not know what things those users are referring to by those sentences. Quine gives the example of a single-word sentence 'gavagai', which is assented to (perhaps accompanied by pointing) if a rabbit is apparently observed, and otherwise dissented from; and contends that, even if we correctly hypothesize that the occasion for use of the word is the observation of a rabbit, we cannot conclude that the words 'gavagai' and 'rabbit' refer to the same things:

Who knows but what the objects to which this term applies are not rabbits after all, but mere stages, or brief temporal segments of rabbits? . . . Or perhaps the objects to which 'gavagai' applies are all and sundry undetached parts of rabbits . . . When from the sameness of stimulus meanings of 'Gavagai' and 'Rabbit' the linguist leaps to the conclusion that a gavagai is a whole enduring rabbit, he is just taking for granted that the native is enough like us to have a brief general term for rabbit and no brief general term for rabbit stages or parts. (Quine 1960: 51–2)

He suggests further that the word could be used as a mass term (like 'water' or 'sugar') to refer to the single though disconnected portion of the world that consists of rabbits, and so on. Further questions could be asked of the natives, but Quine contends that this would not help to solve the problem, because there could be systematic differences between the linguist's understanding of the concepts used in those further questions (such as 'one gavagai', 'the same gavagai') and that of the natives.

Quine considers that, like the problem of induction, his point on the indeterminacy of translation is a case of the under-determination of theory by data, but apparently considers that his problem goes beyond that of induction. Whether or not this is so, in practice linguists do not seem to labour under Quine's problems, and it would appear that here again a process of informal and inconclusive reasoning is taking place which is reasonably reliable and which (Quine's arguments suggest) could not be formalized.

Quine's arguments are used by Davidson to support his thesis of the anomalism of the mental, to show, for example, that 'belief and meaning cannot be constructed from speech behaviour' (Davidson 1981: 351). As pointed out by Kim (1985: 384–5), Quine's 'doctrine of translational indeterminacy can be taken as a denial of the claim that the intentional psychological *supervenes* on the physical', since 'on Quine's view, the fixing of the totality of physical facts does not suffice to fix the intentional' (that is, the mental); but, whereas Davidson takes this 'as ensuring the autonomy of the mental, Quine takes it as showing the illegitimacy of the mental' (aligning the mental with alchemy and astrology!). I say, rather, that if one accepts that there is informal rationality working in translation, Quine's arguments support not merely the legitimacy of the mental (*pace* Quine) but also its efficacy (*pace* Davidson).

3. Reasoning beyond language. Another aspect of the relationship between plausible reasoning, as used by human beings, and language is that such reasoning does not operate only with statements in natural or artificial language: it can, and often does, operate with consciousness-dependent concepts or images; that is, material of the type considered in Chapter 4, which is non-verbal, non-linguistic, and (at least apparently) non-coded. This is so even for mathematical thinking (see Penrose 1989: 424–5). As stated in Chapter 4, I accept that all aspects of conscious experience (appearance, sounds, feelings, emotions) can be encoded in some 'language' of the brain, the actual pattern of physical events in the brain which corresponds to the person's having the conscious experience. However, our plausible reasoning makes no conscious use of *that* language, *that* code.

Not all of our conscious reasoning is done with words or with statements. Further, and perhaps more importantly, even when we do reason with statements, we generally also keep in mind their meaning, our best understanding of the possible reality to which the statements refer: the very uncertainties of language mentioned above make it useful to reason with, or by reference to, the meanings of the statements. It is an advantage to have knowledge and understanding of things and events, and not merely of words or codes, *inter alia* because words do not have fixed and certain meanings. Certainly in legal reasoning, when one is testing various possible applications of words in (say) a statute, one keeps in mind not just forms of words, but what one takes to be the reality to which the various alternatives refer. Reasoning using words alone would be very different: the only 'meaning' which any words would have would be that given by substituting other words, or by reference to the place or role of the words in the network of a formal system.

Artificial intelligence (AI) programs have been devised with a view to meeting the problem of uncertainties in meaning. For example, Lotfi Zadeh has developed programs using 'fuzzy logic', recognizing the fuzzy meanings of words (see Zadeh 1977; Negoita 1985 and works there cited). For example, in relation to the word 'tall' as applied to adult male human beings in Western countries, the program might treat seven feet as 100 per cent tall, with a graph down to (say) five feet as being 0 per cent tall. Such techniques could help a computer to reason in ways apparently similar to human beings, but would not fully overcome the problem. Without the non-verbal knowledge of reality lying behind the words used in reasoning, and continually checking for errors due to lack of precision in meaning, information processing remains tied to words and vulnerable to the effects of their imprecisions.

Another line which mechanists could take is to agree that our reasoning does have the characteristic that it is not limited to language, and that it uses our knowledge of things (through information of the type referred to in Chapter 4: appearance, sound, feel, etc.), but to assert that mechanistic reasoning could have this same characteristic. A computer could be provided with 'sight', 'hearing', and 'touch', which would give it (in its own code) the appearance, sound, and feel of things. From this it could construct representations or models of reality with which words could be associated: these (it could be suggested) would be entirely analogous with representations or models constructed by our brains when we actually see, hear, and feel things.

However, the computer's representations or models would be in its own code, as would any words it might use; and its reasoning would be limited to the manipulation of this coded material. The computer's code is relevantly similar to a language, and I suggest that 'reasoning' limited to manipulation of coded material can be in no better case than reasoning limited to manipulation of words: there is still no non-verbal or non-coded access to reality. I look at this further in Section 8.1.

5.3.2. *The Use of Analogy*

Another characteristic of plausible reasoning is the use of analogy. An analogy is a partial likeness between things, which forms a basis for comparison. Arguing or reasoning by analogy is using known similarities between things and/or events and/or states of affairs to suggest or justify conjectures or conclusions about further similarities between them. (This is, I think, the usual meaning of the term now, although it is somewhat different from the argument from analogy described by Greek philosophers, which had to do with equality of ratios and/or proportions.)

Analogy may (like induction) be useful in a process of discovery. Observed similarities between item *A* and item *B*, when one knows item *A* has property *x*, may suggest as something to be investigated that item B also has property *x*. Subsequently, one may seek to justify a hypothesis that item *B* has property *x*; and in this case the original analogy which suggested the hypothesis may be part of that justification (although it need not be). As stated earlier, I am concerned with justification by plausible reasoning, rather than discovery.

Justification through analogy is closely related to other types of plausible reasoning:

1. An inductive argument, for example, from the observation of many (and only) black ravens to the conclusion that all ravens are black, may be compared to an argument by analogy from the same observation to the conclusion that all other objects which are similar to those observed in being ravens will also be similar to them in being black.

2. The application of a term like 'table' to an uncertain case (say, the counter top mentioned earlier) will be guided to a considerable extent by similarities and differences between this case and things which are clearly tables. In cases of legal interpretation of words in legal documents and statutes, this process is used: indeed, in many areas of legal reasoning analogy is used extensively.

3. Analogy is also relevant in the case of a person seeking to understand an unfamiliar language, as exemplified by Quine's linguist (see Section 5.3.1). He will presumably proceed from observed similarities in circumstances of use of words, phrases, and sentences (as between his own language and that of the native tribe) to conclusions about similarities in meaning.

In some cases of reasoning by analogy to a conclusion, one step is to consider what is the closest or best analogue or analogy to a given item. For example, a judge may be faced with a situation which is not covered exactly by any established legal rule, and there may be two different established legal rules each governing slightly different circumstances: then, one question which the judge may well consider is 'which class of these situations governed by the established rules is the best analogy to the subject situation?'

In some types of informal reasoning, the very object is to find the best analogy. An important case (discussed in Hofstadter 1986: 586–9) is that of translation from one language to another by a person familiar with both languages. There will generally be a range of possible translations, some more literal, some more idiomatic, some which perhaps more than others capture the 'flavour' which the original has by reason of such things as puns, rhymes, consonances, associations, etc. A translator will seek the 'best' translation (or analogue, in the new language, of the original), having regard to the nature of what is translated and the purpose of the translation.

The use in reasoning of the concept of similarity (and thus the use of analogy) has been criticized by philosophers.

For example, Nelson Goodman in 'Seven Strictures on Similarity' (Goodman 1970) contends in effect that the concept is either hopelessly vague or else superfluous. His fifth and seventh strictures are respectively: 'Similarity does not account for our predictive, or more generally, our inductive practice'; and 'Similarity cannot be equated with, or measured in terms of, possession of common characteristics' (pp. 23, 25). In relation to the former, he suggests 'that rather than similarity providing any guidelines for inductive practice, inductive practice may provide the basis for some canons of similarity' (p. 24). In relation to the latter, he points to the indeterminacy and ambiguity of statements that two things are similar, unless the respects in which they are similar are specified. He continues: 'when to the statement that two things are similar we add a specification of the property they have in common, we . . . remove an ambiguity; but . . . we render . . . superfluous' our initial statement about similarity (p. 27).

My own view is rather that judgements of unanalysed similarity, and comparisons of unanalysed similarities, are extremely useful, and indeed that our ability to make such judgements and comparisons is at or near the core of our ability to reason informally. Such judgements and comparisons are fallible, and they can be tested, and perhaps rejected or changed, by analysing the similarities in terms of common properties, identifiable differences, etc. But such analysis will rarely exhaust the original judgement, and will generally itself involve unanalysed similarities. For example, a judgement that a man is like his mother in appearance, or more like his mother than his father, can be analysed in terms of particular features (eyes, nose, build); but the analysis will not cover the field of the original judgement, and will itself involve further judgements of unanalysed similarities.

In my view that analogy is central to our informal rationality, I find an unlikely ally in artificial-intelligence writer Douglas Hofstadter. In Hofstadter (1986) he writes:

what good are analogies? . . . What is the purpose of trying to establish a mapping between two things that *do not* map onto each other in reality? The answer is surely very complex, but the heart of it must be that it is good for our survival (or our genes' survival), because we do it all the time. Analogy and reminding, whether they are accurate or not, guide all our thought patterns. Being attuned to vague resemblances is the hallmark of intelligence, for better or for worse. (p. 556)

Hofstadter goes on to consider the mechanization of analogies, and in particular his own project (which he calls COPYCAT) to develop a computer program to that end. Here we part company: while I accept that a program with sufficient rules of thumb could find analogies quite successfully in many cases, I believe that *we* work *inter alia* with unanalysed similarities, and that this gives us an edge over computers.

5.3.3. *Conflicting Reasons of Different Types*

Another characteristic of plausible reasoning which is relevant to the feasibility of mechanizing it is that very often there are reasons for and against various alternative conclusions (whether these conclusions are alternative actions which could be performed, or alternative judgements about truth or value which could be arrived at); and very often these conflicting reasons are of such widely differing types as to be apparently incommensurable.

1. Scientific reasoning. Even in relation to the evaluation of scientific theories, there is no single scale for assessment. I referred earlier to the various 'good-making' features of such theories identified by Newton-Smith, and it is difficult to see how these features could be reduced to the same scale: for example, how could one systematically calculate a score for the respective merits of two theories, one of which seems preferable on the basis of simplicity, the other on the basis of fertility? This problem is adverted to by Popper (1959: 408), and also in the following passage by Nozick:

There are different virtues of a scientific theory, different dimensions along which it can be evaluated: explanatory power, goodness of fit with the data, breadth and diversity of evidential support, degree of testability, range and diversity of phenomena it covers, simplicity, fit with other accepted theories, and so on. . . . there certainly is no adequate systematic proposal about how these different desiderata of a theory are to be combined in an overall evaluation, about how two competing theories are to be comparatively evaluated or ranked when one is better along some of these dimensions, while the other is better along others. (Nozick 1981: 483)

If this is to be done by mechanized reasoning, the theory must be selected which has 'the highest overall weighted value' (cf. Boden 1972: 224–5). Yet this presupposes a single scale, on which the different virtues of different theories may systematically be assigned 'weights'. No method for doing this has been devised, and our own conscious deliberations in such matters do not appear to be directed towards discovering, by means of algorithms, what is the appropriate 'weight' for each of the opposing considerations. As argued by Nozick: the reasons for and against alternative actions (in which can be included judgements) 'do not come with previously given precisely specified weights; the decision process is not one of discovering such precise weights, but of assigning them' (1981: 294; I would add, 'in each particular case'). Nozick continues: 'The process not only weighs reasons, it (also) weights them. At least, so it sometimes feels.'

It is a feature of plausible reasoning that it deals with incommensurable considerations, and does so without appeal to any higher-order standard by which they may be compared; so there is no need, as supposed in Kane (1985: 83 ff.), to postulate random processes to select between such considerations. His suggestion that this is necessary seems to flow from the hold which the mechanistic view of reasoning has had, and from non-advertence to the reality of plausible reasoning.

2. Practical reasoning. It is perhaps in legal reasoning, where one usually has two (or more) competing contentions, each of which often has substantial incommensurable considerations in its favour, that these problems arise most starkly. I will briefly look at some aspects of this in Section 5.4. However, similar problems arise in practical reasoning generally.

As mentioned earlier, practical reasoning often involves decisions between countervailing considerations, which may be of different types, such that they cannot be reduced to a commensurate scale: examples of such countervailing considerations are self-interest and interests of others; and duty and expediency. In the absence of a common scale, a decision between such considerations can only be on the basis of some poorly defined 'weighing'.

Some years ago, it appeared to me that it might be possible to approach practical reasoning in general, and moral decisions in particular, in a way which involved a single scale only. The one plausible way in which I thought this might be done was to adopt some utilitarian test, probably an act-utilitarian test, so that a right action in any circumstance was the one with consequences at least as good as those of any alternative action. However, on closer examination it seemed to me that this was not plausible, at least as a test which could be applied by persons in deciding what to do. My reason for this was that a person's adoption of such a test as a sole test, rather than accepting that duties may arise from circumstances and relationships with other persons, could itself have bad consequences. Indeed, it seemed to me that to adopt act-utilitarianism and apply it rigorously would involve such problems, in particular with one's close personal relationships, that it was more rational to reject it (see Hodgson 1967). I do not now agree with everything in that book, but its central argument remains, I believe, the only argument which meets head-on the act-utilitarian's most appealing contention, namely that it must be irrational rule-worship to follow a rule where to do so would produce worse consequences than not following it. The argument stated shortly is that being a rule-following person enables one *inter alia* honestly to make commitments to other persons, which are valuable, and which cannot honestly be made by a person who is not a rule-following person: and one cannot at once be a rule-following person and also break rules whenever it has best consequences to do so.

In the result, it seems clear to me that any satisfactory system of morality must allow for cases where there is a clash of considerations of duty (to persons to whom one has a commitment or some special relationship) and expediency (production of best consequences for oneself, or for everyone). Similarly, considerations of justice may clash with considerations of expediency or utility. Unless one says that in such a case one of such considerations always wins (and I have already suggested it cannot be expediency or utility) then one must determine which carries greatest weight in each particular case.

Such considerations cannot, on any precise and generally applicable basis, be reduced to a common scale. How then can a decision between them be made? Only, I would suggest, by informally weighing them in individual cases, in circumstances where there are no previously specified comparative weights for the competing considerations. Perhaps there is some sort of rough scaling of the competing considerations, but this, like the weighing, could not be formalized. The relative weights of the competing considerations are determined by the decision, rather than vice versa.

It might be said that in such cases competing considerations are rated subconsciously by the brain to some sort of common scale of desire or volition to which all opposing considerations are converted; and/or that such a decision is not a case of rational choice but merely the effect of irrational desires.

As regards the former, on what basis could such scaling be performed? And why can it be done subconsciously, when consciously we cannot see any way of doing it?

As regards the latter, it is difficult to see why that sort of decision should not be regarded as rational. It is true that emotional feelings enter into the decision process in these cases, but these feelings themselves can be subjected to rational scrutiny. This is certainly so in the related field of aesthetic judgement, which is widely regarded as a field of rational endeavour.

3. The role of emotion. Indeed, I believe that emotional feelings are an essential part of our general rationality in all fields (see Oatley 1989). For example, scientists talk of the beauty of theories such as the theory of relativity, relying on aesthetic judgements (and thereby on emotional feelings) as indicia of truth. Emotions can be highly irrational; but such irrationality in oneself may be identified, controlled, and perhaps eliminated, by application of one's general rationality (which, as I say, itself includes emotion). In making rational decisions, one attends to 'feelings' of similarity and difference, rightness and wrongness, beauty and ugliness, clarity and confusion, coherence and repugnance, simplicity and complexity, and so on. The totality of rational appraisal comprehends such things as dialectic and rhetoric (to mention some traditional categories) as well as logic.

4. One correct answer? Of course, when what is required for a decision is a choice between factors which cannot precisely and reliably be reduced to a common scale, there may in some cases be no unique 'correct' decision. In some cases, all or most reasonable human beings would agree on the 'correct' decision; in others, there would not be such agreement.

It might be contended that accordingly all that is necessary (and probably all that occurs) is that the brain should instantiate a formal system which decides the obvious cases correctly—that is, in accordance with what most reasonable human beings would decide—and the balance at random. This formal system need only be capable of roughly scaling the competing factors, perhaps assigning a range to each: then if all calculations using the extremities of each range give the same result, it could be treated as correct. Otherwise, the result could either be given by calculations based on averages, or else at random: it would not really matter. At its formal substratum the brain might work that way; and a computer could simulate it.

That is a possibility, but I think it is unlikely. It overlooks *inter alia* what has been called 'the infinity of argument'. That is, that any proposition and any step of reasoning may be questioned and made the subject of plausible reasoning, quite possibly involving competing non-commensurable considerations. Any basis of scaling, any value judgement, can be reconsidered. Conscious decision-making enables one to adopt and change any method of dealing with such competing considerations: such flexibility may depend on people being affective, being able to make value judgements which are in a sense ultimate and unsupported, but which may nevertheless be challenged and changed on the basis of plausible reasoning.

5.3.4. *Reliance on Weighing and Judgement*

It has already been noted that in so far as our ordinary reasoning is not logically valid, it will on examination be seen to involve steps which come down to what is usually referred to as judgement, or weighing alternatives, or the like. I have already suggested that most of our reasoning, in science, philosophy, practical reasoning, and law (*inter alia*), involves such steps; and indeed in many cases those steps are the most significant ones.

If such steps are tested on the basis of formal logical validity, they are seen to be invalid: from that point of view the likelihood that the conclusion is false (given the truth of the premises) is no different from the likelihood that it is true: neither the conclusion nor its negation is entailed, and on the basis of formal logic no more can be said. However, the argument involving these steps is put as being persuasive, and is generally accepted as such. Such persuasiveness cannot depend on logic: it must depend on some informal judgement or weighing.

To avoid the last conclusion, one or both of two propositions could be put:

1. Such steps in argument really involve unstated premises, and when these are supplied, such steps become a valid logical inference.

2. Formal systems with rules of inference wider than the rules of logic could be used, so as to make conclusions, which are not logically entailed by premises, plausible or probable; for example, rules of induction as formalized by Carnap.

As regards (1), this does not seem to be a satisfactory explanation either of how plausible reasoning actually works, or of why it has persuasive force. In relation to induction, it is vulnerable to the Hume–Popper infinite regress. In many, perhaps most, cases, the conclusion of plausible reasoning seems more readily acceptable than any premisses which might be suggested in order to convert the argument into a logically valid one. Particularly is this so where there are two countervailing considerations, and one is judged to have greater weight in the particular case: for example, the convincing demeanour of one witness in a court of law who tells one story, and the plausibility of the different story told by another witness. One may be able to give any number of reasons why a judgement is made in the particular case, and be confident that it is correct; but find it impossible to formulate a statement or rule of more general application which can be mechanically applied in such cases, and which one accepts to be correct as readily as one accepts the result in the particular case.

As regards (2), I have already discussed the problem of induction. Furthermore, this does not reflect how plausible reasoning actually works. Such a system *may* underlie such reasoning and explain its persuasive force. However, I suggest that we could not reasonably be persuaded of this. Any argument seeking so to persuade us will itself be a plausible argument appealing to rational judgement and weighing of reasons: that is, it will depend upon the very sort of argument it seeks to explain away.

The crucial step of judgement or weighing is of its nature inconclusive, as is all plausible reasoning. This is my most fundamental disagreement with Penrose. In Penrose (1989: 426–8) he adopts a Platonic view of mathematical truths, and suggests that 'consciousness is closely associated with sensing of necessary truths' (p. 429). In Section 1.3 I expressed scepticism about necessary truths, and I contend that all knowledge is fallible and provisional. My view is, rather, that consciousness is for plausible reasoning, which can show probability of approximate truth, but is of its nature fallible.

Finally, it will be seen that I have assimilated plausible reasoning about facts (in the case of scientific theories) and about values (in the case of practical and aesthetic reasoning). I believe that the two are much closer than is sometimes recognized. Emotion enters into both areas. And in both areas there may not be a unique correct answer, but, rather, a range of answers more or less (in some cases indistinguishably) rationally justifiable (see my discussion of truth and language in Section 1.1). But, on the other hand, there may be a unique correct answer. For example, in courts of law, often a decision has to be made (involving no problem of conceptualization) about what actually happened, for example whether the accused shot the victim: there is one correct answer, but generally only plausible reasoning can decide it.

5.4. Legal Reasoning

To illustrate some of the points raised in this chapter, I will consider some aspects of legal reasoning.

It is convenient for the purposes of this discussion to consider three processes of legal reasoning, at least one of which is involved in any but the
simplest cases:

1. deciding the facts, i.e. what actually happened;
2. deciding the applicable law; and
3. applying the law to the facts, i.e. deciding what is the appropriate
   description or categorization of the facts for the purposes of the relevant
   rules of law.

5.4.1. *Deciding the Facts*

Facts have to be decided on the basis of evidence given by witnesses, and
documentary and other 'real' evidence in the case. Even if there is no substantial conflict in the evidence, it might be necessary to make a decision
about the accuracy of certain evidence, which (even in the absence of direct
conflict) may raise questions about the accuracy of observation and recollection of witnesses, and about their veracity. Assessment of these matters may
depend on such things as the demeanour of a witness; the answers he gives to
various questions, for example about events not centrally involved in the case
but of which (if he is telling the truth) he should have similarly detailed
recollection; his motives for either telling the truth or misrepresenting the
position in one way or another; the plausibility (as a matter of common sense
and experience) of the account he gives; how well the evidence fits (as a
matter of common sense and experience) with other evidence in the case,
which all must be similarly assessed. The evidence in the case may include
documents prepared at the time of the events in question: these may be
extremely reliable evidence of what happened, but even here the possibility
of accidental or deliberate inaccuracy has to be considered, in the light, for
example, of the means of knowledge of the person preparing the document,
the apparent time and care taken to ensure accuracy, the motives of such
person to record matters truthfully or untruthfully, etc.

It is clear that many of the factors I have outlined could point in different
directions, even in the absence of outright conflict in the evidence. When
there is outright conflict in the evidence, the same factors arise in assessing
all the evidence on both sides, and it is necessary to weigh them all, and
ultimately come to a decision about what in fact happened. The decision can
rarely be absolutely certain: in common-law jurisdictions, it has to be
'beyond reasonable doubt' in criminal cases, and 'on the balance of probabilities' in civil cases. In some cases, this decision has to be made by a judge
or magistrate, in others by a jury with the assistance of legal directions from a
judge.

It is clear that, in reaching a decision on such matters, factors of entirely
different types have to be taken into consideration: demeanour, apparent

ability to observe and remember, motives, plausibility of the story, coherence with other evidence, etc. There is no way in which these factors can be systematically reduced to a common scale, so that points awarded for each can be weighted and added up, and totals for different versions compared. In assessing such matters as demeanour, acuity, motives, plausibility, coherence, one does not and cannot put such factors completely into words. An assessment is made on the basis of one's experience and common sense, the result of which can be partially expressed in words. But such words do not exhibit the whole basis of the assessment: the actual 'weight' to be given to each factor cannot be explicitly stated. In all these matters, the reasoning process ultimately has to be expressed in terms of weighing various factors, and coming to a conclusion on the basis of one's judgement, which one may support by exhibiting as best one can one's reasons. These reasons generally do not support the conclusion as a matter of logic; and if one looks for premises which together with those reasons would do so, generally one cannot find premises which one accepts as readily as one accepts the conclusion.

5.4.2. *Deciding the Law*

In common-law jurisdictions the sources of law are essentially statutes and previous court decisions. Even the application of statutes may involve uncertain plausible reasoning about the meaning of words, as considered in Section 5.3.1: this may be considered as a problem of deciding the law, or of applying it.

In relation to previous court decisions, there is greater room for plausible reasoning. Generally a court is bound to apply a rule stated in a previous court decision only if it both was stated by a superior court in the same hierarchy of courts, and was part of the *ratio decidendi* of the case in which it was stated, i.e. a rule on the basis of which that superior court actually decided the case. (Other rules stated by courts, called *obiter dicta*, generally carry less 'weight'.) Otherwise, the rule has merely persuasive force, which may vary from very slight (e.g. if stated by an inferior court, and not in any event part of the *ratio decidendi* of the case but merely *obiter dicta*) through moderate (e.g. *ratio decidendi* of courts of equivalent status in related hierarchies) and strong (e.g. *ratio decidendi* of courts of superior status in related hierarchies or the same status in the same hierarchy) to overwhelming (e.g. if included in carefully considered *obiter dicta* given unanimously by a superior court, being the highest court in the particular hierarchy).

It sometimes happens that conflicting previous decisions can be found on particular points; and it sometimes happens that previous decisions on related points, while not actually conflicting, do not cohere or make good sense when considered together. It sometimes happens that no previous decision states a rule which applies precisely to the case presently to be decided, but that there are two or more rules which could be extended to cover the case, giving different results; or that two or more rules have been stated in contexts different from each other and from that of the present case, each of which literally applies to the present case, giving different results.

Even from this brief and inadequate outline of what is involved in deciding questions of law, it is obvious that such decisions often involve many of the features I have been discussing. There is obviously considerable indeterminacy as to what is *ratio decidendi* and what is *obiter dicta*, particularly in a decision of a superior court in which more than one judgement is given, and the reasons for the decision are expressed differently. There is also indeterminacy in considering whether rules, which do not actually conflict, cohere or make good sense when considered together.

Thus one may have a rule that is arguably but not certainly part of the *ratio decidendi* of a decision of superior court of a related hierarchy giving one result in the instant case, and something that is only an *obiter dictum* of one judge given in a decision of a superior court in the same hierarchy giving another result. The former may cohere well with some established rules, and not with others; the latter may cohere reasonably well with all established rules. There is no way in which such considerations (and there may be many others) could be reduced to a common scale.

One is certainly reasoning with words here, since all the legal sources are expressed in words. However, when assessing the weight to be given to particular rules according to who stated them and in what circumstances, and assessing how well two rules or groups of rules cohere, one is dealing with ideas which are generally not fully and accurately put into words in one's reasoning, and one's conclusions and reasons for them generally express such ideas only partially and imperfectly. In any event, when one comes to decide what rule or rules to apply to the present case, where countervailing considerations of the type being discussed apply, the most important parts of the reasoning are not logically valid inferences, but matters of weighing the conflicting considerations and coming to a decision on the basis of one's judgement. Further premises which could make the inference a logical one are not stated. Indeed, courts generally avoid basing their decision on rules which are any wider than necessary for deciding the particular case, and often counsel against doing so.

These matters are discussed in a number of books (e.g. Hodgson 1967 and books there cited), and I will not pursue them in detail here. Some discussions tend to treat decisions as based on strict legal reasoning only in so far as the reasoning is logically valid, and to treat the residue as something else, such as the expression of non-rational values or preference. I contend strongly that plausible legal reasoning is involved *all the way through* in such decisions: in some cases there is no unique correct solution, and some examples show better legal reasoning than others, but virtually all exhibit informal rationality.

5.4.3. *Applying the Law*

In many cases, applying the legal rules to the facts involves deciding whether the facts as proved fall within categories such as the following: reasonable care, reasonable time, reasonable notice; consideration (for a contract); merchantable quality; substantial interference with competition. In order to decide whether facts do or do not fall into such categories, it is often necessary to consider countervailing considerations of different types; to envisage, in ways not fully expressible in words, the reality of what has been proved, and actual human beings acting in the circumstances proved; to weigh the various considerations and come to a judgement on them.

Even when the categories involved are apparently more precise, similar problems arise and similar reasoning occurs. The question may be whether a person has been caused loss by fraud. It may be proved that the defendant made a representation to this person which was true in some respects and not in others, which may complicate the question whether the misrepresentation was material. It may not be proved that the defendant knew that the representation was false, and so there may be a question whether the defendant was reckless, that is, knew that the representation might have been false but proceeded to make it not caring whether it was true or false. There may be a question whether the plaintiff relied on the representation, perhaps where he had some suspicions about the matter and/or had some other reasons to act as he did irrespective of his belief in the representation. Then there might be questions concerning the causation of the plaintiff's loss and foreseeability of it. At each stage there may be difficulties in finding primary facts (process (1) at the beginning of Section 5.4), and further difficulties in deciding if they fit in to the relevant legal categories (process (3)). Informal reasoning of the type discussed is involved at each point.

5.5. The Mechanization of Plausible Reasoning

Matters of the kind raised in this chapter have to some extent been considered by cognitive psychologists, computer scientists, and philosophers concerned with artificial intelligence.

Weizenbaum (1984) refers to the 'unavoidable question': 'Are all the decisionmaking processes that humans employ reducible to effective procedures and hence amenable to machine computation?' (p. 67). As mentioned earlier, he considers it an open question. See also Chouraqui (1984: 144–55) and Sloman (1984: 40–1).

There are several recent publications which deal in various ways with the derivation of effective procedures for reasoning by analogy, induction, and other such processes (e.g. Holland *et al.* 1986; Jackendoff 1987; Johnson-Laird 1988; Keane 1988). However, they concentrate mainly on practical procedures for performing something like these processes. There are few attempts to deal in depth with the problems of principle I have identified in relation to induction and plausible reasoning generally: that is, to explain how effective procedures can achieve informal rationality, and to relate our conscious informal rationality to the unconscious effective procedures which (on the consensus view) must underlie it.

Indeed, Holland *et al.* (1986: 6–9) contend that a formal and syntactic approach to induction cannot succeed, and they offer a 'pragmatic resolution' to the paradoxes of Hempel and Goodman, which depends on 'variability conditions' (pp. 233–5). They contend that we can use inductive procedures in relation to such things as 'ravens' and such properties as 'green', because we have background knowledge which bears on their variability; but not in relation to 'non-black things' or 'grue', because we have no such background knowledge about them. The authors accept that the application of this background knowledge cannot be formalized, so (it would seem) they also accept that informal rationality cannot be explained by reference to effective procedures.

There are other writers in this area who contend that human informal rationality is highly fallible and subject to misleading biases, and is inferior to appropriate effective procedures (see, for example, articles in Kahneman *et al.* 1982). There is no doubt that human informal reasoning is fallible, and may be assisted and corrected by formal reasoning; and that, in certain respects, without such assistance and correction it can be inferior to appropriate effective procedures. However, this in no way refutes my contention that there is informal rationality which cannot be reduced to or comprehended in effective procedures.

Some of the best consensus writing on the problems of principle involved here is by Hofstadter, and I will refer to some of it in what follows.

5.5.1. *A System of Effective Procedures as Underlying Rational Thought?*

Most people would accept that human reasoning of the kinds I have discussed is rational; and that such reasoning does not, at least consciously or explicitly, follow valid logical rules, or indeed any system of effective procedures. Also it is clear that any mechanistic reasoning must be in accordance with a system of effective procedures: that is, in accordance with explicit rules which can be applied mechanically. It could be that such a system underlies human reasoning: a mechanistic brain operating according to causal laws would be equivalent to such a system, and is indeed asserted by consensus writers to underlie human rationality.

However, if this is so, then somehow the informal, non-logical reasoning of the kinds discussed must correspond to, and be reducible to, the application of the rules of such a system. And if that is correct, then it is difficult to resist the conclusion that the rationality of the informal, non-logical conscious reasoning is dependent on, and secondary to, rationality-giving characteristics of the system of effective procedures which underlies it and to which it corresponds and is reducible. That is, plausible reasoning (on this view) is rational because there is underlying it a sound system of effective procedures: and what occurs consciously is some sort of approximation or simplified summary of what occurs subconsciously, or outside the realm of consciousness.

These thoughts give rise to the following questions:

1. If a system of effective procedures does so underlie non-logical reasoning, why have the rules of this system (other than logical or mathematical rules) not been established?

2. Why has evolution favoured consciousness, which on this view is unnecessary; and favoured not merely its existence, but also its use for solving difficult problems?

3. Given that there is consciousness, why does it deceive one into thinking that one's conscious non-logical reasoning is rational and efficacious, rather than a non-rational and ineffectual tip of a substantially non-conscious mechanical rationality-supporting iceberg?

It could be said in answer to (1) that non-logical plausible reasoning is far easier to *do* than to *describe* or reduce to algorithms: and of course it is only by describing such reasoning and reducing it to algorithms that the rules of any underlying system could be established. I will pursue this by considering some passages from Hofstadter.

As regards (2), I deal with this in Chapter 6.

In relation to (3), I will be suggesting in Section 5.6 that our conscious thinking is our basic model for rational thinking; and it generally proceeds by non-formal reasoning, dependent on consciousness. Our formulations of rules of logic and mathematics, and our descriptions of non-formal reasoning, are all on the basis of conscious informal rationality.

5.5.2. *Hofstadter's Approach*

In *Gödel, Escher, Bach* (Hofstadter 1980), Hofstadter asks what sort of rules could 'capture all of what we think of as intelligent behaviour'. He continues:

Certainly there must be rules on all sorts of different levels. There must be many 'just plain' rules. There must be 'metarules' to modify the 'just plain' rules; then 'meta-metarules' to modify the metarules, and so on. The flexibility of intelligence comes from the enormous number of different rules, and levels of rules. The reason that so many rules on so many different levels must exist is that in life, a creature is faced with millions of situations of completely different types. In some situations, there are stereotyped responses which require 'just plain' rules. Some situations are mixtures of stereotyped situations—thus they require rules for deciding which of the 'just plain' rules to apply. Some situations cannot be classified—thus there must exist rules for inventing new rules . . . and on and on. (pp. 26–7)

In this passage, there is some recognition of the complexity of the problem, but no hint about *how* it is that informal reasoning can be effected by means of large numbers of rules, and of levels of rules.

Later, Hofstadter invokes the Church–Turing thesis to support an assertion that what is human-computable is machine-computable (p. 429); and in chapter 17 (pp. 559 ff.) he elaborates on this thesis in various ways. He asserts (p. 568) that, 'when one computes something, one's mental activity can be mirrored isomorphically in some FlooP program' (by which he means a computer program written in a language that he calls FlooP, which is of sufficient power to program general and partial recursive functions—it is not necessary to consider such functions here).

He then again introduces the notion of levels of operation of information-processing systems, though not here, it would seem, in the sense of levels of rules: rather, it is in the sense of levels of description, ranging from the bottom level ('neural firings, or perhaps even lower level events') to the top level (where there is a meaningful representation of the real world, which perhaps may be equated with the level of consciousness). He considers whether the processes at the various levels are 'skimmable', that is (in effect) whether they can be simulated by a computer without regard to processes at lower levels.

He suggests (p. 570) that at the bottom level 'there may be no interpretations of the primitive elements'; and continues: 'Yet on the top level, there emerges a meaningful interpretation—a mapping from the large "clouds" of neural activity . . . onto the real world.' He proposes that 'events on the neural level . . . are there purely as the substrate to support the higher level' and says:

Personally, I would guess that such multilevel architecture of concept-handling systems becomes necessary just when processes involving images and analogies become significant elements of the program—in contrast to processes which are supposed to carry out strictly deductive reasoning. Processes which carry out deductive reasoning can be programmed in essentially one single level, and are therefore skimmable, by definition. According to my hypothesis, then, imagery and analogical thought processes intrinsically require several layers of substrate and are therefore intrinsically non-skimmable. (pp. 570–1)

He then asserts that 'a computer simulation of a neural network . . . is in principle feasible, no matter how complicated the network, provided that the behaviour of individual neurons can be described in terms of computations which a computer can carry out' (p. 572); and proceeds to the conclusion 'All brain processes are derived from a computable substrate.'

This is, of course, only a brief selection from the extensive discussions touching on the problem in *Gödel, Escher, Bach*; but it is sufficient, I think, to serve as a basis for an indication of what appear to me to be fundamental difficulties of his approach, and of any similar approach.

5.5.3. *Difficulties of Hofstadter's Approach*

It seems to me that there are two difficulties which can be pointed to, one of a negative and the other of a positive character.

The 'negative' difficulty is that Hofstadter's discussion does not begin to solve the problems of mechanizing informal plausible reasoning, to which I have referred: the assigning of prior probabilities, Goodman's 'new riddle' of induction, the use of ordinary language and analogy, deciding between conflicting incommensurable reasons, the ultimate resort to 'judgement', maintaining the objectivity of reason, and so on. Indeed, when he comes to consider the nature of evidence, Hofstadter almost concedes as much:

Is it possible to define what evidence is? Is it possible to lay down laws as to how to make sense out of situations? Probably not, for any rigid rules would undoubtedly have exceptions, and nonrigid rules are not rules . . . My feeling is that there are guidelines which one can give, and out of them an organic synthesis can be made. But inevitably some amount of judgment and intuition must enter the picture—things which are different in different people. They will also be different in different AI programs . . . My feeling is that the process by which we decide what is valid or what is true is an art; and that it relies as deeply on a sense of beauty and simplicity as it does on rock-solid principles of logic or reasoning or anything else which can be objectively formalized. (pp. 694–5)

However, somewhat inconsistently, he goes on to assert that human intelligence is programmable, but that, when artificial intelligence reaches or surpasses this level, it 'will still be plagued by the problems of art, beauty, and simplicity, and will run up against these things constantly in its own search for knowledge and understanding'.

This leads to the 'positive' difficulty in his approach, which is the way that it points up the elusiveness of informal human reason, and leads to ambivalence and even contradiction in attempts to describe and locate it.

On the one hand, Hofstadter is at pains to deny any source of rationality in the high-level operations of the brain–mind, outside the rationality-giving features of the mechanistic system which (he contends) underlies it. This follows directly from Hofstadter's versions of the Church–Turing thesis. A clear statement to this effect is to be found, given by Hofstadter's *alter ego* Tortoise (in one of his Lewis Carroll-influenced dialogues), in Hofstadter (1986):

Reasons may sound plausible but they are never the essence of a decision. The verbalized reason is just the tip of an iceberg. Or, to change images, conflicts of ideas are like wars, in which *every reason has its army*. When reasons collide, the real battleground is not at the verbal level . . . it's really a battle between opposing armies of neural firings bringing in their heavy artillery of connotations, imagery, analogies, memories, residual atavistic fears, and ancient biological realities. (p. 621)

Thus, in so far as there is rationality at the top level, it must depend upon and be reducible to the rationality-supporting qualities of the computable mechanistic steps at lower levels. Yet, as we have seen, Hofstadter also asserts that 'events on the neural level are there purely as substrate to support the higher level'; and he appears (in Hofstadter 1980: 710) to accept Sperry's contention that events at the top level, namely conscious thoughts, can 'push' neurons.

This ambivalence, or contradiction, is also illustrated by his assertion that, just as a human being reasons informally, and makes errors, an intelligent machine would do similarly. In Hofstadter (1980) he asserts:

let us say you are having a hard time making up your mind whether to order a cheeseburger or a pineappleburger. Does this imply that your neurons are also balking, having difficulty deciding whether or not to fire? Of course not. Your hamburger-confusion is a high-level state which fully depends on the efficient firing of thousands of neurons in very organized ways . . . There is no reason to believe that a computer's faultlessly functioning hardware could not support high-level symbolic behaviour which would represent such high-level states as confusion, forgetting, or appreciation of beauty. (p. 577)

Hofstadter thus makes a virtue (in his approach) of the coexistence of high-level confusion etc. with a logical computable substrate. Yet if, as Hofstadter seems to assert, all rationality *does* reduce to logical steps, then any informality, confusion, or error at the top level would be so much gratuitous 'noise' which could only damage rationality. Why would one introduce it into a computer program? And why would evolution have favoured it in human beings? A more reasonable explanation is, rather, that the possibility of confusion and error is a price which must be paid for the capacity to engage in efficacious informal plausible reasoning, which cannot be mechanized.

5.5.4. *Is it for the Future to Decide?*

One response to my whole line of argument is to say it is premature. AI research is in its infancy. As computer hardware is developed, and programs become more sophisticated, it is likely, or at least possible, that any valuable aspects of human plausible reasoning will be available to computers, and will be seen to be so available.

There is force in this suggestion. My arguments are of a theoretical character, and such arguments can be misleading: it is said, for example, that according to the theory of aeronautical engineering, a bumble-bee cannot fly. The failure of work on artificial intelligence to achieve anything like the results predicted in its early years by no means indicates that it will never do so. The only reasonable course, it may be said, is to suspend judgement until the results are in.

However, I think the suggestion should be rejected, for three main reasons: the present need for a view on the matter, the strength and nature of the arguments now available, and the unsupportability of the contrary view.

1. The need for a view. I suggest that judgement cannot reasonably be suspended for a period which is necessarily indefinite. At the individual level, any person seeking a philosophy of life will need to form a view on the character of the human mind, in particular on whether or not it is no more than a complicated computer. At the level of society, the question bears heavily on important social and ethical questions, such as genetic engineering, euthanasia, abortion, and animal rights. Public opinion has already been heavily influenced by consensus assertions. Continued consensus assertions (such as those by Moravec to the effect that it will shortly be possible to preserve the 'living essence' of human beings in computers) will further influence public opinion, presumably (for example) in the general direction of favouring unrestricted manipulation of human brains for (real and supposed) therapeutic purposes, and unrestricted genetic engineering of human beings. It is necessary, therefore, to consider what view *now* seems most reasonable, recognizing, of course, that it can only be provisional and subject to revision.

2. Available arguments. The arguments which I have put do not relate to matters of technical shortcomings, or complexity, or the like: they are not, in Turing's terms, arguments from 'various disabilities'. They concern matters of principle, which have been closely considered by philosophers such as Hume, Popper, Goodman, and Putnam. Work on AI to date has suggested no solution to these matters of principle which retains any concept of informal rationality; but such work has tended rather to confirm the problems. The most reasonable possible solution which is consistent with the consensus appears to be that based on Hume's appeal to habit, which requires the discounting of any objective informal rationality; namely, that there are just mechanistic procedures used by the brain–mind, which have been selected by evolution as useful for survival and reproduction, and which we take to be rational. The problems with this solution are along the lines identified by Nagel and Putnam, namely that informal rationality *appears* to be far more objective and general than this solution suggests, and that (as asserted in (3) below) the solution is self-defeating.

3. The unsupportability of the contrary view. Any system (or collection of systems) of effective procedures which was propounded as incorporating all the merits of human plausible reasoning could itself be supported (as successfully doing so) *only* by means of plausible reasoning. If the supporting plausible reasoning was exactly as formalized by the proposed system, then the whole question is begged. If the supporting plausible reasoning was *not* as so formalized, then there must be recognition that the formalization is incomplete and inadequate. I consider this further in Section 5.6.

So it comes to this. Either each rational step in our thinking is based on, or reducible to, effective procedures (with or without random steps); or some of our rational thinking is not mechanistic. If the former is correct, we are of course not aware of most of such procedures, just as we are unaware of mechanistic steps in our brain which (for example) help us to see. It has not yet been possible to state what those procedures are, and how they combine to make up our plausible reasoning. My contention is that plausible reasoning cannot without residue be reduced to mechanistic steps; and that such residue involves rational thinking which depends on consciousness.

5.6. Formal Reasoning Based on Plausible Reasoning

In Section 5.5, I looked at the contention that plausible reasoning is the conscious tip, as it were, of the iceberg of a mechanistic brain operating mechanistically, in a way which can be represented by a formal system or a system of effective procedures. I suggested that, if that is correct, the rationality of plausible reasoning must be dependent upon the rationality-giving features of the underlying system; and that this in turn must mean that plausible reasoning must be capable of being formalized, and reduced to a system of formal reasoning.

In this section, I suggest that the truth is quite the contrary. I do not deny that to some extent human reasoning is supported by a mechanistic instantiation of a formal system. But I say that formal reasoning is an invention of human reason; and that this human reason itself transcends formal reasoning, and in its most important aspects involves informal plausible reasoning. Further, although we do use formal logic and other formal reasoning to test and appraise informal plausible reasoning, ultimately formal reasoning is justified by plausible reasoning, rather than vice versa.

5.6.1. *Formal Reasoning Invented and Learnt*

The use of formally valid reasoning is not something undertaken by human beings in their conscious thinking without some process of invention, discovery, and/or learning. The rules of formal logic, and of mathematics, have been invented and/or discovered over the centuries, by application of informal plausible conscious reasoning, and have been learnt by succeeding generations.

Furthermore, when a person who has learnt such rules reasons in accordance with them, he does so fallibly: his memory of the rules is fallible, and he can make mistakes in applying them. For example, when one adds a column of numbers, one knows that mistakes can be made. (That is why one sometimes checks the result by first adding from the top and then adding from the bottom: if the two results coincide, one can be reasonably confident no mistake has been made.) So even in the actual application of formal rules, the conscious reasoning involves some process other than the mere mechanical application of the rules (cf. Marr 1982: 348).

It could be suggested that it can equally be argued that the possibility of a malfunction in the circuits of a pocket calculator means that its operations involve something more than the mere mechanical application of rules. However, the fallibility of conscious human applications of mathematical rules is of a different type: it is not the possible result of a malfunction of the circuits of the brain. Mistakes are made even though the circuits of the brain are functioning correctly; and they can usually be detected and corrected simply by the person concerned attending more closely and carefully to the calculations in question, or perhaps by his writing them down.

I suggest, therefore, that, even in the conscious application of formal rules, a wider rationality is also involved. Is this rationality itself the outcome of the operation of a formal system? Certainly, it is not so consciously. Furthermore, we are confident in our use of formal rules, in particular those of logic and of mathematics, because we can recognize them as valid and correct, and can recognize their limitations, by application of our more general rationality. This is shown, I suggest, in my consideration of the limitations to the 'necessary truths' of logic, in Section 1.3. If and in so far as our rationality is dependent on some further underlying formal system, operating subconsciously, presumably our confidence in that formal system also depends on its being recognized as valid and correct: if so, however, all we have available to do this is our general rationality, which on this hypothesis is itself dependent on that formal system.

Of course, we do recognize that formal logic can be used to appraise and correct our informal reasoning: but this in no way contradicts my contention that formal logic is itself invented, discovered, and/or learnt, and recognized as valid and correct, by application of this same informal plausible reasoning, which is certainly not infallible or incorrigible, but which can be compelling and convincing. Reasonable certainty or assurance about the results of such reasoning is not simply a matter of applying rules of logic to accepted premisses, although this may be helpful. Rather, it is achieved by a process somewhat similar to looking closely and carefully at something, to be sure of what it is. In a similar way, one examines one's reasoning carefully, trying to bring to bear on it as many relevant considerations as possible, in order to be sure about it. Rules of logic may be helpful in this process, but ultimately one can rely only on one's judgement about such matters as what things are relevant, what weight they should be given, and what is the correct conclusion.

5.6.2. *Formal Reasoning Tested by Plausible Reasoning*

A person who accepts the mechanistic view must accept that his own rationality (and thus the rationality of his own acceptance of his mechanistic view) is dependent upon, indeed determined by, a purely formal causal system; which is not itself justified by any further rationality. There simply is no further, or different, rationality which could justify it. Any confidence which such a person might have in his own rationality could be no greater than his confidence in the underlying formal system; and any confidence in the underlying formal system must depend on confidence in his own rationality.

As mentioned earlier, the most plausible answer to this which a believer in mechanism can make is the appeal to evolution-tested habits of thought. An example of such an answer is that given by Stephen Hawking:

if there really is a complete unified theory, it would also presumably determine our actions. And so the theory itself would determine the outcome of our search for it! And why should it determine that we come to the right conclusions from the evidence? . . . The only answer I can give to this problem is based on Darwin's principle of natural selection. The idea is that in any population of self-reproducing organisms, there will be variations in the genetic material and upbringing that different individuals have. These differences will mean that some individuals are better able than others to draw the right conclusions about the world around them and to act accordingly. These individuals will be more likely to survive and reproduce and so their pattern of behaviour and thought will come to dominate. (Hawking 1988: 12)

This is an attempted naturalization of reason, and denial of its objectivity; and it faces difficulties of the kind raised by Nagel and Putnam, which I referred to at the end of Section 5.2. On Hawking's approach, what does one make of debates between great minds, such as that between Einstein and Bohr, which I refer to in Chapter 9? Is it just a matter of two evolution-selected systems giving different results; so that the truth can be judged by a third party (if at all) only on the basis of which of three systems (Einstein's, Bohr's, or the assessor's) was best adapted to survival and reproduction?

A person who rejects the mechanistic view, on the other hand, accepts that confidence in any belief can be supported by an appeal to reasons which are limitless, and (while not conclusive, being always provisional and subject to correction) plausible. Informal conscious reasoning, by appeal to a possible infinity of such reasons, supports both itself and formal reasoning.

5.6.3. *Haldane's Argument*

The argument of this section has affinities with the argument against materialism advanced in 1932 by the biologist J. B. S. Haldane: 'if materialism is true, it seems to me that we cannot know that it is true. If my opinions are the result of the chemical processes going on in my brain, they are determined by chemistry, not the laws of logic'. Haldane recanted from this argument in 1954, for reasons put shortly as follows in Popper and Eccles (1977): 'a computing machine may be said to be determined in its working by the laws of physics; but it may nevertheless work in full accordance with the laws of logic' (p. 76).

In similar vein, the argument is disowned by one of today's best advocates of dualism and of freedom of the will, philosopher Richard Swinburne. In Swinburne (1986), he writes:

This argument has, I believe, no force at all. The mere fact that our beliefs are caused is no grounds for holding them unjustified. Exactly the reverse . . . to the extent that we regarded them as uncaused or self-chosen, we could not regard our beliefs as moulded by the facts and so likely to be true. The point is rather that if we see some belief to be caused by a totally irrelevant factor (e.g. a belief that I am now being persecuted being caused by something irrelevant in my upbringing) then we rightly regard it as unjustified. But a belief that determinism is true could be both caused and justified, if caused by relevant factors, e.g. hearing relevant arguments. (p. 233 n.)

I contend that this is a serious mistake, which renounces an important part of the best case against mechanism; and which arises from the influence (I would say baleful influence) of the mechanistic view of reasoning, and from failure to distinguish between formal reasoning and plausible reasoning.

If it were reasonable to believe a theory on the basis of formal reasoning alone, then a belief in mechanism could be reasonable by its own standards. However, the reasonableness of a belief in a theory must depend on *plausible* reasoning, which has not been and (I contend) cannot be mechanized. Accordingly, one cannot reasonably believe in mechanism, because only formal arguments can be mechanized, and these are insufficient to support any theory.

It has to be conceded to Swinburne that, in order to be reasonable, a belief must be *caused* in some sense by its antecedents: but only in the sense that it must arise by way of reasoning based on such antecedents. This reasoning will be at least partly informal, and therefore not fully mechanistic. So, unless one could show that, contrary to the above, plausible reasoning *is* or *can be* mechanistic, it is not reasonable to believe in mechanism. And one could conceivably show that plausible reasoning can be mechanistic only by engaging in plausible reasoning, involving at best begging the question, or at worst a contradiction.

This reworking of Haldane's argument is somewhat similar to that proposed by Popper in Popper and Eccles (1977: 75–81). He concludes that 'materialism has no right to claim that it can be supported by rational argument' because the standards of rational criticism 'appear from the materialist point of view as an illusion, or at least as an ideology' (p. 81). And there is a similar argument used against determinism in Boyle *et al.* (1976), in which there is an appeal to what the authors call 'rationality norms' (pp. 144 ff.), which is similar to my appeal to plausible reasoning. See also Finnis (1983: 137). There is also an interesting elaboration of this type of argument in Penrose (1989: 417–18), which makes use of Gödel's theorem: I look at it in the next section.

However, I think the argument is clarified by the distinctions I have drawn, particularly that between formal and plausible reasoning.

5.7. Gödel's Theorem

In about 1900, mathematician David Hilbert proposed the complete formalization of mathematics: the creation of a formal system for mathematics which was complete and consistent, and within which any mathematical problem could be decided by a number of algorithmic steps. In 1930, the mathematician Kurt Gödel proved a theorem which undermined this proposal. It showed that no system as proposed by Hilbert could be both complete *and* consistent. (Subsequently, as we saw in Section 3.3, Alan Turing proved that in any event there were problems which could not be decided in any such system in a finite number of steps.)

Gödel's theorem is to the following effect. If you take any formal system, which is finitely describable, consistent, and also sufficiently strong to prove the basic facts about whole-number arithmetic, then there is at least one statement of pure mathematics which is true but which cannot be proved within the formal system. This theorem has been used in support of an argument against mechanism, in particular by Oxford philosopher J. R. Lucas. His argument has been strongly criticized by various writers, and is by no means conclusive. However, it is my contention that Gödel's theorem does provide some support to the argument against mechanism which I have advanced in this chapter.

5.7.1. *Outline of Gödel's Theorem*

The basic idea underlying Gödel's theorem is similar to the liar's paradox. You take any consistent formal system S, and take the sentence G which asserts 'G is not provable within S'; and then consider whether or not G is provable within S. Assume that G is provable within S. This means that it is provable within S that G is not provable within S. So the following would both be true:

1. G is provable within S.
2. It is provable within S that G is not provable within S.

From (1), G is an axiom or theorem of S. From (2), assuming S is consistent, G is not an axiom or theorem of S. The inconsistency within S that these two statements involve means that one must reject the assumption on which they are based, namely that G is provable within S. It follows that G is not provable within S; that is, that G itself is true. So G is true, but is not provable within S.

All the above is of itself of limited significance. What is important, and what Gödel proved, is that, if S is finitely describable, and strong enough to prove the basic facts about whole-number arithmetic, then for any such S the sentence G can be encoded in the language of S as a sentence of pure mathematics stating that a certain polynomial equation has no solution in the whole numbers. That is, Gödel proved that for any formal system satisfying the specified requirements, there is at least one statement of pure mathematics of the type specified which is true but which cannot be proved by the system.

What would happen if one added G to S as an axiom? G would then be provable within the system, simply by pointing to one of its axioms. However, the system would no longer be S but a different system S^*, formed by adding G as an axiom to S. G would be provable within S^*: but there would be a different sentence G^* which would not be, G^* being the sentence which asserts 'G^* is not provable within S^*'. G^* could be encoded in the language of S^* as a sentence of pure mathematics stating that a certain polynomial equation (different, of course, from that associated with G) has no solution in the whole numbers. (Alternatively, if one tried to formulate a system S^* which included as an axiom G^*, that is, the statement 'G^* is not provable within S^*', then S^* would not be a consistent system.)

5.7.2. *Its Application to the Theory of Mind*

Gödel's theorem has been used, in particular in Lucas (1964), to argue against a mechanistic theory of mind, in this way. A mechanistic mind must be equivalent to a formal system. It would presumably be consistent: otherwise any proposition could be proved by it. It would be sufficiently powerful to prove the basic facts about whole-number arithmetic. Therefore, there would be a sentence G which it could not prove, and an equivalent sentence in pure mathematics which similarly it could not prove. However, a human being has proved G, human beings have no such limitations, and therefore the human mind cannot be mechanistic. A recent similar argument is that put by mathematician Roger Penrose in Penrose (1987: 269–70).

There is also an interesting use of Gödel's theorem in Penrose (1989: 417–18), which combines it with an argument along the lines of that in Section 5.6. He supposes that mathematicians do form all their judgements of mathematical truth (or proof) on the basis of algorithms. Such algorithms cannot be inequivalent for different mathematicians, because it is accepted that abstract argument will settle the truth of propositions for all concerned; so there must be one universal formal system which comprehends all the algorithms used by different mathematicians. But, if this were so, *it* would have a Gödel sentence which could be constructed *and* known to be a mathematical truth; but not by the supposedly universal formal system in question. So there is a contradiction.

Before considering objections to this argument, it should be noted that it does not assert any general superiority of a human brain over any mechanistic system S. All it does is to assert that S cannot prove a certain statement about itself, whereas there is no similar statement about a human brain which such a brain cannot prove.

Further, it should be noted that it does not show that all truth cannot be contained in a formal system, only that such a formal system (i.e. one containing all truth) cannot be *finitely describable*. If a system is not finitely describable, then it cannot be proved that *G*, in relation to that system, can be expressed as a statement of pure mathematics of the type referred to, and Gödel's theorem does not apply. Indeed, if one could have an infinite system, with all possible true statements as axioms or theorems within it, then *G* becomes identical with the liar's paradox: that is, '*G* is not provable within the system' becomes equivalent to 'This statement is not true'. According to our earlier discussion, neither *G* nor not-*G* is true, because of the inverse relationship between their truth and what they assert.

5.7.3. *Objections to Lucas's Argument*

Artificial intelligence pioneer Douglas Michie dismisses Lucas's argument simply by asserting that Gödel's theorem applies just as much to human beings as to machines, presumably because he assumes that the human brain is equivalent to a formal system (see Michie and Johnston 1985: 189). With respect, this wholly begs the question. Other objections are more substantial.

Hofstadter and Rucker challenge the assertion that the human brain has no similar limitations to those of formal systems (see Hofstadter 1980: 476; Rucker 1984: 292–4). It is true that some human beings have been able to encode *G* in relation to relatively simple formal systems, and thus to prove that the mathematical sentence thereby produced is true. However, this does not mean that any human being could encode *G* in relation to a formal system as complex as the human brain, particularly his own brain. This, it is said, could be completely impossible for a human brain, which is thus not shown to be other than mechanistic.

However, it must be remembered that the unprovability of *G* in relation to a formal system is not directly related to the *complexity* of *G*'s expression within the system. It is true that the more complex *S* is, the more complex *G* (encoded as a mathematical statement) will be. But the important thing about *G* is not its complexity, but its *logical relationship* with its particular *S*. There is nothing in Gödel's theorem to suggest it is not possible that one system *S1* could prove *G2* (which asserts '*G2* is not provable within system *S2*'), while the other system *S2* could prove *G1* (which asserts '*G1* is not provable within system *S1*').

In relation to a human mind, the question is not whether *G* (that is, '*G* is not provable by *this* human mind') is provable by this particular human mind. Of course, if this human mind operates consistently, it is not. Rather, the question is whether *that G* can be formulated as a mathematical statement of the type discussed. And that in turn depends on whether the human brain–mind is a finite formal system. If someone (or something!) were to present me with a mathematical sentence, and to say 'That is G to your S', why cannot I say: 'Although for me to prove G will prove that I cannot prove G, I can see that as well as you'? Furthermore, what could prevent me from following each step of his argument showing that his mathematical sentence is indeed G to my S?

The only reason which Hofstadter and Rucker can offer as to how a human mind could fail to understand and prove its own G is its degree of complexity. But degree of complexity as such has nothing to do with Gödel's theorem. Its basis is simply that proof by S of G would involve a contradiction; and that G can be formulated as a mathematical sentence of the type discussed in the language of S. That is, Gödel's proof is of a logical impossibility, rather than any contingent impossibility dependent on complexity. Is it plausible to accept that there is a sentence G, expressed as a mathematical sentence of the type discussed, such that by reason, not of complexity, but of its relationship to the formal system instantiated by a human brain, it would be logically impossible for that human brain to prove it? If so, the problem would have to be in the construction of the mathematical sentence. No doubt any brain–mind would have difficulty in recognizing a description of the formal system which (on this assumption) it instantiates, and difficulty in encoding its own G in the language of that system. But if this task could be undertaken by some other person, perhaps with the aid of a computer, it does not seem plausible to suggest that it could not be done by the person himself, with similar aid. That is, any problem indeed seems to be one of complexity, not of logical impossibility.

If (as I contend) the brain–mind is not mechanistic, and can proceed rationally in ways not dependent on formal validity, then Gödel's theorem does not apply. Even in so far as we do use formal systems, and do draw conclusions from them on the basis that they are consistent, our procedure is not vulnerable to Gödel's theorem. This, I suggest, is because there is no problem unless the sentence G is involved, and because we can and do proceed on the basis that our 'axioms' and 'rules' are only provisionally true or provisionally valid.

Other answers to Lucas's argument are, I think, similarly inconclusive, and leave the argument as having some persuasive force. As examples, I refer to arguments of Putnam, Boden, and Dennett.

1. Putnam (1975b: 366) contends that an argument like that of Lucas is a simple mistake, a fallacy. He contends that a system S *can* prove that if S is consistent, then G is true; and that G, which S cannot prove (assuming consistency), a human being cannot prove either unless he can prove that S is consistent, which is unlikely if S is complicated. I think this is too short a way with the argument. If a system is not consistent, then (if it is of sufficient power) it can prove any proposition whatsoever: it therefore seems reasonable to assume that any system claimed to be equivalent to a human brain *is*

consistent, so that for it there would be a *G* which is true but not provable. Since this *G* is expressible as an ordinary (if complicated) mathematical statement, the question is fairly asked, *why* could a human being not prove it to be true?

2. Boden (1977: 434–5) contends that the formal system instantiated by a human brain–mind continually changes as it interacts with its environment, so that any inability to prove a particular *G* would be temporary. However, one would think that, for a short period at least, any interaction with the environment could be controlled to the extent that the human brain–mind in question plus the *relevant* environment, for this period, could be regarded as instantiating a formal system, *if* the brain–mind could be so regarded. The argument would then apply to this totality of brain–mind plus relevant environment.

3. Dennett (1978: 256 ff.) contends ·that arguments invoking Gödel's theorem fail because 'they must implicitly deny an obvious truth, namely that constraints of logic exert their force not on the things in the world directly, but rather on what we are to count as defensible descriptions or interpretations of things'. He specifies what he sees as the essential error of such arguments; namely

supposing that objective and exclusive determinations of the activities and capacities of concrete objects are possible which would determine uniquely which Turing machine specification (if any) is *the* specification for the object . . . if a man were (a realization of) a particular theorem-proving Turing machine with Gödel sentence *S*, then *in his role as that Turing machine* he could not prove *S*, but this says nothing about his capacities in other roles . . . (p. 264)

This approach seeks to resist the suggestion that a mechanistic brain is equivalent to one particular formal system. For reasons given in Section 1.3, I would suggest that (apart from matters arising from interaction with an environment which is not finitely describable) a finite mechanistic brain either is, or could be simulated to arbitrary accuracy by, a particular discrete-state machine; and that such a machine in turn is equivalent to a particular formal system. I do not think that the possibility of different roles or descriptions of such a brain (or such a machine, or such a formal system) means that the *brain* escapes the limitation which Gödel's theorem imposes on the formal system.

I repeat, I am not claiming that Lucas's argument is conclusive: far from it. I am suggesting that it is a plausible argument, which sits well with the main argument of this chapter: indeed, the chapter could itself be regarded as an informal corollary of Gödel's theorem.

6

Consciousness Selected by Evolution

ACCORDING to the theory of evolution, human beings are the result of an evolutionary process beginning millions of years ago with a simple life form. In general terms, each of the physical characteristics of human beings can be related in some way or other (directly or indirectly) to their adaptation for survival and reproduction. It seems reasonable to assert that consciousness, which is presumably also the result of an evolutionary process, is similarly somehow related to the adaptation of human beings for survival and reproduction. As I have already suggested, a mechanistic brain could work without consciousness. Accordingly, unless consciousness is merely a by-product of a mechanistic brain of some complexity, consciousness itself must make a difference, so that the brain is not mechanistic.

This argument has previously been advanced in support of anti-materialist positions (for example, see Popper and Eccles 1977: 72–5, 87–8, 94). However, I think there is more to be said about it. I begin with a general statement of the argument, and then look at various answers to it: in the course of this, I consider what could be the advantages of consciousness which may have led to its selection by evolution.

6.1. General Statement of the Argument

Information processing in accordance with effective procedures or formal systems does not require consciousness. Anything that a computer can do by way of acceptance, storage, and retrieval of information, and processing of information in accordance with unambiguous directions or rules (including rules of logic and rules of mathematics), *can* be done mechanically and without consciousness. Indeed, that is the whole point of the effective procedures which computers use.

Nevertheless, evolution has apparently favoured consciousness, not merely by giving rise to organisms with consciousness, but also by equipping them with mechanisms to ensure that in times of danger or crisis, or otherwise requiring important decisions to be made, full conscious attention is brought to bear on the problem.

The latter point is, I think, significant, especially since conscious attention has disadvantages as well as advantages, particularly in persons who tend to panic or become confused or otherwise less efficient in times of crisis. When a person is confronted with a situation requiring a decision he recognizes as important, as where there is imminent danger, generally his full conscious attention is brought to bear on the problem, automatically, without any effort or even any decision on his part. Sometimes this effect is heightened, in times of real emergency, by the phenomenon of things appearing to happen 'in slow motion', giving the person more apparent time to assess the situation and make the best decision about what action to take. Now if satisfactory decision-making could be achieved without consciousness, surely it would be more conducive to survival to 'shut off' consciousness in emergencies (perhaps producing a state similar to hypnosis), to avoid the possibility of panic and confusion, in much the same way as consciousness of pain is shut off in certain situations involving trauma and shock.

I am not asserting that all useful thinking is done consciously. For example, when one wishes to remember something (such as the name of a person) and cannot, it sometimes helps to think of something else: then, after a time, the name just occurs to one. Even scientific discoveries are sometimes reported as occurring 'unconsciously': a person wrestles consciously for long periods with a problem, and then a solution simply occurs to him or her at a time when he or she is not thinking about the problem at all. Such examples as these do not, I suggest, alter the situation that our brains are so constituted that we are fully conscious and attending when we realize an important decision is required. And, generally, any idea which 'occurs' to a person, in the way I have indicated, would be actually adopted only after being consciously appraised (see Penrose 1989: 418–23).

It seems a reasonable conclusion that consciousness has emerged and been maintained in evolution because it is advantageous to survival and reproduction.

Churchland (1986: 320) suggests that evolutionary biology raises a difficulty for substance dualism, a difficulty which could arguably be applied to my contentions: where does the 'soul-stuff' (or consciousness) come from? However, in suggesting that consciousness has evolved, I am not suggesting that there is something other than the genes encoded in DNA which transmits the products of evolution. The transmission of the products of evolution is by means of the physical structures of DNA, which in turn determines the general physical structures of the resulting organisms. What I am saying is that the physical structures thus determined are such that the organisms have central nervous systems, one property of which is that the organisms are conscious. Whether this consciousness arises because conscious events are just *different aspects of* the appropriate physical events, or are *caused by* the appropriate physical events, does not matter for this discussion. It is sufficient to say that consciousness is associated with the appropriate physical structures and physical events, and that DNA can transmit information which brings about the appropriate physical structures and physical events.

The question then remains: why does DNA promote physical structures and physical events such that consciousness is associated with them, rather than structures and events such that the organism can process information without the 'useless luxury' of consciousness? The answer, I suggest, is that consciousness is *useful*, in ways not achievable by mechanistic information processing, and that consciousness makes a difference to what happens in ways not explicable in terms of mechanistic causation: *the mind matters*.

Before dealing with three possible answers to this argument, there is one very general objection which needs to be dealt with here, namely an objection to the use of the concept 'consciousness' in the argument, and to the assumption that there is a 'sharp qualitative difference' between information-processing systems which are 'merely behavioural' and those which are conscious (see Dennett 1984: 35, 37). Churchland (1986: 321) contends that consciousness probably is not 'a natural kind' or 'a single type of brain process'. She continues: 'The brain undoubtedly has a number of mechanisms for monitoring brain processes, and the folk psychological categories of "awareness" and "consciousness" indifferently lump together an assortment of the mechanisms.'

I have attempted to deal in advance with such views by stating at some length in Chapter 2 what I take 'mental events' and 'consciousness' to be. As I there conceded, there are problems at the borderline; but I do not think there can really be any question about the distinction between my central case (the subjective aspect of fully conscious experiences, thoughts, and actions of normal human beings), on the one hand, and events involving no human (or animal, or similar) consciousness whatsoever, on the other hand. Furthermore, if the behaviour of animals (including human beings) is regarded as fully explicable by mechanistic causal laws, then, prima facie, consciousness *of any kind* appears superfluous, at least as regards such behaviour.

Whether or not this prima-facie view is correct depends, I think, on more particular arguments, a number of possible answers to the argument from evolution.

One is to suggest that consciousness could have emerged and been maintained if it was in itself neither an advantage nor a disadvantage, making no difference; or even if it were a disadvantage, if it was associated, as a by-product, with an attribute which *was* advantageous, such as a complex information-processing brain. Next, it could be suggested that, although consciousness may be useful, and even 'make a difference', this is no more so than other 'global properties' such as solidity and sharpness, which themselves involve no departure from mechanistic causation. Finally, it could be argued that (since it has been shown that in many respects the brain *does* operate mechanistically, in ways which affect the content of consciousness) to suggest that consciousness is selected as useful by evolution, and makes a difference, raises starkly unanswerable questions such as: what (if not the brain) makes choices, and with what equipment (if not the brain); and what ensures there is no gross violation of mechanistic causation?

I consider first the 'no-advantage' and 'by-product' approaches, which lead me to consider in some detail what could be the advantages of consciousness. I then consider the 'global property' approach; and I conclude by looking briefly at the further questions raised by the discussion.

6.2. The No-Advantage and By-Product Approaches

In introducing these objections, I mentioned the possibility that consciousness could even be disadvantageous, if associated as a by-product with a useful attribute. The example is sometimes given of the disadvantage of the weight of a polar bear's woolly coat, which is associated with its useful property of warmth. Another example, closer to home, is the phenomenon of sleep: the properties of brains which require such vulnerable episodes must have compensating advantages.

However, subject to the global property argument which I consider in Section 6.4, a disadvantage of consciousness would be a difference made by consciousness, just as much as an advantage would be. So the real question to be considered is whether, consistently with evolutionary theory, consciousness could (plausibly) be neither an advantage nor a disadvantage; that is, could (plausibly) make no difference at all.

This question can be considered, first, independently of any by-product argument: it could be argued that consciousness could have emerged by a chance mutation of genes, and then survived, because it was no disadvantage.

However, it appears that consciousness is an expensive property, by reason both of the complexity of the systems required to support it, and of the energy required for its actual occurrence. Brains of human beings and (to a lesser extent) of other animals are the most complex objects in the universe; and studies of the human brain suggest that consciousness occurs only when there is high activity in large numbers of neurons. Conscious deliberation is generally engaged in by human beings only where it is advantageous: we develop ways of doing things which require a minimum of conscious activity. Sherrington (1951) writes: 'Habit is a charitable economy relieving the "I's" more costly mental action. The "I" has this labour-saving device of truanting' (p. 160). Accordingly, if consciousness is to be considered as of no advantage, it seems more plausible to argue that consciousness is a by-product of processes which *do* have advantages, namely the operations of a complex information-processing brain.

But consciousness cannot be a *necessary* by-product of any such processes. As we have seen, purely physical processes can be simulated by a machine, which in turn can be regarded as the instantiation of a formal system. A formal system cannot have consciousness as a necessary associate, nor can any instantiation of such a system: any such instantiation can operate mechanistically, so consciousness is not a necessary attribute. Computer science and work on artificial intelligence demonstrate convincingly that consciousness is not necessary for receiving, storing, and processing information; for performing precise and complex physical movements directed by such information; or for displaying and communicating such information. All these things *can* be achieved by means of non-conscious effective procedures carried out by machines. As mentioned in Section 3.3, Johnson-Laird (1987: 257, 1988: 366–7) concedes this, and suggests that consciousness is a property of certain *parallel* (as opposed to serial) computational procedures: but parallel computational procedures do not escape these arguments either.

So if, as seems to be the case, *all* animals of more than a certain sophistication of behaviour are conscious, the question is raised: why are there not animals which use exclusively non-conscious information processing? There seems no reason why such animals would not have emerged by chance, along with conscious animals; and on the by-product approach the former would have been no less successful than the latter at surviving and reproducing. If it is accepted that consciousness, in varying degrees, is enjoyed by (say) at least all animals with eyes, it seems highly improbable that consciousness could be just a chance no-disadvantage attribute: if *that* were the case, surely there would be *some* non-conscious animals of some behavioural sophistication.

It might be thought that this argument is circular: how do we know that animals unlike ourselves *are* conscious? Surely, for example, the eyes of such animals *could* be non-conscious optical detection systems, just as their brains *could* be non-conscious information-processing systems. However, as before, I would argue from similarities of the physical properties of the brain, and of behaviour, as between ourselves and other primates, to the probability of consciousness in the latter; and so on through the animal world. There is no clear discontinuity or difference at any stage which could suggest that one species operates consciously, whilst another, of similar behavioural sophistication, operates non-consciously.

The whole problem is, I think, related to what I suggested was a dilemma for functionalism, particularly in relation to the views of Shoemaker in Section 3.1. According to functionalism, types of mental event can be identified by reference to their function in relation (directly or indirectly) to behaviour. As shown by Shoemaker, this means that either functionalism cannot distinguish between cases where subjective sensations of colour (or pain) are present and cases where they are absent; or else it must assert that such subjective sensations make a difference to what happens. Yet functionalism is supposed to be inimical to any sort of interactive dualism. Similarly, evolutionary biology is supposed to be inimical to dualism: yet either it leaves consciousness (including subjective sensations of colour and of pain) entirely unexplained and mysterious, or else it explains consciousness as being something useful, i.e. something which makes a difference. To put it crudely: if the same results could be achieved by non-conscious mechanisms producing appropriate actions in response to the nerve stimulations which we feel as pain, why do we have to put up with the unpleasant feelings of pain which we sometimes suffer? Why do we feel the pain-ness of pain, instead of just having computational algorithms performed which cause us to take the course most beneficial to survival?

One can approach it another way. I am as sure that other normal human beings enjoy consciousness as I am of almost anything. If our close relatives, the apes, are *not* conscious, then it seems highly implausible to suggest that *our* consciousness makes *no* contribution to our increased sophistication of behaviour, that it is a mere by-product of the somewhat greater complexity of our brains as compared with theirs. On the other hand, if the apes are conscious, and other primates are not, a similar comment applies as between these groups. And so on through the animal kingdom. At each stage, the question can be asked: if increased sophistication of behaviour *could* have been achieved without consciousness, just as it was with it, why did this not happen?

Accordingly, it seems reasonable to conclude that consciousness does make a difference; that the substratum of brain events *serves* consciousness, rather than being of itself, without consciousness, all that is necessary and sufficient to determine bodily movements. However, a complete answer to the no-advantage and by-product approaches requires close consideration of just what the evolutionary advantages of consciousness could be, and this is what I turn to next.

6.3. Advantages of Consciousness

What then are advantages which consciousness could give over a purely mechanistic information-processing system?

Such a question has been asked by various writers (see, for example, Dawkins 1976: 63; Bruner 1983: 201–16; Humphrey 1983, 1986; Dennett 1984: 35–7; Penrose 1989: 409–13). Dawkins, Bruner, and Dennett do not take the matter far; with Dawkins calling the question 'the most profound mystery facing modern biology'. Humphrey (and perhaps Dawkins) asks the question in relation to what I call self-consciousness. Humphrey's point is somewhat related to my argument in Section 7.4, and I will deal with it there. One useful discussion of the question is in Nozick (1981: 333–44). He writes that 'there is evolutionary selection for organisms (brains, constitutions) that reduce rational considerations' (p. 337); and:

So far as I know, little illumination thus far has been shed on the evolutionary advantage of conscious awareness. Is conscious awareness necessary for certain other things, or instead is it an efficient facilitator of them? Although other nonconscious routes to achieving or doing them are imaginable, perhaps these other things actually would not have happened without the evolution of conscious awareness. (p. 341)

One answer to Nozick's question, and to mine, is suggested by the arguments of Chapters 4 and 5: a conscious human being has information not available to a non-conscious entity, and can reason informally in ways not available to such an entity. The very circumstance that human beings *have* the information referred to in Chapter 4 suggests (from an evolutionary viewpoint) that the information is of some use, that it is used. How is it used? Chapter 5 suggests that it is used in plausible reasoning, to assist in making decisions in which the actual appearance, sound, and feel of things, and the actual feel of one's sensations and emotions, play a part in the weighing and judging process.

It could be said that all this is only the mental aspect or dimension of physical events operating causally. I have already given some answers to such suggestion, and more will be given in this and the following sections.

It could also be said that the above suggestion only indicates a way in which consciousness could be of advantage to human beings. If, as appears to be the case, consciousness appeared much earlier in evolution, its advantages should be related to the organisms in which it first appeared, not to human beings.

As mentioned earlier, I think that consciousness probably did appear much earlier in evolution than the emergence of human beings. I believe that the similarities in physical structure and in behaviour between human beings and other primates give very strong reasons for accepting that the latter are conscious. As one moves further away from human beings in the animal world, through other mammals, birds, reptiles, amphibians, fish, insects, etc., the reasons for accepting that the animal in question is conscious become progressively less strong. Furthermore, assuming such animals are conscious, it would seem probable that their conscious experiences are progressively less and less like our own. It is very difficult for us to have any idea of what it is like to be a bat: it is perhaps even more difficult to have any idea of what it is like (if it is 'like' anything) to be a bird, or a fish, or a fly.

However, I do accept that it should be possible to give some account of the advantage of consciousness in quite primitive animals, and I shall attempt to do so.

Dawkins (1976) characterized living things, including ourselves, as 'survival machines for genes'. Accepting for the moment that this is in general terms a fair characterization, it seems likely that a 'machine' would have a better chance of providing survival if it had the ability to respond appropriately to a wide variety of circumstances, including circumstances which neither it nor its evolutionary ancestors had previously encountered. It seems reasonable to suppose that any such advantage would be related to an organism's ability to respond appropriately to features in its environment relevant to its survival and/or reproduction.

Such ability could be provided by a mechanism specifying, or enabling computation of, responses to properties identified as the same as those previously encountered by the organism or its ancestors, plus procedures for computing responses to other properties. Even the former aspect would require some abstraction ability, so as to enable identification of properties in presently encountered circumstances. The latter aspect would presumably require a procedure for further abstracting properties from presently encountered circumstances, so that such properties could be identified in future circumstances; that is, for recognizing that different circumstances are alike in certain respects. The mechanism would presumably require a procedure for adjusting the response when new circumstances encountered are in some respects like circumstances in which one response is appropriate, and in other respects like circumstances where a different (perhaps opposite) response is appropriate. This in turn would presumably require, or at least be assisted by, a procedure for reducing opposing indications of the appropriate response to a common scale, so that an actual response could be computed.

The procedure outlined above could to some extent be performed mechanistically, without consciousness. However, if the organism had also the ability to deal with new circumstances by comparison of wholes, there could be advantages, in particular: (1) detection of similarities and differences not previously abstracted; and (2) weighing of similarities and differences qualitatively, rather than quantitatively on some common scale. There could be evolutionary advantages in fallible qualitative judgement over quantitative computation.

That ability to compare wholes would, I suggest, require consciousness.

Take recognition of food, for example. As I understand it, the most primitive organisms encounter food by chance, and 'recognize' it simply by accepting only appropriate molecular configurations. If an organism can accept as food substances other than particular molecules, this will give it an advantage, so long as it can distinguish what it can use as food from what it cannot. It may be that a conscious organism could recognize substances not previously encountered as being food, or not food, more reliably than a non-conscious organism.

In the competitive situation postulated by evolution theory, it would be an advantage to increase the chance of encountering food, and to increase the variety of substances which serve as food. Dealing with the latter, it could be an advantage to be able to 'try out' substances not precisely the same as any previously used as food, either by the organism itself or by its ancestors; but at the same time to avoid trying out substances harmful to the organism. It would thus be an advantage to have a mechanism for detecting points of similarity to, and points of difference from, substances previously used as food, and for arriving at some probability of whether the substance will be beneficial or harmful. It could be a further advantage if, in addition to detecting points of similarity and points of difference, and (as it were) mechanically computing a probability score, the organism could also use some information about the substance as a whole, to be compared with similar information about substances previously encountered: this information could consist of its appearance (in the case of organisms with sight), its smell, its taste, etc.

How could this come about?

To start with, what would be necessary to make such a probability computation? First, the organism would need to have within it some representation of the substance presently encountered in the external world. Secondly, it would need to have within it some representation of substances previously used as food (by itself or its ancestors), and perhaps of substances previously found harmful (by itself or its ancestors): the origin of such representation could be entirely heredity, or partly heredity and partly learning. Thirdly, it would need to have within it some instantiation of a formal system for two possible responses, one appropriate for relevant *similarity* between the substance then encountered and food, and one appropriate for relevant *difference* (or similarity between the substance encountered and harmful substances).

This instantiation of such a formal system could be such that the outcome is the (certain) result of a mechanical computation based on points of similarity and points of difference. However, it could also be such that the outcome is (objectively) uncertain, by reason (say) of quantum physical indeterminism, with only the *probabilities* of the outcome (rather than the outcome itself) determined by the computation. (I will say much more about this in Part III.) For example, the mechanism for computation of the probability of appropriate similarity could (theoretically) be coupled with a Geiger counter and a quantity of radioactive substance, with parameters appropriately adjusted to give (quantum mechanically) the computed probability of outcome. (No doubt, if this suggestion is correct, the method actually used in the organism's central nervous system would be less cumbersome.)

To have such a mechanism, giving rise to computed probabilities of outcomes via quantum uncertainties, even without anything else, could be favoured by evolution over a mechanism giving a certain outcome in accordance with computed probabilities. The main difference would be that in a minority of cases the less probable outcome would occur, promoting experiment and diversity of response.

This may mean that, in some cases within this minority, the organism in question is damaged or killed; but it may mean, in other cases, that the organism extends the range of its food in a way which can be taught to its kin and its descendants. The disadvantage of some injurious or fatal choices may be outweighed by the occasional successful choice which is beneficial to the organism and genetically related organisms. Certainly, the fact that the uncertainty of outcome is provided by the quantum physics of the organism's central nervous system, rather than a mechanical (approximate) 'random number generator' (as discussed by Dennett in *Elbow Room* (1984: 119–21)), would be immaterial at this stage; although it could well be simpler (and thus more readily achieved by evolution) for quantum physics to be utilized rather than any mechanical approximation to random processes.

However, suppose that, in addition to the above, the organism had a further faculty for selecting between outcomes whose probability had been thus computed, by some sort of holistic comparison which somehow made use of the probability computation, but also made use of information concerning the substance as a whole (appearance, smell, taste, etc.). Such faculty would be fallible, but it could well (if only marginally) increase the likelihood of successful choices being made, and injurious or fatal choices being avoided; and, if so, it would be favoured by evolution.

To make use of information concerning the substance as a whole, I would suggest that the organism would need to be conscious: that is, it would need to have information of the type discussed in Chapter 4, namely, what the substance looks like (smells like, tastes like, etc.). To make use at the same time of the probability computations, I would suggest that these computations too would need somehow to be reflected in the organism's conscious experience, perhaps by way of associations of the substance's appearance, smell, etc. (and/or the alternative responses) with feelings of varying strengths of attraction and repulsion.

Suppose all food previously encountered and consumed by an organism and its ancestors had the properties *ABC*, and these had been abstracted and could be recognized. A substance is encountered with the properties *AB*, but not *C*; and another with the properties *ABCD*, where *D* has not previously been associated with *ABC*. Without consciousness, a correct decision about the suitability of the new substance as food would appear to be at best a matter of probability, and at worst a matter of pure chance. With consciousness, some sort of qualitative appraisal of the difference, and its significance for the whole, could perhaps be made, so that a correct decision would have some slightly greater probability. Of course, once a correct decision in favour of suitability was made, substances with the features of this new substance could be recognized in the future, with advantages to survival. Accordingly, an organism with consciousness, which could thus give an 'edge' in relation to dealing with new substances, could have a survival advantage.

On this approach, it can be suggested that Nelson Goodman (in Goodman 1970: 27–9), in the course of heaping strictures upon the undefined notion of similarity which is important in my approach, in fact made out a case for its significance:

comparative judgments of similarity often require not merely selection of relevant properties but a weighing of their relative importance, and variation in both relevance and importance can be rapid and enormous . . . relative weighting of the different qualities of objects is so variable that even reliable measures of similarity for qualities of each kind will give no constant measure of overall similarity for the objects themselves.

That is, it is only by holistic overall comparisons that reasonably reliable assessments of similarity can be made.

The discussion so far has related only to recognition as food of substances presented to an organism. Similar considerations could apply to recognition of danger, recognition of circumstances likely to give rise to food or to danger, and so on. As the organisms, and their repertoires of responses, become more complex, the problems to which this sort of approach could apply would similarly increase in range and complexity.

Putting this whole matter another way, consciousness may well give an advantage in relation to, and perhaps be necessary for, reasoning by analogy. Even primitive organisms, with consciousness, may be able to 'reason' (in a primitive sense) in this way, giving them a survival advantage over those without consciousness. If human beings can exercise rationality which is not formalizable, by reason of consciousness, then this (it can be argued) gives an evolutionary advantage to consciousness in human beings; and this can be regarded as similar in kind, though different in degree, to the advantage discussed above in relation to more primitive animals. Indeed, the whole range of human informal rationality could have its basis in this kind of analogical 'reasoning'.

In a sense, this approach, suggesting that consciousness is efficacious in the way discussed above, involves attributing a measure of freedom from mechanism even to quite primitive animals, if they are conscious. I do not baulk at that. It is a view shared by the eminent biologist René Dubos (see Dubos 1978: 20); and it could explain the apparent superiority of pigeons over present-day computers in dealing with concepts like 'trees' and 'chairs', noted in Terrace (1984: 270). I do suggest, however, that such freedom from mechanism would fall short of what has been called 'freedom of the will': the expression as used in relation to human beings requires not merely the freedom from mechanism discussed here (involving in particular proceeding by analogy in a primitive way), but also the self-conscious rationality of human beings.

One final point in this section. It will be recalled that in Section 5.2 I referred to and adopted Thomas Nagel's contention that the ability to reason informally is not plausibly regarded as explained by evolution, because such ability appears to apply far beyond the circumstances in which it evolved. It might be suggested that my arguments here oppose this contention. There are at least two answers to such a suggestion:

1. I used Nagel's contention to oppose the view that non-rational habit, as refined by evolution, could explain our informal-reasoning abilities; that is, in substance, to oppose Hume's explanation of induction. If what evolution produced were *not* refined non-rational habits, but rather some genuine

informal rationality, then it is far less surprising that this would apply in circumstances far removed from those in which the ability evolved.

2. A person who denies that mind can make a difference to what happens (that is, who supports mechanism) is far more committed to evolutionary biology as a complete explanation of organisms than is a person who does not deny this. Accordingly, the need for the former person to explain consciousness in evolutionary terms, that is in terms of its having some advantage to survival and reproduction, is correspondingly greater.

For these reasons, I do not think that there is a real conflict between Nagel's contention and the arguments of this section.

6.4. The Global Property Approach

The second main answer to the argument from evolution is along the following lines. Consciousness has indeed been selected by evolution, but only as a global property of successful organisms, not different in principle from other global properties of objects, such as the solidity and sharpness of a knife. It is not suggested that these properties (which have effects which cannot be achieved without such properties) involve any interference with ordinary physical causality. Why should it be suggested that consciousness does?

6.4.1. *Consciousness as a Global Property*

In order to be useful, a knife (say, a bread knife) has to be solid and sharp: solidity and sharpness are 'global properties' of the object as a whole, rather than properties of any of its constituent parts. Without those global properties, the knife could not cut bread. The ability of a knife to cut depends on its having these global properties, and the desired effect of obtaining slices of bread cannot be achieved without using something which has global properties of this kind (see Searle 1984: 26). Similarly, an engine cannot propel a motor vehicle unless it has global properties which give it the necessary power.

Although these effects cannot be achieved without such global properties, no one suggests that this involves any departure from mechanism. Similarly, it can be said, even if our rationality cannot be achieved without consciousness, and even if consciousness has been selected by evolution because of this, rationality and consciousness are just global properties of brains, just as solidity and sharpness are properties of knives; so no departure from mechanism is involved here either.

It is possible in principle to give explanations at different levels of a knife cutting bread. An explanation in terms of the fundamental physics of atoms and molecules will not disclose the knife's properties of solidity and sharpness; and yet these are useful, indeed necessary, properties of the knife. Similarly, it can be said, an explanation of a person's action in terms of the brain's neuron activity will not disclose the property of consciousness; but this also could be a useful property of the brain. The solidity and sharpness of the knife are useful and effective, but they in no way deflect or override the operation of physical laws at the atom–molecule level. Similarly, consciousness is useful and effective; but it does not deflect or override the operation of physical laws at the level of neurons of the brain (or at any other level), or choose between alternatives left open by the operation of such laws.

6.4.2. *Global Effects Require Global Properties*

However, the effects of global properties, such as solidity, sharpness, and power, which require such global properties to bring them about, are all (in general terms) at a level of description and scale similar to that of the global property itself. One requires solidity and sharpness to effect the slicing of bread, not to cause any particular molecule or atom or subatomic particle of the bread to behave in a particular way. Similar comments can be made about power and the propulsion of motor vehicles.

Thus one can understand why global properties are necessary for global effects. However, a choice or decision is not a global effect: its scale or level of description is irrelevant. As I have argued, the primary usefulness of consciousness appears to be to determine what is to happen, by a choice based on reasons which cannot be formalized. Now a determination can be in any sort of code, at any scale: it is scale-less. The advantages suggested for consciousness thus have nothing to do with scale, but everything to do with choice, which is independent of scale.

Reduced to essentials, a choice is no more than a determination that one thing *A* should be made to happen rather than another thing *B*. Although a mentalistic description of a choice requires a certain level of description, it is not (primarily at least) that description which has survival value: what has survival value is merely the determination of *A* rather than *B*, if *A* is more advantageous to survival. Once a determination is made, magnification of it to any requisite scale or level does not require consciousness. Thus the question of earlier sections of this chapter remains: if such an advantageous choice can be made by effective procedures, without consciousness, why have the consciousness? Reference to global properties, and to levels of description, seems irrelevant.

This contention is supported by computer science and by work on artificial intelligence, which shows that consciousness is *not* necessary for such things as the following: receiving, processing, and storing information; making 'determinations' and 'choices' based on the application of effective procedures to such information; performing complicated and precise physical movements based on such information, determinations, and choices; and displaying and communicating such information, determinations, and choices. On one view, then, this shows with exquisite precision that *if* consciousness is a global property required to bring about certain effects, then these effects cannot be the making of determinations and choices by application of effective procedures, or anything else which (as this work shows) does not require consciousness.

6.4.3. *Global Properties Explained by Micro Properties*

A related objection to the global properties approach is that global properties such as solidity, sharpness, and power can be *fully* explained in terms of the micro properties of the entities concerned; whereas it is otherwise in the case of consciousness. Furthermore, the causal properties and effects of such global properties, but not of consciousness, are just those that can be explained, and calculated, from the causal properties and effects of the constituent micro elements.

One cannot conceive of a world in which the micro events associated with (say) a knife cutting bread occur, but not the macro events. The latter are just an aggregation of the micro events; are systematically correlated to the micro events; and are merely a different level of description of the same events.

As pointed out in Nagel (1974), we can see in principle how high-level phenomena not involving consciousness can be correlated systematically with each other, and with associated micro events, in accordance with knowable quantitative rules. Take, for example, heat, and its association with the random motion of molecules. Feelings of heat involve consciousness; but the random motion of molecules can in principle be systematically correlated, in accordance with knowable quantitative laws, with all other high-level aspects of heat, including: expansion of solids and liquids, boiling of liquids, pressure of gases, radiation of heat, convection, conduction, burning of materials, other chemical effects, etc.

In the case of the consciousness, however, it seems otherwise. One *can* conceive of a world in which objective brain events occur, but mental events (such as consciousness of sensations of pain) do *not* occur. Mental events are not (in any obvious or straightforward way, at least) an aggregation of brain events; are not (in any clear way, at least) systematically correlated to brain events; and are not merely a different *level* of description (because the description of mental events does, and that of physical events does not, involve the point of view of a subject). It will be recalled from Section 3.1 that Searle argued persuasively against the systematic correlation of mental events and physical events, although, somewhat inconsistently I think, he elsewhere supports a global property approach to mental events.

Furthermore, high-level descriptions of physical objects, involving their global properties, generally obey quantitative causal laws: this is a corollary of the systematic correlation referred to earlier. Whether or not such an explanation can actually be given, it can readily be envisaged how a machine could be explained as operating on varying levels, obeying causal laws at each level, with each level reducible to and explicable in terms of its operation at lower levels. However, there appear to be no similar laws which govern mental events: this is Davidson's contention referred to in Section 3.1, and it seems correct. Each mental event is unique, and it seems impossible to predict its effects, because it is never possible to *quantify* the differences from other mental events, or the effect of such differences: mental events are just not measurable, even in principle, so cannot (as mental events) be governed by quantitative deterministic laws.

From this, either of two conclusions could follow, if there is to be consistency between the causally determined physical events, and the indeterministic mental events: (1) the former completely determine what happens, so any indeterminism is only apparent (as appears to be Davidson's position); or (2) the latter are at least sometimes efficacious and can in certain circumstances affect physical events in ways not completely determined by quantitative causal laws. The second of these conclusions is supported by the arguments of this chapter, as well as those of Chapters 4 and 5.

6.5. Further Questions

The arguments of this chapter raise a number of further questions. Two of them I will only mention now, but will consider in some detail in Chapter 16, where I outline a theory of mind. The third I will briefly deal with here, and consider further in Chapter 16.

1. How can 'wholes' be 'compared'? I have suggested that mental events, such as awareness of the appearance of objects, must be associated with many spatially separated physical events in the brain or central nervous system. Similarly, an organism's recollection of previously encountered objects, or properties of such objects, must be associated with many spatially separated physical events in the central nervous system. If a choice or decision is made by comparing these two wholes, and is itself associated with one or more physical events in the central nervous system, that comparison would seem to involve some instantaneous correlation of spatially separated physical events. How can that be, particularly when the special theory of relativity precludes signals being sent faster than the speed of light?

2. Who (or what) compares wholes, and with what equipment? The brain or central nervous system is a physical entity, apparently operating in accordance with quantitative causal laws. In so far as it operates in accordance with such causal laws, it is operating mechanistically, and consciousness has no independent role. If and in so far as it does not so operate, so that consciousness has an independent role, what (if not the physical brain) is it that

compares wholes and makes choices, and what equipment (if not the physical brain) is being used to do so?

3. Is there violation of causal laws? If it is the case that consciousness is independently efficacious, so that physical movements occur which might not have occurred if only physical events, operating in accordance with causal laws, were involved, does that not mean that causality is violated? Even if physical events operating in accordance with causal laws leave open alternatives, causality would still be violated unless the conscious choice happened to coincide with one of these alternatives. What (if anything) ensures that this is the case?

On this third point, we know that, in certain respects, the rational operation of the mind seems to be at the mercy of the physical events affecting the brain: certainly personality, memory, and ability to reason generally, can be affected by physical injury to the brain and by chemical alterations in the brain. As argued in Taylor (1985: 166–70), there is a real possibility of conflict between accounts of what happens in terms of mental events (and beliefs, desires, reasons, etc.) and in terms of physical events (and causal laws of nature). How can it be other than miraculous if conscious choices, not determined by physical events, do not involve a violation of causation, a violation which would conflict with our knowledge of the dependence of the mind upon the brain?

To some extent, my answer has already been suggested in Section 6.3. Physical events determine what alternatives are available, and also determine quantum mechanical probabilities as between those alternatives. On this approach, injury to the brain (and indeed anything which can affect physical events within the brain, including heredity and environment) will affect what alternatives are available, and also their quantum mechanical probabilities. Nothing can happen outside these alternatives, so causality is not violated. Within them, however, choices can be made; and it seems reasonable to conjecture that the *reasons* for which such choices are made will somehow be related to the quantum mechanical probabilities.

I will consider this matter further in Chapter 16.

7

Folk Psychology

So far, I have argued against mechanism on grounds generally related to evolutionary advantages of consciousness for plausible reasoning. In this chapter, I turn to grounds related to what has (somewhat slightingly) been called 'folk psychology': the untutored common-sense psychology which we all continually undertake in relation to our own behaviour and the behaviour of other persons. (Incidentally, slighting references to 'folk psychology' have drawn the apt response that this includes the folk psychology of Shakespeare and Tolstoy, which compares not unfavourably with today's 'scientific psychology'!) I will be arguing that, based on such psychology, there are good grounds supporting rejection of mechanism.

In the first place, introspection, or observation or monitoring of one's own mental processes, seems to give a picture of mental processes which is inconsistent in various ways with mechanism. I suggest that some weight should be given to this picture.

Secondly, this picture is deeply entrenched both in our language, and in the attitudes we normally adopt towards the behaviour of ourselves and of other persons. This does not mean that mechanism is incorrect: indeed, this circumstance should put us on our guard against uncritical acceptance of views which are entrenched in these ways. However, our language and attitudes are (in part) a reflection of insights of past generations, and so assertions embedded in them should be given some persuasive weight.

Next, the very fact that we *do* folk psychology is itself a consequence of the occurrence of mental events; and so the very existence of folk psychology appears to be a *difference* made by the occurrence of mental events. In particular, a causal theory of knowledge suggests that we can *know* about mental events only because they have effects.

Finally, folk psychology itself has effects on what happens: it is by doing folk psychology that we have, in our ordinary lives, some (albeit limited) understanding of behaviour, both of ourselves and others. That is (I contend): we can do folk psychology only because mental events have effects; and our doing folk psychology itself has effects on what happens; therefore, mechanism is probably false.

7.1. The Way it Seems

Until one examines the question as a philosopher or scientist, it seems obvious to us that our actions are directly affected (indeed, effected) by our mental events. Our volitions are in one sense *part* of our actions (their 'internal' aspect), but also seem to us to *cause* the bodily movements involved. Furthermore, what we decide to do seems to us to be affected by our consideration of the question, and by our subjective experiences; and how well we perform tasks seems to be affected by such subjective matters as attention, concentration, and effort. We consider ourselves to be active participants in the world, not mere spectators (cf. Bohr 1961: 119).

Is there a good reason to give up this common-sense or folk psychology view, that our mental events play a causative role in our actions? In one sense, even some supporters of the consensus would say no. According to them, mental events do play such a role, precisely the same role as the associated physical events. However, that does not seem to do full justice to the common-sense view. In this section, I consider various aspects of such a common-sense view, and associated considerations arising from both our ordinary attitudes and introspection.

7.1.1. *Experiencing and Doing*

I have earlier suggested that our experiences and volitions generally comprise a (weighted) mixture of two aspects, one passive (experiencing) and one active (doing). In some cases, for example feeling pain, the doing aspect might be minimal or nil. In other cases, for example writing with one's eyes shut, the experiencing aspect might be minimal: one's knowledge of what is happening is derived mainly from what one is doing. Even though in many, perhaps most, cases the two aspects are inextricably mixed, there is a clear distinction between them: we just *know* that there is a fundamental distinction between 'doing' and merely 'experiencing'. It may be that, in relation to 'experiencing', our mental events simply reflect physical events operating causally, but 'doing' seems fundamentally different.

What can be made of the distinction, on the consensus view? It must presumably be contended that the distinction is between different types of experiences: any explanation in terms of the causal role of the experience–volition would undermine the insistence of the consensus that all experience–volition is merely a conscious aspect of physical events proceeding according to physical laws. Now the difference we perceive between experiencing and doing could merely be a difference between different types of experiencing: a 'feeling' of activity, choice, decision, problem-solving, etc., without the reality. But that is certainly not how it seems to us.

It seems to us that the difference does involve a difference concerning the causal roles of the two aspects. Experiencing involves no causal input or throughput from the self or person (considered subjectively); volition involves such an input or throughput, and when the volition relates to bodily movements, it causes them.

It will be recalled that in Section 1.4 I referred to causation in accordance with quantitative physical laws; and also to the possibility of another type of causation, which may be called 'agent causation'. On each occasion that we do a voluntary act, we seem to experience a kind of causation. I do not suggest that we experience 'a *causing* which is not a *doing*' (see French 1985: 79); but rather that doing is experienced as a kind of causing—not in the sense of some law-determined development, but in the sense of an *efficacious* event. Hume contended that the idea of causation cannot be derived from any single occurrence, but only from many occurrences where there is the same sequence of events. This may be correct in so far as the idea of causation involves lawlike regularity; but in so far as the idea of causation (even in the inanimate world) involves the idea of efficacy, I suggest that this derives from our knowledge of causation experienced in individual volitions (see Lucas 1970: 62–3). Our apparent agent causation may be inefficacious, as mechanists would contend, but it certainly does not seem that way.

7.1.2. *Reasons as Motivation*

In addition to the two types of causation referred to in the previous paragraph (lawlike physical causation and agent causation), intentional actions seem to involve a third type of causation or causation analogue, namely the motivating role of reasons for actions and decisions. Indeed, another illustration of folk psychology which suggests a conflict with mechanism is the role accorded to reasons for actions or decisions. When a person acts for reasons, or else makes a decision for reasons, folk psychology accords something like a causal role to these reasons: the reasons are seen as motivating and explaining the action or decision, and (in a sense) as bringing it about or causing it. However, reasons cannot, on a mechanistic view, be causes at all, hence the conflict.

1. No objective existence. Reasons cannot be any kind of cause, on a mechanistic view, because they have no *objective* existence.

In the terminology I have used in this book, this can be put as follows. Mental events involve the interdependent coexistence of a subject and a private conscious world of experiences and volitions. It seems that neither element exists without the other: what certainly does exist is the *combination* of subject and experiences–volitions. This combination is one aspect of brain–mind events: the other aspect is the brain events which somehow encode it. On a mechanistic view, only the combination exists objectively, and so only this combination could operate as a cause: whereas, the folk psychology view is that the experiences influence the subject, which in turn *does* the actions. A person's reasons for actions include the content of beliefs which he has, which may or may not be correct; and the content of his desires, which are in some way reflected in the content of his experiences. The fact that the person has these beliefs and desires, and the occurrence of the relevant mental events and associated physical events in the brain, do have objective existence and may operate as causes. However, *these* are not the person's reasons: his reasons are of the nature of, or are reflected in, the *content* of experience.

Bond (1983: 21–30) gives the example of a person leaving a building because (he or she believes) it is on fire. The person's reason for leaving (what he or she would say if asked why) is 'The building is on fire'. This reason is the same whether or not the building is in fact on fire: the reason itself has no objective existence. What has objective existence is the person's having the belief that the building is on fire; that is, the-person-having-the-reason. The reason itself, therefore, is not the sort of thing that can be an objective cause.

To take another example: I have a headache, and take an aspirin tablet. My reasons for doing so are the pain that I feel, my desire to get rid of it, and my belief that the aspirin tablet will help to do so. None of these things by themselves exist objectively: their objective existence is as a part or aspect of me-feeling-my-pain, and me-having-my-desire, and me-having-my-belief. The corresponding physical events encode the combinations me-feeling-my-pain, me-having-my-desire, and me-having-my-belief. My pain itself, my desire itself, and my belief itself, as they appear to me, exist only in my subjective world; and by themselves (that is, apart from their interdependent coexistence with 'me') do not correspond to any physical events or states. Accordingly, by themselves they are not the sort of things that can be a cause, on a mechanistic view. Nevertheless, as I have said, *my* reasons are the pain, the desire, and the belief; not any conception of their association or combination with me.

Our folk psychology belief is that our reasons *do* motivate us, and thereby, in a sense, act as causes. In my reasoning, I believe that my reasons motivate me, not merely that me-having-those-reasons causes the decision or action. I consider my reasons as real, *inter alia* in the sense of justifying and being the basis for my choice, decision, and action; even though I may believe that those reasons are real only in my subjective world, and that it is only me-having-those-reasons which has *objective* existence.

2. Not conclusive. Folk psychology explanations, in terms of reasons, also conflict with the mechanistic view of causation in that such explanations are generally inconclusive, and irreducibly so.

The mechanistic view is that there is in principle a complete causal explanation of any event, which is such that no other event is possible; or at least, in cases where quantum physics is relevant, is such that only a range of events is possible, with determined probabilities assigned to events within this range. An explanation in terms of reasons, however, cannot generally, even in principle, have this character. It conceivably might do so, if all reasons point the one way, or perhaps if the only reasons pointing a different way are of no different type and are unambiguously weaker. However, generally an explanation in terms of reasons will not be such that no *other* choice, decision, or action was possible (nor such that determined probabilities could be assigned to alternatives): such an explanation is inherently inconclusive. This is related to the point that mental events are not law-governed, *inter alia* because they cannot be given a quantitative description appropriate for the application of precise quantitative laws; and also to the point that plausible reasoning is inconclusive and fallible. Reasons 'incline but do not necessitate' (see Flew and Vesey 1987: 57–71, 174).

3. The relationship to desire. The mechanistic approach to reasons is associated with the view that reasons as such do not motivate, that only *desire* motivates.

This view has also been advanced by non-mechanists. For example, Bond (1983) argues that a reason must be more than a 'motivational ghost', that is, there must be 'something beyond mere belief or cognition' to account for doing something, some 'motivational propensity'; and that therefore an agent having reasons to act in a certain way entails the agent having a desire so to act. The conclusion does not follow from the premiss, although to some extent this is moderated by Bond's taking a wide view of desire, using it in the 'motivational' sense, as opposed to the 'inclinational' sense.

One may accept that to have a reason for an action or decision is not merely to believe a fact but also to have some sort of 'pro-attitude' towards that action or decision (see LePore and McLaughlin 1985: 4). But such an assertion is almost without content (see Swinburne 1986: 115). And to identify this amorphous pro-attitude with desire is misleading, for two related reasons.

First, it obscures that motivational reasons include a wide variety of reasons, many of which would not usually be called 'desires'; for example, a motive associated with a belief that an action is right. Secondly, it suggests that reasons are commensurable, and that one acts in accordance with the strongest desire; whereas I contend that reasons are often incommensurable, and that, if there is a 'strongest' reason, it is so only by being determined to be so by one's decision.

In general, the insistence that only desires motivate suggests that the operation of reasons is mechanical and quantitative, rather than by way of rational inclination. I say that reasons are diverse and often incommensurable; yet also, at the same time, such that many of them, if fully understood in their complete context, similarly motivate most reasonable human beings. Indeed, while it may well be that 'reasons' can be used in a sense such that mere cognition of reasons does not motivate, nevertheless the motivational force of what are generally regarded as reasons would usually arise with cognition of such reasons by a reasonable human being.

4. Implications of the mechanistic view. On the consensus approach, a person is 'motivated by reasons' only in so far as that expression can be considered an appropriate description of the causative operation of the-person-having-those-reasons. The reasons themselves, and their cogency, are relevant to a choice, decision, and action only if and in so far as they reflect the causative operation of the-person-having-those-reasons.

Consider, for example, the case of making a decision, where one alternative is supported by a formally valid argument from accepted premises. Such an argument does not in fact move us in any way significantly different from a merely plausible argument: we can accept or reject a conclusion of either. If we are being rational in such a case, our rejection of the conclusion of the formally valid argument will lead us to question either our acceptance of the premises, or the rule of inference; but this does not alter the circumstance that we *can* reject the conclusion, if, for example, there are *other* arguments against it. In such a case, the formally valid argument will just be one argument with persuasive force.

On a superficial approach, this might appear to support the mechanistic view: the formally valid argument is not itself causally relevant (if it were, it would be conclusive), whereas what is causally relevant is the agent's adoption of the argument as a reason. However, I contend that this example illustrates a difficulty of the consensus view. According to a mechanistic view of rationality, formally valid arguments from accepted premises (axioms or theorems) give rise to theorems: such arguments are conclusive, and their conclusions cannot be rejected. And, as we have seen, a mechanistic view of rationality can give no account of informal plausible reasoning, except in terms of the mechanistic application of rules or procedures which have proved useful in the past; that is, in terms essentially of habit resulting from natural selection.

On the consensus view, then, arguments or reasons *as such* can have either conclusive effect or no effect: formally valid arguments may have conclusive effect, whereas informal arguments can have effect only in combination with habits of thought selected as useful by evolution. Thus, when one believes one is thinking critically in assessing the weight and cogency of arguments for the alternatives which are open for choice or decision, on the consensus view one is doing no such thing: rather, the arguments, together with (unconscious) habits of thought selected by evolution and perhaps developed by one's personal history, operate together to produce a deterministic result, which otherwise has nothing to do with the weight or cogency of the arguments.

This is another illustration of the tendency of the consensus to be self-refuting. It can be seen as another way of putting my development of the Haldane argument, set out in Section 5.6: when a person is purportedly assessing the arguments for the consensus view, he is (on that view) merely being operated on by the combination of such arguments and certain habits of thought, which passed evolutionary tests in vastly different circumstances.

This argument also shows that an explanation of conduct in terms of the person's reasons is *not* just a higher-level description of the same processes as the operation of the brain; although an account in terms of the-agent-having-those-reasons could be such a description.

7.1.3. *Alternatives Open until Decision*

As I will be suggesting in Section 7.2, it seems impossible to adopt a mechanistic stance in relation to one's own actions. Any subject which 'sees' things 'to be done', and has experiences relevant to what is to be done, cannot without confusion regard its own actions otherwise than as being chosen by it (i.e. the subject) on the basis of reasons grounded in the content of its experience. I have also, in Section 7.1.1, referred to the difference between experiencing and doing. The latter involves a belief that 'doing' 'does', i.e. that 'willing' or volition causes the physical movements of the action willed; and that 'willing' itself is one's own performance based on reasons and not determined by anything else.

Even if I believed intellectually that everything must occur simply as it does, unaffected by (for example) whether or not I make an effort, the fact is that my making an effort *does* make a difference, and I *can* make an effort or not make an effort as I choose. In making an effort, I act for reasons and make a difference: otherwise, why try, why make an effort, why think? Swinburne writes: 'It is only if an agent believes that he can make a difference to whether something happens, that he can purpose to do so . . . causation is part of the content of the experience of acting' (1986: 99–100).

Consideration of reasons for and against alternative actions presupposes that both (or all) alternatives are possible: otherwise the reasons are irrelevant to what is to be done. All views accept that consideration of reasons (or associated physical processes) is causally related to what happens. But, in addition, right up to the instant of decision (or action), one believes that the reasons are relevant: yet this can be so only if alternatives are open. If one's decision is determined by physical processes, so that alternatives are never truly open in the sense that either (or any) is possible, then reasons for and against are not relevant. That is, they are not as a matter of rationality relevant; and if this is appreciated by the subject, the subject cannot reasonably consider them to be relevant.

Doing or deciding, we believe, is for reasons; yet the subjective process presupposes that the doing is not mechanically determined by the reasons (or the-agent-having-the-reasons, or the associated physical processes); because otherwise there would be no alternatives in relation to which competing reasons could have relevance.

7.2. **Entrenchment in Language and Attitudes**

The folk psychology theory of action has persuasive force in itself; but furthermore this theory is entrenched in the language we use about human action, and in the attitudes we habitually adopt towards human action.

7.2.1. *Language*

The folk psychology view that actions are explained, and in a sense caused, by reasons involving beliefs and desires, and in ways not wholly consistent with mechanism, is reflected and indeed embedded in our language.

This is suggested particularly in Norman Malcolm's article 'The Conceivability of Mechanism' (Malcolm 1982). He argues *inter alia* that desires and intentions are conceptually linked with the actions which are desired or intended, in that the connection between a desire or intention to do an action, and the action itself, cannot be dependent on any objective contingent regularity; whereas mechanism asserts that the connection between an action and any antecedent states is purely that of objective contingent regularities. Proof of mechanism would show that explanations in terms of desires and intentions (as we understand them, that is, as conceptually connected with actions) are not true.

As I understand it, Malcolm's point is this. If one says that a person has an intention to do something, for example to go shopping this afternoon, then part of what one is *saying* is that, in the absence of countervailing factors, that is what he or she will do. Of course, before this afternoon, the person may change his or her mind, or factors may arise which somehow prevent or override fulfilment of the intention; but if, in the absence of anything like this, the intended act is *not* done, then we would consider that it had been incorrect to attribute the intention at all. That is, the link between intention and action is, at least in part, conceptual, and bound up in the meaning of words; and not merely a matter depending on laws or regularities of nature which we might discover, which could have been otherwise, and about which we could be mistaken.

As Malcolm concedes, this does not show that mechanism is false: it could be that our concepts of desire and intention just do not in fact apply to states and/or events in the real world. States and/or events in the brain which are precursors of actions would (on the mechanist view) be connected with actions only by contingent regularities, and so could not be desires or intentions as we understand them; and so presumably it would be necessary to (at least) modify our concepts of desire and intention if mechanism were shown to be true.

Malcolm goes further (p. 145), and contends that mechanism is incompatible with the existence of any intentional behaviour; and that since it is intentional behaviour to assert anything, no one could (consistently) assert that mechanism is true. This has considerable force, but is not conclusive: the concepts of intentional behaviour and of assertion could perhaps be modified so as to fit in with a mechanist view of the world; and in that modified sense one could perhaps consistently 'assert' that mechanism is false.

However, it is surely significant that folk psychology views of desire and intention are embedded in language. I suggest that much accumulated wisdom is reflected in the actual use of language (cf. Armstrong and Malcolm 1984: 212–13), and that we should not lightly reject it. However, it must be conceded that ordinary language may embody and perpetuate factual mistakes: on one view, this has been the case in relation to the concepts of 'parallel lines' and 'straight lines', at least prior to the development of non-Euclidean geometry and the reflection of non-Euclidean geometry in ordinary language (if this has in fact yet occurred).

7.2.2. *Attitudes*

In Section 2.5, as one distinction between mental events and physical events, I mentioned that there were *preferred* descriptions in the case of mental events: that is, descriptions in terms of the *significance* which an action or experience has for the agent or experiencer, a factor emphasized, for example, by Charles Taylor:

We define the action by the significance it had for the agent (albeit sometimes unconsciously), and this is not just one of many descriptions from different observers' standpoints, but is intrinsic to the action *qua* action . . . It is just the principal feature of agents that we can speak about the meanings things have for them in this nonrelative way, that, in other words, things *matter* for them. (Taylor 1985: 197)

Taylor calls this the significance factor, and contends that 'the crucial difference between men and machines is that the former have it while the latter lack it'. Whether or not this is the crucial difference, it is, I think, an important expression of folk psychology, and is one way in which folk psychology is embedded in our attitudes: we just cannot help thinking of actions primarily in terms of this significance factor.

More generally, in our consideration of our own actions and those of other persons, we generally adopt what Dennett called the intentional stance (Dennett 1978: 3–6; see Section 3.1.3): we view actions as being done in terms of systems of mental concepts, such as beliefs, desires, and intentions. It is possible for us to adopt one of the other two stances identified by Dennett: we can, for example, take the physical stance, and consider the physical movements involved in actions as caused mechanistically by physical events and states. However,

1. As noted in Section 7.1, such a stance seems impossible to maintain in relation to one's own actions. In the case of one's own actions, it seems that one can do no other than choose how to act on the basis of reasons, which one

feels free to accept or reject, or to accord whatever weight one considers appropriate. When actually acting consciously, one cannot regard one's action (or even just one's bodily movements) as mechanistically caused by physical events. Even Dennett concedes that 'we, *as persons*, cannot *adopt* exclusive mechanism' (1978: 254).

2. Such a stance is rarely in fact used in relation to others. Even psychiatrists treating patients rarely abandon the intentional stance entirely. Generally our moral discourse about, and attitudes towards, ourselves and others is in a framework of mental explanations of actions in which freedom and responsibility are assumed. Hence, *inter alia*, our shame (and pride) in relation to our own conduct, and our gratitude (and resentment) in relation to the conduct of others. As philosopher Sir Peter Strawson puts it in Strawson (1982), we use a 'participant attitude' or 'ordinary moral reactive attitude' rather than an objective attitude.

Thus our ordinary attitudes both to ourselves and to others assume that mental events and states cause actions; and that a mechanistic explanation of actions is not complete.

The entrenchment of non-mechanistic views in our attitudes, as in our language, does not prove that mechanism is false. However, this entrenchment is very much bound up with language and its use, and it may similarly be regarded as reflecting human wisdom and experience over a long period of time. Its anti-mechanist implications should not be rejected without reasons which are more persuasive than mechanist arguments have turned out to be.

7.3. Folk Psychology as a Consequence of Consciousness

As a further argument against mechanism, let us consider a particular class of assertions and beliefs, namely those which are themselves *about* one's own mental events and states, and the mental events and states of other persons. It seems clear that concepts of mental events and states (such as pains, beliefs, desires, intentions, emotions) are in fact used to enable thought and communication concerning human (and indeed animal) behaviour. That is, understanding and discourse about human behaviour is promoted by use of such concepts: by attributing the referents of such concepts (that is, pains, beliefs, intentions, etc.) to ourselves and others, and by taking such referents to affect behaviour.

There are two aspects to this argument. The first, which I consider in this section, is this: if one accepts a causal theory of knowledge, then the very circumstance that we can know of the occurrence of mental events and mental states in ourselves and (I contend) in others, shows that such events and states must have at least *some* consequences: namely, those consequences which are necessary to enable them to be known. The second, which I consider in

Section 7.4, is that the circumstance that we know of and use words for such events and states has further consequences, in enabling us to have, and act upon, some understanding of the behaviour of ourselves and others.

As asserted in Shoemaker (1984: 191, quoted in Section 3.1.1), 'a causal theory of knowledge implies that states or features that are independent of the causal powers of the things they characterize would be in principle unknowable'; and to deny a causal theory of knowledge undermines all knowledge. I cannot *know* that I am in pain unless the subjective qualitative character of pain, the feeling of pain, has some consequences: unless my knowledge is a consequence of what it is knowledge *of*, then it cannot be soundly based, it cannot *be* knowledge. Therefore, a state which lacks such a subjective feeling of pain cannot be functionally identical to a state which has it.

Similarly, Swinburne writes:

I have beliefs, not only about the physical world but about my sensations them-selves—that they have such and such a shape or colour or taste, and beliefs on some occasions that I am then having a sensation. If sensations are purely epiphenomenal, these beliefs will not be caused by the sensations but by brain-states . . . And what goes for me, goes for everyone else as well. But if that is so, everyone's belief that there are sensations will be totally without justification. (Swinburne 1986: 39–40)

This argument from knowledge is a strong one. I suggest that I do know that my sensations (of pain etc.) exist or have existed, as much as I know anything: no other knowledge of mine is more certain than that. For any belief in something's existence to count as knowledge, it must be justified, *inter alia* by being caused by that something. So, if that something has no con-sequences, one *cannot know* of its existence.

If mechanism were true (so that physical events developed over time purely in accordance with unambiguous rules and random jumps, and so could be simulated to arbitrary accuracy by a machine carrying out effective proce-dures), then I could conceive of a world in which physical events occurred which (1) were identical with those that are associated in my world with feelings of pain, but (2) occurred in that other world without the feelings of pain. I could then know that my world is not such a world only if feelings of pain had consequences different from, or at least additional to, those of their associated physical events, that is, if mechanism were not true. I *do* know that my world is not such a world, because I know that I have feelings of pain; therefore, mechanism is not true.

I see three possible objections to this argument. First, it could be said that my knowledge that I have sensations of pain (and other experiences) is itself only a mental state or mental event; and that mechanism is not inconsistent with one mental state or event having consequences (additional to those of associated physical events) for other mental states and events (as distinct from physical events). Secondly, it could be contended that Wittgenstein has shown that our language uses public concepts, and does not refer at all to private subjective events and states, as I have suggested. Thirdly, it could be suggested that the global properties argument (see Section 6.4) applies, and does so more strongly than in relation to evolution; because beliefs in the existence of sensations are at the level of description of the sensations themselves.

I will consider these in turn.

1. My knowledge of my own pains (and other sensations, and beliefs and intentions), coupled with the naming of them, assist me to have some understanding of my own behaviour, incomplete though such understanding may be. Further, such knowledge is part of the basis for my attributing to others sensations and beliefs and intentions, and thus of my (again limited) understanding of the behaviour of others. This understanding affects my behaviour, and thus affects physical events. I look at this further in the next section.

2. Wittgenstein did not show (or arguably even contend) that words such as 'pain' do not refer at all to subjective private experiences; but rather that there must be some public criteria for use of such words. As indicated earlier, I accept that the criteria for use of such words include objective observable behaviour, but I contend that what such a word refers to is, primarily, the subjective experience. When I take an aspirin for my headache, I may be wanting to make myself less inclined to rub or hold my head, and less irritable; but primarily, I think, I want this nasty feeling to go away. When I flinch under my dentist's drill, and he sympathetically asks if it hurt, I take him to be interested in what I subjectively felt. When a court awards compensation for pain and suffering, I believe it is attempting to compensate for feelings.

3. Most of the arguments advanced in Section 6.4 concerning global properties apply here: in particular, the conceivability of the existence of the relevant physical events without the mental events, the lack of any complete systematic correlation between the two, and the non-availability of a complete deterministic account at the level of the supposed global property. The only argument which does not apply is that concerning the scale of the relevant consequences, and I contend that the others are good enough.

7.4. Consequences of Folk Psychology

Our knowledge of mental events and mental states, referred to in the previous section, has further consequences for physical events; in particular in that we base our actions to some extent on our beliefs about the beliefs, desires, intentions, etc. of ourselves and other people.

As regards other people, if we did not have those beliefs about their mental states and events, we would not understand their behaviour in the way that we do, and our actions towards them (including our physical movements) would be different. Accordingly, it makes a difference to our behaviour that we can attribute intentions and motives to other people. If other people were non-conscious, our behaviour towards them would be the same as it actually is only if we (incorrectly) attributed consciousness to them.

Similarly, we reason about our own wants and intentions: our decisions (and therefore actions) are sometimes different because we take into account certain of our own mental states and events. It appears, therefore, that our own mental states and events have effects on our actions in that way.

One finds a foreshadowing of this argument in Nagel (1974):

It is often possible to take up a point of view other than one's own . . . There is a sense in which phenomenological facts are perfectly objective: one person can know or say of another what the quality of the other's experience is. They are subjective, however, in the sense that even this objective ascription of experience is possible only for someone sufficiently similar to the object of ascription to be able to adopt his point of view . . . (pp. 441–2)

This can be taken as asserting that we can know what the conscious experiences of others are like only because we have conscious experiences ourselves. It is a smallish step from this to asserting that we can *understand* the actions of others only because we can know the conscious experiences underlying and motivating them, and thus only because we ourselves have such conscious experiences.

A somewhat similar argument is advanced more elaborately by psychologist Nicholas Humphrey (in Humphrey 1983, 1986). In these books, Humphrey discusses the function of 'consciousness', from an evolutionary viewpoint, *but* using 'consciousness' as meaning what I call 'self-consciousness' (see, for example, Humphrey 1986: 52). The essence of his argument can be gleaned from the following:

My thesis . . . is that Nature's solution to the problem of doing psychology has been to give to every member of the human species both the power and the inclination *to use a privileged picture of his own self as a model for what it is like to be another person.* (Humphrey 1983: 6)

When we watch the behaviour of our fellow human beings, we seldom, if ever, see merely a mosaic of incidental acts: we see beneath it a deeper causal structure—the hidden presence of plans, intentions, emotions, memories, etc.—and it is on that basis that we can claim to understand what they are doing. We have in other words a picture, a kind of conceptual model of the human mind, and we should not be natural psychologists without it. (Humphrey 1986: 66)

He goes on to point out that the human brain is 'unimaginably complex', so that we could not understand behaviour by modelling its operation as such: our understanding of behaviour requires a model of the subjective operations of the mind.

In some ways, it may be that both Nagel and Humphrey suggest limits on this kind of reasoning which are too narrow. Notwithstanding what Nagel in particular says, I think that we do understand animal behaviour, to some extent at least, by attributing mental properties to them, even though their subjective experiences (assuming they have them) are probably very different from ours. Perhaps even more significantly, it appears that animals may attribute mental properties to *us*: see, for example, the material in Hearne (1987) suggesting that dogs are interested in, and respond to, *intentions* of their trainers.

However, Nagel and Humphrey do support the point I am trying to make: that mental events and states have consequences, because it is only by considering our own mental events and states, and those which we attribute to others (at least partly on the basis of our knowledge of our own mental events and states), that we can achieve some understanding of the behaviour of ourselves and others (cf. Kim 1985: 386). And such understanding affects our actions, and thereby affects physical events.

It seems to me that the only way to oppose this argument is to deny the thesis of the previous section: that is, to deny the causal theory of knowledge. To do this, that is, to suggest that knowledge can be acquired without any causal influence from what is known, would undermine all knowledge.

Another approach to this matter is from the point of view of evolution. It has apparently proved useful for survival for an organism to develop a central nervous system capable of using high-level descriptions of objects, states, and events, and in particular of (subjective) mental events. This does not necessarily itself *require* subjective mental events, because non-conscious computers can certainly at least *use* such descriptions; and just as human beings have programmed computers to do so, evolution and natural selection could similarly have programmed human beings. Further, as Dennett and Boden point out, human beings can be helped in understanding activities of computers by taking an intentional stance towards them; that is, by attributing to computers mental properties such as beliefs, desires, intentions, etc. (which I, of course, contend are purely fictional or, at best, metaphorical).

However, if human beings behave in accordance with physical laws operating on physical states and events, that is mechanistically, the question arises: why is the useful high-level description of the operations of human beings, which has been developed in the course of evolution, one which is in terms of mental events and states operating non-mechanistically? Surely if mental events and states are not causally efficacious, evolution would have developed high-level mechanistic descriptions of human behaviour. Twentieth-century psychology, in particular behaviourist psychology, has attempted to develop high-level mechanistic descriptions of human behaviour. However, it seems generally accepted that this endeavour has had only limited success; and, in any event, my point is that, had such a description been available, then surely it would have had survival value for human beings to develop and use it long before such a project was devised by the behaviourists.

This whole argument suggests that there may be some incoherence in Boden's apparently plausible position of distinguishing two kinds of reductionism, and adopting one while rejecting the other (noted in Section 3.3.2). She attributes significance, and so presumably consequences, to psychological descriptions: yet surely the existence of such descriptions must itself be a consequence of the existence of psychological phenomena, that is, of mental events. The descriptions and their consequences would never have arisen but for the occurrence of mental events, and are therefore a *difference* made by the occurrence of mental events. If so, then mechanism (and with it the form of reductionism which Boden advocates) is false.

Finally, I note that the argument of this section has some affinity with two other arguments.

First, there is the so-called *verstehen* position, which, according to Philip Pettit (Gregory 1987: 786–7), claims that our working conception of human agents (involving the use of 'mentalistic concepts, such as those of intention, desire . . . and belief') is indispensable to our understanding of human beings, and distinctive in the sense of 'not allowing for the sort of amendment and development which characterizes scientific theory'. My argument does not start from this position, although it tends to support it. I do not (initially at least) contend that we could not possibly understand human beings without 'mentalistic concepts', but, rather, I argue that we do *in fact* use such concepts in order to understand human beings: I argue that our knowledge of the referents of such concepts (that is, of mental states and events) means that these referents have consequences; that our use of such knowledge has further consequences (namely, through our understanding, such as it is, of human behaviour); that the referents of the concepts therefore make a difference to what happens; and that accordingly mechanism is false. It seems that some version of the *verstehen* position would *then* follow.

Secondly, there is Popper's argument based on the influence of World 3 (creations of the human mind) on World 1 (see my discussion in Section 1.2.2). In Popper and Eccles (1977: 47–50), he contends that World 3 objects can be grasped only by the human mind, that is, in World 2; and that, since what happens in World 1 is obviously affected by World 3 objects, this must be via World 2; and that therefore World 2 must influence what happens in World 1. However, it seems to me that his argument takes insufficient account of a computer's ability to process (and possibly produce) World 3 entities, and to affect World 1 as a result.

8

Transcending the Code

I HAVE suggested that conscious mental events, the events of the mind, can be considered as being to some extent encoded in physical events of the brain. However, the arguments of the previous four chapters suggest that mental events have properties, *inter alia* causal properties, which are not themselves fully captured by the code of physical events; so that mental events and mind somehow transcend the physical events which encode them. In this chapter I support this suggestion in two other ways.

First, I consider intentionality, the apparent power of the mind to treat words or perceptions as referring to objects and events in the real world. I conclude that there *is* something about intentionality in the human brain–mind which distinguishes it from a mechanistic information-processing system; but that this difference substantially comes down to the same points as argued in Chapters 4 and 5.

Secondly, I consider the central, and indispensable, role of mind in the life and world of every human being. In an important sense, the totality of each person's world comprises his or her mental events and states. Such events and states (including perception and conscious reasoning) are basic to all knowledge. Apart from mind, external reality may be considered as little more than a 'cosmic code': an abstract structure which can be decoded into the substantive reality common to human beings only by minds. Does mind occupy this central role, and achieve so much, only to abdicate totally to the rule of matter?

I conclude this chapter, and this part of the book, by considering where the arguments of Part II have led, and foreshadowing the next stage of the enquiry.

8.1. Intentionality

The problem of intentionality is discussed by Hilary Putnam at the beginning of *Reason, Truth and History* (Putnam 1981). He supposes that an ant, crawling on some sand, traces a line which is a recognizable caricature of Winston Churchill. He notes that 'the line is not "in itself" a representation of anything', so that it 'may seem that what is necessary for representation is *intention*'; and he notes further that this gives rise to the following line of argument:

No physical object can, in itself, refer to one thing rather than to another; nevertheless, *thoughts in the mind* obviously do succeed in referring to one thing rather than another. So thoughts (and hence the mind) are of an essentially different nature than physical objects. Thoughts have the characteristic of *intentionality*—they can refer to something else; nothing physical has 'intentionality', save as that intentionality is derivative from some employment of that physical thing by a mind. (p. 2)

Putnam goes on to reject this argument, as involving what he calls 'magical theories of reference'; and to give an account of reference which suggests that mental representations are 'of the nature of *concepts* and not of the nature of images', where concepts are not mental objects, but 'are (at least in part) *abilities* and not occurrences' (pp. 16–21).

Similarly, Daniel Dennett in *Brainstorms* (Dennett 1978: 122–6), in discussing artificial intelligence, considers what he calls Hume's problem: 'nothing is intrinsically a representation of anything; something is a representation only *for* or *to* someone; any representation or system of representations thus requires at least one *user* or *interpreter* of the representation who is external to it'. Thus, in doing psychology, when one postulates an internal representation, one needs also to postulate an interpreter of it, some sort of little person in the mind, or 'homunculus', which can understand and act on it. Dennett proceeds to argue that work on artificial intelligence has shown how to deal with this problem: namely, by considering how the task performed by this homunculus can be broken down into a number of simpler tasks, which can be performed by 'more stupid' homunculi; and similarly with these simpler tasks, and also with the yet simpler tasks into which they in turn are broken down; until one has only tasks which are so simple (and can be performed by homunculi which are so stupid, indeed by simple machines) that all homunculi can be 'discharged'.

Another aspect of representation and reference concerns meaning: it has been suggested that for an item to mean something, there needs to be someone to whom it has that meaning. According to Paul Churchland, this suggestion is answered by the network theory of meaning:

Since meaning arises from an item's place in a network of assumptions . . . therefore our mental states can have the propositional contents they do because of nothing more than their intricate *relational* features. This would mean that there is no problem in assuming that physical states could have propositional content, since in principle they could easily enjoy the relevant relational features. (Churchland 1984: 66)

Thus, on the one hand, Putnam, Dennett, and Churchland give us reason to believe that intentionality can be explained as a property which computing machines can have; and, on the other, suggestions that it can be a property only of minds seem to depend on making it a mysterious, even magical, property. Accordingly, I would hesitate to suggest that intentionality is an exclusive property of minds, at least unless I could explain precisely what intentionality was, and how and why it was a property of minds, and not of anything else.

However, I think that intentionality does have some relevance to the mind–matter question.

We believe, with justification, that our words and thoughts can mean, refer to, and/or represent, objects and events of a substantive reality external to us, which is common to all human beings and at least partly understandable. We believe, with justification, that we have some knowledge of that reality, which knowledge in part comprises abilities (knowing how), but also in part comprises representations or models of that reality (coupled with assertions that the representations or models *are*, or are *of*, reality). Indeed, it seems that to deny these beliefs is self-refuting.

These models include those of actual present perception; but also include recollections of perceptions, and (more generally) beliefs of all kinds. Even non-perceptual models are, to some extent, based on perception, and have or display or assert perceived properties, which we take to be properties of the external reality which the models represent. These perceived properties are essentially those which are detected by the senses: shape, size, weight, position and orientation, motion, colour, texture, solidity or fluidity, hardness or softness, heat or cold, sound, taste, smell, etc.

Some of them, the secondary qualities (such as colour, heat (as *felt*), taste, smell) we recognize as being due to the effect *on us* of more fundamental properties of the objects (selectivity of energy or wavelength of light absorbed, motion of molecules, structure of molecules, etc.); while even primary qualities (such as shape, size, weight, motion), although apparently more fundamental than secondary properties, *may* similarly be due to the effect on us of even more fundamental properties of reality. All the perceived properties may, as Kant suggests, be those of 'things-for-us' rather than of 'things-in-themselves'. (As we will see, this view has considerable support from the implications of quantum mechanics for non-locality.)

Notwithstanding this, the fact remains that the perceived properties are central to our models of reality: we take them to be (when our models are accurate) properties of real objects and events in the external world. Our theories, which contribute to our perception of properties, also allow us to infer further properties which are not so directly perceived (such as mass, energy, electric charge, etc.), and which may be, in Kant's terms, properties of things-in-themselves; but, even in relation to these, our understanding of them requires, or at least is greatly assisted by, an understanding of the relationship of these inferred properties to perceived properties. (Part of the difficulty of understanding quantum physics is due, I think, to the difficulty of understanding the relationship of properties postulated by the theory of quantum physics to perceived properties of the world.)

Apart from what I have called perceived properties and inferred properties, our models of the world use what may be called mental properties, being

properties we detect in our own conscious experiences; such as those involving beliefs, desires, intentions, feelings, pains, etc. As discussed in Sections
7.3 and 7.4, we are aware of such properties in ourselves, and we infer that
they (really) exist in others.

I contend that our best, perhaps only, access to any external reality is via
these models. In so far as they are not accurate, so that the properties they
have or display or assert are not properties of the world external to us (either
because they do not truly correspond to the world as conceptualized by us, or
because our conceptualizations are unsatisfactory), we believe we can extend
and improve our models so that they do, at least, more closely approximate to
reality.

Thus, the reality, which we consider our words and thoughts can mean
and/or represent and/or refer to, is a reality conceived of as having properties
like the perceived properties, inferred properties, and mental properties of our
models; and of actually *having* the properties of our models, if and when the
models are accurate. Thus, *our* intentionality, the ability of our minds to refer,
is very much bound up with our ability to construct models that have or
display or assert properties which depend upon perception of external reality
and upon access to our own mental events; that is, upon the information
discussed in Chapter 4, involving consciousness. Furthermore, our beliefs in
the accuracy or approximate accuracy of our models can be assessed and
justified, if at all, only by plausible reasoning, as considered in Chapter 5.

On the other hand, while I do not contest that computers can construct
models (or representations) of external reality, can in some sense interpret
such models, and can in some sense refer to an external reality taken to be
represented by the models, I do question whether these models can have
anything other than formal properties, and whether the external reality can be
taken by the computer to have anything other than formal properties. It has
been said that 'content' is just 'fancy form'; that is, that sufficiently complex
and organized formal properties can be 'the same as' properties of substance,
such as the perceived and mental properties to which I have referred. I have
already considered this kind of view in Chapter 4, and indicated my disagreement; and I will say more here.

Let it be assumed that a computer can in principle encode any form of
information; that is, not merely sentences of natural languages or of mathematics or other artificial languages, but also (through its own detectors) all
kinds of visual, auditory, and tactile information. Then, no doubt, it can
encode relationships between these kinds of information; and it can process
this information, and display the results. A computer could with this information make a model of reality, and other information encoded in the computer
could include assertions concerning that model of reality. This 'reality' (i.e. as
modelled by the computer) must be in the computer's code, and its relationship with the 'outside' reality would presumably be one of cause and effect,
plus isomorphism; that is, such that the model is caused by the reality which it

models, encodes it, and accordingly has elements which in some way correspond to elements of the relevant reality. The relationship of isomorphism may be exemplified by that of the sound of a musical composition (the reality) with the digital code in a compact disc which encodes it (the model).

The precise code used by the computer to encode the model of reality, and any assertions concerning it or the reality which is modelled, could be *any* code which the computer can use: so long as the code can encode the necessary information, and so long as the computer can perform the necessary information processing in that code, then (questions of efficiency aside) one code is as good as another; and any differences between codes are immaterial.

It is difficult to see how all this could amount to the sort of intentionality which our minds have. The computer's model, as used in its information processing, would not have, or manifest, any perceived properties, or properties somehow based on them; but would be in some (indeed any) code. On the other hand, the models of reality which our minds construct do not seem to be in code at all. Much less do we think that our models could equally be in any code whatsoever, so long as our brains could process information in that code.

Furthermore, whereas we believe in an external reality common to all of us, having the properties of our best models, and whereas such beliefs are accepted as having rational basis, I do not think that a computer could be considered as having a rational basis for any particular beliefs in an external reality. Particular beliefs could be programmed into the computer, and further beliefs could be derived through interaction with the environment and by effective procedures; but the rationality of *our* beliefs apparently involves: (1) the ability to challenge any belief whatsoever (so that there are no axioms); (2) the availability of limitless plausible arguments (not just logical arguments) for and against such beliefs; and (3) the ability to weigh such arguments, and reach a well-supported, though inconclusive, decision on them.

As I suggested earlier, all this is essentially another slant on the arguments of Chapters 4 and 5, but it does, I think, take them a little further. If it is the case that we have some access to reality and its substantive properties (and so transcend the encoding of such reality and properties in our physical brain events), whilst computers do not have such access, then it seems reasonable to assert that it must make a *difference* for us to have such access, rather than not have it. From another viewpoint, it seems reasonable to assert that the brain–mind is not mechanistic, because a mechanistic brain could not have well-grounded beliefs in aspects of a substantive external reality, as we do in fact have.

8.2. Mind and Reality

I turn now to consider the central role which mind has in the life and world of every human being: in an important sense it is the totality of each person's world, it is basic to all knowledge, and may well be the constructor (not merely the knower) of the common external reality as we know it.

8.2.1. *Mind as the Totality of Each Person's World*

All human experience consists of what I call mental events. It seems clear that things do happen in the world which are never reflected in any subjective human experience—and indeed things may happen *to a person* which are not reflected (at least directly) in any mental events of that person. So, the world is not only (at least in part) other than and external to mind, but also (at least in part) beyond even reflection in human minds.

However, from the point of view of each human being, his or her conscious experiences are the totality of his or her world, in the sense that the occurrence of such experiences is necessary for there to be *any* world, *any* reality, for that person; that any acquaintance of each person with the world and reality either is by reason of its being the object of such experiences, or else is derived or at least sifted through the medium of such experiences; and that the whole significance of the world for each person is to be found in or through his or her conscious experiences.

Things and events which are *not* reflected in any human experience are, to adopt the words of quantum physicist Erwin Schrödinger, 'played to empty benches' (Schrödinger 1967: 100); except, of course, to the extent that they may be reflected in the conscious experiences of other conscious beings (such as animals, or God).

So, I suggest, for each human being, indeed each and every conscious being, the world has no significance not dependent on the totality of his, her, or its conscious experiences. What would a world without any mind, any consciousness, amount to? Consensus writers, when they do consider consciousness at all, tend to treat it as a small anomaly or embarrassment in an otherwise perfect mechanistic physical world; whereas I say that consciousness is of central importance—without it, there could be no point to anything.

8.2.2. *Mind as Basic to All Knowledge*

Next, all knowledge which we do have is derived, or at least filtered, through our conscious experiences. If it is accepted that knowledge is true belief, appropriately justified, then I suggest that for each person knowledge requires conscious perception and/or conscious reasoning.

I do not overlook such things as a priori knowledge, reliance on other persons or sources, and apparent non-conscious perception (such as blindsight). As to these:

1. I accept that truths may come to us a priori, without any perception or process of conscious reasoning. However, I contend that they cannot count as

knowledge unless and until assessed and justified by a process of conscious reasoning. In a sense, the ability to reason plausibly and informally is itself a kind of a priori knowledge (that is, of knowledge how); but any process of such reasoning is itself subject to assessment, and is corrigible, by the same kind of reasoning.

2. Similarly, I accept that we may know things that we have not ourselves perceived, and have not justified by our own reasoning, but, rather, have accepted on the authority of other persons and sources. Here too, however, I contend that our justification for doing so, and hence the appropriateness of calling this knowledge, depends on our consciously assessing the reliability of the source.

3. Finally, I accept that persons without conscious sight have proved able to detect or point to objects in front of them. However, again I suggest that this could count as knowledge in the person concerned only if that person had, in conscious experimentation and reasoning, satisfied himself or herself regarding the nature and extent of the reliability of such detection.

8.2.3. *Mind as Creating Substantive Reality*

I argued in Section 8.1 that only conscious minds can be acquainted with, and refer to, the substantive external reality which we take to be common to all human beings. I suggest here that there are grounds for going further, and contending that in an important sense this substantive reality is *created* by minds.

This idea has some history. It is supported by part of the argument for idealism advanced by philosophers such as F. H. Bradley (which in turn has similarities to my argument in Chapter 4). As described by Sprigge, it goes as follows:

Whenever you really bring home to yourself the character you conceive a physical thing as having, you find that this includes characteristics it can only have within an experience . . . you cannot form a, so to speak, positive conception of what a physical thing would be like denuded of all qualities which reflect a mind's awareness of it, and thus your belief that there may be a physical thing denuded of such qualities is merely a verbal belief in something of which you have no real conception. (Sprigge 1984: 64)

My suggestion here concedes that there is a real ground of things, independently of subjective experiences; as argued in Section 1.1., on any other view the success of science, and indeed the general consistency of the observations of different people, would be a miracle. It has some similarity to Kant's distinction between things-for-us and things-in-themselves: the former being the way things (external reality) appear to us (organisms with the sensory and cognitive apparatus of the human species), and thus being dependent in part on the nature of that apparatus; and the latter being the way things are in themselves, independently of any interaction with that apparatus.

Kant's view was that our knowledge of things was via our sensory and cognitive apparatus, so we could have no knowledge of things-in-themselves.

As mentioned earlier, quantum physics has something to say about this distinction; and I will elaborate on this later. Here, I merely say that quantum physics suggests that, at some deep level, spatial separation (and therefore spatial extension) can be disregarded, and (perhaps) is non-existent. This suggests that Kant may have been right to suggest that things-in-themselves have properties which are *very* different from the properties of things-for-us. However, it also suggests that perhaps he was wrong in so far as he says that we can know nothing about how they are in themselves; that rather, by experimentation and reasoning, we can know *something* about this.

Now if for things-in-themselves spatial separation and spatial extension are non-existent, then things-in-themselves have properties which are *very* different from those of things-for-us. I am not here saying that our knowledge of things-for-us is misleading or deceptive: the substantive properties of things-for-us can be considered as objective properties (at least in the sense that they are much the same for all normal human beings), about which true statements can be made. I am saying, rather, that things-in-themselves, as best we can conceive them, seem to have complex and rather abstract properties which are (to our way of thinking) dimensionless (lacking in spatial separation and extension), shapeless, featureless, colourless, and silent.

There is force in the view expressed by physicist Heinz Pagels that the world is a 'cosmic code' (Pagels 1982); and in the contention that the substantive reality of our experience, which in so many ways depends on spatial separation and spatial extension (as well as sound, colour, etc.), is a translation or construction from the cosmic code by our minds. This approach should not be taken too far, however: the world, untranslated by our minds, is not merely formal, because its basic properties, such as position (in the sense of quantitative position coordinates rather than actual location in three-dimensional space), momentum, energy, mass, electric charge, etc., are substantive properties which correlate in various ways with the substantive properties of things-for-us. We can *know* about things-in-themselves only through discoverable correlations with things-for-us; and we can *talk* about things-in-themselves only with the assistance of our natural languages, which have their basis in things-for-us.

On this approach, the physical world, apart from its interaction with conscious minds, consists of what we might regard as abstract properties; although its code is such that our minds *can* translate it into the sort of substantive reality with which we are acquainted.

8.2.4. *So What?*

None of this says much directly about mechanism: all the above could be correct, and yet mental events have no irreducible effect on what happens.

However, to me it seems implausible that what is so central and important to the life of every human being should be completely under the dominion of objective physical processes and objective physical laws. Does mind occupy this central position only to establish that it is nothing but what brains do, only to abdicate from any independent causative role?

8.3. Where to from Here?

I have now completed my major arguments against mechanism. To me, they are strong arguments, and they considerably outweigh the opposing contention that work in cognitive psychology and artificial intelligence has resolved the mind–matter question in favour of a mechanistic view. However, there are problems with the anti-mechanist position. I outlined some in Section 6.5; and I think the main ones can be put as follows:

1. The physical sciences. As we have seen, one of the main arguments for mechanism stems from the view associated with Laplace to the effect that the movement of physical objects must be in accordance with physical laws of nature. The nineteenth- and twentieth-century success of the physical sciences is sometimes regarded as having confirmed this view; and, as we have seen, the formulation of quantum physics has not widely been considered as undermining it. If all physical objects behave in accordance with laws of nature, which are either fully deterministic or else partly deterministic and partly random, how *can* mental events as such affect what happens? There might seem to be no room for such effects, and no plausible means by which 'mind–matter interaction' could take place. These considerations lead me to try to understand (in some detail) the theory of quantum physics, the implications of that theory for the nature of matter, and its implications for the mind–matter question. This is undertaken in Part III, and completed in Part IV.

2. A theory of conscious choice. The other major problem I see is the difficulty in giving an account of conscious choice which does not reduce it to determination by physical events, on the one hand, or require the assumption of mysterious ghostly entities, on the other. I think some contribution to this is made by the arguments in this part, in particular the idea of comparison of consciously presented wholes as providing non-conclusive and fallible, but plausible and persuasive, reasons for decision and action. However, there remains the severe problem of identifying and describing who (or what) it is that makes the choice, and with what equipment. I look at this problem in Part IV.

III
Quantum Mechanics

To some readers, it may seem odd that one whole part (amounting to about one-third of the whole) of a philosophical book on mind and matter should deal with quantum mechanics, and that much of this should simply give a fairly straightforward account of some basic physics and mathematics.

There are strong reasons for this.

1. The arguments of Part II, and particularly questions such as those posed in Sections 6.5 and 8.3, suggest that the indeterminism of quantum mechanics may be relevant to the mind–matter question.

2. My consideration of quantum mechanics has persuaded me that it is important to this question, not merely because of indeterminism, but also because of what it tells us about matter. This is by reason *inter alia* of the postulated involvement of observers in physical processes (the measurement problem) and of the non-locality of certain physical processes. I believe that some understanding of quantum mechanics is essential to any attempt to deal with metaphysical questions concerning the nature and existence of matter generally, as well as the relationship of mind and matter.

3. Understanding the implications of quantum mechanics requires, or at least is greatly assisted by, some understanding of the mathematics of the theory. To most people outside the field, the mathematics is not easy. Most non-specialist works avoid it altogether. I found no simple exposition of it and, as outlined in the Introduction, such understanding as I have acquired was the result of some struggle with a number of sources.

4. There is no generally accepted interpretation of quantum mechanics among those physicists and philosophers who have grappled with the question of interpretation. This makes it even more desirable for philosophers to acquire some understanding of the mathematics, so that they can reach soundly based views on interpretation. It also increases the problems of giving a comprehensible introduction to the mathematics; because once one adds some explanations in order to assist understanding, one necessarily introduces some measure of interpretation, which will not be universally accepted.

5. I believe that it is a defect of most philosophy on the mind–matter question that it barely touches on quantum mechanics, particularly where (as I have noted) there is no generally accepted interpretation of it, and no readily available simple exposition of the relevant mathematics.

So, I decided that it was not sufficient in this book to discuss implications of quantum mechanics: although I have no claim to be an authority on the subject, I thought it appropriate to give an exposition of some basic physics and mathematics of the theory. I have done so with some explanations, in order to make it easier to follow the exposition; and these explanations themselves (as indicated earlier) to some extent manifest matters of interpretation and assumption.

The result (in Chapters 9 to 13) may seem difficult to some readers, and elementary to others. To the former, I suggest that they persevere, because even a partial understanding of the more mathematical chapters (10 to 13) will assist them in understanding the discussion of implications in Chapters 14 and 15, and their application to the mind–matter problem in Chapter 16. To the latter, I suggest that they at least skim Chapters 9 to 13 in order to detect my interpretations and assumptions, because this will similarly assist them in evaluating Chapters 14, 15, and 16.

I also hope that my exposition of quantum mechanics will fill a gap which I think exists between popular (and non-mathematical) accounts of that topic on the one hand, and university textbooks in physics on the other; and in that way also will be of use to philosophers and others interested in reality, matter, and mind.

9

Historical Outline

BY the end of the nineteenth century, tremendous advances had been made in the understanding of the physical world; and classical physics as developed up to that time provided powerful and coherent models for a wide range of phenomena. Many scientists then would have agreed with A. A. Michelson (whose experiment with E. W. Morley in 1887, *failing* to detect differences in the speed of light as measured in different directions, led to the theory of relativity), writing in 1902, that 'the more important fundamental laws and facts of physical science have all been discovered and those are now so firmly established that the possibility of their being supplanted in consequence of new discoveries is remote' (see Brown 1986: 66). Furthermore, although classical physics was in certain respects not in accordance with untutored common sense, it was such that common sense easily adapted to conform to it. Indeed, the nineteenth-century biologist T. H. Huxley wrote that 'Science is nothing but trained and organized common sense.'

We shall see that Michelson's statement was shortly shown to be profoundly wrong; and that within a short time new 'fundamental laws and facts of physical science' did supplant those he referred to. We shall also see that these new laws and facts were far from being 'trained and organized common sense', and that common sense has not yet adapted to conform to this new physics.

In order to suggest the range and power of classical physics, and also its consistency with common sense, I will start by reviewing briefly some areas of classical physics, and pointing out certain assumptions about the world and about measurement which underlie and are reflected in classical physics. I will then outline, as an extension of classical physics and as part of pre-quantum physics, aspects of the theory of relativity.

In the remainder of the chapter, I will try to make it clear why the reasonable and common-sense views of classical physics *had to be* discarded; and to give some understanding of the historical development of quantum physics, and of the refutations of common-sense views involved.

9.1. Classical Physics

9.1.1. *The Atomic Theory of Matter*

The word 'atoms' originally referred to postulated basic indivisible particles. One view of the material world was that it was made up of such particles, while another was that matter was infinitely divisible.

By the end of the nineteenth century, it was recognized that certain substances could not be created or destroyed in chemical reactions. Ninety-two of such substances had been identified, and they were called elements. It was considered that any pure quantity of an element comprised a collection of identical particles characteristic of that element, and these particles were called atoms. Although atoms had originally been postulated as indivisible, it became known prior to the emergence of the quantum theory in the early twentieth century that atoms, conceived of as the identical particles characteristic of elements, were divisible into yet smaller particles. I will return to this later.

Progress had been made in classifying atoms in accordance with their relative weights and their properties. What is known as the periodic table had been prepared, which showed how similarities in chemical properties recurred periodically in relation to grouping of atoms in accordance with their relative weights (see Snape 1989: 153–4). Apart from the elements, there were other substances which could be created and destroyed in chemical reactions, which were considered as made up or compounded from elements. The smallest unit of such chemical compounds which could have independent existence was called a molecule; this word in fact applied to any group of atoms joined by chemical bonds, including groups of identical atoms.

All this might be considered part of chemistry, rather than physics. However, it was believed that the properties of atoms and molecules, and thereby of substances made up of atoms and molecules, might be explicable in terms of physics: that is, in terms of the behaviour of particles of matter under the operation of physical forces; in particular electromagnetic forces, which I will shortly consider. Further, the atomic theory of matter entered in various ways into other areas of physics, in particular those dealing with heat and with electromagnetism. Before looking at those areas, it is convenient first to look briefly at classical mechanics.

9.1.2. *Classical Mechanics*

One great insight of classical or Newtonian mechanics was that contained in Newton's first law of motion, namely that 'a body continues in a state of uniform motion in a straight line unless it is compelled to change that state by a force impressed on it'. Acceptance of that law removed the need to explain, for example, why planets kept moving: so far as the motion of planets was concerned, it was necessary to explain only why they moved in orbits and not in a straight line. And that was substantially achieved by Newton's second law of motion and his law of universal gravitation.

The former may be stated: when the resultant force on a body is not zero, the body changes its state of motion by acceleration in the direction of the force, and for a given force the acceleration is inversely proportional to the mass of the body. The latter may be stated: every particle in the universe attracts every other particle in the universe with a force that is directly proportional to the product of the masses of the particles, and inversely proportional to the square of the distance between them. These two laws explained why planets orbited around the sun, with the gravitational force exerted by the sun on each planet providing an acceleration towards the sun. These laws enabled accurate calculation of the orbits.

Although the spectacular early success of Newtonian mechanics was in relation to planetary orbits, the application of the laws was perfectly general. They were considered as applying to all objects, of whatever size, shape, and composition: to the smallest particles, even to atoms, as they did to planets and stars. Indeed, the entirely general application of mechanical laws was an important insight of Newton. In everyday situations, of course, objects do not in general move forever in a straight line: usually, if not pushed along, an object slows down and stops; but this is because of forces causing it to do so, generally arising from friction. Further, in relation to the motion of ordinary objects, it is often necessary to take into account rotation, as well as the motion from place to place of the whole object; but laws governing the rotation of bodies can be derived from Newton's laws.

An important concept used in Newtonian mechanics is that of energy. Energy is a numerical quantity, calculated according to various formulae, such that (according to classical physics) its form can change but not its overall quantity. One form of energy (called kinetic energy) is associated with motion: for a given mass, it is proportional to the square of the speed. Another form (called potential energy) is associated with position, either in relation to fields of force or in relation to mechanical contrivances (such as springs). Other forms of energy were identified (such as heat, chemical energy, electrical energy), and it came to be realized that they reduce in various ways to kinetic energy and/or potential energy.

So far as conservation of energy is concerned, it was shown that, where the speed of a body was slowed by friction, the loss of kinetic energy associated with the reduction of speed was balanced by an increase of heat energy caused by the friction. And it was shown that, if friction was disregarded, changes of kinetic energy of bodies moving under gravitational forces were balanced by changes in gravitational potential energy. Thus, when an object falls some distance under gravity, the increase in its kinetic energy due to its increased speed is balanced by the decrease in potential energy due to loss of height, except to the extent to which friction (air resistance) has operated against the direction of motion; and that extent is accounted for by increased heat energy in the object and the air (and perhaps some kinetic energy in non-random motion of the air).

9.1.3. *Heat and Statistical Mechanics*

A great generalization was achieved in the first half of the nineteenth century, when it was shown that heat consisted of random motion of the atoms and/or molecules making up a substance; while temperature was proportional to the average kinetic energy of such atoms and/or molecules. Accordingly, it became possible to represent all heat and temperature effects in terms of the laws of mechanics, with the aid of statistical laws.

This provided an explanation for the different states of matter: solid, liquid, and gas. When a substance is in a solid state, its atoms and/or molecules are held in a lattice structure or array by electromagnetic forces, permitting only limited mutual movement. There *is* movement of the atoms and/or molecules, because (at least at temperatures above absolute zero) solids have heat: but the movement of each atom and/or molecule is within its place in the array.

However, as the solid is heated, the movements of the atoms and/or molecules increase, until their motion is such that the binding forces can no longer maintain the array: the substance melts and becomes a liquid. However, the binding forces remain sufficient to prevent the atoms and/or molecules flying apart. If the substance is heated further, the motion increases further; and eventually the binding forces are no longer sufficient to hold the atoms and/or molecules together: they fly apart, and the substance becomes a gas.

When matter is in a gaseous state, the atoms and/or molecules (not being bound to each other) will keep hitting the walls of any vessel containing it: this constitutes the pressure exerted by the gas on the walls of its container, or indeed on any surface it comes in contact with. The motion of the atoms and/or molecules of a gas may be partly co-ordinated, and partly random. In so far as the motion is random, as we have seen, it constitutes heat. In so far as it is co-ordinated, it may constitute a flow of the gas (where the motion is in one direction, on the average); or it may constitute a wavelike disturbance (as where the gas is carrying sound-waves).

Statistical laws were developed dealing with the behaviour of the huge quantities of atoms and molecules in detectable quantities of substances. With the aid of such laws, it was shown, for example, that the number of atoms or molecules of a gas occupying a certain volume at a certain temperature and pressure was always the same, for any gas.

In the middle of the nineteenth century, it was shown that, where heat is used to do mechanical work, energy is conserved; and this was later generalized to the assertion that (as stated earlier) although energy can take many forms, it cannot be created or destroyed. This law of conservation of energy is also called the first law of thermodynamics. And, at about the same time, the second law of thermodynamics was also developed. It was shown that, whenever heat was used to do work, there had to be a transfer of heat from a hotter body to a cooler body; and that conversely work (that is, an imparting of energy) was required to bring about a transfer of heat from a cooler to a hotter body. More generally, the second law asserted that in any physical or chemical process the amount of heat available for work decreases, or (at least) does not increase. A quantity called entropy was identified, being a measure of disorder of a system and also a measure of the unavailability of heat for work: according to the second law, the entropy of an isolated system always tends to increase.

9.1.4. *Light*

In the early part of the nineteenth century, experiments by Thomas Young appeared to resolve a long-standing controversy about the nature of light. Some (including Newton) had contended that light consisted of a stream of particles—the 'corpuscular' theory. Others contended that light consisted of waves, presumably involving disturbances of some universal medium, called the ether.

Young's famous two-slit experiment in 1800 not only seemed to decide the question in favour of the wave theory over the corpuscular theory: it also established the actual wavelengths of the waves associated with light of different colours. Since this experiment took on great significance in relation to the ideas of quantum physics, it is useful to look at it in some detail.

Monochromatic light from a single source was made to pass through a screen with a narrow slit. It was then made to pass through a further screen with two narrow parallel slits, close together; and to fall on a further screen. With either of the two slits in the middle screen blocked, an oblong patch of light appeared on the third screen. With the two slits open, there appeared on the third screen, not a combination or sum of the oblong patches, as one would expect if light consisted of a stream of particles; but rather a series of light and dark bands. The explanation for this was found in the wave nature of light. Where waves (for example, in water) of equal amplitude and wavelength meet, they can interfere constructively and destructively. Where the phases of the waves are the same where they meet, so that two peaks or two troughs coincide, they reinforce one another, and there results a heightened peak or deepened trough. Where the phases of the waves where they meet are opposite, so that a peak and trough coincide, they cancel out, leaving no wave at that point. The bright centres of the light bands, then, were where the waves passing through the two slits interfered constructively so that the light wave was intensified; while the centres of the dark bands were where they interfered destructively, so that the light wave was destroyed.

The spacing of the bands differed according to the colour of the light used: they were wider, and wider apart, in the case of red light than in the case of blue light. This enabled calculation of the wavelength of light of different colours. The geometry is as shown in Fig. 9.1.

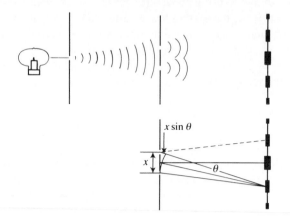

FIG. 9.1. The geometry of the two-slit experiment

The brightest band is directly opposite the two slits: the centre of that band is equidistant from the two slits, so that an equal number of wavelengths of the light occurs between this point and each of the two slits. The centre of the next bright band, then, is where there is a difference of one in the number of waves of the light between this point and each of the two slits. This one wavelength can be calculated: it is to a close approximation $x \sin \theta$, where x is the distance between the two slits, and θ is the angle subtended, at the point midway between the two slits, by the centre of the bright band directly opposite the slits and the centre of the next bright band.

In this way Young showed that red light had a wavelength of about 700 nanometres (where 10^9 nanometres equals one metre, so that $1 \text{ nm} = 10^{-9} \text{ m}$); that violet light had a wavelength of about 400 nm; and that other pure colours had various intermediate wavelengths.

9.1.5. *Electromagnetism*

In the latter half of the nineteenth century, another great generalization was achieved when it was shown that electricity, magnetism, and light were all different manifestations of the same thing: electromagnetism. Electromagnetism has to do with the forces created and felt by particles carrying what is called an electric charge, a physical quantity similar in some ways to mass, but different from it *inter alia* in that it comes in two types, called positive and negative. Such forces accounted for the binding together of atoms and molecules, and of constituent parts of atoms; for the phenomena of electricity and magnetism; and for the whole range of electromagnetic radiation, one part of which is visible light. These forces made up the second fundamental force recognized by classical physics (the first, of course, being gravity), to which other forces apparently reduced. (Twentieth-century physics has, in addition, recognized two further fundamental forces, which have to do with the binding together and decay of the nuclei of atoms; and has also recognized the possibility of reducing some or all of the four fundamental forces to even more basic forces.)

One aspect of the electromagnetic force is like gravity, in that it varies inversely with the square of the distance; but is unlike gravity in that it is far more powerful, and in that it is either an attractive or repulsive force, depending on whether the particles involved have unlike or like charges. As explained in Feynman *et al.* (1963, vol. i, p. 2.3), atoms generally consist of equal numbers of positive and negative charges, and accordingly they exert very little force on distant charges, because the forces of attraction and repulsion largely cancel out. However, if a charge is brought close to an atom, 'the repulsion of likes and the attraction of unlikes will tend to bring unlikes closer together and push likes further apart', so that the attraction becomes greater than the repulsion, and there is a net attractive force. Feynman continues:

This is the reason why the atoms, which are constituted out of plus and minus electric charges, feel very little force when they are separated by appreciable distance (aside from gravity). When they come close together, they can 'see inside' each other, and rearrange their charges, with the result that they have a very strong interaction. The ultimate basis of an interaction between the atoms is *electrical*. Since this force is so enormous, all the plusses and all minusses will normally come together in as intimate a combination as they can. All things, even ourselves, are made of fine-grained, enormously strongly interacting plus and minus parts, all neatly balanced out.

Feynman goes on to illustrate the strength of the forces involved by postulating two grains of sand, a millimetre across and 30 metres apart; and pointing out that if the electromagnetic force was wholly attractive (irrespective of whether charges were the same or different), there would be a force of 30 million tons (or tonnes) between the two.

The electromagnetic force we have been considering so far is exactly inversely proportional to the square of the distance only if the charges concerned are stationary in relation to each other and undergoing no acceleration: this is Coulomb's law. If the charges are moving in relation to each other, an adjustment has to be made to the strength and direction of the force; and also there is another (second) force operating at right angles to the line joining the particles and also to the motion, the force of magnetism.

Perhaps more importantly, if a charge is accelerated by forces acting on it, it exerts a (third) force which varies inversely, not with the square of the distance, but just with the distance; and which, accordingly, can be detected at great distances from the source. This is the force associated with electromagnetic radiation; and, in the important case where the charge is oscillating, this electromagnetic radiation moves as a wave outwards from the source. Such a wave delivers energy which varies inversely as the square of the distance. This means that the total energy which can be extracted from the wave remains the same, at whatever distance from the source charge it is extracted; and accordingly that the charge loses energy which it cannot recover.

The equations dealing with the radiation show that such a wave propagates with the speed of light c. Its frequency v is that of the oscillation of the charge. Its wavelength λ is such that the frequency times the wavelength equals the speed of light: $v\lambda = c$. It came to be realized that visible light is a particular species of this electromagnetic radiation, namely that whose wavelength lies between 400 nm and 700 nm, and whose frequency accordingly lies in the vicinity of 10^{15} cycles per second (written 10^{15} Hz). Radiation with shorter wavelengths (and higher frequencies) comprises ultraviolet light (down to 10 nm), X-rays (down to 10^{-3} nm), and beyond that gamma rays and cosmic rays. Radiation with longer wavelengths comprises infrared light (up to 10^6 nm), short radio waves, including those used for radar and FM and TV broadcasts (up to 10^{11} nm or 100 m), medium radio waves (up to 10^{12} nm), and long radio waves (up to and exceeding 10^{16} nm or 10^7 m).

The force exerted by a charge on another charge at various points in space can be considered as arising from a field (or rather two fields, the electric field and the magnetic field); and equations were developed, in particular by Maxwell, for calculating the value of those fields at any point. The resultant electromagnetic force at any point, on a charged particle, could be considered as arising from two fields, made up of all the fields produced by all the charges, apart from that acted upon, at the point in question.

9.1.6. *Constituents of the Atom*

As mentioned earlier, atoms were originally thought of as indivisible. However, before the development of the quantum theory, it had been shown that atoms were made up of a positively charged nucleus, in which almost all of the mass of the atom was concentrated, and one or more negatively charged electrons.

The first step was the discovery of the electron by J. J. Thomson in 1897. He established that the radiation produced from a negatively charged metal plate in a vacuum tube comprised negatively charged particles; and he calculated the ratio of the charge and the mass of such particles. Since similar particles were produced whatever metal was used in the plate, he concluded that such particles, called by him electrons, were parts of atoms, and that different atoms contained identical electrons.

This led to a picture of an atom as comprising a substance through which a positive charge was spread, and in which the negatively charged electrons were embedded, like fruit in a fruit-cake. That picture was destroyed by experiments carried out by Ernest Rutherford in about 1911, using high-energy alpha particles emitted by radioactive substances.

Rutherford had previously studied emissions from radioactive atoms, and had identified two types of such emission, calling them alpha and beta radiation. Alpha radiation comprised particles with mass about four times that of a hydrogen atom, and a charge double that of the electron, but positive rather than negative (and such particles were later shown to consist of two protons and two neutrons lost by the decaying nuclei, and to be the same as helium nuclei). Beta radiation consisted of electrons (and later was shown to involve decay of the nucleus of an atom, whereby it came to have one more proton and one less neutron than previously). (A third type of radioactivity was later identified, and called gamma radiation: this consisted of highly energetic electromagnetic radiation, given off in transitions of nuclei from higher to lower energy states).

In the 1911 experiments, beams of alpha particles were directed at a very thin gold foil, and detected on fluorescent screens. Most of the particles changed direction very little or not at all; but a very few were deflected through very large angles, some even bouncing back towards the source of the beam. As Rutherford put it, 'It was almost as incredible as if you fired a 15-inch shell at a piece of tissue paper and it came back and hit you' (1938: 68). Since an alpha particle had a mass more than 7000 times that of the electron, such particles could not be deflected measurably by electrons. If the positive charge(s) and the remaining mass of the gold atoms (that is, apart from the mass of the electrons) were *spread* throughout the atom, then all the alpha particles should have behaved quite similarly. Rutherford's explanation for what in fact happened was that the positive charge(s) and the remaining mass of the atoms must be *concentrated* in a tiny central region, which he called the nucleus; and that alpha particles hitting this directly could bounce back, while less direct impacts could cause large deflections, and near misses could cause small deflections through the mutual repulsion of the positive charges.

It came to be shown that if the nucleus was considered to be a roughly spherical particle, its diameter must be of the order of 10^{-14} m; while if an atom was so considered, its diameter must be of the order of 10^{-10} m. Accordingly, if a circular playing field with a diameter of about 100 m was taken as representing a cross-section of an atom, the nucleus could be represented by a small pebble with a diameter of the order of 1 cm. There are differing views on the size to be attributed to an electron, if similarly considered to be a roughly spherical particle: on one view, it is effectively a point particle, while, on another view, its diameter may be taken as about 10^{-13} m, in which case it could be represented in our example by a tennis ball with a diameter of the order of 10 cm. In any event, it would seem that, on this approach, an atom must consist almost entirely of empty space! (To complete the impression of the scales involved here: if the whole atom, whose cross-section I have treated above as being represented by the playing field, were instead considered as being represented by a grain of sand with a diameter of the order of 1 mm, then on that scale, a disc of 1 cm diameter, say a very small button, would have to be represented by a circle with a diameter of the order of 100 km.)

All this raised two related puzzles: how could atoms occupy such comparatively vast volumes, as compared with their component parts; and if it was by means of the electrons, why did the electrons of an atom not collapse into the nucleus (having regard to the great attractive forces between negative and positive charges)? A suggestion by Rutherford was that the electrons must travel at extremely high speeds, so that the attractive electrical force merely caused them to orbit the nucleus (like planets around the sun). This suggestion had the major difficulty that the continuous acceleration of an electron towards the nucleus, to provide the orbit, would (according to classical electromagnetic theory) give rise to electromagnetic radiation, and therefore continuous loss of energy; so that the speed of the electron would be progressively reduced, until it was insufficient to prevent it falling to the nucleus. This difficulty was a major problem of the pre-quantum approach to the atom, and as we shall see it gave rise to one of the early developments of the quantum theory.

9.1.7. *Classical Assumptions*

Two groups of important assumptions which underlie and are reflected in classical physics concern the mode of existence of physical objects, and the nature and effect of observation and measurement. There are also assumptions concerning determinism and reductionism, but I have already looked at these in Section 1.4.

1. The existence of physical objects. It is assumed that all physical objects, of whatever size: exist continuously over time (though not necessarily unchanging); exist independently of being observed or interacted with; have at any particular time definite dimensions and mass; have at any particular time a definite mechanical state, including a position in space (both location and orientation) and motion (both velocity and rotation); and have motion which is continuous over time and (accordingly) infinitely divisible. Consistently with this, the (mechanical) state of a system of particles at a particular time is taken to involve a definite position in space and a definite motion for each of the particles.

These assumptions are in accordance with common sense, and are difficult to abandon. However, the third (relating to dimensions and mass) is significantly modified by the theory of relativity; and all the others are flatly contradicted by the quantum theory, and have to be abandoned, at least in relation to objects at the micro scale of atoms and their constituents.

2. Observation and measurement. The associated assumptions about observation and measurement are that any observation or measurement made of the dimensions, mass, position, and/or motion of a physical object is of properties (or 'observables') which exist independently of such observation or measurement; that, while such observation or measurement may not be absolutely accurate in practice, there are no theoretical limits on accuracy; that there is no theoretical limit on the smallness of the disturbance caused to the object by observation or measurement, or on the accuracy to which any such disturbance can itself be measured or calculated; and that any imprecision in the results of observation and measurement, giving uncertainty about the measured position and/or motion of a physical object, does not mean that its actual position and/or motion is itself uncertain or imprecise.

Consistently with the impact of the theory of relativity and the quantum theory on the assumptions about existence, they also contradict these assumptions about measurement and observation. According to the theory of relativity, the mass and dimensions of a physical object, as measured, will vary according to its motion relative to the frame of reference with respect to which the measurement is made; and the mass and dimensions of a physical object cannot be considered as having definite values except in connection with a particular motion relative to the frame of reference adopted.

More importantly, according to the quantum theory, generally neither the position nor the motion of a physical object (particularly on the micro scale of atoms and their constituents) actually has a precise value; and it is impossible for both position and motion together to have precise values. One can measure one such observable (say, position) to an arbitrarily high degree of precision, even if prior to the measurement such an observable did not have that degree of precision: if so, however, the measurement will cause the position (if that is the observable so measured) to have greater precision than before the measurement, and at the same time cause the motion of the object in question to become less precise than before the measurement.

9.2. Relativity

One of the two great revolutions of twentieth-century physics was the theory of relativity. Radical though it was, it disturbed the classical assumptions less than did the quantum theory; and it can be considered as extending classical physics rather than overturning it.

The special theory of relativity established that measurements of time, distance, and mass (and hence of velocity and energy) varied according to the motion of the frame of reference against which the measurements were made;

and this in turn involved some merging of time and space, and of mass and energy.

9.2.1. *Origins*

The special theory of relativity was published by Albert Einstein in 1905. Two particular historical developments contributed to its formulation: one concerned Maxwell's equations, the other the speed of light.

1. Maxwell's equations and the Lorentz transformation. According to classical mechanics, when physical laws are applied to the motion of objects, the same results should be given no matter what inertial frame of reference is used: that is, so long as the frame of reference is (because it is either at rest, or moving uniformly in a straight line) such that there are no apparent forces due to the motion of the frame. In the latter part of the nineteenth century, it was seen that Maxwell's equations for the electromagnetic field did *not* satisfy this requirement; and it seemed that this indicated some defect in these equations.

H. A. Lorentz found that if coordinates were transformed as between inertial frames by means of certain equations, Maxwell's equations did give the same results in different inertial frames of reference. These equations used a factor $1 / \sqrt{(1 - v^2 / c^2)}$, where v is the relative speed of the frames and c is the speed of light (about $3 \times 10^8 \, \mathrm{m \, s^{-1}}$); and the transformation was called a *Lorentz transformation*. However, if such a transformation was applied to Newton's laws, they did not give the same results. As we will see, the theory of relativity indicated that it was Newton's laws, not Maxwell's equations, which were defective, leading Poincaré and Einstein to postulate that *all physical laws* should be such that their effect in inertial frames of reference is unchanged or invariant under a Lorentz transformation.

2. The speed of light. In 1887, Michelson and Morley showed that the speed of light measured the same in any direction, so that if light propagated as a wave in some medium (whether this medium was considered as some material ether, or as a force field), its speed was not affected by any motion of the earth through that medium. Later experiments showed that this could not be explained by postulating that the medium moved with the earth. In 1905, Einstein postulated that an observer in any inertial frame of reference would measure the same speed for light; and produced his special theory of relativity as a solution to the problem.

9.2.2. *Formulation of the Special Theory*

The special theory of relativity has many aspects, but at its heart is a correction to Newton's second law of motion: this involves recognition that the mass of an object (as measured in relation to a frame of reference) is greater when the object is moving with respect to that frame than when it is at rest with respect thereto, by Lorentz's factor of $1 / \sqrt{(1 - v^2 / c^2)}$. When that correction is made, Newton's laws become invariant under Lorentz transformation. It also follows from this correction that the length of an object (as measured in relation to a frame of reference) is similarly shortened in the direction of travel by $\sqrt{(1 - v^2 / c^2)}$, the reciprocal of Lorentz's factor, when the object is moving with respect to the frame of reference; and that time on an object (as measured in relation to a frame of reference) passes *more slowly*, by the same factor, when the object is moving with respect to that frame.

Further matters follow. With the above adjustments to time and length, and applying the Lorentz transformation, the theory of relativity indicates that the speed of light will indeed measure the same speed c in any inertial frame. No object having mass can be accelerated to the speed of light, because if it did its mass would become infinite. Increasing the kinetic energy of an object will cause the mass of the object to increase. Mass and energy are equivalent: $E = mc^2$.

None of this is observable at speeds with which we are familiar in ordinary life. The relevant factor, $\sqrt{(1 - v^2 / c^2)}$, is close to 1 except at extremely high speeds. At a speed as high as 10 km per second (about the speed required to escape earth's gravity), it gives a correction of only one part in over two thousand million; while even at $c/2$, it gives a correction of only about 15 per cent.

9.2.3. *Space-Time*

More importantly to the discussion of this book, special relativity indicates that, where two separate events (each considered as occurring at a moment of time, in a point of space) are measured in relation to different inertial frames, the intervals of space and of time between them, as so measured from each frame, may be different. Even the *order* in time of two spatially separated events can be different. (Einstein went further, and asserted that inertial frames of reference were all equivalent, that no one or more of them had any claim to accuracy of preferred status over any others; although, as we shall see in Chapter 18, later developments throw some doubt on this.)

However, it was possible to identify an interval between events which was *not* different as measured in relation to different inertial frames of reference; namely, by considering space and time as merged in a four-dimensional continuum ('space-time'), consisting of the usual three dimensions of space, and a fourth dimension involving time. (I say 'involving time', because the units used are units of space, obtained by multiplying time by the speed of light.) If the respective intervals between events in the four dimensions are given by x, y, z, and ct, then the interval in space-time between the events is given by $\sqrt{(x^2 + y^2 + z^2 - c^2 t^2)}$; and this interval will be the same as measured in relation to any inertial frame (although, of course, the *x*, *y*, *z*, and *t* may each be different).

This led Einstein and Minkowski to deny any fundamental distinction between space and time: they postulated that our view of things as happening over time in three-dimensional space could be considered as a projection from the more basic four-dimensional space-time. This approach is graphically represented by Minkowski diagrams, which reduce the spatial dimensions to one (or sometimes two), and represent the dimension involving time as the vertical dimension on the page, as shown in Fig. 9.2.

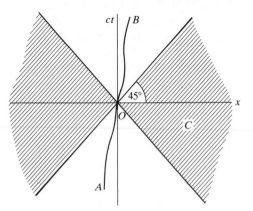

FIG. 9.2. A world-line in a Minkowski diagram

A particle is represented on such a diagram as a line such as that from *A* through *O* to *B*, called a world-line. If the particle is not moving, the world-line will be vertical. If it is moving at a constant speed, the world-line will be straight, but at an angle to the vertical. If it is accelerating, the world-line will be curved. The lines shown as going at 45 degrees to the vertical, from point *O*, represent light passing through point *O*: in the time represented by a distance *ct*, the light will move a similar distance in space (represented in Fig. 9.2 by the *x* axis).

According to special relativity no signals and no causal connections can propagate faster than the speed of light. Accordingly, events in the area within the segments generally above the 45-degree lines could be affected by what happens at *O*, and events in the area within the segments below the continuation of such lines below *O* could affect what happens at *O*. However, events in the shaded segments to the right and left of *O* can neither affect, nor be affected by, what happens at *O*: such events are said to have spacelike separation from *O*. An event *C*, which has spacelike separation from *O*, may be measured as earlier than, later than, or simultaneous with *O*, with reference to different inertial frames of reference, depending on the motion of those frames.

Sometimes Minkowski diagrams are drawn to show three dimensions, two of space and one of time, with the second dimension of space generally shown as if projecting from the x axis towards and away from the reader. In such diagrams, the regions of space-time in which events can affect or be affected by events at the origin O are represented by two cones, with their apexes meeting at O. The surfaces of the cones represent the paths of light passing through O, and the cones are called light cones.

9.2.4. *General Relativity*

One important implication of special relativity is the rejection of absolute space and absolute time, Newton's cosmic framework: the implication that space is not an unchanging arena in which things exist and events occur over time. Space and time become themselves in some sense not only interwoven, but also active and changing: not merely a setting for the world, but parts of it. This aspect is further emphasized in the general theory of relativity, published by Einstein in 1915.

It is sufficient here to note that the general theory of relativity gives a geometrical explanation of the force of gravity, as resulting from curvature of space-time caused by mass. Einstein pointed out that no measurement could be made within a frame of reference which would distinguish between (1) its being an inertial frame of reference on which a certain resultant gravitational force operated, sufficient to give to each object an acceleration a; and (2) its being a frame of reference actually undergoing acceleration a in the opposite direction. He developed a comprehensive mathematical theory according to which these two apparently different situations are manifestations of the same underlying reality.

9.3. The Origins of Quantum Mechanics

Four important developments can be identified prior to the actual formulation of quantum mechanics in the mid-1920s by Heisenberg and Schrödinger: these are associated respectively with Max Planck, Einstein, Niels Bohr, and Louis de Broglie.

9.3.1. *Planck and the Quantum*

Classical physics had identified the heat of an object with the random motion of its constituent atoms and/or molecules. In the case of solids, this motion consists of oscillations of the atoms and/or molecules in their places in the lattice structure of the solid. Such oscillations, according to classical electromagnetic theory, give rise to electromagnetic radiation. Experiments and observation showed that, when the temperature of a solid was below a certain level, this radiation was principally at frequencies below that of visible light. As the temperature of the solid was raised, this radiation came to include frequencies at the low end of the visible spectrum, that is, those of red light. At that stage, the object would appear red hot. At higher temperatures, the radiation extended to higher frequencies of light, and the object might ultimately become white hot.

This radiation associated with heat was called black body radiation. In the late nineteenth century, calculations were made on the basis of statistical mechanics of the distribution of frequencies to be expected in such radiation, in particular in the case of radiation from a so-called 'perfect' black body, such as an enclosed cavity in thermal equilibrium. Such calculations accorded with observation and experiment in relation to lower frequencies; but not in relation to higher frequencies, in particular those above the range of visible light (ultra-violet radiation): the calculations suggested that the distribution should be weighted towards the high frequencies, to the extent of approaching infinity as the frequency did similarly. This result, suggested by these calculations, was called the ultra-violet catastrophe.

In 1900, Max Planck postulated that electromagnetic radiation could be emitted only in discrete packages or quanta rather than continuously as assumed in classical mechanics. According to classical mechanics, electromagnetic radiation could be given off at any frequency and in any quantity, however small: Planck showed that calculations concerning black body radiation could be made to accord with observation if such electromagnetic radiation could be emitted only in packages whose energy E was equal to the product of the frequency of the radiation ν and a constant h which he calculated: $E = h\nu$.

The constant in question, the famous universal constant named Planck's constant, and conventionally represented by the letter h, is a very small quantity of action (that is, that quantity in classical mechanics whose units are the same as those of the product of momentum and distance, or energy and time): about 6.6×10^{-34} joule seconds. One joule (or newton-metre) is the amount of energy imparted by a force of one newton operating in the direction of motion over a distance of one metre. A newton is the force required to give a body of mass one kilogram an acceleration of one metre per second per second (1 m s^{-2}). Thus, for example, according to Planck, visible light of frequency 10^{15} Hz can be radiated only in quanta each having energy equal to 6.6×10^{-19} joules.

It will be seen that the quanta associated with higher frequencies involve higher energies, so that higher energy is required for each quantum emitted; and it is this which enabled the calculations to give results falling off in relation to frequencies higher than a certain level, and thus to accord with observation and experiment.

9.3.2. *Einstein and Light as Particles*

Although Planck introduced the idea of emission of energy in quanta or packages, he did not suggest that the electromagnetic field itself comprised such packages. In 1905, however, Einstein did make this suggestion. In his famous paper, he developed the idea of light quanta (which later came to be called photons), relying on a number of indications, most notably the photoelectric effect.

In 1887, Hertz had observed that ultra-violet light falling on metals produced the emission of sparks; and it was later shown that these were electrons. It was also established, prior to 1905, that if the incident light was below a certain frequency, no electrons at all were emitted, irrespective of the intensity of the light; that when this threshold frequency was exceeded, the number of electrons emitted (but not the energy with which they were emitted) varied with the intensity of the light; and that increasing the frequency of the light increased the energy (but not the number) of emitted electrons.

Einstein explained this so-called photoelectric effect by extending Planck's ideas. He postulated that electromagnetic radiation was not merely *emitted* in discrete quanta, but also *interacted* with substances as discrete quanta, indeed as if it comprised particles. Thus, in the photoelectric effect, each emission of one electron was caused by the collision of one such particle (or photon) with one electron in the metal. If the frequency of the light was below a certain threshold, no photon would have enough energy to cause the emission of an electron; and increasing the intensity of the light (and thereby the number of photons) would not alter this. If the frequency was above the threshold, so that the photons would each have sufficient energy to cause the emission of an electron, then increasing the intensity of the light (and thereby the number of photons) would increase the number of electrons emitted, but not their energy. Further increasing the frequency, and thereby the energy, of each photon, would cause electrons to be emitted with greater energy.

9.3.3. *Bohr and Atomic Orbits*

In 1913, Niels Bohr used the ideas of Planck and Einstein to suggest a solution to the difficulties of the Rutherford picture of the atom (mentioned in Section 9.1.6), which at the same time provided an explanation for the distinct spectral lines (bands of colours of particular wavelengths) of light given off by different substances in certain circumstances.

As early as 1859, the spectroscope had been developed, whereby atoms could be identified by the light which they gave off when heated. This instrument used a prism to disperse the light into its component colours, whose wavelengths could be measured: each different element was found to have its own characteristic set of spectral lines. In 1885, an amateur scientist Joseph

Balmer made an extraordinary discovery concerning the spectral lines of hydrogen, namely that they were connected by a simple numerical relationship:

$$\lambda = An^2/(n^2 - 2^2),$$

where λ is the wavelength of each line, A is a constant, and n can take values 3, 4, 5, 6, ... Subsequently, other series of spectral lines for hydrogen were discovered, in relation to radiation outside the visible spectrum: these were connected by numerical relationships similar to those of the Balmer series. Somewhat similar series were discovered for other elements.

Bohr noted that the units of Planck's constant h were the same as those of angular momentum (momentum times distance), and supposed that the angular momentum of an electron orbiting a hydrogen atom could only be in packages of $h/2\pi$ (itself a constant used so often that it is given a symbol of its own, namely $\hbar$). On that hypothesis, such angular momentum would always be given by $n\hbar$, where n equals 1, 2, 3, ... : only orbits coinciding with such values of angular momentum were possible, the lowest value being that associated with the orbit closest to the nucleus, and with the lowest energy level of the electron. While remaining in any such orbit, the electron's energy would remain the same: this was called by Bohr a 'stationary state'. When an electron jumped from a more distant to a closer orbit, it lost energy, and this energy would be emitted as a photon of electromagnetic radiation. Similarly, if a photon of the correct frequency was absorbed by the atom, an electron would gain its energy and jump to a more distant orbit.

On this basis, and assuming the electrons to have circular orbits, Bohr proceeded to apply classical mechanics (using the charge and mass of the electron) to calculate the radius of the electron orbit for each value of n, and the total energy of the electron for each different orbit. It turned out that the differences between the second lowest energy level (associated with the second closest orbit), and the third lowest, fourth lowest, and higher energy levels, were (almost exactly) such as to account for the Balmer series: that is, if the frequencies of the light in the lines of the Balmer series were given as v_1, v_2, etc., the differences between the energy which an electron would have in the second closest orbit and that which it would have in the third, fourth, etc. orbits were respectively hv_1, hv_2, etc. The differences between the lowest energy level and higher energy levels, and those between the third lowest level and higher levels, and so on, were found to account for the other series (outside the spectra of visible light).

This view of the hydrogen atom thus gave an explanation for the Balmer series and the other series of spectral lines. It also suggested a solution to the difficulties of the Rutherford picture of the atom: if the angular momentum (and so the energy) of the electron could not fall below a minimum level, the electron would not collapse into the nucleus. Further, electromagnetic radiation would not involve a continuous loss of energy, but, rather (consistently with the theories of Planck and Einstein), discrete transitions between possible orbits and possible energies.

9.3.4. *De Broglie and Matter Waves*

Although Bohr's model of the atom gave plausible explanations of the Balmer series and other series of spectral lines, and also of the stability of atoms, it was nothing like a complete theory: it was an *ad hoc* combination of classical mechanics (as regards the orbits) and some undeveloped new mechanics (as regards jumps between orbits). Important progress towards a more general theory came in 1924, when Louis de Broglie postulated that, just as electromagnetic radiation (considered since the time of Young as consisting of waves) had a particle aspect as photons (following Einstein), so also particles such as electrons had a wave aspect.

He noted Planck's formula $E = h\nu$, which made the energy of a photon equal to h times the frequency of an associated wave process. He noted further that, according to classical electromagnetic theory, the energy of an electromagnetic wave equalled the magnitude of its momentum p times the speed of light c: $E = pc$. He combined these two equations to conclude that, for a photon, $p = h\nu/c = h/\lambda$ (where λ is the wavelength of the associated wave process, and is equal to the speed of light divided by the frequency). He suggested that, just as a photon or particle of electromagnetic radiation was associated with a wave of frequency equal to its energy divided by h, and of wavelength equal to h divided by its momentum, so it should be similarly for a particle of matter such as an electron. That is, such a particle should be associated with a wave of frequency ν equal to its energy divided by h (E/h), and of wavelength λ equal to h divided by its momentum (h/p).

De Broglie developed this idea by considering properties of this associated wave, having regard to Einstein's special theory of relativity. He sought to reconcile the frequency of a postulated internal periodic process of the particle, and the frequency of the associated wave when the particle was moving, the latter being adjusted according to relativity theory. In so doing, he deduced properties of 'matter waves', including a 'phase velocity' greater than the speed of light, and a 'group velocity', which, importantly, he showed to be equal to the velocity of the associated particle. The matter waves also were shown to have the same energy and momentum as the associated particle.

A further aspect of de Broglie's association of momentum with wavelength was as follows. If one took Bohr's postulate of an electron circling a hydrogen atom with angular momentum given by $n\hbar$, and de Broglie's association of momentum with h divided by wavelength, and then calculated the wavelength of the electron for each energy level, this wavelength turned out to be related to the circumference of the circular orbit which Bohr had calculated for each energy level. At the first level, the associated wavelength was equal to the circumference; at the second level, it was half the circumference; at the third level, it was one-third the circumference; and so on. The analogy with standing waves was striking, and suggested a reason why only certain orbits should be possible.

A wave aspect of electrons, as suggested by de Broglie, was demonstrated experimentally in 1927, when Davisson and Germer in the United States showed that electrons could be scattered from a nickel crystal in a way indicating wavelike behaviour, the relevant wavelength being that postulated by de Broglie. Similar diffraction experiments were conducted at about the same time in England by G. P. Thomson, the son of J. J. Thomson, who discovered the electron. (It is said that the father proved the electron was a particle, the son proved it was a wave!)

9.4. The Formulation of Quantum Mechanics

The formulation of a theory which drew together the strands which I have mentioned commenced in 1925 with work by Werner Heisenberg, and a quite different approach by Erwin Schrödinger. Schrödinger soon showed that the two approaches were equivalent, and Paul Dirac developed a more abstract theory which comprehended both approaches. At the same time as the mathematics of the theory was developed, important contributions were made to its interpretation by Max Born, Heisenberg, and Bohr. By about 1930 a comprehensive theory had been developed, which has needed little subsequent change; although, as we will see, subsequent work has extended its range, particularly in relation to the interaction of matter and radiation (quantum electrodynamics) and the nucleus (quantum chromodynamics).

9.4.1. *Heisenberg and Matrix Mechanics*

Heisenberg set out to build a theory strictly based on what could be observed. The postulated orbits of electrons could not be observed, but the emission of radiation (indicating transitions between energy levels as suggested by Bohr) could be. According to Heisenberg, therefore, the various energy levels and the jumps between them, and the thickness and intensity of the spectral lines (indicating energy levels 'preferred' by electrons), should be the basis of a mechanics of the behaviour of electrons in the atom. Heisenberg looked for a way in which a mechanics so based could incorporate classical equations, such as those relating to motion and energy. He used the analogy of Fourier analysis of more complicated functions in terms of simple harmonic functions. (I will say something about this in Section 10.2.4, but here it is sufficient to note that the mathematician Joseph Fourier demonstrated around 1800 how single-valued functions, and associated graphical representations, can be expressed as weighted sums or superpositions of simple harmonic functions, associated with simple repeated undulating sine and/or cosine waves.)

Heisenberg wrote that the idea came from the principle of correspondence, which required that, in large or highly energetic systems, the new physics should correspond to classical physics:

One had to give up the concept of the electronic orbit, but still had to maintain it in the limit of high quantum numbers, i.e. for large orbits. In this latter case, the emitted radiation, by means of its frequencies and intensities, gives a picture of the electronic orbit; it represents what the mathematicians call a Fourier expansion of the orbit. The idea suggested itself that one should write down the mechanical laws not as equations for the positions and velocities of the electrons, but as equations for the frequencies and amplitudes of their Fourier expansions. (Heisenberg 1989: 26–7)

However, the basic elements to be dealt with here were more complicated than those usually dealt with in Fourier analysis: rather than being simple series like $\cos \theta$, $\cos 2\theta$, etc., the elements included the jumps from the first energy level to the second, third, fourth, etc. levels (and back again), from the second energy level to the third, fourth, fifth, etc. levels (and back again), and so on. Whereas the weighting of the elements in a Fourier analysis could be expressed as a simple list of numbers (a_1, a_2 etc., where the full series was $a_1 \cos \theta + a_2 \cos 2\theta + ...$), the weighting of these elements could best be expressed as an array called a matrix:

$$\begin{bmatrix} a_{11} & a_{12} & .... \\ a_{21} & a_{22} & .... \\ .... \end{bmatrix}$$

Here a_{11} would be the weighting associated with the first energy level, a_{12} that associated with the jump to the first from the second level, and so on. The diagonal elements represented the weighting (and thereby the probability) of a particular energy level, and the off-diagonal elements represented the weighting (and thereby the probability) of transitions between the energy levels.

Heisenberg developed a way of expressing position as one such array, and momentum as another. He found that such arrays could be used with certain equations of classical physics to calculate the energy levels of the electron of the hydrogen atom, and the weighting of such levels. The results were consistent with the frequencies and the weighting of frequencies shown by the spectrum of the hydrogen atom.

He found one strange result of using these arrays, which at first led him to question his methods. This was that the product $x \times p$ (where x was the position matrix and p the momentum matrix) was different from the product $p \times x$. However, it turned out that this asymmetry is a feature of quantum mechanics, and that Heisenberg's methods were indeed correct.

9.4.2. *Schrödinger's Wave Function and its Interpretation*

At about the same time as Heisenberg was developing his matrix mechanics, Schrödinger built on the ideas of de Broglie and produced a quite different version of quantum mechanics.

De Broglie had associated an electron of momentum p with a wave whose wavelength was equal to h/p and had proceeded to develop properties of such a wave having regard to the theory of relativity. Schrödinger used the wave idea, shorn of relativity considerations, to produce an equation for determining possible energy levels of a system. I will discuss this equation in Chapter 11: here, it is sufficient to note that this equation enabled calculation of energy levels for the electron of the hydrogen atom, which coincided with the Balmer series and the other related series. Schrödinger also devised an equation of motion, that is, to determine the development over time of quantum systems. This is discussed in Chapter 12.

In Schrödinger's equations, the state of a particle was represented by a mathematical object, namely a wave function for which he used the Greek letter psi (ψ), which contained information about the position and the momentum of the particle. This function generally appeared to indicate a 'smeared out' position (and also momentum) for the particle, certainly not a well-defined location or even a well-defined orbit. Further, the more closely the position was defined by this function, the less closely the momentum was defined; and vice versa.

Notwithstanding what was indicated by Schrödinger's wave function, the fact was that, whenever an experiment was conducted in a way appropriate to locate an electron precisely, the electron was found to have a precise position. Accordingly, the function was interpreted not as indicating a 'smeared' electron but, rather, as giving the probability of finding the electron in various locations, or of finding it to have various momenta: many similar experiments would then give a distribution of positions or momenta reflecting this probability. This interpretation of the wave function was first suggested in 1926 by Max Born. It is associated with the characteristic indeterminism of quantum physics: for individual measurements, generally quantum physics can only give probabilities, not certainties.

I discuss the wave function in some detail in Chapter 11.

9.4.3. *Unification and Dirac*

Soon after formulating his wave mechanics, Schrödinger demonstrated that it was equivalent to Heisenberg's matrix mechanics.

A more fundamental unification of quantum physics was achieved by Dirac, who created an abstract mathematical formalism which comprehended both systems as special cases. Dirac used the idea of vectors in multidimensional space to represent particles and systems of particles. I outline this approach briefly in Chapter 11.

In addition to this important contribution to the nonrelativistic quantum mechanics invented by Heisenberg and Schrödinger, Dirac laid the foundation for later developments by extending the theory to take account of relativistic effects. In so doing, he also postulated the existence of an anti-particle of the electron, with a positive charge (later discovered, and called the positron).

9.4.4. *The Uncertainty Principle*

I noted that Schrödinger's wave function appeared to indicate that the more closely the position of a particle was defined, the less closely its momentum was defined. The same followed from Heisenberg's matrix mechanics and from Dirac's system of vectors. In fact, as will be seen in Chapter 11, the mathematics of quantum physics indicates that the product of the uncertainty of position in any direction (Δx) and the uncertainty of momentum in that direction (Δp) is at least of the order of Planck's constant h. When uncertainty is defined in precise statistical terms, the mathematics demonstrates that $\Delta x \Delta p \geqslant \hbar/2$ (or $h/4\pi$). Either position or momentum can (in principle) be made precise to any desired degree, but only at the expense of loss of precision of the other; and elimination of uncertainty in regard to one would mean infinite uncertainty in regard to the other. The mathematics also shows a similar relationship between uncertainty in regard to energy (ΔE) and uncertainty in regard to time (Δt).

These relationships are generally referred to under the name 'Heisenberg's uncertainty principle', because it was Heisenberg who first articulated them and considered their implications. The mathematics indicated a limit to the precision with which position and momentum can simultaneously be known: if position and momentum could in fact simultaneously be measured with greater precision than allowed by the mathematics, that would suggest that the mathematics was not appropriate to the way the world actually was and that the quantum theory was defective. Heisenberg devised a series of thought experiments to show that measurement could not give greater precision than allowed by the mathematics of the quantum theory.

The best known of these thought experiments concerned the measurement of the position and momentum of an electron by using a microscope. Heisenberg pointed out that the precision of such a position measurement depended on the resolving power of the microscope, which in turn depended on the wavelength of the light used and the aperture of the microscope. The longer the wavelength of the light, and the narrower the aperture of the microscope, the less precise could be the measurement of position. If, in order to obtain a precise measurement of position, light of a short wavelength is used (perhaps beyond the visible spectrum, such as ultra-violet light or even gamma rays), then the energy of each indivisible quantum of light (or photon) is necessarily higher than for light of a longer wavelength. Accordingly, the irreducible disturbance caused by the interaction of any one photon with the electron to the motion or momentum of the electron is greater. It could be possible to calculate that disturbance if one could know precisely where the photon went after it bounced off the electron, that is, precisely where it entered the microscope. But, to do this, the aperture of the microscope would have to be narrow, involving low resolving power and so low accuracy regarding position. Combining all these considerations, Heisenberg showed that the uncertainty of position times the uncertainty of momentum, as measured (and calculated) by these means, was of the order of h.

At the macro scale, the effect of the uncertainty principle is negligible. For a body of mass 1 kg, an uncertainty of position of the order of 2×10^{-17} m (much less than the diameter of the nucleus of an atom) would require an uncertainty of velocity only of the order of 2×10^{-17} m s^{-1} (or less than 1/1000 mm per century). However, at the micro scale it is different. The rest mass of an electron is about 9×10^{-31} kg, and if the uncertainty of position of an electron is of the order of the diameter of an atom (say, 10^{-10} m), then its uncertainty of velocity would have to be of the order of 10 000 km s^{-1} (1/30 the speed of light). We will see that this last statement is not quite correct, because in quantum physics the concept of velocity does not apply to objects such as electrons in the same way as in classical physics; but the statement gives a fair impression of the scale of the uncertainty principle.

9.4.5. *Bohr's Role*

Throughout the late 1920s and early 1930s, Niels Bohr made a great contribution to the interpretation of quantum physics, without being responsible for any single discovery or invention of similar significance to his 1915 theory of the atom (which was itself largely displaced by the quantum mechanics of Heisenberg, Schrödinger, and Dirac).

1. The correspondence principle. One principle associated with Bohr from the time of his theory of the atom, and of great importance throughout the development of quantum mechanics, was the correspondence principle: that for large systems quantum mechanics should give the same results as classical mechanics (which had, after all, been so successful in dealing with large systems).

2. The principle of complementarity. Another principle even more closely associated with Bohr is the principle of complementarity. This principle is to the effect that there are alternative descriptions of reality available, which are complementary in the sense that both are necessary to make up a full description; but which are mutually exclusive, in that the experimental arrangements appropriate to manifest reality under one description exclude its manifestation under the other description. Thus, one can know (and describe reality in terms of) the precise positions of particles, in which case there can be no

knowledge or description in terms of their precise momentum; and vice versa. In a somewhat similar way, one can treat electrons or photons as particles, in which case their wave aspect will be obscured; or vice versa. This can be illustrated with reference to Young's two-slit experiment.

We saw how that experiment demonstrated the wave nature of light, and how it enabled calculation of the wavelengths of the colours of the spectrum. However, according to the quantum theory, light comes in packages or quanta, called photons. The intensity of light used in a two-slit experiment can be lowered to the extent that only one photon at a time passes the screen with two slits; and (seemingly) it must go through one slit or the other. If a photon detector is placed at each slit, it will detect only complete photons, at one slit or the other. However, if a photographic plate is placed over the detection screen, when both slits are open, eventually the interference pattern will emerge on that plate, demonstrating a contribution of both slits depending on the wavelength of the light. If the photons pass one at a time, through one slit or the other, how does such interference occur?

A similar experiment can be performed with electrons, with the slits much closer together, because of the electron's shorter wavelength. Electrons are sprayed on the screen with two slits, and some means of detecting them placed at the second screen. With one slit closed, the electrons form an oblong pattern at the detector screen. With two slits open, a banded interference pattern is formed. However, each electron arrives at the detector screen discretely, one at a time. If light is used to illuminate the electrons as they pass through the slits, then (if the light is of sufficiently short wavelength) this can disclose which slit each electron goes through. However, doing this, it turns out, destroys the interference pattern.

On the complementarity approach, an interference pattern will occur only if photons (or electrons) are permitted to behave as waves between the source and the detector screen. Then, each individual photon or electron which passes through the two-slit screen does so as a wave, dividing into two waves on the far side of the screen, causing constructive or destructive interference depending on phase relationships; and this gives rise to a probability distribution at the screen, which eventually builds the interference pattern. However, if a detector is placed near the two-slit screen, so that the position of the photon or electron is determined with some precision, its particle aspect is manifested, and this precludes its behaving as a wave and precludes the interference pattern.

Thus photons and electrons can be considered as waves or particles: the two aspects are complementary in that both are necessary for a full account; but they are mutually exclusive, in that they cannot be fully manifested simultaneously. Bohr, and others, saw this approach as following from the requirement to accept the quantum postulate (involving discontinuous change), while at the same time having to continue to use classical concepts (which *inter alia* assume continuous existence and continuous change) to describe the very observations which confirm the quantum theory.

3. The Copenhagen interpretation. We have seen that Schrödinger's wave function generally gives only probabilities for finding a particle such as an electron to be in a particular position, or to have a particular momentum. According to the quantum theory, this is not because of any incompleteness in the information contained in the representation: as suggested by the uncertainty principle and the principle of complementarity, there just is an irreducible uncertainty and indeterminacy in the world. This suggests questions: what exactly is an electron doing between measurements, and how is it that measurement can make definite what was previously only a probability?

I will be considering these questions in some detail later, particularly in Chapter 14. I note here that the predominant approach to these questions, the so-called Copenhagen interpretation, was developed at the Niels Bohr Institute in Copenhagen, with Bohr himself making a major contribution. According to this interpretation, quantum physics is to be regarded as a means for predicting the results of experiments, performed with the aid of instruments which, by reason of their scale, operate in accordance with classical physics. There is just no need to speculate on what happens in the absence of, or in between, such measurements; or on when or how a measurement makes definite what was previously only a probability.

4. The Bohr–Einstein debate. One aspect of Bohr's work in supporting and interpreting the new quantum physics was his continuing debate with the most notable critic of the theory, Albert Einstein. Although Einstein had contributed significantly to its development with his work on electromagnetic radiation as quanta, he continued to resist the notions of indeterminacy and indeterminism inherent in quantum physics. Over a number of years, Einstein formulated thought experiments with which he attempted to overturn aspects of quantum physics, in particular the uncertainty principle (by showing how a precise measurement could be made of momentum and position, or of time and energy, simultaneously). These were submitted to Bohr, who in each case was able to demonstrate how it was that the uncertainty principle prevailed.

Einstein's final effort in this direction was contained in an article he wrote in 1935 in collaboration with Boris Podolsky and Nathan Rosen (Einstein *et al.* 1935). This famous article, widely known under the initials of its authors, 'EPR', was answered by Bohr, though perhaps not in an entirely satisfying way (see Bohr 1935). The EPR article gave rise to further expositions of extraordinary implications of quantum physics in the 1960s and afterwards, particularly with the 1964 theorem of John Bell ('Bell's inequality') and experiments culminating in those of Alain Aspect in the early 1980s. This will be discussed in Chapter 15.

9.4.6. *The Overturning of Classical Assumptions*

This brief outline of quantum mechanics suggests why many of the classical assumptions had to be abandoned.

The assumption of continuous existence and motion of physical objects was contradicted by Bohr's 1913 theory of the atom: this theory did not assign a trajectory to an electron as it passed from one orbit to another (and any such trajectory would be inconsistent with the Newtonian mechanics on which the orbits were based). The theory was overtaken by the full quantum mechanics of Heisenberg, Schrödinger, and Dirac, which, particularly in its application to systems of more than one particle (which I look at in Chapters 13 and 15), involves even greater departures from the classical assumptions.

The assumption of definite position and motion of physical objects was clearly contradicted by quantum mechanics: the theory necessarily involved mathematics according to which a particle such as an electron *cannot* at the same time have both precise position and precise motion.

As to measurement, the standard interpretation of quantum mechanics is to the effect that in many situations a particle's 'observables' of position and motion do not exist, at least with precision, independently of their being measured. In such cases, measurement of precise position or precise motion (or momentum) will cause the observable measured to become precise, often at the expense of making other observables less precise than previously. There is an irreducible minimum to the imprecision of measurement of both position and motion, and (in some cases) to the disturbance which measurement causes to those observables.

9.5. Later Developments

Non-relativistic quantum mechanics, as developed in the late 1920s and early 1930s by Heisenberg, Schrödinger, Dirac, Born, and Bohr, dealt superbly with the behaviour of electrons under the influence of potential energy due to the electromagnetic field, and in particular in relation to the nucleus. In so far as it was a non-relativistic theory, it fell short of complete accuracy: however, it enabled explanation of the chemical properties of matter in terms of the physics of the atom, and the development of such things as the laser and the transistor. Later developments in quantum physics concerned such matters as the discovery of new fundamental particles and forces; the development of quantum electrodynamics, dealing with the interaction of the electromagnetic field and matter; and the development of quantum chromodynamics, dealing with the forces within the nucleus, and pointing towards a unification of the fundamental forces. I will deal with these developments very briefly. They are of vast importance; but they did not greatly affect the problems of the interpretation and philosophical implications of quantum physics, and I will for the most part be considering only non-relativistic quantum mechanics in dealing with these problems (see d'Espagnat 1989: 192 ff.).

9.5.1. *New Particles and Forces*

By 1932, it had been discovered that the nucleus consisted of particles of two types: the positively charged proton, and the neutral neutron. In the case of atoms other than hydrogen, the nucleus included two or more protons; and, since the electromagnetic force between them was strongly repulsive, it came to be realized that there must be a very powerful attractive force operating between them, to hold them together in the nucleus. This force was named the strong nuclear force or the strong force; however, attempts to model it mathematically had little success until the 1960s.

Also in the 1930s, a fourth fundamental force (called the weak force) was identified, and shown to be responsible for the decay of certain particles, including that responsible for beta radiation. It, too, was not well understood until recent years.

I have already mentioned the discovery of the positron. Further experiments led to the discovery of many more particles, some extremely difficult to detect (such as the neutrino) and some with extremely short lifetimes. This has continued up to the present day, in association with efforts to understand and unify the fundamental forces.

9.5.2. *Quantum Electrodynamics*

This theory, formulated shortly after the Second World War, gave a procedure for calculating the results of any interaction involving photons and electrons. One important step towards this theory was the invention by Richard Feynman of a new formulation of quantum mechanics, sometimes called the sum-over-histories version.

Feynman noted that, according to the various versions of quantum mechanics, where an event can occur as a result of alternative processes, each of which consists of a succession of intermediate processes—for example, in the two-slit experiment, the passage of a photon from the source to one or other slit, and then passage from there to the detecting screen—the probability of the event is calculated *not* by multiplying and adding the probabilities of intermediate processes but by multiplying and adding what are called probability amplitudes. As we will see in Chapters 10 to 13, these are complex numbers containing information relating to probability, and also relating to phase (and thus to whether wavelike interference between alternative processes would be constructive or destructive).

Feynman then considered in quite general terms the calculation of probability amplitudes for the passage of a particle from one position to another. He postulated that every possible path for the particle between the two positions, considered individually (that is, without reference to other possible paths), had equal probability. He then showed that the probability amplitudes of possible 'wild' paths, far from the path which classical physics would attribute to the particle, were generally out of phase with those of adjoining wild paths, so that on addition these probability amplitudes tended to cancel each other out; while the probability amplitudes of possible direct paths, near the classical path, were generally in phase with those of adjoining direct paths, so that on addition these probability amplitudes tended to reinforce each other. This approach gave mathematical results equivalent to those given by application of Schrödinger's equation of motion.

This sum-over-histories approach was not only consistent with earlier approaches, but also proved more suitable for application to the interaction of electrons with the electromagnetic field.

Quantum electrodynamics uses the notion of what are called virtual photons, and takes them to be the carriers of certain electromagnetic forces. The earlier theory had identified photons with electromagnetic radiation, that is, as carriers of those electromagnetic forces recognized by classical physics as being produced by accelerating charges. The new theory recognized, in addition to such 'real' photons, 'virtual' photons as being carriers of other electromagnetic forces, such as those which operate according to the inverse square law between static charges. According to quantum electrodynamics, each electron can be considered as continually emitting, and as being accompanied by, clouds of such virtual photons. These virtual photons may be absorbed by other particles; if so, there is a transmission of electromagnetic force; but, if not, the virtual photons are considered as reabsorbed by the electron (as they must be, to avoid violating laws requiring conservation of energy and momentum). The energy of such virtual photons can be considered as 'borrowed', the justification for that being the energy–time uncertainty relationship: the more energetic such virtual photons are, the less will be the time of their existence, so as to ensure that the product of time and 'borrowed' energy stays under the Planck constant h.

A general picture of the processes involved is given by Feynman diagrams, devised by the same Richard Feynman. Thus the scattering of two electrons could be roughly depicted as in Fig. 9.3.

The paths of the electrons are shown (as in a Minkowski diagram) moving in time up the page. The wavy line depicts a virtual photon emitted by the particle on the left (causing it to recoil to the left) and absorbed by the particle on the right (causing it to divert to the right). In the case of an interaction between particles of different charges, say an electron and a proton, the virtual photon is emitted and absorbed in the direction *away* from the other particle, so that the particles tend to come together.

These diagrams do not reflect the sophisticated mathematics of the theory; and must not in any event be taken too literally, because electrons do not have a well-defined path as the diagrams suggest. The paths shown by such

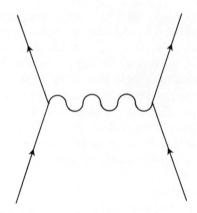

FIG. 9.3. A Feynman diagram showing electron repulsion

diagrams represent *possible* paths, and what actually happens depends upon probability amplitudes arrived at by adding probability amplitudes for *all* possible paths.

9.5.3. *Towards Unification*

The success of quantum electrodynamics caused it to become the model for quantum descriptions of other forces of nature. Messenger particles called gravitons were postulated for the force of gravity. However, a successful quantum theory of gravity has yet to be developed.

As regards the weak force, a theory was developed in the 1960s and 1970s according to which the electromagnetic force and the weak force are two parts of a single force, which was called the electroweak force. This theory required the existence of three messenger particles, which unlike photons have mass, and which are respectively negatively charged, positively charged, and electrically neutral. Because of their mass and (accordingly) high energy content, the energy–time uncertainty relation means that the time of their existence is short; they travel at less than the speed of light; and so the range of the force is small.

As regards the strong force, it now appears to result from forces operating between postulated component parts of nuclear particles, called quarks. The inter-quark force is supposed to be carried by messenger particles, called gluons, of which there are considered to be eight different types. The quantum theory dealing with quarks and the inter-quark force is called quantum chromodynamics; the name chromodynamics was chosen because the property of quarks which interacts with the gluon field (as charge interacts with the electromagnetic field) was called 'colour'.

Work is currently proceeding with a view to giving a unified account of all forces: some of this work postulates a multidimensional reality (with up to eight extra dimensions of space), and some uses the idea of 'strings'. It is unnecessary for the purposes of this book to pursue these matters.

10

Some Mechanics and Mathematics

IN order to prepare for consideration of some basic mathematics of quantum physics, in this chapter I consider first some basic mathematics of classical mechanics, and then some mathematical ideas used in quantum physics.

10.1. Some Aspects of Pre-Quantum Mechanics

I will deal first with Newton's laws, then with the concept of energy, and finally with Hamilton's equations (which have some affinity with the approach of quantum mechanics).

10.1.1. *Newton's Laws*

Newton's three laws of motion concern relations between motion and forces generally. His law of universal gravitation concerns just one particular force. I will deal with these laws in turn.

1. Newton's first and second laws of motion. The motion, and/or change of motion, of physical objects is determined by the forces acting on it, in accordance with these two laws:

    (i) Every body continues in a state of uniform motion in a straight line or of rest, unless caused to change that state by forces impressed upon it.

    (ii) When the resultant force on a body is not zero, the body changes its state of motion by acceleration, and for a given force the acceleration is inversely proportional to the mass of the body.

The latter is symbolically expressed by the equation:

$$\mathbf{F} = m\mathbf{a}.$$

In this equation, $\mathbf{F}$ is the resultant force, m is the mass (which can be considered the measure of inertia), and $\mathbf{a}$ is the acceleration (or rate of change, with respect to time, of the velocity). $\mathbf{F}$ and $\mathbf{a}$ are in bold type, because they represent quantities having direction as well as magnitude. Such quantities are called vectors, whereas quantities which have magnitude only (such as mass) are called scalars. The magnitude of vectors can be written in italic type (F, a), and also by placing vertical lines round the vector symbols, as in

| **F** | and | **a** |. The above equation indicates a relation of magnitude ($F = ma$), and also indicates that the vectors **F** and **a** have the same direction.

Such vectors can be resolved into component vectors with the respective directions of three orthogonal axes (that is, axes at right angles to each other) conventionally called the x, y, and z axes (see Section 11.3.1). Newton's laws apply separately to the components of vectors along each axis; and, in relation to vectors whose direction is constant, the three axes can be chosen so that one of them lies in that direction (so that there is no component of such vectors in the direction of the other axes). It simplifies the discussion to consider the laws in one dimension only, that is, as applying to motion and forces in the direction of one axis (say the x axis). In such discussion, the vectors can be dealt with as scalars: if in any case the vectors have components in the direction of the y and or z axes, then a similar discussion applies in relation to each.

Acceleration I have said to be the rate of change, with respect to time, of velocity. Velocity, in turn, is the rate of change, with respect to time, of position. In order to do calculations based on these ideas, use is made of what are called functions, and of the branch of mathematics known as calculus. A function can be considered as a set of rules for deriving a quantity or value (called the dependent variable) from each possible value of one or more independent variables. Thus, position may be expressed as a function of time: say,

$$x(t) = a_0 + a_1 t + a_2 t^2,$$

where a_0, a_1, and a_2 are constants. Then velocity can also be expressed as a function of time, by calculation of the rate at which $x(t)$ changes with respect to time.

This is done by an operation of calculus called differentiation: graphically, this finds the function (called the derivative) which gives, for any t, the slope of the curve representing $x(t)$: the rate of change of a function at any point is the slope of the graph of the function at that point. This operation is written dx/dt or $d/dt\, x(t)$, and in the example given would produce the function $a_1 + 2a_2 t$. I cannot here set out the rules for differentiation. However, it will be seen that a_0, the part of the function which did not vary with t, has disappeared in the derivative: this is because its rate of change with respect to t is zero.

When one thus has velocity as a function of time, acceleration can be calculated by a further process of differentiation. Thus we have the equations:

$$v = dx/dt$$
$$a = dv/dt = d^2x/dt^2.$$

Here x represents the position coordinate on the x axis, v represents the velocity along that axis, and t (a scalar) represents time; and d^2/dt^2 represents two successive operations of differentiation with respect to t.

If one is given the acceleration a as a function of t (which can be written $a(t)$), one can calculate the velocity v as a function of t by integration (the reverse process to differentiation):

$$v = \int a \, dt + C.$$

This function is called the integral of a with respect to t. C is an unknown constant of integration. As we have seen, parts of functions which do not vary disappear on differentiation; so the result of integration is a range of functions, which differ only by their constant term.

One can then find the change in velocity between two times (say t_1 and t_2) by calculating the above function for $t = t_1$ and for $t = t_2$ and subtracting, thereby eliminating the unknown constant. This can be written:

$$\text{Change in } v \text{ (between } t_1 \text{ and } t_2) = \int_{t_1}^{t_2} a \, dt$$

It is represented graphically by the area under the curve representing $a(t)$ between $t = t_1$ and $t = t_2$, as shown in Fig. 10.1. The average of the acceleration

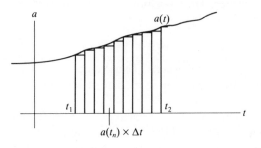

FIG. 10.1. Integration as the limit of a summation

over this time can be arrived at by dividing this integral by the elapsed time $(t_2 - t_1)$, the range over which the integral is calculated. An integral between two values of the independent variable (here t) can be considered as related to a summation of products of equal small increments in the value of the independent variable between these two values (such increments being written Δt) and the value of the dependent variable (here a) at each incremental point. This summation can be written $\sum_{t_1}^{t_2} a(t_n) \, \Delta t$, where the $a(t_n)$ are the values of the function $a(t)$ at the successive incremental points; and it gives an approximation of the area under the curve between the two values. If one then considers the increments Δt to approach zero, so that the number of elements in the summation approaches infinity, then at the limit the summation becomes the integral referred to above, giving the exact area under the curve, rather than an approximation to it.

Similarly, from v as a function of t, the position x as a function of t can be calculated:

$$x = \int v \, dt + C.$$

The change in position between two times (again, say t_1 and t_2) is given by $\int_{t_1}^{t_2} v \, dt$.

Newton's second law can be expressed in terms of position and time rather than acceleration:

$$F = m \, d^2x/dt^2.$$

It can also be expressed in terms of a quantity called momentum (conventionally represented by p), which is the product of mass and velocity:

$$p = mv.$$

Then Newton's second law can be expressed:

$$F = dp/dt.$$

This formulation is of some importance, *inter alia* because in any interaction momentum is conserved: that is, the sum of the momenta of all objects involved is not altered by any interaction between them. (Conservation of momentum has some association with Newton's third law of motion, dealt with below.) Momentum is also significant for us, because it plays an important part in the equations of quantum physics, although, as we shall see, it is a somewhat altered concept in quantum physics.

2. Newton's third law of motion. If one is given the mass, position, and velocity of an object at any time, and all forces acting on it over a period including that time, it is possible by using Newton's first and second laws of motion to calculate its position and velocity at any time within that period. In many cases, however, calculations are simplified, and can be made on the basis of different data, by using Newton's third law:

(iii) Whenever one body exerts a force on another, the latter always exerts a force on the former that is equal in magnitude, is opposite in direction, and has the same line of action.

If one has two interacting particles, then the forces between them arising from the interaction are equal and opposite; and accordingly (if one leaves aside the effect of any other forces, i.e. external to the interaction) the rate of change with respect to time of the momentum p_1 of one particle is equal to minus the rate of change of the momentum p_2 of the other particle:

$$dp_1/dt = -dp_2/dt.$$

It follows that the rate of change of the sum of p_1 and p_2 is zero:

$$d(p_1 + p_2)/dt = 0.$$

Thus the total momentum is unchanged by the interaction: so that Newton's third law is consistent with the conservation of momentum. The same applies to interactions involving more than two particles.

3. Newton's law of gravitation. The three laws so far considered say nothing about calculation of forces acting upon a body. One of the fundamental forces recognized by classical physics (and of particular importance for the motion of planets, and for the motion of objects near the surface of the earth) is the force of gravity. Newton formulated a law by which such force can be calculated:

(iv) Every particle in the universe attracts every other particle in the universe with a force that is directly proportional to the product of the masses of the particles, and inversely proportional to the square of the distance between them.

This law can be expressed by the equation:

$$F = Gm_1 m_2/r^2.$$

This equation gives only the magnitude of the force. The direction of the force is from the particle it operates on towards the other particle. The masses of the two particles are represented in the equation by m_1 and m_2, and r is the distance between them. G is a constant, called the gravitational constant. If the force is expressed in newtons (one newton being that force which gives to 1 kilogram an acceleration of 1 metre per second per second), the masses in kilograms and the distance in metres, then G is equal to 6.670×10^{-11} newton $m^2 \, kg^{-2}$.

Newton's law of gravitation refers to the force between particles: in this context, this means objects whose mass is concentrated at a single point. It can be proved that the force of gravity exerted by or on an object which is a homogeneous sphere, with respect to any object external to it, is the same as if the entire mass of the former object were concentrated at its centre. The earth is not exactly a homogeneous sphere; but it can be approximated to such a sphere, and accordingly the force of the earth's gravity acting on an object of mass m_0 near the earth's surface is approximately as follows:

$$F_G = - Gm_0 m_E /r^2.$$

Here F_G is the magnitude of the force due to the earth's gravity, m_0 is the mass of the object, m_E is the mass of the earth, and r is the distance of the object from the centre of the earth (and approximates the radius of the earth). This force F_G is called the weight of the object. I have expressed the force as negative, because if direction is taken into account, and r is considered to be positive, the force of gravity causes motion which would reduce r.

10.1.2. *Energy*

I have said that momentum is important because it is conserved, and because it is used extensively in quantum physics. The same applies to another quantity, energy. Energy is not a vector, but it can be calculated for, and is conserved in, each dimension; so in general it is convenient to continue the one-dimensional discussion.

1. Forms of energy. Classical physics distinguished between the kinetic energy of an object, which can be considered as an *actual* energy, and which in general terms is the energy which an object is considered to have by reason of its motion; and its *potential* energy, which in general terms is energy which a body is considered to have by reason of its position. Other forms of energy are recognized, such as heat; but this can be considered as equivalent to the kinetic energy due to random motion of the molecules of the hot object. As we saw, this motion is what constitutes the heat. The theory of relativity recognizes energy constituted by mass ($E = mc^2$), and this can be treated as a form of actual energy of objects, alongside kinetic energy. Classical physics recognized that electromagnetic radiation (as well as objects) could be also considered as having energy.

2. Kinetic energy and gravitational potential energy. The conservation of energy, and also an important characteristic of potential energy, can be illustrated by reference to an object moving under the influence of the earth's gravity. The kinetic energy K of an object of mass m moving with velocity v and momentum $p(= mv)$ is given as $mv^2/2$ or $p^2/2m$. Potential energy is conventionally represented by the letter V, and the gravitational potential energy of an object near the surface of the earth (assuming, as is often the case, that gravitational forces acting on it due to all objects other than the earth can be disregarded) is given by the equation $V = -\int F_G \, dr$, where r is the variable representing the position coordinate of the object with respect to the centre of the earth, and F_G is the gravitational force acting on the object (i.e. $-Gm_0m_E/r^2$, where m_0 is the mass of the object and m_E is the mass of the earth).

Then, if such an object moves vertically at velocity v, under the influence of the earth's gravity and no other force, it can be seen that the total of its kinetic and potential energies is conserved, in the following way.

The rate of change of potential energy with respect to r is as follows (mass being constant in non-relativistic mechanics):

$$dV/dr = -F_G.$$

It is a rule of calculus that if you have three variables x, y, and z, and x is a function of y, and y is a function of z; then $dx/dz = (dx/dy)(dy/dz)$. So the rate of change of potential energy with respect to time t is as follows:

$$dV/dt = (dV/dr)(dr/dt) = -F_G v.$$

The rate of change of kinetic energy with respect to time is as follows:

$$(d/dt)mv^2/2 = (d/dv)mv^2(dv/dt)/2 = mv(dv/dt)$$

$$= m(dv/dt)v \qquad = F_G v.$$

(Since no other force is operating, $m(dv/dt)$ must equal F_G.)

Accordingly, if one takes the total energy E to be the sum of kinetic energy $mv^2/2$ (or $p^2/2m$) and potential energy V, we have:

$$E = mv^2/2 + V$$

$$dE/dt = (d/dt)\,(mv^2/2 + V) = F_G v - F_G v = 0.$$

Therefore, the total energy does not change over time: it is conserved.

Gravitational potential energy thus illustrates a significant property of potential energy, namely that it is associated with a resultant force, whose magnitude and direction at any particular time does not depend at all on the motion of the object, but does depend on its position. In the one-dimensional case considered, the magnitude of the resultant force is the negative of the derivative of the potential energy (itself a function of the position coordinate r) with respect to r.

3. Potential energy and fields. The above discussion can be generalized in two ways: first, to apply to cases where one considers the effect, in three dimensions, on a body of gravitational forces exerted by many other bodies; and secondly, to apply to the other fundamental force recognized by classical physics, namely that associated with electromagnetism.

Where one must take into account gravitational forces exerted on a body by several others, one can use the notion of a gravitational field, producing a resultant force at each point in space. The vector representing this field can be ascertained by vector addition (on which see Section 11.1.3) of the vectors representing the force exerted by each of the other objects A, B, C, etc. at this point in space:

$$\mathbf{F_R} = \mathbf{F_A} + \mathbf{F_B} + \mathbf{F_C} + \ldots$$

This resultant force in turn can be resolved into components along three orthogonal axes:

$$\mathbf{F_R} = F_i \mathbf{i} + F_j \mathbf{j} + F_k \mathbf{k}.$$

Here, $\mathbf{F_R}$ is the vector representing the resultant force; and F_i, F_j, and F_k are scalars representing the magnitude of its components along the x, y, and z axes; and $\mathbf{i}$, $\mathbf{j}$, and $\mathbf{k}$ are unit vectors along such axes.

The gravitational potential energy V of the object can then be expressed as a function of the object's three coordinates (x, y, and z), and so can be written $V(x,y,z)$; and it will be such that the magnitude of the components of the resultant force along the x, y, and z axes are the negatives of the partial derivatives of V with respect to x, y, and z respectively. (Functions with a number of independent variables can be differentiated with respect to any single one of those variables, with the others considered as remaining constant—this is called partial differentiation—so each such partial derivative is obtained by differentiating V with respect to one variable, while considering the other two as remaining constant.) This can be written as follows:

$$F_i = -\partial V/\partial x, \; F_j = -\partial V/\partial y, \; F_k = -\partial V/\partial z.$$

The resultant force is given by the following equation:

$$\mathbf{F_R} = -[(\partial V/\partial x)\mathbf{i} + (\partial V/\partial y)\mathbf{j} + (\partial V/\partial z)\mathbf{k}]$$

$$= -\nabla V\,(x,y,z).$$

The symbol ∇ is an operator, which instructs, firstly, the application in turn, to a function of x, y, and z, of the partial differential operators $\partial/\partial x$, $\partial/\partial y$, and $\partial/\partial z$; and, secondly, the multiplication of each result by the unit vectors $\mathbf{i}$, $\mathbf{j}$, and $\mathbf{k}$ respectively; and, thirdly, the vector addition of the results. It thereby produces a vector from a function of x, y, and z: in this case, it produces $\mathbf{F_R}$ from $V(x,y,z)$.

In dealing with objects on the small scale of molecules, atoms, and their constituents, it is the other fundamental force recognized by classical physics, namely electromagnetism, which is more important. The law governing this force in the case of static objects (known as Coulomb's law) has some similarities with that governing gravitation, in that (in principle) it operates between particles at any distance, and its strength as between any two particles varies directly with the product of a quantity associated with each particle, and inversely with the square of the distance between them. However, it differs in that it is much stronger; in that the relevant quantity is electrical charge rather than mass; and in that the force may be one of either attraction or repulsion, depending on whether the charges of the two particles are different (one positive, one negative) or the same. As we saw, this last distinction explains why this force can often be disregarded in larger-scale calculations, in that in many cases it tends to be cancelled out.

In relation to an electromagnetic field associated with a number of particles, there will generally be a resultant force on an electrically charged object, associated with a potential energy V, which is a function of the position coordinates of the object, and from which the resultant force can be calculated. A similar discussion applies as in relation to gravitational potential energy.

This gives a broad idea of the idea of potential energy V, which in three dimensions is a function of position coordinates x, y, and z, but in relation to which calculations limited to one dimension can usefully be made. Generality requires the introduction of one more variable into this concept, namely time. If the field is changing over time, by reason of the motion of massive objects (which give rise to a gravitational field) and/or charged objects (which give rise to an electromagnetic field), then an object's potential energy will be a function not only of position, but also explicitly of time. The resultant force at any particular time is given by calculating V as a function of x, y, and z at that particular time, and then applying the operator ∇ as discussed above.

10.1.3. *Hamilton's Equations*

Before moving on to consider another area of particular importance for quantum mechanics, the mathematics of waves, it is worth while to look briefly at some equations of classical mechanics formulated by the nineteenth-century Irish mathematician William Hamilton, which have some affinities with quantum mechanics. I will revert here to the one-dimensional case.

We have seen that total energy E of an object, the sum of its kinetic energy $p^2/2m$ and its potential energy V, is conserved if no force acts on the body apart from the resultant force associated with the potential energy: that is, E does not change over time (or with changes in the other variables p and x, as those changes occur over time). However, kinetic energy considered alone changes, and its rate of change with respect to p is equal to the object's velocity:

$$(\mathrm{d}/\mathrm{d}p)p^2/2m = p/m = v.$$

Potential energy considered alone also changes, and its rate of change with respect to x is the negative of the resultant force on the object due to potential energy:

$$\mathrm{d}V/\mathrm{d}x = -F = -ma.$$

Accordingly, if one takes partial derivatives of the total energy E, with respect to p and x respectively, in either case holding the other variable (or variables, if V is a function also of t) constant, we have:

$$\partial E/\partial p = v = \mathrm{d}x/\mathrm{d}t$$

$$\partial E/\partial x = -ma = -\mathrm{d}p/\mathrm{d}t.$$

The equations $\partial E/\partial p = \mathrm{d}x/\mathrm{d}t$ and $\partial E/\partial x = -\mathrm{d}p/\mathrm{d}t$ are known as Hamilton's equations. They distil the same information as discussed above in relation to Newton's laws; but they foreshadow quantum mechanics in two respects:

  (i) the central importance given to total energy, or $E(=p^2/2m + V)$; and
  (ii) the near symmetrical place given to momentum and position, the variables p and x.

10.2. Some Mathematics of Waves

In order to understand the mathematical ideas of quantum mechanics, it is necessary to have some acquaintance with sines and cosines; imaginary and complex numbers; the exponential function; and waves and superposition.

10.2.1. *Sines and Cosines*

In trigonometry, the sine of an angle θ (sin θ), where θ is an angle in a right-angled triangle, is the ratio which the side opposite the angle θ bears to the hypotenuse; while the cosine of that angle (cos θ) is the ratio which the side adjacent to the angle θ (not being the hypotenuse) bears to the hypotenuse. This definition is satisfactory only for angles between 0° and 90°.

Sines and cosines are extensively used in algebra, with the angles generally being expressed in radians rather than degrees. (One radian is the angle subtended at the centre of a circle by an arc equal in length to the radius; so that one radian is 360°/2π, that is, about 57°; 2π radians is 360°, π radians is 180°, and π/2 radians is 90°.) Sin θ and cos θ are more generally defined by reference to a graph using Cartesian coordinates, and in particular to the x and y coordinates of points on the circumference of a circle of unit radius centred at the origin. If θ is the angle through which the radius to such a point on the circumference has passed in moving anticlockwise from the positive x axis, then as shown in Fig. 10.2 the x coordinate of that point is cos θ, and the y coordinate is sin θ.

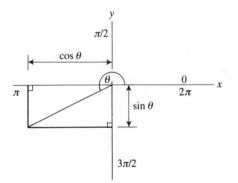

FIG. 10.2. A graphical definition of sines and cosines

Thus, where θ lies between π and 3π/2, as shown in Fig. 10.2, both cos θ and sin θ are negative. Cos θ is 1 when θ = 0, falls to zero when θ = π/2, then to -1 when θ = π, returning to zero at θ = 3π/2, and to 1 when θ = 2π. The cycle is then repeated, so that cos (θ + 2π) = cos θ . Sin θ varies periodically in the same way, but π/2 behind: so that cos θ = sin (θ + π/2) . Accordingly, sin θ is zero when θ = 0, 1 when θ = π/2, zero when θ = π, -1 when θ = 3π/2, and zero when θ = 2π. The cycle is then repeated, so that sin (θ + 2π) = sin θ .

Cos θ is symmetrical about θ = 0, so cos θ = cos (– θ) . Sin θ is symmetrical about θ = π/2, so sin (π/2 + θ) = sin (π/2 – θ); while sin θ = – sin (– θ) . The value of sin θ and cos θ becomes opposite in sign each time θ increases by π, so cos θ = – cos (θ + π) and sin θ = – sin (θ + π) . By Pythagoras's theorem, it is clear that $\sin^2 θ + \cos^2 θ = 1$.

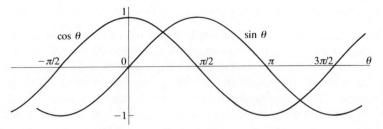

FIG. 10.3. Sine and cosine waves

The graphs of cos θ and sin θ as functions of θ are as shown in Fig. 10.3. The rates of change with respect to θ of these wave functions (called simple harmonic functions) are as follows:

$$d \cos \theta/d\theta = - \sin \theta$$

$$d \sin \theta/d\theta = \cos \theta.$$

10.2.2. *Complex Numbers*

The square of a negative number, as of a positive number, is a positive number. No 'real' number is the square root of a negative number. However, it has been convenient for many purposes to use an imaginary number $i (= \sqrt{-1})$, so that one can give a square root of a negative number: thus the square root of -64 is $\pm 8i$. It has also been convenient to combine real and imaginary numbers to give complex numbers of the form $x + iy$ (where x and y are real numbers). Complex numbers are extensively used in quantum mechanics.

Any complex number may be represented by a point in what is called an Argand plane, similar to an ordinary plane with Cartesian coordinates, but with the horizontal x axis representing the real part of the number, and the vertical y axis the imaginary part (see Fig. 10.4). The point A shown in Fig. 10.4 represents the complex number $z = x + iy$, which can also be written

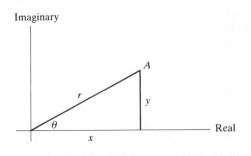

FIG. 10.4. An Argand diagram

$z = r (\cos \theta + i \sin \theta)$. r is called the modulus of the complex number, and θ is called the argument.

Each complex number z has what is called a complex conjugate number $z*$, obtained by changing the sign of the imaginary part, so that if $z = x + iy$, $z* = x - iy$. The product of a complex number and its complex conjugate $(zz*)$ is the square of the modulus (r^2):

$$(x + iy) (x - iy) = x^2 + y^2 = r^2.$$

This is sometimes called the absolute square of z, and written $|z|^2$.

There is an important relationship between sines, cosines, complex numbers, and a number called e, which equals about 2.7, and which is defined as follows: e^x is the limit of $(1 + x/n)^n$ as n approaches infinity. This function e^x, which is called the exponential function and is also written $\exp(x)$, can be written as an infinite power series:

$$e^x = 1 + x/1! + x^2/2! + x^3/3! + x^4/4! + \ldots$$

Here, $2! = 2 \times 1$, $3! = 3 \times 2 \times 1$, and so on. It so happens that $\cos \theta$ and $\sin \theta$ also can be written as infinite power series:

$$\cos \theta = 1 - \theta^2/2! + \theta^4/4! - \theta^6/6! + \ldots$$
$$\sin \theta = \theta/1! - \theta^3/3! + \theta^5/5! - \theta^7/7! + \ldots$$

If x is made to equal $i\theta$, e^x becomes:

$$e^{i\theta} = 1 + i\theta/1! - \theta^2/2! - i\theta^3/3! + \theta^4/4! + i\theta^5/5! - \ldots$$
$$= \cos \theta + i \sin \theta.$$

This important (and surprising) equality is called Euler's formula. It means that any complex number z can be written $re^{i\theta}$, where r is the modulus and θ the argument of the number. The complex conjugate of $re^{i\theta}$ is $re^{-i\theta}$ (or $r(\cos \theta - i \sin \theta)$), so that $|re^{i\theta}|^2$ is $r^2 e^{i\theta - i\theta}$, that is r^2. Incidentally, if θ is equal to π, we have:

$$\exp(i\pi) = \cos \pi + i \sin \pi = -1; \text{ or } \exp(i\pi) + 1 = 0.$$

The last equality links the five most important numbers in mathematics: 0, 1, e, π, and i.

As we will see, in quantum physics $e^{i\theta}$ is used extensively, with both the real and the imaginary parts having significance. Quite apart from that, many calculations concerning sines and cosines can be made more simply by making calculations with $e^{i\theta}$, then disregarding the imaginary (or the real) part of the answer. For example, it is simple to calculate useful equalities based on expansions of $\cos(\theta + \phi)$ and $\sin(\theta + \phi)$, using the equality $\exp[i(\theta + \phi)] = \exp(i\theta) \exp(i\phi)$.

$$\exp(i\theta) \exp(i\phi) = (\cos \theta + i \sin \theta)(\cos \phi + i \sin \phi)$$

$$= \cos \theta \cos \phi - \sin \theta \sin \phi + i(\cos \theta \sin \phi + \sin \theta \cos \phi)$$
$$\exp[i(\theta + \phi)] = \cos(\theta + \phi) + i \sin(\theta + \phi).$$

Comparing the real and the imaginary parts respectively of the right sides of these equalities, we get:

$$\cos(\theta + \phi) = \cos \theta \cos \phi - \sin \theta \sin \phi \qquad (10.1)$$
$$\sin(\theta + \phi) = \cos \theta \sin \phi + \sin \theta \cos \phi. \qquad (10.2)$$

It follows similarly that:

$$\cos(\theta - \phi) = \cos \theta \cos \phi + \sin \theta \sin \phi. \qquad (10.3)$$

By adding and subtracting (10.1) and (10.3):

$$2 \cos \theta \cos \phi = \cos(\theta - \phi) + \cos(\theta + \phi) \qquad (10.4)$$
$$2 \sin \theta \sin \phi = \cos(\theta - \phi) - \cos(\theta + \phi). \qquad (10.5)$$

From (10.4) and (10.5), by putting $x = \theta + \phi$ and $y = \theta - \phi$, so that $\theta = (x + y)/2$ and $\phi = (x - y)/2$, we have:

$$\cos x + \cos y = 2 \cos(x + y)/2 \; \cos(x - y)/2 \qquad (10.6)$$
$$\cos y - \cos x = 2 \cos(x + y)/2 \; \sin(x - y)/2. \qquad (10.7)$$

10.2.3. *Harmonic Oscillation*

In many physical situations, objects vibrate or oscillate about an equilibrium position, under the influence of a force towards that position which is (at least approximately) proportional to the displacement from it: for example, the vibration of a tuning-fork. This is called harmonic oscillation or simple harmonic motion. The mathematics of this motion is important in quantum mechanics.

If one considers a mass m hanging on a spring, it would not in reality give harmonic oscillation, in particular because air resistance and friction within the spring would mean that the resultant force on the mass would not always be proportional to the displacement, and any oscillation would quite quickly reduce to zero. However, it is instructive to consider an 'ideal' mass on a spring, in relation to which friction can be disregarded, as being a simple one-dimensional example of harmonic oscillation. Now, the acceleration of the mass will be equal to the restoring force at any displacement y from the equilibrium position:

$$m \, d^2y/dt^2 = -Ky.$$

Here K is the (constant) ratio of the force to the displacement, and the force is negative because it is in the direction opposite to the displacement y. A general solution to this equation is:

$$y = A \cos{(\omega t + C)}.$$

Here, A and C are arbitrary constants, and $\omega^2 = K/m$. The quantity $(\omega t + C)$ is called the phase of the motion; and since the cosine function repeats itself each time it increases by 2π, the mass completes one oscillation each time ωt increases by 2π (C is constant). Accordingly, the time taken by (or period of) one complete oscillation is $2\pi/\omega$, or $2\pi \sqrt{(m/K)}$. It will be seen that increasing the mass increases the period (slows the oscillations), and increasing the force (by increasing K) reduces the period (quickens the oscillations).

It will also be seen that the period of the oscillation does not depend at all on the size of the oscillation, the maximum displacement from the equilibrium position: this maximum displacement is in fact A (because $\cos{(\omega t + C)} \leq 1$), and it is called the amplitude of the oscillation. I noted above that A is an arbitrary constant: its size can be determined by the initial position and speed of the mass. For example, if the mass is initially displaced a certain distance A_0 and released at zero speed, then A_0 will be the amplitude. (There is of course a practical limit to A: if a spring is extended beyond a certain length, it is distorted and there will no longer be a restoring force proportional to the displacement from the original equilibrium position.) Subject to the practical limitation noted in parenthesis, and disregarding friction effects, the period of the oscillation is the same irrespective of the size of the amplitude: for larger amplitudes, the mass accelerates more quickly from its extreme positions, and reaches a higher maximum speed as it passes the equilibrium position.

I have noted that the time taken by one oscillation is $2\pi/\omega$. This means that the frequency of the oscillations (number of oscillations per unit time) is $\omega/2\pi$. ω is called the angular frequency, being the number of radians by which the phase changes per unit time: it equals $2\pi\nu$, where ν is the frequency of oscillations (cyclic frequency).

The second constant contained in the solution, C, is just an adjustment to the phase to allow for different starting positions (that is, positions at time 0). Thus, for example, if one treats the starting position as $y = A$ (that is, the maximum displacement in what is treated as the positive direction of oscillation), then C is zero, and the displacement y is simply $A \cos{\omega t}$. If one treats the starting position as $y = 0$ (the equilibrium position, and also the position of maximum speed), then C is plus or minus $\pi/2$, depending on the direction of the motion at time 0. Of course, if $C = -\pi/2$, the displacement y can also be written $A \sin{\omega t}$ (since $\sin{\omega t} = \cos{(\omega t - \pi/2)}$).

There is a relationship between harmonic oscillation and circular motion. If a point moves anticlockwise in a circle with a constant speed, the angle between the radius to the moving point at time 0, and the radius to the moving point at time t, will be the phase ωt, where ω is the number of radians through which the radius to the point moves, per unit time. If the centre of the circle is taken as the origin, and the radius to the moving point at time 0 as lying along the positive y axis, and A is taken as the length of the radius, then the projection of the moving point on to the y axis is $A \cos \omega t$. Accordingly, one can consider harmonic oscillation as being a projection, on to the diameter of a circle, of a point moving at constant speed around that circle. Thus in Fig. 10.5 the point undergoing harmonic oscillation moves along the y axis

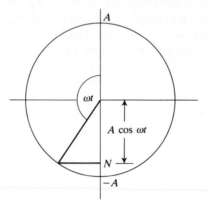

FIG. 10.5. Circular motion, harmonic motion, and phase

between $+A$ and $-A$. Its speed is $d/dt \, (A \cos \omega t)$, that is, $-A \sin \omega t$; and its acceleration is $-A\omega^2 \cos \omega t$. At points $+A$ and $-A$, its speed is zero, but its acceleration is at its maximum (plus or minus $A\omega^2$); while, at the origin, its speed is at its maximum (plus or minus $A\omega$), and its acceleration is zero. To picture harmonic oscillation in this way helps one understand the phase of such oscillation: in the diagram, when the phase is ωt as shown, the point undergoing simple harmonic motion is at position N, and moving in the negative y direction.

If harmonic oscillation is shown on a graph as a function of time, the graph is a sine or cosine wave, as shown in the previous section, but with the maximum and minimum values as A and $-A$ rather than 1 and -1.

Fig. 10.6 shows the graph of $A \cos \omega t$, being a graph for harmonic oscillation as a function of time t, with the position at time 0 being $y = A$. At time 0, the phase of the oscillation is 0. When y falls to zero (at time $\pi/2\omega$) the phase

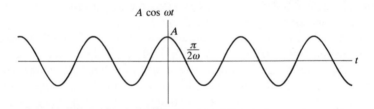

FIG. 10.6. A cosine wave of harmonic oscillation

is $\pi/2$; when it falls to $-A$, the phase is π; when it rises to 0, the phase is $3\pi/2$; and so on. The phase changes by 2π for each complete oscillation; the angular frequency ω of the oscillation, as noted earlier, is 2π times the frequency ($\omega = 2\pi\nu$).

10.2.4. Fourier Analysis

Just as harmonic oscillation through space of an object can be represented graphically as a sine or cosine wave, so also can harmonic oscillation in the one place of quantities such as air pressure, or intensity of an electric or magnetic field.

When a musical tone is sounded there is produced, at each location where the tone can be heard, a periodic variation in air pressure which is the physical basis of the sound. If the tone is pure, as from an ideal tuning-fork, the periodic variation can be represented graphically as a simple harmonic function; that is, a sine or cosine wave, like that shown above. The pitch of the tone corresponds to the frequency of the pressure variations. For middle C, the time from one peak pressure to the next (that is, the period of the oscillation and the 'wavelength' of the corresponding wave function) is about 1/264 seconds. So the frequency ν is about 264 Hz, and, as before, the angular frequency ω of the wave function is $2\pi\nu$. The loudness of the tone corresponds to the magnitude of the pressure changes, that is, to the amplitude A of the wave function.

1. Superposition of harmonic waves. Where the musical tone is not pure, it has another characteristic, namely its quality or 'sound', giving rise to the differences in sound between different musical instruments and between different voices. The physical basis of the tone is still a periodic variation in air pressure, but such variation is not such as can be represented by a simple harmonic function. Its graph as a periodic function of time may be as shown in Fig. 10.7. Moreover, according to what is sometimes referred to as Fourier's theorem, such a graph can be obtained by addition or superposition of graphs of simple harmonic functions.

If this periodic function repeats itself ν times per unit time (i.e. has frequency ν), it can be expressed as a sum or superposition of simple harmonic functions whose angular frequencies are ω, 2ω, 3ω, 4ω, etc., where $\omega = 2\pi\nu$. This means that if y is a periodic function which repeats ν times per unit time, then y has an expansion like:

$$y = A_1 \cos \omega t + A_2 \cos 2\omega t + \ldots$$

This does not cover every possible case, because the phases of the component simple harmonic functions may not coincide. However, instead of using functions like $\cos(\omega t + \theta_1)$, $\cos(2\omega t + \theta_1)$, etc., one can use the fact that $\cos(\omega t + \theta_1) = \cos\theta_1 \cos\omega t - \sin\theta_1 \sin\omega t$ to arrive at a completely general expansion, to cover all cases, as follows:

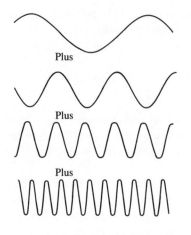

Plus

Plus

Plus

Equals

FIG. 10.7. A summation or superposition of waves

$$y = A_0 + A_1 \cos \omega t + B_1 \sin \omega t + A_2 \cos 2\omega t + B_2 \sin 2\omega t + \ldots$$

The term A_0 is inserted because, if only sines and cosines are used, the average value of the function for any whole number of wavelengths must be zero: I say more about this later.

In the case of musical sounds, the quality of sound of a musical tone is determined by the relative amounts or weighting of the various harmonics. As indicated previously, a tone with only the first harmonic is a pure tone (such as produced by an ideal tuning-fork); different musical instruments produce tones with different weightings of the second and higher harmonics. The sounds of different musical instruments can be produced by appropriate combinations of tuning-forks (or other instruments capable of producing pure tones) sounding at appropriate relative volumes, which together produce tones with the appropriate weighting of the various harmonics. This is the principle on which an electronic music synthesizer operates.

It can be shown that not merely functions for musical tones, but any periodic function which is continuous and has a single value for the dependent variable (y in the series given above) based on each value of the independent variable (t in the series given above), can be expressed as such a series (called a Fourier series). This is so, however jagged or irregular each period of the function may be. And the coefficients A_0, A_1, A_2, B_1, etc. can in all such cases be calculated in a way which I will discuss.

Even if the function is not periodic, it can still be expressed as such a series, with the total range or period of the independent variable giving the wavelength of the basic 'first harmonic' function. In some cases, one might wish to make the range of the independent variable infinite: in the case of sound and air pressure, one may wish, for example, to represent by the function that a particular sequence of sounds occurred over a particular period, and not at any other time during the history of the universe (considered as being infinite into the future, if not into the past). As the relevant period approaches infinity, the frequency and angular frequency of the first harmonic function approach zero; so at the limit the Fourier series, involving multiples of that angular frequency, becomes an integral. (I will illustrate this shortly in connection with Fourier transforms.) It may be that only a limited range of angular frequencies need be used, but within that range *all* angular frequencies must be used: the values of such angular frequencies must be continuous, not discrete, if the function is to represent an infinite period. To put this another way, if the values of angular frequencies used are discrete, then after some finite period the function will repeat: to prevent this, frequencies with a continuous range of values must be used.

2. Calculation of Fourier coefficients. It is possible, given a function (say, y as a function of t in the case of air pressure), to calculate the Fourier series. To make the discussion more general, it is better to represent the phase of the basic first harmonic function as θ (so that $\theta = \omega t$ in the air pressure case):

$$y = A_0 + A_1 \cos \theta + B_1 \sin \theta + A_2 \cos 2\theta + B_2 \sin 2\theta + \ldots$$

The coefficients can then be calculated as follows.

In order to find (say) A_2, one multiplies both sides by the harmonic function of which it is the coefficient, that is, by $\cos 2\theta$, and integrates both sides with respect to θ over a complete period (for example, from $\theta = -\pi$ to $\theta = \pi$); and then considers what happens to the various A and B terms. We saw in Section 10.1.1 that the integral of a function over a range, divided by the value of that range, gives the *average* of the function over that range: and it can be seen from Fig. 10.3 that the average (and therefore the integral) of any sine or cosine function over a range of 2π, or any multiple thereof, is zero.

Accordingly, looking first at the A_0 term, $\int_{-\pi}^{\pi} A_0 \cos 2\theta \, d\theta$ is zero. As regards the A_1 term, $\int_{-\pi}^{\pi} A_1 \cos \theta \cos 2\theta \, d\theta$ is similarly zero. This can be seen in the following way. From equation (10.4):

$$\cos \theta \cos 2\theta = 1/2 \ \cos(\theta + 2\theta) + 1/2 \ \cos(\theta - 2\theta)$$
$$= 1/2 \ (\cos 3\theta + \cos - \theta) .$$

As before, the average (and so the integral) of $\cos 3\theta$ and of $\cos(-\theta)$ from $\theta = -\pi$ to $\theta = \pi$ is zero.

However, as regards the A_2 term, the position is different:

$$\cos 2\theta \cos 2\theta = 1/2 \ (\cos 4\theta + \cos 0) .$$

The average of $\cos 4\theta$ from $\theta = -\pi$ to $\theta = \pi$ is zero; but $\cos 0$ is a constant (equal to 1), so its average is 1. Thus:

$$\int_{-\pi}^{\pi} \cos^2 2\theta \, d\theta = 2\pi \times 1/2 \times (0 + 1) = \pi .$$

The remaining A terms follow the discussion of the A_1 term. So far as the B terms are concerned, it can be seen that the average of $\sin(n\theta)\cos 2\theta$ from $\theta = -\pi$ to $\theta = \pi$ is zero, because $\sin(n\theta) = \cos(n\theta - \pi/2)$; so the discussion is essentially the same as for unequal cosines. Generally,

$$\int_{-\pi}^{\pi} \cos(m\theta)\cos(n\theta)\,d\theta \text{ is zero for } m \neq n, \text{ and } \pi \text{ for } m = n;$$

and

$$\int_{-\pi}^{\pi} \cos(m\theta)\sin(n\theta)\,d\theta \text{ is zero for either } m \neq n \text{ or } m = n.$$

Accordingly, after multiplication by $\cos 2\theta$ and integration from $\theta = -\pi$ to $\theta = \pi$, we have:

$$\int_{-\pi}^{\pi} \cos 2\theta\, y\, d\theta = \int_{-\pi}^{\pi} A_2 \cos^2 2\theta\, d\theta$$
$$= \pi A_2$$
$$\therefore A_2 = 1/\pi \int_{-\pi}^{\pi} \cos 2\theta\, y\, d\theta.$$

In a similar way, one can find A_1 by multiplying both sides by $\cos\theta$, and proceeding as before; B_1 by multiplying both sides by $\sin\theta$, and proceeding as before; B_2 by multiplying both sides by $\sin 2\theta$; and so on. It can be shown that generally:

$$A_n = 1/\pi \int_{-\pi}^{\pi} \cos(n\theta)\, y\, d\theta \qquad (10.8)$$

$$B_n = 1/\pi \int_{-\pi}^{\pi} \sin(n\theta)\, y\, d\theta. \qquad (10.9)$$

Since A_0 is the average of the function y, we have:

$$A_0 = 1/2\pi \int_{-\pi}^{\pi} y\, d\theta. \qquad (10.10)$$

So we can write:

$$y = A_0 + \Sigma A_n \cos(n\theta) + \Sigma B_n \sin(n\theta), \qquad (10.11)$$

where A_0, A_n, and B_n are as shown above.

3. Fourier transforms. The ideas discussed above are important in quantum mechanics. However, in considering wave functions in quantum mechanics, we will be dealing with cases where, although the independent variables (for which symbols such as x, y, p, and so on, are often used) are real, the function or dependent variable (for which symbols such as ψ, ϕ, and so on, are often used) are complex. An important case is where the complex function $\psi(x)$ is expressed as a Fourier series of complex exponential functions:

$$\psi(x) = \Sigma c_n \exp(ik_n x). \qquad (10.12)$$

Here, the Fourier coefficients c_n can be complex numbers, and this means that there is no need for two series of coefficients to deal with phase variations.

Each complex wave $\exp(ik_n x)$ in this series is equal to $(\cos k_n x + i \sin k_n x)$. One can visualize such elements by showing two separate graphs for the real and imaginary parts, as in Fig. 11.2; or (as suggested in Penrose 1989: 244–6) by combining them in a three-dimensional graph which can be visualized as a spiral or 'corkscrew' passing through an infinite succession of Argand planes, as shown in Fig. 10.8: the separate graphs are given by the projections from

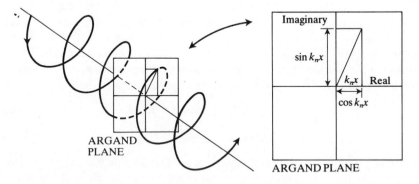

FIG. 10.8. A complex harmonic wave as a corkscrew through Argand planes

the spiral on to the planes constituted by the real and imaginary axes of the Argand planes.

A mathematical procedure which is particularly important in quantum mechanics is Fourier transformation; and in order to show its mathematical basis, one can proceed as follows. The different phase coefficients k_n are set at $2\pi n/L$, where L (which can be a multiple of 2π) is the total range or period of the function $\psi(x)$; that is, the range after which the function repeats; and n can take successive integer values (1, 2, 3, etc.), generally from $-\infty$ to $+\infty$. Then, if c_n is expressed in terms of another series of coefficients ϕ_n, where $c_n = \sqrt{(2\pi)}/L \ \phi_n$, we have:

$$\psi(x) = \sqrt{(2\pi)}/L \ \Sigma \ \phi_n \exp(ik_n x). \tag{10.13}$$

To calculate the coefficients ϕ_n, one proceeds in a somewhat similar way as before: one multiplies both sides in succession by $\exp(-ik_n x)$ for each value of n, and integrates with respect to x over the range of $\psi(x)$, that is, from $-L/2$ to $L/2$. As before, in each case, all terms on the right-hand side disappear, except for that whose coefficient corresponds to the respective value of n. So one has, for each n:

$$\int_{-L/2}^{L/2} \exp(-ik_n x) \ \psi(x) \ dx = (\sqrt{2\pi/L})(L/2\pi) \ \phi_n$$

$$\therefore \phi_n = 1/\sqrt{(2\pi)} \ \int_{-L/2}^{L/2} \exp(-ik_n x) \ \psi(x) \ dx. \tag{10.14}$$

Next, if we note that each increment in n (which can be written Δn) is 1 (since the n are just all the whole numbers), so that each increment in k (which can be written Δk) is $2\pi/L$ times Δn, or just $2\pi/L$, we can rewrite equation (10.13) as follows:

$$\psi(x) = \sqrt{(2\pi)}/L \quad \Sigma \, \phi_n \exp (ik_n x) \, (L/\, 2\pi) \, \Delta k$$
$$= 1/\sqrt{(2\pi)} \quad \Sigma \, \phi_n \exp (ik_n x) \, \Delta k \qquad (10.15)$$

Now, if we want $\psi(x)$ to have an infinite range (that is, if we do not want it to repeat), it is necessary to consider the limits of the equations (10.15) and (10.14) as the total range L of the function approaches ∞, that is, as Δk approaches zero. The summation in equation (10.15) becomes an integral, as mentioned in Section 10.1.1: the discrete numbers represented by ϕ_n become a continuous function $\phi(k)$, and the equations become respectively:

$$\psi(x) = 1/\sqrt{(2\pi)} \quad \int_{-\infty}^{\infty} \exp (ikx) \, \phi(k) \, dk \qquad (10.16)$$

$$\phi(k) = 1/\sqrt{(2\pi)} \quad \int_{-\infty}^{\infty} \exp (- ikx) \, \psi(x) \, dx. \qquad (10.17)$$

These important (and beautiful) equations are Fourier integrals, as mentioned earlier; and they are called Fourier transforms of each other. We will encounter them again in Section 11.2, where we will see that they can be used to transform a function of position (x) into a function of momentum ($\hbar k$, where $\hbar$ is Planck's constant divided by 2π).

10.2.5. *Travelling Waves*

So far, the wave functions considered have been for oscillations of position about a single point in space, or of intensity at a single point in space: these functions have had only one independent variable, generally time. Wave functions can also represent travelling waves, using two or more independent variables: if one is considering only a single dimension of travel, there are two independent variables, namely position in that dimension, and time. The function will then enable calculation of the value of the oscillation at any position in the dimension of travel, and at any time. If the oscillation at each point is a simple harmonic oscillation, and if at any time the values of oscillation along the dimension of travel form a simple harmonic wave, then the function of the travelling wave may be given by:

$$y = A \cos (\omega t - kx). \qquad (10.18)$$

Here x is the coordinate of the dimension of travel, and k is the (angular) wave number, that is, 2π times the number of oscillations (or wavelengths) per unit distance. As before, ω is the angular frequency, and t the time. I have included no constants, because I am assuming that the coordinate system is arranged so that the value of the oscillation of y at $t = 0$ and $x = 0$ is A. At any particular value of x (say $x = 0$), y as a function of t will behave as discussed earlier. At any particular time (say $t = 0$), y as a function of x will have the familiar shape of a simple harmonic wave, as shown in Fig. 10.9. y will reduce to zero when $kx = \pi/2$, that is, when $x = \pi/2k$. A complete cycle will occur each time kx increases by 2π, that is, each time x increases by $2\pi/k$.

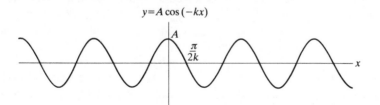

$$y = A \cos(-kx)$$

FIG. 10.9. A simple harmonic travelling wave

The velocity of the wave (that is, the rate of change of x with respect to t, for any constant value of y, such as the peak of the wave at $y = A$) is ω/k: since for constant y, $(\omega t - kx)$ is constant. Since $\omega = 2\pi\nu$ (ν being the frequency), and $k = 2\pi/\lambda$ (λ being the wavelength), the velocity of the wave (ω/k) equals $\nu\lambda$, which is to be expected: each oscillation moves the wave one wavelength, so the speed of the wave must be the wavelength times the number of oscillations per unit of time. This is sometimes called the phase velocity, to distinguish it from what is called the group velocity, which I referred to in connection with de Broglie, but which will not concern us further.

This function represents a wave whose amplitude does not diminish with travel. In physical situations such as the propagation of sound or electromagnetic radiation, the amplitude of the associated wave does diminish as it travels from the source, as it spreads in space. At a sufficient distance from the source, however, the rate of spreading (and therefore the diminution in amplitude) becomes small compared to the wavelength: at such a distance, the wavefront is very nearly a plane. Waves whose wavefront moves as a plane are called plane waves; and sound-waves and electromagnetic waves, at a sufficient distance from the source, can be considered as plane waves.

The wave function $y = A \cos(\omega t - kx)$ can represent the intensity of sound or of electromagnetic radiation spreading in the x direction as a plane wave, that is, sufficiently far from the source. In either case, it must be the result of a simple harmonic oscillation at the source, such as a tuning-fork (for sound) or a charge oscillating harmonically at right angles to the x direction (for electromagnetism). In quantum mechanics, plane waves are used to represent particles which have definite momenta; but such plane waves are complex, having both a real and an imaginary part. They are therefore written, not in terms of $\cos(\omega t - kx)$, but rather of $\exp[i(\omega t - kx)]$, as follows:

$$\psi = N \exp[i(\omega t - kx)]. \tag{10.19}$$

In the more general case, where the oscillation of the source is more complicated, the function of the travelling wave will be more complicated. However, just as the intensity of complicated oscillations in one place can be analysed as sums or superpositions of harmonic oscillations, so also complicated travelling waves can be represented as sums or superpositions of harmonic travelling waves.

In the cases of sound and of electromagnetism, the speed of travel in air is very nearly independent of frequency; and if one can disregard any small dependence on frequency, it can be shown from the laws of mechanics (in the case of sound) and from the laws of electromagnetism, that the function describing a plane wave (of sound or electromagnetism) moving in the x direction satisfies the equation

$$d^2y/dx^2 = 1/c^2 \; d^2y/dt^2,$$

where y is the intensity of the wave, and c is the phase velocity in the x direction. One solution to this equation is $y = A \cos(\omega t - kx)$, where $c = \omega/k$. ω and k can take different values (for different frequencies), maintaining this relationship with c; and A can take any value.

Now the equation $d^2y/dx^2 = 1/c^2 \; d^2y/dt^2$ is linear in x: that is, if y_1 and y_2 are solutions, so also is $y_1 + y_2$. Accordingly, if $y = A_1 \cos(\omega_1 t - k_1 x)$ and $y = A_2 \cos(\omega_2 t - k_2 x)$ are solutions, then so also is $y = A_1 \cos(\omega_1 t - k_1 x) + A_2 \cos(\omega_2 t - k_2 x)$. This is consistent with my assertion that complicated travelling waves can be represented by superpositions of harmonic travelling waves.

10.3. Probability

One other mathematical idea which is important in quantum mechanics is probability.

10.3.1. *A Definition*

The mathematics of probability is elaborate, and widely accepted. However, there is no widely accepted definition of just what probability is.

I will take it that probability can be considered as a numerical relationship between one set of events and/or states of affairs which are known and/or determined and/or specified and/or actual (which I will call the known) and another set of events and/or states of affairs which are unknown and/or uncertain and/or unspecified and/or future (which I will call the unknown). I will take this relationship to involve the following:

1. If, given the known, the unknown is certain or determined, the probability of the latter with respect to the former is 1.

2. If, given the known, the unknown is precluded, the probability of the latter with respect to the former is 0.

3. If, given the known, the unknown is certain or determined to be one (but not both) of two possibilities; and there is, in the known, rational basis for not believing (and no rational basis for believing) that the unknown is or will be a particular one rather than the other; then the probability of each with respect to the known is 1/2 or 0.5.

4. Generalizing (3), if, given the known, the unknown is certain or determined to be one (but not more) of y possibilities; and there is, in the known, rational basis for not believing (and no rational basis for believing) that it is or will be a particular one rather than any other; then the probability, with respect to the known, of the unknown being one or other of any x of such possibilities is x/y.

As an example of (3), if a fair coin is tossed, the probability of either heads or tails is 1/2. As examples of (4), if a fair six-sided die is thrown, the probability of any one number is 1/6; while if two fair six-sided dice are thrown, the probability of various possible totals is as shown in Table 10.1.

TABLE 10.1

Total	No. of ways	Probability
2	1	1/36
3	2	1/18
4	3	1/12
5	4	1/9
6	5	5/36
7	6	1/6
8	5	5/36
9	4	1/9
10	3	1/12
11	2	1/18
12	1	1/36

The respective probabilities in this table are arrived at as follows. There are 36 different possible results of the throw, since each of six different results of one die could be combined with any one of six different results of the other. Each of the 36 is equally probable (as discussed above) with respect to the known. However, some different results give the same totals: for example, 6 is given by five different results, namely 1 and 5, 5 and 1, 2 and 4, 4 and 2, and 3 and 3. In the table, the totals in the first column can be given respectively by the number of different results shown in the second column: the second column gives the number of different ways in which each total can be produced. The probability for each total is arrived at by dividing the number of different results which give that total, by the overall number of possible results (36). The total of the probabilities is 1, because it is certain that one or other of the totals in the first column will be given.

The above is sufficient to give a meaning to any probability expressed as a rational number. Any probability which can be expressed as a fraction x/y can be said to be the same as that probability which exists for the unknown being one or other of x possibilities out of a total of y possibilities, all of which are equally probable (as discussed above) with respect to the known. So, for example, if something is said to have the probability 5/36 with respect to the known, this means that it has the *same* probability as does (say) obtaining a total of 6 in throwing two fair six-sided dice.

In the case of probabilities not expressed as fractions (i.e. those expressed as irrational numbers), these cannot simply be equated with probabilities as defined above. However, one can find two fractions very close to, and spanning, any irrational number; and can then say that the probability shown by the irrational number is that probability which is greater than the lower fraction and also less than the greater fraction. In that way, one can give meaning to any irrational probability, to any desired degree of approximation.

What then do probabilities convey?

Clearly probabilities 1 and 0 convey respectively that, given the known, the unknown is certain or precluded. Any number between 0 and 1 conveys that the unknown is neither certain nor precluded; that is, that it is possible, given the known. The size of the number between 0 and 1 gives some measure of the degree of belief or assurance which an observer, who is aware of the known, may reasonably have in the existence or happening of the unknown. Thus, for example, a probability of 1/2 for the unknown tells us that, given the known, it is objectively reasonable to have the same expectation for the unknown as for the result 'heads' in a single toss of a fair coin.

Very importantly, for our purposes, probabilities also have a statistical significance. If the circumstances constituting the known are repeated a large number of times, and the unknown ascertained on each occasion, then the statistics of these experiments should approximately reflect the relevant probability. Thus, if two dice are thrown 36 000 times, one would expect the total 12 (or 2) to appear something like 1 000 times, 6 (or 8) something like 5 000 times, and so on.

Many definitions of probability are more subjective than my suggestion (in that they refer to expectation or belief), and/or depend on statistical ideas, and/or are circular (using words such as 'probable' or 'likely': see e.g. Feynman *et al.* 1963, vol. i, ch. 6). I have attempted to make my definition as objective as possible, because in quantum physics probability seems to be objective. The subjective element in my account, namely the use of 'rational basis for not believing (and no rational basis for believing)' is, I think, unavoidable. I have also attempted to give probability some meaning for *single* events, because, although in general probabilities greater than 0 and less than 1 are manifested as differing from each other only as statistical effects over many events, quantum physics (on one view at least) asserts probabilities in relation to single events.

In some classical physics, probability could only be seen as depending on a limited viewpoint, as, for example, reflecting limited knowledge of the facts. Even the result of tossing a coin, on some views, is a matter of probability only because all relevant factors are not (cannot be, as a practical matter) known in sufficient detail. As we will see, some views of quantum physics (those which postulate 'hidden variables') take a similar approach. My account of probability can be used with such an approach (because 'the known' may be less than all there is to know), but is not limited to it: my account still applies if 'the known' is *all* there is to know.

10.3.2. *Statistical Considerations*

The mathematics of probability gives information about the probabilities of the spread of actual results about those numbers which precisely reflect the initial probability: this can often be represented graphically as a bell-shaped curve, known as a Gaussian distribution. This is in fact the spread to be expected in relation to all random processes. Barrow and Silk write:

If you went out into the street and gathered information for a long period of time, say, on the height of everyone passing by, you would inevitably find that a graph of the number of persons versus height would result in a characteristic bell shape called the 'normal', or Gaussian, distribution by statisticians. . . . This curve is characteristic of the frequency of occurrence of all truly random processes, whatever their specific origin. The resulting curves differ only in their width and the mean on which they are centered. (Barrow and Silk 1984: 214)

If, in particular cases, one does not find statistical results which approximate those predicted in this way, this is an indication that the probability assigned is incorrect. If one had assigned probabilities on the ground that there was no rational basis in the known for believing the unknown to be one possibility rather than another, one would need to re-examine this: for example, one might question whether a die being thrown was a fair die.

If one threw two dice on a large number (N) of occasions, one could derive a mean or average (A) of the totals obtained, which would be as follows:

$$A = (n_1 2 + n_2 3 + \ldots + n_{11} 12)/N.$$

Here, n_1, n_2, etc. are the number of times when the totals 2, 3, etc. were respectively obtained, with $n_1 + n_2 + \ldots + n_{11}$ equalling N. One would expect the ratios n_1/N, n_2/N, etc. to be roughly equal to the probabilities of the respective results; and one can accordingly identify an expectation value for A (written $\langle A \rangle$) arrived at as follows:

$$\langle A \rangle = 2(1/36) + 3(1/18) + \ldots + 12(1/36).$$

Here $\langle A \rangle$ is 7 because, apart from 7 itself, the components comprise pairs of totals with equal probability and averaging 7 (for example, 2 and 12, each with probability 1/36; and 3 and 11, each with probability 1/18).

More generally, if one is dealing with a case where there are N possible unknowns that are themselves numbers (say A_1, A_2 ... A_n), and where the probabilities of the unknowns are respectively c_1, c_2, ..., c_n, an expectation value $\langle A \rangle$ can be defined as follows:

$$\langle A \rangle = c_1 A_1 + c_2 A_2 + \ldots + c_n A_n. \tag{10.20}$$

In a large number of experiments, in each of which the known is produced and the unknown ascertained, the average of the results could be expected to approximate to $\langle A \rangle$ (with the total of the results of N experiments approximating to $N\langle A \rangle$).

One can also identify a number which gives an impression of the *spread* of the results. A possible way to do this would be to find the average of the absolute values of the deviations of the actual results from the average result (which involves changing the sign of negative deviations). However, the number generally adopted to indicate the spread of results is slightly more complicated than this: it is the square root of the average of the squares of such deviations. It is called the root-mean-square (rms) deviation. It is used because it has certain advantages over a simple average deviation, one of which is that there is no need to worry about changing the sign of negative deviations: all squares of deviations will be positive. The rms deviation also indicates a spread which includes more of the results than would an average deviation.

The expectation value of the rms deviation (which I will write ΔA), in my general example, will be given by the following:

$$(\Delta A)^2 = c_1(A_1 - \langle A \rangle)^2 + c_2(A_2 - \langle A \rangle)^2 + \ldots + c_n(A_n - \langle A \rangle)^2.$$

It turns out that the right-hand side is equal to $\langle A^2 \rangle - \langle A \rangle^2$, where $\langle A^2 \rangle$ is the expectation value of the squares of the results. This can be shown as follows. Writing the right-hand side as $\Sigma c_n (A_n - \langle A \rangle)^2$, we have:

$$\begin{aligned}
\Sigma c_n (A_n - \langle A \rangle)^2 &= \Sigma c_n A_n^2 - 2\langle A \rangle \Sigma c_n A_n + \langle A \rangle^2 \Sigma c_n \\
&= \langle A^2 \rangle - 2\langle A \rangle\langle A \rangle + \langle A \rangle^2 \\
&= \langle A^2 \rangle - \langle A \rangle^2 \\
\therefore \Delta A &= \sqrt{(\langle A^2 \rangle - \langle A \rangle^2)}. \tag{10.21}
\end{aligned}$$

This result is another advantage of the use of the rms deviation: such deviation is simply the square root of the difference between the average of the squares and the square of the average.

Sometimes the unknowns, that is the possible results of experiments in each of which the known is produced, are not a finite number of discrete alternatives, but, rather, can fall anywhere within a continuous range. In such a case, the probability may be represented by a function of a variable representing the unknown: thus, $P(x)$ may be the probability function concerning an unknown x. The probability of x taking any *particular* value will be zero (because the number of possible values is infinite), but there will be a finite probability of x falling between any two values, for example, within the range x_1 to x_2. This probability is given by the integral of the function between those two values: $\int f(x) \, dx$ from x_1 to x_2.

11

The Quantum Mechanical State

As we saw, in classical physics the 'state' of a particle, at any particular time, is taken to involve a definite position in space and a definite motion; and the state of a system of particles is taken to involve a definite position in space and a definite motion for each of the particles.

For the purposes of making calculations, such quantities, or 'observables', as position and momentum can be represented mathematically by symbols indicating variable scalar and vector quantities. The state of a particle, so far as position and motion is concerned, may be represented by the vector **r** (or coordinates x, y, and z) representing position; and the vector **v** representing velocity (or **p** representing momentum). If the magnitude and direction of these vectors for a particle in relation to a given coordinate system is known, then its state (so far as position and motion is concerned) is known. The particle actually *has* the position and motion indicated, and the vectors correctly represent or indicate the position and motion.

Furthermore, the actual value of each of these vectors can be ascertained by measurement to arbitrary accuracy. If calculations are correctly made on the basis of such measured values, then results can be arrived at representing a state different from that measured; and there is *certainty* that measurement of the calculated state would, to an accuracy related to the accuracy of the original measurement, coincide with the result of the calculation.

The situation in relation to quantum mechanics is completely different. As in classical physics, calculations can be made concerning the position and motion of a particle, such as an electron, a proton, or a neutron. And, as in classical physics, for the purpose of these calculations there is a mathematical representation of the 'state' of a particle, which relates to the quantities or 'observables' of position and momentum. However, this representation is not by means of symbols for scalar or vector quantities which directly indicate position and momentum: it is by a more complex mathematical object, the nature of which I will discuss shortly.

Furthermore, this mathematical object does not indicate or represent position or motion in any direct way: what it does in substance is to enable calculation of the probability of the particle in question being found to have a position or momentum (to a greater or lesser degree of precision) *if* an appropriate measurement is made. What if anything this mathematical object actually represents, in the absence of any measurement being made (that is, what the quantum physical state *really is*) is a matter of controversy, as we will see: certainly, however, it does *not* represent a particle having a definite position and motion as contemplated by classical physics and common-sense views of the world. And this is not to say that the mathematical object is in any sense incomplete: the view generally accepted by physicists is that it contains all the information which there can be concerning the particle's position and motion.

11.1. Representation of the State of One Particle

There are alternative versions of quantum mechanics, which use different mathematical objects to represent the quantum mechanical state of a particle; but these objects are in substance equivalent to each other. The mathematical object which has general application to all kinds of quantum mechanical states is called a vector or a state vector. Such vectors are not of the type previously discussed, namely quantities involving magnitude and direction in ordinary three-dimensional space. Rather, they are an elaborate mathematical extension of such ordinary three-dimensional vectors: as we will see, their 'magnitudes' (and particularly their 'inner products') involve complex numbers; and their 'directions' are in a fictional space which may be of infinite dimensions.

I will commence, however, by considering a more familiar mathematical object which is often used to represent the state of an electron and/or a nuclear particle, namely a function (called a state function, or wave function). This is often represented by the symbol ψ, the Greek letter psi.

We have seen that a function can be regarded as a set of rules for deriving a quantity or value from each possible value of one or more variables. A state function in quantum physics is a *complex* function of *real* variables: that is, the quantities on which the rules operate are real, but the rules are such that the quantity derived by application of such rules is generally complex. It is often called a wave function, because it has a periodic wavelike character, and can generally be considered as the sum or superposition of simple harmonic waves.

The real variables in question will often be variables representing position and a variable representing time. In this chapter, I will consider a state function as representing a quantum physical state *at a particular time*; and for such a function time is not treated as a variable. Thus the function at a particular time may be a function of position coordinates (x, y, and/or z) or of a position vector ($\mathbf{r}$). For the most part, I will deal with the function as a function of one position coordinate only: the same discussion will apply separately to each dimension, and in some situations calculations can be made separately in relation to each dimension. Alternatively, with somewhat more sophisticated mathematics, calculations can be made with coordinates of three dimensions at once, or with a position vector; but we will not need to consider this.

A state function can also be expressed as a function of momentum (either components of momentum on the x, y, and/or z axis or a momentum vector **p**). As we will see, momentum in quantum mechanics is not simply mass times velocity (as in classical mechanics), in particular because velocity has no straightforward counterpart at the micro level in quantum mechanics. However, momentum in quantum mechanics has similarities to momentum in classical mechanics, *inter alia* in its relation to energy.

Taking the state function to be a function of position, one can calculate the value of the function for any position (that is, in the one-dimensional case we are considering, for any value of the x coordinate) by applying the rules of the function to this value of the x coordinate. What the state function of a particle then indicates is as follows. In relation to those values of x for which the value of the function is zero (i.e. where $\psi(x) = 0$), there is no possibility that the particle represented by the state function would be found, by a measurement of position, to be in a position with any of those x coordinates. In relation to those values of x for which the value of function is not zero, it is certain that the particle would be found, by an appropriate measurement of position, to be in a position with an x coordinate somewhere or other within those values.

Where the function is not zero, its value $\psi(x)$ will generally be a complex number. This number can be called the amplitude (or probability amplitude) of the wave function at the x coordinate in question. Like any complex number, it can be expressed in the form $Ne^{i\theta}$, where N is the modulus and θ the argument of the complex number. The absolute square of this complex number (i.e. $|\psi(x)|^2$), which is the same as the square of the modulus (N^2), has the following physical significance: it is proportional to the probability that the particle would be found, by a position measurement, to be in a position with that x coordinate. The other part of the complex number, $e^{i\theta}$, is called the phase factor. It has no immediate physical significance, but is of importance in relation to calculations where wave functions have to be added to each other: it affects the interference of such functions.

The absolute square of the amplitude I have said to be 'proportional to the probability': to assign a number to the probability, which must, of course, be positive and less than or equal to 1, some further procedures are necessary. Generally, the state function of a particle does not indicate a finite number of discrete positions where the particle may be found: rather, it indicates a continuous range of positions, anywhere within which the particle could be found by a position measurement. Thus, the state function generally indicates an infinite number of possible positions, so that the probability of finding the particle at any precisely defined position will generally be zero. What one can calculate from the state function is the probability for the particle to be found within any small part of the possible range; and this is done by integrating the

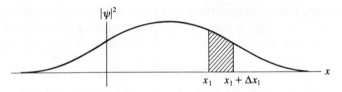

FIG. 11.1. The integral of a probability function from x_1 to $x_1 + \Delta x_1$

function which expresses probability as a function of x (i.e. $|\psi(x)|^2$) over the part of the range in question (say from x_1 to $x_1 + \Delta x_1$). Graphically, this gives the area under the curve of the function $|\psi(x)|^2$ over this part of the range, as illustrated in Fig.11.1. The shaded area is given by $\int |\psi(x)|^2 dx$ from x_1 to $x_1 + \Delta x_1$, which I will call $P(\Delta x_1)$. The total area under the curve is $\int_{-\infty}^{\infty} |\psi(x)|^2 dx$, which I will call P (all x): it represents the probability that the particle will be found to have an x coordinate somewhere between $x = -\infty$ and $x = \infty$, if an appropriate position measurement is made. Now since the particle must be found somewhere, P (all x) should be equal to 1. If in any calculation it turns out not to equal 1, the state function must be adjusted to ensure that it does equal 1: for example, if P (all x) turns out to be 10, then the state function must be divided by $\sqrt{10}$. This is called normalization. Assuming the function has been normalized, then $P(\Delta x_1)$ will be the probability that the particle would be found to have its x coordinate within Δx_1, if a position measurement were made.

This process of integration (finding the area under the curve of the probability function) is necessary because the state function indicates a range of positions, anywhere within which the particle could be found by a position measurement. As we will see, in the case of some other observables, the state function may indicate instead a finite number of discrete possible values: there are then probability amplitudes $(c_1, c_2, \ldots, c_n)$ and accordingly probabilities $(|c_1|^2, |c_2|^2, \ldots, |c_n|^2)$ for such values $(a_1, a_2, \ldots, a_n)$ which do not form a continuous function (as did $|\psi(x)|^2$, the probability function for position). And, so long as the state function is normalized, so that $\Sigma |c_n|^2$ (that is, the sum of the probabilities $|c_1|^2 + |c_2|^2 + \ldots + |c_n|^2$) equals 1, the probability that the observable will be found by appropriate measurement to have the value a_n (say) will be simply $|c_n|^2$. Integration is not necessary.

Generally, for momentum as for position the state function is considered as indicating a range of possible values. The amplitude or probability amplitude for any particular momentum p in the x direction can be found from the state function $\psi(x)$ (expressed as a function of position) by a process based on Fourier analysis. By this means, the state represented by $\psi(x)$ can be represented by a function of momentum rather than position, which can be written $\phi(k)$ (where $p = \hbar k$). I will discuss how this is done in the next section. Two things should be noted here: first, that these two functions are different representations of the same state, each containing all the same information in a different form; and secondly, that the amplitude of the function of momentum has (for momentum) the same significance as the amplitude of the function of position has (for position). That is, in relation to those values of momentum p for which the amplitude $\phi(k) = 0$, there is no possibility that the particle would be found, by a measurement of momentum in the x direction, to have any of those values of momentum in that direction. In relation to any value of p for which $\phi(k) \neq 0$, the amplitude of $\psi(k)$ will generally be a complex number; and the absolute square of the amplitude is proportional to the probability that the particle would be found, by a measurement of momentum in the x direction, to have that value of momentum in the x direction.

Consistently with the above discussion (and generalizing to three dimensions), the state function of a particle will generally not give a definite position or a definite momentum for the particle. It will generally contain the information that the probability of finding the particle in some volume(s) of space is zero, and (consistently) that the probability of finding it by measurement of position within the totality of the remaining volume(s) of space is 1, a certainty. It will give the probability (above zero, not more than 1) of finding it, by a position measurement, within any selected volume within such remaining volume(s). The same (*mutatis mutandis*) applies to momentum.

The state function for a particle *can* assume a form which gives certainty as to a precise position; that is, it can indicate probability 1 of finding the particle, by a position measurement, in a precise location. A function in this form is called the Dirac delta function, which is written $\delta(x - x_1)$, and which has the following properties:

$$\delta(x - x_1) \quad = 0 \quad \text{for } x \neq x_1$$
$$\int_a^b \delta(x - x_1)\, dx = 1 \quad \text{for any } a < x_1 < b.$$

It is not a function as usually understood, but it has the properties necessary to indicate that a measurement of position is certain to locate the particle at x_1.

However, the state function in this form will give equal probability to finding the particle with any momentum whatsoever in the x direction. Similarly, the state function for a particle can assume a form which gives certainty in relation to precise momentum (a form discussed in the next section); but, if so, it will give equal probability to finding the particle in any position in space whatsoever. That is, if the state function is such as to give absolute determinacy to position (or momentum, as the case may be) on the one hand, then it is such as to make momentum (or position) on the other hand wholly indeterminate.

Indeed, the nature of the mathematical objects used to represent the quantum mechanical state of a particle is such that it can be shown that there is a reciprocal relationship between the determinacy or certainty of the position of a particle as disclosed by such a mathematical object, and the determinacy or certainty of its momentum as so disclosed. It can be proved that if the state function shows that the position of a particle will be found on measurement to be within a volume, any one dimension of which is Δx, and that its momentum in the same direction as Δx will be found on measurement to lie within a range Δp, then:

$$\Delta x \Delta p \geqslant \sim h.$$

This is an expression of Heisenberg's uncertainty principle. Broadly, it asserts that the uncertainty of position of a particle in any direction times the uncertainty of its momentum in the same direction always exceeds a quantity of the scale of Planck's constant h (which as we saw is a very small quantity of action, namely about 6.6×10^{-34} joule seconds). Thus, consistently with the prior discussion, nil uncertainty in relation to one involves infinite uncertainty in relation to the other. However, because h is so small, it is possible to have very small uncertainty in relation to both: although, as noted in Section 9.4, in relation to particles such as electrons the uncertainty can be significant.

It should be noted carefully that the uncertainty principle follows mathematically from the mathematics of quantum mechanics, and in particular from the nature of the mathematical representation of the state of a particle. It is a necessary consequence of the quantum theory itself. It is not, as some discussions might suggest, merely a practical consequence of the disturbance caused to a particle by measuring its position or momentum. Of course, such practical considerations relating to measurement are important in relation to the uncertainty principle: if it were possible simultaneously to measure the position and momentum of a particle to a greater degree of accuracy than permitted by the uncertainty principle, this would indicate either that the quantum theory was incorrect, or at least that it was incomplete.

This is the reason why thought experiments concerning practicalities of measurement, such as those suggested by Heisenberg, and those discussed by Einstein and Bohr, were so significant. It was perceived that the quantum theory would be damaged if it could be shown that measurement conflicting with the uncertainty principle was possible. In so far as the thought experiments suggested that such measurement was not possible, these thought experiments protected the quantum theory.

Before proceeding to consider more closely wave functions for single particles, I should note that, following Heisenberg and Bohr, I am assuming that the formalism of quantum physics *does* refer to single particles. There is another view, which I will refer to again in Section 14.5, that quantum physics only deals with 'ensembles' of large numbers of particles or 'systems'; but I think that the view I am presenting is more generally accepted, and I think it is the preferable view.

11.2. The Wave Function of a Single Particle

Understanding how a state function of a particle operates is assisted by a closer consideration of the wave functions used to represent states of a particle, such as an electron. I will continue for the most part to limit the discussion to one dimension.

11.2.1. *Harmonic Waves*

It will be remembered that de Broglie associated particles with waves in accordance with the following relation:

Wavelength (λ) = Planck's constant (h)/momentum (p).

Experiments confirm that an electron having momentum p exhibits behaviour consistent with association with a wave of wavelength λ, equal to h/p. For this discussion, it is convenient to work with additional symbols, introduced in Section 10.2, in particular k and ω; and also with the symbol $\hbar$. k is the symbol for what is called the wave number or angular wave number (or, in vector form, the wave vector), and is equal in magnitude to 2π divided by the wavelength λ. ω is the symbol for the angular frequency of the wave, which is the frequency of the wave multiplied by 2π. $\hbar$ is Planck's constant h, divided by 2π. Thus:

$$p = h/\lambda = hk/2\pi = \hbar k.$$

Then, if a particle such as an electron were to have a constant precise momentum p in the x direction, it would be appropriate to represent it by a function for a simple harmonic plane wave moving in the x direction with wave number k and angular frequency ω. For the purposes of quantum mechanics, the wave function has to be complex. As we saw in equation (10.19), such a wave is represented by the following function ψ (expressed as a function of the position coordinate x and time t):

$$\psi(x,t) = N \exp[i(kx - \omega t)].$$

N is a constant, representing the amplitude of the wave. As we will see, it has no physical significance, except where wave functions are combined or superposed. This function gives certainty regarding momentum: it conveys that if the momentum of the particle in the x direction is measured, it will be found to be $\hbar k$ with probability 1, that is, with certainty.

At any particular time (say, time $t = 0$) this function is a function of x alone, $\psi = N \exp(ikx)$ [$= N(\cos kx + i \sin kx)$]. It is a complex function, comprising a real part, which can be written $[R]\psi$, and an imaginary part, which can be written $[I]\psi$. These parts may be graphically represented as shown in Fig. 11.2. As mentioned in Section 10.2.4, one can visualize a combination of

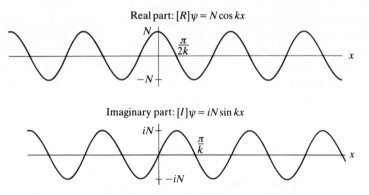

Real part: $[R]\psi = N \cos kx$

Imaginary part: $[I]\psi = iN \sin kx$

FIG. 11.2. The real and imaginary parts of complex harmonic wave

these graphs, in three dimensions, as a corkscrew passing through a succession of Argand planes.

The amplitude of the wave for any coordinate x on the x axis is $N \exp(ikx)$, so (from the previous discussion) the probability of finding the particle to have such a coordinate by a measurement of position is proportional to $| N \exp(ikx) |^2$, that is to N^2. This probability does not depend at all on the value of x, but, rather, is equal for all x. Therefore, consistently with what was said before, it is possible that the particle could be found by measurement to have any x coordinate, and the probability is the same for all positions in the x direction. This is because the momentum p is precise: certainty in relation to momentum involves total uncertainty in relation to position.

Where the momentum p is not precise, so that the particle could on measurement be found to have some momentum p_n within a range of possible momenta, the state function of the particle could be expressed as a weighted sum or superposition of the harmonic wave functions associated with all such possible momenta. It could take the form:

$$\psi(x) = \Sigma\, c_n \exp(ik_n x). \qquad (11.1)$$

Here, the k_ns are the different values of k associated with the possible different values p_n of p, and the c_ns are numbers giving the weighting (or probability amplitudes) for the different simple harmonic waves and the associated momenta.

As was noted in the previous section, generally the state function is considered as indicating a *continuous* range for possible momenta, so that the state function should not be expressed as a sum (as above) but, rather, as an integral. However, it is helpful to consider it as a sum, and indeed it may even be strictly correct: if the universe is finite, the maximum wavelength λ in the x direction will be the distance L required to circle the universe in that direction; and, according to Fourier analysis, any function of x could then be expressed as a weighted sum of simple harmonic functions $\exp(ik_n x)$, where

$k_n = 2\pi n/L$. Such a function would repeat after distance L, but this in the circumstances would be appropriate: $L + x$ would indicate the same position on the x axis as x. On this approach, momentum in the x direction could only take discrete values $\hbar k_n$ (n being an integer, and k_n being $2\pi n/L$), though the intervals between the values of k_n (namely $2\pi/L$) is *very* small. The state function is then $\Sigma\, c_n \exp(ik_n x)$, where from equation (10.14):

$$c_n = 1/\sqrt{(2\pi)} \ \int_{-\infty}^{\infty} \exp(-ik_n x)\, \psi(x)\, dx. \tag{11.2}$$

That is, the c_ns are the coefficients indicated by Fourier analysis. It will be seen that if one writes $\exp(ik_n x)$ as $\psi_n(x)$, then these coefficients take the general form $\int \psi_n^*(x)\, \psi(x)\, dx$: in fact, the form $\int \psi_n^*(x)\, \psi(x)\, dx$, called the overlap integral, and written (ψ_n, ψ), is of general application in quantum mechanics, as giving the amplitude for the state represented by the function $\psi(x)$ to be found by appropriate measurement to be in the state represented by the function $\psi_n(x)$.

The more usual approach is to treat L as infinite, and so to treat the k_ns as being continuous. Then, as we saw in Section 10.2, $\psi(x)$ becomes the integral:

$$\psi(x) = 1/\sqrt{(2\pi)} \ \int_{-\infty}^{\infty} \exp(ikx)\, \phi(k)\, dk.$$

As we also saw in Section 10.2, it can be shown that:

$$\phi(k) = 1/\sqrt{(2\pi)} \ \int_{-\infty}^{\infty} \exp(-ikx)\, \psi(x)\, dx.$$

The last two equations are the same Fourier transforms as given in equations (10.16) and (10.17). The latter gives k (and therefore momentum $p = \hbar k$) as a function of x, from which probability amplitudes for different values of momentum can be calculated, as discussed in Section 11.1.

11.2.2. *Superposition and Interference*

Now let us return to the view of a wave function $\psi(x)$ as a sum or superposition of a finite number of harmonic wave functions (each of which would represent a particle with a definite momentum along the x axis of $p_n = \hbar k_n$). Suppose that the component wave functions are associated with momenta lying within the range Δp, and that their wave numbers lie within a corresponding range Δk. Such a wave function at a particular time could be expressed as in equation (11.1):

$$\psi(x) = \Sigma\, c_n \exp(ik_n x).$$

The weighting factors c_n will generally be complex. However, it will be recalled that any complex number can be expressed in the form $re^{i\theta}$, where r is the modulus and θ the argument of the complex number. Further, to multiply a harmonic wave function $\exp(ik_n x)$ by $e^{i\theta}$ merely shifts the phase to

$$[R]\psi_n = a \cos k_n x$$

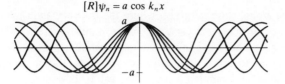

FIG. 11.3. Interference of harmonic waves

$\exp(ik_n x + i\theta)$; and this in turn can be represented graphically simply by moving the wave sideways to the extent of $\theta/2\pi$ of one wavelength. Thus, to multiply a harmonic wave function by a complex number c $(= re^{i\theta})$ alters the amplitude of the function by a factor of r (the modulus) and shifts the phase by θ (the argument).

Accordingly, the coefficients c_n may be considered as being real numbers a_n multiplied by phase factors $\exp(i\theta_n)$. If, as may be the case, the phases of all the component waves coincide at some point in the x direction, then one can choose a coordinate system such that $x = 0$ at this point: one can then disregard these phase factors altogether, and the real part of each harmonic wave will be just $a_n \cos k_n x$, and the imaginary part $a_n i \sin k_n x$. Although generally the a_ns will range from a minimum at the extremities of the wave numbers to a maximum around the mean of such numbers, the general effect of a superposition of such waves can be seen most clearly by means of a graph showing a number of such waves with equal amplitudes and with phases coinciding at $x = 0$. Then, the real part of such waves could be represented as in Fig. 11.3 (I show only a small number within a range). It will be seen that at $x = 0$, all the components are at the maximum value a; and that, on either side, their value drops off at differing rates: so that, when the components are added, there is maximum reinforcement (or constructive interference) at $x = 0$. From the point where the wave with the shortest wavelength crosses the x axis, generally some of the components are negative, and some positive; so that when the components are added there is some destructive interference. At some distance on either side, the components tend to cancel each other out.

The real part of the combined wave function produced by adding the superposed waves (which can be written $[R]\psi$ or $[R]\,\Sigma\psi_n$) could look like Fig. 11.4.

$$[R]\psi$$

$$[R]\psi = \Sigma a_n \cos k_n x$$

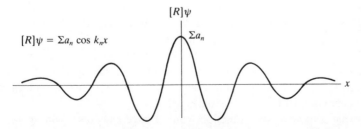

FIG. 11.4. A wave produced by combining superposed harmonic waves

This could be an appropriate graph where the a_ns vary as in the general case, and where the intervals between the wave numbers are very small. If the intervals between the wave numbers is as small as $2\pi/L$, where L is the distance required to circle the universe, the cancellation beyond a certain distance would be complete, and the value of the resultant function everywhere outside these limits would be zero.

The graphs of the imaginary part of each of the components, the functions $a_n i \sin k_n x$, and of the combined state function, would look somewhat similar to Figs. 11.3 and 11.4; but with small lateral displacements of the components like the displacement shown in Fig. 11.2. However, since the phases would coincide where $x = 0$, and thus where $a_n \sin k_n x = 0$, the maximum reinforcement would be less than with the cosine series, but would occur in two places, one on either side of the y axis. As noted in Section 10.2, the complex function can be visualized in three dimensions as a spiral passing through a succession of Argand planes; but here with the diameter of the spiral varying as shown in Fig. 11.4.

The absolute square of the combined state function $|\psi|^2$ would then appear graphically as in Fig. 11.5. This graph no longer has the wave form of the

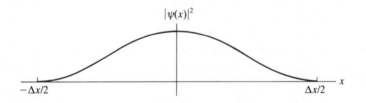

FIG. 11.5. The probability function of a wave packet

earlier graphs, because the absolute square of complex numbers is always positive, and the contribution to it of the imaginary part smooths out the fluctuations. (The suggestion to the contrary in the corresponding diagrams in Pagels (1983: 81, 138) is, I think, somewhat misleading.) It will be remembered that the magnitude of $|\psi|^2$ for any position x is a measure of the probability of finding the particle by an appropriate measurement to be in that position. It will be seen that this probability is at a maximum at $x = 0$, and decreases to zero at points which I have marked as $-\Delta x/2$ and $\Delta x/2$. Thus there is no possibility that the particle would be found with x coordinates outside the total interval Δx, and there is certainty that by an appropriate measurement it would be found somewhere within that interval. The greatest probability is that it would be found in the vicinity of $x = 0$, and the probability decreases with distance from $x = 0$.

Thus the combined state function which I have been discussing gives some certainty concerning the location of the particle in the x direction: and it does so because the component plane wave functions (each associated with a different momentum) cancel each other out by destructive interference beyond this interval Δx in the x direction. As stated earlier, each of the component wave functions is associated with a possible momentum which could be found by an appropriate measurement of momentum of the particle, with the range of possible momenta being within Δp. It is this uncertainty regarding momentum, associated with component waves of varying wavelength that cancel out outside the range Δx, which thereby gives some certainty regarding position. A wave function comprising a superposition of plane waves associated with a range of momenta Δp, which confines the position of the associated particle to a small range Δx, is called a wave packet.

11.2.3. *The Uncertainty Principle*

This discussion gives some indication of how it is that the mathematical object which represents the state function gives rise to the uncertainty principle. Certain momentum involves complete uncertainty of position: some certainty of position involves less certainty of momentum. Furthermore, the discussion indicates why it is that, in order to reduce the length of Δx and thereby to reduce the uncertainty of position, it is necessary to widen the range of wavelengths of the component waves, that is, to increase the uncertainty of momentum.

There is in fact a theorem of Fourier analysis concerning the range of simple harmonic functions which are needed to be added or 'superposed' to give a function of x the value of which is zero outside an interval Δx, namely:

Extension of function times range of or wavenumbers $\geqslant$ about 1.

$$\Delta x \times \Delta k \geqslant \sim 1.$$

As expressed in this theorem, k is not the angular wave number which I have called k, but $1/2\pi$ times this angular wave number. Thus, the k expressed in this theorem, times h, equals momentum p: so

$$\Delta p = \Delta k \times h$$
$$\therefore \Delta x \Delta p \geqslant \sim h.$$

This is a rough derivation of Heisenberg's uncertainty principle for a single particle (see Born 1951: 148, 159–60).

This discussion can be generalized to three dimensions. Each of the other dimensions (that is, in the y direction and in the z direction) can be separately dealt with in the same way as the x direction. (Incidentally, if the momentum were (certainly) zero in any direction, this would be certainty relating to momentum in that direction, which would involve complete uncertainty relating to position in that direction.) Alternatively, as mentioned earlier, state functions can be expressed as functions of position and/or momentum in all three dimensions, either by giving the three components (position coordinates x, y, and z, and momentum components p_i, p_j, and p_k), or by using the position vector $\mathbf{r}$ and momentum vector $\mathbf{p}$.

11.2.4. *Energy*

So far, I have discussed the state function of a single particle (such as an electron, proton, or neutron) principally in relation to two observables, namely position and momentum. The state function of a single particle, ex-pressed as a function of position, also gives information about other observ-ables, of which the most important is the energy of the particle.

In relation to this observable, if the particle is confined in some way, there is not a continuous range of possible energies; rather, there are a number of discrete possible energies which the particle may by an appropriate measure-ment of energy be found to have. It will be recalled that the notion of discrete possible energies was at the heart of Bohr's theory of the atom, formulated around 1913 in order to explain the stability of atoms.

Accordingly, in the case of a confined particle, a state function can be expressed as a weighted sum of the state functions associated with all pos-sible energies:

$$\psi(x) = \Sigma c_n \, \psi_n(x). \tag{11.3}$$

Here each $\psi_n(x)$ is the state function associated with a particular energy E_n: that is, if the energy of a particle with state function $\psi_n(x)$ is appropriately measured, it is *certain* to be E_n. Each c_n is the probability amplitude for the energy E_n, so that (if the state function is normalized) $|c_n|^2$ gives the prob-ability that the particle whose state function is $\psi(x)$ will be found to have energy E_n if an appropriate energy measurement is made. Further, the value of each c_n is given by the overlap integral $\int_{-\infty}^{\infty} \psi_n*(x)\,\psi(x)\,dx$: this can be written (ψ_n, ψ). The summation $\Sigma c_n \, \psi_n(x)$ is not an imperfect expression of what should strictly be an integral (as is said to be the case with momentum), because only discrete states $\psi_n(x)$, each having a specific energy E_n, are possible.

To complete this part of the discussion, it is necessary to introduce con-sideration of the effect of measurement. I have noted that the state function of a particle shows (or enables calculation of) the probability of a particle being found by appropriate measurement to have a position or momentum within any range, or to have a particular energy. If a measurement is made, and a value is found for one of these observables; and if a further measurement is then immediately made of the same observable; then (experiments show) the *same* value will again be measured (unless the measurement destroys the particle, or appreciable time development occurs between the two measure-ments). What was previously only a probability has become a certainty. So, as a result of the first measurement, the state of the particle has changed from one represented by a function which showed the measured value as a probability only to one which can be represented by a function which shows the measured value as a certainty: this change is called the reduction or collapse of the quantum state or state function. Thus, to use the symbols in the previous paragraph, if a particle with state function $\psi(x)$ is found by measurement to have energy E_n, its state function is thereby 'reduced' to the function associated with E_n, namely $\psi_n(x)$. As we will see, this function is called an eigenstate of the measured observable (here, energy), and the measured value is the corresponding eigenvalue.

A final note. It is well known that there are devices which display and/or record the paths of particles such as electrons: for example, cloud chambers and spark chambers. These apparently show successive positions of an electron and also its motion. How does this accord with the discussion of state vectors, eigenstates, and the uncertainty principle? It is true that the track of a particle as shown on such a device gives information about both its position and its momentum. However, by reason of the *scale* of the track, the information is approximate only. The track is best regarded as a succession of approximate position measurements, which because they are only approximate can convey information about motion, and thus about momentum.

11.3. State Vectors

The mathematical object of most general application in quantum mechanics to represent states is the vector or state vector. It is necessary to have some understanding of this mathematical object; and this can usefully be approached by first considering ordinary vectors in three-dimensional space.

11.3.1. *Vectors in Three-Dimensional Space*

Vectors are quantities having direction as well as magnitude. In the three-dimensional space of our experience, any position can be represented by a vector **r** which specifies the distance and direction from a particular point in space, called the origin. Such a vector can be expressed as the sum of three vectors, one in the direction of each of three orthogonal axes (that is, axes at right angles to each other), generally called the x, y, and z axes. If **i**, **j**, and **k** are vectors of unit length in the x, y, and z directions respectively, then:

$$\mathbf{r} = x\mathbf{i} + y\mathbf{j} + z\mathbf{k}.$$

This resolution is shown in Fig. 11.7, with all four vectors shown as having their tails at the origin. However, it can be seen that if the tail of $y\mathbf{j}$ were instead placed at the head of $x\mathbf{i}$, and the tail of $z\mathbf{k}$ were then placed at the head of $y\mathbf{j}$ (in its new position), then the head of $z\mathbf{k}$ would coincide with the head of $\mathbf{r}$: this illustrates the way vector addition works.

The scalar (or inner) product of two vectors $\mathbf{r}$ and $\mathbf{a}$ is that scalar which is the product of the lengths of the two vectors and the cosine of the angle which would be made between them if they were placed tail to tail. It is written:

$$\mathbf{r} \cdot \mathbf{a} = |\mathbf{r}| |\mathbf{a}| \cos\theta,$$

where θ is the angle between them. It is clear that

$$\mathbf{r} \cdot \mathbf{a} = \mathbf{a} \cdot \mathbf{r}.$$

In the important case where one of the vectors is a unit vector, the inner product (say of $\mathbf{r}$ and $\mathbf{i}$) can be thought of as the projection of $\mathbf{r}$ on $\mathbf{i}$; that is, if the two vectors are placed tail to tail, and a perpendicular dropped from the end of $\mathbf{r}$ on to $\mathbf{i}$ (or its prolongation) the inner product is the distance from the tails to the foot of this perpendicular. This distance, a scalar quantity, equals $|\mathbf{r}| \cos\theta$, as shown in Fig. 11.6.

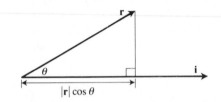

FIG. 11.6. The scalar product of two vectors

The lengths of the component vectors $x\mathbf{i}$, $y\mathbf{j}$, and $z\mathbf{k}$ referred to above can be expressed as inner products:

$$x = \mathbf{i} \cdot \mathbf{r}; \quad y = \mathbf{j} \cdot \mathbf{r}; \quad z = \mathbf{k} \cdot \mathbf{r}.$$

Accordingly, as shown in Fig. 11.7,

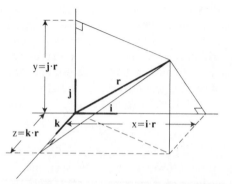

FIG. 11.7. The resolution of a vector into three orthogonal vectors

$$\mathbf{r} = (\mathbf{i} \cdot \mathbf{r})\,\mathbf{i} + (\mathbf{j} \cdot \mathbf{r})\,\mathbf{j} + (\mathbf{k} \cdot \mathbf{r})\,\mathbf{k}.$$

The set of base vectors $\mathbf{i}, \mathbf{j}$, and $\mathbf{k}$ is said to be complete, because any vector in the relevant space (here, three-dimensional) can be expressed as a sum or 'linear combination' of such vectors, with scalar multipliers. It is orthogonal, as we have seen; and this orthogonality can be expressed as follows:

$$\mathbf{i} \cdot \mathbf{j} = \mathbf{j} \cdot \mathbf{k} = \mathbf{k} \cdot \mathbf{i} = 0$$

(because $\cos \pi/2 = 0$, and each of these vectors has zero projection on to each of the others). The set is also said to be orthonormal, because the norm of each of the orthogonal vectors (its inner product with itself) is equal to 1:

$$\mathbf{i} \cdot \mathbf{i} = \mathbf{j} \cdot \mathbf{j} = \mathbf{k} \cdot \mathbf{k} = 1.$$

There are in fact an infinite number of complete orthonormal sets of base vectors in three-dimensional space: so long as the three vectors in each set are at right angles to each other, each set can be orientated in any way whatsoever. If the vectors represent a quantity other than position (or distance and direction), then the same mathematics and diagrams can be used, but the 'space' of those diagrams is a fictional mathematical space. The *direction* of the vectors can indicate a direction in the real space of our experience: however, the *length* of the vectors does not indicate a distance in that real space, but rather a *quantity* which can have a point location in that real space (such as force, acceleration, velocity, momentum, etc.).

Before moving on to consider the extension of these ideas to multidimensional space and complex numbers, it is useful to note the suitability of unit vectors in a three-dimensional mathematical space to represent the probabilities of various combinations of three mutually exclusive events (such as one horse winning a three-horse race, with rules to eliminate ties). Such events can be represented by the orthogonal vectors $\mathbf{i}, \mathbf{j}$, and $\mathbf{k}$, with tails meeting at the origin as shown in Fig. 11.7. If there is another event which can give rise to at least one, but not more than one, of such events (such as running the race), this other event can be represented by a unit vector $\mathbf{r}$ from the origin. Then the projections of $\mathbf{r}$ on to the other three vectors (that is, its inner products with them) can be considered as probability amplitudes for the events respectively represented by $\mathbf{i}, \mathbf{j}$, and $\mathbf{k}$; so that, given event $\mathbf{r}$, the probability for each of the events $\mathbf{i}, \mathbf{j}$, and $\mathbf{k}$ is given by the square of the respective projections. Pythagoras's theorem shows that the sum of the probabilities is 1, as it should be; and, since $\mathbf{i}, \mathbf{j}$, and $\mathbf{k}$ are orthogonal, there is no projection of one of these on to any other of them, and so no probability of any event represented by one of them giving rise to an event represented by another of them. In that sense they are mutually exclusive.

Furthermore, given the three base vectors $\mathbf{i}, \mathbf{j}$, and $\mathbf{k}$, the vector $\mathbf{r}$ is uniquely identified by the scalar numbers which are its inner products with those base vectors. There are an infinite number of possible sets of orthogonal base vectors which can be joined at the same origin. The same vector **r** can then give the probabilities for the events represented by each of these sets (say, one or other of the horses leading 100 metres from the finish); and its mathematical properties can be identified by specifying any one of these sets, and by its inner products with each unit vector in that set.

11.3.2. *Vectors in Multidimensional Space*

In quantum mechanics, the state of a particle or system can be represented by a vector in a multidimensional mathematical space. Such a vector is generally taken to be of unit length, and as being equal to the sum of vectors whose 'directions' are those of the members of a complete set of orthogonal base vectors of unit length, and whose magnitudes are respectively the vector's projections on to (inner products with) such members. As in the three-dimensional case, there can be many such complete sets of base vectors: there is in fact one set for each of the observables of the particle or system represented by the state vector, generally with one base vector in each set corresponding to each state associated with a possible value of that observable.

The differences from the three-dimensional case I have looked at are as follows:

1. the number of dimensions of the space is equal to the number of base vectors, and therefore no less than the number of possible values of relevant observables; and it may therefore be infinite; and
2. the relevant inner products are generally complex numbers.

Accordingly, the state vector can be thought of as being a direction in its multidimensional space; but a direction defined not by three base vectors plus three real-number inner products, but by up to an infinity of base vectors plus an infinity of complex-number inner products.

In three-dimensional space, any sum or 'linear combination' of vectors (not necessarily base vectors) will make a further vector in the same space:

$$\mathbf{r} = a_1 \mathbf{r}_1 + a_2 \mathbf{r}_2 + \ldots + a_n \mathbf{r}_n + \ldots$$

Here, the $\mathbf{r}_n$ s are any vectors in three-dimensional space, and the a_n s are any real numbers. In the multidimensional linear vector space used for quantum physics, the state vectors are generally symbolized in a notation invented by Dirac, that is, by the $|\,\rangle$, generally with an identifying number or symbol inside. As in ordinary space, any linear combination of vectors will make a further vector in the same space:

$$|\psi\rangle = c_1 |\psi_1\rangle + c_2 |\psi_2\rangle + \ldots + c_n |\psi_n\rangle + \ldots$$

Here, the $|\psi_n\rangle$s are any vectors in the space, $|\psi\rangle$ is a further vector in the same space, and the c_n s are any real or complex numbers. The order of addition does not matter:

$$| \psi_1 \rangle + | \psi_2 \rangle = | \psi_2 \rangle + | \psi_1 \rangle.$$

Ordinary linear rules apply for combining multiplications of vectors by numbers:

$$c(| \psi_1 \rangle + | \psi_2 \rangle) = c | \psi_1 \rangle + c | \psi_2 \rangle \qquad (11.4)$$

$$(c_1 + c_2) | \psi \rangle = c_1 | \psi \rangle + c_2 | \psi \rangle. \qquad (11.5)$$

In general, there is a distinct 'space' used for each system: for example, if one is dealing with two particles, there would be one 'space' for one particle, another 'space' for the other; and also a 'space' for the two particles together, which is a combination (called a tensor product) of the 'spaces' of the individual particles. I will say more about this in Chapter 13.

Any two vectors in each linear vector space can be combined so as to form an inner product, analogous to the scalar product of three-dimensional vectors. This inner product is a scalar, that is, a number; but it may be complex. In Dirac's notation, the inner product of two vectors $| \phi \rangle$ and $| \psi \rangle$ is written $\langle \phi | \psi \rangle$: it can be thought of as some sort of projection of the vector $| \psi \rangle$ on to the vector $| \phi \rangle$. The order is important: the projection of $| \phi \rangle$ on to $| \psi \rangle$ is the complex conjugate of the projection of $| \psi \rangle$ on to $| \phi \rangle$.

$$\langle \psi | \phi \rangle = \langle \phi | \psi \rangle *. \qquad (11.6)$$

In writing an inner product, the state vector $| \psi \rangle$ or $| \phi \rangle$ has been combined with a different vector symbol $\langle |$. Dirac called a vector written in the form $| \rangle$ a 'ket' vector, and a vector written in the form $\langle |$ a 'bra' vector, so that an inner product $\langle \phi | \psi \rangle$ constituted a 'bra–ket'. For each space of ket vectors, there is a corresponding (but distinct) 'space' of bra vectors, such that if the ket vectors $| \psi_n \rangle$ correspond to the bra vectors $\langle \psi_n |$, then the ket vector made up of the summation $\Sigma c_n | \psi_n \rangle$ corresponds to the bra vector made up of the summation $\Sigma \langle \psi_n | c_n *$. Just as $\langle \phi | \psi \rangle$ can be considered as the projection of $| \psi \rangle$ on to $| \phi \rangle$ in ket vector space, it can also be considered as the projection of $\langle \phi |$ on to $\langle \psi |$ in bra vector space.

Inner products also obey normal distribution rules, so that, if $| \psi \rangle = c_1 | \psi_1 \rangle + c_2 | \psi_2 \rangle$, then:

$$\langle \phi | \psi \rangle = c_1 \langle \phi | \psi_1 \rangle + c_2 \langle \phi | \psi_2 \rangle . \qquad (11.7)$$

The inner product of a vector $| \psi \rangle$ with itself, namely $\langle \psi | \psi \rangle$ (called its norm), is like the square of a real number (and the absolute square of a complex number), in that it is always positive (or zero, if $| \psi \rangle$ is zero). Where $\langle \psi | \psi \rangle = 1$, the state vector is normalized (like a vector of unit length in three-dimensional space). Note that if the vector $| \psi \rangle$ is normalized, so is the vector $e^{i\theta} | \psi \rangle$: the inner product of $e^{i\theta} | \psi \rangle$ with itself is $\langle \psi | e^{-i\theta} e^{i\theta} | \psi \rangle$, which is $\langle \psi | \psi \rangle$.

In quantum physics, each possible state of a particle is represented by a vector in a particular state space (and, similarly, each possible state of a number of particles: see Chapter 13). However, if the vector $|\psi\rangle$ represents a particular state of a particle, then $c|\psi\rangle$ (where c is any complex number) does not represent a different state: either it represents the same state, or alternatively one may say that states may be represented only by normalized vectors, so that if $|\psi\rangle$ represents a state, then $c|\psi\rangle$ will represent a state only if $c = e^{i\theta}$. I will generally adopt the latter view, and assume that the state vectors are normalized. Even on the former view, it should be noted that multipliers of state vectors cannot be disregarded, because $|\phi\rangle + |\psi\rangle$ is not the same state as $|\phi\rangle + c|\psi\rangle$: the relative weightings in a linear combination (also called a superposition) are significant.

If one is dealing only with normalized vectors, then $e^{i\theta}|\psi\rangle$ is generally considered as representing the same state as $|\psi\rangle$: no difference between such states is experimentally detectable. However, again, in a linear combination or superposition, the change in *phase* involved in multiplying only one element by the phase factor would involve differences in interference effects, which in turn would be experimentally detectable. Thus one may say that $|\phi\rangle + |\psi\rangle$ represents the same state as $e^{i\theta}(|\phi\rangle + |\psi\rangle)$, but not the same state as $|\phi\rangle + e^{i\theta}|\psi\rangle$.

One may then take a complete orthonormal set of base vectors for an observable of a particle (say energy): these base vectors might be written $|\psi_1\rangle$, $|\psi_2\rangle$, ..., $|\psi_n\rangle$, ... and so on. Because they form an orthonormal set, one can write:

$$\langle \psi_m | \psi_n \rangle = \delta_{mn}. \tag{11.8}$$

The symbol δ_{mn} is the Kronecker delta, and it is defined by:

$$\delta_{mn} = 1 \quad \text{if } m = n$$
$$= 0 \quad \text{if } m \neq n$$

That is, the inner product of any two different base vectors is zero (this is the condition of orthogonality); and the inner product of any base vector with itself, that is its norm, is 1 (making the set orthonormal). Because the set is complete, any vector $|\psi\rangle$ can be expressed as a sum or linear combination of these base vectors, with scalar (complex) multipliers:

$$|\psi\rangle = c_1|\psi_1\rangle + c_2|\psi_2\rangle + \ldots + c_n|\psi_n\rangle + \ldots$$

This can be written:

$$|\psi\rangle = \Sigma c_n|\psi_n\rangle. \tag{11.9}$$

As with vectors in three-dimensional space, the scalar multiplier of each component base vector is the inner product of that base vector with the resultant general vector $|\psi\rangle$:

$$c_n = \langle \psi_n | \psi \rangle. \tag{11.10}$$

This can be shown by multiplying both sides of equation (11.9) by $\langle \psi_n |$. Then, applying equations (11.7) and (11.8), we get:

$$\langle \psi_n | \psi \rangle = c_n \langle \psi_n | \psi_n \rangle = c_n.$$

Now a bra–ket in the form $\langle \psi_n | \psi \rangle$ is said to represent the *amplitude* for the state $| \psi \rangle$ to change to the state $| \psi_n \rangle$. The inner product $\langle \psi_n | \psi \rangle$ is, as noted above, a complex number; and so it can be considered as the product of a modulus N and a phase factor $e^{i\theta}$. The probability for a particle whose state vector is $| \psi \rangle$ to be found by an appropriate measurement to be in the state $| \psi_n \rangle$ will be N^2, i.e. $|\langle \psi_n | \psi \rangle|^2$. (The measurement which could find the particle to be in the state $| \psi_n \rangle$ would be a measurement of the particular value, of the particular observable, associated with $| \psi_n \rangle$.)

In bra vector space, the equivalent equations to (11.9) and (11.10) are the following:

$$\langle \psi | = \Sigma \langle \psi_n | c_n* \tag{11.11}$$

$$c_n * = \langle \psi | \psi_n \rangle. \tag{11.12}$$

As in the three-dimensional case, a bra or ket vector is suitable to represent the probabilities of measurement of the system to be in one of the different base states. Because the inner products are projections from a vector of unit length on to other vectors, all of which are orthogonal, the sum of the absolute squares of these inner products is equal to 1. This can be seen mathematically, as follows: if one multiplies both sides of equation (11.9) by $\langle \psi |$, then, applying equations (11.7) and (11.12),

$$\langle \psi | \psi \rangle = \Sigma c_n \langle \psi | \psi_n \rangle = \Sigma c_n c_n*.$$

Therefore, since the vectors are normalized,

$$\Sigma | c_n |^2 = 1. \tag{11.13}$$

Accordingly, the vector can convey that it is certain that a measurement will disclose one of the possible values of each observable; and that if the system is in one of the base states, it is certain that measurement will disclose the value associated with that state, and no other.

11.3.3. *Comparison with Wave Functions*

The analogy with state functions is as follows.

The quantum physical state represented by the resultant vector $| \psi \rangle$ can also be represented (at a particular time) by the function $\psi(x)$. The base states associated with different values of an observable (say, energy) represented by the vectors $| \psi_n \rangle$ may also be represented by the functions $\psi_n(x)$.

As we saw, if E_n is the value of the observable energy associated with $\psi_n(x)$, the probability for the particle whose state function is $\psi(x)$ to be found by an appropriate measurement to have energy E_n is (assuming the function has been normalized) the absolute square of amplitude given by the overlap integral $\int_{-\infty}^{\infty} \psi_n*(x)\, \psi(x)\, dx$, or (ψ_n, ψ). Similarly, if E_n is the value of the observable energy associated with $|\psi_n\rangle$, the probability for the particle whose state vector is $|\psi\rangle$ to be found by appropriate measurement to have energy E_n is the absolute square of the amplitude $\langle \psi_n | \psi \rangle$. The inner product $\langle \psi_n | \psi \rangle$ is equivalent to the overlap integral (ψ_n, ψ), both giving the amplitude for the state $|\psi\rangle$ (or ψ) to change on measurement to $|\psi_n\rangle$ (or ψ_n).

The requirement that base vectors be orthogonal is reflected, as regards the functions representing states associated with particular values of observables, in the requirement that, where such functions are represented by ψ_n, the overlap integrals (ψ_m, ψ_n) must equal zero for $(n \neq m)$. This is because, if a particle has state function ψ_n, so that an appropriate energy measurement is certain to show that its energy is E_n, the amplitude for the state function to change by reason of an energy measurement to a different function ψ_m, associated with a different energy E_m, has to be zero.

For many purposes, a state function $\psi(x)$ or ψ can be considered as equivalent to the corresponding state vector $|\psi\rangle$. In particular, many of the algebraic operations which are performed on state functions can also be performed on state vectors. The two notations can often be used interchangeably; and I will sometimes do so. When discussing the interpretation and implications of quantum mechanics, I will often just refer to state functions, and mean thereby state functions and/or state vectors.

11.4. Operators, Eigenstates, Eigenvalues

I have noted that in some cases an observable can take a value anywhere within a continuous range of values, and that in other cases an observable can only take one of a number of discrete values. However, so far I have not said how the mathematics of quantum physics enables the possible values of observables to be calculated. This requires consideration of another type of mathematical object, the operator.

Speaking generally, the point is as follows. In classical mechanics each observable has a single representation in the mathematics, generally a variable number or vector which stands for the observable and also for the possible and actual values of the observables. However, in quantum mechanics the situation is different. Although in functions or equations variables appear which in a sense represent observables (as, for example, a wave function expressed as a function of position x, from which can be calculated the probability of finding the particle in the vicinity of x), this is not the only representation of observables in the mathematics. Observables are also represented by operators; and it is the relationship between the operator representing an observable, on the one hand, and the state function (or state vector), on the other, which determines the possible values which that observable can take.

11.4.1. *Operators on State Functions*

In mathematics, an operator (generally written as a letter with a circumflex: Â) is simply an instruction to perform a specified mathematical operation or series of operations. Examples of operators are:

$$2 + \quad \text{add 2 to}$$
$$3 \times \quad \text{multiply by 3}$$
$$d/dt \quad \text{differentiate with respect to } t.$$

In quantum mechanics, various systems are possible; but, within each system, one operator is associated with each observable. In the system generally used in association with state functions, the operators associated with momentum, energy, and position (in one dimension) are as follows:

Momentum $\hat{p} = - i\hbar \partial/\partial x$

Energy $\hat{H} = - \hbar^2/2m \; \partial^2/\partial x^2 + V(x, t)$

Position $\hat{x} = x$.

The meaning of these operators, a plausible derivation of them, and the way they work will now be given. It is convenient to start with momentum.

11.4.2. *The Momentum Operator*

It will be recalled that a particle of constant definite momentum p in the x direction can be represented by a wave function $\psi \{ = N \exp [i (kx - \omega)] \}$, where k is the wave number of the wave, and is such that p equals $\hbar k$; while ω is the angular frequency of the wave, and is such that the total energy E of the particle equals $\hbar \omega$. If one takes a partial derivative of the function with respect to x (that is, holding t constant), one obtains:

$$\partial/\partial x \; \psi = ik N \exp [i (kx - \omega t)].$$

If one then multiplies both sides by $- i\hbar$:

$$- i\hbar \; \partial/\partial x \; \psi = \hbar k N \exp [i (kx - \omega t)]$$

$$= p\psi. \tag{11.14}$$

Thus, application of the operator $- i\hbar \; \partial/\partial x$ to ψ has the effect of multiplying the function by p.

When, as here, the effect of applying an operator $\hat{A}$ to a function ψ is to multiply the function by a number n, it is said that ψ is an eigenfunction of the operator $\hat{A}$ with eigenvalue n. The German word 'eigen' means 'own'; and the idea is that each function (and its associated value) of which the above is true is special to and characteristic of the operator in question. The application to quantum mechanics is as follows: the possible values which an observable may take, and the state functions associated with them, are respectively the eigenvalues and eigenfunctions of the operator associated with that observable.

Thus the momentum operator $\hat{p}$ is $-i\hbar\ \partial/\partial x$ (or $-i\hbar\nabla$ in three dimensions). The eigenfunctions of momentum (as we have seen) take the form $N\exp[i(kx - \omega t)]$. The eigenvalues p are equal to $\hbar k$, where k is the wave number of the wave represented by the function; and generally (subject to considerations arising from the size of the universe) they can take any value in a continuous range, since k can do similarly.

11.4.3. *The Energy Operator*

In classical mechanics, the kinetic energy of a particle having momentum p in the x direction is $p^2/2m$, where m is the mass of the particle. The operator associated in quantum mechanics with kinetic energy is obtained by performing a similar operation on the momentum operator:

$$\hat{p}^2/2m = (-i\hbar\ \partial/\partial x)^2/2m = -\hbar^2/2m\ \partial^2/\partial x^2.$$

If the particle is not free, but subject to external forces, this fact can be expressed in terms of another element of the total energy of the particle, namely potential energy. If these external forces vary only according to the location of the particle, the potential energy can be expressed as a function of position $V(x)$ (or $V(x, y, z)$ in three dimensions). If these forces vary also with time, independently of varying with position, the potential energy will be a function of position *and* time $V(x, t)$ (or $V(x, y, z, t)$ in three dimensions). The operator in quantum mechanics associated with this aspect of energy is simply 'multiply by the potential energy function'.

The operator for total energy then is the 'sum' of these two operators: it is called the Hamiltonian (after the mathematician mentioned in Section 10.1), and is written $\hat{H}$:

$$\hat{H} = -\hbar^2/2m\ \partial/\partial x^2 + V(x, t). \tag{11.15}$$

In three dimensions:

$$\hat{H} = -\hbar^2/2m\ \nabla^2 + V(x, y, z, t).$$

We can take the 'sum' of these two operators in this way, because they are linear operators, as are all operators associated with observables in quantum physics. This means essentially that if $\hat{A}$ and $\hat{B}$ are linear operators used with respect to a function ψ, then:

$$(\hat{A} + \hat{B})\psi = \hat{A}\psi + \hat{B}\psi .$$

To find what values the total energy of a system may take, and to find what function is associated with each of those values, it is necessary to find solutions to the equation

$$\hat{H}\psi = E\psi. \tag{11.16}$$

The solutions of this equation in particular cases will be the possible energy levels in those cases (the energy eigenvalues $E_1, E_2, \ldots$) and the state functions associated with them respectively (the energy eigenfunctions $\psi_1, \psi_2, \ldots$). I shall say more about this, and give an example, when I come to deal with time development of the quantum physical state. It will there be seen that, when a particle is confined, the above equation requires that energy levels be discrete.

I am here dealing with states as functions of position (or momentum) only, with time considered a constant. In the more general situation, one has states as a function of position (or momentum) and time; and the eigenstates may then similarly be functions of position (or momentum) and time, although, as we shall see, the time dependence may only relate to the phase factor. Generally, on the Schrödinger approach, which I will for the most part be following, the operators themselves do not vary with time; so there is no question of the eigenvalues and eigenfunctions (as functions) being different at different times. However, the potential energy V may vary with time; and in such cases the energy operator $\hat{H}$ will similarly vary with time. Then, the eigenvalues and eigenfunctions (as functions) will similarly generally be different at different times: this introduces complications, so in general I will be discussing cases where the potential (and so the operator $\hat{H}$) does not vary with time.

11.4.4. *The Position Operator*

The position operator is simply 'multiply by the variable representing position coordinate' (or in three dimensions, 'position vector'). The functions of which it can be said that multiplication by x involves multiplication by a particular value of x (say x_0) are just those functions which disappear everywhere except at that precise value of x: that is, the delta function $\delta(x - x_0)$, and functions differing from it only by multiplication by some factor (enabling normalization to the delta function by dividing by the same factor). Functions in that form are thus the position eigenfunctions, and position eigenvalues may generally be found anywhere within a continuous range.

11.4.5. *Operators on State Vectors*

In the more abstract formulation of quantum physics in terms of state vectors, a more general account is given of operators, which comprehends but is not restricted to the algebraic operators on state functions which I have just discussed. Many properties of operators in quantum physics can usefully be considered in relation to this more general approach.

As in the case of algebraic operators on state functions, there can be constructed for any observable a corresponding linear operator $\hat{A}$, which will mathematically represent the observable. Thus, suppose that a_1, a_2, etc. are eigenvalues of this observable, and $| \psi_1 \rangle$, $| \psi_2 \rangle$, etc. are a complete set of eigenstates, and $| \psi \rangle$ is a state vector, so that:

$$| \psi \rangle = c_1 | \psi_1 \rangle + c_2 | \psi_2 \rangle + \ldots$$

(with c_1, c_2, ... being complex numbers, the probability amplitudes, equal respectively to $\langle \psi_1 | \psi \rangle$, $\langle \psi_2 | \psi \rangle$, etc.). Then, the eigenvalues a_n of the observable $\hat{A}$ are given by the eigenvalue equation

$$\hat{A} | \psi_n \rangle = a_n | \psi_n \rangle. \tag{11.17}$$

Accordingly,

$$\hat{A} | \psi \rangle = c_1 a_1 | \psi_1 \rangle + c_2 a_2 | \psi_2 \rangle + \ldots$$

Sometimes, it is convenient to use the expression $| a_n \rangle$ instead of $| \psi_n \rangle$ as referring to the eigenstate associated with the eigenvalue a_n. This is satisfactory so long as there is a single eigenstate associated with each eigenvalue. Sometimes, however, this is not the case: where one eigenvalue a_n is associated with more than one eigenstate $| \psi_{n1} \rangle$, $| \psi_{n2} \rangle$, etc., the eigenvalue and eigenstates are said to be degenerate; and of course $| a_n \rangle$ would not uniquely represent one particular eigenstate. I shall for the most part ignore the problems of degeneracy, and assume that there is just one eigenstate for each eigenvalue.

It is possible to develop the mathematics of operators on vector space, and to relate this to properties of quantum physical states, without distinguishing the operators which are appropriate for different observables, or giving any details of the mathematical structure of different operators; and I shall be doing some of this. However, when applying quantum physics to actual physical problems (such as the structure and properties of the hydrogen atom), it is necessary to distinguish operators for particular observables.

One approach is to consider state vectors as just being functions, and using algebraic operators such as those discussed in relation to state functions. Another is to consider state vectors as comprising arrays of (generally complex) numbers, which represent the amplitudes for the eigenstates of some observable; and to consider operators as similarly being arrays of (generally complex) numbers, which when combined with the state vector arrays give appropriate numerical results. On this approach, the state vectors are represented by arrays called column and/or row vectors, while the operators are represented by arrays called matrices.

For example, suppose that the eigenstates of the observable total energy $\hat{H}$ are $|\psi_1\rangle$, $|\psi_2\rangle$, etc., and that one is dealing with two different states $|\phi\rangle$ and $|\psi\rangle$ such that

$$|\phi\rangle = b_1|\psi_1\rangle + b_2|\psi_2\rangle + \ldots + b_i|\psi_i\rangle + \ldots$$
$$|\psi\rangle = c_1|\psi_1\rangle + c_2|\psi_2\rangle + \ldots + c_i|\psi_i\rangle + \ldots$$

Then the ket vectors $|\phi\rangle$ and $|\psi\rangle$ can be represented, in relation to these eigenstates, by column vectors written

$$\begin{bmatrix} b_1 \\ b_2 \\ \ldots \\ b_i \\ \ldots \end{bmatrix} \text{ and } \begin{bmatrix} c_1 \\ c_2 \\ \ldots \\ c_i \\ \ldots \end{bmatrix}$$

The corresponding bra vectors $\langle\phi|$ and $\langle\psi|$ can be represented by row vectors $(b_1{}^*, b_2{}^*, \ldots, b_i{}^*, \ldots)$ and $(c_1{}^*, c_2{}^*, \ldots, c_i{}^*, \ldots)$. An operator $\hat{A}$ (not necessarily $\hat{H}$, the operator of which the $|\psi_i\rangle$ are the eigenstates) can then be represented by a matrix, each of whose elements A_{ij} gives the number $\langle\psi_i|\hat{A}|\psi_j\rangle$. If written in full, this matrix would look like this:

$$\begin{bmatrix} A_{11} & A_{12} & \ldots & A_{1n} \\ A_{21} & A_{22} & \ldots & A_{2n} \\ \ldots\ldots\ldots\ldots\ldots\ldots\ldots \\ A_{n1} & A_{n2} & \ldots & A_{nn} \end{bmatrix}$$

(I am assuming there are n eigenstates $|\psi_i\rangle$, where n may be infinite.) Then A_{12}, for example, gives the (generally complex) number $\langle\psi_1|\hat{A}|\psi_2\rangle$. Using this and the row and column vectors of $\langle\phi|$ and $|\psi\rangle$, the number $\langle\phi|\hat{A}|\psi\rangle$ can be calculated, using the rule for matrix multiplication, which is as follows. If one is multiplying two matrices, the element D_{ij} in the product (in the ith row and the jth column) is calculated by adding the products arrived at by multiplying each item in the ith row of the first matrix with the corresponding item in the jth column of the second matrix. That is, if one is multiplying one $n \times n$ matrix B by another $n \times n$ matrix C ($B \times C$) to arrive at a matrix D, then D is also an $n \times n$ matrix, and:

$$D_{ij} = B_{i1}C_{1j} + \ldots + B_{in}C_{nj} = \sum_k B_{ik}C_{kj}.$$

The application of this rule where one or both of the components is a row or column vector means that the product $\hat{A}|\psi\rangle$ of a matrix $\hat{A}$ and a column vector $|\psi\rangle$ is itself a column vector, of which the element in the ith row is the sum of the products of each item in the *i*th row of the matrix with the corresponding item in the (only) column of the vector:

$$A_{i1}c_1 + A_{i2}c_2 + \ldots + A_{in}c_n = \sum_j c_j A_{ij} .$$

The product $\langle \phi \,|\, \hat{A} \,|\, \psi \rangle$ of a row vector $\langle \phi \,|$ with this column vector $\hat{A} \,|\, \psi \rangle$ is a number, being the sum of the products of each item of the row vector with the corresponding item of the column vector. So:

$$\langle \phi \,|\, \hat{A} \,|\, \psi \rangle = \sum_i b_i{}^* (A_{i1}c_1 + \ldots + A_{in}c_n)$$

$$= \sum_{ij} b_i{}^* c_j A_{ij} \qquad (11.18)$$

Note that the order of writing vectors and operators is important, but *not* the place or order of numbers.

The use of matrices as observable operators goes back to the original Heisenberg approach to quantum mechanics.

11.4.6. *Hermitian Conjugation and Unitary Operators*

Certain important properties of operators concern what is called hermitian conjugation. The hermitian conjugate of an operator $\hat{A}$, written $\hat{A}^{\dagger}$ ('$\hat{A}$ dagger'), is defined by the equality, in relation to any states $|\,\phi \rangle$ and $|\,\psi \rangle$:

$$\langle \phi \,|\, \hat{A} \,|\, \psi \rangle = \langle \psi \,|\, \hat{A}^{\dagger} \,|\, \phi \rangle {}^*. \qquad (11.19)$$

Since $\langle \phi \,|\, \hat{A} \,|\, \psi \rangle = \sum_{ij} b_i {}^* c_j A_{ij}$, it is clear that, in terms of matrices, $\hat{A}^{\dagger}$ is that matrix whose elements can be produced from those of $\hat{A}$ by transposing them and taking the complex conjugate of each of them, so that:

$$A_{ij}{}^{\dagger} = A_{ji}{}^*. \qquad (11.20)$$

An operator which is its *own* hermitian conjugate is said to be hermitian. An important property of hermitian operators is that their eigenvalues are real. And so it is that the operators representing observables, as well as being linear, are also hermitian: the eigenvalues of observable operators, being the possible results of precise measurement, must be real. Otherwise the mathematics would not give appropriate values for the results of measurements, which must be expressible in real numbers. To show this property of hermitian operators, suppose that $|\,\psi_i \rangle$ is an eigenstate of such an operator $\hat{A}$, with eigenvalue a_i: then

$$\hat{A} \,|\, \psi_i \rangle = a_i \,|\, \psi_i \rangle$$

$$\therefore \langle \psi_i \,|\, \hat{A} \,|\, \psi_i \rangle = a_i \langle \psi_i \,|\, \psi_i \rangle = a_i.$$

Since $\langle \psi_i | \hat{A} | \psi_i \rangle = \langle \psi_i | \hat{A} | \psi_i \rangle*$ (because $\hat{A}$ is hermitian), therefore $\langle \psi_i | \hat{A} | \psi_i \rangle$ must be real; and accordingly so must a_i.

Apart from the hermitian operators, which can represent observables, there is another important class of operators in quantum physics, namely unitary operators. An operator $\hat{U}$ is said to be unitary if the result of the application of it, followed by that of its hermitian conjugate, is identity: that is, where

$$\hat{U}\hat{U}^{\dagger} = \hat{U}^{\dagger}\hat{U} = 1. \tag{11.21}$$

This means that $\hat{U}^{\dagger}$ can also be written $\hat{U}^{-1}$. An important unitary operator, which I will mention in Chapter 12, is the operator representing time development.

11.4.7. *Functions of Operators*

In quantum physics, use is also made of functions of operators. If $\hat{A}$ is an operator with eigenstates $| \psi_i \rangle$ and eigenvalues a_i, then generally a function of $\hat{A}$ (written $f(\hat{A})$) is an operator with the same eigenstates, and with eigenvalues $f(a_i)$. It will be recalled that the energy operator for a free particle was obtained from the momentum operator by using the relationship between kinetic energy and momentum ($p^2/2m$). The energy operator for a free particle is thus a function of the momentum operator, has the same eigenstates, and its eigenvalues are the appropriate function of the momentum eigenvalues.

11.4.8. *Expectation Values*

If the same quantum physical state, represented by a state vector $| \psi \rangle$, is prepared many times, and a measurement of a particular observable made, the results will reflect the probability of the results of individual measurements calculated in the way indicated above. Indeed, the conformity of the results of repeated measurements to such probability calculations is the experimental confirmation of the probability interpretation of the state vector.

A good indication of the likely result of such measurements is given by an average or mean value, which is called the expectation value of such observable. This can usefully be combined with another figure which gives an indication of the likely *spread* of results around such an average.

If there are a finite number of eigenvalues a_n of an observable $\hat{A}$, the probability for each of which is $|c_n|^2$, then the expectation value (written $\langle A \rangle$ or $\langle \hat{A} \rangle$) is:

$$\langle \hat{A} \rangle = \Sigma |c_n|^2 a_n. \tag{11.22}$$

In vector notation, this is given by:

$$\langle \hat{A} \rangle = \langle \psi | \hat{A} | \psi \rangle. \tag{11.23}$$

This can be seen from the following. We know that:

$$\hat{A} \mid \psi \rangle = \Sigma\, c_n a_n \mid \psi_n \rangle.$$

If both sides are multiplied by $\langle \psi \mid$, and using equations (11.6) and (11.11), we have:

$$
\begin{aligned}
\langle \psi \mid \hat{A} \mid \psi \rangle &= \Sigma\, c_n a_n \langle \psi \mid \psi_n \rangle \\
&= \Sigma\, c_n \langle \psi_n \mid \psi \rangle * a_n \\
&= \Sigma\, c_n c_n * a_n \\
&= \Sigma \mid c_n \mid^2 a_n.
\end{aligned}
$$

The equality $\langle \hat{A} \rangle = \langle \psi \mid \hat{A} \mid \psi \rangle$ holds good even if the eigenvalues form a continuous spectrum, so that an integral rather than a sum has to be used.

The measure of deviation from the expectation value is often called ΔA (and I will write it $\Delta\hat{A}$), and, in accordance with equation (10.21), is given by the square root of the difference between the mean of the square, and the square of the mean:

$$\Delta\hat{A} = \sqrt{(\langle \hat{A}^2 \rangle - \langle \hat{A} \rangle^2)}$$

The great bulk of cases will then be within $\langle \hat{A} \rangle \pm \Delta\hat{A}$.

11.4.9. *Commutation and Compatibility*

We saw earlier that if a particle is in a state such that its momentum in one direction has a precise value (that is, in a momentum eigenstate), then there will be complete uncertainty regarding its position in that dimension; and vice versa. We also saw that if a precise measurement of one or other of these observables is made on a system, then the system is caused to go into an eigenstate of that observable; namely, that eigenstate associated with the value disclosed by the measurement. It follows that it is impossible simultaneously to make a precise measurement of a particle's momentum in one dimension and a precise measurement of its position in the same dimension: the particle cannot be caused to go into an eigenstate of momentum in one dimension and at the same time an eigenstate of position in the same dimension, because these two eigenstates are different. Thus, these two observables are not compatible. This incompatibility is associated with a mathematical property of the operators associated with these observables: they do not commute.

Operators are said to commute if the order of their application to a state vector (or function) is immaterial. Thus, $\hat{A}$ and $\hat{B}$ commute if $\hat{A}\hat{B} = \hat{B}\hat{A}$, and do not commute if $\hat{A}\hat{B} \neq \hat{B}\hat{A}$. (It will be recalled that it was Heisenberg's discovery of the non-commutation of the matrix operators he was using for position and momentum which at first led him to doubt the correctness of his work.) A mathematical object called the commutator of two operators, which is itself an operator, is identified: in relation to observables $\hat{A}$ and $\hat{B}$, it is written $[\hat{A}, \hat{B}]$, and it is equal to $\hat{A}\hat{B} - \hat{B}\hat{A}$. If the commutator is zero, the observables commute, and are compatible; while if the commutator is not zero, the observables do not commute, and simultaneous precise measurements are impossible.

It is sometimes said that the observables 'position along one axis' (say, the x axis) and 'momentum along another axis' (say, the y axis) are compatible, and that the corresponding operators do commute. In one sense this is so: the mathematics of quantum physics does not preclude simultaneous precise measurement of such observables. However, as we will see in Chapter 13, the quantum physical states of a particle associated with its position and momentum along different axes can be regarded as distinct systems: in terms of state vectors, the different state vectors and operators belong to different vector spaces, so the question of commutation and compatibility does not really arise.

If one considers commutation and compatibility of operators in the same vector space (say, representing the state of motion of a particle in one dimension), such operators commute and are compatible if and only if they have a complete set of eigenvectors in common. A precise measurement of an observable puts the system into an eigenstate of that observable: so a precise simultaneous measurement of two observables can be made only if the system can be put into an eigenstate of *both* observables. In such a case, if the measurements are made in quick succession, so that there is no time development of the state between measurements, the order of the measurements does not matter, in the sense that in any event the probability of the result of *both* measurements is as indicated by the pre-measurement state, and the post-measurement state is an eigenstate of *both* observables.

Where, however, measurements are made, in quick succession, of incompatible observables, the order *does* matter. The pre-measurement state gives the probability of the result only of the *first* measurement, not that of the second: the latter is given by the eigenstate into which the first measurement puts the system. The post-measurement state is an eigenstate only of the *second* observable measured: the second measurement changes the system from an eigenstate of the first observable measured to an eigenstate of the second observable measured.

The immateriality of the order of measurement in the case of compatible observables is associated mathematically with the equality $\hat{A}\hat{B} = \hat{B}\hat{A}$ in the case of commuting operators; while the materiality of the order of observation in the case of incompatible observables is associated mathematically with the inequality $\hat{A}\hat{B} \neq \hat{B}\hat{A}$ in the case of non-commuting operators. In a general way, the application of an operator to a state vector can be considered as a mathematical representation of the precise measurement of that observable.

11.4.10. *Uncertainty Relations*

By considering commutators of observables, a mathematically precise statement of Heisenberg's uncertainty principle in relation to expectation values can be proved.

If one takes a state vector $| \psi \rangle$, and considers two observable operators $\hat{A}$ and $\hat{B}$, and a further state vector $| \phi \rangle$ which is equal to $(\hat{A} + ix\,\hat{B}) | \psi \rangle$, where x is an arbitrary real number; then $\langle \phi | = \langle \psi | (\hat{A} - ix\,\hat{B})$, and so:

$$\langle \phi | \phi \rangle = \langle \psi | \hat{A}^2 | \psi \rangle - x \langle \psi | i\,(\hat{A}\hat{B} - \hat{B}\hat{A}) | \psi \rangle + x^2 \langle \psi | \hat{B}^2 | \psi \rangle$$
$$= \langle \hat{A}^2 \rangle - x \langle i\,[\hat{A}, \hat{B}] \rangle + x^2 \langle \hat{B}^2 \rangle.$$

Now $\langle \phi | \phi \rangle \geq 0$ for any x, so $\langle i\,[\hat{A}, \hat{B}] \rangle^2 \leq 4 \langle \hat{B}^2 \rangle \langle \hat{A}^2 \rangle$ (since $b^2 \leq 4ac$ where, for all x, $ax^2 - bx + c \geq 0$), and therefore:

$$\langle \hat{A}^2 \rangle \langle \hat{B}^2 \rangle \geq 1/4 \; \langle i\,[\hat{A}, \hat{B}] \rangle^2 . \tag{11.24}$$

(Despite appearances, $\langle i[\hat{A}, \hat{B}] \rangle$ is real!) Now if one substitutes, for $\hat{A}$ and $\hat{B}$ in the above inequality, the operators $(\hat{A} - \langle \hat{A} \rangle)$ and $(\hat{B} - \langle \hat{B} \rangle)$, we obtain:

$$\Delta\hat{A}\, \Delta\hat{B} \geq 1/2 \; | \langle i\,[\hat{A}, \hat{B}] \rangle | \tag{11.25}$$

This inequality, called the general uncertainty relationship, follows from equation (11.24), because by definition $\langle (\hat{A} - \langle \hat{A} \rangle)^2 \rangle = (\Delta\hat{A})^2$ and $\langle (\hat{B} - \langle \hat{B} \rangle)^2 \rangle = (\Delta\hat{B})^2$; and, since $\langle \hat{A} \rangle$ and $\langle \hat{B} \rangle$ are just numbers:

$$[(\hat{A} - \langle \hat{A} \rangle), (\hat{B} - \langle \hat{B} \rangle)] = [\hat{A}, \hat{B}].$$

Applying the general uncertainty relationship to the algebraic operators associated with the observables position and momentum on the x axis (namely, $\hat{x} = x$, and $\hat{p} = -i\hbar\, \partial/\partial x$), and using the rule for differentiation of a product (that is, $d/dx\, yz = z\, dy/dx + y\, dz/dx$), we find the following:

$$\hat{p}\hat{x}\, \psi(x) = \hat{x}\hat{p}\, \psi(x) - i\hbar\, \psi(x).$$

Since this is true for any $\psi(x)$, we have:

$$[\hat{x}, \hat{p}] = \hat{x}\hat{p} - \hat{p}\hat{x} = i\hbar. \tag{11.26}$$

Accordingly, from equation (11.25):

$$\Delta\hat{x}\, \Delta\hat{p} \geq 1/2 \; | \langle i \times i\hbar \rangle |$$
$$\geq \hbar/2. \tag{11.27}$$

This is the most usual mathematical expression of Heisenberg's uncertainty principle, in terms of a spread of expectation values, rather than in relation to any single measurement. Pagels (1983: 88–90) suggests that the only valid expression of the uncertainty principle is in such statistical terms. Such a view is consistent with the view that state functions deal only with ensembles of large numbers of particles: the ensemble or statistical view of quantum mechanics. However, if one accepts that state functions represent individual systems, then, as shown *inter alia* by the previous discussion of the wave representation of a single particle, the mathematics of quantum physics *does* involve a somewhat similar uncertainty in individual measurements, as indicated by equation (11.5): this is the view taken by Heisenberg in formulating his microscope thought experiment, and by Bohr in his debate with Einstein.

11.4.11. *Density Operators*

In classical statistical mechanics, calculations are often made concerning what are called statistical mixtures. Such mixtures are represented by mathematical objects which can indicate that one or other of a number of possible states of affairs actually exists, and also indicate their respective probabilities on the basis of what is known about them.

These objects differ from quantum mechanical state vectors in that they convey that there is a deficiency in knowledge: one of the possibilities does *in fact* exist, but *which one* is not known. All that is known is respective probabilities for the various alternatives. On the other hand, while quantum mechanical state vectors show (or enable calculation of) probabilities for various possible states of affairs, no deficiency of knowledge is conveyed: unless and until one of the possibilities is established as a certainty by measurement, no one of them actually exists, except as a possibility. What exists is a superposition of all the possibilities, weighted by their probability amplitudes, with mutual interference.

However, in quantum mechanics as in classical mechanics, it is often necessary to make calculations in terms of statistical mixtures. In classical mechanics, a mixture M can be given by the following equation:

$$M = \Sigma \, d_n S_n \, ,$$

where the S_ns are the possible states of affairs, the d_ns are their respective probabilities, and $\Sigma \, d_n = 1$. However, in quantum mechanics a mixture M of states $| \psi_n \rangle$ cannot be expressed as $\Sigma \, d_n | \psi_n \rangle$ because such a summation of states in quantum mechanics represents a superposition of states, which is itself just another 'pure' state (about which there is nothing more to know), not a mixture.

In order to represent a mixture in quantum mechanics, it is necessary to use, not a state vector or function, but an operator; an operator which is different from the observable and unitary operators so far discussed.

First, it can be noted that a state represented by a vector $| \psi \rangle$ could also be represented by the mathematical object $| \psi \rangle \langle \psi |$. This object contains all the information which the vector $| \psi \rangle$ contains, although different procedures are necessary in order to extract that information. This object is an operator; and mixtures can be represented by means of such operators. Suppose that a system is in fact in one of the states which can be represented by the orthogonal vectors $| \psi_n \rangle$, or by the operators $| \psi_n \rangle \langle \psi_n |$; but that it is not known which one, except to the extent that probabilities d_n for each are known. Then one has a statistical mixture which can be represented by a density operator $\hat{\rho}$, where:

$$\hat{\rho} = \Sigma \, d_n \, | \, \psi_n \rangle \langle \, \psi_n \, | . \qquad (11.28)$$

It can be seen that in the particular case where one of the d_n is 1, so that all the others are 0, the density operator does not represent a mixture but a pure state.

Now, if $| \, \psi_j \rangle$ is any one of the $| \, \psi_n \rangle$,

$$\hat{\rho} \, | \, \psi_j \rangle = \Sigma \, d_n \, | \, \psi_n \rangle \langle \, \psi_n \, | \, \psi_j \rangle .$$

Since the $| \, \psi_n \rangle$ are orthogonal, we have $\langle \, \psi_n \, | \, \psi_j \rangle = 0$ if $j \neq n$, and $= 1$ if $j = n$. So:

$$\hat{\rho} \, | \, \psi_n \rangle = d_n \, | \, \psi_n \rangle .$$

That means that the states $| \, \psi_n \rangle$ are the eigenstates of the operator $\hat{\rho}$, and the probability weightings d_n are the corresponding eigenvalues.

One can derive an expectation value for an observable $\hat{A}$ for a mixture represented by a density operator. This requires use of the idea of the trace of an operator, which is the sum of its eigenvalues. It is in fact the sum of the diagonal elements of its matrix in any representation: although the matrix for an observable operator is different in relation to different sets of base states, the sum of the diagonal elements of the matrix is the same for all of them. Thus where $| \, \psi_1 \rangle, | \, \psi_2 \rangle, \ldots | \, \psi_n \rangle$ is any set of orthogonal base states:

$$\text{trace } (\hat{A}) = \Sigma \, \langle \, \psi_n \, | \, \hat{A} \, | \, \psi_n \rangle .$$

Then, if $\hat{\rho} = \Sigma \, d_n \, | \, \psi_n \rangle \langle \, \psi_n \, |$,

$$\begin{aligned} \text{trace } (\hat{\rho}\hat{A}) &= \Sigma \, \langle \, \psi_n \, | \, \hat{\rho}\hat{A} \, | \, \psi_n \rangle \\ &= \Sigma \, \langle \, \psi_n \, | \, \Sigma \, d_n \, | \psi_n \rangle \langle \, \psi_n \, | \, \hat{A} \, | \, \psi_n \rangle \\ &= \Sigma \, d_n \, \langle \, \psi_n \, | \, \psi_n \rangle \langle \, \psi_n \, | \, \hat{A} \, | \, \psi_n \rangle \\ &= \Sigma \, d_n \, \langle \, \psi_n \, | \, \hat{A} \, | \, \psi_n \rangle . \end{aligned} \qquad (11.29)$$

Now if the $| \, \psi_n \rangle$ are eigenstates of $\hat{A}$,

$$\begin{aligned} \text{trace } (\hat{\rho}\hat{A}) &= \Sigma \, d_n \, \langle \, \psi_n \, | \, a_n \, | \, \psi_n \rangle \\ &= \Sigma \, d_n a_n . \end{aligned}$$

And if the $| \, \psi_n \rangle$ are not eigenstates of $\hat{A}$, then trace $(\hat{\rho}\hat{A})$ equals the sum of the expectation values of $\hat{A}$ for $| \, \psi_n \rangle$, weighted in accordance with the d_ns. In either case, then, trace $(\hat{\rho}\hat{A})$ gives the expectation value of $\hat{A}$ for $\hat{\rho}$.

There are two broad situations where density operators can be used to represent mixtures in quantum mechanics. First, as mentioned above, if a system is in one or other of a number of pure states $| \psi_n \rangle$, but it is not known which, the system may be represented by the density operator $\hat{\rho} = \Sigma d_n | \psi_n \rangle \langle \psi_n |$. Secondly, if a system is not in a pure state at all, because it is only a component of a larger system (which is in a pure state) and has correlations with other parts of that larger system (see Sections 13.1 and 13.3), then it may be appropriate to represent it as a mixture by the density operator $\hat{\rho}$. Mixtures of this second kind are sometimes called 'improper mixtures' (see d'Espagnat 1976, ch. 6 and Sudbery 1986: 190; but see also Krips 1987: 93–6). In this second situation, the operator does not contain all possible information about the component system—only the representation of the combined system can do this—but it may contain all the information that there can be about the component system considered in isolation.

Some philosophical discussions make considerable use of the density operator formalism; and Krips (1987; chs. 4 and 5) in particular suggests that it helps to provide a solution to the measurement problem of quantum mechanics. However, I do not agree: see Section 14.2.

11.5. Spin and Polarization

The discussion so far has concerned the state of a particle, such as an electron, proton, or neutron, in so far as it relates to position, momentum, and energy. It is now to be extended in two directions.

First, it is necessary to refer to another important observable property of such 'matter-like' particles, which is not dealt with by the state vector or function as so far discussed. This is the spin of such a particle, its 'internal' or intrinsic angular momentum: it is a quantized angular momentum, which does *not* arise (as does angular momentum in classical physics) from any motion around a centre of mass.

Secondly, it is necessary to note that quantum physics also deals with the states of the quantum of electromagnetic radiation, the photon. However, since photons 'travel' at the speed of light, treatment of the state of a photon, so far as concerns position and momentum, must take account of relativity effects. As noted earlier, I do not undertake this here. However, there is an observable property of photons which is of considerable theoretical interest, and which I shall discuss. This is polarization, which is dealt with in classical physics, and is indeed a matter of some common knowledge. It is recognized in quantum mechanics as a property analogous to the spin of matter-like particles, with differences related to the circumstances that photons travel at the speed of light, and cannot be measured without being destroyed.

11.5.1. Spin

To represent the complete quantum physical state of a particle such as an electron, it is necessary to have a state vector representing position, momentum, and energy as discussed above (in three dimensions), and also a state vector representing spin—or else a single state vector representing all these observables. As noted above, spin is an intrinsic angular momentum. In particles such as electrons, its magnitude is always $\hbar/2$. It can be measured on any axis, and when so measured will be found to be either $+\hbar/2$ (if in one direction, namely clockwise looking from the negative to the positive direction along the axis in question—called spin 'up') or $-\hbar/2$ (if in the other direction—called spin 'down').

As with other quantum physical states, the spin state of a particle can be expressed as a sum of or superposition of amplitudes to be found in each of a set of base states, which is complete and orthonormal. In the case of spin, such a complete set of base states is provided by the two states, spin up and spin down, in any direction: often, the z direction of the frame of reference being used is chosen. Thus, any spin state of a particle (which I will write $|S\rangle$) can be expressed as the amplitude to be found in the up state in the z direction (which I will write $|+z\rangle$ or simply $|+\rangle$) plus the amplitude to be found in the down state in the z direction (which I will write $|-z\rangle$ or $|-\rangle$). Then we have:

$$|S\rangle = c_1|+z\rangle + c_2|-z\rangle.$$

Here, the amplitudes c_1 and c_2 are generally complex numbers, given by the inner products $\langle +z|S\rangle$ and $\langle -z|S\rangle$ respectively. Also, because $|+z\rangle$ and $|-z\rangle$ make up an orthonormal set of base states:

$$\langle +z|-z\rangle = \langle -z|+z\rangle = 0$$
$$\langle +z|+z\rangle = \langle -z|-z\rangle = 1.$$

Given $|S\rangle$ expressed as above, it is possible to express $|S\rangle$ in terms of amplitudes for base states of spin up and spin down in any direction, including, of course, the x and y directions in the same frame of reference. In the particular case where $|S\rangle$ has been measured in the z direction and found to be in the state $|+z\rangle$, the following results obtain for the x and y directions:

$$|+z\rangle = 1/\sqrt{2} \ |+x\rangle - 1/\sqrt{2} \ |-x\rangle$$
$$= 1/\sqrt{2} \ |+y\rangle - i/\sqrt{2} \ |-y\rangle.$$

Thus, when there is certainty regarding the spin in the z direction (here, that it is spin up), the uncertainty regarding spin on the other two axes is maximized: the probabilities of measurements of spin up and spin down in the x direction are each 1/2, and similarly in the y direction. Spin in each of the three directions of the coordinate system is an incompatible observable, as regards spin in the direction of each of the other two axes: just as there cannot be simultaneous certainty about position (on any axis) and momentum (on the same axis), so also there cannot be certainty about spin on more than one axis.

A state vector which fully represents the state of an electron would thus have to give the amplitudes for it to be found in each of a set of base states, comprising base states associated with its state of motion (such as energy base states $|\psi_n\rangle$) and, for each of such states, the two base states associated with its spin in some direction:

$$|\psi\rangle = \Sigma c_n |\psi_n +\rangle + \Sigma d_n |\psi_n -\rangle.$$

Here, c_n gives the amplitude for $|\psi\rangle$ to be found to be in energy state $|\psi_n\rangle$ *and* also spin state $|+\rangle$ in (say) the z direction; and d_n the amplitude for $|\psi\rangle$ to be found to be in energy state $|\psi_n\rangle$ and also spin state $|-\rangle$.

Alternatively, the state vector can be considered as a function ψ having two parts, one associated with spin up in the z direction, and one with spin down. I will say more about combination of state functions (and of state vectors) in Chapter 13.

11.5.2. *Polarization*

1. In classical physics. According to classical physics, light is propagated as an electromagnetic wave, comprising electric and magnetic fields oscillating at right angles to each other and to the direction of propagation. At every point of a light ray, the electric field (which determines the force it exerts) can be represented as a vector (of the ordinary three-dimensional kind) lying in the plane which is perpendicular to the direction of propagation. If, at each point on the ray, this vector oscillates in the same direction, the light is said to be polarized in that direction. At least, this is in accordance with common usage: in scientific usage, the light is said more precisely to be plane polarized (because the lines along which the vector oscillates are parallel with each other and together make up a plane), to distinguish the case from other possible forms of polarization, namely various kinds of elliptical and circular polarization, to which I will come.

Light which is plane polarized in a certain direction will be passed entirely by a polarizer (such as a piece of polaroid, as used in some sun-glasses) with its axis in the same direction. However, if the polarizer is set with its axis at an angle θ to the direction of polarization, not all the light is passed: the intensity of the light is reduced to $\cos^2 \theta$ times the original intensity. If the axis of the polarizer is perpendicular to the direction of polarization (so that $\theta = \pi/2$ and $\cos^2 \theta = 0$), no light is passed. Light that is passed by a polarizer becomes polarized in the direction of the axis of the polarizer. Light not passed is absorbed by the polarizer, and its energy raises the temperature of the polarizer.

(Light can also be polarized by being passed through a calcite crystal: in this case, *all* the light is passed, but in two separate beams, one plane polarized in one direction, and the other plane polarized at right angles to this direction. Then, if the light was initially plane polarized at an angle θ to the axis of the crystal, the intensities of the two beams are respectively $\cos^2 \theta$ and $\sin^2 \theta$ times that of the original. For the most part, I will consider polarizers which absorb some of the light rather than such crystals.)

This is dealt with in classical physics, by considering the electric vector as being resolved into component vectors perpendicular to each other. Thus if the electric vector $\mathbf{E}(t)$ oscillates immediately in front of the polarizer in accordance with $\mathbf{E}_A \cos \omega t$, then $\mathbf{E}_A$ (the amplitude of the oscillation) may be considered as being made up by $(\mathbf{i} \cdot \mathbf{E}_A)\,\mathbf{i} + (\mathbf{j} \cdot \mathbf{E}_A)\,\mathbf{j}$, where $\mathbf{i}$ is a unit vector in the direction of the axis of the polarizer and $\mathbf{j}$ is a unit vector perpendicular to such direction (and to the direction of propagation). If the angle between the direction of polarization and the axis of the polarizer is θ, then $\mathbf{i} \cdot \mathbf{E}_A$ equals $\mathbf{E}_A \cos \theta$ and $\mathbf{j} \cdot \mathbf{E}_A$ equals $\mathbf{E}_A \sin \theta$. Passing through the polarizer eliminates the $\mathbf{j}$ component of the vector, leaving a vector in the $\mathbf{i}$ direction, with amplitude $\mathbf{E} \cos \theta$. The intensity of the light is proportional to the square of the amplitude of the electric vector, so it is reduced to $\cos^2 \theta$ times the original intensity.

The above discussion deals with a case where the oscillation has a single angular frequency ω, so that the light is monochromatic: it can be extended to plane-polarized light which is *not* monochromatic.

Other states of polarization are possible. In the case of monochromatic light, which is not plane polarized, the electric vector can be resolved into components in the $\mathbf{i}$ and $\mathbf{j}$ directions which have different phases:

$$\mathbf{E}(t) = E_i(t)\,\mathbf{i} + E_j(t)\mathbf{j},$$

where $E_i(t) = \mathbf{E}_A \cos \theta \cos(\omega t + \phi_i)$ and $E_j(t) = \mathbf{E}_A \sin \theta \cos(\omega t + \phi_j)$. This means that at any point the tip of the electric vector can be envisaged as moving round an ellipse in the plane perpendicular to the direction of propagation. (Where $\phi_i = \phi_j$, the oscillations are in phase, and the light is plane polarized.) Where $\cos \theta = \sin \theta$ and $\phi_i - \phi_j = \pi/2$, the light is said to be in a state of right-handed circular polarization; and where $\cos \theta = \sin \theta$, and $\phi_i - \phi_j = 3\pi/2$, the light is said to be in a state of left-handed circular polarization.

If the direction of oscillation of the electric field is random, the light is unpolarized: and if unpolarized light meets a polarizer with its axis set in any direction, then the intensity of the light is reduced to one-half (or $\cos^2 \pi/4$) of its previous intensity; and again, the light which is passed becomes polarized in the direction of the axis of the polarizer.

2. In quantum physics. In quantum physics, light is considered as being made up of photons, the quanta or packages of electromagnetic radiation. If a beam of light is plane polarized in (say) the x direction, then the state of polarization of each photon in the beam can be considered to be in that direction. I will use the notation $|P\rangle$ to represent a general state of polarization, and $|x\rangle$ to represent plane polarization in the x direction; so in respect of each photon:

$$|P\rangle = |x\rangle.$$

If such a beam meets a polarizer with its axis in the x direction, each photon will be passed; and its state of polarization will be unchanged. However, if a beam of light is plane polarized at an angle θ to the x direction, and meets a polarizer with its axis in the x direction (perpendicular to the direction of propagation), the classical results indicate that the intensity of the light is reduced to $\cos^2 \theta$ times its original intensity, and that the direction of polarization becomes that of the axis of the polarizer. In quantum physics, this is taken to mean that some photons are passed by the polarizer (and have their direction of polarization changed to that of the polarizer), and some are absorbed by it: the classical result concerning intensity indicates that the proportion of those passed must be close to $\cos^2 \theta$. Each individual photon is either absorbed or passed, yet there is nothing relevantly to distinguish one photon from another: each is plane polarized in a direction at an angle θ to the x direction.

Quantum physics deals with this by asserting that the state of polarization of each photon is a superposition of amplitudes to be found in each of two orthogonal base states, one of which can be chosen as plane polarization in the x direction, in which case the other is plane polarization in the y direction (similarly perpendicular to the direction of propagation, and also perpendicular to the x direction):

$$|P\rangle = c_1|x\rangle + c_2|y\rangle.$$

As before, c_1 represents the amplitude for a photon in the state $|P\rangle$ to be found to be in the state $|x\rangle$; and similarly for c_2 and $|y\rangle$. The photon will be found to be in the state $|x\rangle$ if it is found to have passed the polarizer whose axis is in the x direction; and will be found to be in the state $|y\rangle$ if it is found to have been absorbed by that polarizer.

The probability of the alternative results will then be respectively $|c_1|^2$ and $|c_2|^2$. As before, c_1 and c_2 can be complex, but in the case of plane polarization the complexity lies only in a possible common phase factor, and c_1 and c_2 can be taken as $\cos \theta$ and $\sin \theta$ respectively. Thus the probability for any photon in the state $|P\rangle$ to be found to have the state $|x\rangle$, that is, be found to have passed through the polarizer, is $\cos^2 \theta$; and, out of a large number of photons in that state, a proportion of about $\cos^2 \theta$ will be found to have passed, consistently with the classical result.

In accordance with the previous discussion, the amplitudes c_1 and c_2 can be expressed as inner products $\langle x|P\rangle$ and $\langle y|P\rangle$; and, also in accordance with that discussion, $\langle x|x\rangle = \langle y|y\rangle = 1$, and $\langle x|y\rangle = \langle y|x\rangle = 0$.

States of polarization other than plane polarization can be dealt with similarly. If there is a beam of monochromatic light which is elliptically polarized, the state of polarization of individual photons can still not be distinguished; and the state of each can be written as a superposition of amplitudes to be found to have plane polarization in the x direction and in the y direction:

$$|P\rangle = c_1 |x\rangle + c_2 |y\rangle.$$

In the case of elliptical polarization, however, the c_1 and/or the c_2 will be complex. The general form will be:

$$|P\rangle = \cos\theta \exp(i\phi_i) |x\rangle + \sin\theta \exp(i\phi_j) |y\rangle.$$

In the particular case of states $|R\rangle$ and $|L\rangle$, representing right-handed and left-handed polarization respectively, $\theta = \pi/2$, and the phase difference $\phi_i - \phi_j$ is $\pi/2$ (in the case of $|R\rangle$) or $3\pi/2$ (in the case of $|L\rangle$). Then, if ϕ_j is set at $\pi/2$ (in other words, if a common phase factor of $\exp[i(\phi_j - \pi/2)]$ is ignored), we have:

$$|R\rangle = 1/\sqrt{2}\,(|x\rangle + i|y\rangle)$$
$$|L\rangle = -1/\sqrt{2}\,(|x\rangle - i|y\rangle).$$

It can then be shown that $|R\rangle$ and $|L\rangle$ can also be chosen as base states: they can be shown to be orthogonal, and all other states of polarization can be represented in terms of them. For example, by adding and substracting the above, we get:

$$|x\rangle = 1/\sqrt{2}\,(|R\rangle + |L\rangle)$$
$$|y\rangle = -i/\sqrt{2}\,(|R\rangle - |L\rangle).$$

It will also be seen that plane polarization and circular polarization are incompatible observables; and that certainty regarding one gives maximum uncertainty regarding the other. If a photon is known to be in the state $|x\rangle$ (or the state $|y\rangle$), then the probability of its being found to be in the state $|R\rangle$ is the same as that of its being found to be in the state $|L\rangle$, namely 1/2. Similarly, if a photon is known to be in the state $|R\rangle$ (or in the state $|L\rangle$), then the probability of its being found to be in the state $|x\rangle$ is the same as that of its being found to be in the state $|y\rangle$, namely (again) 1/2.

12

The Development of the Quantum State

In Chapter 11, I considered at some length the representation of the quantum state of a particle at a particular time, and especially how that representation relates to values obtained by measurement of certain observables. In doing so, I mentioned one way in which the quantum mechanical state of a particle can change, namely by measurement: according to the quantum theory, when an observable of a particle is precisely measured, the state of that particle (if it was not previously an eigenstate of that observable) will change to an eigenstate of that observable, with the probability for any particular eigenstate being indicated by the state vector prior to measurement. This sudden, partly unpredictable, and indeterministic change to the quantum physical state of a particle—the reduction of the quantum state, which the mathematician von Neumann called 'process 1'—will be further considered in Chapter 14.

Quantum theory also postulates a second way in which the quantum mechanical state of a particle can change, namely by development over time in the absence of measurement: this process—called by von Neumann 'process 2'—is, according to the quantum theory, entirely deterministic, taking place in accordance with 'equations of motion' analogous to those of classical physics. Using these equations, if one knows the state vector at one time, and also knows sufficient about the forces acting on the system, one can calculate the state vector at a later time, and thereby ascertain the probabilities of the results of various measurements, should they be made at such later time.

12.1. The Schrödinger Equation

The 'equation of motion' most generally used in order to calculate the development over time of a quantum mechanical state is that formulated in 1926 by Erwin Schrödinger as applying to state functions. It is not possible to prove the validity of this equation mathematically: its justification is that the results it gives accord with the results of measurements. It can perhaps best be introduced by a discussion showing its plausibility, which builds on the previous discussion concerning momentum and energy eigenstates and eigenvalues.

12.1.1. *A Plausible Derivation of the Schrödinger Equation*

It will be recalled from equation (10.19) and Section 11.2 that the state function ψ for a free particle of momentum p $(= \hbar k)$ in one dimension is given by:

$$\psi = N \exp [i (kx - \omega t)].$$

If one takes a partial derivative of each side with respect to t (holding x constant), and multiplies each side by $i\hbar$, one gets:

$$i\hbar(\partial/\partial t)\psi = \hbar\omega\,\psi.$$

Now the energy of a photon is given by $h\nu$ $(= \hbar\omega)$; and, using the de Broglie analogy, one can suggest that the energy E of a particle is similarly $\hbar\omega$. That is, one associates the angular frequency ω of the wave with total energy. Then, one obtains:

$$i\hbar(\partial/\partial t)\psi = E\psi. \tag{12.1}$$

From earlier discussion of eigenvalues, we can use the energy eigenvalue equation $\hat{H}\psi = E\psi$ to obtain an equation of motion:

$$\hat{H}\psi = i\hbar(\partial/\partial t)\psi. \tag{12.2}$$

We began the discussion considering a free particle (i.e. one in relation to which the potential $V = 0$), so the conclusion is limited to the case of a free particle (where $\hat{H} = - (\hbar^2/2m)\partial^2/\partial x^2)$. However, it is reasonable to generalize it to cases where the particle is not free (where $\hat{H} = - (\hbar^2/2m)\partial^2/\partial x^2) + V(x, t))$. One thereby obtains the equation:

$$[- (\hbar^2/2m)\partial^2/\partial x^2 + V(x, t)]\psi = i\hbar\,\partial\psi/\partial t. \tag{12.3}$$

This is the Schrödinger equation, sometimes called the time-dependent Schrödinger equation (to distinguish it from the energy eigenvalue equation (11.16), which is sometimes called the time-independent Schrödinger equation). It can be generalized to three dimensions:

$$[- (\hbar^2/2m)\nabla^2 + V(\mathbf{r}, t)]\psi(\mathbf{r}, t) = i\hbar(\partial/\partial t)\psi(\mathbf{r}, t). \tag{12.4}$$

If one can solve this equation, by finding ψ as a function of x (or $\mathbf{r}$) and t, then one is in a position to calculate the value of ψ (and thereby the position probability function $|\psi|^2$ and other probability functions discussed earlier) for different positions and times.

In order to show this equation in its most general form, I have shown the potential energy V as time-dependent. This introduces major complications, and in the remainder of my discussion I will assume that potential energy depends only on position, as can be assumed to be the case in dealing with many problems.

It will be observed that the time evolution of the quantum state is governed by the Hamiltonian operator. In this respect, there is an analogy with Hamilton's formulation of classical mechanics. According to this formulation, the time development of the classical state is governed by the Hamiltonian H, here generally being the total energy $p^2/2m + V(x, t)$, in accordance with the equations given at the end of Section 10.1:

$$\partial H/\partial p = dx/dt$$
$$\partial H/\partial x = - dp/dt.$$

12.1.2. *Stationary States*

As we have seen, the energy eigenstates satisfy the equation (11.16):

$$\hat{H}\psi = E\psi.$$

From the previous section, the energy eigenstates also satisfy the equation (12.1):

$$i\hbar(\partial/\partial t)\psi = E\psi.$$

It can be shown from this that any time dependence of energy eigenstates is purely a phase factor $\exp(- i\omega t)$. Suppose that $\psi(x, t)$ can be separated into a product of separate functions $\phi(x)f(t)$. Then from the above equation:

$$i\hbar(\partial/\partial t)f(t)\phi(x) = E f(t)\phi(x)$$
$$\therefore \ i\hbar \ df/dt = E f(t)$$
$$\therefore \ df/dt = - iE/\hbar \ f(t)$$
$$= - i\omega f(t).$$

Now the general solution to the equation $dy/dx = ia \ y$ is $y = \exp(iax)$. So we have:

$$f(t) = \exp(- i\omega t).$$

Thus, if $\psi(x, t)$ is an energy eigenstate:

$$\psi(x, t) = \phi(x) \exp(- i\omega t).$$

It follows that $|\psi(x, t)|^2$ is equal to $|\phi(x)|^2$, which means that, in the case of energy eigenstates, the probability function for position is independent of time. For this reason, energy eigenstates, the states for which the energy of a particle is definite, are called stationary states. This means that if a particle has a definite energy, that is, is in an energy eigenstate rather than a superposition of such eigenstates, then the probabilities for position measurements remain constant over time.

12.1.3. *Time Operator*

The time evolution of the quantum state can also be expressed in terms of an operator $\hat{U}(t)$ or $\hat{U}$, which is such that the application of the operator to the state function (or vector) at time t_0 gives the state function at time t.

$$\psi(x, t) = \hat{U}(t)\psi(x, t_0). \qquad (12.6)$$

The form of $\hat{U}(t)$ can be derived as follows. If the above is substituted into the Schrödinger equation, one gets:

$$\hat{H}\hat{U}(t)\psi(x, t_0) = i\hbar \, \partial/\partial t \quad \hat{U}(t) \, \psi(x, t_0).$$

Since this is to be true for *any* $\psi(x, t_0)$, we get:

$$i\hbar \;\; d/dt \, (\hat{U}(t)) = \hat{H}\hat{U}(t)$$
$$\therefore \;\; d/dt \, (\hat{U}(t)) = -i\hat{H}/\hbar \; \hat{U}(t)$$
$$\therefore \;\; \hat{U}(t) = \exp(-i\hat{H}t/\hbar). \qquad (12.7)$$

Thus $\hat{U}(t)$ is a power series in the operator $\hat{H}$ (*not* a number): it is not easy to apply generally, but it does have a quite simple application with respect to energy eigenstates.

If $\psi_n(x, t)$ is an energy eigenstate, with eigenvalue E_n, then $\hat{H}\psi_n(x, t)$ equals $E_n\psi_n(x, t)$. Now, in accordance with rules concerning functions of operators, this in turn means that:

$$\exp(-i\hat{H}t/\hbar) \;\; \psi_n(x, t) = \exp(-iE_nt/\hbar) \;\; \psi_n(x, t).$$

Accordingly, if we have a general state function written as a combination of energy eigenstates $\Sigma c_n\psi_n(x, t)$, the time development of the system can be given a direct numerical expression:

$$\psi(x, t) = \Sigma c_n\psi_n(x, t)$$
$$= \Sigma c_n \exp(-iE_nt/\hbar) \;\; \psi(x, t_0). \qquad (12.8)$$

It may be noted that, in terms of my previous discussions of operators, the time operator is *not* hermitian, is not an observable operator, and does not have real eigenvalues. It is a unitary operator.

It may also be noted that the conclusions of the above discussion can be considered as applying to state vectors $|\psi\rangle$, when those state vectors are considered as functions, and operators are considered as algebraic operators. The effect of time development on a state vector can be pictured in the following way. The state vector is a unit vector pointing in a particular direction in multidimensional space, and the probability amplitudes for different measurements of an observable are given by the projection of the state vector on to each of the orthogonal base vectors for that observable. Process 2 time development rotates the state vector, thus altering its projections on to the base vectors, and thereby altering the probability amplitudes for different measurements. If a measurement is made of an observable, then the state vector 'collapses' on to the particular base vector for that observable which is associated with the measured value: this is the collapse or reduction of the quantum state.

12.2. The Heisenberg Picture

It will be apparent that the discussion so far has proceeded on the assumption that what changes with time is the state vector (or function); that the observable operators generally do not change with time (the exception being the Hamiltonian, in those cases where the system is subject to forces which vary explicitly with time, and not merely with location); and that similarly the eigenvalues and eigenstates generally do not change (the exception again being energy eigenstates, in those cases where the Hamiltonian varies with time). The change with time in the state vector involves changes in the inner products of the state vector with the vectors of the various eigenstates; so that thereby the possibilities and probabilities of the results of various measurements similarly change. This essentially is the Schrödinger picture of time development of the quantum physical state.

In the Heisenberg picture, the mathematical object representing the quantum physical state does not change. What are considered as changing with time are the observable operators, and it is the changes to these operators which involve changes in the possibilities and probabilities of the results of various measurements. An idea of how this works can be given by the following.

12.2.1. Bra–Operator–Ket Sandwiches

In his brief explanation of the Heisenberg picture, Polkinghorne (1984: 88–9) asserts that the physical interpretation of the theory is all expressed in terms of 'bra–operator–ket' sandwiches of the form $\langle \phi \mid \hat{A} \mid \psi \rangle$. At first sight, this seems wrong, because at least two aspects of such physical interpretation do not appear to require such 'sandwiches':

1. the eigenvalues of an observable operator $\hat{A}$, that is, the possible results of precise measurements, are given by the equation $\hat{A} \mid \psi_n \rangle = a_n \mid \psi_n \rangle$; and

2. the probability of measuring a state $\mid \psi \rangle$ to have a particular eigenvalue a_n is given by $\mid c_n \mid^2$, where $c_n = \langle \psi_n \mid \psi \rangle$, $\mid \psi_n \rangle$ being the eigenstate associated with that eigenvalue.

However, there is a sense in which the assertion is correct. Unless and until events occur which can be mathematically represented by a bra–operator–ket sandwich, the matters represented by the mathematical objects used by the quantum theory are (so far as the ordinary physical world is concerned) purely hypothetical: that is, such objects indicate merely what *could* be the result of measurement *if* measurement were to occur.

Thus, in relation to a system represented by $|\psi\rangle$, the information that the observable $\hat{A}$ has eigenstates $|\psi_n\rangle$, and eigenvalues a_n, indicates only the following: that *if* $|\psi\rangle$ is subjected to a precise measurement of $\hat{A}$, *then* the result will be one of the eigenvalues, and the system will be left in a corresponding eigenstate. Further, the information that the state $|\psi\rangle$ is equal to $\Sigma c_n |\psi_n\rangle$, where the $|\psi_n\rangle$ are the eigenstates of an observable $\hat{A}$, and the c_n are given by $\langle \psi_n | \psi\rangle$, indicates only the following: that the amplitudes for the $|\psi_n\rangle$ are c_n (this having consequences in relation to the expression of $|\psi\rangle$ in terms of the eigenstates of *other* observables, and also in relation to its time development); and that *if* $|\psi\rangle$ is subjected to a precise measurement of $\hat{A}$, *then* the probability of the result a_n is $|c_n|^2$. The latter links to physical reality only hypothetically; while the former does not directly link to reality at all, since it only gives rise to other expressions of the state function or to further state functions.

A bra–operator–ket sandwich, on the other hand, can be regarded as mathematically representing an actuality. For example, $\langle \phi | \hat{A} | \psi\rangle$ can be regarded as representing an application to the state $|\psi\rangle$ of an apparatus appropriate to measure $\hat{A}$, and a determination that the state $|\phi\rangle$ has resulted. If it is so regarded, the vector $|\phi\rangle$ will in fact be an eigenstate of the observable $\hat{A}$, which can be written $|\psi_n\rangle$. We know that, where $|\psi\rangle = \Sigma c_n |\psi_n\rangle$, $\hat{A}|\psi\rangle = \Sigma a_n c_n |\psi_n\rangle$, so that $\langle \psi_n | \hat{A} | \psi\rangle = a_n c_n$ (because $\langle \psi_n | \psi_n\rangle = 1$, and $\langle \psi_n | \psi_m\rangle = 0$ where $m \neq n$). One can therefore express both the eigenvalue a_n, and the amplitude c_n, in terms of the sandwich $\langle \psi_n | \hat{A} | \psi\rangle$, as follows:

$$a_n = \langle \psi_n | \hat{A} | \psi\rangle / \langle \psi_n | \psi\rangle$$

$$c_n = \langle \psi_n | \hat{A} | \psi\rangle / a_n .$$

Another way of expressing the idea that $\langle \psi_n | \psi\rangle$ is hypothetical is to say that a state does not *spontaneously* jump into an eigenstate of an observable: it will make such a jump only if a precise measurement is made of the observable in question; and such a measurement can be represented by the application of the relevant observable operator to the state vector, and the representation of the eigenstate which the system is then found to be in. (We will see that one suggestion made to overcome the problem of measurement, which I mention in Section 14.8.5, is to the effect that spontaneous jumps into eigenstates do occur; but this is not a generally held view.)

As an example of this idea, consider a photon passing through a calcite crystal, and thereby being put into a superposition of two polarization states. If the original polarization state was $|P\rangle$, one can represent the calcite crystal by a polarization operator $\hat{A}$, and the process can be represented by:

$$\hat{A} \mid P \rangle = c_1 \mid x \rangle + c_2 \mid y \rangle .$$

(There is no a_1 or a_2 involved here, because the eigenvalues of the states of polarization are simply unity.) If one places a photon detector in the path of the component with the $\mid y \rangle$ polarization, and no photon is detected, it is thereby established that the photon's polarization is $\mid x \rangle$; and the whole process can then be represented by $\langle x \mid \hat{A} \mid P \rangle$. This expression equals c_1, the amplitude for $\mid x \rangle$ of $\mid P \rangle$. Merely to pass the photon through the crystal (a process represented by $\hat{A} \mid P \rangle$)) does not give a physical result unless and until it is determined whether the polarization is in fact (say) $\mid x \rangle$ rather than $\mid y \rangle$ (making the sandwich $\langle x \mid \hat{A} \mid P \rangle$)); while the transition $\langle x \mid P \rangle$ does not occur spontaneously, so the number $\mid \langle x \mid P \rangle \mid^2$ gives only the probability of such a transition *if* a polarization measurement is made.

Apart from the eigenstate–operator–state sandwich considered above, there is another sandwich which links to reality, namely the state–operator–state sandwich $\langle \psi \mid \hat{A} \mid \psi \rangle$, which, as we have seen, gives the expectation value $\langle \hat{A} \rangle$ of observable $\hat{A}$ for the state $\mid \psi \rangle$. This cannot be interpreted as simply representing the application of an apparatus represented by $\hat{A}$ to $\mid \psi \rangle$, with $\mid \psi \rangle$ as the resultant state; because $\mid \psi \rangle$ is not generally an eigenstate of $\hat{A}$. It could be regarded as representing a repeated application of $\hat{A}$ to $\mid \psi \rangle$, with the distribution of the resultant eigenstates being weighted in accordance with the original state $\mid \psi \rangle$; thereby giving a mean or expectation value, as mathematically shown earlier.

12.2.2. *Time-Dependent Operators*

In the previous section, I discussed two important cases of bra–operator–ket sandwiches, namely $\langle \psi_n \mid \hat{A} \mid \psi \rangle$, giving the product of a_n (the eigenvalue associated with eigenstate $\mid \psi_n \rangle$) and c_n (the amplitude of state $\mid \psi \rangle$ to change to eigenstate $\mid \psi_n \rangle$); and $\langle \psi \mid \hat{A} \mid \psi \rangle$, giving the expectation value $\langle \hat{A} \rangle$ of the observable $\hat{A}$ for state $\mid \psi \rangle$.

According to the Schrödinger picture, $\mid \psi \rangle$ will generally vary with time t, in accordance with the Schrödinger equation; so that c_n and $\langle \hat{A} \rangle$ will similarly vary. However, according to the Heisenberg picture, the state $\mid \psi \rangle$ does not vary with time, but rather the operator $\hat{A}$ does; and it is the time development of the operator which results in time variations of c_n and $\langle \hat{A} \rangle$.

This can readily be seen in relation to expectation values. We know from equation (12.7) that a state $\mid \psi \rangle$ at time t can be expressed in terms of the state $\mid \psi_0 \rangle$ at time 0 by means of the time operator $\hat{U}(t)$ or $\hat{U}$, that is, $\exp(-i\hat{H}t/\hbar)$:

$$\mid \psi \rangle = \hat{U}(t) \mid \psi_0 \rangle = \exp(-i\hat{H}t/\hbar) \mid \psi_0 \rangle .$$

The hermitian conjugate of $\exp(-i\hat{H}t/\hbar)$ is $\exp(i\hat{H}t/\hbar)$, so the equivalent equation for bra vectors is:

$$\langle \psi | = \langle \psi_0 | \exp(i\hat{H}t/\hbar).$$

Accordingly, the bra–operator–ket sandwich $\langle \psi | \hat{A} | \psi \rangle$ can be written $\langle \psi_0 | \exp(i\hat{H}t/\hbar) \hat{A}_0 \exp(-i\hat{H}t/\hbar) | \psi_0 \rangle$. (I have replaced $\hat{A}$ by $\hat{A}_0$ to indicate that this is the operator at time 0). One can then write the sandwich as $\langle \psi_0 | \hat{A}(t) | \psi_0 \rangle$ so that the time-dependence has shifted from the bra and ket vectors to the operator $\hat{A}(t)$, where

$$\hat{A}(t) = \exp(i\hat{H}t/\hbar) \hat{A}_0 \exp(-i\hat{H}t/\hbar) = \hat{U}^{-1} \hat{A}_0 \hat{U}. \qquad (12.9)$$

Then, on both the Schrödinger and the Heisenberg approaches, it can be said that $\langle \psi_0 | \hat{A}_0 | \psi_0 \rangle$ gives the expectation value $\langle \hat{A}_0 \rangle$ for the state $| \psi_0 \rangle$ of the observable $\hat{A}_0$, at time 0. According to the Schrödinger approach, at time t the expectation value $\langle \hat{A} \rangle$ for the (time-dependent) state $| \psi \rangle$ of the time-independent observable $\hat{A}$ (which is the same as $\hat{A}_0$) is given by $\langle \psi | \hat{A} | \psi \rangle$. According to the Heisenberg approach, at time t, the *same* expectation value $\langle \hat{A} \rangle$ is given; but this is an expectation value for the time-independent state $| \psi_0 \rangle$ of the time-dependent observable $\hat{A}(t)$, and is given by $\langle \psi_0 | \hat{A}(t) | \psi_0 \rangle$. The expectation value is the same, in both cases, because:

$$\langle \psi | \hat{A} | \psi \rangle = \langle \psi_0 | \hat{U}^{-1}\hat{A}_0 \hat{U} | \psi_0 \rangle = \langle \psi_0 | \hat{A}(t) | \psi_0 \rangle.$$

When we turn to the eigenstate–operator–state sandwich, the matter becomes somewhat more complicated. This is because, on the Schrödinger approach, the eigenstate portion of the sandwich does not change over time under the influence of the time operator which operates on the state; while, on the Heisenberg approach, the relevant eigenstate *does* change, because the observable *operator* changes. However, here too it can be shown that an approach which uses time-independent states and the time-dependent operator $\hat{A}(t)$ previously described gives the same results as does the Schrödinger approach previously considered.

12.2.3. *Heisenberg's Equation of Motion*

The Heisenberg approach is more difficult to apply for solving many problems. However, it does have advantages in some areas, and it also gives rise to equations of motion which are similar to equations of classical physics.

Heisenberg's equation of motion gives the rate of change of the operator $\hat{A}(t)$ (or $\hat{U}^{-1} \hat{A}_0 \hat{U}$) with respect to time t. Because of the exponential form of $\hat{U}$, $i\hbar\, d\hat{U}/dt = \hat{U}\hat{H}$ and $i\hbar\, d\hat{U}^{-1}/dt = -\hat{H}\hat{U}^{-1}$; and therefore:

$$i\hbar\, d\hat{A}/dt = \hat{A}\hat{H} - \hat{H}\hat{A} = [\hat{A}, \hat{H}]. \qquad (12.10)$$

This is Heisenberg's equation of motion. We see again that if $\hat{A}_0$ commutes with $\hat{H}$, and thereby with $\hat{U}$ (and thus also with $\hat{A}(t)$), then $\hat{A}$ is constant $(d\hat{A}/dt = 0)$: again, an indication of conservation of energy. Heisenberg's equation of motion is very similar to an equation of classical Hamiltonian mechanics, namely:

$$dA/dt = \{A, H\} .$$

Here H is the classical observable total energy, A is any classical observable, and the expression $\{A, H\}$ is called the Poisson bracket of two observables, which has properties similar to those of the commutator $[\hat{A}, \hat{H}]$ in quantum mechanics.

12.3. Ehrenfest's Equations

One can derive from Heisenberg's formulation equations of motion for expectation values; and thus confirm that quantum mechanics will generally give results which correspond to those of classical mechanics where large numbers of particles are involved, and where the indeterminacy of individual quantum events is not significant. Thus, for any observable $\hat{A}$,

$$
\begin{aligned}
d\langle \hat{A} \rangle/dt &= d/dt \langle \psi_0 | \hat{A}(t) | \psi_0 \rangle \\
&= \langle \psi_0 | (i\hbar)^{-1} [\hat{A}, \hat{H}] | \psi_0 \rangle \\
&= \langle i/\hbar [\hat{H}, \hat{A}] \rangle .
\end{aligned}
\tag{12.11}
$$

If this is applied to a single particle moving in the x direction in a potential for that direction of $V(x)$, we find the following. Since $\hat{H} = \hat{p}^2/2m + V(x)$, and recognizing that V and $\hat{x}$ commute (so that $[V, \hat{x}] = 0$) and using equation (11.26), we have:

$$
\begin{aligned}
[\hat{H}, \hat{x}] &= (1/2m)[\hat{p}^2, \hat{x}] + [V, \hat{x}] \\
&= (1/2m)([\hat{p}, \hat{x}]\hat{p} + \hat{p}[\hat{p}, \hat{x}]) \\
&= (- i\hbar/m)\hat{p} .
\end{aligned}
\tag{12.12}
$$

Since from (12.11), we have $d\langle \hat{x} \rangle /dt = i/\hbar \langle [\hat{H}, \hat{x}] \rangle$, we can derive from (12.12):

$$d\langle \hat{x} \rangle/dt = \langle \hat{p} \rangle/m .\tag{12.13}$$

Also:

$$[\hat{H}, \hat{p}] = [V, \hat{p}] .$$

Applying $[V, \hat{p}]$ to ψ, an arbitrary function of x, and using the rule relating to differentiation of a product:

$$
\begin{aligned}
[V, \hat{p}]\psi &= V(- i\hbar \, d\psi/dx) + (i\hbar \, d/dx)V\psi \\
&= i\hbar \, (dV/dx)\psi \\
\therefore [\hat{H}, \hat{p}] &= i\hbar \, dV/dx .
\end{aligned}
\tag{12.14}
$$

Again from (12.11), we have $d\langle \hat{p} \rangle/dt = \langle i/\hbar \ [\hat{H}, \hat{p}] \rangle$; so we can derive from (12.14):

$$d\langle \hat{p} \rangle/dt = -\langle dV/dx \rangle. \qquad (12.15)$$

If one then defines an operator $\hat{F} = - dV/dx$, as being the operator for that observable which (in classical terms) is the force on a particle due to its potential energy V, one gets

$$d\langle \hat{p} \rangle/dt = \langle \hat{F} \rangle. \qquad (12.16)$$

The two equations (12.13) and (12.16) are known as Ehrenfest's equations: they indicate that 'equations of motion' involving expectation values $\langle \hat{x} \rangle$, $\langle \hat{p} \rangle$, and $\langle \hat{F} \rangle$ can be obtained simply by substituting those expectation values for terms in classical equations of motion.

Equation (12.13) shows that, although momentum is defined for quantum physics by the de Broglie relationship $p = h\lambda$ (where λ is the wavelength of the associated wave), it is associated via expectation values with motion and mass in a way analogous to the association of momentum with motion and mass in classical physics. *If* a state vector $|\psi\rangle$ could indicate a precise position x, and also a precise momentum p (so that for this $|\psi\rangle$, $\langle \hat{x} \rangle = x$ *and* $\langle \hat{p} \rangle = p$), then for $|\psi\rangle$, dx/dt and p would be related exactly as in classical physics; but we know that a state vector cannot do this, because there has to be uncertainty in position and/or uncertainty in momentum, such that the product of these uncertainties is of the order of Planck's constant h. So the difference here between quantum physics and classical physics (and the error of classical physics) can be considered to arise from the circumstance that $h \neq 0$: if h were 0, classical physics would be correct.

Equation (12.16) (with equation (12.13)) makes it possible to show that, if $|\psi\rangle$ disappears outside a small region Δx, and the value of $\hat{F}$, which I will call $F(x)$, can be treated as the same throughout that region, then the particle (which can be regarded as a wave packet in that region) behaves like a classical particle with position $\langle \hat{x} \rangle$ obeying the classical equation of motion:

$$m(\mathrm{d}^2/\mathrm{d}t^2) \langle \hat{x} \rangle = F(\langle \hat{x} \rangle). \qquad (12.17)$$

From (12.13) and (12.16), we have:

$$m(d^2/dt^2) \langle \hat{x} \rangle = \langle \hat{F} \rangle.$$

Now, we have taken $F(x)$ to be the same throughout the region Δx, and $\langle \hat{x} \rangle$ must be within that region; therefore $F(x)$ takes the value $F(\langle \hat{x} \rangle)$ throughout the region, so $\langle \hat{F} \rangle$ within that region must be $F(\langle \hat{x} \rangle)$, giving (12.17).

In the case of macroscopic measurement, any uncertainty (or spread of possible results of measurements) can be disregarded, so the classical equations and the quantum physical equations coincide. This is one important aspect of the correspondence principle mentioned earlier.

It should be noted, however, that if the condition for (12.17) is satisfied at one time, then (at least on the generally accepted view of quantum physics and of measurement) it will generally not remain satisfied, because if a state $|\psi\rangle$ is restricted to a small wave packet, it will spread with time development. This can be seen intuitively by considering the wave packet as a superposition of harmonic waves associated with a spread of momenta. The most compact form of the wave packet depends upon a coincidence of crests (or troughs) of all components at one point. These crests (or troughs) will be moving at a speed ω/k, which will be different for each of the component waves; and hence the coincidence of crests will not last. Mathematically, it can be shown that for a free particle (for which $V = 0$), the following relationship exists between $\Delta\hat{x}$ and $\Delta\hat{p}$ (here used in the statistical sense):

$$d^2/dt^2 \ (\Delta\hat{x})^2 = 2/m \ (\Delta\hat{p})^2.$$

So $\Delta\hat{x}$ tends to increase.

I qualified the above by reference to generally accepted views. I will be noting in Section 14.8 views to the effect that the tendency of wave packets to spread may be repeatedly checked by interactions which operate like measurements.

12.4. An Example

The application of quantum mechanics to real situations, or realistic models, requires more complicated mathematics than I am undertaking in this book. However, some idea of how it works can be given by considering its application to a highly idealized situation: that of a single particle confined in one dimension to a 'box' which has impenetrable walls, but no force operating (that is, no 'potential') within it.

According to classical physics, such a particle would at any time have a definite position within the box, and a definite motion and energy; and if no more is known about the situation than the above, this could be any position, motion, and energy.

According to quantum mechanics, however, the particle might not have any definite position or motion or energy; and if it does have a definite position, it cannot have a definite momentum or energy. Further, the states of motion which the particle can have are subject to constraints: if, for example, it does have a definite energy, then the value of such energy must be one or other of a number of discrete values, which can be calculated.

The constraints arise because of the requirement that the state function ψ of the particle must be capable of satisfying both the time-independent Schrödinger equation (the eigenvalue equation (11.16), $\hat{H}\psi = E\psi$) and also the time-dependent Schrödinger equation (equation (12.2), $\hat{H}\psi = i\hbar \ \partial\psi/\partial t$). The latter requirement means that the function ψ and (for all realistic situations) its first derivative $\partial \psi / \partial x$ must be continuous. Otherwise, the second derivative $\partial^2 \psi / \partial x^2$ (which is involved when one applies $\hat{H}$ to ψ) would be infinite at points of discontinuity, giving an infinite term in the equation. The equation could then be satisfied only if there were another infinite term; and there is no such term, unless potential energy V is infinite, which it cannot be in realistic situations. (However, in the idealized case I am considering, V is put at infinity in certain regions; and this means that only ψ has to be continuous, while $\partial \psi / \partial x$ need not be.)

To represent mathematically a one-dimensional box with impenetrable walls, with no force operating within it, one sets potential energy V at 0 between $x = 0$ and $x = L$ on the x axis, and at ∞ elsewhere on that axis. This means that the state function of a particle in the box must be 0 otherwise than from $x = 0$ to $x = L$; and that, since ψ must be continuous, it must be zero at $x = 0$ and $x = L$: these are called the boundary conditions. Between $x = 0$ and $x = L$, since V is zero in this region, the energy eigenvalue equation $\hat{H}\psi = E\psi$ takes the form

$$-\hbar^2/2m \;\; \partial^2 \psi / \partial x^2 = E\psi.$$

If one introduces a new variable k, where $k^2 = 2mE/\hbar^2$, this equation becomes

$$-\partial^2 \psi / \partial x^2 = k^2.$$

All solutions to this equation take the general form

$$\psi = A \sin kx + B \cos kx,$$

where A and B are numbers, which may be complex. However, in this case, the boundary conditions impose constraints on possible solutions. Since $\psi = 0$ at $x = 0$, B must be zero. Further, since $\psi = 0$ at $x = L$, kL must be $n\pi$, where n is any integer. (n cannot be zero, because there would then be no non-zero function at all.) So the energy eigenstates must be

$$\psi_n = A \sin (n\pi x/L), \tag{12.18}$$

where $n = 1, 2, 3, \ldots$

Since $E = \hbar^2 k^2/2m$, the energy eigenvalues are $n^2\hbar^2\pi^2/2mL^2$, for $n = 1, 2, 3, \ldots$ Thus, if the particle has a definite energy, it must be one of these discrete values: the smaller the size L of the 'box', the greater the separation between them; and, as L approaches ∞, the separation approaches zero (which would give the possibility, accepted in classical physics, of energy taking any value).

It is apparent that the particle cannot have a definite momentum: no function $A \sin (n\pi x/L)$, and no linear combination of such functions with different integer values of n, can equal a complex plane wave $N \exp (ikx)$. The particle cannot have a definite momentum, because the position is defined to the extent of being within the range $x = 0$ to $x = L$.

One can determine the coefficient A by a process of normalization. Since the particle must be somewhere within the box, we have, in the case of the first energy level,

$$\int |\psi_1|^2 \, dx = 1$$

$$\therefore |A|^2 \int \sin^2 kx \ dx = 1.$$

Since $\sin^2 kx + \cos^2 kx = 1$, it follows from equation (10.1) that $\sin^2 kx = 1/2 \ (1 - \cos 2x)$. So:

$$|A|^2 \int \ 1/2 \ (1 - \cos 2x) \, dx = 1$$

$$\therefore |A|^2 \, L/2 = 1$$

$$\therefore A = e^{i\theta} \sqrt{(2/L)} \, . \qquad (12.19)$$

In cases where one is not concerned about superposition and interference, ψ represents the same state as $e^{i\theta} \psi$; so that, in those cases, the normalized eigenstates can be taken to be simply $\sqrt{(2/L)} \sin (n\pi x/L)$. The graphs for the eigenstates ψ_1 and ψ_2 for the first two energy levels are as set out in Fig. 12.1.

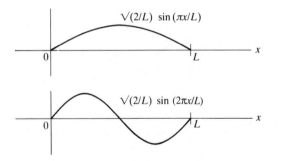

FIG. 12.1. The state functions of the first two energy levels of a particle in a box

It will be seen that in each case there is no chance of the particle being detected at $x = 0$ or $x = L$, and that, in the case of the second energy level, there is no chance of the particle being detected at $x = L/2$.

If the time-development operator $\exp(- i\hat{H}t/\hbar)$ is applied to an energy eigenstate, one obtains the following:

$$\psi(t) = \exp(- iEt/\hbar)\psi_0$$
$$= \exp(i\theta - iEt/\hbar) \sqrt{(2/L)} \sin (n\pi x/L) \, .$$

Thus only the phase factor varies, and $|\psi|^2$ remains the same. Accordingly, time development of a particle at the second energy level would not alter from zero the probability of its being found at $x = L/2$.

The state of the particle need not be an energy eigenstate. A general state ψ can be expressed as a superposition of such eigenstates:

$$\psi = \Sigma_n c_n \sin(n\pi x/L) \ .$$

If a particle has a location within a small region Δx within the box, then its state will be such a superposition. In that case time development will alter $|\psi|^2$, because the phase relationships between the eigenstates ψ_n will be changed, because the time-development factor $\exp(-iEt/\hbar)$ will be different for each energy level.

I will not consider further examples. However, I do note that if, at the extremities of such a 'box', potential energy V is set at a finite level, the energy eigenfunctions are generally such as to give a finite probability of the particle being found outside the box, even if the energy of the particle is not sufficient, according to classical physics, to overcome the barrier of the potential energy. This is associated with the phenomenon of quantum tunnelling, which is the basis for a number of electronic devices, and more recently for the scanning tunnelling microscope.

13

Combined Systems

So far, I have for the most part considered systems involving just one aspect of one particle. In particular: position, momentum, and energy of a particle in one dimension; the spin of a particle; and the polarization of a photon.

I have noted that the discussion can be extended to deal with all aspects of one particle (that is, position etc. in three dimensions, plus spin), without as yet descending to any detail of how this can be done. In fact, the principles are the same as those applying to the application of quantum physics to more than one particle: and, since the latter is more important for my consideration of the implications of quantum physics, I shall concentrate on it. That is, I shall for the most part discuss the application of quantum physics to one-dimensional motion (etc.) of multiple particles, and indicate how the principles apply to dealing at once with all aspects of one particle.

13.1. State Functions for Multiple Particles

In considering the application of quantum physics to several particles, four distinct situations need to be considered. First, there is the situation generally encountered with a beam of particles, where there are a large number of particles which can be regarded as having the same state function, and whose mutual interactions can be disregarded. Secondly, there is the situation of two or more particles whose states are independent of each other, that is, are unaffected by any mutual interaction. Thirdly, there is the situation of two or more particles whose states are not independent of each other, having been correlated by interaction. Fourthly, there is the particular case of indistinguishable particles.

13.1.1. *Beams of Particles*

Many experiments consist in the preparation and subsequent detection of beams of particles, such as electrons, in such a way that:

1. each of the particles can be regarded as being in the same state following preparation and immediately prior to detection; and
2. particle density is sufficiently low that mutual interactions of the particles can be disregarded.

In those cases, the state vector representing the state of each particle can be considered as representing the beam, in a straightforward way. The state vector can in such cases be 'normalized' so that the total of the probabilities is not 1, but rather the total number of particles in the beam. The probabilities calculated from the state vectors for the various eigenvalues of observables will then be the expectation values for the *numbers* of the particles which would be found to have the respective eigenvalues. The expectation values for various possible results of measurement, as indicated by the state vector immediately prior to measurement, will (if the number of particles in the beam is sufficiently large) be closely reflected in the distribution of actual measurements.

If the interaction between particles in a beam is not negligible, this approach is not valid, and the other approaches will have to be used.

13.1.2. *Non-interacting Particles*

Next, I consider the situation where more than one particle is involved, whose states can be considered as not affected by any mutual interaction (either direct, or through other particles), but cannot be considered as identical; and where no two particles are indistinguishable. In such cases, a state vector can be constructed, for the state of the ensemble of particles, from the state vectors of the individual particles: the combined state vector can be regarded as a kind of product (by simple multiplication) of the individual state vectors.

The idea can perhaps most readily be grasped by first considering the state functions for a number of particles (in one dimension, omitting spin) $\psi_1(x_1)$, $\psi_2(x_2)$, etc. The combined state function $\psi(x_1, x_2, \dots)$ for all the particles is then $\psi_1 \times \psi_2 \dots$. For two particles, we have:

$$\psi(x_1, x_2) = \psi_1(x_1)\,\psi_2(x_2)\,.$$

Then, just as a probability function $P(\Delta x_1)$ can be derived from ψ_1 to give the probability that the particle represented by ψ_1 will be found by appropriate measurement to be within the region Δx_1, and so on, so also a combined probability function $P(\Delta x_1, \Delta x_2, \dots)$, that is, $P(\Delta x_1) \times P(\Delta x_2) \times \dots$, will give the probability that the particle represented by ψ_1 will be found within Δx_1, and at the same time the particle represented by ψ_2 will be found within Δx_2, and so on.

Thus if the probability of finding one particle within Δx_1 is (say) 0.1, calculated from its separate function ψ_1; and the probability of finding another particle within Δx_2 is (say) 0.05, calculated from its separate function ψ_2; then the probability of finding one particle within Δx_1, and at the same time finding the other particle within Δx_2, as calculated from the combined wave function $\psi_1 \times \psi_2$ will be 0.005. This is, of course, just the result to be expected *if* the probability of one particle being found to be within Δx_1 is not correlated to the state of the other particle, and is unaffected by where such other particle may be found by a position measurement.

The individual probabilities, as calculated from the individual state functions, can also be recovered from the combined function: the probability of finding the first particle within Δx_1, will be the probability of finding the first particle within Δx_1, and finding the second somewhere (anywhere!). If each of the component functions has one independent variable, and if there are n such functions, then the combined function will have n independent variables. If the component functions each have three independent variables (one for each spatial dimension), then the combined function will have $3n$ independent variables. It is then sometimes said to be in a $3n$-dimensional 'space'.

Putting the above in terms of state vectors, the vectors $|\psi_1\rangle$, $|\psi_2\rangle$, etc. can be combined to form a vector $|\psi\rangle$ (or $|\psi_1, \psi_2, \ldots\rangle$) which will represent the state of all the particles: when the particles represented by $|\psi_1\rangle$, $|\psi_2\rangle$, etc. are distinguishable and not correlated by interaction, $|\psi\rangle$ can be written as a product $|\psi_1\rangle|\psi_2\rangle, \ldots$. (The order is significant here, essentially to keep track of the different particles: when functions are multiplied, the order of multiplication is not significant—$\psi_1(x_1) \times \psi_2(x_2) = \psi_2(x_2) \times \psi_1(x_1)$—but the variables have to be kept distinct in the expression of the product function $\psi(x_1, x_2)$; and this is generally expressed by the order in which the variables are stated, so that $\psi(x_1, x_2)$ generally does not equal $\psi(x_2, x_1)$). If the component vectors are each in an n-dimensional space (a space with sets of n orthonormal base vectors), and if there are m such components, then the combined vector will be in an $m \times n$-dimensional space (with sets of $m \times n$ orthonormal base vectors).

If $|\psi_{1i}\rangle$, $|\psi_{1j}\rangle$, etc. are eigenstates of observables $\hat{A}_1$, $\hat{A}_2$, etc. with eigenvalues a_{1i}, a_{2j}, etc. in the respective spaces of $|\psi_1\rangle$, $|\psi_1\rangle$, etc., then $|\psi_{1i}\rangle|\psi_{2j}\rangle \ldots$ will be an eigenstate of a combined observable $\hat{A}$ in the space of the combined vector $|\psi\rangle$. The amplitude for $|\psi\rangle$ to be measured as $|\psi_{1i}\rangle|\psi_{2j}\rangle \ldots$ is then given by the inner product of the combined eigenstate $|\psi_{1i}\rangle|\psi_{2j}\rangle \ldots$ and the combined vector $|\psi_1\rangle|\psi_2\rangle \ldots$: this in turn is given by the product $\langle\psi_{1i}|\psi_1\rangle\langle\psi_{2j}|\psi_2\rangle \ldots$. The probability of measuring $|\psi_1\rangle$ to have eigenvalue a_{1i}, *and* at the same time $|\psi_2\rangle$ to have eigenvalue a_{2j}, and so on, is then given by the absolute square of the above amplitude, that is $|\langle\psi_{1i}|\psi_1\rangle\langle\psi_{2j}|\psi_2\rangle \ldots|^2$; which is the same as the product of the individual probabilities $|\langle\psi_{1i}|\psi_1\rangle|^2, |\langle\psi_{2j}|\psi_2\rangle|^2$, etc.

One complete set of base vectors in the combined space will be given by all combinations of the members of the sets of base vectors of which $|\psi_{1i}\rangle$, $|\psi_{2j}\rangle$, etc. are members. Thus such a complete set could be written $|\psi_{1i}\rangle|\psi_{2j}\rangle \ldots$, with i, j, etc. taking any value from 1 to n. The combined state could then be expressed as a superposition:

$$|\psi\rangle = \sum_{ij\ldots} c_{ij} \ldots |\psi_{1i}\rangle|\psi_{2j}\rangle \ldots \tag{13.1}$$

In the case we are considering of distinguishable, non-interacting, particles:

$$c_{ij} \ldots = c_i d_j \ldots , \tag{13.2}$$

where:

$$c_i = \langle \psi_{1i} \mid \psi_1 \rangle ,$$
$$d_j = \langle \psi_{2j} \mid \psi_2 \rangle ,$$

etc.

13.1.3. *Particles Correlated by Interaction*

A combined system represented by a state function ψ or state vector $\mid \psi \rangle$ will be a simple product of state functions (i.e. $\psi_1 \times \psi_2 \times \ldots$) or of state vectors (i.e. $\mid \psi_1 \rangle \mid \psi_2 \rangle \ldots$) representing the component particles *only* if the probabilities of results of any measurements carried out on each component can be considered as unaffected by correlations with the states of the other components. As we shall see in Section 13.3, such correlations arise when there are interactions between component systems.

Even where there are such correlations, however, the combined state can still be considered as a superposition of its eigenstates, which are themselves simple products of eigenstates of the component systems. Thus, if the component systems are $\mid \psi_1 \rangle$, $\mid \psi_2 \rangle$, etc., respectively with eigenstates given by $\mid \psi_{1i} \rangle$, $\mid \psi_{2j} \rangle$, etc., then the combined system $\mid \psi \rangle$ can be written.

$$\mid \psi \rangle = \sum_{ij\ldots} c_{ij} \ldots \mid \psi_{1i} \rangle \mid \psi_{2j} \rangle \ldots .$$

However, the coefficients $c_{ij} \ldots$ are themselves generally *not* simple products of corresponding coefficients in the superposition of eigenstates in the component systems (namely, $c_i = \langle \psi_{1i} \mid \psi_1 \rangle$, $d_j = \langle \psi_{2j} \mid \psi_2 \rangle$, etc.) as in the case of non-interacting particles.

One important case of a combination of two systems is that involved in measurement. One system (which may be represented before measurement by a vector $\mid \psi \rangle$) is the system to be measured, the other (which may be represented before measurement by a vector $\mid \phi \rangle$) is the measuring apparatus: the former could be an electron, the latter could be a screen which gives an approximate measurement of position by displaying a small spot where it is hit by an electron. (Clearly, the latter is itself a combined system of vast numbers of component systems, each of which would be in a vector space of infinite dimensions: so the space of the combined system would be of dimensions equal to the product of all the (infinite) dimensions of the component systems.) Before measurement, the system to be measured would generally be in a superposition of position eigenstates; and the measuring system would be in a state such that it displayed no spot. In order to be effective, the measuring system would have to be such that, upon interaction with the measured system, it would change to a state such that it displayed a spot at the position where it detected an electron.

If one assumes that the measurement of an observable of any system *including combined systems* involves the system being in an eigenstate of the observable measured, then the detection of a spot at a point on the detector involves the measuring system being in an eigenstate corresponding to this result for the relevant observable. This eigenstate would presumably be highly degenerate: there would presumably be enormous numbers of combinations of base states of the component systems, any one of which would give the same result for the observable corresponding to any particular position of the spot.

If the state of the measuring system which shows a spot at a position identified by the letter n can be written $| \phi_n \rangle$ (ignoring degeneracy), and if the eigenstate of the system being measured (the electron) corresponding to its being at position n can be written $| \psi_n \rangle$, then the condition for an effective measurement is that immediately following measurement the combined system must be in a state $| \psi_n \rangle | \phi_n \rangle$ or $| \phi_n \rangle | \psi_n \rangle$: particularly, there must be excluded any combined states of the form $| \psi_m \rangle | \phi_n \rangle$ or $| \phi_n \rangle | \psi_m \rangle$, where $m \neq n$. This is necessary in order to ensure that the existence of state $| \phi_n \rangle$ as disclosed by the appearance of the spot at position n does show that the electron is in fact at position n (and therefore in the state $| \psi_n \rangle$). Accordingly, even if $| \psi \rangle$ could be measured individually, and found to be in state $| \psi_m \rangle$ (i.e. being in position m); and $| \phi \rangle$ could similarly be measured individually, and found to be in state $| \phi_n \rangle$ (i.e. displaying a spot at position n, not position m); nevertheless, the interaction between the systems would exclude the possibility of there being any state $| \psi_m \rangle | \phi_n \rangle$ (or $| \phi_n \rangle | \psi_m \rangle$), where $m \neq n$.

In other words, if before measurement

$$| \psi \rangle = \sum_i c_i | \psi_i \rangle$$

$$| \phi \rangle = \sum_j d_j | \phi_j \rangle ,$$

then the combined system $| \psi, \phi \rangle$ (which, as we saw, can be written $\sum_{ij} c_{ij} | \psi_i \rangle | \phi_j \rangle$) will, in the case when a measurement occurs, in fact be $\sum_i c_i | \psi_i \rangle | \phi_i \rangle$. That is, in the superposition there will be no terms $| \psi_i \rangle | \phi_j \rangle$, where $i \neq j$.

13.1.4. *Identical Particles*

If any two particles of a combined system are identical, there is an additional complication: the circumstance that (for example) one electron cannot be distinguished from another electron affects the form of a combined state vector involving identical particles. This is perhaps easiest to discuss in terms of state functions.

Suppose the individual state functions for position etc. of two electrons in one dimension are $\psi_1(x_1)$ and $\psi_2(x_2)$, and that the combined state function of the two particles is $\psi(x_1, x_2)$. Then, assuming the individual functions of the two electrons are *otherwise* identical (that is, in relation to position etc. in the other two dimensions, and in relation to spin), it will be impossible to distinguish between $|\psi(x_1, x_2)|^2$ and $|\psi(x_2, x_1)|^2$ by measurements made on any number of identically prepared systems which could be represented by those state functions. Accordingly

$$|\psi(x_1, x_2)|^2 = |\psi(x_2, x_1)|^2$$
$$\therefore e^{i\theta}\psi(x_1, x_2) = \psi(x_2, x_1).$$

That is, $\psi(x_1, x_2)$ differs from $\psi(x_2, x_1)$ only by a phase factor $e^{i\theta}$. However, since the particles are identical, to change $\psi(x_2, x_1)$ back to $\psi(x_1, x_2)$ is the same operation, again involving multiplication by the same $e^{i\theta}$. Thus:

$$(e^{i\theta})^2\,\psi(x_1, x_2) = \psi(x_1, x_2)$$
$$\therefore e^{i\theta} = \pm 1.$$

That is, the phase factor $e^{i\theta}$ which provides the only difference between $\psi(x_1, x_2)$ and $\psi(x_2, x_1)$ must equal either 1 or -1 (so that the θ in the $e^{i\theta}$ is either 0 or π or 2π or ...). Therefore the combined state function $\psi(x_1, x_2)$ must differ from $\psi_1(x_1)\,\psi_2(x_2)$ because it is *correlated* to $\psi(x_2, x_1)$, in that either:

$$\psi(x_1, x_2) = \psi(x_2, x_1)$$

or

$$\psi(x_1, x_2) = -\psi(x_2, x_1).$$

Neither of the above two conditions is satisfied by the equation which was given for non-identical non-interacting particles, namely:

$$\psi(x_1, x_2) = \psi_1(x_1)\,\psi_2(x_2)\,.$$

Instead, for two identical non-interacting particles, the combined wave function must take the form

$$\psi(x_1, x_2) = 1/\sqrt{2}\quad[\psi_1(x_1)\,\psi_2(x_2) + \psi_1(x_2)\,\psi_2(x_1)] \tag{13.3}$$

or

$$\psi(x_1, x_2) = 1/\sqrt{2}\quad[\psi_1(x_1)\,\psi_2(x_2) - \psi_1(x_2)\,\psi_2(x_1)]. \tag{13.4}$$

The former function is called symmetric and the latter is called antisymmetric. It is the antisymmetric function which applies to electrons. It will be seen that if you put $x_1 = x_2$ in that function, $\psi(x_1, x_2)$ becomes zero, so that the amplitude (and therefore the probability) for finding an electron becomes zero: this means there is no possibility of finding two electrons in the same state. (It will be recalled that we have *assumed* that the states of the two particles are identical for the two other spatial dimensions and for spin.) This is the mathematical expression of what is known as the Pauli exclusion principle, which was proposed by Wolfgang Pauli in 1925 to explain why atoms did not collapse: because no two electrons can occupy the same quantum state, electrons with different 'quantum numbers' stack up in shells of progressively increasing energy levels. It is this in turn which enables explanation of the chemical properties of different elements.

Such an antisymmetric combined function or state of two objects in fact applies to all elementary 'matter-like' particles, and to all composite objects containing an *odd* number of such elementary particles. Such particles and objects are called fermions. Thus, electrons and quarks are fermions, as are protons and neutrons (because they each contain three quarks). I have indicated earlier that the magnitude of spin of electrons is always $\hbar/2$, and this is the case with all elementary fermions: they are accordingly called spin one-half particles.

There are also objects such that combined state functions for the state of two such objects are symmetric: these include 'radiation-like' particles such as photons. Although I have not considered how states for position etc. of photons are represented, in fact something like the above symmetric function does apply to photons, with the result that where $x_1 = x_2$ the probability amplitude is $\sqrt{2}$ times that of a simple product of the probability amplitudes of the individual functions, and the probability of finding two photons in the same state is double what it would have been for two different non-interacting particles. This means that, whereas two or more electrons *cannot* be in the same state, two or more photons will tend to be in the same state, rather than not. This characteristic of photons is part of the theoretical background of the laser, a device for producing coherent light (involving many photons in the same quantum state) by stimulated emission.

Such symmetric combined functions or states apply also to composite objects containing an even number of matter-like fermions, such as helium atoms. Objects to which such symmetric combined functions or states apply, and which accordingly can occupy the same quantum state, are called bosons. They comply with what are called Bose–Einstein statistics; and the quantum mechanical phenomenon of many bosons being in the same state is called Bose condensation.

13.2. Different Aspects of a Single Particle

Similar considerations to those considered in Sections 13.1.2 and 3 apply to combined systems each representing one aspect of the state of a single particle.

If $|\psi_i\rangle$, $|\psi_j\rangle$, $|\psi_k\rangle$, and $|S\rangle$ respectively represent the state of motion of a particle on the x, y, and z axes, and its spin state on the z axis, then the complete state of the particle $|\psi\rangle$ can be regarded as a combined state, of which the first-mentioned states are components.

If it is the case that the probability of the result of any measurement, of any observable, of any of the component states, is unaffected by the other component states or by the making of any measurement upon them, then the combined state will be a simple product of the component states:

$$|\psi\rangle = |\psi_i\rangle |\psi_j\rangle |\psi_k\rangle |S\rangle .$$

Then, the probability of a measurement of Δx_1 on the x axis, and Δy_1 on the y axis, and Δz_1 on the z axis, and spin up on the z axis, will simply be the product of the individual probabilities of each of these measurements.

In many instances, this will not be so. The function $|\psi\rangle$ will be such that the probability of measurements of one component system will be affected by the states of, and measurements made upon, other component systems: and accordingly it will not be a simple product.

For example, if (as will generally be the case) the potential energy which a particle in a field would have at coordinate x on the x axis is not the same for all positions on the y and/or z axes, then its time development in that field will bring about correlations between $|\psi_i\rangle$, and $|\psi_j\rangle$ and/or $|\psi_k\rangle$. For this reason, when making calculations about a particle in three dimensions, it is often not convenient to deal separately with each dimension, as I have done; rather, it is convenient to express both the state vector $|\psi\rangle$ and the potential V as a single function (either of three variables x, y and z or of a single vector variable $\mathbf{r}$), not as three separate functions.

It will often be the case, too, that the position of a particle will not be independent of its spin. For example, when spin is measured by what is known as a Stern–Gerlach device, position and spin are correlated, so that measurement of a particle to be in one position will indicate spin up, and measurement of it to be in another position will indicate spin down.

13.3. The Time Development of Combined Systems

In general terms, the same equations apply to the time development of combined systems as to individual systems. That is, if $|\psi\rangle$ represents a combined system, involving any number of particles or individual systems, then its time development (von Neumann's process 2) in the absence of measurement (von Neumann's process 1) is governed by the equation (12.2), which can be written using Dirac's notation:

$$\hat{H}|\psi\rangle = -i\hbar\,\partial|\psi\rangle/\partial t .$$

Similarly, if $|\psi_0\rangle$ represents a combined system at time 0, then the state of the system at time t will be represented by $\hat{U}|\psi_0\rangle$, where, from equation (12.7):

$$\hat{U} = \exp\left(-i\hat{H}t/\hbar\right).$$

In these equations, just as $|\psi\rangle$ will be more complicated than in the case of a single system, so also $\hat{H}$ will be more complicated than in such case.

If the combined system $|\psi\rangle$ consists of non-identical particles which can be regarded as not interacting, and as not having interacted (so that $|\psi\rangle$ can take the form $|\psi_1\rangle$, $|\psi_2\rangle, \ldots$, where $|\psi_1\rangle$, $|\psi_2\rangle$, etc. are the state vectors representing the component systems), then the Hamiltonian $\hat{H}$ of the combined system will be a simple combination of the Hamiltonians $\hat{H}_1$, $\hat{H}_2$, etc. of the component systems. The operation prescribed by $\hat{H}$ will be to apply $\hat{H}_1$ to $|\psi_1\rangle$, $\hat{H}_2$ to $|\psi_2\rangle$, etc; so that if $\hat{H}_1|\psi_1\rangle$ is written $|\psi_{1m}\rangle$, $\hat{H}_2|\psi_2\rangle$ is written $|\psi_{2n}\rangle$, etc., then:

$$\hat{H}|\psi\rangle = |\psi_{1m}\rangle|\psi_{2n}\rangle\ldots$$

Where two systems which can be considered as not having interacted commence to interact, the Hamiltonian $\hat{H}$ of the combined system cannot be regarded as a simple combination of the Hamiltonians $\hat{H}_1$ and $\hat{H}_2$ of the component systems operating individually on such systems. If the Hamiltonians of the component systems $|\psi_1\rangle$ and $|\psi_2\rangle$ immediately prior to the commencement of the interaction are written $\hat{H}_1$ and $\hat{H}_2$, then immediately after such commencement the Hamiltonian of the system $|\psi_1\rangle$ will have an additional term $\hat{H}_{12}$ (representing the potential energy of $|\psi_1\rangle$ due to its interaction with $|\psi_2\rangle$)), and the Hamiltonian of the system $|\psi_2\rangle$ will have an additional term $\hat{H}_{21}$ (representing the potential energy of $|\psi_2\rangle$ due to its interaction with $|\psi_1\rangle$ and accordingly being the negative of $\hat{H}_{12}$).

The time development of $|\psi_1\rangle$ will therefore be governed by $\hat{H}_1 + \hat{H}_{12}$; while the time development of $|\psi_2\rangle$ will be governed by $\hat{H}_2 + \hat{H}_{21}$, that is, by $\hat{H}_2 - \hat{H}_{12}$. The existence of the common term in the Hamiltonians of the component systems means that the two states will come to be correlated to some extent, so that the combined system can no longer be represented as a simple product $|\psi_1\rangle|\psi_2\rangle$. The correlations mean that only the combined system is in a (pure) state which can be represented by a state function or state vector. The component systems considered separately cannot be so represented: they are regarded as mixtures, and may be represented by density operators as discussed in Section 11.4.11.

In the particular case of an interaction giving rise to a measurement, it would appear that there must be some combination or combinations of von Neumann's process 2 and process 1. When the system to be measured $|\psi\rangle$ begins to interact with the measuring system $|\phi\rangle$, a common term appears in the Hamiltonian of each system (representing the potential energy arising from the interaction). This common term has the effect of correlating the measured system and the measuring device as they develop continuously over time in accordance with process 2. For measurement to occur, the correlation must eventually be such that any eigenstate of the observable being measured in the measured system becomes associated with just one eigenstate (or group of eigenstates with the same eigenvalue) in the measuring device. However, in fact only one eigenvalue is observed in the measuring device, indicating the corresponding single eigenvalue in the measured system, and thus completing the measurement. Accordingly, at some stage (or stages), a process 1 development must apparently have occurred, whereby the combined state of the measured system and the measuring device has jumped discontinuously from a superposition of eigenstates to just the single eigenstate disclosed by measurement. I discuss the problems associated with this in the next chapter.

14

The Measurement Problem

IN the discussion of quantum mechanics to this point, I have said that the information given by the state function (or state vector) of a system comes down to this: that *if* a measurement of any observable $\hat{A}$ is made, then there are certain values of that observable which could possibly be found (all other values being impossible), and the respective probabilities of those values which *are* possible are as shown by the state function. Of course, much can be built on this information, and virtual certainty can be reached where vast numbers of particles are involved: but this hypothetical information is the basis of it all.

So, the state function expresses information only hypothetically, concerning what will be disclosed *if* a measurement is made. Further, the result of a measurement is generally a sudden partly unpredictable change of the state of the system—the reduction of the quantum state—which does not accord with the rules of quantum mechanics concerning the progressive and deterministic development of quantum states. However, no part of the mathematics of quantum theory defines what *constitutes* a measurement. This would not be a severe problem if there were a clear demarcation between a domain in which quantum theory operated (for example, in relation to atoms and their constituents) and a domain in which it did not operate. However, there is no such demarcation: there is no level at which quantum effects (such as interference) suddenly disappear; and no level at which representation of systems by state functions or state vectors suddenly becomes inappropriate. Accordingly (it would seem), there is no reason why measurement (like any other interaction) should not be explicable, and expressible, in terms of quantum physics.

There have been various attempts to resolve this 'problem of measurement': I will consider some of the main ones.

14.1. The Copenhagen Interpretation

The interpretation of quantum mechanics in general, and of the measurement problem in particular, which was substantially adopted in about 1930 by most of the founders of quantum mechanics, is called the Copenhagen interpretation. It was the work particularly of Niels Bohr at the Bohr Institute in Copenhagen.

The 'Copenhagen interpretation' means different things to different people, and it may be considered as embracing aspects of interpretation of quantum mechanics not directly involving the measurement problem as I have defined it: these include the probability interpretation of the state function, the complementarity of wave and particle views of matter, and the correspondence of quantum physics with classical physics in systems where h (because of its comparative magnitude) can be regarded as zero. These aspects I have assumed in my general account of quantum mechanics; and, although some theories of measurement may to some extent call them into question, they are largely uncontroversial.

So far as the problem of measurement is concerned, the Copenhagen interpretation requires that measuring systems be considered as classical objects, operating according to classical physics; and that the rules of quantum physics be regarded as rules for predicting the outcome of measurements. In broad terms, it postulates a 'cut' between the system being measured, and the system doing the measuring: on one side of the cut, quantum physics applies; on the other, classical physics. So, a measurement is treated as a classically describable event, with the measuring device acting according to classical physics. Quantum physics then correlates the results of such measurements. As to what 'happens' (so far as a measured system is concerned) between or in the absence of such measurements, one can only refer to the mathematical objects used in quantum physics: one should not otherwise attempt to describe what, if anything, 'really happens'.

The main reason given for this approach is that the only language available to us for description is the language of classical physics: that language alone can describe measurement, but it *cannot* describe what happens between or in the absence of measurements (see Folse 1985: 139–41). Heisenberg (1989) refers to the paradox 'that we describe our experiments in the terms of classical physics and at the same time from the knowledge that these concepts do not fit nature accurately' (p. 44). He goes on to assert that any suggestion that one should depart from classical concepts rests on a misunderstanding in that the 'concepts of classical physics are just a refinement of the concepts of daily life and are an essential part of the language which forms the basis of all natural science'. And later he writes:

> The demand to 'describe what happens' in the quantum-theoretical process between two successive observations is a contradiction *in adjecto*, since the word 'describe' refers to the use of the classical concepts, while these concepts cannot be applied in the space between the observations; they can only be applied at the points of observation. (p. 133)

There is force in this contention, but it perhaps underestimates the capacity of language to be adapted to describe previously unfamiliar processes, and to develop under the influence of scientific discovery. Even Heisenberg did not fully adhere to his views stated above, being prepared to describe the unmeasured world as a superposition of possibilities or *potentia* (see Herbert 1985: 194–5).

The Copenhagen interpretation has proved satisfactory in practice: the predictions of quantum mechanics do indeed correspond to the results of measurement which can be described in the language of classical physics. But it avoids rather than answers the problems of measurement: it certainly does not explain in quantum mechanical terms what a measurement is. In particular:

1. It gives crucial importance to the distinction between the system being measured and the measuring device, that is to the cut between these systems; yet does not specify in quantum mechanical terms where this cut is to be placed.

2. It accepts that interactions of systems, including systems being measured and measuring devices, *can* be represented in the quantum mechanical formalism, even though *that* representation involves only deterministic development of the state function, and not the sudden and partly unpredictable change of the state function which results from measurement.

3. The sudden and partly unpredictable change to the state function brought about by measurement is treated as part of the quantum theory, yet there is no explanation why *measurement* has this effect and other interactions apparently do not: it seems wrong to suggest that this effect occurs only in measurement, and does not occur if interactions similar to those involved in measurement occur spontaneously; yet if the effect arises whenever certain *kinds* of interaction occur, there is no identification of what kinds of interaction have this effect.

Indeed, there is something of a paradox at the heart of the Copenhagen interpretation. As put by d'Espagnat, it asserts 'that any valid description of quantum phenomena must ultimately refer to the primary concept of classical objects, more specifically to that of "the experimental set-up" '; yet 'we cannot avoid seeing macroscopic objects as consisting ultimately of microscopic, or quantum, objects' (1989: 156–7). Similarly, Davies writes: 'The fact that the Copenhagen interpretation is founded upon acceptance of the prior existence of the classical macroscopic world appears circular and paradoxical, for the macroworld is *composed of* the quantum microworld' (1989: 12).

There are difficulties in considering these questions, not least being the dependence of language on classical concepts. However, I do not think that these difficulties require that the questions not be considered: rather, I would agree with the observation in Redhead (1987: 51) that the main objection to the Copenhagen interpretation 'is the finality with which Bohr prohibits even asking certain questions about QM [quantum mechanical] systems'. I believe it is worth while pursuing such questions, for several reasons. In particular: the problems, if unsolved, really question the validity of quantum physics itself (see Leggett 1987: 169–73); pursuit of these problems is itself a line of enquiry which may lead to advances in quantum physics; and the problems are of profound philosophical interest, particularly to persons like myself trying to understand the nature of matter, and its relationship to mind.

In fact consideration of such questions has led to developments from the Copenhagen interpretation in two main directions, which I will consider separately. The first takes as crucial the concept of measurement (involving participation of a human being or at least a conscious entity): and I will consider it forthwith. The second takes as crucial the occurrence of particular kinds of interaction (whether or not involving human beings or consciousness): this is probably the approach tacitly assumed by most working scientists, and I will consider it in Section 14.8.

14.2. Von Neumann and Schrödinger's Cat

One of the most systematic early discussions of the measurement problem was undertaken by von Neumann in his 1932 work on the mathematics of quantum mechanics (von Neumann 1955: 417–45). He approaches the problems discussed in relation to the Copenhagen interpretation by drawing an analogy with classical mechanics. He suggests that, in classical mechanics, measurement involves two kinds of processes: (1) objective causal processes and (2) processes whereby a human observer becomes aware of the result. He argues that in classical mechanics the 'cut' between (1) and (2) can be placed anywhere between the system being observed, and the 'conscious ego' of the observer: the principle of psychophysical parallelism means that processes (1) could be pursued into the brain of the observer, but at some stage it is necessary to conclude by saying 'and this is perceived by the observer'.

Von Neumann contends that, just as with classical mechanics the principle of psychophysical parallelism means that the boundary between the observed system and the observer can be displaced arbitrarily, so also with quantum mechanics that principle would be violated 'so long as it is not shown that the boundary between the observed system and the observer can be displaced arbitrarily'. He sets out to show mathematically that this boundary can be so displaced, and (it would seem) he treats this as resolving the measurement problem.

That is, von Neumann seems to assume that the distinction in quantum mechanics between interactions other than measurements, on the one hand, and measurements, on the other hand, is just the same as the distinction in classical mechanics between objective causal processes, on the one hand, and the observation of those by a human observer, on the other hand; and that the 'measurement problem' in quantum mechanics arises because it is not clear there that the cut between causal processes and observation by a human observer can be arbitrarily displaced, i.e. placed anywhere between the system being observed and the 'conscious ego' of the observer.

Von Neumann introduces his discussion by referring to 'the peculiar dual nature of the quantum mechanical procedure'. He distinguishes two processes:

1. 'process 1', whereby a state ψ undergoes in measurement a non-causal change in which each of the states ψ_1, ψ_2, ... can result, and in fact does result, with respective probabilities $|(\psi_1, \psi)|^2$, $|(\psi_2, \psi)|^2$, ... (which von Neumann writes $|(\psi, \psi_1)|^2$, $|(\psi, \psi_2)|^2$, ...)).

2. 'process 2', whereby a state ψ is transformed causally into the state ψ^1 under the action of an energy operator $\hat{H}$ in the time t such that:

$$\psi^1 = \exp(-i\hat{H}t/\hbar)\psi .$$

He asserts that quantum mechanics describes events in the observed portions of the world, so long as they do not interact with the observing portions, with the aid of process 2: however, as soon as a measurement occurs, it requires the application of process 1.

In order to discuss the measurement problem, von Neumann suggests a division of the world into three parts:

(I) the system actually observed;
(II) the measuring instrument;
(III) the actual observer.

He supposes that $\hat{A}$ is the quantity to be measured in (I), and that its eigenstates are ψ_n.

Then, if (I) is taken as the observed portion of the world, and (II) and (III) are taken together as the observing portion, application of (II + III) to (I) involves a process 1 change in (I) from the state ψ into one of the states ψ_n, the probabilities for which states are the respective values of $|(\psi_n, \psi)|^2$. That is, whereas previously $\psi = \Sigma c_n \psi_n$, where $c_n = (\psi_n, \psi)$, after application of (II + III), (I) goes into a statistical mixture in which only just one of the ψ_n obtains, with probability $|c_n|^2$.

Von Neumann then considers how the measurement is to be described if (I + II) is taken as the observed system, and only (III) as the observer. For a measurement to take place, (II) must manifest the relevant value of the observable $\hat{A}$ in (I); and such manifestation (whether it is the position of a pointer etc., or even some physical event in the brain of the observer) must be by means of a physical quantity $\hat{B}$ in (II) such that:

If $\hat{A}$ has values a_1, a_2, ...
then $\hat{B}$ has values b_1, b_2, ...
and a_n corresponds to b_n.

Before the interaction, (I) is in the state ψ, and (II) is in the state ϕ, so that (I + II) is in the state $\psi\phi$. The interaction between (I) and (II) is the process 2, whereby (I + II) develops by application of the time operator $\exp(-i\hat{H}t/\hbar)$. For measurement to occur, as viewed by the observer (III), the application of (III) to (I + II) must measure by process 1 the simultaneously measurable quantities $\hat{A}$ and $\hat{B}$; and this requires that the pair of values a_m and b_n have probability 0 for $m \neq n$, and $|(\psi_n, \psi)|^2$ for $m = n$.

In order to prove that this can occur, von Neumann supposes that a complete orthonormal set ψ_n is given in (I); and he shows that there can be found a set ϕ_n in (II), a state ϕ in (II), an energy operator $\hat{H}$ in (I + II), and a time t, so that for an arbitrary state ψ in (I), the application of the time operator $\exp(-i\hat{H}t/\hbar)$ to $\psi\phi$ changes (I + II) to $\Sigma\, c_n\psi_n\phi_n$, where $c_n = (\psi_n, \psi)$. That is, the process 2 interaction between (I) and (II) brings about a correlation of eigenstates in (I) with eigenstates in (II), such that ψ_n in (I) is correlated to eigenstate ϕ_n in (II); so measurement of b_n in (II) necessarily indicates a_n in (I), and has the same probability $|(\psi_n, \psi)|^2$ as does measurement of a_n in (I).

Therefore, von Neumann concludes, to measure $\hat{A}$ in (I) it is sufficient to look at $\hat{B}$ in (II). The cut is shifted from between (I) and (II + III) to between (I + II) and (III). Since these divisions, in particular the division between (II) and (III), are arbitrary, the cut can be made *anywhere* between (I) and the consciousness of the observer, without affecting the result.

This, of course, does not solve the problems of the Copenhagen interpretation, but it does to some extent defuse them: if it does not *matter* where the cut is made, so far as the result of measurement is concerned, then why worry?

One possible shortcoming of von Neumann's discussion is that it does not (as I read it) deal with any question of time development during the measurement process. Thus if there is some time lapse between the application of (II) to (I), and the application of (III) to (I + II), then there could well be a difference in the result which obtained depending on whether, on the one hand, the wave function of (I) was 'collapsed' by application of (II), or, on the other hand, there was no 'collapse' of any wave function until the combined wave function of (I + II) was collapsed by application of (III). The interference effects during the time development between the two applications could be different in the two cases.

However, the main shortcoming is that it just does not solve the problem. Its failure to do so is well illustrated by a notorious thought experiment suggested by Schrödinger to illustrate the measurement problem of quantum mechanics; the 'ridiculous' example (as he calls it—see Wheeler and Zurek 1983: 157) of Schrödinger's cat. A cat is placed in a box with a device designed to release a poison gas if a Geiger counter is activated within the space of one hour (after which the device switches itself off); and a radioactive substance is placed in the box, such that there is a 50/50 chance of one of its atoms decaying, and thereby activating the Geiger counter, within one hour. The box is closed, and opened some hours later by the experimenter. In von Neumann's terms, we can consider the radioactive substance as (I), the box with the Geiger counter and the cat as (II), and the experimenter as (III).

Then, the state vector of the radioactive substance after one hour would be to the effect:

$$1/\sqrt{2} \quad |\text{decayed}\rangle + e^{i\theta}/\sqrt{2} \quad |\text{not decayed}\rangle$$

($e^{i\theta}$ is a possible phase difference introduced by the interaction). If the Geiger counter plus the cat is regarded as part of the observing portion of the world, then the decay or non-decay of the particle after one hour is measured by the state of the cat, dead or alive.

However, the Geiger counter and the cat can be considered as part of the observed portion of the world, whose states after one hour are correlated by the quantum physical (process 2) interaction of (I) and (II): that is, $|\text{dead cat}\rangle$ is correlated with $|\text{decayed}\rangle$, and $|\text{live cat}\rangle$ is correlated with $|\text{not decayed}\rangle$. The state of (I + II) would thus be relevantly:

$$1/\sqrt{2} \quad |\text{decayed, dead cat}\rangle + e^{i\theta}/\sqrt{2} \quad |\text{not decayed, live cat}\rangle.$$

On this approach, this would continue until the box was opened by the observer, when measurement would occur, and (I + II) would disclose either the value 'dead cat' or 'live cat', in each case with probability 1/2. Accordingly, although the device switches itself off after one hour, it would not be determined then whether the cat does or does not survive. Rather the cat would remain in a superposition of live and dead states until the box was opened. This seems absurd.

Furthermore, as pointed out by physicist Eugene Wigner, the person who opens the box could also be regarded as part of system (II), that is, of the observed portion of the world, so that on the von Neumann approach no measurement need take place until this person reports what he sees to another person, the latter then being regarded as system (III), with his involvement constituting the measurement. Until the involvement of this other person, the relevant quantum physical state (unmeasured) of (I + II), including the person who opened the box, would presumably be:

$$1/\sqrt{2} \quad |\text{decayed, dead cat, dead cat observed}\rangle$$
$$+ e^{i\theta}/\sqrt{2} \quad |\text{not decayed, live cat, live cat observed}\rangle.$$

Now it is difficult to believe that a living macro object such as a cat could be put into a superposition of live and dead states: surely it must be dead or alive, not in some combination of these states. It is even more difficult to believe that a human being could be put into a superposition of states (of having observed a dead cat, and of having observed a live cat) which is resolved only by a 'measurement' constituted by a report to a further person.

It is perhaps more difficult again to believe that whether the cat is dead or alive, or in some combination of these states, depends on where one (arbitrarily) chooses to make the cut between the observed system and the observing system.

The relativism referred to by the last comment seems to involve this difficulty. If the application of system (II) (not including the box opener) to system (I) is regarded as the measurement, then the measurement was completed after one hour, by which time the cat was either dead, or alive. Let us suppose that the cat was in fact dead. However, if measurement is not regarded as occurring until the box is subsequently opened, then there would *at this time* still be a 50/50 chance for the cat to be alive. Yet the choice of what is to be regarded as the measurement is supposed to be arbitrary. If to avoid this it is said that there can be no measurement before a human observer is involved, the same point can still be made: the person who opened the box may (if this is regarded as the measurement) have 'collapsed' the cat's state to | dead cat ⟩, whereas the later 'measurement' by the person to whom the result is reported could nevertheless (with probability 1/2) still collapse the box-opener's state to | live cat observed ⟩.

Henry Krips (1987: 112–15) attempts to resist this conclusion, and also to maintain that there is no reduction of quantum states in measurement. He says that the measurement interaction produces correlations between systems (I) and (II) so that, while (I + II) is a pure state which may include a superposition of live and dead cats, (I) and (II) considered separately are mixtures. This is not controversial: see Section 13.1.3 above and von Neumann (1955: 437). However, he contends that this means that if one considers system (II) separately, its density operator tells us that the cat is either live or dead, but which is not known. This *is* controversial: it seems inconsistent with the quantum theoretical principle that the state function for the system (I + II) contains all possible information about the system.

Furthermore, if the system (II) considered alone has a definite value (say, cat dead) at the time of one measurement, how can the state function for the combined system (I + II) continue to indicate a 50/50 chance of a later measurement giving the value 'cat living'; and yet still be a correct representation of the combined system? The need to postulate a quantum state reduction is not avoided.

Krips also (pp. 116–18) relies on the circumstance that quantum theory itself requires that, in the absence of time development or destruction of the measured system, two successive measurements of the same observable must give the same result: so that there is zero probability that the cat will be measured as dead at one time and alive at a later time. But this means that after the first measurement the relevant state function is either reduced or else does not correctly represent the system.

To get over these problems, two general approaches have been taken.

One is to say in effect that any collapse or reduction of quantum states is only apparent. This is associated with the idea that the whole universe could be regarded as a quantum physical system, and there is nothing outside the universe which could be the observing system by means of which a measurement of the universe could be made. The main elaboration of this approach, which seeks to explain how it is that states appear on measurement to 'collapse' to give definite values, is the 'many worlds interpretation', which I will come to shortly.

The other approach is to postulate that measurement takes place, and a quantum state collapses, when and only when the result of a measurement is *first* observed by a human (or other) consciousness. This is a significant approach to the measurement problem, and I will now consider it separately.

14.3. Measurement by Consciousness

The discussion to date of the Copenhagen interpretation, and of von Neumann's contribution, has brought us with seeming inevitability to the view first put expressly in 1939 by London and Bauer (and espoused at various times by distinguished physicists such as Wigner) that measurement takes place, and the quantum state collapses, when the result of measurement is first observed by a human consciousness. It is, I suppose, for this reason that this view is sometimes said to be part of the Copenhagen interpretation (for example, by physicist Sir Rudolf Peierls, in Davies and Brown 1986: 70–82). I do not think this is so, however, as should be clear from what I have said up to this point.

In the English translation of London and Bauer, we find:

it is not a mysterious interaction between the apparatus and the object that produces a new ψ for the system during measurement. It is only the consciousness of an 'I' who can separate himself from the former function $\psi(x, y, z)$ and, by virtue of his observation, *set up a new objectivity* . . . (London and Bauer 1983: 252)

Certainly this view does deal with some of the difficulties which I have so far discussed. If measurement is effected by the first registration on human consciousness, then it is not surprising that the mathematics of quantum physics, dealing with the objective world, does not represent it. Further, a reasonably clear distinction is drawn between measurement, on the one hand, and the physical processes which are represented by the mathematics of quantum physics, on the other. A reasonably clear indication is given of where the cut between 'observed systems' and 'observing systems' is to be drawn.

As regards Schrödinger's cat, the implausibility of a cat somehow being in a combination or superposition of dead and living states is not avoided (although a modification of the view, whereby measurement is made by the first registration on *any* consciousness, including that of an animal, could avoid this). However, there is no obvious ambiguity in the resolution of the problem: the measurement is made, and the fate of the cat is resolved, when the contents of the box are first observed by a human observer.

However, the view has problems of its own:

1. One may perhaps be ready to accept that registration of a measurement on the consciousness of one person could 'collapse' a quantum physical state, so as to show a definite value, *for that person.* However, to avoid solipsism, on the one hand, and different values of observables being disclosed to different persons, on the other hand, one has to suppose that registration of a measurement on the consciousness of one person reduces the state so as to show a definite value *so far as everyone is concerned.* When a person opens the box containing Schrödinger's cat, and observes it to be dead, that observation must (apparently) make the cat dead for *everyone* who thereafter looks at it. This seems prima facie implausible: in particular, it raises the question how this conscious mental event of one person can somehow reach out to the observed world and/or to the minds of other persons, so as to collapse the state for them too (cf. Putnam 1979*a*: 165). A further aspect of this problem is raised by John Bell (in Davies and Brown 1986: 54–5): if the interaction between the mind and the rest of the world, which on this view reduces the quantum state, occurs at an instant in time, then, for consistency with special relativity, it must also occur at a single point in space; and this seems highly unlikely.

2. This problem is heightened when the possibility of error is taken into account. What if the first person who opens the box sees what (but for some aberration of his brain–mind) would be interpreted as a dead cat, but which is in fact interpreted by him as a living cat? Is the state reduced, and if so to which alternative? If one seeks to say that mistakes are not possible, in that the state perceived (for whatever reason) is that realized, then the implausibility of this affecting the external world and other minds is emphasized. Further, what if the mistake lies in some malfunction of equipment (as, for example, if the box is not opened, but a monitor of the cat's vital systems is read, and in a particular case gives an erroneous indication of death)? Surely the observation which is thereby mistaken does not determine the value to which the state collapses; and equally surely it could not reduce the state to the *correct* value which is *not* observed. Again, if the measurement is of an observable with many (perhaps continuous) possible values, so that there can be *degrees* of accuracy in reading an apparatus, what degree of accuracy in reading the apparatus is necessary to collapse the state?

3. The difficulty of this view is further illustrated by consideration of what could happen in relation to mechanical recordings, say by photographs, of the result of a measurement (see e.g. Davies 1982*b*: 134). A measuring instrument is applied to a system, no one looks at the reading, but two photographs are taken, one after the other. A person then looks at the second photograph taken.

Does that reduce the state of the original system, the measuring device, *and* the first photograph taken? Suppose that both photographs are removed to places which are far distant from each other and from the measuring device, and three different persons then (at a pre-arranged time) look (one each) at the two photographs and at the measuring device: the pre-arranged time may be such that the three events have spacelike separation, so that according to the special theory of relativity none can be considered prior in time to either of the others. Again, it seems prima facie implausible that some one of these three events could reduce the state function for all persons and all purposes.

These arguments seem sufficient to justify rejection of this approach to the measurement problem, at least if it is understood in a literal and straightforward way. However, I believe that this view can be put in a way which deals with these arguments, and leaves it as a plausible contender among possible solutions to the measurement problem.

One can approach the matter in this way. It is our perceptions which we *know* to be actualities and not mere potentialities, and which we know to be determinate rather than being superpositions of potentialities. If (as seems likely) our perceptions are identical with (being different aspects of) certain physical events, then presumably *those* physical events will, like their associated mental events, also be determinate. However, conceivably *all else* could be indeterminate, could be superposed potentialities. Thus, when a perception occurs, its associated (determinate) physical events occur: it is possible that *at that time* one element of a superposition of potentialities becomes an actuality, and all other elements of that superposition are eliminated.

Now, if one has a perfectly operating chain of connection between a micro observable to be measured, and a conscious entity such as a human observer, then perception of the result of measurement will reduce the quantum state to one involving a definite value of the measured observable, namely that perceived. On the other hand, if one does not have such an error-free connection, then, while the occurrence of a perception in the human observer will in some way or other reduce a quantum state by eliminating inconsistent possibilities, there will not be the same simple connection between what is perceived and a particular value of the micro observable. One can say that some potentialities are eliminated, but not necessarily that a particular measured value of a micro observable is thereby established.

Consistency of the mental events of different persons can be ensured, because of the non-locality of quantum processes, which I consider in Section 15.2. This means that, despite the theory of relativity, correlated distant potentialities can be eliminated instantaneously: this could solve both the problem of reducing quantum states for other persons, and Bell's problem about simultaneous interactions at different places in the brain. It also means that it is not wholly inconceivable that the taking of photographs of the reading of a measuring device could give rise to a single widely extended quantum state, which could in turn be reduced by spacelike separated events in a way which does not involve the assigning of time order to those events.

As for the question of *what* consciousness can reduce quantum states, my suggested answer would be *any* consciousness. The more primitive the consciousness, however, the less would be its power to reduce quantum states. A mental event will eliminate only potentialities which are excluded by its associated physical events; and the more such physical events are adapted so as to discriminate between alternatives in the 'external world', the greater the scope for eliminating possibilities and thereby reducing quantum states. Returning to Schrödinger's cat: on this approach, the cat's awareness of the click of the Geiger counter or the breaking of the poison container would (assuming error-free connection to the micro observable) eliminate the potentiality of non-decay of the radioactive substance—although the cat would not know *this*!

14.4. Hidden Variables

The problems of the Copenhagen interpretation, together with the aversion of some scientists (of whom Einstein is the most notable example) to a physical theory which is not deterministic, led to the formulation of various 'hidden variables' theories.

According to these theories, the reason why the state function or vector enables only prediction of probabilities is that quantum theory as at present formulated is (at least) incomplete. There 'must be' factors, at present unknown, which do determine the outcome of each measurement: these are the 'hidden variables'. As Einstein put it, 'God does not play dice.' On this view, the state function gives incomplete information because of our ignorance, and this in turn gives rise to the apparent paradoxes of measurement. Once the hidden variables are understood, a complete theory could be formulated: this would take account of both the deterministic development of the state function in the absence of measurement, and the change of the state function (which is only *apparently* indeterministic) occurring in measurement.

There is little support for these theories now. Von Neumann had attempted to prove that such theories were impossible; but the main present-day proponent of them, David Bohm, has shown that this proof is based on an assumption which need not be made. However, for such a theory to explain (even) the two-slit experiment, complicated mathematics is required, which compares unfavourably with the simple elegance of the mathematics of quantum theory (see Section 15.1).

As we saw in the historical outline, Einstein and his collaborators sought to support a hidden variables approach in the famous EPR thought experiment; but a variant of this thought experiment was turned, via Bell's theorem and a series of experiments culminating in the 1982 Aspect experiments, into a powerful case in favour of quantum mechanics as presently formulated, and against hidden variables theories. I will deal with these matters in the next chapter: as will be seen, at the very least they show that any hidden variables theory would have to involve non-locality or 'action at a distance'.

There is no evidence in favour of any objective physical hidden variables theory. The one thing possibly in its favour is that, if such a theory could be formulated, it could outflank the measurement problem: this is hardly enough to justify its acceptance. However, I will be contending in Chapter 16 that subjective mental events can sometimes determine, by choosing, which out of a number of outcomes (that are possible according to quantum physics) actually occurs: this is not what is usually considered to be a hidden variables theory, and I do not put it forward as a solution to the measurement problem.

14.5. The Ensemble or Statistical Interpretation

Another view of measurement which is sometimes associated with the Copenhagen interpretation, and sometimes (on the contrary) associated with the hidden variables view, is the ensemble or statistical or minimal statistical interpretation. One exponent is mathematician John Taylor, who discusses this approach in Davies and Brown (1986: 106–17).

On this approach, quantum physics does not describe individual systems (whether they are of single objects such as electrons, or of composite objects such as Geiger counters or cats); rather, it describes the results which will be obtained from a measurement performed on an aggregate or ensemble of many identically prepared systems, giving a probability distribution of particular values for that measurement.

The approach has some similarities to the Copenhagen interpretation, in restricting the questions that can be asked and the answers that can be given in relation to systems described by the formalism of quantum mechanics. However, the Copenhagen interpretation, as I understand it, accepts that the formalism of quantum mechanics does describe individual systems: this is shown *inter alia* by Heisenberg's thought experiments and by Bohr's contribution to the Bohr–Einstein debate. On the Copenhagen approach, what cannot be asked is, essentially, what 'really' happens to systems between measurements, and when (in quantum mechanical terms) does measurement take place? These restrictions are imposed because we have to use language appropriate to classical physics to describe what happens (we *have no other* language), and this language is not appropriate to describe what happens between measurements; whereas the formalism of quantum mechanics, which does apply to what happens between measurements, is not appropriate to describe or otherwise represent measurement.

The statistical interpretation proscribes questions about individual systems. One may ask why. If the state function indicates (say) a 50 per cent probability of one or other of two values for some measurement, surely this tells us, about each individual measurement of each individual system, that no *other* value will be measured. Surely it also tells us that one may reasonably approach each individual measurement with the same expectation for either result as one would have for either possible result of a single toss of a fair coin; and this must be equally so whether the individual measurement is one of a series of such measurements which are made, or the only measurement which is made. Similarly, it tells us that it would be *un*reasonable to approach each individual measurement with the same expectation for either result as one would have (say) for a six to be the result of a single throw of a fair die. As I understand it, the only justification for denying this is that to do so avoids the paradoxes which otherwise arise in relation, for example, to the EPR thought experiment; and, to my mind, this is no justification at all.

If one accepts that the state function tells us *that* much about individual systems, questions then arise about what it is that makes one's expectation regarding the result of the individual measurement reasonable: if the expectation is reasonable, then there must be something about the system and/or its relationship with the world which makes it reasonable. This could be either wholly something described by quantum physics (relevantly, the propensity or probability indicated by the state function), or else at least partly something not described by quantum physics. If one takes the former view, then one is faced with the measurement problem as I have formulated it; and any proscription of further questions brings one back to something like the Copenhagen interpretation. If one takes the latter view, then one is suggesting that quantum physics is incomplete, and that there are 'hidden variables'.

Accordingly, it seems to me that the statistical interpretation does not stand as an independent solution to the measurement problem. Either it evades the problem by simply not tackling legitimate questions, without sufficient justification for this; or else it reduces substantially to another interpretation. Taylor suggests (Davies and Brown 1986: 106) that Einstein in the end settled for the ensemble interpretation: however, he quotes Einstein's denial that 'the statistical quantum theory is in principle capable of producing a complete description of an individual system', that is, a denial which itself points strongly to the existence of 'hidden variables' not included in the description provided by quantum theory.

A new book by astrophysicist David Layzer advocates a version of the statistical interpretation (Layzer 1990, ch. 7), on the basis of what the author calls the Strong Cosmological Principle—namely, that a complete description of the universe contains no information that would serve to define a preferred position or direction in space (p. 47). Such a description, Layzer says, 'contains *only* statistical information' (p. 300). So, it would assign a planetary system like ours some frequency of occurrence, and that is all that can be demanded of a description satisfying the Strong Cosmological Principle. Obvious as the distinction between one place and another may seem, the Strong Cosmological Principle implies that it is merely a prejudice, just as the Principle of Relativity implies that the obvious distinction between rest and uniform motion is merely a prejudice. (p. 48)

As regards non-statistical information, Layzer says this:

Of course, nonstatistical properties exist and can be *measured* . . . And yet, paradoxically, the kind of information that appears in atlases and astronomical catalogues couldn't appear in a complete description of the astronomical Universe. Just as we leave behind an aspect of subjective experience when we take up the objective point of view of natural science, so we leave behind the particular, nonstatistical data of astronomy and earth sciences when we take up what is literally, in Thomas Nagel's phrase, 'the view from nowhere,' a view that excludes all reference to particular places. (p. 300)

Thus, he claims that the measurement problem is solved, by asserting that any particular occurrences figure in complete theoretical descriptions only as possible outcomes having some statistical frequency of occurrence. This puts the description of 'actual' events (such as a particular experiment) on a wholly different level of discourse from the quantum formalism, so that there is no need to bring the two into harmony in any *common* description.

I think this is no solution. I believe that a theory should fit with particular occurrences, to the extent of providing answers to reasonable questions about them, not limited to their statistical frequency: for example, the question of when it becomes certain whether Schrödinger's cat lives or dies. And I do not think a description of the universe could be complete if it wholly excluded the actual particular history of our galaxy, our solar system, our earth, its life, and humankind.

14.6. The Many Worlds or Relative State Interpretation

I come now to an interpretation which is nothing if not extravagant, yet which has had considerable support from well-qualified people. In addition to the basic articles in DeWitt and Graham (1973), see Jammer (1974: 517); Davies (1982*b*, ch. 7); Gribbin (1985, ch. 11); Smolin (1985: 42–3); Penrose and Isham (1986: 204); and Barrow and Tipler (1988: 472–89).

This is the interpretation which in effect suggests that any 'collapse' of quantum states by measurement is only apparent. It originated in a thesis of Hugh Everett III in 1955–7. The approach commences by noting that the quantum theory can deal with interacting systems without having to invoke the idea of an observer or of measurement. A quantum state function can be constructed for the systems after interacting, and this (like that for the systems before interacting) will give probabilities for the results of various measurements or observations. This will be so even if one of the systems is a measuring system (or a human observer). The result of an interaction with a measuring system will be to correlate certain states of the measured system with corresponding states of the measuring systems (as discussed by von Neumann).

So far, the approach is relatively uncontroversial: it really does no more than express accepted doctrine concerning ordinary quantum physical inter-actions (von Neumann's process 2) coupled with von Neumann's analysis of correlation of eigenstates in a measurement interaction. The next step, how-ever, is controversial: it is to assert that no process 1 occurs at all. Even when a human observer becomes involved, all that happens is that 'whereas before the observation we had a single observer state, afterwards there were a num-ber of different states for the observer, all occurring in a superposition' (De-Witt and Graham 1973: 68 n.). Thus, when a person opens the box containing Schrödinger's cat and looks in, the single observer state becomes two states in superposition, $1/\sqrt{2}$ | dead cat observed ⟩ and $e^{i\theta}/\sqrt{2}$ | live cat observed ⟩, each correlated with the *relative state* of the cat (hence, one of the names of this interpretation). There is no collapse of any state.

What this means for that observer, according to the many worlds interpreta-tion, is that the world splits into two nearly identical worlds, in one of which the observer sees a dead cat and in the other of which he sees a live cat. Once the split has occurred, there can be no interaction between the two worlds, and so the observer seeing the dead cat is entirely unaware that a copy of himself in another world is seeing a live cat. Some expositions (for example, Barrow and Tipler 1988: 475–7) say that it is only the observer, the measuring apparatus, and the measured system which split—the rest of the universe is unchanged—but for the most part this will not affect my discussion.

Thus, on this view, the quantum state describes all possible results of measurement, and all possible responses of all measuring devices, and sup-plies correlations between them. These possibilities exist in superposition, evolving progressively in accordance with Schrödinger's equation. Whenever necessary, the state divides into separate branches, each carrying possibilities which have by reason of the division become distinct. Presumably such divisions must be occurring frequently, all over the world, at least whenever a person observes an outcome which according to the laws of quantum mechanics could occur in different ways. Thus the world must be continu-ously splitting into near-identical copies of itself.

Notwithstanding the extravagance of this view, it has had considerable support. It once had the support of John Wheeler, although he later found it carried 'too great a weight of metaphysical baggage'. It is claimed to be mathematically impeccable, especially in that it takes literally the mathe-matics of quantum physics, including the notion of superposition of states. It is claimed to avoid the necessity of thinking about 'half-dead' cats.

However, I suggest that it can confidently be rejected, for two main reasons. First, it cannot reasonably stand with the probability interpretation of the quantum physical state. Secondly, it does not in any event answer the problems of measurement.

The first problem can be illustrated by a variant on the Schrödinger's cat thought experiment. The experiment as previously discussed had the radio-active substance and the device with the Geiger counter adjusted so that the probability of each result was one-half. However, they could be adjusted (for example, by having the device switch off much earlier than in one hour) so that, according to quantum physics, the probability of the cat being found dead is any number between 0 and 1.

Suppose that the probability of finding the cat dead is 0.01; and suppose that the experiment is repeated many times (say 100 times). (It must be remembered that this is a thought experiment: I do not suggest that anyone would actually do this!) Suppose that, on each occasion the box is opened, the world splits into two, in one of which the observer sees a dead cat and in the other of which he sees a live cat. At the end of the series of experiments, in the majority of the 2^{100} worlds thus created, the results of the 100 experiments would be grouped around a 50/50 result, and the statistical predictions of quantum mechanics would be violated. Our living in a world where the statistical predictions of quantum physics hold good would be an unlikely accident.

A many worlds advocate could assert that the worlds in which the statistical predictions of quantum mechanics do not hold good are 'less probable' worlds—this may be DeWitt's position in DeWitt and Graham (1973: 163, 186)—but what could this *mean*, and how could one *know* if one was in a less probable world? One could know this only by finding that in some particular series of experiments the statistical predictions of quantum mechanics did not hold good: indeed that would be precisely what *makes* it a less probable world. This seems viciously circular. Such a finding would say nothing about whether such predictions would or would not hold good in any other experiments, past or future. The question remains: why should the statistical predictions of quantum mechanics consistently hold good in our world, and why should our world be different in this respect from most other worlds?

The only way to avoid the incoherence of postulating such unknowable variations in the probability of worlds would be to suggest that, each time the box is opened, the world must split into 100 worlds (or some multiple there-of), in one of which the observer sees a dead cat and in 99 of which he sees a live cat. The results after 100 experiments would then conform to the predictions of quantum mechanics in the great majority of the 100^{100} worlds thus created. (The probability of finding oneself in a world where the dead cat was observed on all 100 occasions would then be one in 100^{100}; that is, the same as the probability of such a thing happening in our world.) However, the idea that the number of worlds created must depend in this way on the probabilities of the outcome seems absurd.

The absurdity is highlighted when one considers that in some situations quantum mechanical probabilities can be given by irrational numbers (not expressible as a fraction), so that in those cases (on this approach) the determination of the number of worlds to be created would have to be the result of some approximation chosen by Nature. (Would this approximation have to be accurate to 2 decimal places; or 6; or 23?)

This argument can be taken further, in relation to observables such as position and momentum, which can take a value anywhere within a continuous range. There is in those cases no limit in principle to the precision of measurement of one of those observables, so that the probability of any particular result can be made infinitesimal, while the probability of any particular result *not* being obtained can be (virtually) 1. Would the making of such a measurement (as between the particular result, and not obtaining that result) divide the world into two, or into a near-infinity of worlds (in only one of which the particular result is obtained)?

An attempt has been made to grapple with this sort of problem by Neill Graham (in Graham 1973). His approach is to postulate a 'two-step' measurement, 'in which a macroscopic apparatus mediates between a microscopic system and a macroscopic observer' (p. 236). In the first step 'an apparatus measures the relative frequency with which a given event occurs in a collection of independent, identically prepared systems' (p. 229). In the second step, when the apparatus has returned to thermal equilibrium, it is read by an observer. That interaction, in the second step, is considered as causing the state of the observer and the apparatus to split into 'Everett worlds'; and Graham seeks to show that the probability interpretation will hold good in the great majority of those worlds.

His method is to consider the relative frequency, in a series of measurements, of any value a of an observable $\hat{A}$: this relative frequency is itself an observable, which I will call $\hat{B}$. Thus, if 100 measurements of $\hat{A}$ were made, and a particular result a_1 were to be obtained 10 times, then the relative frequency of this result would be 10/100, i.e. 0.1. Now, suppose that N such measurements of $\hat{A}$ are made without giving rise to any collapse of the state function (that is, to any von Neumann process 1, or to any Everett world-splitting), and suppose that the apparatus can give a reading of the relative frequency observable $\hat{B}$. Graham seeks to show that if, when this reading is 'measured' by an observer, an Everett world-splitting *then* takes place, then the value which would be shown on the apparatus in most of the resulting Everett worlds would be close to that predicted by the probability interpretation of the state function.

I am not certain that he shows even this. He does show that the standard deviation $\Delta\hat{B}$ from the average $\langle\,\hat{B}\,\rangle$ will be relatively small if the number N of measurements is large. However, surely this is because the state function of the apparatus (according to quantum physics) after many measurements is such that the amplitudes for it to be found in states associated with the average $\langle \hat{B} \rangle$, and with values close to this average, are large; whilst those to be found in states associated with values distant from $\langle \hat{B} \rangle$ are small. If that is correct, then the same problem arises: when worlds split, is there just one world for each possible eigenstate (in which case the probability interpretation fails), or do the more probable eigenstates get more worlds? And if they get more worlds, to what degree of precision does Nature take the probability comparison, in order to decide how many worlds (in all) should occur?

However, even if Graham *does* show what he sets out to show, any substantial appeal of the many worlds theory, and any pretence it has to solve the measurement problem, is lost. If world-splitting occurs, at least in the case of repeated measurements, *only* when an apparatus giving a reading of relative frequency is observed, then the many worlds interpretation apparently says nothing about all other cases of measurement. Further, it gives us no account of *why* the world would split *then, and only then*. It apparently gives no account, for example, of the case where an observer reads the apparatus after each measurement, instead of only reading a relative frequency indication at the end of many measurements.

This leads me to the second main reason for rejecting the many worlds interpretation: it does not in any event answer the real problem of measurement. It does not, any more than the Copenhagen interpretation, explain precisely what amounts to a measurement: just as the Copenhagen interpretation cannot define (in quantum physical terms) the circumstances in which there is a reduction of the quantum state, so also the many worlds interpretation cannot define (in quantum physical terms) the circumstances in which worlds split. A *fortiori*, it gives no explanation why in some circumstances state functions develop without worlds splitting, while in other circumstances worlds split. The many worlds interpretation introduces the 'metaphysical baggage' of other worlds, and the difficulties with the probability interpretation of the wave function, without any significant countervailing advantage so far as quantum theory is concerned.

There are, however, what some may see as advantages in other directions. It (like some hidden variables views) avoids the rejection of strict determinism otherwise required by quantum physics: every possibility is in fact realized, in different worlds. It also provides a neat way of dealing with problems based on the extreme improbability of a universe providing the precise stable conditions capable of supporting life: by providing countless millions of universes, it enables the answer that some improbable universes are only to be expected, and that (of course) we can only observe a universe which is such as to support intelligent life. To others, on the contrary, the rejection of strict determinism is an advantage of quantum theory; whilst the improbability of a universe capable of supporting life, and indeed of all the 'cosmic coincidences', can be considered a not unwelcome pointer to a religious outlook.

In Oxford philosopher Michael Lockwood's recent book *Mind, Brain and the Quantum* (1989, chs. 12 and 13) there is a vigorous case presented for a version of this interpretation; and this despite Lockwood's recognition (pp. 225, 230–2) of something like my first main objection. He makes two points which are relevant here:

1. He asserts that it is misleading to talk of worlds or universes splitting: all that happens is that (as postulated by von Neumann) the different possible eigenstates of an observed system become correlated to different states of the human observer, so that each eigenstate of the former is associated with a relative state of the latter. Thus the version does not postulate splitting worlds: the difference from other versions is just that it denies any state reduction, so that macroscopic superpositions (including superpositions of conscious experiences) occur.

2. The role of probability is discussed at pp. 230–2. Lockwood presents a picture-model in which a developing state (including both observed system and human observer) is represented by a long cylinder, with its long dimension representing time. At any cross-section of the cylinder, the respective probabilities at a particular time of various components of a superposition are represented by component areas of the cross-section. Any progression or succession of conscious experiences (which Lockwood calls a biography) can be represented by an arbitrary line parallel to the sides of the cylinder: then the experiences within any such biography will tend to occur consistently with the probability predictions of quantum mechanics.

These points do not overcome the problems which I have identified, as I believe is shown by the following considerations.

We are all familiar (either directly or indirectly) with the chattering response of a Geiger counter brought into proximity with a radioactive substance. However, quantum mechanics gives a (very small) finite probability that none of the billions of atoms in a piece of highly radioactive material will decay in any determinate period of time, say one particular minute. The quantity and radioactivity of the substance may be such that this probability is of the order of (say) one in 10^{10000}. Now according to the many worlds–relative state view, in such cases there is at least one observer-state for whom this is exactly what does occur. One 'biography' associated with this observer-state will be to the effect that a wildly chattering Geiger counter in the vicinity of the substance will fall silent for exactly this one minute, then suddenly resume chattering as before.

According to this view, there will also be other biographies of the observer which are similar to that one, except that a single click occurs at some specific time within the minute's silence; and there will be others in which two clicks occur at specific times within the minute; and so on. And there will be others in which something similar happens during periods different from that specific one-minute period. Each of these observer biographies would be regarded by its subsequent observer-states as just (wildly improbable) memories of an ordinary human being.

I will wager that none of the readers of this book has any such memories, or indeed any memories so wildly at odds with the statistical predictions of quantum mechanics. (It is possible to construct even more wildly improbable scenarios involving, say, the behaviour of the photons by means of which we perceive the world, which nevertheless still have a finite probability, and so on this view are each associated with at least one observer biography.) Yet if the many worlds–relative state interpretation is correct, there must be a near-infinity (at least) of persons or person-versions with many such wildly improbable memories. Lockwood seeks to deal with this sort of problem by postulating (at p. 232) a continuous infinity of biographies or streams of consciousness within his cylinder, so that the numbers of the biographies which are generally in line with the statistical predictions of quantum mechanics can be appropriately greater than the numbers of those which are not.

What this means, however, is that there must be an infinity of observer-states for every outcome for which there is a finite probability, even a probability as small as one in 10^{10000}. (Infinity divided by 10^{10000} is still infinity!) This is, I suppose, one way of trying to deal with the problem I raised earlier of how many worlds must occur in order to provide adequately for the probability predictions of quantum mechanics: but at what cost? It requires an infinity of worlds (or observer-states) for every outcome for which there is a finite probability, with relative probabilities corresponding to ratios among all these infinities. That is both highly implausible (an infinity of different versions of me for every finitely possible outcome, however wildly improbable!) and mathematically unsatisfactory (infinities are, to say the least, terribly tricky to work with).

And why would one want to suggest this? Only to avoid the problematic reduction of quantum states, and to maintain determinism. As noted earlier, the former problem is not really avoided: even on Lockwood's account, the question still arises 'When do observer-states split?' Lockwood's answer seems to be 'Whenever they become correlated to different elements of a superposition of quantum states.' If so, then one can equally say it is just then that one observer-state–quantum-state combination is actualized, while all others of the quantum states previously in superposition are eliminated. One would then have the plausible version of the measurement-by-consciousness interpretation, and the statistics would be taken care of without postulating Lockwood's implausible infinities.

Finally, I should note that there seems to be a moral danger in views such as Lockwood's and, to a lesser extent, Layzer's (noted at the end of Section 14.5), which should cause us to withhold assent unless really convincing reasons are advanced in their favour. They carry the suggestion that our decisions and actions really do not matter very much, because what appears to follow from them is always just one of a multitude of equally existing alternatives, many of which are very different. I say rather that our decisions and actions are important; what we do has real and unequivocal consequences; there are no other versions of our world, or of the people who flourish and suffer in it, which could in any way dilute the significance of our acts and their effects. In any event, I contend that the objections I have raised justify rejection of the many worlds interpretation.

14.7. Quantum Logic

Before returning to consider the other direction of development from the Copenhagen interpretation, it is necessary to consider a view which has been advanced to the effect that the problem of measurement can be dealt with by applying a different logic to the propositions of quantum mechanics. Quantum logic is a large topic, and a technical one. I will attempt to deal in a non-technical way with its possible application to the problem of measurement.

In my account of quantum mechanics to date, I have said that the information given by the state function relates to what *would* happen *if* certain measurements were made. It is this that makes it particularly unsatisfactory that no adequate account of measurement is given. If an account of the state function could be given which avoids this hypothetical character (that is, according to which the state function gives information about the values of observables which is not conditional on a measurement being made), then to some extent at least the problem of measurement would be avoided.

According to the approach of quantum logic, as set out, for example, in Putnam (1979b), one can interpret the state function as giving such unconditional information, so long as the logic applicable to such information is appropriately altered. For example, if a system is in an eigenstate of momentum, with eigenvalue p_n, and if possible results of position measurements are $x_1, x_2, \ldots, x_n$, and so on (generally, to an infinite number of alternatives), then the system can be considered as *having* momentum p_n and position x_1 or x_2 or $\ldots$ or x_n or $\ldots$ (and so on). One can then consistently regard a measurement of position (say x_n) as *discovering* rather than *creating* this value. However, once position is measured as x_n, the momentum is made uncertain by this measurement, and its representation will become p_1 or p_2 or $\ldots$ or p_n or $\ldots$ (and so on).

Thus, prior to such measurement, the system *did* have position x_n (since, as we have said, the measurement discovered this position). However, one cannot infer from the above that the system prior to measurement could have been represented as having momentum p_n *and* position x_n. If p is the assertion that the system has momentum p_n, and x is the assertion that it has position x_n, then p can be true, and x can be true, but their conjunction 'p and x' cannot be true: the mathematics of quantum physics shows this. In logical terms, 'p and x' is treated as not being a well-formed proposition (or at least as false).

Further, although prior to measurement the system could be represented as being in the state (so far as values of position and momentum are concerned):

p_n and (x_1 or x_2 or ... x_n or ... and so on)

it could not be represented as being in the state (so far as values of position and momentum are concerned):

(p_n and x_1) or (p_n and x_2) or ... or (p_n and x_n) or ... and so on.

This is because each of the alternatives in the latter expression is impermissible, while the conjunction in the former expression is permissible. The rule of logic which permits making a transition such as that from the former expression to the latter does not apply to representations of quantum states.

Thus it appears that the quantum logic approach allows a particle to have a definite position and also to have a definite momentum: what it does not allow is that the representation of the particle, for the purpose of the quantum physical formalism, *assign* both a definite position *and* a definite momentum to the particle. The representation of the particle (that is, in effect, the state function or state vector) *cannot* do this: and it is the representation of the particle to which the causal laws of quantum mechanics (such as Schrödinger's equation) apply. This might be thought to be a hidden variables version of quantum mechanics, but it is not necessarily such: the disturbance caused to momentum by a position measurement (or vice versa) *might* be determined by hidden variables; but this is not required by the quantum logic approach, and such disturbance could be random.

However, this approach can, I think, also be rejected.

In the first place, if a particle has a definite position and a definite momentum, presumably it could be represented either by a state function assigning a definite position and uncertain momentum, or else by a state function assigning a definite momentum and uncertain position. Although the two representations would appear equally to be available, the time development of such representations would differ. The point can perhaps be most clearly seen in relation to a comparison of a representation giving a definite position, and another giving a definite energy.

Consider a particle confined in the one-dimensional 'box', discussed in Section 12.4. If it had a definite energy, this could be the second energy level: as we saw, this would give a zero probability of the particle ever being found in the centre of the box; and this would not alter under time development. However, if the particle could have a definite position (as well as that definite energy), then, no matter where that position was within the box, time development of the state function representing the particle having that position would eventually give a finite probability of the particle's being found in the centre of the box.

In the second place, if the quantum logic approach is to solve the problem of measurement by explaining how measurement merely finds, and does not create, values of observables, then it seems vulnerable to Bell's theorem and the Aspect experiments. I will discuss these matters more fully in the next part. Here it is sufficient to note that Bell's theorem shows that, if two particles each have three separate well-defined properties (which may be values of observables), there is a particular upper limit to certain correlations that can occur between them. Quantum theory predicted, and Aspect's experiments confirmed, that such a limit would in some cases be exceeded. This is consistent with the conventional approach of the quantum theory to the effect that prior to measurement particles do not have well-defined properties, at least not in respect of more than one of a number of incompatible observables: for other incompatible observables, the value measured is *created* by measurement. This escape is not available if it is asserted that all values measured are *found*, not created, by the measurement. Accordingly, it would seem, quantum logic either does not answer the problem of measurement, or else it conflicts with Bell's theorem and the Aspect experiments.

In the third place, again taking the version of quantum logic which purports to solve the problem of measurement, it would involve an extraordinary complexity in relation to such observables as the state of polarization of a photon. If a photon is plane polarized in a particular direction, then there is $\cos^2 \theta$ probability that it will be passed by a polarizer orientated at angle θ to the direction of polarization (and $\sin^2 \theta$ probability that it will be absorbed by the polarizer). Meeting such a polarizer can be regarded as a constituent part of a measurement of polarization in the θ direction; and the conventional approach of the quantum theory would say that such a measurement changes the polarization to polarization either in the θ direction or in the $\theta + \pi/2$ direction, with respective probabilities $\cos^2 \theta$ and $\sin^2 \theta$. However, if quantum logic is to avoid measurement having such effect (and therefore needing explanation), it must assert that the photon is (prior to such measurement) already polarized (or at least *potentially* polarized) either in the θ or the $\theta + \pi/2$ direction, so that the measurement merely discovers this. Thus each photon would have to be polarized (at least potentially) at the same time in many directions, with the distribution of (potential) polarization directions conforming to the requirement that its density must be proportional to $\cos^2 \theta$, where θ is the angle with the principal (or actual, or measured) polarization direction. Furthermore, if there are many photons polarized in the same direction, then each must have such a distribution of (potential) polarization directions: and *these* distributions cannot all be identical, but must differ in such a way that measurement of polarization in the θ direction of many such photons will (for *any* angle θ) give a proportion of approximately $\cos^2 \theta$ which *are* so polarized.

The above comments only apply in so far as quantum logic is said to answer the measurement problem, and say nothing about the merits of quantum logic generally.

14.8. Measurement by Types of Interaction

I return now to the other direction of development from the Copenhagen interpretation, which I mentioned earlier. This is to suggest that 'measurement' (or reduction of quantum states) is effected by particular *types* of interaction or event, irrespective of whether any human observer (or indeed any conscious entity) is undertaking a measurement, or indeed is involved in any way (see e.g. Heisenberg 1930: 58; Bohr 1958: 73; Feynman *et al.* 1963: 3.9). For this approach to be satisfactory, it must be possible to identify the *types*: that is, to identify what objective properties of measurement interactions explain why there are, in such interactions, sudden partly unpredictable changes in quantum systems. A number of different suggestions have been made.

14.8.1. *Macroscopic Events*

One general suggestion is that measurement is effected by macroscopic events. Such events have not been defined with precision. They are variously said to be: macroscopic events; events of a scale to be readily observable by human beings; events by means of which information enters irreversibly into the macroscopic world; irreversible entropy-increasing events. Examples of such events include the clicking of a Geiger counter and the appearance of a mark on a photographic plate; but such events extend to virtually all processes in the physical world that human beings actually observe.

One approach takes such events to be the data, which are to be explained, correlated, and predicted by the formalism of quantum mechanics. The formalism is then taken as providing such explanations, correlations, and predictions. Similarly, entities such as electrons, protons, neutrons, and photons (as well as quarks, gluons, and the rest of the particle 'zoo') are taken as convenient labels, the use of which in combination with the formalism assists in ascertaining and understanding connections between the detectable events in the observable physical world.

This approach can be seen, for example, in Watson (1967: 64, 94), and Rae (1986, chs. 9, 10). In relation to particles such as electrons and their associated wave fields, Watson says:

Thus the particle exists in space-time as a localised entity only in the events that mark its creation, its disappearance or its interaction with some other physical system. . . . The wave field is in effect a statistical invention; it applies to connecting the detectable events in which physical effects actually occur. These are the only physical reality to be observed. They would be there if we cared to look. Whereas in the absence of physical effects that change the odds for possibilities not yet realised, there is, strictly speaking, nothing to observe. It has not happened. (Watson 1967: 63–4)

A somewhat similar approach is taken by Rae: he emphasizes the irreversible nature of macro events, and (at p. 116) advocates the view that regards subatomic processes represented by the functions and vectors of quantum mechanics as 'illusion', or at least no more than an approximation to reality.

There are problems with this approach. I do not think sufficient reason is given to deny reality to entities represented by the quantum mechanical formalism. I look at this further in Sections 15.1 and 15.4; but, in general terms, even if such entities are 'only' connections, I do not see why connections cannot be real, particularly where they enable a better explanation of observable phenomena than do the detectable objects and events themselves. There is also the paradox referred to earlier that somehow the detectable objects and events are *made of* quantum objects and events.

More generally, no satisfactory definition of measurement in terms of the quantum theory is given. To say that measurement is effected by irreversible events is not very helpful: virtually all quantum theorists accept that measurement is irreversible, so that it is the *identification* of *what* (in quantum physical terms) constitutes an irreversible measurement (rather than a reversible time development) that is at the heart of the measurement problem. The other criteria suggested—that the event should be macroscopic and readily observable—although conveying some information which can be applied in a general sort of way in a classical description of what happens, are imprecise and do not greatly assist in a quantum mechanical description of measurement.

14.8.2. *Bohm*

An attempt to give an account in quantum physical terms of what distinguishes a measurement event was made by Bohm in his book *Quantum Theory* (Bohm 1951), prior to his adoption of the 'hidden variables' approach. He contended that measurement interactions are those whose effect, on each eigenstate of the measured observable which is superposed in the measured system, can be represented as multiplication by a different unpredictable phase factor; so that thereafter the representation excludes interference effects as between these eigenstates. Bohm contended that this makes measurement irreversible as a practical matter, and also explains why the superposition thereafter behaves indistinguishably from a (classical) statistical mixture. He does not give a detailed mathematical proof that this happens: rather he gives a qualitative argument for it, and contends that it must happen if quantum mechanics is to make sense.

If Bohm's contention is correct, it would explain the cessation of inter-ference effects as between the elements of the superposition; and thereby, for example, provide a possible answer to my minor objection to von Neumann's analysis (Section 14.2). However, this could at best be only part of the story. It does not tell us how or why in the real world (as distinct from the mathe-matical representation of it) eigenstates which were previously objective potentialities, having detectable interference effects, are altogether elimin-ated; or how or why one such eigenstate which was similarly a (mere) poten-tiality is elevated to being an actuality. Accordingly, it does not explain why a reading of a measuring device gives a single result, and it does not explain why successive readings of the same measuring device in an individual case give the same result.

Nevertheless, it seems to me that Bohm's approach may well be correct, as far as it goes, having regard to the following plausible considerations.

In the first place, the measurement interaction (viewed quantum mechani-cally) presumably must affect the quantum state of the measured system, yet it must not scramble the eigenstates of the observables measured. The out-come of a precise measurement must be one of the eigenstates of the observ-able measured, and in particular must be one which was in the superposition of such eigenstates which existed prior to measurement: the measurement interaction must not *introduce* any eigenstate of the observable measured which was *not* included in the prior superposition, as otherwise the result of measurement could be an eigenvalue which, prior to measurement, had nil probability; that is, was not a possible result of measurement. This charac-teristic of the measurement interaction will be assured *if* the interaction can be represented mathematically as doing no more than multiplying each ele-ment of the superposition of eigenstates of the observable measured by some number, and not otherwise changing the state function.

In the second place, there is an analogy in quantum mechanics between the measurement of an observable, on the one hand, and the application of the operator representing that observable to the state function, on the other hand. The celebrated difference (first noted by Heisenberg) between the results of 'multiplying' the position and momentum operators, depending on which is placed first, is an example of this analogy: this difference is said to cor-respond to the different results derived from measuring first position and then momentum, and vice versa. Another example is that in the vector formulation of quantum mechanics, the 'sandwich' $\langle \phi \,|\, \hat{A} \,|\, \psi \rangle$ can represent the applica-tion to a system represented by $|\psi\rangle$ of an apparatus appropriate to measure the observable $\hat{A}$, and the production thereby of a system represented by $|\phi\rangle$. And, of course, the result of applying an operator representing an observable to a state function, expressed as superposition of eigenstates of that observ-able, is to do no more than multiply each element of the superposition by a number, namely the respective eigenvalue. Thus if $|\psi_1\rangle$, $|\psi_2\rangle$, etc. are eigenstates of the observable $\hat{A}$, and a_1, a_2, etc. are the corresponding eigenvalues; and if c_1, c_2, etc. are probability amplitudes associated with the respective eigenstates, so that $| \psi \rangle = \Sigma c_n | \psi_n \rangle$; then:

$$\hat{A} | \psi \rangle = \Sigma a_n c_n | \psi_n \rangle$$

Clearly, no additional eigenstate is introduced.

In the third place, however, the von Neumann analysis shows that the end result of the measurement interaction (considered as process 2) is that eigenstates of a corresponding observable $\hat{B}$ of the measuring apparatus are so correlated with the eigenstates of the measured observable $\hat{A}$ of the measured system that the probability of the eigenstate associated with the value b_n of the relevant apparatus observable is $| c_n |^2$. It would seem, therefore, that the analogy suggested in the previous paragraph is not precise: it is difficult to see how the correlation postulated by von Neumann between an eigenstate of the measured system and an eigenstate of the apparatus could be consistent with the former having a probability amplitude $a_n c_n$ following the measurement interaction, and the latter having a probability $| c_n |^2$. And this could not be overcome by normalization, because the eigenvalues a_n are generally different from each other. On the other hand, if the interaction with the measuring apparatus merely multiplied each eigenstate by a different phase factor $e^{i\theta}$ as suggested by Bohm, then at least the probabilities $| c_n |^2$ are unaltered, consistently with the correlation postulated by von Neumann.

14.8.3. *Daneri, Loinger, and Prosperi*

Later approaches have tended to concentrate on the macroscopic nature of measuring devices, and/or the notion of thermodynamic irreversibility. An example of the former is the approach of Daneri, Loinger, and Prosperi (1983).

They take the case of a macroscopic measuring device which reaches thermal equilibrium after a measurement interaction, and they consider the differences in the predictions for observation given by representations of such a device first as a quantum mechanical superposition of states (consequent on a von Neumann process 2 interaction with the measured system), and secondly as a classical mixture of such states (a statistical combination of states representing our knowledge about which single state does in fact obtain). They show that, while the two representations will make different statistical predictions about measurements of some observables, they will make the same statistical predictions about all macroscopic observables, in particular the observable giving the result of the measurement.

So, if one measures a number of identically prepared systems, the same statistics of results will be predicted whether one considers the macroscopic measuring system to end up after measurement in a quantum physical superposition of states, or in just one state represented by a classical mixture. For that purpose, the question of the collapse of the wave function is irrelevant. As with Bohm, however, Daneri, Loinger, and Prosperi do *not* show that in the former case the *same* result will be given by two *successive* readings of the macroscopic measuring device which measures just *one* of the systems (see Cartwright 1983: 169–71).

Thus, if the Schrödinger's cat 'experiment' were to be prepared identically 100 times, and the result observed 100 times, the same statistics of the results of observation would be predicted whether one regarded the cat as ending up in a superposition of live and dead states, or as ending up either live or dead in accordance with the probabilities indicated by quantum physics. However, if one looked at any single cat on two successive occasions, and if on each occasion it was in a superposition of live and dead states, one could observe a dead cat on the first occasion and a live cat on the second occasion. Thus, the collapse of the wave function cannot be dispensed with if one is to have an orderly history of macroscopic objects.

It seems to me, therefore, that this approach does not really take the question much further than did von Neumann and Bohm.

14.8.4. *Thermodynamic Irreversibility*

One current approach is to associate measurement with thermodynamic irreversibility and entropy: this is suggested in Rae (1986: 81–2, 94–118). However, there are problems here too. In particular, no satisfactory quantum mechanical description of thermodynamically irreversible events has yet been provided. An entropy superoperator has been proposed by Misra, Prigogine, and Courbage (1979); but, as they define it, it cannot exist for quantum systems consisting of finite numbers of particles enclosed in a finite volume, and so (it would seem) could not account for a measurement performed on a system by an observer, where both are enclosed and isolated (for practical purposes) from the rest of the world (see also Coveney 1988.) Furthermore, even if one did establish a precise criterion for irreversible events in the detectable world, still it seems one would not account for measurement by *non-events*, such as the non-clicking of a Geiger counter, and the non-death of Schrödinger's cat (see Jammer 1974: 495–9).

That is, measurement can be effected by the non-occurrence of macro events, as well as by their occurrence. Thus, in the case of Schrödinger's cat, the absence of any click or other reaction by the Geiger counter, and the non-death of the cat, measures the radioactive substance to be in the state of not-decayed. The part of the state function of that substance associated with its decay by the emission of a radioactive particle is eliminated by the non-occurrence of macro events.

Measurement by a non-event involves the occurrence of a quantum mechanical interaction (von Neumann's process 2), plus the non-occurrence of an event which according to quantum physics is a possible event; and such non-occurrence involves von Neumann's process 1. If the measurement is to determine between two possible states $|a_1\rangle$ and $|a_2\rangle$, then prior to measurement the system to be measured will be in the state $c_1|a_1\rangle + c_2|a_2\rangle$, where c_1 and c_2 are the (complex) probability amplitudes. Suppose that the measuring system relevantly has two states $|b_1\rangle$ and $|b_2\rangle$, corresponding to $|a_1\rangle$ and $|a_2\rangle$ respectively. Then, on the von Neumann approach, after the measurement interaction (viewed quantum mechanically) the combined system will be in the state $c_1|a_1\rangle|b_1\rangle + c_2|a_2\rangle|b_2\rangle$. Now suppose the measuring system, before the measurement interaction, is already in the state $|b_1\rangle$, which could be (for example) | cat living ⟩. Then if, after the measurement interaction, the system *still* displays the same state $|b_1\rangle$, that is, if *nothing has happened*, then the measured system has been measured to be in the state $|a_1\rangle$. Of course, if something happens, and the measuring system displays state $|b_2\rangle$, for example | cat dead ⟩, then the measured system has been measured to be in the state $|a_2\rangle$.

14.8.5. *A Quantitative Limit on Superposition*

Having regard to all the above problems, it seems to me that if there is to be an objective solution to the measurement problem—that is, one not involving consciousness and subjectivity—then it may well lie in some limitation on what kinds of states can exist in superposition. This has been considered by Schlegel (1980: 198–228), but the limitations suggested by him do not appear sufficient to solve the measurement problem.

All measurement involves a coupling of the (small) system to be measured to another (presumably larger) system, the measuring device. On the von Neumann analysis, eigenstates of the relevant observable of the measured system become correlated to eigenstates of a corresponding observable of the measuring device—for example, pointer positions. However, the latter does *not* persist in a superposition of such eigenstates: one only of such eigenstates persists, and this in turn apparently puts an end to the superposition of eigenstates in the measured system. The single eigenstate, which corresponds to the eigenstate that persists in the larger system, is selected, and the rest are eliminated.

It seems reasonable to conjecture that the superposition does not persist in the measuring device because it *cannot*—there is some quantitative limit placed by Nature on what state can persist in superposition. If there is such a limit, it must presumably have something to do with scale; but Heisenberg's uncertainty principle suggests that it cannot depend on just *one* aspect of scale, since the minimum indeterminacy of any single aspect of scale can in theory approach infinity (as the indeterminacy of the complementary observable approaches zero). This leads me to speculate that such limitation may be encapsulated in a maximum value for the *product* of the indeterminacies in the values of certain observables. Before looking at this speculation of mine, I will briefly mention two other suggestions.

1. Ghirardi, Rimini, and Weber. A recent proposal for an objective description of measurement (or quantum state reduction) appears in Ghirardi, Rimini, and Weber (1986), and is discussed in Bell (1988*b*: 201–12). The proposal is that quantum systems from time to time spontaneously jump to reduced quantum states, in accordance with certain probability parameters involving two new constants of nature.

The probability per unit time of such a jump is N/T, where N can be taken as the number of matter-like particles in a quantum system, and T is a new constant of nature which the authors suggest to be of the order of 10^{15} seconds (10^8 years). In a small system being measured, with relatively few matter-like particles, there is negligible probability of any jump occurring while the system is effectively isolated; but in a measuring device, with of the order of (say) 10^{20} particles, the mean lifetime before a jump would be about 10^{-5} seconds.

The suggested jumps in the quantum states are collapses *away from* locations in space which are randomly determined in a manner depending partly on another new constant of nature. As I understand the proposal, it would mean that, when a measured system becomes coupled to a measuring device so that the latter goes into a superposition (say) of two pointer positions, there would be a jump or succession of jumps which would quickly eliminate one of the two elements of that superposition, by establishing nil probability for finding any particle in the region of one pointer position.

To me, this proposal has some plausibility, but it would require much working out.

2. Penrose. In Penrose (1986, 1989: 367–71), Roger Penrose suggests that the reduction of quantum states is a gravitational phenomenon, and that understanding such reduction really requires a satisfactory theory of quantum gravity, which has yet to be developed.

He suggests that quantum state reduction may occur when the superposed states of a measuring device are such that 'the difference between the gravitational fields of the various alternatives reaches the one-graviton level' (Penrose 1989: 369). The graviton is the postulated quantum carrier of the force of gravity, just as the photon is the quantum carrier of the force of electromagnetism; and, as I understand him, Penrose puts the one-graviton level at about 10^{-7} grams.

As Penrose acknowledges, his proposal needs a lot of development. One matter that puzzles me is this. If I understand him correctly, the difference between superposed states which (he suggests) brings about reduction is measured in terms of mass (or its relativistic equivalent, energy). However, Heisenberg's uncertainty principle allows for substantial indeterminacies of of energy (and therefore mass) for sufficiently short periods of time. I wonder, therefore, if Penrose's criterion really requires some *combination* of differences or indeterminacies in energy *and* time (or space-time, or space) if it is to be consistent with Heisenberg's principle.

More generally, it seems to me possible that a superposition cannot persist where it would involve indeterminacies in two or more observables (say, total energy E and another observable O) such that their *product* would exceed some limit imposed by Nature. What happens whenever a superposition involving such indeterminacies occurs is that one or more elements of such a superposition are immediately eliminated, so that the permissible maximum is not exceeded for any finite time: just *which* elements are eliminated is a matter the probabilities of which may be derived from the state vector at the stage of time development when such superposition first occurs.

As to what this limit could be, Penrose's proposal that gravity is somehow involved is appealing, especially in suggesting a link between two unsolved mysteries, quantum measurement and quantum gravity.

A different idea which has occurred to me is that some one or more known universal constants could be involved: Planck's constant h would be a very likely candidate, as would the speed of light c. The product hc gives units which are the same as those of energy by distance. This gives rise to the speculation that perhaps this very product provides a maximum for some product of indeterminacies for quantum systems which cannot be exceeded for any finite time: perhaps the product of the indeterminacy of total energy and the indeterminacy of position around any point. In one dimension, this could be written $\Delta E \Delta x \leq 2hc$ (or $\Delta |E| \Delta x \leq 2hc$ to emphasize that one is not dealing with any resolution of energy along the x axis). For many-particle systems, there could be some ambiguity in Δx particularly, but this could be overcome: for example, it could be the position indeterminacy of the centre of mass (although this approach could require some further parameter to deal with rotational indeterminacy).

This limit may seem far too small, and perhaps it is: however, many systems involve symmetries, such that great indeterminacy of momentum can be associated with little or no indeterminacy of total energy. (Perhaps also the proposed limit could be too small merely by a factor of some pure numerical constant, such as the fine structure constant.) The limit would (if correct) indicate that quantum states cannot persist in superpositions such that the indeterminacy of energy exceeds the energy of a photon with wavelength equal to the indeterminacy of position around any point.

This suggestion is highly speculative; and, even if it has any merit, it would, like the two other proposals, require much working out.

14.8.6. *Conclusions*

Whether or not a solution can be found along these lines is an open question. In his careful and deep consideration of quantum physics and reality, *Reality and the Physicist* (d'Espagnat 1989), Bernard d'Espagnat suggests that such a solution is improbable (e.g. p. 245), particularly one which has strong objectivity, involving no reference to human observers (pp. 75–9, 85–6). If there is no objective solution, then I believe that the only plausible solution is along the lines of the version of 'measurement by consciousness' which I outlined in the latter part of Section 14.3.

Otherwise, I think, one must be content with something like the Copenhagen interpretation: this seems to be d'Espagnat's position. He suggests that quantum physics is a theory which does not have strong objectivity, but only weak objectivity, or intersubjectivity: some of its 'basic statements . . . mention the observer, *but only on the clear understanding that these statements are deemed to be true for any observer'*.

In order to pursue these matters, I will need to look at some other aspects of the relation between quantum theory and reality; and this I undertake in the next chapter.

15

Quantum Theory and Reality

THE problem of measurement as discussed in the previous chapter is only part of the overall problem of reconciling quantum mechanics with our other knowledge of the world. There are other aspects, closely related to the problem of measurement and sometimes discussed as part of this problem, which also need to be considered: I am particularly concerned with three matters, which were touched on in the previous chapter, but which I will now consider in more detail. First, there is the question of what a quantum particle *is*, and how it behaves *between* measurements. Secondly, there is the matter of the curious correlations which exist between particles distant from each other, involving the Bell inequality and the Aspect experiments. Thirdly, there is the general problem of reconciling the quantum mechanical view of macro objects with our common-sense view of such objects. I will deal in turn with each of these topics, and will conclude this chapter by drawing some conclusions about the implications of quantum physics for the nature of matter and of reality generally.

15.1. The Nature and Behaviour of Quantum Particles

The classical view was that the ultimate constituents of matter are particles; and quantum physics takes a similar approach. But, according to classical physics, each particle has a definite position (and in that position occupies no more space than its own size) and a definite (and continuous) motion. Quantum mechanics is inconsistent with that view. But what then *are* quantum 'particles'?

15.1.1. *What Is a Quantum Particle?*

It has been said that a quantum particle is sometimes a particle and sometimes a wave: in particular, it is a particle when its position is measured, so that the particle-like property of definite location is manifested; and it is a wave (with wave number k) when its momentum is measured, manifesting a definite momentum $\hbar k$. However, as I see it, it is misleading to regard a quantum particle as *ever* being a classical particle or a classical wave, or even as being some sort of mixture of the two.

What it is, is perhaps best expressed in terms of its being something described by a quantum mechanical state function, which (according to the rules of quantum mechanics) will manifest properties which are more or less particle-like, and more or less wavelike, depending upon what 'measurement' of it occurs (and I use 'measurement' here in the wide sense, so as to include all quantum state reductions which manifest values of observables). This means in turn that, when measurements are not being made, a quantum particle should be regarded (like a state function) as a matter of potentialities, of possibilities (or, better, quantified probabilities) of manifesting various values of observables *if* measurements occur.

In cases where, according to quantum theory, a particle such as an electron is adequately represented by a single-particle state function, one can give a fairly straightforward realist account of what such a particle is. It can be considered as a sort of density or intensity, simply located in that volume (or those volumes) of space where there is a possibility that it would be found by a measurement of position. The state function gives the value of this density or intensity at each point in this volume of space; and also an 'expectation value' for position, being in effect the point at which the particle is most likely to be found.

The value of the density or intensity is a complex number, which can be written $re^{i\theta}$. The fact that it is complex, involving the imaginary number i, helps to give quantum mechanics its air of mystery and unreality: however, there is a straightforward reason for this. While the probabilities of *position* measurements are given by the real number r (in fact, by r^2), the probabilities of various *momentum* measurements depend in part on the phase factor $e^{i\theta}$. It is this which indicates the phase relationships which are necessary for calculation of the momentum probabilities. As we shall see in further discussing the two-slit experiment, in cases where a single-state function is divided into two parts which are superposed, the phase factor also indicates phase relationships between the parts which give rise to interference effects. These phase relationships must be considered real, because the interference effects which they give rise to are reflected in the calculation of probabilities, which in turn are reflected in measured values. However, since the phase relationships cannot be *directly* observed, there is no reason why they cannot be represented mathematically by imaginary and complex numbers; and it so happens that the mathematical properties of the function $e^{i\theta}$ are ideally suited to dealing with phase relationships.

Phase relationships *could* be dealt with by other mathematical techniques not involving complex and imaginary numbers, but not so conveniently: what would be needed, in effect, instead of complex numbers, would be groups of two real numbers, and rules to ensure that operations with such groups give similar results to those given by similar operations with the real and imaginary parts of complex numbers.

So, what corresponds to motion for a classical particle is in part represented (on this 'local densities' account) by the phase factor $e^{i\theta}$. As well as giving the probabilities of various momentum measurements, the state function will also give an 'expectation value' for momentum; and, as we saw in Section 12.3, there is a relationship between this expectation value for momentum, and the time development of the expectation value for position, which is analogous to the relationship between momentum and motion in classical physics. Thus, the volume of space in which the particle could be found, and the 'density' distribution within that volume, will develop over time so that the expectation value for position will move in the way suggested (classically) by the expectation value for momentum: it is this time development which is the quantum equivalent to the classical concept of motion for a single particle.

This general approach is also appropriate where a single-particle state function can be used to represent beams of particles, because each particle can be considered as having the same state function, and mutual interactions can be disregarded. However, as we shall see, it is not appropriate for many-particle state functions where mutual interactions cannot be disregarded.

The approach can be illustrated by considering the experiment which (despite its origin in the early nineteenth century) is above all others the classic illustration of quantum physics and its weirdness: the two-slit experiment.

15.1.2. *The Two-Slit Experiment*

It will be recalled that this experiment was devised by Thomas Young as a demonstration of the wave nature of light, and as a means for calculating the wavelength of light of different colours.

A monochromatic beam of light from a point source is directed towards an opaque screen with two parallel slits, and the light passing through the slits is allowed to fall on a further screen on the far side. If one slit is blocked, a roughly oblong patch of light appears on the further screen generally in line with the open slit. Similarly, if the first-mentioned slit is left open and the other blocked, a similar patch appears in a slightly different position, generally in line with the slit that is now open. When both slits are left open, one might expect that there would be just the two patches, overlapping somewhat. However (if the slits are narrow enough and correctly placed close together), there is instead a pattern of alternating dark and light stripes.

As we saw, the explanation for this lies in the wave nature of light. Where the 'peaks' of the waves from one slit coincide with the 'troughs' of the waves from the other slit (this is a matter of phase relationships between two parts of the same state function), they cancel each other out (giving rise to nil position density), so that no light appears on the screen. Where the 'peaks' of the waves from both slits coincide, they reinforce each other, so that more intense light appears on the screen.

However, the quantum theory asserts that light is made up of photons, each of which is in some respects like a particle: if a precise measurement is made of its position, it will be found at one precise position. The source can be turned so low that only one photon will be passing through the screen with the slits at any one time; yet if the display screen is prepared so as to be able to detect the arrival of single photons, over time the same interference pattern will be built up.

Indeed, as mentioned earlier, the same experiment can be performed using electrons rather than photons: the short wavelength associated with electrons requires the slits to be so close together as to be very difficult to realize in practice, but it has now been done (see *New Scientist*, 27 May 1989). If electrons are directed from a point source to the screen with slits, and a detection plate of some sort placed on the far side, the results are similar to those with light: with one slit blocked, the electrons fall in a single band; and with both open they fall in a pattern of stripes, similar to the interference pattern produced by light. If the electrons are sent one at a time, the same pattern builds up.

Returning to the case of light, it is apparent that some parts of the display screen are *darker* with *both* slits open than with one slit open. If photons were regarded as having a definite trajectory, one would have to say that each photon passed through either one slit or the other: it would then be inconceivable that fewer photons could arrive at parts of the display screen with both slits open than with one slit open. If steps are taken to determine which hole each photon (or electron) passed through, it is found that, while measurements to this end can be made, the effect of doing so is to destroy the interference pattern.

The mathematics of quantum mechanics gives an explanation. Ignoring time development (it is not relevant to this question), the state function ψ of each electron on the far side of the slits can be considered as made up of contributions ψ_1 and ψ_2 from slit 1 and slit 2 respectively: $\psi = \psi_1 + \psi_2$. The probability of locating an electron at any point on the screen (and thus the probability distribution of many electrons in a beam) is given by the absolute square of the relevant state function applied to the point in question. Thus, if only slit 1 is open it will be $|\psi_1|^2$; if only slit 2 is open it will be $|\psi_2|^2$; and if both slits are open it will be $|\psi|^2$, that is $|\psi_1 + \psi_2|^2$. Now, ψ_1 and ψ_2 are each made up of an amplitude (which we can call r_1 and r_2 respectively) and a phase factor (which we can call $\exp(i\theta_1)$ and $\exp(i\theta_2)$ respectively); and while $|\psi_1|^2 = r_1^2$, and $|\psi_2|^2 = r_2^2$ in general $|\psi_1 + \psi_2|^2$ does *not* equal $r_1^2 + r_2^2$ Rather:

$$
\begin{aligned}
|\psi_1 + \psi_2|^2 &= [r_1 \exp(i\theta_1) + r_2 \exp(i\theta_2)] \times [r_1 \exp(-i\theta_1) + r_2 \exp(-i\theta_2)] \\
&= r_1^2 + r_2^2 + r_1 r_2 \{\exp[i(\theta_1 - \theta_2)] + \exp[i(\theta_2 - \theta_1)]\} \\
&= r_1^2 + r_2^2 + 2r_1 r_2 \cos\phi .
\end{aligned}
$$

Here, ϕ is the phase difference $\theta_1 - \theta_2$. Now, where $\phi = \pi/2$ or $3\pi/2$, $\cos \phi = 0$, so that, for those cases only, $|\psi|^2$ will be $r_1^2 + r_2^2$. However, where $\phi = \pi$, $|\psi|^2$, will be $r_1^2 + r_2^2 - 2r_1r_2$, so that, if r_1 and r_2 are nearly equal, $|\psi|^2$ will be approximately zero. Where $\phi = 0$, $|\psi|^2$ will be $r_1^2 + r_2^2 + 2r_1r_2$, so that, if r_1 and r_2 are nearly equal, $|\psi|^2$ will be approximately double $r_1^2 + r_2^2$. The former case corresponds to, and accounts for, the areas between the stripes; while the latter corresponds to, and accounts for, the areas of maximum intensity within the stripes.

On the other hand, in those cases where the electron is known to have gone through one hole, then (leaving aside the question of disturbance by the measurement), its state function on the far side of the slit will be ψ_1 *or* ψ_2 (subject to normalization), and the probability of locating it at any point will be given by r_1^2 or r_2^2. Accordingly, the probability distribution of all such electrons will be given by r_1^2 for those found to have gone through slit 1, and by r_2^2 for those found to have gone through slit 2, a total of just $r_1^2 + r_2^2$.

Accordingly, until detection, the state function of each single electron on the far side of the slits, when both are open, can be considered as comprising a sum of contributions from each slit. The electron itself, then, until detection, is best regarded as a matter of potentialities, of probabilities quantified by the state function, that various values of observables such as position will be manifested if an appropriate measurement is made (or an appropriate interaction occurs). These probabilities are contributed to by both slits; and if the measurement of position cannot determine which slit gave rise to the potentiality actualized by the measurement, then in a sense the electron has 'gone through' both slits.

15.1.3. *Wheeler Delayed-Choice Experiment*

This approach is useful for analysing a variant of the two-slit experiment, which is sometimes said to undermine realism and/or to demonstrate reverse-time causation.

Wheeler has pointed out that the display screen in the two-slit experiment (with light) could be replaced by a venetian blind, and that a lens could be placed behind this, focusing the light on to a further screen. When the venetian blind is open, the lens will display an image of the two slits on the further screen, making it seemingly obvious which slit it was through which the light making up each image has come. However, no interference pattern is displayed: each photon has (apparently) definitely passed through just one slit. If the venetian blind is closed, the interference pattern appears on the blind, made possible (as we have seen) because (in a sense) each photon has gone through both slits.

If the venetian blind is closed, then opened after a photon has traversed the slits but before it reaches the blind, the lens will tell us which slit it passed through. However, at the time it traversed the slits, the venetian blind was closed; and if it had been left closed, interference would have occurred by reason of the photon 'passing through both slits'. It has been suggested from this that there is no objective reality in which the photon passes through either both slits or one only; or, alternatively, that opening the blind retrospectively causes the photon to go through one slit only.

There is, however, a simpler explanation in terms of potentialities. The image caused by the lens does *not* in fact tell us which slit a photon passed through, except in the sense that the potentiality which gave rise to the detection of the photon on the further screen was due to the opening of a particular slit: this detection was a manifestation of ψ_1 (say) rather than ψ_2. However, until that manifestation, both ψ_1 and ψ_2 existed, so that an appropriate measurement (say, by a late reclosing of the venetian blinds) could have resulted in a manifestation contributed to by both and exhibiting the interference pattern. In particular, if the detection of the photon on the further screen is a manifestation of ψ_1 (that is, of a potentiality due to slit 1), this does *not* mean that *if* photon detectors had been placed at the slits, this photon would have been detected at slit 1: on the contrary, it could have been detected at slit 2 with probability $| \psi_2 |^2$.

Thus, where a photon is detected in such a way that you can say it was a manifestation or realization of a potentiality arising from slit 1 only, interference effects due to slit 2 are absent. These interference effects themselves are, until manifested or realized, mere potentialities which will be realized by an appropriate measurement or interaction, which must be such as not to permit detection of only one slit being involved in the particular manifestation.

15.1.4. *Many-Particle State Functions*

A state function which represents two or more particles cannot necessarily be considered in the fairly straightforward realistic way which I outlined for single-particle systems. It was previously noted that a state function for two particles will give the probability of (both) finding one particle at position *A* and (at the same time) finding the other particle at position *B*.

As pointed out in Squires (1986: 128–9), such a function is 'a function of *two* positions' and so 'is not like a density', and 'does not have a value at each point of space'; although, where a two-particle function can be written as a simple product of two state functions, each depending on only one position, it can be considered as 'two "somethings" which have densities at all points in space'. However, this is the case only if the probabilities of where one particle would be found are independent of where the other particle is found; that is, if the particles have no correlations arising from interaction.

In other cases, where a many-particle state function cannot be written as a simple product of single-particle state functions, the straightforwardly realistic account of quantum particles as densities, simply located in space, is not available. It is still possible to assign to each location in space a probability for finding a particle at that location (or rather, within a small distance from that location) *if* one looks *only* in that location: but such probabilities (and any associated phase factors) are only a small part of what is represented or conveyed by the state function. In particular, such state functions give interdependent probabilities for *simultaneous* measurements of any number of the constituent particles at all relevant locations in space; and this cannot be considered as involving simply located densities.

This is a striking example of the holistic character of quantum physics. When one is dealing with a system of particles, it is not merely the case (as in classical physics) that every particle exerts forces (gravitational and electrical) on every other particle; but also generally the actual result of a measurement at one place (which is unpredictable) will be correlated with actual results of simultaneous measurements at other places (which are similarly unpredictable). I look at this further in Section 15.2.

This point is related to another aspect of quantum mechanics which gives it an air of mystery and unreality: the suggestion that the 'waves' of state functions for many-particle systems are waves, not in ordinary three-dimensional space, but in space of $3n$ dimensions, where n is the number of particles concerned. However, this 'space' is just a mathematical concept: the state function will always give information from which can be calculated probability amplitudes, and probabilities, for the manifestation of the particles comprised in the system at locations in ordinary three-dimensional space. One can still regard the state function, in the absence of measurement, as describing *real potentialities* for measurement (or measurement-like interactions). What one cannot do, however, is to consider such potentialities as being something like simply located densities. The potentialities of multiparticle systems, involving correlations through interaction, do not have simple location; and this element of non-locality makes it particularly difficult to envisage in simple terms what the particles of the system 'really' are.

So, although in general terms quantum mechanics still treats particles as the ultimate constituents of matter, in any but the simplest case such particles cannot be considered as having either separate identities or simple location, except when they are manifested as having such identities and/or location in measurements or measurement-like interactions. In other cases, in the absence of such interactions, they are potentialities without individual existence or simple location, with no better description than that given by a many-particle quantum state function or state vector.

Finally, I should relate this discussion to the other type of multidimensional 'space' used in quantum mechanics which, like the $3n$-dimensional space referred to earlier, gives it an air of unreality. This is the multidimensional space used in relation to the representation of quantum mechanical states by vectors: here, the number of dimensions is equal to the number of possible eigenstates of the system, which may be varying levels of infinity where the eigenvalues fall within a continuous spectrum. This, too, is a fictional, mathematical space; and its use does not indicate any unreality in the quantum physical state. As before, probabilities can be calculated for real measurements of values of observables in the ordinary three-dimensional world; and the vectors in multidimensional space are an alternative way of describing the real potentialities which exist in between measurements.

15.2. EPR Correlations and the Bell Inequality

The existence of correlations between systems that have interacted, and are spatially separated, is a general feature of the mathematics of quantum mechanics. However, it was a 1935 paper by Einstein, Podolsky, and Rosen (1983) that particularly highlighted some of the extraordinary implications of this: the EPR article, as it is known, argued on the basis of these correlations that quantum mechanics was incomplete. However, in 1964 came the proof by J. S. Bell that certain correlations predicted by quantum mechanics exceeded what could be explained in terms of pre-existing properties of the systems: this proof suggested either that quantum mechanics was incorrect, or that spatial separation was irrelevant to the correlations, in which case the EPR argument would be undermined. Finally, in a series of experiments culminating in those by Aspect in 1982, the predictions of quantum mechanics, along the lines considered by Bell, were confirmed, and correlations were observed exceeding those which could be explained in terms of pre-existing properties of the systems. In effect, non-locality was demonstrated and the EPR argument indeed undermined. I will consider these developments in turn, and conclude with some discussion of their implications.

15.2.1. *The EPR Article*

The article, entitled 'Can Quantum-Mechanical Description of Physical Reality Be Considered Complete?', appeared in the *Physical Review* of May 1935. It begins by asserting a criterion for the reality of a physical quantity: 'If, without in any way disturbing a system, we can predict with certainty . . . the value of a physical quantity, then there exists an element of physical reality corresponding to this physical quantity.' It sets out to show that a quantum particle can have both a real position *and* a real momentum, in this sense; and concludes that, because quantum mechanics cannot account for this, it must be incomplete.

The authors point out that quantum physics permits a state function for two particles which have interacted both (1) to give a definite value for the total momentum of the particles and (2) to specify that their position vectors are equal and opposite. The particles can be allowed to move far apart before any measurement is made, so that (according to the authors) any measurement made on one could not affect the other. Then, the measurement of the momentum of one particle enables the momentum of the other to be known with certainty: therefore, the momentum of the latter particle is a real physical quantity, and (since the measurement of the former particle would not have affected the latter particle) must have been a real physical property immediately *prior* to that measurement. But exactly the same can be said of position. Measurement of the position (rather than momentum) of the one particle would have enabled the position of the other to have been known with certainty: therefore, the position of the latter particle is a real physical quantity, and was so immediately prior to measurement. Therefore, the EPR article concluded, quantum mechanics is incomplete, because it cannot account for the simultaneous reality of *both* the position and momentum of the latter particle: the Copenhagen interpretation made such reality 'depend upon the process of measurement carried out on the first system which does not disturb the second system in any way. No reasonable definition of reality could be expected to permit this.'

The point of divergence between the EPR approach, on the one hand, and the approach of standard quantum mechanics, on the other, lies in the assertion of the former that, when two correlated particles have moved far apart, a measurement made on one could not affect the other. According to the quantum mechanical description of these events, where, for example, the state function for the two particles shows a definite value for the total momentum p of the system, the measurement of the momentum of one particle as having the momentum p_1 will result in the two-particle system going into a state $|p_1\rangle|p_2\rangle$, where $|p_1\rangle$ is a momentum eigenstate of the first particle associated with the momentum p_1, and $|p_2\rangle$ is a momentum eigenstate of the second particle associated with the momentum p_2, where $p_2 = (p - p_1)$; and this will be so whatever the spatial separation of the particles may be. That is, the quantum mechanical description implies that the momentum measurement of one particle does instantaneously affect ('disturb') the other particle, irrespective of spatial separation. And similarly for position measurements.

This quantum mechanical implication of instantaneous associations between distant events, involving some sort of faster-than-light connection, does not sit comfortably with Einstein's theory of special relativity, and the EPR article was a clear and forceful statement in opposition to the quantum mechanical view. However, Bell's theorem and the Aspect experiments have since established that the quantum mechanical view is not refuted; and that in the case of correlated systems, irrespective of separation, the measurement of the one system *does* in a sense 'disturb' the other system. (They have thereby also, in my view, refuted those versions of the quantum logic interpretation of quantum mechanics which similarly assert the simultaneous reality of position and momentum, but merely deny the possibility of their conjoint *assertion*.)

15.2.2. *Bohm's Formulation*

In 1951, David Bohm gave a modified formulation of the EPR thought experiment, which was later used by Bell in creating his theorem (see Bohm 1951: 614–23). He supposed a molecule containing two atoms, in a state such that the total spin was zero and the spin of each atom was $\hbar/2$; and that the molecule was distintegrated by a process which did not change the total angular momentum. The atoms could then separate to an arbitrary distance. Quantum theory predicts, and experiments establish, that, if one particle is then measured to have spin up on any axis, the other will be found to have spin down on that axis—and vice versa.

Thus, a measurement of spin on the z axis of one atom would give a definite result (say, spin up); and this would mean that the other atom had a definite spin on the z axis (spin down). Since (on the EPR view) the measurement of the first atom could not have disturbed the (distant) second atom, then the latter must have had a definite spin on the z axis prior to the measurement of the first atom.

However, the measurement *could* have been made of the spin of the first atom on the y axis, or on the x axis, and in either case a definite spin obtained. So, according to EPR, the second atom must have had, prior to any measurement of the first atom, a definite spin on each of these axes also. However, a quantum mechanical description of an atom can assign a definite spin only on *one* axis (in which case it gives maximum uncertainty regarding spin on the other two orthogonal axes); therefore, the quantum mechanical description must be incomplete.

15.2.3. *Bell's Theorem*

In 1964, John Bell proved that the statistical predictions of quantum mechanics were inconsistent with the thesis of the EPR article: in particular, he proved that, if such statistical predictions were correct, then a particle could not, prior to measurement, have definite spin on three axes (Bell 1988*a*).

The proof is based on a simple numerical relationship, which has come to be called Bell's inequality. For one version of it, one may suppose that an entity has three properties (say, 1, 2, and 3), each of which can take either of two values (say, + or –) so that eight combinations are possible ($1^+2^+3^+$, $1^+2^+3^-$, $1^+2^-3^+$, $1^+2^-3^-$, $1^-2^+3^+$, $1^-2^+3^-$, $1^-2^-3^+$, $1^-2^-3^-$). One then considers the case of a large number of such entities, and the relations between the numbers of them which have the particular values of *two* properties 1^+2^+, 2^-3^+, and 1^+3^+. These numbers can be written $N(1^+2^+)$ etc.; while the numbers in relation to possession of all three properties can be written $N(1^+2^+3^+)$ etc. Bell's inequality is:

$$N(1^+2^+) + N(2^-3^+) \geqslant N(1^+3^+).$$

The proof is simple:

$$N(1^+2^+) = N(1^+2^+3^+) + N(1^+2^+3^-)$$
$$N(2^-3^+) = N(1^+2^-3^+) + N(1^-2^-3^+)$$
$$N(1^+3^+) = N(1^+2^+3^+) + N(1^+2^-3^+)$$
$$\therefore\ N(1^+2^+) + N(2^-3^+) = N(1^+3^+) + N(1^+2^+3^-) + N(1^-2^-3^+)$$
$$\therefore\ N(1^+2^+) + N(2^-3^+) \geqslant N(1^+3^+).$$

Applying this to spin, it means that, in a large population of atoms, if each had a definite spin (or properties giving certainty regarding spin measurement) on the *x*, *y*, *and z* axes, then: the number of atoms with spin up on the *x* and *y* axes *plus* the number of atoms with spin down on the *y* axis and spin up on the *z* axis *must* exceed or equal the number of atoms with spin up on the *x* axis and spin up on the *z* axis. However, in certain situations quantum mechanics predicted measurements inconsistent with this inequality; so that, if the predictions of quantum physics could be proved correct, then this would prove that an atom *cannot* have a definite spin on all three axes, as the EPR article (as reformulated by Bohm) suggested.

The significance of this in relation to Bohm's formulation of the EPR thought experiment would be as follows. If the two-atom molecule with zero total spin disintegrates, and the atoms separate to an arbitrary distance, then measurement of spin on *any* axis of one particle will give certainty that the other particle would be measured to have the opposite spin on that axis. If prior to measurement neither particle could have a definite spin (or even properties giving certainty of spin measurement) on more than two axes, so that the spin of both particles on all axes apart from two could be no more than matters of probability, then in the general case the measurement of spin on an axis of one particle (changing *that* spin from a probability to an actuality or certainty) must *instantaneously* change the spin on the same axis of the other (distant) particle from a probability to an actuality or certainty.

15.2.4. *Application to Photons*

It is in relation to polarization of photons that the predictions of quantum mechanics have been proved correct. So I will briefly discuss how Bell's inequality can be applied to the polarization of photons.

It will be recalled that, according to quantum theory, a photon plane polarized in one direction (say, vertically) will *certainly* pass through a vertically orientated polarizer, and *may* pass through a polarizer orientated at an angle θ from the vertical, with probability $\cos^2 \theta$; and there are no other objective properties of the photon (or the world) which determine whether or not it will pass through the latter. The EPR argument, as applied to photons, would (if correct) show that the photon (and/or the world) has definite properties which determine whether or not it would pass through a polarizer with any orientation; and thereby would show that the quantum physical description is incomplete.

Suppose (in accordance with the EPR contention) that a photon (considered alone or in relation to the rest of the world) has three properties (which I will number 1, 2, and 3) such that 1 relates to its ability to pass through a polarizer with vertical orientation, and can have values '+' where it has such ability and '−' when it does not; 2 relates to its ability to pass through a polarizer with orientation 2θ from the vertical; 3 relates to its ability to pass through a polarizer with orientation θ from the vertical; and 2 and 3 can similarly have values '+' or '−'. Then a photon with properties such that it would pass through a polarizer with vertical orientation, *and also* one with orientation 2θ from the vertical, has the values 1^+2^+; one with properties such that it would *not* pass through a polarizer orientated 2θ from the vertical, but would pass through one orientated at θ from the vertical, has the values 2^-3^+; and one with properties such that it would pass through a polarizer with vertical orientation, *and also* one orientated at θ from the vertical, has the values 1^+3^+. Then, by the same reasoning as before, in any large population of photons with either + or − values for each of these properties:

$$N(1^+2^+) + N(2^-3^+) \geqslant N(1^+3^+) \, .$$

Calcium atoms can be caused to emit pairs of photons, so that each of them travels in opposite directions. Each can then be made to encounter a polarizer, with a detector on the far side. Quantum theory predicts, and experiments establish, that, if the polarizers have the same orientation (whatever it may be), then if one photon of such a pair is detected as having passed its polarizer, the other will certainly be detected as having passed the other polarizer. If the polarizers are at an angle of θ to each other, then, according to quantum theory, the number of photon pairs detected as having passed both polarizers will approximate $\cos^2\theta$ times the number of single photons detected as having passed either individual polarizer. (As I understand it, the quantum physical formalism is not appropriate in this case to treat pairs of successful detection events at the polarizers as simultaneous: but, whichever of a pair is treated by the formalism as occurring first, the result is the same.)

On the EPR approach to such an experiment, the contention would be that, if the photons of such a pair are allowed to separate to such an extent that a measurement of polarization performed on one 'could not affect' the other, then measuring the polarization of one to be at any orientation would determine that the other had properties such that it would pass through a polarizer at that orientation. Accordingly, if one such photon is detected after passage through a polarizer orientated vertically, while the other of the same pair is detected after passage through a polarizer orientated 2θ from the vertical (with these two events having spacelike separation), then (on the EPR approach) *both* photons prior to their respective measurements must have had properties such that they would pass through polarizers with vertical orientation *and* through polarizers with parallel orientations 2θ from the vertical: so both photons had values 1^+2^+. And similarly for other orientations.

Suppose that very large numbers of randomly orientated pairs of photons are emitted from calcium atoms, and the pairs in three very large equal groups are thus measured for values 1^+2^+, 2^-3^+, and 1^+3^+ respectively. Then, on the EPR approach, Bell's theorem shows that the numbers measured to have the values 1^+2^+ and 2^-3^+ in the first two groups would together exceed the number having the value 1^+3^+ in the third group. (This is not a logical necessity, because the respective numbers are not measured within a single group: however, since the three groups are large, equal, and indistinguishable groups of randomly orientated photon pairs, the probabilities are such as to make it a practical necessity.) Results consistent with this will be obtained, according to quantum mechanics, for *some* values of θ, but *not* for others: for example, where $\theta = 30°$, as shown below and in Fig. 15.1.

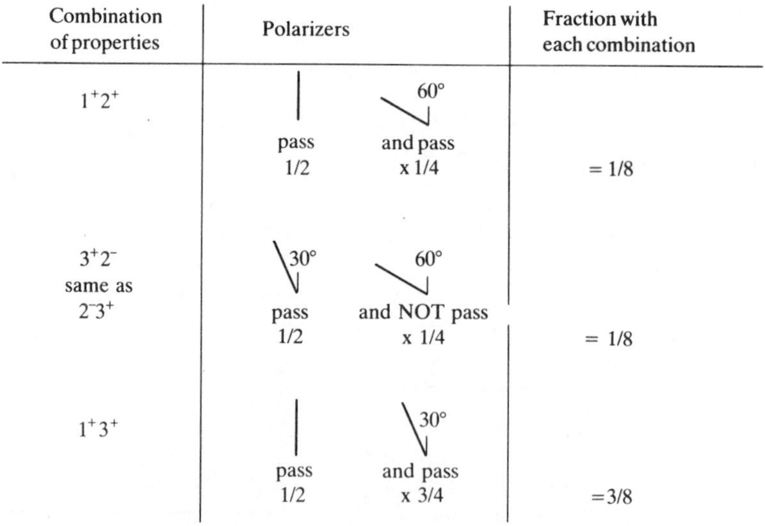

Combination of properties	Polarizers		Fraction with each combination
1^+2^+	pass 1/2	60° and pass x 1/4	= 1/8
3^+2^- same as 2^-3^+	30° pass 1/2	60° and NOT pass x 1/4	= 1/8
1^+3^+	pass 1/2	30° and pass x 3/4	=3/8

Fig. 15.1. The violation of Bell's inequality

According to quantum mechanics, the number of photon pairs which would be detected as having passed both polarizers, where they are at an angle of $60°$ to each other, is approximately $\cos^2 60°$ (that is, 1/4) times the number detected as having passed either one; and the number of photons which would be detected as having passed through either one (say, the one orientated vertically) is approximately 1/2 the number of pairs measured (which I will call T). So, for a large number T of randomly orientated photon pairs, quantum mechanics predicts that about $(1/8)T$ would be measured consistently with their having the value 1^+2^+. Similarly, according to quantum mechanics, the number of photons which would be detected as having passed a polarizer orientated at 30° from vertical is approximately $(1/2)T$; and in about 1/4 of the pairs which do include such a photon, the *other* photon would *fail* to pass through a polarizer orientated at 60° from the vertical ($\sin^2 (60° - 30°) = 1/4$). So, out of T of randomly orientated photon pairs, quantum mechanics predicts that about $(1/8)T$ would be measured consistently with their having the value 2^-3^+. And the number of photon pairs which would be detected as having passed both polarizers, where one is vertically orientated and the other is orientated at 30° from the vertical, is about 3/4 of the number detected as having passed through either one. So, out of T of randomly orientated photon pairs, quantum mechanics predicts that about $(3/8)T$ would be measured consistently with their having the values 1^+3^+. Thus, according to quantum mechanics, where $\theta = 30°$ the measurements would indicate:

$$N(1^+2^+) + N(2^-3^+) = (1/4)T$$
$$N(1^+3^+) = (3/8)T$$
$$\therefore N(1^+2^+) + N(2^-3^+) < N(1^+3^+) .$$

Bell's inequality would be violated.

If experiments confirmed these predictions of quantum mechanics, and the violation of Bell's inequality, then one would have to conclude, contrary to the EPR conclusion, that prior to measurement the photon pairs did *not* have definite properties determining whether or not they would pass through three differently orientated polarizers; and that, accordingly (contrary to the EPR premiss), in some cases at least the measurement of one photon must 'disturb' the other photon, however far apart they may be.

15.2.5. *The Aspect Experiments*

These matters were tested in a number of experiments commencing in the 1970s, and culminating in experiments in France by Alain Aspect, which concluded in 1982. It is generally accepted that these experiments have confirmed the predictions of quantum mechanics, and the violation of the Bell inequality; and that the conclusion argued for by the EPR article is thereby refuted. It is also generally accepted that the premiss in the EPR article which is in turn refuted is the premiss that, where the particles or photons in a correlated pair are widely separated, measurement of one will not affect ('disturb') the other. It is thus established that a photon cannot have properties such that it will certainly pass through a polarizer, for any more than two orientations in each case (quantum theory in fact asserts only *one*); that in respect of all *other* orientations, the polarization of a photon is a matter of potentialities only; and that when such a potentiality becomes (by reason of measurement) an actuality for one photon in a correlated pair, instantaneously the same actuality is established for the other photon of the pair. Where there are measurement events for both photons in a pair, which events are space-like separated, it does not matter which event is considered as occurring first; although (as mentioned earlier), if the measurements are of *different* orientations, they must be considered as taking place successively, because the quantum mechanical formalism does not allow the two members of a correlated pair of photons simultaneously to manifest different polarizations.

The Aspect experiments in fact showed a violation of a slightly different form of Bell's inequality, using angles which were multiples of $22\frac{1}{2}°$, but the principle is the same. The polarizers and detectors were located up to 15 metres apart. In order to ensure that the results violating Bell's inequality were not due to some causal influence operating between the detectors at no more than the speed of light, a device was used which effectively changed the orientation of the detectors about 100 million times per second, thereby ensuring one or more changes *after* each photon pair separated from the source.

These experiments not only refute the contention of the EPR article, and the premiss that measurement of one particle *cannot* disturb a distant particle. They also show that if the result of measurements is *not* a matter of chance, in accordance with probabilities indicated by the state function, then the 'hidden variables' which determine the outcome of measurement must operate non-locally, that is, in a co-ordinated way on spacelike separated events.

15.2.6. *Implications*

It has been contended that Bell's theorem and the Aspect experiments do not contradict the special theory of relativity, because they indicate, not faster-than-light causation or communication, but, rather, non-local correlations; and that, since the results obtained at each 'end' of the experiments are only random sequences, the correlations cannot be *used* to achieve faster-than-light communication. (There is, however, a variant of the EPR experiment suggested by Popper, which may suggest otherwise: I will consider it in the next section.)

What is indicated, however, is that, at the level of quantum systems (that is, of potentialities), spatial separation may be irrelevant: the possibilities in different locations are instantaneously correlated. This is in fact a feature of single-particle quantum mechanics, quite apart from any consideration of correlations between two particles or systems. If a quantum state function for a single particle gives a finite probability of finding the particle over a volume of space, and it is found by measurement in a particular part of that volume, then this instantaneously puts an end to any possibility of its being found anywhere else in that volume: this is part of what is involved in the 'collapse' of the wave function. Indeed, if a function is such that a particle must be either in the region *A* or in the distant region *B*, an appropriate measurement in region *A* which is unsuccessful will instantaneously increase to 1 (that is, to certainty) the probability that the particle will be found in region *B* if an appropriate measurement is made there.

But it is, of course, in relation to systems involving more than one particle that this instantaneous adjustment of probabilities has striking implications, as demonstrated by the Aspect experiments. Here too, however, what happens can be regarded as involving *elimination* of possibilities: for example, measurement of θ polarization for one photon eliminates the possibility of measurement of θ + π/2 polarization for the correlated photon.

However, these experiments do raise questions about special relativity. If for any purpose spatial separation is irrelevant, then special relativity's insistence on the relativity of simultaneity becomes suspect. As pointed out by John Bell (in Davies and Brown 1986: 48–50), if there is one frame of reference according to which there are simultaneous non-local connections between spacelike separated events, then there will be other frames of reference according to which such connections operate backwards in time; so, if one wishes to say there is a real causal sequence, one has to deny the equivalence of frames of reference and to prefer the frame of reference disclosing simultaneity. And if one says that for quantum systems involving non-locality there can be absolute simultaneity of spatially separated events (because these events are *as if* there was *no* spatial separation), then it would seem that there must be simultaneity of any classical observable events which correspond to these quantum events.

It can be suggested that this simultaneity (and corresponding preferred frame of reference) is only relative to the system under consideration, so that there is no substantial inroad into relativity's insistence on the general equivalence of inertial frames of reference. However, according to quantum mechanics all systems which have interacted have correlations, so that generally the whole universe will be a system as to which there can be simultaneity of distant events, and so a preferred frame of reference.

This does not mean that faster-than-light signals are possible: if they were, we could signal to our own past, and this seems unacceptable; and there are proofs by Philippe Eberhard and others that according to quantum mechanics any *measurable* influence must travel at the speed of light or slower. It would seem that the instantaneous correlations shown by Bell's theorem and the Aspect experiments are, in the words of Nick Herbert, 'private lines accessible to nature alone'. This thought leads him to ask the question: 'Why . . . does nature need to deploy a faster-than-light subatomic reality to keep up merely light-speed macroscopic appearances?' (Herbert 1986: 44). In the next chapter, I will argue in support of an answer to this, namely that it does so to make *consciousness* possible.

15.2.7. *Popper's Variant of the EPR Experiment*

Notwithstanding the proofs by Eberhard and others, there have been proposals for experiments to demonstrate a direct conflict between standard quantum theory and special relativity on the question of faster-than-light signalling. One of the simplest is that proposed by Karl Popper (1982: 28 ff.). Popper proposes that pairs of particles with EPR correlations of position and momentum should each be passed through a slit of finite width Δy in the y direction, to be detected by one of an array of detectors arranged round the slit. The general set-up is shown in Fig. 15.2. Popper notes that quantum theory predicts that, as a slit is narrowed and Δy is *reduced*, Δp in the y direction is increased, so that particles will be detected by detectors at greater angles from the slit. Popper then suggests that, if only one of the two slits is narrowed, the EPR correlation means that (according to standard quantum theory) this must reduce Δy at *both* slits, so that detections of particles at more widely angled detectors will occur even behind the slit which is not narrowed. In this way, a message could (according to standard quantum theory) instantaneously be sent from one screen to the other.

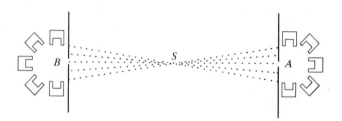

FIG. 15.2. Popper's variant of the EPR experiment

Sudbery (1985) contends that Popper's suggested experiment is misconceived, because it assumes that the particles *approach* the screens with a small range of momenta in the y direction; but, for this to be the case, the particles must be collimated, and this would destroy the EPR correlation. However, I doubt if this is correct. If the source of the particles is sufficiently far from the screens, then there is (without any collimation) a high probability that those particles which pass through the slit will have approached the slit with a small range of momenta in the y direction (cf. Feynman *et al.* 1963, iii. 2.2 f.). Accordingly, I do not think that Popper's proposed experiment suffers the suggested defect.

However, I think there is another problem with it. It assumes that, at the macro level of screens, one can say that the event which collapses the state function at the screen with the narrowed slit (to a smaller Δy) and thereby creates a greater Δp, also collapses the other part of the state function precisely *at the other screen* (that with the unaltered slit) so that macro events (photon detection at wide angles) occur. However, even accepting that the screens are equidistant from the source, one cannot assume this without already contradicting special relativity at the macro level; that is, by asserting the occurrence of macro events which manifest an absolute simultaneity of events.

If one provisionally accepts the opposite assumption, namely that absolute simultaneity is not disclosed at the macro level, then one cannot say that the combined wave function encounters both screens at the same time. One could equally say that, at the time when one part of the combined function is collapsed by the narrowed slit, the other part has already encountered the detectors beyond its (unaltered) slit. And, of course, in that event, no difference would be detected at the unaltered slit, and no faster-than-light message passed.

I suspect that there is 'a conspiracy of nature' which prevents signalling into one's own past; and which, in so doing, prevents any faster-than-light communication *and* any disclosure (at the macro level) of absolute simultaneity.

Thus, even if Popper's experiment did not disclose faster-than-light communication, this would certainly not contradict standard quantum theory, as understood following the Aspect experiments. It would only indicate that quantum systems obey special relativity in so far as they give rise to macro events (so they avoid faster-than-light signals); and the lack of absolute priority in time as between the macro events at the two screens permits each to develop consistently with being unaffected by the other. The result of measurement ·at each screen will be compatible with the predictions which quantum mechanics makes for the screen in question, without regard to what occurs at the other screen.

15.3. Quantum Descriptions of Macro Objects

What description can quantum theory give of the macro objects of our everyday world? I will suggest that quantum theory does not deny the existence or reality of macro objects; but that it does give an account of such objects, of their ultimate nature and of the laws governing their behaviour, which differs from (while accounting for) common-sense views.

A macro object (or 'thing'), on the quantum physical approach, is, to a very good approximation, a multi-particle system which could in principle be represented by a single very complicated state function. I say 'to a very good approximation', because macro objects are continually interacting with their environment, and so on a strict quantum theoretical view should be represented by a state function for the object plus the relevant environment. And according to standard quantum theory a state function connects with actual observations only by giving the possibilities and probabilities of the values of various observables *if* measurements should be made.

Now it might be said that a state function could not be an adequate representation of a macro object, because a macro object is surely not just a matter of possibilities and probabilities: it is an actuality, it exists. Such a representation would be even further from our common-sense view of macro objects than (say) Eddington's account of his table as consisting mainly of the spaces between nuclear particles and electrons (see Eddington 1929: xii). However, unless a macro object is itself conscious, it is only by its interactions with *other* objects or systems that it can either be perceived by or otherwise known to a conscious entity, or indeed make any difference to the rest of the world apart from itself. So, leaving aside questions of consciousness, macro objects are manifested only by their interactions: their existence between, and/or apart from, their interactions could well be just a matter of possibilities and probabilities. So long, therefore, as a state function can account for the *interactions* of a macro object, it can be an adequate representation of it (leaving aside questions of consciousness).

I am not recommending that we cease to think and talk of macro objects as things having a 'real' existence (not merely an existence of potentialities) apart from their interactions. Indeed, there is surely a sense in which existence (apart from interactions) as a matter of potentialities *is* an actuality: this is an area where the adequacy of our concepts is doubtful, to say the least, and thus an area where rational acceptability rather than correspondence to reality is the touchstone of truth.

In any event, for the most part macro objects *can* be regarded as having what very closely approximates common-sense 'real existence', quite apart from their interactions. States represented by state functions are demonstrated to be mere potentialities only when their interactions are such as to discriminate between superposed elements of such functions. For example, we saw that if a quantum state is an eigenstate of an observable, then a measurement of that observable will give a particular value with certainty; so, as suggested in the EPR article, the state can be regarded as 'really' having that value of that observable prior to measurement. Measurements or observations of macro objects cannot generally discriminate between elements superposed in the many-particle quantum system which can be considered as being the object. The macro observables of (macroscopically sharp) position, motion, shape, colour, etc. would generally be established by the state function with practical certainty: in the case of states involving millions upon millions of particles, the standard deviations around the expectation values for such macro observables would for the most part be so small that sharpness by macro standards was not prejudiced.

The observation or measurement of macro observables of macro objects involves statistical effects derived from the huge numbers of particles comprising the relevant quantum system. In cases where the macro object is a device which can measure micro observables themselves involving a super-position of eigenstates prior to measurement, and the macro observable is the relevant reading of the indicator of the device, then (as we have seen) some-where along the line potentialities must be eliminated and/or elevated to being actualities. In other cases, where measurement or observation does not involve discrimination between values of micro observables, it is by no means clear that any elimination or elevation of potentialities occurs. If an interaction between the macro object and the observer is such that it cannot discriminate between the various potentialities of the macro object's quantum state, then it would appear that no reduction of the quantum state needs to take place. The macro object can reasonably be regarded as actually existing, with the observed properties, prior to the observation.

The reason why macro observables can be sharp, by macroscopic standards, may be approached in the following way.

According to quantum physics, interaction between two systems causes correlations. If two interacting systems are regarded as being parts of, or sub-systems within, a wider system, then the correlations caused by their mutual interaction will in turn affect the interactions of the wider system with further systems. On this approach, a macro object may be considered (quantum mechanically) as a many-particle system, with strong mutual interactions among the subsystems of which it is composed. The numbers of subsystems and the strength of their mutual interactions involve significant correlations, such that:

1. in interactions between the system comprising the macro object and other systems, macroscopically sharp values of macro observables can be manifested; and
2. such values exhibit the substantial permanency and consistency of be-haviour characteristic of a macro object.

The mathematics of quantum mechanics is consistent with this approach. Certainly, Heisenberg's uncertainty principle is consistent with macro objects exhibiting relatively definite values of observables. We saw that an individual particle has in any dimension an indeterminacy of position (Δx) and of momentum (Δp) such that $\Delta x \Delta p \geqslant \sim h$. Consistently with this, however, a group of n interacting particles (perhaps held in the lattice structure of a solid object) may have an indeterminacy of position (Δx_n) and of momentum (Δp_n) such that $\Delta x_n \Delta p_n \geqslant \sim h$; and this notwithstanding that the mass m_n of the n particles will be of the order of n times the mass m of one particle. This suggests that, in macro objects which display motion (such that motion times mass equals momentum), the indeterminacy of position times motion may be (absolutely) about n times less in the case of the n particles, as well as being *relatively* less by a further factor of about n. This is explicable in terms of correlations between strongly interacting particles, which may be such (for example) that a high value of momentum for one correlates to a low value for another, and vice versa.

I do not mean by this to suggest that quantum physics, at its present stage of development, is capable of explaining all macro properties of macro objects. Indeed, even the success of quantum physics in explaining the shape and chemical properties of molecules is not complete: as discussed in Woolley (1988), at present this explanation involves an uncomfortable amalgam of classical and quantum ideas. Woolley contends that quantum theory says nothing about the structure and shape of molecules. However, I suggest that a preferable statement is that, when applied to anything other than the simplest systems, the mathematics of quantum physics is too complicated to yield solutions; so that approximations and compromises involving classical ideas have to be adopted.

My suggestion then is that the correlations produced by strongly interacting systems organize events, explicable (in principle, at least) in terms of quantum mechanical state functions, which in turn account for the solidity, the appearance, the continued relatively stable existence, and behaviour of macro objects like tables. On this approach, a macro object, or thing, could in principle be adequately represented by a state function (questions of consciousness aside) because a macro object needs to be considered only in relation to its interactions; and its state function can adequately account for all its interactions with other systems.

However, if a macro object is conscious, then to deal with *that* property one has to have a representation of such a macro object which does more than account for its interactions with other systems. A state function of a conscious macro object (such as a human brain) has not been interpreted so as to account for either consciousness itself, or the occurrence and sequence of conscious events. On the other hand, neither has a classical representation of such an object. Accordingly, one need not suppose that the representation of a brain by means of a state function is any less adequate to account for consciousness than is the classical representation of it as a material object.

Thus, if one tries to give an account of consciousness in terms of the brain as a classical object, then presumably one must postulate that some patterns of events involving its component parts somehow also involve conscious events. I would think one could suggest with (at least) equal plausibility that it is, rather, that some patterns of quantum potentialities involve conscious events; and this is part of the thesis of the next chapter.

15.4. Conclusions

In drawing conclusions about the implications of quantum physics for the nature of matter and of reality generally, it is necessary to look at two broad alternatives. One of them accepts that there is an *objective* solution to the measurement problem of quantum mechanics, presumably along the general lines considered in Section 14.8. The other does not accept that there is such a solution, and therefore (as I see it) accepts something like the neo-Copenhagen approach of d'Espagnat, or the measurement-by-consciousness approach of Section 14.3.

I will look at these in turn, and note that even the former view has profound implications for the nature of matter and of reality.

15.4.1. *Objective Solution*

Even if there is an entirely objective solution to the measurement problem, quantum theory involves not only indeterminism, but also 'non-material' views of matter, following from the indeterminacy and non-locality of the quantum world.

1. Indeterminism. Consideration of quantum physics confirms that there is genuine indeterminism in quantum systems. Physical measurements, physical events, and physical laws can at best give probabilities for individual micro events; and, while that does not necessarily involve indeterminism for macro events, it can do so.

2. The 'non-materiality' of matter. I suggested in Section 15.3 that quantum mechanics does not deny reality to the macro objects and macro events of our experience, but that it does suggest that in certain respects their fundamental nature is not as we assume it to be.

The entities described by quantum mechanics are very different in many respects from the substantive reality of our experience: they are both indeterminate, consisting at least in part of superposed potentialities, quantifiable probabilities for observable properties; and also non-local, capable of operating by way of instantaneous correlations between spatially separated events.

I noted earlier the question whether the quantum physical descriptions represent entities and events which are *real*, or whether at best they are merely *rules* giving some sort of connection between the macro objects and events which are the 'true' reality. I suggested that the quantum physical descriptions do (at least approximately) represent entities and events which are real; even though these entities and events are difficult to describe and comprehend in our ordinary language, dependent as it is on concepts associated with macro objects and classical physics. As we saw, a rather different view was expressed in Watson (1963), and Rae (1986), which accorded primary reality to the detectable world of our experience, and which suggested that the quantum physical formalism is merely an invention systematizing connections between the objects and events of that world, and thereby providing explanations and predictions of such objects and events. On this view, the formalism does not provide representations of real entities or events at all.

My view is based in part on the detectable effects from the probability amplitudes, phase factors, EPR correlations, and the like, which are represented by the quantum mechanical descriptions: even if these things are 'only' connections, I see no reason to deny existence or reality to connections. In any event, since the quantum physical descriptions make possible a fuller and more reliable account of the macro objects and events of the detectable world than do any descriptions limited to the macro objects and events themselves, it seems reasonable to think that the quantum physical descriptions approximate more closely to objective reality than do descriptions restricted to macro objects and events.

Further, as mentioned earlier, the world of our experience must be *composed* of the micro objects which only quantum theory can describe in a satisfactory manner. On this approach, the substantive reality of our experience, the macro objects and events of our experiential world, is *based on* the reality of the quantum world. The macroscopic properties which we observe are relatively sharp and stable because they manifest the statistics of huge numbers of states and events of the quantum world: we perceive such properties because our perceptual apparatus in general responds to such statistics.

However, I think there is an element of truth in the Watson–Rae view, which links with the main topic of this book. The quantum physical descriptions cannot be complete descriptions of reality, because (on the 'objective solution' approach) they are descriptions only of *objective* reality; and the character of the quantum world (as consisting of non-local potentialities) confirms my suggestion in Section 8.2 that objective reality is a code which has only abstract properties in so far as it is not 'infected' by the meaning-giving processes of consciousness. One of my contentions is that reality includes also the subjective world of mental events, and it is characteristic of *that* world that conscious subjects conceive of and experience the objective world in terms of the 'substantive reality' of macroscopic things and events, and not the abstract reality of a 'cosmic code' represented by the quantum physical formalism.

So, for the intersubjective world of human beings, their relationships, and their language, it is the substantive reality of objects and events which is primary, and the quantum world of codes which is secondary and derivative. The matter is put this way by d'Espagnat:

The sensory data of various individuals generally converge in such a way that they can be described all together by means of a model which is realistic on the macroscopic scale and which is based on the notion of separable macroscopic objects. Presumably this circumstance constitutes the reason why mankind has elaborated a language essentially based on the concept of such objects. Again, constructed in this way, empirical reality is obviously not identifiable with Being, since the idea on which it rests, that of macroscopic objects, is a vague one and is itself definable only with reference to the community of human beings. Moreover, as soon as man's thinking leaves the domain of the macroscopic, he can no longer rely on the notion of separable objects and he can *only* predict the results of observations (even though he still does this wonderfully well). (d'Espagnat 1983: 166)

There is a hint at the end of this passage of d'Espagnat's neo-Copenhagen approach, which I look at shortly. But the general approach holds good, so that matter is radically 'non-material', even if there is an objective solution to the measurement problem.

15.4.2. *No Objective Solution*

The view that there is an objective solution to the measurement problem is not universally accepted, even by those who do not adopt the measurement-by-consciousness approach. For example, d'Espagnat writes that the mathematical descriptions of the quantum theory 'refer not exclusively to Reality, but, to a great degree to our minds as well' (1983: 157). This is consistent with his neo-Copenhagen approach in d'Espagnat (1989), to the effect that the quantum formalism is weakly objective, and thus dependent on reference to the community of human observers.

Although I have not excluded an entirely objective solution to the measurement problem, and indeed have ventured a speculation of my own about such a solution, on the whole I am now inclined to doubt that there is such a solution. I think there are reasons for questioning whether references to consciousness can be eliminated from *any* mathematics-based theory which is as satisfactory and comprehensive as the quantum theory. In addition to the problems discussed in Chapter 14, I note the following:

1. Built-in inaccuracy. From a strict quantum theoretical point of view, there cannot be a wholly accurate representation of anything less than the whole universe. Any part of the universe which one selects to be represented in quantum physical formalism will have interacted with other parts of the universe so as to create correlations of potentialities with such other parts: so the quantum physical representation of part of the universe will be inaccurate in not providing for the effect of those correlations. On the other hand, there is in perception a *natural* separation of an object of observation from the rest of the universe, and this object is represented in perception as an actuality: there is no representation of superposed potentialities, and so no *mis*representation of potentialities because of failure to correlate potentialities to the whole of the universe.

2. The basis of the measurement problem. The measurement problem itself may be the result of another (perhaps related) inaccuracy: quantum theory may be inaccurate in so far as it suggests that there is a strongly objective dichotomy between (deterministic) time development and (random) state reduction, which gives rise to the measurement problem. In objective reality, the development of events may not be in accordance with such a dichotomy. It may also be that no mathematics-based theory *can* accurately represent such development, that the best such a theory can do is to predict the results

of observations by means of a formalism which involves this inaccurate dichotomy. Of course, so long as the theory does give accurate predictions of all observations, so that no experiment can disprove it, it may be flawless as a theory of physics. However, in so far as there is *no* solution to the measurement problem, such a theory must fail as a strongly objective theory: this may be 'merely' a matter of metaphysics; but it may also indicate the inability of objective science to deal with consciousness. (This is, I think, roughly d'Espagnat's position.)

3. The need for reduction. There is in general no need to postulate any quantum state reduction when dealing with the statistics of huge numbers of quantum entities and events (as in the case of perception) *unless* physical quantities of small numbers of such entities and events are linked to those of the huge numbers in such a way as to defeat the levelling effect of the statistics: this is what happens in the case of measurement. There may similarly be no need to postulate state reduction *unless* the occurrence of conscious mental events requires such reduction in order to exclude perception of superposed alternatives.

4. The power of consciousness. I have already suggested that, in the perception of a macro object such as a photograph, objective reality provides only abstract properties, which are non-local and include superposed potentialities; but that (normally at least) such superposed potentialities do not involve any indeterminacy in macroscopic properties of the photograph. In conscious perception, these abstract properties are translated or decoded into the substantive properties of spatial extension, shape, colour, etc. The measurement problem can be expressed as involving the question whether objective reality always wholly determines in advance the content of perceptions, or whether sometimes the perceived phenomenon is determined in part by the conscious perception itself. Since the perception *does* provide the spatial extension, shape, colour, etc., it may not be a large step to say that sometimes, for example in cases of measurement, it also provides determinacy. Viewed that way, it may not seem so surprising if it is perception (accurate or inaccurate) which completes measurement; whether this be Schrödinger's cat hearing the click of a Geiger counter, or three spacelike separated persons looking at photographs, or whatever.

If it *is* accepted that the best theory of matter requires references to consciousness, whether that of individual human beings (or animals) in the measurement-by-consciousness approach, or that of a community of human beings in some neo-Copenhagen approach, then the consensus project of capturing mind and consciousness in terms of matter seems fatally flawed: what is strongly suggested is that mind and matter are interdependent and complementary, rather than that one is secondary to the other (cf. d'Espagnat 1989: 212–13, 269–70). I am rather inclined to think that this is indeed the case.

IV
Mind and the World

THE arguments of Part II made a case against mechanism, but left un-answered some questions (outlined in Sections 6.5 and 8.3) about how a non-mechanistic mind could work. In Chapter 16, I try to answer those questions by outlining a theory of mind, which makes use of the discussion of quantum physics in Part III. This theory is in one sense dualist–interactionist, in another sense monist. It also gives the beginnings of an account of free will. However, a full account of free will requires an account of the self and of time, on both topics of which volumes could be written. In the following chapters, I offer some views on these matters, but also suggest that, at least for the present, the notion of complementarity can usefully be applied. In the final chapter, I make some suggestions for a world-view based on the approaches, arguments, and conclusions of the book.

16

Outline of a Theory of Mind

THE initial interest in quantum mechanics as being relevant to the mind–matter problem concerned its indeterministic character, and the possible 'room' it could leave for freedom of the will. My discussion of quantum mechanics has confirmed its indeterministic character; and has also suggested that quantum mechanics shows that matter is ultimately 'non-material' and non-local, and (perhaps) that mind and matter are interdependent.

My basic hypothesis is that (consistently with some consensus views) mental events and associated physical events are (both of them) aspects or manifestations of the same (comprehensive) events of the brain–mind, with some discoverable correlations between them; but that (contrary to consensus views):

1. just as the macroscopic physical events of neural firings are manifestations of micro events of the quantum world, so also mental events are related more directly to those quantum events than to the neural firings themselves;
2. even the best objective description of the events *as physical events* (that is, in their *objective* character), comprehending all the insights of quantum theory, cannot account for all the properties of mental events, in particular all their causal properties; and
3. the best description of the events *as mental events* (that is, in their *subjective* character) must use the language and concepts of folk psychology, which can, of course, be improved and refined.

16.1. Brain, Mind, and Quantum Reality

On this approach, mind and brain are both manifestations of the same underlying reality. Mind can to some extent be said to be a function of the brain, but only if the brain here is understood not as the detectable macroscopic object, but as the quantum reality underlying *both* this object *and* the mental events of consciousness. Mind and brain are two manifestations of, and viewpoints towards, a single reality; but with important differences, in particular in relation to the development over time of this reality and (specifically) the causes and explanations of such development.

Quantum physics confirms that the world, uninterpreted by the mind, can be considered as a cosmic code; but shows that the things that are detectable by us, and interpreted by us as the objects and events of our perception, are not the fine details of this code, but rather its gross statistical properties. This is true of the brain itself and of macroscopic events within the brain, considered as objects of perception. These macroscopic events (and *their* statistical properties) will, as a matter of fact, have extensive correlations with the mental events of subjective experience and action: however, my suggestion is that such mental events must relate more directly to the quantum level than to the macroscopic level of gross statistical properties, *inter alia* (1) because mental events seem to involve the instantaneous correlation of spatially separated physical events, and (2) because of the arguments against mechanism in Part II.

16.1.1. *Elaboration of Conjecture*

The general idea is not new. For example, in Barrett (1987) a similar idea is attributed to Leibniz, in the following terms: 'What we call body and what we call soul are abstractions, aspects of one unitary reality and process' (p. 26). However, its elaboration with reference to quantum physics is of recent origin.

One important difference between this conjecture and the consensus position lies in the denial that any identity between brain and mind can be adequately considered at the level of neurons and neural firings. My suggestion is that the mind is *not* a function of neurons and neural firings, but rather that both mental events and neural firings are 'functions' of the development of the underlying state of the brain.

Thus, I am conjecturing that there can be no adequate type–type identification between categories of mental events and categories of detectable macro physical events, whether in terms of functions or in terms of other properties. I suggest rather that, because of the common underlying substratum, there will be significant correlations between certain types of macro physical events (such as patterns of firings of neurons in the visual cortex) and certain types of mental events (such as perception of particular shapes and colours); but that these correlations will not amount to type–type identities. In particular, even if patterns could be artificially created which apparently have the same functional role as do the natural patterns in a neural network, and apparently have the same other relevant properties as do such natural patterns, the same types of mental events will not occur *unless* (at least) appropriate developments of quantum states also occur.

To give a crude analogy. If one plays a videotape of a person speaking, one has a correlation between the moving picture and the sound of the words spoken. However, this is because both are manifestations of the underlying substratum of the videotape, the video machine, and the television set. There is no type–type identity between the picture and the sound; and clearly one can occur without the other.

Thus, as regards my seeing my red pen, I suggest that the standard account in terms of light reflected from the pen's surface entering my eyes, an image formed on the retinas giving rise to electrical–chemical signals to my brain, and further electrical–chemical signals in neurons of the cortex, is inadequate to ground a satisfactory account of the mental events involved, *inter alia* because it is not the most complete and fundamental account of the physical events involved.

If it were possible to give it, the most complete and fundamental account of the physical events would comprehend the time development of combined quantum physical states; but the complexity of the many-particle systems involved is such as to make such an account a practical impossibility. In fact, at each stage of the process, up to the stage of events within the cortex, the developments of the quantum physical states are such that indeterminacies, interference effects, EPR correlations, and suchlike quantum physical properties make no detectable difference to what happens; so that an account in terms of classical physics, perhaps with some quantum mechanical trimmings, is quite adequate.

At the stage of events within the cortex, however, I suggest that an account in terms of classical physics is substantially inadequate, if one wishes to explain the mental events involved. A description in terms of macroscopic matter and events is not only insufficient: it is also possibly misleading, *inter alia* in suggesting a gulf between the physical and the mental. In order to identify the physical types with the best correlation to mental events, it is necessary to go to the quantum level.

I will support this hypothesis in Section 16.2 with reference to the arguments of Part II, by attempting to show how it conforms to the anti-mechanistic arguments of that part, while at the same time maintaining consistency with physical causation and also giving appropriate scope to cognitive psychology. However, in the remainder of this section, I will support it primarily by reference to another important aspect of quantum reality, namely non-locality. For the most part, in this chapter I do not rely on the suggestion that quantum physics shows that matter is dependent on mind; although clearly, if this *is* the case, it would strongly support my general approach.

16.1.2. *Non-locality*

In my view, a very strong indication of the close relationship between mental events and the development of quantum physical states is the element of non-locality in both. This can be considered under a number of headings.

1. Extension of relevant macroscopic physical events. Single or unified mental events have some association with (at least roughly) simultaneous

macroscopic neural firings occurring in specific, but spatially extended and even separate, regions of the brain. What would be considered a single, coherent, apparently unified and indivisible conscious experience is associated with a pattern of physical events which are substantially contemporaneous and spatially extended.

For example, perception of an object involves events in the brain associated with detection of many features of the appearance of the object, and with recognition of (and consequent beliefs about) the object: such events must involve many neurons and accordingly some spatial extension. This must be so even when what one perceives is as simple as (say) a red circle. Subjectively, the perception of an object is a unified experience, which at any instant of time includes detection of many features of the object's appearance together with beliefs about what the object is. Somehow, it would seem, the subjective experience has to take in, all at once and non-sequentially, contributions from extended and perhaps separate regions of the brain.

In general, every experience–action involves physical brain events extending in space, including some at least of the following: sensation events, cognition events, other association events (involving memory and understanding), affective events (appreciation, enjoyment, pain, emotion), and action events. All of these events are associated with signals passing round the brain at less than the speed of light, yet apparently may be combined non-sequentially in association with a unified conscious experience–action.

2. The unity of conscious experience. As noted in the previous point, a conscious experience appears to be unified, to comprise many aspects presented all at once, to embrace many features which must be contributed to by events spanning appreciable space. Not only does a complete experience appear to be present to consciousness at each instant, but also changes to different aspects of that experience appear similarly to be simultaneously present to consciousness, together with the remainder of the experience continuing unchanged. If I am watching a moving object, I see its movement and the still background at the same time.

It may be said that this is explained by short-term memory: different aspects of experience only *seem* to be present at the one time, since some of them are there merely due to short-term memory. Indeed, the so-called specious present (or psychological present) of experience appears to span time, as illustrated by the recognition of a melody involving successive notes. However, this just restates the problem: any contribution to experience from short-term memory is itself part of the experience, and is itself associated with many neuron events in spatially extended portions of the brain.

Similarly, when a decision or choice is made, or action is done, it seems to be based on many aspects of the experience giving rise to it. An evaluation of a work of art, for example, is based on many features of the work, and indeed (at least in difficult cases) one tries to hold many of its features in the forefront of one's mind, all at once, as the basis for a judgement. The features so held and assessed must be associated with many separated neuron events in the brain: yet they all seem to contribute simultaneously to the decision. The point is similar to some of the views on informal reasoning made in Part II, but it is made here with a different objective: in so far as informal reasoning involves assessing wholes, it seems to require *simultaneous* awareness of such wholes and their constituent parts or aspects, notwithstanding that such parts or aspects are associated with spatially separated physical events.

3. The non-locality of mental events. Thus I suggest that mental events bring together, non-sequentially, elements associated with spatially separated physical events, and that in that respect they are indifferent to spatial separation. This indifference to spatial separation is also supported by the apparent non-locality of the mental events themselves. I recall the point made in Section 2.4 that visual perception, for example, seems to place images in space around an observer, with the experiencer–subject being placed, if anywhere, behind the eyes of the person in question.

4. The non-locality of quantum states. All the above suggests that mental events somehow span space, so as to enable simultaneous experiencing of, and acting upon, matters associated with spatially separated physical events. As noted in the previous chapter, indifference to spatial separation is shown by quantum states: indeed, consistently with the theory of relativity, there can be (instantaneous) correlations effected between spacelike separated events *only* in the quantum world, that is, in the world of potentialities comprised in quantum states. The existence of EPR correlations between such states, and also the non-local correlations of probabilities associated with any 'collapse' of a quantum state, show that to some extent quantum states are indifferent to spatial separation, in a way which (consistently with the theory of relativity) macroscopic physical events cannot be.

These considerations, it seems to me, make it plausible to associate mental events closely with the quantum physical states manifested by brain events. Such a view proposes an answer to a question suggested by the non-local character of quantum states, as shown by Bell's theorem. *Question* (as put in Herbert 1986: 44): 'Why . . . does nature need to deploy a faster-than-light subatomic reality to keep up merely light-speed macroscopic appearances?' *Answer*: to make possible consciousness and mental events.

16.1.3. *Previous Views*

The point that conscious mental events apparently correspond to spatially separated physical events in the brain has been remarked upon previously. It is instructive to consider some examples of how it has been dealt with.

1. Köhler. An early consideration of the point is found in Köhler (1961):

if it is a process which underlies our experience, say, of a certain visual distance between two points, then this process must arise after the local messages corresponding to the two points have arrived, and must now translate their merely *geometrical* relation into an aspect of its own spatial distribution as a *function*. A physicist will be inclined to assume that the process in question is a 'field' which relates those points across their distance, and in doing so expresses this difference in functional terms. . . . Some interactions in the brain occur across considerable distances, and yet very fast. In the brain, only one kind of process can operate so fast, namely the electric field and the current which it establishes. (p. 29)

It seems to me that in requiring fast interactions, this exposition understates the problem: any causal interaction, however fast, involves temporal sequence; yet the relationship between different aspects of a visual experience (such as the shape and colour of the object seen) is such that they apparently combine without temporal order.

Of course, the above passage was written before Bell devised his theorem, and well before the non-local properties of quantum physics were established by experiment. Hence it is perhaps not surprising that Köhler chose the electric field as the medium for correlating events in separate parts of the brain. However, leaving aside quantum physical non-locality, events in one part of the electric field can be detected in another part of the field only by means of perturbations spreading at no greater than the speed of light. We know now that spatially separated events can be correlated instantaneously, or non-locally, at the quantum level; so that if different aspects of (say) a visual experience are indeed present non-sequentially to consciousness, it seems reasonable to invoke quantum non-locality to explain this.

2. Barlow. A more recent approach to the problem is found in Barlow (1985):

The main gap in the perceptual apparatus that a physiologist can point to is the means of tying together different aspects of our sensations. The mechanisms we know about are terribly local in their scope: a pattern-selective retinal neuron picks up from about a square millimetre or so of retina, corresponding to only a few degrees in the visual field. The situation is no better in the primary visual cortex, where the processes of cortical cells may spread further, but the magnification in mapping from retina to cortex means that a millimetre only corresponds to a fraction of a degree in the region of central vision. What mechanisms can 'look' simultaneously at remote parts of the visual field? What gives unity to our perceptions and prevents them consisting of many small, isolated fragments?

The most promising possibility here is non-topographic mapping. The neuroanatomical maps that we understand securely involve the establishment of a set of regular connections from one array of nerve cells to another, arranged in such a way that the order and neighbourhood relations of the first are maintained in the second. Now if the developmental mechanisms can perform this feat of mapping one array on to another according to the physical location of cells in the two arrays, they can surely form maps depending upon properties of cells other than their physical location—for example, their selective properties of motion, colour or orientation . . . The point is that, in such non-topographic ways, information from topographically remote regions would be accessible at one region, and hence the coincidence-detecting, relative entropy-enhancing mechanisms that seem to be present in the cortex could undertake the task of combining remote parts. (pp. 36–7)

The solution proposed here seems to be to the effect that non-topographic mapping could bring all the information together to 'one region'. However, even then this one region would have to involve huge numbers of events in huge numbers of cells, with some spatial separation; and the problem remains of combining all these events non-sequentially in a single experience. Again, the proposed solution of quantum non-locality seems preferable.

3. Wolf and Schumacher. The suggestion that quantum non-locality has something to do with the operations of the mind is to be found in Wolf (1984) and Schumacher (1986). I find Wolf's writing obscure; while Schumacher seems to be suggesting that vision involves quantum correlations not only within the brain, but also incorporating the eye and the thing seen as well. Schumacher may be correct *if* the measurement-by-consciousness solution to the measurement problem of quantum mechanics is correct; but my argument is not limited to this: it is directed essentially to quantum correlations which are entirely within the brain.

16.1.4. *Comparison with the Computer*

My approach may be considered by comparing the operation of a computer. In a computer, its 'knowledge' or 'awareness' of any substantial information comprises many states and/or events in spatially separated parts of the computer in which such information is encoded: any operation which uses such information requires causal input (transmitted at no more than the speed of light) involving all of such separate locations. There is no need to postulate, and (I suggest) no good reason to believe in, any subjective aspect of the computer which can know or be aware of all such information (from the states or events in various locations in the computer); and, in particular, know or be aware at the same time of changes to different parts of that information in different locations in the computer. The time required to co-ordinate information and changes in information in different locations in a computer may be measured in millionths of seconds: but such co-ordination can never be instantaneous and non-sequential. On the other hand, it seems to be the case that in the brain there can, via conscious experience, be instantaneous knowledge of (and two-way correlation between) events in distant parts of the brain.

For a decision to be based on all available information, such information must be co-ordinated, either in stages or all at once. A computer achieves this in stages by cause and effect. This is perhaps most obvious in relation to a Turing machine, where the different pieces of (coded) information are correlated by steps dictated by the information itself and by the organization of the machine; but the same applies to any computer, including one with parallel processing. The consequence of the correlation of such information can only then be used for computation or displayed in output.

However, if in the brain all information can be instantaneously correlated, so that (for example) data X and data Y, and changes occurring in each, are together present, then this data can be used all at once to base action. Indeed, if, as I contend, conscious experience makes an irreducible difference, then the whole experience *must* enter into the causal order at whatever location or locations in the brain the choice becomes manifest; and for this to happen its parts and their correlations must be simultaneously effective, so that each part can simultaneously contribute to the one action or decision. And this in turn suggests the instantaneous correlations which do exist between spatially separated quantum potentialities.

In this discussion of computers, I am referring to computers as we know them now, which do not operate with quantum physical correlations or indeterminacies. In Deutsch (1985) there appears a description of an idealized quantum computer, which could mix together quantum states in ways that have no classical analogues; although Deutsch does not suggest that it could operate non-algorithmically. Perhaps our brains–minds are such 'machines', but I would say with the difference that they *can* operate non-algorithmically.

16.1.5. *Summary*

In short, then, I suggest an association between mental events and the development of quantum states, because the content of consciousness has properties, corresponding to spatially separated events, which are nevertheless present together; and because this 'togetherness' is not plausibly regarded as macroscopic cause and effect connecting the separated events, but is plausibly regarded as associated with the sort of correlation between distant events which exists in quantum states. I am not asserting that the unity of conscious experience is provided specifically by EPR correlations, or indeed any particular kind of quantum non-locality; merely that quantum states have this property of non-locality in various respects, and this general property seems to be what is necessary to explain the unity of consciousness.

16.2. Conscious Choice

The other main support for my hypothesis is that it can provide a plausible theory of conscious choice: it can accommodate the anti-mechanism arguments of Part II, and at the same time accept many of the ideas of cognitive psychology; it can accept that from the physical viewpoint the brain is a physical object operating in accordance with physical laws, that from the mental viewpoint a person can make rational indeterministic choices, and that no contradiction or conflict is involved; and it makes possible an account of choice which gives an appropriate role to our elaborate brains, and does not postulate some ghostly entity which, without the assistance of the brain, makes the real decisions.

16.2.1. *General Account*

I do not seek to infer a theory of choice from quantum indeterminism: at best, quantum indeterminism makes room for such a theory. Rather, I approach it this way.

A brain–mind (or a person) is a physical–mental object. Its behaviour seems to be determined to some extent by mental events, choices based on beliefs, desires, etc.; and to some extent by physical events, the objective brain processes of neural firings, etc.

The success of the objective sciences suggests that the behaviour of this object might be completely determined by the physical events, so that the apparent determinative role of the mental events either is illusory or else simply coincides with the role of physical events. This gives rise to the project of abstracting the measurable physical properties of the object, and seeking quantitative physical laws of nature which are sufficient, together with the measurable physical properties, to determine the behaviour.

However, when that project is pursued to the limit, it becomes clear that the physical properties and laws are not sufficient to determine completely the behaviour of the brain–mind, because of quantum indeterminism. It may still be possible to exclude independent mental determination, however, by showing that quantum indeterminism has no *significant* impact on the behaviour of the brain–mind: for example, by showing that the firing of neurons cannot be affected by quantum indeterminism, or by success in cognitive psychology and/or artificial intelligence research in accounting for all purposive behaviour. This has not been done, so one may reasonably believe on the basis of the arguments of Part II that mental events *do* have an independent determinative role in behaviour.

An account can be given of how this could work, as follows.

1. Cognitive psychology and choice. The brain–mind can be regarded from a physical viewpoint and a mental viewpoint.

From the physical viewpoint, it can be considered as a macroscopic object, operating in accordance with laws appropriate to such objects; and for many purposes that will give a sufficient approximation to the true position. However, in cases where conscious subjective choices are being made (that is, all cases of conscious decision and action), I suggest that an adequate physical account of the brain would have regard to quantum mechanical effects. Even then, however, I suggest that the physical account could not, even in principle, predict or explain *which* choice is made: it would at most show the *alternatives* and their *respective probabilities*. So, the brain–mind can be considered (consistently with the approach of cognitive psychology) as a mechanistic (though indeterministic) computer; but only in so far as it throws up alternatives for choice.

Where, for example, a choice involved determining the application of a word whose meaning could encompass a range or spectrum, the identification of the range and of probabilities within that range could be achieved mechanistically: it may be an operation of the kind undertaken by the 'fuzzy logic' programs mentioned earlier. It could take account of many factors bearing on the appropriateness of various alternatives within the spectrum. Ultimately, this mechanistic process could provide a range (either continuous or discrete) of possibilities, with probabilities within that range: rather like the range shown by a quantum physical state function for observables such as position and momentum. The choice itself, from a physical viewpoint, would appear as a random reduction of these possibilities.

There could be a similar process in relation to any and all of the conscious choices which we make. The process could be of great complexity, having regard to the number of neurons and connections in the brain: and choices could arise at many stages of dealing with a particular problem. The general point is that computational procedures plus quantum physics would seem appropriate to give rise to probability-weighted alternatives. The number of alternatives could be finite, if the possibilities are discrete; or infinite, if they are in a continuous spectrum. Each choice would appear as a random state reduction.

From the mental viewpoint, there would be little if any consciousness of the computer-like processing which gives rise to the alternatives. There would be some consciousness of alternatives (even if only the alternatives of doing something and not doing it), and consciousness of vaguely weighted considerations for and/or against each alternative: these considerations may be felt as various kinds and degrees of inclination and aversion, of obligation and inhibition, and so on. The felt weight of the considerations, the mental effort required to give effect to one set of considerations rather than another, and the difficulty of coming to a decision, may perhaps be related to the probabilities indicated by the quantum physical viewpoint.

However, on my suggested approach, any prior weighting of the considerations is associated only with probabilities, and does not *determine* the choice: it is only the conscious choice which determines which considerations prevail in the particular case, and thereby precisely determines their weighting *inter se*. A somewhat similar idea was proposed in Nozick (1981) using the analogy of quantum mechanical measurement:

a person before decision has reasons without fixed weights; he is in a superposition of (precise) weights, perhaps within certain limits . . . The process of decision reduces the superposition to one state . . . but it is not predictable or determined to which state the decision (analogous to a measurement) will reduce the superposition. (p. 298)

He goes on to assert that 'uncaused' does not entail 'random' (p. 299): that is, that choice or decision need not be either random or wholly determined.

Consistently with my discussion of plausible reasoning in Chapter 5, I contend that rational decisions are indeed like this: they give effect to rational considerations in ways which cannot be formalized, and which are accordingly not mechanistic or predetermined. They are *fallible*, but may have a probability of being correct greater than the mechanistic probability suggested by the physical viewpoint.

2. An objection. A possible difficulty for this kind of approach is raised in Nagel (1986):

> an autonomous intentional explanation cannot explain precisely what it is supposed to explain, namely *why I did what I did rather than the alternative that was causally open to me.* It says I did it for certain reasons; but does not explain why I didn't decide not to do it for other reasons. . . . At some point this question will either have no answer or it will have an answer that takes us outside of the domain of subjective normative reasons and into the domain of formative causes of my character or personality. (pp. 116–17)

That seems reasonable, at first blush; but I suggest it is fundamentally incorrect. I do not deny that one *can* look for further explanations in such formative causes; and these could either be mechanistic physical explanations or plausible explanations involving mental terms. However, I strongly disagree that without such further explanation there is no answer to the question of explanation posed by Nagel. If one accepts the rationality of plausible reasoning, as contended in Chapter 5, then one must accept that there can be reasoning to a rationally based conclusion which is not compelled by its premisses; and that other conclusions may be less rational, or even irrational, although not excluded by the premisses or indeed by any weighing of commensurable reasons. (By 'less rational', I am suggesting a qualitative rather than a quantitative judgement.) In that sense, a complete explanation of action *can* be given, without any need to go to 'formative causes' of one's character. Nagel's point is good only if one rejects the rationality of plausible reasoning and says, with Hume and others, that it is only a matter of useful habit selected by evolution; and that approach, as I have suggested, undermines *all* reason and all knowledge.

My disagreement here with Nagel is close to the heart of the whole problem. His unstated assumption is that an explanation must either be conclusive (and so algorithmic, mechanistic, etc.) or else no explanation at all; whereas our whole experience of reasoning and acting is to the contrary, as I have tried to show in Chapter 5. It is of the nature of most of our justifications and explanations of action that they are not conclusive—but, nevertheless, they may be rational, and different ones may be less rational, or irrational. The pervasiveness of the mechanistic assumption made by Nagel has led, I believe, to mistakes such as that of Swinburne noted in Section 5.6; and also to endeavours such as that of Kane (1985) to find free will in randomness rather than rational choice.

3. The relationship to quantum probabilities. The hypothesis of a close association of mental events with the time development of quantum physical states of the brain suggests a natural explanation of the difference we feel between experiencing and doing. Quantum physics identifies two kinds of time development: the deterministic development of such states in accordance with the relevant rules of motion, notably Schrödinger's equation, and the sudden partly unpredictable changes which occur upon state reduction. Actions, including decisions and choices, may be identified with certain developments of the second kind, in which possibilities thrown up by previous time development are eliminated. Prior to any particular action, this action was possible (with a probability calculable in principle from the prior quantum state), as were alternative actions. The occurrence of one action, rather than any of the alternatives, would be, from an objective physical point of view, random. However, from the subjective mental point of view, it could be chosen.

On this approach, the quantum physical probabilities of the alternatives may be related to the consciously felt weight of competing reasons for the different actions. Where the alternative which occurs is an action which was objectively highly probable, one might have a case of an action with small 'mental input', an action done virtually by habit or as of course. Where the alternative which occurs is an action which was objectively improbable, perhaps one could have a case of concentration, effort, the exercise of 'will-power'. Where a decision has to be made between alternatives of objectively similar probability, perhaps the weighing, judgemental aspect of decision-making is especially exercised.

The choice does not in fact occur *at random* in accordance with some quantum probability: the apparent random occurrence of one alternative is simply the manifestation of the choice to the physical viewpoint. There is a striking statement in Wilber (1983) that 'the Heisenberg uncertainty principle represents all that is left of God's radical freedom on the physical plane' (p. 169); and that is substantially what I am saying about quantum indeterminism and human choice. Penrose (1989: 431) appears to overlook this approach when he questions whether random state reduction can have anything to do with freedom.

In similar vein, there is a reference in Gomes (1978: 450) to an argument by Schrödinger to the effect that quantum physics is in fact inconsistent with free choices being made between superposed alternatives of quantum states, because those free choices could violate the statistical predictions of quantum physics. Even if this were correct, it would not be conclusive: it could simply mean that, when choices are made, the 'known' as represented in the relevant state function is not all there is to know, because there is a mental element involved which cannot be so represented. In any event, the argument seems to overlook that every choice is a unique event: each person is unique, and a matter for choice cannot be precisely one which has previously faced the same person (that would itself be a difference!). Accordingly, the quantum physical superposition of alternatives corresponding to each choice must itself be a single *unique* highly complicated quantum state; so that there never could be a series of *like* state reductions in which statistical effects could be disclosed. In my view, the linking of quantum probabilities to the felt strength of reasons is very plausible.

16.2.2. *What Chooses, and How?*

How, then, does this approach deal with what I have suggested to be a problem of dualist approaches such as that of Eccles; that is, the postulation of some immaterial entity which makes the real decisions, using some other faculty apart from the human brain?

On my approach, the human brain viewed purely as a physical object, even a quantum physical object, does not choose (or explain the choice) between the alternatives which it throws up for decision. However, the human brain at the macro level is a manifestation of the underlying reality described by the corresponding quantum physical state function, which reality is also manifested in the subjective world of consciousness. So, both the chooser and a faculty by which the choice is made can be located in just this same underlying reality. As stated earlier, the most complete objective physical description of this reality (if it could be given) would be in terms of a multi-particle quantum physical state; while the best subjective description would be in terms of the language of folk psychology (which can, of course, be progressively refined and improved). This reality, in its subjective manifestation, does comprehend the choice, and also explain it, to the greatest extent that an explanation can be given.

Looked at subjectively, the reality appears to consist of both a subject and the experiences–actions of which the subject is conscious. One cannot separate out the subject from this combination: as noted in Section 2.5, mental events involve the interdependent existence of both an experiencer–actor and the experience–action. Indeed, as noted there, it seems that one may with equal justification regard either the subject as the substance to which the experience–action is adjectival, or vice versa.

In either case, one may in general terms regard the subject, this experiencer–actor, as being what makes the choices; and one may regard the quantum reality underlying both physical and mental events as providing the faculty for making these choices. I do not contend that the experiencer–actor is necessarily a continuing unchanging self, much less an immortal soul. Indeed, as discussed further in Section 16.3, it may be that the conscious self, which each of us takes to be a single experiencer–doer, is some sort of combination of many such entities; and it may be that there are many such entities ('conscious subsystems') associated with each of us, whose experiences and actions are not always fully integrated into those of the self-conscious being each of us takes himself or herself to be.

Thus, on my approach, one could suggest that a decision or action is partly the result of physical mechanistic causes, and partly the result of choices between alternatives left open by those causes. However, one would normally not mix objective and subjective viewpoints in this way; and it would generally be difficult or impossible in practice to identify the choices. One would normally take either an objective approach, and say that the decision or action is caused by physical laws operating upon physical events, in the sense of being the outcome of deterministic developments plus random steps; or alternatively take a subjective approach, and say that the decision or action is made or done for reasons. From either viewpoint, the decision or action could have been otherwise. On the objective approach, the random steps could have been other than they turned out to be. On the subjective approach, the reasons are not conclusive, and the person acting could have weighed them differently.

In this way, one has the beginnings of an account of freedom of the will. To develop such an account, it is necessary in particular to consider in more detail problems pertaining to the self, which will be pursued in the next section and in Chapter 17.

16.2.3. *Primitive Choices*

So far, I have been considering the human brain–mind. It will be recalled that in Section 6.3 I argued that consciousness could have been an advantage to animals at quite an early stage in evolution: I suggested that quite primitive organisms could have the capacity to make a choice based on qualitative comparison of wholes.

It seems reasonable to propose an account of the central nervous system of such animals similar to that given of the human brain–mind, namely that both the macroscopic physical events and the conscious experiences are different manifestations of the same underlying events. From the objective physical viewpoint, again the most complete description would be in terms of a many-particle quantum physical state, giving rise to alternatives which according to the laws of quantum physics have certain probabilities. From the subjective mental viewpoint, the organism may (for example) be 'deciding' whether or not to consume a substance which is in some respect like, and in some respect unlike, a substance previously used as food; and making a choice amounting to a simple qualitative judgement of 'like' or 'unlike'.

What precisely about such an organism's central nervous system could give rise to consciousness, and the ability to choose between wholes?

This is something which I looked at briefly in Section 6.3: it relates to one of the fundamental questions of this enquiry, namely by virtue of what properties of brains and of certain physical events in brains does it come about that such events are associated with conscious mental events? My suggestion is that in order to be conscious a system must be such as to provide for both:

1. representation within the system of some part of the world presently encountered, such as the potential food; and
2. creation within the system of at least two alternative possible processes consequent upon that representation, which are individually linked with the goals of the system and are in quantum mechanical superposition.

I suggest that if a brain or other physical system does not have properties which provide for both (1) and (2), then it will not be conscious. I say this, on the grounds that the usefulness of consciousness appears to lie in the capacity it gives to make choices on the basis of fallible qualitative comparisons of wholes; and that this in turn seems to require that the wholes to be compared be in quantum physical superposition, in order both (1) to enable comparisons unaffected by spatial separation and (2) to allow for an outcome which is not mechanistically determined. I contend therefore that the emergence and existence of consciousness must be explained in evolutionary terms by the selection of physical structures which make possible its useful operation.

Biologist Marian Dawkins argues in Dawkins (1987: 159) that it is reasonable to believe that animals feel pain just to the extent to which this has survival value; that is, to the extent that pain can be a ground for useful action. Accordingly, she argues, it is unlikely that an organism will feel pain unless it has both some mobility and some intelligence. I think this argument extends to consciousness: an organism is unlikely to be conscious of pain or anything else, unless this has survival and/or reproductive value; mechanistic response to pain or any other stimulus or any representation of the world does not require consciousness; so consciousness is probably associated only with physical structures of the kind I have outlined, they being the physical structures in association with which consciousness can be useful.

In relation to the first requirement, namely representation of part of the world presently encountered, it would seem that, without this, there would be no possibility of a system making a decision or taking action which is useful for survival or reproduction: that is, such a decision or action must in some way be relevant to the situation in which the system is placed, and therefore must be based on some representation of that situation.

In relation to the second requirement, the production of alternative processes in quantum mechanical superposition, this could occur mechanistically; although not to a single outcome but to a superposition, because the quantum mechanical indeterminacies would not all cancel out. The alternatives so produced would, for this whole process to have survival or reproductive value, need to be individually linked with goals or instructions instantiated within the system. The individual linkages to the goals or instructions of the system would be such as to quantify the quantum physical probabilities represented in the superposition, in terms of some mechanistic computation of the weights of the considerations supporting each of the alternatives.

The suggestion, then, is that if these necessary requirements are met, the system *might* be conscious; that is, it might be aware of the representation of part of the external world and/or of the availability of alternative processes and/or of the linkages of such processes to its goals (as feelings of desire or aversion, or as more developed reasons for action); and it might then be able to choose between the superposed processes, so that one (or more) is eliminated and the remaining one promoted to an actuality. Such a choice would be made on the basis of consciously felt 'reasons' (essentially the 'feelings' mentioned above), which do not determine the issue, but the ultimate effect of which, on the contrary, is determined by the choice.

If physical structures appropriate for systems thus capable of conscious choice resulted from mutations in the course of evolution, they may have proved advantageous to survival and reproduction, and thereby been preserved and promoted by evolutionary processes. However, unless a system had at least the two features I have identified, there would appear to be no survival or reproductive value in consciousness; and accordingly, I suggest, it is unlikely that a system without both these features would be conscious.

16.3. Unity of Mind

I mentioned in the previous section that there may not necessarily be just a single conscious subject in each person, but that rather there may be a community of co-operating subsystems (cf. Ornstein 1986*a*: Gardner 1987: 132–3: Minsky 1987). On the other hand, each of us sees himself or herself as a single subject, with identity and continuity over time, and with no other or rival subject involved in the same brain.

I will consider in the next chapter the philosophical question of the identity or continuity of the self over time. Here, I will look at whether each person should be considered as comprising a number of co-operating conscious subsystems, rather than as being always one single, undivided conscious system.

16.3.1. *Conscious Subsystems*

The possibility that there is not just one centre of consciousness in human beings, but rather a collection of subsystems each of which may be conscious, and more or less integrated into a single system, is suggested by split-brain cases and certain performances of the subconscious.

I suggested in Section 2.2 that there appear to be two centres of consciousness in patients whose brains have been divided by cutting the corpus callosum. Indeed, consideration of such cases led Nagel to write:

If I am right, and there is no whole number of individual minds that these patients can be said to have, then the attribution of conscious, significant mental activity does not require the existence of a single mental subject . . . our own unity may be nothing absolute, but merely another case of integration, more or less effective, in the control system of a conscious organism. (Nagel 1976: 124)

Similarly, Gilling and Brightwell report the following contentions of Michael Gazzaniga, based on observations of split-brain patients:

that we have to quit viewing man as a single psychological entity, that in fact his psychological self is a multiple self. He has a variety of mental systems existing in his brain, most of them non-verbal, like the one in his right hemisphere tends to be. They have emotions, they have memories, they have incentives, they have destinies and they are able to control the motor apparatus, to make movements. They're able to precipitate behaviours on the part of someone, and once that action is carried out, the left language centre must interpret the action. It must give an explanation to itself why the system behaved in that way. (Gilling and Brightwell 1982: 175)

(The assertion that the 'left language centre' interprets to itself actions really performed by other systems seems to suggest that it thereby deludes itself into believing itself to have performed them: this is similar to contentions of Restak based on experiments by Libet, to which I will come.)

Observers, and also the verbally communicating dominant hemisphere of split-brain patients, do not for the most part notice any problems arising from the division of the brain; and this does suggest that the existence of conscious subsystems in normal persons might well pass unnoticed. Certainly, such cases do seem to suggest that subsystems in the human brain *can* be conscious.

Furthermore, in Section 2.2 I gave the example of a traffic accident drawing a person's attention, and enabling him to describe what traffic was doing just prior to the accident; and similar to this is the 'cocktail party syndrome', where hearing a keyword (such as a familiar name) spoken in a crowded room brings to consciousness words spoken just *preceding* that word. Such cases suggest that there may be some sort of consciousness of the earlier events *at the time they occurred* which is somehow not integrated immediately into the full consciousness of the person concerned, but becomes so retrospectively when attention is drawn.

If there are conscious subsystems, it may be that 'decisions' can be made by such systems without participation of the full integrated self-conscious mind. Indeed, I have suggested that an essential characteristic of consciousness *is* the possibility of making decisions between superposed alternatives on the basis of some kind of holistic comparison. If animals have consciousness in this sense, it may not seem surprising that the same may be true of *parts* of the human brain; and that the consciousness of such parts may at different times be (or not be) integrated into a single consciousness.

Such a view may derive some support from experiments of Libet concerning the timing of the perception of stimuli (see Libet 1966, 1978: Libet *et al.* 1979). These experiments show that: there is no conscious sensation of (say) stimulation to the skin unless there is appropriate neuronal activity in the cortex for a substantial minimum period of time, of up to about half a second; such a skin sensation can be masked by direct stimulation to the cortex occurring during this period; but if there is a (non-masking) stimulation to the cortex (say) three-tenths of a second *before* the skin stimulus, the subject reports that the skin stimulus came first. Libet postulates that there is a subjective referral of the skin sensation backwards in time to when it first evoked a cortical response, about one-hundredth of a second after the skin stimulation. He suggests that this creates problems for theories involving the co-occurrence of mental and physical events: I question this because, just as perception can distort space in useful ways, it may also be able to distort time in useful ways.

More relevantly to the present topic, he also observes (in Libet 1966: 176, 1978: 80) that behavioural responses can occur much more quickly than half a second after stimulus, indeed as soon as one-twentieth of a second after stimulus; and he suggests that in such cases conscious free choice could not be exercised (see also Cotterill 1989: 261–8).

The matter is put more forcefully by Restak:

In one notable experiment, Libet and Feinstein measured the time it took for a touch stimulus on the patient's skin to reach the brain as an electrical signal. The patient was also requested to signal the arrival of the stimulus by pushing a button. Libet and Feinstein found the first detectable electrical signal on the brain's surface occurred in 10 milliseconds. The patient's response—the button pushing—took place in one-tenth of a second. But strangely, the patient didn't report being consciously aware of the stimulus and response for close to half a second. Remarkably, the data indicated that the patient's conscious actions were somehow referred back in time so that they helped create the comforting delusion that the stimulus *preceded* the action instead of the other way around. (Restak 1983: 52)

However, it may be no 'delusion' that the stimulus preceded the action. The response may be by a conscious subsystem, which is integrated into and adopted by the overall conscious self only after the lapse of half a second. If one accepts the idea of conscious subsystems of the brain–mind, which may or may not be integrated into the overall conscious self, then there would be nothing very surprising about a simple response to a stimulus being performed by such a subsystem, and the subsystem's conscious experience and response being subsequently integrated into the consciousness of the overall conscious self.

Libet (1978: 79) postulates evolutionary purposes for the delay period, namely 'as a filter mechanism in keeping much ongoing sensory inputs from reaching conscious levels' and to 'provide an opportunity for modifying or modulating a perception'. So if, during the half-second delay, the integrated conscious mind has to deal with a more important matter, it would not need to be distracted by awareness of a stimulus (or indeed any response). On the other hand, in so far as Gazzaniga and Restak suggest that the conscious self is in some general way deluded into believing itself to be responsible for actions, this seems to make little evolutionary sense. If consciousness *is* efficacious, this is no general delusion; and if it is not efficacious, why is there any evolutionary use for a comforting delusion?

16.3.2. *What Makes One Mind?*

Even if one accepts that 'choices' can be made by conscious subsystems without participation of the full self-conscious mind, this does not mean that there is no unity of mind. It seems clear that there is in every normal human being a substantially integrated consciousness, which is engaged for most important experiences and actions of that person.

As pointed out by Sir Charles Sherrington, a strong indication of the unity of mind is provided by the circumstance that a person at any one time does only one main thing. In Sherrington (1951) he writes: 'we can have no surer evidence of the integration of the individual than the doing of one main thing at a time. And what then is a main thing? It is always one of those acts we call intentional' (p. 144).

The question is raised of what could be the conditions under which there can be *one* consciousness; and also the related question of what *separates* one consciousness from others.

On my approach, it is necessary for mind that there be locality-independent correlations between spatially separated events which are associated with the experiences–actions of that mind. It seems plausible to say that these correlations can generally exist only within a single neural network, when that network is active in the ways associated with consciousness in animals.

Presumably, whatever it is that can make up a single mind must have some spatial limitations, certainly as regards possible *outputs* from that mind, so as to ensure that faster-than-light communication, at the macro scale of detectable events, is avoided. The distances involved within a human or animal brain would be unlikely to cause any such problem. However, if a single mind could be constituted by a neural network extending some large distance, say millions of kilometres, which could act at its extremities, then its ability to so act could give rise to there being instantaneous information, put out at one extremity, that a certain action had occurred at the other extremity, millions of kilometres away. To avoid paradoxes such as signalling into one's own past, it appears that the spatial extension of the neural network giving rise to a single mind would have to be limited, or at least that the spatial separation of possible *outputs* from that mind would have to be limited.

This could follow, I suppose, if the correlations necessary for mental events require signals transmitted throughout a neural network at less than the speed of light, which quickly die out if not constantly renewed in all relevant parts of the network. (This may be necessary, for example, to restore quantum correlations manifested, and thereby destroyed, in neural activity.) This would limit the spatial extent of a neural network which could support the locality-independent correlations necessary for a mind, and it would also prevent such correlations existing between distinct neural networks.

16.4. Some Questions

Finally in this chapter, I consider the extent to which my suggestions are vulnerable to the consensus criticisms of the use of quantum indeterminism to support freedom of the will; and whether my suggestions can be falsified by experiment.

16.4.1. *Consensus Criticisms*

It will be recalled that in Section 3.3 I noted consensus arguments dismissing the relevance of quantum physics to the operation of the brain–mind, on the grounds of the scale of neural activity, its statistical character, and the conflict between randomness and rational choice.

I suggested there that the first two points were not cumulative, but were to some extent mutually destructive. It appears that the operation of the brain is more robust than it would be if it were liable to disruption by individual quantum fluctuations; but it also appears that the operation of the brain, at the level of neurons, has a statistical character, so as not to be affected significantly by indeterminism of individual neural firings resulting from spontaneous random activity at the synapses. It is therefore possible both that individual macroscopic events of neural firings are indeterministic, for the very reason that they magnify quantum mechanical indeterminism at the synapses; *and* that robustness is provided by the statistical character of neural firings.

A recent consensus book on the brain–mind, Rodney Cotterill's *No Ghost in the Machine* (1989), categorically asserts the contrary. Cotterill says that quantum uncertainty 'could have no influence on the will, because it makes itself felt at much too small a scale' (p.274). He goes on:

A single neuron is composed of millions of atoms, and the quantum phenomena of many individual atoms cooperate to give a macroscopic effect only under very special conditions, conditions which would not prevail in biological cells.

But this is just wrong: it is plainly refuted by the well-established fact that 'Under appropriate conditions, a rod cell in the human retina signals the absorption of a single photon, which activates only one of the 100 million rhodospin molecules in the rod' (Schnapf and Baylor 1987: 35). Of course, the circumstance that rod cells respond macroscopically to single quantum events does not necessarily mean that neurons in the brain itself do the same. Penrose (1989: 400) suggests that they may not; while Zohar (1990: 61–2) asserts that some 10^7 of the brain's 10^{10} neurons are believed to be capable of responding to quantum-level phenomena. However, even if neurons other than retinal cells cannot be triggered by single quantum events, neurons characteristically have of the order of 1 000 incoming connections, so quantum-level events in all or many of these connections could very plausibly affect neuron response.

This raises the issues of statistics, and of co-ordination of many quantum events. It is significant that the same experiments in the early 1940s, which showed the response of retinal rods to a single quantum of light, also showed that sensation did not occur unless there were about seven such responses within a short time, confirming the statistical character of neural activity. Of course, statistics involving only seven events might seem inadequate to ensure robustness of operation; but if the resolution of quantum indeterminacies in relation to many quantum events (perhaps thousands or hundreds of thousands) could be co-ordinated so as to affect the statistics of neural firings, then such co-ordinated resolution of indeterminacies could plausibly both make a detectable difference to macroscopic operations of the brain dependent on the statistical properties of neural firings, and also ensure robustness of operation. The non-local character of reality at the quantum level suggests that there is no reason in principle why there could not be co-ordination of the resolution of indeterminacies affecting many neural firings. Indeed, a possible mechanism for this, associated with Bose condensation, is conjectured in Lockwood (1989: 251–60) and Zohar (1990: 63–88). See also Eccles (1990).

As discussed earlier, all this would appear random from the physical viewpoint, because that viewpoint can take no account of subjective mental processes, in so far as they transcend physical processes. However, from the mental viewpoint, this co-ordinated resolution of indeterminacies could be a matter of choice.

Accordingly, I contend that the consensus arguments are by no means overwhelming; and that the arguments of Part II, and those based on non-locality, make out a strong case for the general approach of this chapter.

16.4.2. *Can the Approach be Tested?*

I have contended that there is not a hard-and-fast line between science and philosophy, but that it is rather a matter of degree: the less one relies on uncertain inference, and the more one relies on experiment, the more scientific (and the more dependable) become one's conclusions. Scientific advances progressively extend the area amenable to experiment. I would think that experiments could be devised to test at least some aspects of my suggested approach.

For example, there could theoretically be experiments to test whether or not the brain (whether of human beings or of lower animals considered to be conscious) is so constructed that quantum uncertainties can have macro effects of the type postulated. If such effects were excluded, then the approach would be disproved. If, on the other hand, experiments suggested that the possibility of such effects was systematically provided for in the physical and chemical structure of the neural networks, then the approach would (*pace* Popper) have some positive support.

Again, the development of a computer whose operation involved no utilization of quantum physical indeterminacies, but which showed a general rationality equal to that of a normal human being, would be some evidence against my position. On the other hand, the failure at any time to have produced such a computer would not, I think, give very much support to my position: the complexity of the brain, and in particular the vast extent of the connections between neurons, is such that it could perhaps be for ever beyond computer science to model even the mechanistic operation of such a system at the macro level.

If my position could be used to formulate a strategy which would be assured of distinguishing, in a Turing test, between a normal human being and a computer, this would strongly support it. However, I have no confidence that such a strategy could be formulated: once any strategy is formulated and disclosed, a computer can be programmed to perform plausibly in dealing with it.

It may well be, therefore, that the choice between the mechanistic consensus approach and the position which I suggest will for a long time depend on uncertain plausible considerations such as those advanced in this book. I think these considerations justify adoption, at least tentatively, of the non-mechanistic position.

17

The Self

IN Section 16.3, I noted that each person tends to see himself or herself as a single conscious subject or self, with identity and continuity over time, and with no other or rival subject involved in the same brain; but I suggested, none the less, that there may not be just one centre of consciousness in human beings, but rather a collection of conscious subsystems more or less integrated into an overall system.

It is necessary to pursue this matter further, for the following reasons. I am attempting to outline a theory of mind, based on the considerations in Parts II and III; and any such theory must give some account of the nature of the subject of consciousness, of the nature of the 'self' of each person, and of what constitutes the identity and/or continuity over time of such subjects and selves. Particularly, such an account is necessary if one wishes to pursue such questions as freedom of the will, and any moral and/or religious implications of the theory.

There is a vast literature on the topic of personal identity and the self, and I cannot hope to give a comprehensive account of the topic. I will commence by attempting to justify my preoccupation with conscious subjects or selves, rather than complete physical–mental persons. I will then look briefly at Descartes's famous argument for the existence of selves, and at how this fares from the consensus viewpoint. Next, I will outline philosopher Derek Parfit's reductionist view of the self, which seems to be the plausible outcome of the consensus approach. Finally, I will give reasons for holding that, contrary to Parfit's view, there *is* a deep further fact of personal identity or continuity, over and above physical and psychological continuity as generally understood.

17.1. Persons and Selves

In dealing up to this point with the self as the subject of experiences–actions, I have generally focused rather narrowly on what I have called the 'subject' aspect of mental events. It has been suggested (for example, by Strawson—see the discussion in Popper and Eccles 1977: 115–18) that one should, rather, take as primary the ordinary notion of a *person*, a complete physical–mental being; and that questions of identity and continuity over time (and even of subjectivity) apply to that concept more appropriately than to the concept of a subject or self, narrowly conceived as the subject of mental events.

Certainly, in everyday situations we are concerned with complete persons; and we find no need to focus on the conscious subject of mental events, as distinct from the complete person. We consider that the person, the whole physical–mental organism, just *is* the subject which experiences the perceptions and the pains, and does the actions; and there is generally no particular difficulty in deciding questions of identity and continuity over time of such organisms.

However, even ordinary talk and speculation raises questions concerning which the concept of a whole person is inadequate: for example, questions about life after death and reincarnation. Furthermore, there are real-life situations, such as destruction or disease of significant parts of the brain, or the cutting of the corpus callosum, which cannot be satisfactorily discussed without focusing specifically on the conscious subject or self. And finally, in order to bring out the implications of various views on the mind and the self, one can formulate 'thought experiments' in relation to which, again, the concept of a whole person is insufficient.

I will look in turn at these areas.

17.1.1. *Ordinary Speculations*

People do ask if there is life after death, if they and their loved ones will somehow survive their own deaths. I do not think that these questions are incoherent, although some philosophers may argue otherwise: I believe that we have a reasonable idea of what the questions mean, and that most of us would be prepared to answer to the effect 'I believe yes', 'I believe no', or 'I just don't know'. If this is right, it must mean that we readily understand references to persons as being references not to the complete physical–mental beings, but to selves or conscious subjects.

The same can be said about reincarnation, although here there may be stronger ground for arguing that reincarnation with no memories of a previous life is incoherent. However, the very fact that reincarnation can be discussed at all indicates, I think, that we readily refer to and think about persons as selves, not just as whole physical–mental persons.

I am not arguing here that speculation about reincarnation, or even life after death, is plausible; only that it can to some extent be understood, and that therefore we do have a concept of selves, relating to which we do ask questions concerning identity and continuity.

17.1.2. *Medical Problems*

There are detailed descriptions in the literature of effects of destruction or disease of various parts of the brain; and, in some cases, this is such that, although there is substantial physical continuity of the person, a real question arises concerning personal identity. Consider, for example, the descriptions of Korsakov's syndrome patients in neurologist Oliver Sacks's book *The Man who Mistook his Wife for a Hat* (Sacks 1986, chs. 2 and 12): patients who have virtually no memory of much of their pasts, and who can remember nothing new for more than a few seconds or minutes. Consider also the case of persons severely affected by senile dementia. Real questions arise about whether such a person is the same person, completely or partly, as before the onset of the disease; and the concept of a whole physical–mental person again seems inadequate for consideration of these questions.

Human beings have survived the loss of many parts of the body; and if brain function is unaffected few people would question that it is the same person who survives. Human beings have also survived the destruction of as much as a whole hemisphere of their brains, apparently retaining a substantial part of their memories and character; and many people would accept that here too it is the same person who survives. These considerations have led to the suggestion that a person survives so as to preserve identity or continuity as long as enough of his or her brain continues as the living brain of a human being: again, we are a long way from a complete physical–mental person.

Although it cannot now be done, and may never be done, it is conceivable that a brain could be transplanted from one body into another. (Such a thing might even be attempted some day if, for example, in a road accident one person's body was largely destroyed, but his brain was undamaged; while another's brain was largely destroyed, but his body undamaged.) In such a case, if the resulting person lived, we would, I think, readily conclude that he was the same person, or at least the same conscious subject or self, as the person whose brain was undamaged.

From these examples, it can be seen that we attribute particular importance to the conscious subject or self, which we take to be intimately connected with the brain; and, when circumstances require it, we are prepared to identify the person with the conscious subject, rather than the complete physical–mental organism. This is consistent with the attitude suggested by speculation about life after death and reincarnation.

Another area where the concept of a person needs refinement concerns cases where there seem to be more than one conscious subject in the one person. I have already mentioned those cases where to control epilepsy the corpus callosum has been cut. If, as appears to be the case, there are two, at least partially independent, conscious subjects in such persons, meaningful questions can be asked about whether the original person survives, and, if so, as either or both of such subjects.

There have also been well-publicized cases in which a single human being has apparently, at different times, exhibited a number of different personalities. One example is the case of 'Eve', recounted in the book and film *The Three Faces of Eve*. Eve's initial personality as an adult was that of a somewhat submissive, repressed, and withdrawn person (persona *A*). Episodes then occurred in which a highly extroverted, uninhibited, and somewhat irresponsible personality was displayed. This manifestation (persona *B*) claimed to know what persona *A* did and experienced, and yet (as if persona *A* was a different person) to be quite unfeeling about any pain or unhappiness of persona *A*; whereas persona *A* was wholly unaware of persona *B*, and regarded the episodes when persona *B* took over as black-outs, periods of which she had no recollection. Later a third, well-balanced, personality (persona *C*) began to be displayed. Persona *B* had no awareness or recollection of periods when persona *C* took over. Ultimately, persona *C* became firmly established, and personas *A* and *B* no longer appeared; and this development was apparently associated with conscious recollection of a particular traumatic incident in the woman's childhood.

Here again, the question can be asked whether there was here one person, or three; and even if the question itself is unclear and stands in need of explanation, we readily accept it as a real question. Such a question cannot be understood, much less answered, if one takes a person as a complete physical–mental organism and nothing else.

17.1.3. *Thought Experiments*

Our concepts of persons, and of what constitutes identity and continuity of persons, are perhaps most dramatically tested by various thought experiments. I will outline a few here, without attempting at this stage to discuss them in any detail.

1. Division and fusion. If a person can survive loss of a hemisphere of the brain, conceivably the brain could be divided in two, and each half housed in a new body (although I believe it is by no means clear that the brain-stem is divisible, or that there could be brain function without it). Parfit (1984: 254–5) proposes the case of three identical triplets: the body of one is fatally injured, as are the brains of the other two; and the remaining brain is divided, and each half successfully transplanted into one of the remaining bodies. Each of the resulting persons believes he is the person whose brain survived, and has generally the memories and character of that person. Does that person survive? It appears that a person survives if a hemisphere of his brain is destroyed, and also if his brain is transplanted into another person's body; and so, Parfit contends, the triplet whose body is destroyed survives, and (if, as may be the case with some people, each hemisphere has the same full range of abilities) does so as two people, neither with a better claim to be him.

Conceivably also, two brain hemispheres of different persons could be fused, producing a person with some of the memories and some of the character of both original persons; and here again there would be severe problems of survival and identity.

2. Brain wiping. Suppose that it became possible to erase from a brain all memories, beliefs, intentions, and characteristics, and to replace those of someone else. Williams (1976) imagines that two persons *A* and *B* are to be so treated, with such material to be extracted from the brain of each and transposed into the brain of the other; and further imagines that *A* is told that subsequently one of the resulting persons is to be tortured, and the other given $100 000. *A* is asked to choose (on selfish grounds) which of the resulting persons is to have which treatment. Williams suggests that *A* might well regard this experiment as involving an exchange of bodies, and might well choose that the *B*-body person be given the $100 000, so that it is the *A*-body person who is to be tortured. If, after the experiment, *A*'s choice is carried out, the *B*-body person (with *A*'s memories, character, and intellect) could be expected to be pleased that before the experiment he (as *A*) made the right choice: this would apparently confirm the interpretation of the experiment as an exchange of bodies.

Williams then asks us to consider something apparently different. *A* is told that he is going to be tortured. He is further told that, before this is done, something else will be done so as to cause him not to be able to remember anything which he now remembers; and so as to give him quite different memories and mental characteristics, which exactly fit those of another person *B*. Williams suggests that *A* would quite reasonably be very fearful, and not at all consoled by the prospect of losing his own memories, and having them replaced by those of another person.

This apparently different situation could be considered to be just another way of describing the transposition of *B*'s memories etc. to the *A*-body person in the experiment previously outlined: yet, in relation to the experiment, it seemed reasonable for *A* to choose to the effect that it would be the *A*-body person with *B*'s memories who would be tortured.

There seem to be two differences between the two descriptions, which could explain the difference in *A*'s attitude. First, in the second description the torture is represented as going to happen to *A*; and secondly, in the second description there is no reference to the fact that another person will end up with *A*'s memories and character, and $100 000. However, neither seem sufficient to give a rational basis for any difference in *A*'s attitude. Whether or not in the second case *A* is told that it is he who is to be tortured, that is a conclusion he could rationally reach from a neutral description of what is to happen. And the fact that a person would then exist with his memories and $100 000 would be little cause for consolation.

Williams draws from these examples the suggestion that it is physical continuity which is more important, so that perhaps *A*, choosing selfishly in the experiment first considered, should rather choose that the *A*-body person be given the $100 000.

3. Replication and teletransportation. Parfit (1984: 199–201) supposes a Teletransporter, which works as follows. The traveller enters and loses

consciousness in a Scanner, which destroys the traveller's brain and body, while recording every detail of it. This information is transmitted by radio to a Replicator, which uses it to create, from new matter, a qualitatively identical brain and body, with the same memories and mental life. The Replica would believe himself to be the traveller, and would have memories of the traveller's life up to the time when he became unconscious in the Scanner.

However, it may be questioned whether the Replica *is* the traveller, or whether the traveller was killed in the Scanner. What if the Replicator used the information to create *several* Replicas? What if the Scanner obtained the necessary information without destroying the Original? As we will see, Parfit argues that such questions about identity do not really matter: all that really matters is the survival of the psychological properties of the Original, and survival of such properties by way of a Replica is 'just about as good as' ordinary survival.

17.2. From Descartes to the Consensus

The considerations of the previous section point up the fact that we tend to think of the self and personal identity as involving more than the continuity of a physical object, and as raising questions of a different kind from questions about the identity or continuity of a physical object. We readily accept that in the case of a physical object there may or may not be a definite answer to whether or not a particular object today is the same as a particular object some time in the past: for example, a loose-leaf manual all of whose pages have been progressively replaced by updating material. In borderline cases, it is a matter of degree, of definition of words, of choice. However, each of us tends to think that it is a matter of objective fact whether he or she will exist tomorrow, and that this is a question which must (tomorrow) have a definite Yes or No answer.

It was contended by Descartes that each person is a unique immortal soul, whose identity over time is simple and unproblematic, and which will continue to exist irrespective of what happens to the body: this is sometimes called a Cartesian ego. However, as we will see, his famous argument for this view is by no means conclusive; and this view certainly does not sit well with the consensus approach to the brain–mind question.

It will be recalled that the consensus approach is to treat mental events and physical events as identical, or as two aspects of the same events; and in that sense to treat the mind not as something distinct from the brain, but as a function of it. (On these matters, my own approach is not very different.) The relevant physical events are events of a physical object, the human brain. The identity and/or continuity over time of this physical object would appear to be of the same nature as for physical objects generally; and therefore in some cases at least (for example, where the object is divided, or changes, or where some of its constituent parts are replaced, etc.) to be a matter of degree. Accordingly, questions are raised about whether the subject of the mental events is in any different case: not only about whether such a subject can survive the destruction of the brain, but also about whether the subject of successive mental events of a person is or may be the *same* subject, and if so what does this sameness consist in.

I will here look briefly at Descartes's argument, and at the very different approaches suggested by Hume and by Kant. I will then say a little in introduction of consensus views on the question. In the next section I will look at what might be considered as being implied by the consensus approach, the thoroughgoing reductionism of Derek Parfit.

17.2.1. *I Think, Therefore I Am*

Descartes's famous one-line argument seems prima facie to be a plausible argument for the existence of a unique and determinate continuing subject or self. However, Hume countered by suggesting that thinking (or any conscious experience or activity) is no more than 'a bundle or collection of different perceptions' (thoughts, sensations, images); and that there is not found in introspection, over and above such perceptions, a subject or self which has them:

when I enter most intimately into what I call *myself*, I always stumble on some particular perception or other, of heat or cold, light or shade, love or hatred, pain or pleasure. I never can catch *myself* at any time without a perception, and never can observe any thing but the perception. (Hume 1965: 252)

Richard Swinburne comments:

It may well be that Hume never catches himself without a 'perception' (i.e. a conscious episode) but his bare datum is not just 'perceptions', but successions of overlapping 'perceptions' experienced by a common subject. If it were not so, we would have no grounded knowledge of succession. Hume says that he fails to find the common subject. One wonders what he supposed that the common subject would look like, and what he considered would count as its discovery. Was he looking for a common element in all his visual fields, or a background noise which never ceased? . . . Yet the self which he ought to have found in all his mental events is supposed to be the subject, not the object of perception. And finding it consists in being aware of different mental events as had by the same subject. (Swinburne 1986: 157)

This is at least a partial answer to Hume. But it is by no means conclusive. Consider Kant's argument, taken up by Sydney Shoemaker in Shoemaker and Swinburne (1984: 123–4). Kant considers the case in which one elastic ball communicates its motion to a second, which in turn communicates it to a third, and so on; and continues by imagining a whole series of substances of which the first transmits its state together with its consciousness to the second, the second its own state with that of the preceding substance to the third, and this in turn the state of all the preceding substances together with its own consciousness and with their consciousness to another. The last substance would then be conscious of all the states of the previously changed substances, as being its own states, because they would have been transferred to it together with consciousness of them.

Shoemaker notes that 'Supposing that such a succession of substances is possible, nothing in the nature of one's self-consciousness shows that this is not what we have in ordinary cases of what we count as personal identity'.

In other words, Swinburne's suggestion that a subject is 'aware of different mental events as had by the same subject' can be countered by pointing out that if the different mental events were in fact had by a succession of different subjects, each passing on its experience and consciousness and memories to the next, no difference could be detected, in introspection by any of these subjects, from the case of a single subject having all the mental events. So, although it appears to me now that I am a single subject who has had and is continuing to have, over time, a long series of experiences, I may just as well be merely one briefly existing subject in a succession of subjects, each passing on its experiences and/or consciousness and/or memories to the next: nothing in my experience can assure me that I am not.

Accordingly, at least when one accepts something like an identity or dual aspect theory, Descartes's argument does not demonstrate a long-continuing identical subject, much less an immortal soul. All that 'I think' proves, as put by Nozick (1981: 87), is that 'thinking is going on' by 'this act's very doer'; and this 'doer' could be as ephemeral as the thought itself.

17.2.2. *Physical and Psychological Continuity*

Notwithstanding the arguments of Hume and Kant, each person does have a strong sense of identity and continuity, both of self and of other persons; and each person's thinking and actions are thoroughly permeated by the belief that persons have identity, or at least continuity, over time. The notion of some irreducible personal or subjective identity or continuity tends to conflict with consensus views; and consensus writers seek to reduce this to some kind of an impersonal or objective physical continuity and/or psychological continuity.

1. Physical continuity. It seems clear that for a person to survive, or continue, it is not necessary that the whole of his or her body continue in existence: it is sufficient if enough of his or her brain continues to function satisfactorily as the brain of a living person. So long as this is the case, the loss of arms or legs, or indeed any part of the body, would not be regarded as preventing survival and continuity of the person, or at least of the conscious subject.

Some consensus writers contend that it is this, the continued existence of enough of the brain, which is constitutive of survival and continuity; and that this is all there is to the identity over time of a person or conscious subject.

This view does not sit well with a principle (mentioned in Section 2.6) widely held by consensus writers: the supervenience of the mental on the physical. This asserts that, given two entities with identical physical properties, if one has mental properties, the other must have the same mental properties—the *history* of two entities is irrelevant. If the mental properties of the two entities are qualitatively identical, how can physical continuity *per se* be of significance?

Further, some (generally those who emphasize the functionalist approach) argue that the physical instantiation of mental states and events is only incidental: what is important is the functional role of those states and events. If the complete functional role of the mental states and events of a person can be instantiated in some medium other than his or her own brain, then that person would continue and survive. We saw a reflection of that approach in Parfit's Teletransporter thought experiment; and also, more realistically perhaps, in the suggestion by computer scientist Hans Moravec that the complete contents of a person's mind could be put into a computer, and that thereby the person (or his or her 'living essence') could become immortal.

In support of this approach, it can be pointed out that physical continuity is a highly indeterminate concept. I referred earlier to the case of a loose-leaf manual. Similarly, if the planks of a rowing-boat were progressively replaced over a period of years, until none of the original remains, we would probably still consider it the same boat. If the neurons of a brain could similarly be progressively replaced, without interfering with its function, we would consider it the same brain, and so (it would seem) the brain of the same person. If a silicon chip could perform the functions of a single neuron, presumably the neurons could be replaced progressively by silicon chips, without affecting the functioning of the brain; and so without interrupting the continuity of the brain or (it would seem) of the person. In fact, molecules in the brain are continually being replaced by the metabolism of the cells; and it seems that eventually there are few (if any) of the original molecules left: yet the brain continues. Why should it make a difference if such physical changes occurred all at once, rather than progressively?

These considerations suggest that psychological continuity may be more important than physical identity or continuity.

2. Psychological continuity. One of the factors which causes each of us to regard himself or herself as a unique continuing self is psychological continuity: the amalgam of generally consistent memories of past involvement in actions and experiences, and of continuity of other mental properties including qualities of character and intellect.

Problems have arisen in this area because the concept of memory to some extent presupposes continuity of the subject: in ordinary talk, nothing can truly be *my* memory of actions and experiences *unless* it was indeed *me* who underwent the experiences, or did the actions, which are remembered. Accordingly, a proposition that identity or continuity of the self is indicated by memories may be true by definition: if I remember doing something in the past, then it must have been me, the same person, who did it; otherwise this would not count as remembering.

To avoid this circularity, the notion of 'quasi-remembering' has been suggested: this notion includes ordinary remembering; and is like it, except that it does not presuppose that experiences and actions which are 'quasi-remembered' were necessarily experienced or done by the person doing the 'quasi-remembering'. The content of the memory experience is the same: it is of experiences and actions 'from the inside'; but use of the concept leaves open the possibility that a different subject may have undergone the experiences, and done the actions, and then passed the consciousness of having done so to a successor subject (in the way suggested in Kant's argument referred to earlier). Rather than adopt the terminology of quasi-remembering, I will use remembering and memory in this wide sense; that is, as not ruling out that the experiences and actions remembered were those of a subject different from that doing the remembering.

If remembering and memory are used in this way, then there is no circularity in saying that personal identity is indicated by a collection of generally consistent overlapping memories. And, indeed, I do take my own memories of past experiences and actions as evidencing identity or continuity between (on the one hand) the person who underwent the experiences and/or did the actions, and (on the other hand) me. Furthermore, if there are experiences and actions which I no longer remember, but which were remembered by 'me' at the time when 'I' underwent an experience and/or did an action which I now remember, then I readily accept that there is identity or continuity between (on the one hand) the person who underwent *those* experiences and/or did *those* actions, and (on the other hand) me. This is the significance of the word 'overlapping' used above.

This approach also has problems, some of which will be looked at later. For the moment, it is sufficient to note that, on one view, it appears to deny continuity in cases of complete amnesia. If a person, through brain damage or other cause, wholly loses his or her memory, then on this view it is not merely that he or she does not know who he or she is: he or she is no longer in fact the same conscious subject as before, or even any continuation of that conscious subject.

3. Not just evidence. The last paragraph points up an important feature of some consensus views on physical and/or psychological continuity: they are *not* just taken as evidence of identity or continuity of the self. That would be wholly uncontroversial. Rather, they are used as indicating what is *constitutive* of identity or continuity of the self. Some consensus writers contend that one or other, or some combination of the two, is just what identity or con-

tinuity of the self *is*. Since physical and psychological continuity are both matters of degree, these consensus writers contend that identity or continuity of the self is also a matter of degree.

This can also be expressed negatively: that there is no *deep further fact*, beyond physical and/or psychological continuity, involved in the identity of the self. The denial of any such deep further fact is at the forefront of the views of Derek Parfit, whose book *Reason and Persons* (Parfit 1984) is perhaps the most thoroughgoing expression of the consensus view of the self. (It may, however, not be wholly typical of consensus views on the self, because it suggests implications which even some consensus writers might regard as a *reductio ad absurdum* of the denial of any deep further fact of identity or continuity.)

17.3. Parfit's Reductionist View

Parfit (1984) puts a case for what he calls (p. 210) the reductionist view of personal identity: that the fact of identity over time just consists in the holding of certain more particular facts, which can be described in an impersonal way. He contrasts this with the non-reductionist view, which he seeks to refute: that identity involves a further fact which cannot be reduced to particular impersonal facts. He contends that in any event personal identity as such does not matter: what matters is psychological connectedness and/or continuity. (Parfit draws distinctions between psychological connectedness and psychological continuity which need not concern us here; and I will generally refer just to psychological continuity.)

Parfit attacks a number of interrelated beliefs, some or all of which many of us accept:

1. that persons are separately existing entities (of the nature of Cartesian egos) distinct from their brains and bodies and experiences;
2. that the identity and continuity of such entities is a 'deep further fact' beyond physical and psychological continuity, which holds either completely or not at all;
3. that accordingly, for any person, the question 'Will I exist?' (say, at future time *t*) always has a definite answer (at least, when time *t* arrives), which must be Yes or No.
4. It is this identity and/or continuity of persons which explains the unity of consciousness at any time, and the unity of a life: these unities are of different experiences had by the same person.
5. Similarly, this identity and continuity is of great importance; and it is this which particularly matters in relation to such things as survival, responsibility, and compensation.

Parfit's contentions in relation to these beliefs are as follows:

1. Persons are not separately existing entities. Their existence just involves the existence of their brains and bodies, and various interrelated physical and mental events, all of which can be described in an impersonal way.
2. Identity and continuity over time just involves psychological continuity, and (in the case of identity) there being no *other* person with similar continuity. There is no deep further fact. Persons exist, but only as clubs or ships exist.
3. It is not true that our identity is always determinate. Sometimes the question 'Will I exist?' does not have a definite answer Yes or No. Indeed, sometimes it is an empty question; and if sufficient impersonal facts concerning physical and psychological continuity are known, there is nothing else to know.
4. The unity of consciousness, and the unity of a person's life, cannot be explained by saying that all his experiences are had by one person; but rather by describing the relations between these experiences, and their relations to this person's brain, in an impersonal way.
5. Personal identity has no importance as such. What matters, particularly in relation to such things as survival, responsibility, and compensation, is not personal identity, but psychological continuity.

Perhaps the central tenets of Parfit's thesis are his adoption of the psychological criterion both for personal identity and for 'what matters'; and his denial of any deep further fact of identity over and above impersonal psychological and physical continuity.

He commences the defence of these views by arguing that the psychological criterion can be described in such a way as does not presuppose personal identity, somewhat along the lines of the previous section. He contends, further, that the carrier of psychological continuity is just a person's brain and body, and not any separately existing entity. He then presents what appear to be the two main positive arguments in support of his views:

1. arguments based on the consideration of spectra of continuity of human beings, both psychological and physical;
2. arguments based on consideration of the division of human brains and minds.

The former, he claims, supports his view on belief (3), that the existence of a person in the future cannot be an all-or-nothing question, at least unless beliefs (1) and (2) are true and persons are separately existing entities whose identity is determinate; and it also makes beliefs (1) and (2) less plausible. The latter, he claims, supports his view on belief (5), that it is psychological continuity which matters; and it similarly makes beliefs (1) and (2) less plausible.

I will consider briefly in turn Parfit's arguments based on spectra of continuity, and on division of brains. I will conclude this section by looking briefly at some implications of Parfit's views.

17.3.1. *Spectra of Continuity*

Parfit begins by presenting his version of the brain-wiping thought experiment proposed by Williams. Parfit postulates that he is the prisoner of a callous neurosurgeon, who proposes to disrupt his psychological continuity by tampering with his brain while he is still conscious and therefore in pain. The surgeon tells Parfit that he will first cause him to lose all his memories; then cause him to have apparent memories of Napoleon's life; and finally change his character so that it becomes just like Napoleon's. As noted in Parfit (1976: 149), this and other examples given in Williams (1976) show how natural it is to believe that the question 'Shall I survive?' must have an answer Yes or No (that is, personal identity is determinate); and that there is a *risk* of our reaching the wrong answer.

However, Parfit then introduces what he calls the psychological spectrum, which he explains by reference to his callous neurosurgeon. Near one end of the spectrum, only one or two memories and character traits are changed; and near the other, almost all memories and character traits are changed. The spectrum thus ranges continuously from no psychological change at all, to the complete psychological change postulated by Williams; in each case with complete physical continuity. Parfit suggests that, if one considers cases throughout the spectrum, three possibilities suggest themselves:

1. that, in all cases, the resulting person is the same (because of the physical continuity);
2. that, in *some* cases, the resulting person is the same, in others not (requiring a sharp borderline between the two classes of cases); and
3. that there are cases in which no definite answer can be given (that is, accepting Parfit's reductionist view).

Parfit contends that (2) is not plausible, in that a borderline between the resulting person being the same and not the same cannot plausibly be drawn somewhere along such a continuous spectrum. Williams suggested that (1) is correct; but Parfit contends that consideration of what he calls the physical spectrum and the combined spectrum suggests that this, too, is not plausible.

The physical spectrum postulates the possibility of breaking physical continuity to various extents, without prejudicing psychological continuity. Near one extreme, one or two neurons are replaced with new material. At the other extreme, there is complete destruction of the brain and creation of an exact replica, having all the memories and qualities of character and intellect of the original. This spectrum ranges continuously from no physical change, through replacement of various fractions of the brain, to complete replacement by an exact replica; in each case with complete psychological connectedness and/or continuity.

Again, Parfit suggests, there are the same three possibilities. He suggests that it is not plausible to suggest a definite borderline; so that either one has identity in the case of *all* resulting persons, or else one must accept the reductionist view.

In the case of the combined spectrum, one considers the possibility of both psychological and physical continuity being broken to various degrees, ranging (in two dimensions) from nil change in both to complete change in both. Now, it is not plausible to think that where one has no physical continuity, and also no psychological continuity at all, one could still have the same person. Yet, here again, it seems implausible that a definite borderline be drawn between those degrees of physical and psychological continuity which preserve the same person completely, and those which do so not all. Only the reductionist view is left.

Thus, Parfit claims, consideration of the psychological spectrum shows that psychological continuity is not necessary for determinate personal identity; while consideration of the physical spectrum shows that physical continuity is not necessary for determinate personal identity. Parfit accepts both conclusions; and contends that, particularly having regard to the combined spectrum, personal identity cannot be determinate. Put shortly: physical and psychological continuity are matters of degree, so personal identity over time cannot be all or nothing.

17.3.2. *Divided Minds*

Parfit refers to cases where the corpus callosum is cut, and points to the apparent existence of two conscious subjects in such persons. He contends that it is not plausible to consider such a person as a single Cartesian ego; nor as somehow involving two such egos, one or both of them coming into existence upon the division of the brain.

To further undermine the latter view, Parfit refers to the possibility that, instead of severing the corpus callosum, a means might be found of temporarily rendering it inoperative. Whether or not this is likely to become possible technically, there seems no reason in principle why it could not be done. Then, not only would one have the situation that what had previously (apparently) been one conscious subject becomes two conscious subjects; but also, there would be the possibility that these two conscious subjects could be reunited into a single subject, having at least some of the memories of both the previously distinct conscious subjects.

Before the operation which rendered the corpus callosum inoperative, the person involved would reasonably be particularly concerned about the future flourishing of both the conscious subjects which were to result. This is confirmed by the circumstance that, when the corpus callosum again became operative, he or she would presumably remember experiences of both of the separate conscious subjects during the time of separation.

Parfit supposes the case of a person who could at will render his or her corpus callosum inoperative, and subsequently at will render it operative again; and who finds it convenient to use this ability during a physics examination, so that he or she could work on two things at once. (Parfit assumes hemispheres with the same abilities: otherwise, perhaps the left hemisphere could tackle the equations, while the right could draw the graphs and diagrams!) He suggests that each hemisphere would, after 'separation', have memories of the events leading up to the separation, followed by the events involving its own separate work. After reunification, the student would have memories of the separate events involving each hemisphere.

Parfit goes on to consider his triplets thought experiment. He contends that the triplet whose brain is not destroyed does survive, but that neither of the two resulting persons is the *same* person as this triplet: identity in this sense has to be a one–one relation. However, this survival is at least as good as if the triplet had survived alone with half a brain, in which case the survivor would have been considered identical with the triplet. Accordingly, he contends, personal identity is not what matters: rather, survival matters, and particularly survival involving psychological continuity.

17.3.3. *Some Implications*

Parfit draws various conclusions from his views, in particular his denial of any deep further fact of personal identity, and his assertion that what matters is psychological continuity. These views, at their lowest, place less importance on the distinctions between persons: they suggest that it is rational to be more concerned about the quality of experiences, and less concerned about whose experiences they are.

Parfit says (1984: 281) that his views have made him less concerned about the rest of his own life (and about his inevitable death), and more concerned about the lives of others. To this extent, his views seem in accordance with many moral outlooks. However, they have other implications which are less so.

1. Responsibility. Since, on Parfit's view, personal identity does not matter, but psychological continuity does, there is less reason to hold persons responsible for past wrongdoing. It would appear that if a Replica were created of a wrongdoer, on Parfit's view it would be rational to hold the Replica responsible for the wrongdoing, just as much as the Original wrongdoer. Indeed, the Replica would be preferred for punishment (say) if, by reason of some disease of his brain, the Original had a weaker psychological connection to the wrongdoing than the Replica.

2. Commitments. Similar comments apply to commitments. Since the identity of the person making a commitment, and that of the person to whom a commitment is made, do not as such matter, the obligation to fulfil commitments must similarly be reduced.

3. Compensation. There is less scope for compensation within a life: burdens at one stage of a person's life cannot be compensated, or fully compensated, by benefits at another stage. Again, this can be seen by considering the case of a Replica: given equal (or greater) psychological connectedness to the person who suffered the burdens, the Replica would have an equal (or greater) claim to the benefits.

4. Distributive justice. Since the quality of experiences matters more than the identity of the persons who have them, there is less reason to worry about the distribution of benefits among different persons.

Parfit concedes that, on his approach to personal identity, it is a defensible position that there is *no* reason for any concern about one's own future, and *no* basis at all for responsibility, commitments, compensation, distributive justice; indeed, for any concern at all for others as persons (rather than for impersonal aggregates of experiences). However, he contends that it is also a defensible position that his views merely *reduce* such reason and such basis; and this fits in well with his utilitarian moral philosophy.

17.4. A Deep Further Fact

Contrary to Parfit, I contend that personal identity and/or continuity does matter, and that there is a 'deep further fact' involved, beyond physical continuity and psychological continuity, at least as these are generally understood.

17.4.1. *Presupposed in Experience and Reasoning*

Descartes asked if there was anything that he could not doubt; and he answered that he could not doubt his own existence, which was revealed in the very act of doubting. We saw in Section 17.2 that this view has been opposed *inter alia* by Hume's reference to bundles of perceptions, and by Kant's argument based on postulated successive selves. However, I suggest that there is still force in Descartes's argument, and extensions of it.

1. Unity of consciousness. In the first place, there is the question of unity of consciousness *at one time*. Schrödinger (1967: 96) writes about the canvas, or ground-stuff, upon which experiences are collected. In *Reasons and Persons*, Parfit contends that the unity of consciousness needs no such explanation:

It is simply a fact that several experiences can be *co-conscious*, or be the objects of a single state of awareness. It may help to compare this fact with the fact that there is short-term memory of experiences within the last few moments: short-term memory of what is called 'the specious present'. Just as there can be a single memory of just having had several experiences, such as hearing a bell strike three times, there can be a single state of awareness both of hearing the fourth striking of this bell, and of seeing ravens fly past the bell-tower . . . Since there can be one state of awareness of several experiences, we need not explain this unity by ascribing these experiences to the same person, or subject of experiences. (Parfit 1984: 250–1)

However, when experiences are 'co-conscious', as Parfit puts it, they surely do have the same conscious subject. It does not matter whether one considers that it is the 'co-consciousness' which causes the experiences to have the same subject, or that it is the circumstance that experiences (occurring at the same time) have the same subject which makes them 'co-conscious': the one seems both necessary and sufficient for the other. It seems that there could be nothing more, or less, involved in co-consciousness than that the experiences be those of a single subject, at the same time. Certainly, it is not sufficient for co-consciousness that experiences occur at the same time: if different conscious subjects have experiences at the same time, the experiences are not co-conscious. Further, it seems to be not necessary for co-consciousness that the experiences involve physical events at the same place, because there can apparently be co-consciousness of experiences involving different areas of the brain.

Parfit compares co-consciousness at a single time with the short-term memory of what is called the specious present. Any substantive experience takes *some* finite time, so it is in fact hard to make sense of any sort of consciousness unless it is considered as lasting for some time. Whitrow (1980: 73–4) suggests that the minimum duration for a conscious experience is of the order of 50 milliseconds, that is, one-twentieth of a second. Parfit writes:

The unity of consciousness at one time is not a deeper fact than psychological continuity over time. This seems to be shown when we consider our short-term memories of the last few moments, or of the *specious present*. There cannot be a deep difference between this short-term continuity, and the unity of consciousness at one time. (Parfit 1984: 521 n. 112)

So, if co-consciousness at one time is that of a single subject, it would seem that co-consciousness spanning the specious present, or whatever time is necessary to constitute an experience, is similarly that of a single subject. And in relation to experience of the specious present, there is the further point that it is often of a *succession* of events (such as the successive notes of a tune) presented to a single subject. Whitrow notes the realization of William James 'that the specious (or psychological) present is not an interval of fixed duration, but is a variable stretch of time with its content perceived as having one part earlier and another part later' (1980: 76). And Swinburne observes: 'one of a subject's basic data is of the continuity of experience, which means the continuity of the mental events of a common subject' (1986: 157).

On this approach, it can plausibly be contended that Kant's argument about successive subjects or 'substances' operates only *beyond* this stage. It may be accepted that a subject cannot know from introspection that its memories are not of experiences of another subject which have been passed on; but if a subject is to have *any* experience at all (whether of present perceptions, or recollections, or some combination), this presupposes *identity or continuity of the subject for whatever time is necessary to constitute that experience.* To make sense of Kant's supposition of a substance being 'conscious of all the states of the previously changed substances, as being its own states', one still has to assume identity and continuity of *this* substance for however long is necessary for *this* consciousness. One could postulate that an experience commenced by one 'substance' could be completed by a second 'substance'; but unless the second 'substance' persisted for long enough for it to have *some* experience in its own right (albeit one partially constituted by short-term memory of whatever the first 'substance' experienced), there would be no experience at all of the second 'substance' by which it could be deceived into believing that some more extensive experience was entirely its own.

Whatever identity or continuity of a subject is necessary thus to span the experiences of the specious present cannot be reduced to psychological or physical continuity. Psychological continuity comes down to qualitative identity or similarity of characteristics of subjects and their experiences, and in particular their memories, and this can be satisfied by Replicas; whereas co-consciousness of two experiences cannot be constituted by one Replica having one experience and another Replica having another. Physical continuity *of some kind or another* may as a matter of fact be involved in the identity or continuity of the subject; but the identity or continuity of the subject involved in co-consciousness of experiences in the specious present (which is, as much as anything can be, presupposed and unquestionable) cannot be reduced to the ordinary physical continuity of physical objects (which is contingent and can be indeterminate).

If there is an identity or continuity of the subject involved here, which is more than psychological or physical continuity as generally understood, then Parfit's argument can be applied in reverse to suggest that there can similarly be an identity or continuity of the subject over time, which is more than psychological or physical continuity. At the lowest, a *type* of identity or continuity is suggested, in relation to which one can meaningfully ask, 'Does it persist over time?'

2. Reasoning. I have argued that plausible reasoning involves decisions or choices, made on the basis of non-conclusive reasons, which themselves may involve or depend on conscious experiences. If this is correct, there appears to be presupposed, in this approach, a subject or self which is identical or continuous over the time involved in making such decisions or choices. This is partially conceded by Kant but, as pointed out by Barrett (1987: 64), only to a very limited extent: 'How much of the ego persists from today to tomorrow? Only as much, [Kant] tells us, as is required to give continuity and meaning to the particular process of thought—in short, a formal, or, in the Kantian terminology, a transcendental, ego.'

However, although in an extended process of reasoning one can readily conceive of stages in the process being carried out by successive subjects or selves (with each subject or self persisting only for so long as necessary to constitute an experience of a 'specious present'), one might ask *why* should one give any credence to such a conception? If there is an irreducible identity or continuity of the self involved in experience of the specious present, it seems reasonable to suppose that it is *this* identity or continuity which supports a process of reasoning, rather than a mere 'formal' ego (which may be consistent with Kant's series of successive selves).

The same argument as Kant used to support scepticism of an identical or continuing self can, with similar force, be used to support scepticism of the very happening of prior experiences and prior events. The memories which a person has of past experiences may indeed conceivably be of past experiences of some other person or subject, as Kant supposes; but, by the same token, they may conceivably be of experiences which *no one* has had at all. Conceivably, the person (and indeed the world) may have just sprung into existence, complete with memories of an apparent past.

It is surely more reasonable to accept the testimony of memory, and to accept that the remembered experiences (including those of the commencement of a particular process of reasoning) were those of the 'same' person who now has the memories and is completing the process of reasoning; just as it is the 'same' person who has all the co-conscious experiences which are combined in the specious present.

So, on this approach, one gets back to Descartes's contention. When I doubt and deliberate on what exists, and take this to be a process of reasoning, I presuppose some identity and/or continuity of a subject which is doing the doubting and deliberating, at least for the duration of the doubting and deliberating; an identity and/or continuity which appears logically prior to, and independent of, both psychological and physical continuity. It would seem that the advocacy of any position, even those of Hume and Parfit, involves the adoption of a point of view and the exercise of a process of reasoning, both being activities presupposing a relatively stable and continuous subject which undertakes them. Barrett writes thus of the view of Hume and the British empiricists:

This is the view that the nature of our human consciousness is essentially additive and atomistic: its function consists in combining one discrete datum, or bits of data, with others; and mind itself is but an aggregate of such data. . . . But . . . their disposition to see facts in a certain way is not merely one more separate datum in the list of facts but, rather, a point of view that provides the structure for the whole. (Barrett 1987: 165)

3. Contrary presupposition. The above quotation suggests a further argument. So far, I have accepted, with Hume, Kant, and Parfit, that it is appropriate to consider experiences as particulars or objects (in the sense of

being bearers of properties, and being such as can be the agent or object of change or activity): one can then consider the conscious subject of experiences as merely in effect a property or attribute of the experience, and dependent upon it. However, to accept this is already to concede, perhaps unnecessarily, part of their case.

As already noted in Section 2.5, one can take a different view of mental events, namely that it is the conscious subject which is the relevant particular or 'object' or 'substance', in the sense just explained, to which the experience happens (or, in the case of actions, which does the action). If one takes this latter view, which is perhaps the more plausible from the viewpoint of the subject in question, the continuance and identity of the subject seems to be taken for granted, and not to be dependent on what the subject experiences or does, that is, on the content of the experiences–actions.

It is perhaps of interest to recall that some consensus writers adopt this latter approach: particularly, supporters of functionalism such as Lycan (1987), who seek to explain away the qualitative character of experiences (such as pains) as being mere adverbial modifications of activities of or happenings to a person. That is, in order to support their view that only material objects exist, they deny that experiences (such as pains) exist as objects, in the above sense; and this points towards a view of persons as being the bearers of experiences, and as *not* being identified by the content of such experiences: that is, it points away from psychological continuity as the sole criterion of the identity or continuity of the self.

17.4.2. *Personal Continuity Matters*

The second main area of argument for a deep further fact proceeds on the basis that we believe strongly that personal or subjective identity or continuity matters, in ways which cannot be accounted for by impersonal objective physical and/or psychological continuity.

1. One's own future. Shoemaker writes that 'a person's future history is the primary focus of his desires, hopes and fears'; and he continues in a footnote:

This is not to deny the possibility or occurrence of unselfish attitudes and emotions. Even the most unselfish man, who is willing to suffer that others may prosper, does not and cannot regard the pleasures and pains that are in prospect for him in the same light as he regards those that are in prospect for others. He may submit to torture, but he would hardly be human if he could regularly view his own future sufferings with the same detachment (which is not indifference) as he views the future suffering of others. (Shoemaker 1984: 48)

This particular concern for one's own future does not appear to be rationally justified either by psychological continuity as such or physical continuity as such: so either it is not rationally justified at all, or else it is rationally justified by some deep further fact of personal identity or continuity.

So far as psychological continuity is concerned, the mere fact that some future human being might happen to have my memories and beliefs, and to have qualitatively identical mental characteristics and capacities, would not of itself rationally justify me in having particular concern for that human being, unless that human being also happened to *be* me. Conceivably, some other person (having very similar mental characteristics) could be brainwashed into having my memories and beliefs; and I would not have the particular concern for that person's future experiences which I have for my own.

The point is further illustrated by consideration of replication. One can conceive of a replica of oneself being created: if it *is* an exact Replica, with a qualitatively identical physical structure, then it would have all the memories, beliefs, and mental characteristics and capacities of the Original, and thus have complete psychological continuity with the Original. Although the Original and the Replica would thus be indistinguishable, and each would believe himself to be the Original, each would see the other as a different person; and neither would have any access to the contemporary mental events of the other.

The situation would be somewhat similar to that of identical twins. They are genetically identical, but are different persons, and each sees the other as being someone else. There may be a feeling of close and special affinity between them, but generally there is no mutual access of each to the mental events of the other. Even if twins had been treated indistinguishably from conception, and remained almost identical physically and mentally to each other, they would still be different and separate persons; and they would remain so, even if one somehow acquired all the beliefs and memories of the other.

It would seem, therefore, that while the Original would reasonably have particular concern for the future of the Original, he would not (before or after the replication) reasonably have the same concern for the future of the Replica: his concern for the future of the Replica would reasonably be similar to the concern of one identical twin for the future of the other twin.

Parfit's contention is in effect that his arguments show that the Original's special concern for the future of the Original, and not for that of the Replica, is not rationally justified; and is to be explained by evolutionary conditioning. Natural selection has caused human beings to be conditioned to seek to survive and to perpetuate their own genes, and the particular concern for one's own future is part of this conditioning. This may be correct; but Parfit's arguments, including this consideration, do not eradicate one's particular concern for one's own future. I contend that it is more reasonable to see one's ineradicable concern for one's own future as pointing, along with the other arguments of this section, towards a deep further fact of personal identity or continuity, which does rationally justify such concern.

As regards physical continuity, somewhat similar considerations apply. The mere fact that a future human being might have physical continuity with me would not of itself rationally justify me in having particular concern for that human being, unless that human being was in fact me.

The relationship of physical continuity comes down to a succession of physical events, with certain close causal relationships. The physical events manifesting the existence of an object or organism at one time, and the developing quantum state underlying such events, have a close causal connection with the relevant events and quantum state at another time. Such connections, and the relationship of physical continuity, are matters of degree.

Again, thought experiments suggest that impersonal physical continuity (either alone or in combination with psychological continuity) does not exhaust personal identity or continuity. When one considers Williams's brain-wiping proposal, or Parfit's case of the triplets, one finds it very difficult to accept that the impersonal descriptions are all there is to know. A person A is told that he (A) and another person (B) are to undergo mutual 'brain-wipes', so that the A-body person ends up with B's memories, beliefs, and qualities of character and intellect, and vice versa. Alternatively, A is told that his brain is to be bisected by a mad surgeon, with one hemisphere transplanted into one body, and the other into another body. In either case, A is told that one of the resulting persons is to be tortured, and that the other is to be given a large sum of money. One instinctively feels that, in either case, A needs to know *more* than the objective, impersonal facts concerning physical and psychological continuity; that, in addition to those facts, he needs to know a further fact, the answer to the question which of the resulting persons will be A; and that if he does not know this, A runs the risk of making the wrong choice (see Swinburne 1986: 150).

2. Other persons. Personal identity and continuity also matter in relation to other persons, in ways which mere physical and psychological continuity do not account for.

We have already noted Parfit's acceptance that his views at least reduce the importance of responsibility, commitments, compensation, and distributive justice; and that his views make him more concerned about the quality of experiences, and less concerned about whose experiences they are. I suggest that this puts it too low.

The full implications of reductionism, such as Parfit's, in relation to other persons can again be brought out by considering replication. Suppose that a Replica is made of the person with whom I have shared my life for twenty-five years. Then, assuming Parfit's view is correct, it should make no rational difference to my attitude to the human being now before me to know whether she is the Original (who has gone through life's ups and downs with me, made sacrifices for me, borne our children, worked with me to raise them, and experienced all sorts of joys and sorrows with me) or the Replica (who was created five minutes ago). Of course, assuming (as I must) that the replication is exact, the Replica not only will have the physical and mental characteristics of the Original, but also will believe that she is the Original, and have the memories of the Original; and to that extent will justify my particular concern. But it is very difficult to accept that it just does not matter at all which is which.

Similarly, assuming replication of a person who has committed a terrible crime, or of someone who has benefited humankind through heroic self-sacrifice, Parfit's view means that (appearances aside) it is just as rational to punish the Replica of the former, and to reward the Replica of the latter, as so to treat the Original in each case.

Reducing continuity of the self to mere physical causation and overlapping memories would seem to destroy any rational basis for the overwhelming moral significance that most of us ascribe to each and every individual human being. Such significance would seem to be linked with a view of human beings as primarily unique continuing conscious selves with personal identity or continuity, and only secondarily as marvellous physical organisms with impersonal physical and psychological continuity.

Of course, concern for each individual human being may not be rationally justified: the thesis of Parfit's *Reasons and Persons* may be correct, negating that concern for each individual, as an individual, which is assumed as a first principle in many ideas of justice or fairness, such as those considered in Rawls's *Theory of Justice* (Rawls 1971). However, unless such concern can be shown to be rationally unsupportable, surely we should not abandon it. If one ceases to ascribe overwhelming moral importance to each individual human being, this could in turn arguably lead one, for example, to countenance the painless killing of innocent individuals for 'good' ends. To go along this track, on the basis of theoretical arguments which must of their nature be inconclusive, would appear to involve (to put it at its lowest) unacceptable intellectual arrogance.

17.4.3. *Limits to Physical Explanations*

The third main area of argument for the deep further fact draws on the arguments and conclusions of this book. In particular, I contend that these arguments and conclusions show limits to what can be explained from a physical, objective, impersonal viewpoint; and therefore support and protect a view of personal identity which cannot be so explained.

It seems clear that a purely physical viewpoint cannot explain consciousness and mental events: indeed, it is arguable that this viewpoint cannot on its own (that is, without the aid of consciousness, and reference to the substantive reality disclosed in consciousness) go beyond explaining abstract relationships in a cosmic code. More specifically, in Part II, I argued that the physical viewpoint cannot explain plausible reasoning, and human decision and choice. Accordingly, it would not be surprising that the physical viewpoint cannot explain the personal identity or continuity of the self.

Thus I accept, on the arguments of this book, that such things as choice, conscious actions, decisions, reasons, etc. cannot fully be explained in terms of objective physical events and laws connecting them (even in terms of quantum physical states and their development). The objective physical events can in theory go so far as to explain the available alternatives, and to give probabilities concerning the outcome: however, where the actual outcome is chosen or done for reasons, there is, from the objective physical viewpoint, an unexplained residue. It is only from the subjective viewpoint that the explanation is complete, though not conclusive, in terms of the person's choice or action made or done for reasons.

Similarly, it seems to me, continuity of the person or the self is not fully explained by physical causation or continuity, or by overlapping memories (which themselves are physically based). There is a residue here as well, which is, I suggest, closely associated with the residue in the other case; and more specifically with that subjective aspect of the person which makes the choices and does the actions. I have suggested that both physical and mental events manifest an underlying reality, and this underlying reality involves a conscious subject which makes decisions not fully explicable on the basis of physical events: it seems reasonable to suggest that the continuity of this subject involves the full scope of the underlying reality, and not merely the physical manifestations of it.

What can be said about the properties of this residue; or, more accurately, the properties which this residue contributes to the whole person?

Since my capacities, inclinations, and characteristics in general, indeed everything that makes me unique and distinguishes me as one individual from all other individuals, seem to be physically manifested (such physical manifestation being the outcome of heredity, environment, and previous decisions), the residue, considered in isolation, may not have or contribute properties peculiar to me. This residue, in so far as it can be considered apart from what is physically manifested, may be undifferentiated in different persons: simply, as it were, a 'piece' of a universal undifferentiated 'something'. In the case of human beings such as myself, this 'piece' combined with my physical (biological and environmental) heritage develops into a unique whole, in which the respective contributions (of residue, genes, environment, and decisions made by the whole) cannot be distinguished.

I think our ordinary common-sense view of persons is that each individual comprises a physical organism with a capacity for conscious experience and conscious action: a complete physical–mental being. The argument of this book is that the capacity to act (and in particular to decide, to choose, to reason informally) cannot be fully explained by objective events and laws. If that is correct, it will not be surprising if the continuity of each person similarly cannot be fully accounted for by objective events and laws (that is, by physical continuity and/or by memory, which itself has a physical basis). Indeed our resistance to the Parfit conclusion, suggesting that there is something more to our continuity than can be explained physically, gives some support to the view of this book that there is something more to our capacity to decide than can be explained physically. I suggest that each of us comprises a totality which is not exhausted by (in the sense that it is not fully explicable in terms of) one's physical being: there is something more, a residue, which may be undifferentiated, at least in origin, but which is essential to two vital aspects of one's being, namely subjectivity and continuity.

17.4.4. *Is it All or Nothing?*

It may be that the residue which I argue for does not provide an all-or-nothing identity, much less survival after death in any simplistic sense. I think Parfit's arguments do strongly suggest that, if there are selves which involve such residues, they can be divided and perhaps also can be aggregated or combined, and that, in extreme cases, continuity is a matter of degree. Further, the whole constituted by the physical and the mental (including the residue) changes as the physical aspect changes; and perhaps all that distinguishes one individual from another is manifested in the physical aspect, does not exist prior to an individual's life, and will not (in any straightforward way) survive his or her death. Whether or not an undifferentiated 'residue' may pre-exist the individual's life, and/or survive his or her death, and if so what significance this would have, I will touch on in Chapter 19.

What I do suggest is that this residue, rather than mere physical or psychological continuity, is essential to the continuity of the whole which rationally justifies one's particular concern about one's own future. One needs the memories to know one's identity and one's past, but what I call the residue is also needed to give reason to *care* particularly about one's past and one's future.

Consistently with what I have said before, I accept also that animals which are conscious are physical–mental beings, whose nature and behaviour are not fully explained by their physical characteristics; so perhaps they too have a residue which goes to complete this explanation, and also contribute to the continuity of each individual.

It may also be that if there are conscious subsystems within each individual person which can make decisions independently of the fully integrated 'self', there is some sort of residue associated with each of these, too. Perhaps it is the case that the residue can divide and reunite, as in the case of Libet's experiment: if the response to the skin stimulation is decided by a conscious subsystem, and the sensation and response are only later integrated into the overall integrated self, it seems plausible to regard the subsystem as involving a residue which can divide from, and reunite with, the integrated self. Again, when the corpus callosum is cut, what was the residue for the whole person is divided between the 'selves' associated with each hemisphere. If the corpus callosum could be rendered inoperative, and then restored, one would expect that the divided residues would again unite.

So, I accept that Parfit's arguments do make it hard to view my continued existence as an all-or-nothing matter, not admitting of degrees. Quite apart from his arguments based on the psychological, physical, and combined spectra, I am inclined to accept that, if I were to be severely brain-damaged, so as substantially to change my intellectual functions and change my personality, the result, I think, would not be the complete continued existence of my present self; similarly the onset, for example, of senile dementia. My identity, and my continuity, do seem very closely linked to the physical manifestation of myself.

However, I am persuaded by the arguments of this section that there is a deep further fact of personal identity or continuity. It is difficult to reconcile all the arguments for the deep further fact, and all the arguments for the relativism of identity and continuity. This is another area where I think our language and our concepts may be inadequate; and perhaps one must at present be content with complementary views which are not wholly consistent.

17.4.5. *Conclusions*

What then is the 'self' of a human being? I think it is best regarded as the aspect or aspects of a human being which consciously experiences and acts. Unless there is particular reason to look at it otherwise, the self is simply the human being having conscious experiences and acting consciously. The self so considered generally continues so long as the human being continues; though in the extreme cases considered by Parfit it may be that it can be divided and reunited. The self or some part of it will continue so long as sufficient of the brain continues; and if it is to be equated with anything objective, it is with the quantum state of the relevant part(s) of the brain, at least when the brain is active to a sufficient extent (so that the relevant quantum state is developing in an appropriate way).

The objective description, whether in terms of the brain or the relevant quantum state, does not account for all properties of the self. It can account for the physical continuity of the brain, the psychological continuity of overlapping memories, and the occurrence of alternatives between which choices are made. It cannot account for the choices actually made, or for the deep further fact of continuity.

My view has dualistic features. It involves a dualism of aspects of:

1. events: namely, physical and mental events;
2. things: namely, the brain, and the self with its experiences/actions;
3. causation: namely, mechanistic and random causation (on the one hand) and causation by choice for reasons (on the other);

4. continuity: superficial physical and psychological continuity (on the one hand) and deep continuity involving the 'residue' (on the other).

The second aspect of each category cannot satisfactorily be described or explained by a purely objective account. A satisfactory description and explanation require terms appropriate to a subjective account.

17.5. Postscript on Replication

I have to this point accepted that although the creation of exact Replicas of human beings may never be a practical possibility, it has no deep theoretical impossibility. My arguments for the deep further fact, and my conclusions, lead me to question this.

I believe that to allow for the possibility of identical replication is to accord undue primacy to the physical, and to make the mental secondary and dependent upon the physical (in a way in which the physical is not dependent on the mental). The thesis of this book qualifies the principle of supervenience at least to the extent of saying that identity of mental properties requires not merely identity of detectable physical properties, but also identity of quantum states. It further suggests that one should accept as prima facie correct one's intuitions about one's own continuity and the continuity of other persons; and also accept that there is more to the quantum state underlying the brain than is manifested in the detectable physical objects and events of the brain, namely (at least) the capacity to be conscious and to choose. It then becomes reasonable to suggest that linked with this capacity is what provides the continuity of the self; and that the properties which provide this capacity and this continuity are no less properties of the underlying quantum state than are physically detectable and measurable properties.

This leads on to the view that the making of a Replica may be impossible in principle, because it would require replication of the underlying quantum state, including the properties which constitute *inter alia* continuity, and would accordingly violate that continuity. Although when dealing with ordinary artefacts, we readily accept that matter can be manipulated so as to produce exact replicas, there may be limits in principle to such manipulation: there may be an exclusion principle which operates here. We saw that the Pauli exclusion principle decrees that there cannot be more than one matter-like quantum particle in the same quantum physical state. There could perhaps be another exclusion principle which operates in the area of subjective continuity, such that physical structures which would interfere with subjective continuity are excluded. Thus it may be impossible in principle to create an exact Replica of a person, at least so long as the Original continues to exist, because the personal continuity of the Original excludes the existence of a Replica.

If the main thesis of this book is correct, and the brain is so constituted that choices can be made between possibilities thrown up by developments of the quantum state of the brain, one may readily accept that it is impossible in principle ever to know, much less reproduce, the full details of the quantum state of any brain. Having regard to quantum indeterminacy, and to the implications of chaos theory, it would seem that an infinity of information would be required. On this approach, the impossibility of knowing, and therefore of reproducing, the quantum state of the brain, may 'protect' the theory that this quantum state involves properties related to continuity, which preclude replication. This situation can be compared with the way quantum physics is 'protected' by the absolute limits on measurement discussed by Heisenberg. It enables one to assert that the world created by, and constituted by, one human self has its own status and identity, and is not merely secondary to its physical manifestation.

There is a similar (and perhaps stronger) point made by Roger Penrose, first in Penrose (1987: 275), and recently in Penrose (1989: 269–70). He argues that it is impossible to produce a copy of a quantum state without destroying the original, and also impossible to produce more than one copy—because otherwise non-measurable indeterminate quantum states could be multiplied so as to be macroscopically measurable. This gives further support to the non-replication thesis.

18

Time

THE subject of time is examined in many major works of philosophy and science; and a detailed treatment of it is beyond the scope of this book. However, it is necessary to say something about it, for this reason. There is a widespread opinion that science requires a view of time which accords reality to *time* (to ascription of time *order*, to notions of earlier and later); but denies reality to *tense* (to the distinctions between present, past, and future). This view is not necessarily inconsistent with my account of mental events, mind, choice, and rationality, but it does not sit easily with it.

I will discuss this view of time, and will contend that science by no means requires it. I will contend briefly for a contrary view of time, according to which the content of reality is (really) changing, the past is gone and no longer real, the future is to come and not yet real.

Such a view, if correct, would provide support for the general approach of this book. It also is relevant to the world-view which I will outline in the last chapter.

18.1. Time and Tense

At the heart of what is sometimes considered the scientific view of time is the notion that each event has its location in space-time, its existence or happening being considered tenseless. This does not mean one can say that each event is always happening, because the word 'is' has connotations of *tense*, and the word 'always' suggests that the event is not confined to its own temporal location. However, one can use 'is' tenselessly (as comprehending 'was', 'is', 'will be', without connotation of tense); for this use, I will use capitals: 'IS'. Then one can say, on this view, that each event of the past, present, and future IS happening at its location in space-time.

This view denies objective reality to the passage of time. It suggests that it is wrong to limit reality, or to attribute any special status of being, to 'now', to the present; that, rather, the past, present, and future ARE all equally real, of equal ontological status. On this view, nothing changes: things only appear to change, as seen from a viewpoint limited in relation to time. In reality, there ARE simply different states of things at earlier and later times.

18.1.1. *Reasons for the Tenseless View*

There are a number of reasons advanced for this approach.

In the first place, in order to distinguish past, present, and future, one needs to be able to identify the present. But every event is in the present, when it happens; and no measuring instrument is either necessary or useful in detecting the present. Laws of physics refer to time, but only as a dimension, like space: earlier and later times, and quantities of time, are referred to, and can be measured. However, the laws of physics have nothing to say about past, present, and future. From the viewpoint of physics, all events simply ARE.

This approach fitted well with the thoroughgoing determinism suggested by classical physics. However, it is seen as receiving particular confirmation by twentieth-century physics, especially the theory of relativity (see e.g. Putnam 1979e and Davies 1983: 124). This theory seemed to preclude any idea of an objective universe-wide lapse of time. There is no absolute simultaneity of spatially separated events, independent of the frame of reference adopted, and any frame of reference is as valid as any other: so, it seemed there could be no unequivocal universe-wide 'present'; and physical reality could not be regarded as a universe-wide temporal progression of events or states.

The theory of relativity gave rise to the view expressed by Herman Weyl, and apparently held by Einstein, that the world is a four-dimensional continuum (as illustrated by Minkowski diagrams), which is progressively exhibited to conscious beings: the 'block universe' view, as William James described it. Weyl writes:

The objective world simply *is*, it does not *happen*. Only to the gaze of my consciousness, crawling upward along the lifeline of my body, does a section of the world come to life as a fleeting image in space which continuously changes in time. (Weyl 1949: 116)

A further reason for denying reality to the passage of time, and for accepting a tenseless view, is found in quantum electrodynamics, in particular as illustrated in the diagrams (based on Minkowski diagrams) developed by Feynman. These diagrams and the associated mathematics not only show a symmetry between directions in time (as indeed does Newtonian mechanics), but also indicate an equivalence between particles (such as electrons) travelling forwards in time, and anti-particles (such as positrons) travelling backwards in time.

The view has also been supported by philosophical arguments, most notably that advanced by the British philosopher J. M. E. McTaggart. McTaggart (1908) argued that tense involves events having three predicates, namely past, present, and future: thus, an event happening now would be present (with respect to present events), future (with respect to past events), and past (with respect to future events). These three predicates are incompatible. The incompatibility is not avoided by suggesting that the predicates merely indicate relations, respectively indicating a relation to events of different times; because *these* latter events would similarly have the same three predicates. And so on *ad infinitum*. The conclusion is that there is no solid ground, as it were, to give such relations as may be suggested by the predicates past, present, and future, any content. The predicates are therefore either incompatible (if they are not mere relations) or devoid of content (if they are).

18.1.2. *The Arrow of Time*

Although there is symmetry between directions in time in the equations of Newtonian mechanics, and in some aspects of quantum mechanics (such as the Schrödinger equation and the interactions illustrated by Feynmann diagrams), it is generally recognized that such symmetry is broken in systems involving many particles. This is expressed by the second law of thermodynamics, which is stated in various ways:

1. in a closed system, the amount of usable energy tends to decrease;
2. a closed system tends to move from a state of greater order to a state of lesser order;
3. in a closed system, entropy tends to increase (where entropy is a particular measure of disorder, often represented by the letter S: it is defined to equal $k \log P$, where k is a constant, called Boltzmann's constant, and P is the number of ways in which a particular state of the system can be achieved).

The second law can be understood as suggesting that irreversible thermodynamic changes occur towards states of increasing probability (because the number of ways of achieving them increases). It is well illustrated by the example of two dogs, one with more fleas than the other, where there is equal probability at any time of any flea jumping from one dog to the other. The tendency will be for the number of fleas on each dog to equalize, because there is a greater probability at any time of a flea jumping from the dog which then has more fleas on to that with fewer fleas, than vice versa.

At one time, the second law was considered of practical importance, but not of great theoretical significance, in that it was believed that, given sufficiently comprehensive and accurate information, the same results could be calculated on the basis of Newton's laws of motion. However, as we saw in Section 1.4, it has in this century become clear that to obtain such comprehensive and accurate information is impossible; and not merely practically impossible but theoretically so.

Accordingly, it seems that the second law and associated statistical laws are not in any way secondary to laws dealing with apparently reversible processes, such as Newton's laws of motion: they indicate irreversible processes, which do not reduce to reversible processes.

These considerations suggest that there are irreversible processes which indicate a direction of time, the so-called 'arrow of time' which distinguishes later states from earlier states. However, this by no means requires the rejection of the tenseless view of time: it merely gives the earlier–later distinction a significance it did not have according to Newtonian mechanics. It indicates general respects in which later states differ from earlier states; but it does not give any significance to *tense* distinctions between past, present, and future.

18.1.3. *Time and Consciousness*

From the viewpoint of human beings, however, and presumably also from the viewpoint of other conscious entities, the distinctions between past, present, and future seem both real and significant. Time seems essentially different from space, in that it seems to pass irreversibly; and this seems necessarily so, because by choices, decisions, and actions a conscious entity affects the future, on the basis of experience of the past. If a conscious entity were purely passive, on the other hand, there would appear no reason why time could not be reversed, and events 'replayed' as on a video machine.

To a person, the past, the future, and the present mean more than just time order:

1. The past means not merely periods earlier than the present, but regions of time (or space-time) the events of which the person can know or be informed of or (if sufficiently close) perceive, but cannot intervene in or affect. Once events are past for a person, they are always past: they no longer exist or happen, and they are unchangeable. For each person, the past is continually expanding.

2. The future means not merely periods later than the present, but regions of time (or space-time) the events of which the person cannot yet know or perceive, but can intervene in and affect, at least indirectly. Events of the future do not yet exist or happen, they are uncertain, and for each person the future is continually contracting.

3. The present is the interface between the past and the future. It is a meeting-place of experience (looking to the past) and action (looking to the future). It appears to involve movement in time: the conscious entity seems to move towards the future, the events done and/or experienced seem to slip into the past. The present appears to be real in a way in which the past and future are not: the past was real, but is so no longer, while the future is not yet real.

All this seems to amount to more than just saying that events can happen earlier, later, or at the same time as each other. For one thing, it suggests that future events are uncertain and may be affected by action, while past events are unchangeable. It suggests also that the content of reality is changing; and that what was once the content of reality, at some time in the past, is no longer such content or any part of it.

18.2. Against the Tenseless View

18.2.1. *Criticism of Arguments for Tenseless Reality*

On examination, many of the reasons for denying reality to tense and to the passage of time do not amount to much.

1. Equations of physics. The fact that many equations of physics (such as Newton's laws of motion, and Schrödinger's equation) are indifferent to time direction says very little, especially now that it is recognized that other equations, representing irreversible processes and not indifferent to time direction, are no less fundamental.

2. Quantum electrodynamics. Much the same can be said about the equivalence of particles 'travelling forwards in time' and anti-particles 'travelling backwards in time'. It might seem a desirable simplification, required by Occam's razor, to assert this equivalence; and thus to assert the possibility, for fundamental particles at least, of travelling backwards in time. This, in turn, would appear to require denial of reality to the passage of time. However, one may accept that the recognition of such an equivalence in the mathematical representation of micro processes is a useful simplification, without accepting that this requires recognition of the reality of such equivalence, in the sense that fundamental particles and anti-particles really can and do travel backwards in time.

In particular, it should be noted that there is no proof of time-reversal: there is nothing like the proof of non-locality constituted by the Aspect experiments on the basis of Bell's theorem. It will be recalled that these experiments proved non-locality by showing that quantum events at location A can 'know about' (that is, be correlated with or affected by) quantum events at location B, instantaneously and without any light-speed (or less) causal connection. There is absolutely no proof that a positron at time t can 'know about' (be correlated with or affected by) events which happen at the later time $(t + x)$ either to it or to an electron with which it then interacts. It is merely a matter of mathematical equivalence and convenience, and that is far short of proof.

3. McTaggart's argument. Philosophical arguments such as those by Mc-Taggart seem to assume some at least of what they are supposed to prove. The attribution of incompatible predicates 'past', 'present', and 'future' to events depends upon first assuming that events ARE (i.e. exist tenselessly); and that 'past', 'present', and 'future' can be regarded as properties which such tenselessly existing events may have. If that assumption is not made, then one can deny that events can be said to be past or future, and still be considered to exist or to EXIST. When an event is past, *the fact that it happened* may be considered as still part of reality, and so as (in some sense) existing: but the event itself may be considered as not existing or EXISTING. As regards a future event, the fact that such an event has not yet happened may be considered as

part of reality, and as (in some sense) existing: but the event itself may be considered as not existing or EXISTING in any sense at all. On this approach, one may consider that only present events, events which are now happening, exist. (There may be some flexibility in defining 'now' or 'the present', and I will return to this.) The view that time really passes, that things really change, denies the tenseless existence which McTaggart's argument assumes. And if there is no tenseless existence, one can never get to the stage of attributing the incompatible predicates 'past' and 'future' to events conceived of as actually existing or EXISTING.

4. The merging of space and time. The remaining arguments against the reality of tense are those associated with the theory of relativity. One part of these arguments, namely the merging of time with space, which is said to be suggested by special relativity, faces a curious problem. It will be recalled that special relativity postulates a space-time interval between events which is the same for all inertial frames of reference, given by $\sqrt{(x^2 + y^2 + z^2 - c^2t^2)}$. If $x^2 + y^2 + z^2 < c^2t^2$, the interval is given by an imaginary number (the square root of a negative number), and the events have timelike separation; and each is inside the light-cone of the other, and one of the events can have a macroscopic effect on the other. And if $x^2 + y^2 + z^2 > c^2t^2$, the space-time interval is given by a real number, and the events have spacelike separation; so that each is outside the light-cone of the other, and neither can have any macroscopic effect on the other.

Now, in order to treat the time dimension as a dimension just like space (and to make the space-time interval analogous to a Pythagorean hypotenuse in four-dimensional space), time t must be multiplied not only by the speed of light c, but also by the imaginary number i; so that the interval can be expressed $\sqrt{\{x^2 + y^2 + z^2 + (cit)^2\}}$. (Some formulations give the interval as $\sqrt{(c^2t^2 - x^2 - y^2 - z^2)}$, so that it is the spatial dimensions which are imaginary; but since we are discussing the assimilation of time to a spacelike dimension, this can be disregarded.)

So the time dealt with in the four-dimensional continuum of space-time is *not* the 'real' time which we experience, but an 'imaginary time'. Hawking (1988: 139) suggests that it is meaningless to ask which is real, this mathematical 'imaginary' time or the 'real' time of our experience: it is 'simply a matter of which is the more useful description'. However, I suggest that the fact that it is an imaginary time which is merged with space into the four-dimensional space-time suggests a fundamental distinction between space and time, rather than their assimilation. Indeed, it suggests that space-time (or at least its time component) is a mathematical model which does *not* correspond to reality.

5. The denial of a universe-wide present. The strongest arguments suggested by the theory of relativity are associated with the denial of any universe-wide 'now', from which it appears that the limitation of reality to what exists or is happening 'now' must be incoherent. However, while the

theory of relativity has substantial experimental support, and while certain aspects of it seem unlikely to be overthrown, there is now reason to question at least its assertion of the equivalence of all frames of reference.

For one thing, as pointed out in Whitrow (1980: 307), the discovery of a universal background radiation, considered to be left over from the Big Bang, seems to provide a universal frame of reference, namely that according to which this radiation appears isotrophic, that is, the same in all directions. One then has reason to attribute particular significance to this frame of reference, and to simultaneity of distant events according to this frame of reference.

More fundamentally, the denial of locality established by Bell's theorem and the Aspect experiments strongly suggests another way in which aspects of relativity theory may be relevantly undermined. It has been shown that inter-action with a quantum system comprising two separated particles apparently instantaneously affects spatially separated parts of the system: quantum theory thus suggests simultaneity of distant (quantum) events, and accord-ingly it suggests some preferred frame of reference according to which such distant events *are* simultaneous.

Quite apart from the above matters, however, it can be contended that special relativity does not in any event require the denial of the reality of tense. The rejection of a universe-wide 'now' does mean that the specification of what is past and so no longer real, what is present and real, and what is future and so not yet real, is less straightforward than it would otherwise be. However, as I will attempt to show in Section 18.3, no incoherence or incon-sistency or even implausibility is involved.

18.2.2. *Problems of the Block Universe View*

On the other hand, the denial of the reality of tense does involve very substan-tial problems in relation to our conscious experiences and actions. It will be recalled that the view of conscious experience associated with Weyl is that of the world as a four-dimensional continuum, which is progressively exhibited to conscious beings. It has been said that the mind is like a torch beam progressively lighting up different parts of this 'block universe'.

This view seems untenable. Any reasonable view of mind and conscious-ness requires a close association between subjective mental events and object-ive physical events. On the Weyl view, the physical events are given a tenseless existence in a four-dimensional world, yet the associated mental events ('the gaze of my consciousness') are supposed in some way to move (in time) through this world. If physical events, existing tenselessly, are associated with consciousness, then presumably the gaze of consciousness would be similarly tenseless. One would not have the world *progressively* exhibited to consciousness, or something like a beam of torchlight moving through the four-dimensional world. Rather, the gaze of consciousness, the beam of torchlight, would be tenseless, in its locations in space-time, to the same extent as its associated physical events. A similar (but perhaps less fundamental) point is made by Whitrow:

If past, present, and future did not apply to events in the physical world but only to mental events, a peculiar difficulty would arise when we consider the interaction of these kinds of events. For, whereas physical events would neither come into existence nor cease to exist but would just be, mental events certainly come to be and cease to be in our personal experience. (Whitrow 1980: 350)

In other words, it seems hard to understand how physical events, in relation to which time is said to be merely one of four dimensions of space-time, could be closely associated with, or a different aspect of, or interact with, conscious experiences and actions, in relation to which time passes.

If one denies the reality of tense, and asserts a tenseless existence in which time is merely one of several dimensions, one must surely assert this of mental events as well as physical events. One can argue then that each instant of consciousness EXISTS at its location in space-time (or the location of associated physical events): it merely does not *seem* that way, because the *content* of consciousness is such that awareness is only of earlier events, there is no awareness of future events, there is apparent affecting of future events by action, and there is apparent movement of the self to the future while experiences and actions appear to slip into the past. On this view, my *other* instants of consciousness (that is, apart from what I regard as my 'present' instant of consciousness) are inaccessible to me at 'present', except by memory or inference: but those other instants of consciousness none the less EXIST in the same way as the 'present' instant of consciousness. The other instants of consciousness ARE real, existent, just as are (and ARE) the instants of consciousness of other persons, whether 'present', 'past', or 'future'.

Some understanding of this idea can be had from the following consideration. I could repeatedly experience the event whereby I write these words; and if, on each occasion, the *content* of my consciousness is the same, and if I never remember or infer more than one such occasion, I will never be aware that the event occurs more than once: only if the content of my consciousness was *different* on a 'subsequent' occasion, by reason of having a recollection of a 'previous' occasion, or I otherwise remembered or inferred more than one such occasion, would I have such awareness. The view I am considering does not postulate such *repeated* occurrence of events, but rather their continued tenseless existence; but the concept is similar.

This view seems to be quite happily accepted by physicist and cosmologist Stephen Hawking: see his explanation in Hawking (1988: 146–7) of why human beings remember events in the past, and not events in the future. The view is also developed at some length in Lockwood (1989, ch. 15). It is, I think, less implausible than the previous one considered, whereby consciousness 'moves' in time through a tenseless universe; but it still appears implausible. It seems to be an essential part of conscious experience that its content is continually *changing* over time: such change is as much part of the content of consciousness as things, events, experiences, and actions. In our experience of the specious present, we experience events as ordered in time and as passing, with later events coming into our experience as earlier ones pass out of it. It could be suggested that the change is only apparent: just as a moving picture is made up of a succession of still frames, our apparently changing experiences could be made up of a succession of closely occurring 'still' momentary experiences. Each of these 'still' momentary experiences could then be considered as EXISTING, with the content of each including the memory of many of the immediately earlier experiences and thereby giving the impression or illusion of change. Such a view is a possible one but not, I suggest, a readily acceptable one.

A notion of repeated, or continually EXISTING, momentary experiences, certainly seems counter-intuitive: it is not how experiences seem to us, and it involves making them more extended and more complex than they seem to be. It is surely a view which one would adopt only if there is a convincing reason for doing so.

Further, the appearance of the passage of time in which the self moves to the future, and experiences and actions move to the past, is very deeply rooted, and is very difficult to give up. It seems essential to our minds that we can understand a situation and act to affect it: this seems built in to our understanding of the world. Of course, the main thesis of this book is that such understanding is substantially correct; and, if so, the tenseless view is probably incorrect. But, quite apart from this, the fact that it conflicts with deeply rooted views of ourselves is a reason not to accept it unless there are convincing reasons in favour of doing so.

To approach the matter another way, when I consider what exists, or what EXISTS, it seems clear that my previous experiences do not exist, or even EXIST: if they did, it surely would not be 'I' who is having (or IS HAVING) them, because I am having my present experiences. It is therefore reasonable to believe that their associated physical events do not EXIST, and that similarly all past experiences and physical events do not EXIST. In this way, the unity and continuity of the self seems to be associated with the passage of time.

Another reason for doubting the tenseless view is that it makes laws of nature superfluous. They can have no causative or formative role because (on this view) everything just IS. Laws of nature would merely be regularities linking earlier and later events in the pattern of events. It might be suggested that they would still be useful in enabling conscious entities to have some understanding of the world, and to exercise some control over it: but there is no point to this either, as the total existence of conscious entities (on this view) similarly just IS. It may be contended that to look for a role or purpose in laws of nature is a futility: there is no reason to think they have a role or purpose. But it seems legitimate to ask why the world is constituted as it is, that is with laws of nature, rather than being chaotic and without such laws.

There may ultimately be no answer, but that is surely a position to be driven to rather than to assume.

Indeed, it is implicit in much scientific endeavour that laws of nature are not mere correlations between earlier and later states and events, but are laws concerning cause and effect; so that earlier states and events together with such laws are seen as causing later states and events (but not vice versa). The laws are seen as having a causative and efficacious role, not merely a role of correlation. Most scientific work on cosmology (the origin and development of the universe), evolutionary biology (the origins and evolution of life), chemistry and biology generally, and indeed much of physics, takes this approach. This may be because scientific experiments must have a before and after, cause and effect, approach, and because it is so difficult to think in any other way. However, this circumstance does point to the artificiality of the tenseless viewpoint.

All the above reasons lead me to think that the view which accords reality to tense, and to the passage of time, is the preferable one. However, an exposition of such a view, if one fully accepts the theory of relativity and its denial of a universe-wide present, is not straightforward. I will attempt a brief exposition in the next section.

18.3. A Changing Reality

The view I suggest is that the content of reality changes over time, in a way that it does not change over space; and that it is possible to identify what is present and real, what is past and no longer real, and what is future and not yet real.

If one does not accept the equivalence of all inertial frames of reference, but rather accepts that there is a unique or preferred universe-wide frame of reference according to which a universe-wide 'now' can be determined, then there is no problem. As we saw, such a view has support from the existence of background radiation seemingly from the Big Bang, and particularly from the non-locality of quantum states as demonstrated by Bell and Aspect; but it conflicts with some aspects of the theory of relativity.

I want to suggest that, even if one completely accepts the theory of relativity and the equivalence of inertial frames of reference (and so denies the existence of any unique or preferred universe-wide frame of reference), one can still give an account which adequately identifies what is present and real, what is past and no longer real, and what is future and not yet real.

As I have suggested, such an account is not straightforward. The difficulty of giving such an account is illustrated by Putnam (1979*e*), where 'the man on the street's' view that 'All (and only) things that exist *now* are real' is shown to be inconsistent with special relativity, on the assumptions (made at p. 198) that I-now am real, that at least one other observer (who may be in motion relative to me) is real, and most importantly that 'If it is the case that all and only the things that stand in a certain relation R to me-now are real, and you-now are also real, then it is also the case that all and only the things that stand in the relation R to you-now are real'. (This last assumption Putnam calls the principle that There Are No Privileged Observers.)

Putnam shows that if 'relation R' is taken to be simultaneity in the observer's coordinate system, there is an inconsistency between special relativity and his assumptions; and that, while the inconsistency can be avoided by deleting 'and only' from the No Privileged Observers (NPO) principle, it can then be shown that future things and past things are real.

Thus, suppose that I-now am real, and you-now are spatially separated from me-now, but simultaneous with me-now in my coordinate system. Then, even if you-now are moving relative to my coordinate system, you-now stand in relation R to me-now, so that you-now are real. However, since you-now are moving relative to my coordinate system, it follows from special relativity that in your coordinate system I-now may not be simultaneous with you-now, in which case I-now do not stand in relation R to you-now; whereas something with the same space coordinates as me-now, but earlier or later in time than me-now, may be simultaneous with you-now in your coordinate system, and thus stand in relation R to you-now.

So, I-now am both real and (according to the NPO principle) not-real; and if to avoid this one deletes 'and only' from the NPO principle, then by appropriately choosing the position and motion of you-now, one can show that past and future things are real.

This is quite a strong argument. It seems reasonable to accept some kind of NPO principle. Although the significance of tense relates to each person's relationship with the past, present, and future, there does seem something wrong with a view according to which you-now can be real for me-now, whilst by the same criterion I-now am not real for you-now. Such a view is a kind of solipsism. It seems reasonable to require of a theory of tense that it accord present reality to other minds, and at the same time provide that I-now am similarly real for those other minds. Yet Putnam's argument suggests that if one accepts an NPO principle, then one has to accept the reality of past and future things.

To avoid these conclusions, it is necessary to modify the 'man on the street's' view, or the NPO principle, or both. I think there are plausible ways of doing this.

For example, one can say that for me-now, all things (which were) located entirely on the surface of or within the light-cone extending from me-now towards the past are no longer real; while all things (which will be) located entirely on the surface of or within the light-cone extending from me-now towards the future are not yet real; and all things in the region of spacelike separation from me-now are present and real.

Then, if you-now are within the region of spacelike separation from me-now, I-now am real for you-now (because spacelike separation is independent of coordinate systems). However, there will be *some* differences between what is real for you-now and what is real for me-now. Parts of my past and future light-cones will be spacelike separated from you-now, and vice versa; so that, for example, some things (and minds) which are not yet real for me-now will be present and real for you-now.

I do not think this is an unreasonable view:

1. It accords present reality to other minds, and provides that I-now am real to those other minds on the same criterion.

2. The significance of tense relates to each person's relationships with what can affect him or her (the past), what he or she can affect (the future), and the interface between the two (the present). This significance is not disturbed by the suggested approach, which recognizes the plain fact that each person can be affected by different regions of the past and can affect different regions of the future.

3. The degree of fuzziness introduced into the present is not great, for ordinary purposes. The timelike width of the region of spacelike separation from me-now at the most distant point on earth (that is, about 13 000 km from me-now) is only about 26 000 (i)km, or less than one-tenth of a second times ic: so, in relation to things on the earth, the fuzziness of the present extends up to a maximum of less than one-tenth of a second.

4. The approach has some support from the mathematics of special relativity. If one takes the spacelike intervals of space-time as being real (which seems a reasonable approach, because the intervals are expressed in units of space), then, as we saw, timelike intervals are imaginary: and it seems appropriate that the interval between two things, one of which is real (because present to me-now) and one of which is not real (because past or future to me-now), should be expressed as an imaginary number.

I do not see it as a fatal objection to this approach that there is residual observer-dependence in what is present and real: since it is the consciousness of individual persons which gives significance to the passage of time, there is no incongruity in this position.

So, even if all inertial frames of reference are equivalent, I think the view which accords reality to tense is preferable to any block universe view; and, as I have said, there are in any event good reasons to doubt the equivalence of all frames of reference.

18.4. Timeless Existence

Is it possible that, consistently with the reality of tense and the other views put forward in the previous section, there could be some sort of timeless or tenseless existence?

This is a matter on which I cannot say much. I prefer the view which accords reality to tense over that which does not. However, the topic is one where our language and ideas may be inadequate to express the truth; and so it may be one where it is appropriate to apply Bohr's idea of complementarity. From one point of view, perhaps, tense is real; from another, perhaps, it is not. Both views may in some limited way be true.

Something similar occurs in relation to space. We know that in one sense the world is non-local, by reason of EPR correlations which are indifferent to distance. However, access from the non-local quantum world to the world of macro events is restricted, and thus the possibility of faster-than-light communication is excluded.

Conceivably, there could be a timeless or tenseless existence, so long as access to and/or from it is restricted, so that the alteration of the past is precluded. Further, to be consistent with the main theses of this book, one would have to contend that, even though a timeless existence would permit knowledge of what is now (in this timed existence) the future, this does not make it any less true that the future will come about partly by reason of choices still to be made by conscious agents. Such a view is possible, I think: it is easier to maintain than compatibilism (of determinism with free will), because determinism by quantitative cause and effect seems inconsistent with choice for non-conclusive reasons. As we saw, such determinism means that rationality is wholly based on logic and habit, so that 'weighing' non-stringent reasons and 'judgement' based on such reasons must merely be misleading expressions of some logical and/or habit-based process.

19
Sketches for a World-View

In this book I have argued for a particular approach to the brain–mind question, involving a rejection of mechanism. In this final chapter, I will begin by making something of a summary of this approach, and some general remarks about it. I will then move into more speculative areas. On the basis of the views of this book, I briefly consider such matters as morality, the soul, God, and the purpose of life.

19.1. A Dualism of Causation

As suggested by the title of this section, I consider the approach of the book to be dualistic, though not in the sense of Descartes's dualism of substance. The starting-point is my distinguishing of mental events and physical events. These may be merely two aspects of the same events, or two manifestations of the same underlying events, rather than entirely different and distinct classes of events: but at least, I suggest, they are different aspects, one subjective and the other objective. This distinction between two different classes of events, or different aspects of events, is itself hardly enough to justify the label dualism. No doubt many such distinctions could be drawn. What justifies the label for my approach is that the distinction is associated with two different types of causation: that is, two different ways in which earlier events give rise to later events, or (to put it another way) in which there is development over time of states.

So far as physical events are concerned, earlier events give rise to later events according to wholly deterministic quantitative rules, combined with random 'jumps' for which only probabilities are given by quantitative rules. That is, from the physical viewpoint, time development of states occurs in two ways: some is continuous and deterministic, governed by rules such as those represented by the Schrödinger equation; and some is discontinuous and indeterministic, comprising sudden changes for which only probabilities can be derived from the relevant rules.

So far as mental events are concerned, earlier events give rise to later events, in some cases at least, by decision, choice, action; and the linkage is then not in terms of deterministic rules and/or random jumps, but rather in terms of action by conscious subjects on the basis of reasons. From the mental viewpoint, time development in such cases is influenced (not determined) by the reasons on the basis of which the relevant conscious entity decided, chose, or acted; but these reasons do not reduce without residue to the application or operation of deterministic rules and/or random probabilistic steps.

Of course, time development of the two classes of events must coincide. It seems clear that mental events and certain physical events are closely associated: on my approach they are different manifestations of the same developments of underlying quantum states. Even more clearly, certain physical events (such as the upward motion of my arm) are sometimes intended by mental events (such as the subjective intentional raising of my arm), and may be considered either as a consequence of the mental event or as an external aspect of the mental event. The physical event or events involved in the upward movement of my arm must presumably follow, in the way appropriate to physical events, from other physical events. The mental event constituted by the intentional raising of my arm (considered subjectively, internally) must presumably arise in the way appropriate for mental events, that is, I must do it for reasons.

My contention is that the coincidence of the two forms of time development arises in the following way. The time development of physical events in the brain operates computer-like to give rise to quantum mechanical superpositions of alternatives, among which (according to the physical viewpoint) quantum physics could in principle assign probabilities. The decision, choice, or action which is the relevant mental event is done by a conscious subject for reasons, with the interaction of the subject and the reasons in effect spanning the computer-like development of alternatives and the probabilistic occurrence of one of such alternatives. In theory, the interaction of the subject and the reasons could be analysed in terms of a logical production of alternatives and a judgemental weighing of them (or, more usually, a series of such steps), in which each judgemental weighing may come down to a simple holistic judgement of 'like' or 'unlike', or something similar. However, in practice such analysis would be extremely difficult, if not impossible.

The outcome of the judgemental weighing of and selection among alternatives (from the subjective viewpoint) corresponds to the probabilistic occurrence of one such alternative (from the objective viewpoint). I have suggested that in normal conscious intentional action, where there is little 'mental effort', a highly probable alternative occurs; that mental effort may correspond to the occurrence of less probable alternatives; while difficult decisions, between apparently evenly matched alternatives, may correspond to cases where associated quantum probabilities are similarly evenly matched.

Although the dualism of this book does not depend upon the existence of two different substances, the distinction drawn between the physical and the mental is of sufficient moment to make it reasonable to follow Popper's terminology, and to identify two 'worlds': the World 1 of the physical or objective, and World 2 of the mental or subjective.

I have suggested that states considered as states in World 1 develop mechanistically, according to deterministic rules plus random probabilistic steps; whereas states considered as states in World 2 develop in accordance with decisions based on reasons. Corresponding to this difference is a difference in approach which may be taken to achieving results: the World 1 approach of manipulating matter, and the World 2 approach of discussion, reasoning, persuasion, etc. Other associated differences between the two worlds may be summarized as follows:

1. Within or from the viewpoint of World 1, human beings are physical organisms, whose identity and continuity can be considered only in terms of physical continuity and/or psychological continuity (as realized physically); while within or from the viewpoint of World 2, they may be considered persons or selves, with some deeper identity and continuity.

2. Within or from the viewpoint of World 1, there is no basis for regarding time as other than a dimension, or for selecting particular times or periods or volumes of space-time as 'the present'; while, within or from the viewpoint of World 2, there is basis for regarding time as passing, and for selecting particular times as 'the present'.

3. In World 1, physical states and events as manifested (i.e. on the basis of statistics of the possibilities–probabilities world of quantum states), special relativity holds good and precludes faster-than-light communication or causation; while, in World 2, in certain respects space is irrelevant, time orders of events are not alterable by Lorentz transformations, and in some sense at least faster-than-light communication and/or causation occurs.

4. Most generally, World 1 without World 2 is not only a play staged before empty benches, as Schrödinger (1967: 100) would see it, but an abstract code. It is only World 2 which provides meaning.

Some of this World 1 coded material is manifested both by particular types of physical events, namely events of the brain, and also by mental events, the subjective experiences–actions of conscious entities. The only mental events we directly know of are matter-dependent to this extent, and perhaps all mental events are (although I argue to the contrary in Section 19.4). However, from the last paragraph, matter as we know it is mind-dependent in certain respects: for its appearance, for its characteristics as we perceive them, perhaps for its extension in space, though probably not for its place in time, and probably not for its existence as code. On the approach of this book, mind or World 2 transcends the code of World 1 by 'creating' matter as we know it out of abstract code, and by determining by reason between alternative quantum possibilities to which the code gives rise.

The approach is somewhat Kantian, in suggesting an underlying reality very different from our perceived reality. However, it differs from Kant in suggesting that we need not be entirely ignorant about the underlying reality: not only can we say it is sufficiently rich and complex to encode reality as we perceive it, but also science, and in particular quantum physics, can tell us quite a lot about it. See d'Espagnat (1983: 157).

These views are different from what I have suggested is the present consensus. The consensus tends to deny many of what I have suggested to be characteristics of World 2. In general terms, it asserts that the world (not just World 1) is in substance physical and objective; that time development of events and states is mechanistic (deterministic plus random probabilistic steps); that there is no time development of states decided upon for reasons and not reducing to mechanism; that persons have no identity or continuity other than physical continuity and psychological continuity; that time does not really pass. Some consensus views allow the existence of mental events, of some sort of World 2; but they do not allow for it the characterization which I suggest, in particular, for time development by non-mechanistic choices based upon non-conclusive reasons.

I have found it possible to reconcile the two worlds, as I view them, through quantum physics. My reconciliation is one which I think could stand even if quantum physics was superseded as a theory of matter, because any superseding theory would have to account for the relevant features of quantum physics, in particular indeterminism and non-locality. Further, even if scientific developments did raise problems for my reconciliation, this would not necessarily refute my view of World 2. The arguments for it are strong: I do not think there is any other satisfactory answer to what I believe are *hard* questions for the consensus position, in particular:

1. *Why* do we have consciousness-based information (Chapter 4)?
2. How could there be plausible reasoning which is rational *and* mechanistic *and* plausibly justified (Chapter 5)?
3. What is consciousness *for*, in evolutionary terms (Chapter 6)?
4. How can we *know about* and *act upon the basis of* mental properties, if mental properties make no difference to the world (Chapter 7)?
5. How can basic physics be expressed without reference to *observers*—either individual consciousnesses or a community of human observers (d'Espagnat 1989, and Chapters 14 and 15)?
6. What explains the *unity* of conscious experience; and *why* does Nature provide faster-than-light quantum connections in order to maintain light-speed appearances (Chapters 15 and 16)?

Rather than abandon my view of World 2, I could well adopt something like Bohr's complementarity: this would accept the existence of World 1 and World 2, with the characteristics indicated, as complementary aspects of the world. In so far as they were inconsistent, this could indicate an inadequacy of the language and/or the concepts used in relation to either or both worlds.

19.2. Morality

Morality as I understand it concerns primarily the rightness and wrongness of actions (which may include thoughts). It also concerns virtues and vices of character, and perhaps also the rightness or wrongness or goodness or badness of events and things and states of affairs; but I think that actions are central.

The importance of morality is presently under challenge in two main ways. First, it is often said that morality is only a matter of emotions or preference: it has no objective truth or validity, and is outside the domain of reason. Secondly, it is said that since all events including actions are determined mechanistically in accordance with laws of physics, morality is pointless: what will be will be. The arguments of this book are relevant to both these contentions.

Its relevance to the second contention is obvious. My suggestion is that, although from the physical point of view actions may be determined mechanistically (with random steps), from the mental point of view they may be *done* through decisions based on non-conclusive reasons. If so, then obviously morality may be an important aspect of those reasons, and thus play an important part in what is decided, and thus in what happens.

The first contention involves a number of related points. A distinction is often drawn between fact and value, with morality being an aspect of the latter. Morality, then, like other matters of value, is not regarded as concerning facts or matters to which the concepts of truth and falsity are applicable. Morality, like other questions of value, is not in the domain of reason, which relates to facts: it is, rather, in the domain of emotion or preference, in which each individual can make a choice. Indeed, if any person is not concerned about morality, not interested in being moral, then there are no reasons which can persuade him otherwise. Moral conclusions, concerning what 'ought' to be done, can never be derived from factual premisses, concerning what 'is' the case. For all the above reasons, there cannot be consensus on matters of morality, as there can generally be on matters of fact.

In various ways, the arguments of this book are relevant to different aspects of this contention. In general, they can be used to challenge the supposed distinction between fact and value, and to support a contention that certain matters supposedly on the 'value' side of that distinction may be matters of fact, so that truth and falsity are relevant.

If matters of value were purely matters of (non-rational) emotion and preference, then there would be grounds for maintaining a sharp distinction between fact and value. However, questions in the realm of value, concerning morality and the rightness of actions (and indeed also concerning aesthetics and the merits of works of art, literature, and music) are matters amenable to reasoned consideration and debate. Initial emotional responses can be modified by reason, and one can attempt to come to views on such matters in which emotion and reason are in harmony, and in which one's particular prejudices or preconceptions play as little a role as possible. The circumstance that value statements ('ought' statements) cannot logically be derived from statements about value-free facts ('is' statements) does not mean that value statements cannot be facts, cannot be true or false. The arguments of this book are relevant here in at least three ways.

1. Plausible reasoning. The view that one cannot derive an 'ought' statement from an 'is' statement was forcibly stated by Hume. Equally, however, he pointed out that a universal proposition cannot be derived logically from any number of particular premises (the problem of induction). I have contended that by fallible plausible reasoning, which requires consciousness, the exercise of judgement, the weighing of alternatives, etc., one can pass from particular premises to general propositions; not of course with certainty of truth, but, rather, aiming at a likelihood of approximate truth. Similarly, I suggest, one can pass from premises about value-free facts to value judgements by fallible plausible reasoning, aiming for likelihood of approximate truth. Just as some consensus can be achieved in relation to general factual propositions, so also some consensus can be achieved in relation to some value judgements. In particular, there can be consensus that certain actions are wrong, for example killing people because of their race. More mundanely, many people would agree with Nagel when he defends 'the unsurprising claim that sensory pleasure is good and pain bad' (1986: 156). As with general propositions, finality and certainty of truth is probably unattainable: reasons are potentially infinite, and further relevant reasons can always be found.

2. The role of emotion. Even in reasoning on matters which are generally regarded as factual, emotion plays a part: for example, the role of beauty in assessment of scientific theories. Generally, I contend that emotion, while it can be irrational, is a part of rationality; so that the involvement of emotion in value judgements does not make them non-rational.

3. Matter as mind-dependent. I have argued that the world *as we know it* does not exist, valueless, independently of our minds. What does exist, independently of our minds, can be regarded as some sort of code for the world as we know it, the latter being created from the code by our minds. However, in the world so created by our minds, facts and values are entangled: for example, one cannot separate the objective features of a painful sensation and its abhorrence. Values are said to be subjective, and not to be objective matters of fact, because they are created by our minds; but on this approach facts about the world are similarly so created.

It might be said that none of this answers the point that different people give different weight to various plausible arguments; and that at the extreme some persons give no weight whatsoever to moral considerations.

The former point applies also, of course, to plausible arguments about scientific theories, and explains why different opinions can be held by experts even on what would generally be considered matters of (value-free) fact. In relation to morality, as in relation to matters of scientific fact, one can try to be as objective as possible, and to recognize and avoid being influenced by one's own peculiarities.

The latter point assumes, I think, a narrow view of morality, and of moral considerations. I take morality in a wide sense, as being concerned with finding answers to the question 'What shall I do?', which continually faces us all, and which we all are continually answering, if only by action: it is for this reason that moral reasoning is sometimes called 'practical reasoning', or considered as one type of practical reasoning. The question is not expressly asked in relation to every individual action; nor is it asked only immediately prior to individual actions, or in relation to individual actions. We may ask, for example:

What shall I do now?
What shall I do next week?
What shall I do in circumstance *x*?
What shall I do with my life?

It is sometimes suggested that morality concerns only *some* considerations relevant to these questions, namely those other than selfish considerations; or possibly those which relate to what one ought to do rather than what one wants to do. I do not think that such restrictions are appropriate: I think that proper regard of self is part of morality, and also that one may want to do unselfish things.

Thus, I think that when any person asks 'What shall I do?' he or she is seeking the 'right' action, not in any narrow sense of 'right' which excludes consideration of self-interest, but simply in the sense of 'the thing to do'. He or she can then bring to bear on the question *any* relevant consideration, including short, medium, and long-term self-interest, facts about the world and about human beings, suggested moral rules, commitments to others, interests of others, and so on. In adopting this approach, I am not unmindful that Nagel warns us 'that the convergence between rationality and ethics should not be achieved too easily, and certainly not by a simple definition of the moral as the rational or the rational as the moral' (1986: 200). However, I am not here attempting a comprehensive account of morality, but merely expressing some views as being related to the main arguments of this book.

On that approach, the right action might be considered an idealization of what a highly rational human being would judge to be 'the thing to do', having regard to all relevant considerations. The problem sometimes raised about morality to the effect that there is a choice whether to be moral or not, and that there is no argument which could compel a person to choose to be moral rather than amoral, does not really arise. All that is required is that a person be prepared to 'listen to reason', and to apply reason to the question of what to do.

That may not be a short or simple matter. There is no limit to reasons relevant to the question of what to do. In particular cases, appreciation of vast amounts of material may be necessary for a satisfactory decision. For example, a person wishing to come to a fully considered view on the place to accord self-interest in practical reasoning may find it necessary *inter alia* to read and understand the arguments concerning the nature of the self and its implications contained in Parfit's *Reasons and Persons* (Parfit 1984), and also counter-arguments such as those briefly outlined in Chapter 17 of this book.

It might be objected that this still does not get to grips with the position of a person who says 'I am only concerned about looking after my own interests' (perhaps also those of a limited number of other persons) 'and am simply not concerned about anyone else, or about any so-called moral considerations.' However, what I say is that there are good plausible arguments against that position, which would carry weight with any person willing and able to examine the matter in sufficient depth. These arguments are particularly in two areas to some extent along the lines put in *Reasons and Persons*: first, to the effect that such position is likely to be (at least indirectly) self-defeating; and secondly, to the effect that what *is oneself* (and so one's own interests) is not as simple as it appears.

It might be further objected that such arguments would not make the person moral, but would only cause him to look differently at what is in his own interests; whereas a moral person is one who is prepared to do the right thing because it is what he ought to do, not because it would be in his own interests, properly understood. There is some force in that objection, but I think it on the one hand underestimates the change in attitude that arguments in the two areas could bring about, and on the other perhaps overestimates the importance of conscientiousness. Willingness to do the right thing, just because it is what one ought to do, is important in morality: but if it is coupled with a misguided view of what one ought to do, and an unwillingness or inability to examine this view rationally, it can be dangerous, to say the least.

If it is the case, as I contend, that certain answers to the question 'What shall I do?' specify (or are) actions which are in truth wrong, while other answers are actions which are in truth right, how does one go about deciding what to do? It is obvious from what has gone before that I say that one should be prepared to reason about the matter, to look for and evaluate plausible arguments in relation to the possibilities. A number of things can be said about such arguments:

1. In difficult cases, it is likely that there will be conflicting considerations, and it is also likely that they will be non-commensurable: that is, there will be no way in which they can be reduced to a single scale. I have already referred briefly to my contention in Hodgson (1967) that the one and only plausible

candidate for such a single scale, namely the value of consequences of the alternatives, cannot reasonably be adopted: that contention was (shortly) that the adoption of such a utilitarian view was inconsistent with the making of personal commitments which most of us regard as a necessary part of valuable human existence. This book provides a further argument to the same conclusion: because strict determinism does not hold good, and because of the great differences which can quickly result from the most minute differences in initial conditions, it cannot be said that the hypothetical consequences of actions which are *not* done are determinate. At best, one can deal only in foreseeable probable consequences, and this further robs utilitarianism of plausibility.

2. In any but the clearest cases, one will never have certainty of truth: one can only use fallible plausible reasoning, and there are likely to be conflicting, non-commensurable reasons. This consideration immediately points strongly to the rationality of tolerance and humility. One must act oneself, and one must therefore decide what one is to do, and come to judgements on what is the right thing to do. However, since these judgements are fallible, one must be careful before either seeking to impose one's own views on other people, or undertaking actions harmful to other people simply because one believes (arrogantly, it might be thought) that it is right to harm them. Where one's views differ from those of another, it may of course be appropriate to engage in dialogue, this being conducive to the evaluation of the plausible arguments for and against the different views; but in general it is not appropriate to seek to impose one's views on others.

3. Moral rules may be involved in such arguments in various ways. They may be put forward as having authority (perhaps divine authority, as with the Ten Commandments; or perhaps the authority of some revered person); or as giving guidance, in that they embody what has been learnt through long experience; or as the terms on which people live together in communities, each person giving compliance in return for the benefit of compliance by other persons in the community; or as a necessary part of a rational morality, associated with the view that an action which is right for one person must be right for any person in relevantly similar circumstances. I would suggest that plausible moral arguments may involve rules in any of the above ways, and that no single one of them exhausts the significance of rules. I would also suggest that not all moral arguments involve rules: in particular, arguments about facts, about likely consequences, about attitudes.

4. The involvement of moral rules in such arguments may be complex. For example, suppose that it is necessary for the good of a particular society that for most of the time a sufficient number of people live law-abiding and productive lives, and that children be raised in family circumstances. Then, this may not require *universal* observance of generally accepted rules about compliance with the law, the work ethic, and sexual behaviour, but it would seem to require widespread respect for such rules. If the society is a modern

Western society, such rules are unlikely to be considered to have divine authority or otherwise to have universal validity; and it may well be that the existence of a minority which questions or rejects these rules, and indeed occasional breaches of them by the majority, is positively beneficial (in preventing dull uniformity of behaviour and promoting social experimentation and reform). However, it may also be that in such a society general respect for some such rules needs somehow to be maintained and promoted. What then would be the appropriate attitude to these rules? Should it be such as, on the one hand, to promote general respect for the rules; while, on the other hand, avoiding mere lip-service and hypocrisy? And if so, how?

Without attempting here to develop any substantial moral theory, I will conclude by suggesting that some features of such a theory would be:

1. the fundamental role of rationality;
2. the importance of caring about oneself, others, and the world;
3. the importance of an attitude of reverence for life and nature in all its aspects, to counter the tendency to seek to dominate and manipulate nature, and to counter materialistic and hedonistic values;
4. the importance of humour, to prevent reverence becoming inappropriate or pompous;
5. the importance of honesty, and of using one's abilities to the full.

19.3. The Soul

In Chapter 17 on the self, I argued for the view that there was some 'deep further fact' of identity and/or continuity of the self, apart from physical and psychological continuity. I contended that this was necessary to make sense of what we understand a person (including oneself) to be, and of a person's role in mental events. However, I did not elaborate much on what this deep further fact involved, and I did concede that arguments such as Parfit's made it unlikely that the deep further fact was one of all-or-nothing one–one identity.

In this section, I consider briefly some possible implications of my approach for the notion of the soul, which seems to include the self but to go beyond it, in suggesting some existence which is not matter-dependent. So far, I have been content to assume that mental events, and therefore the self, are matter-dependent, at least in the sense that they only occur in conjunction with certain quantum states, which are at the same time manifested in physical events. I now wish to consider whether or not there is reason to think that the self or soul can exist otherwise.

In the next section, on God, I will be considering a number of arguments for the view that some sort of mind (and so, some sort of self) has existed at least as long as matter has existed, and (having regard to what science tells us about the beginning of time and matter, the Big Bang) has probably existed in a way not dependent on matter. That would suggest the existence of at least one 'soul'. In this section, I approach the question more from the viewpoint of individual persons.

I pursue two main lines: first, I argue against the likelihood of a straightforward individual survival after death of each person, and against the existence, in or for each person, of an individual soul capable of existence independently of matter; and secondly, I look at the possibility of regarding each person as an expression of some more universal underlying soul or mind or consciousness, which transcends the life of individual persons.

The first point is supported by several of the views considered in Chapter 17 on the self:

1. that personal identity is not always a matter of all-or-nothing one–one identity;
2. that selves can be divided, and (at least in theory) combined;
3. that everything which makes an individual person unique seems to have a physical manifestation, which is itself the outcome of heredity, environment, and previous decisions;
4. that within the life of a person, his or her self may change greatly along with changes in his or her age and health.

These considerations suggest a view of the self as being, as a matter of fact, the subjective aspect of a person, and accordingly as:

1. changing;
2. manifested by the person's physical make-up and subjective aspect—the result of heredity, environment, and previous decisions;
3. making decisions between alternatives presented and weighted by the physical make-up, but not determined by it;
4. subject to affection by damage to the physical make-up, and even to division.

If a person *were* to survive death in a straightforward way, a question would arise of what version of the person it would be. Would it be the person as he or she was just before death, perhaps suffering from senile dementia? Would it be as he or she was at some earlier stage of life, and if so what stage? What of a person who dies as a young child? It may be suggested that what survives is the 'essence' of the person, not the person as at any particular time of life. But what could this 'essence' be? The particular characteristics of each person at any time apparently have a physical basis, and that physical basis is continually changing: there seems no ground for postulating an essence which is particular to the person, but not manifested in the person's changing physical make up.

On the other hand, and this brings us to the second point, I have argued that there is ground for postulating a 'residue' (over and above physical and psychological continuity as usually understood) which is essential to the deep further fact of identity or continuity; and which (over and above the objective physical events of the brain) enables completion of the subjective explanation of conduct. The very fact that decisions are made between alternatives suggests an input from something non-physical. I have suggested that this residue may not contribute characteristics peculiar to me, but may be, as it were, a 'piece' of an undifferentiated 'something'. This leads to the speculation that the residue is provided by some more universal mind or psyche.

This might be suggested also as follows. We postulate that there is a common reality which contributes to, and is represented by, experiences of different persons. Appearances of things exist in Popper's World 2; but not 'free-floating', only as seen by a conscious entity. And it is the seeing of something by someone which is associated with physical events in the brain. We infer a common world, which provides the appearances for all of us, and which the appearance relates to or is 'of'. Might we not also postulate a common reality which contributes to, and is represented by, the self of each of such persons. Just as the physical brain provides to the self the experience of a common material world, may it not also provide to the experience a self, which is an expression, a particular limited shaping or form, of some more universal subject ('us'!)? The brain shapes experience from (coded) material provided by the physical world: may it not also shape the self from material provided by another common world?

On this view, each person may be considered as a unique node of connection between a more universal mind and what we consider to be objective reality. Then, when the person dies, what is destroyed is a unique structured link between the reality behind the self (that is, the underlying mind) and the reality behind the experiences (that is, the common objective world). On this approach, I as a person with particular characteristics (personality, outlook, feelings, abilities, interests, indifferences, everything which goes to make me an individual, different from others) did not exist prior to my conception and will no longer exist after my death: all my characteristics seem too closely dependent on my physiology. However, there may be a more universal psyche of which I (and each person, maybe each conscious entity) am an expression, and a node of connection with the material world. In so far as I am constituted by *that* underlying psyche, I existed before conception and will exist after my death.

A similar approach could be expressed as follows. Reality—and specifically the quantum world of possibilities–probabilities—is such that the occurrence of certain patterns (or patterns of change) involves consciousness. One might say that the 'stuff' of this world is the 'stuff' of consciousness. When such patterns occur, the consciousness is *active*, to varying degrees: the stuff of consciousness is such that the patterns involve activity, in varying degrees. However, this stuff is indistinguishable for all persons and animals: only the patterns are distinguishable. The stuff may therefore be, or be a medium of, a common or universal consciousness. Perhaps it is itself a bearer of a consciousness with wider experiences and activities, with access to the world as we know it only through the links which constitute conscious entities. Perhaps such limits to access are what avoid conflict with relativity theory. Such a consciousness might be analogous to a mainframe computer, with conscious entities as the terminals giving access to and from the material world as we know it.

On this sort of view, the 'I' who thinks, feels, acts, and decides may be considered as some sort of amalgam of my physiology and the underlying consciousness (or psyche) giving rise in combination to my particular psyche, my total subjective aspect. This is not solely produced by my genes and my environment and my previous decisions, but also by my piece or aspect of a universal psyche. It is this *totality* which decides, and is (within the limits of my peculiarities) free.

On this approach, each person constitutes a link between what might be called a 'universal mind', and 'matter', such link being structured in a way unique to that person. The unique structure of each link is what makes each person, each self, unique—and, it may be asserted, of immeasurable value. The self is limited in time to each individual's life span, but may, nevertheless, have eternal significance: (1) as a unique expression or manifestation of the universal mind; and (2) because it can make a unique contribution to the mental and the material world.

On the latter aspect, one can say that the flourishing of each person can enrich the mental world (that is, the universal mind and its individual manifestations) and the material world, both directly and through promoting the flourishing of other persons. For example, adopting Popper's terminology, World 3 (creations of World 2, the mental world, which on my approach would include the universal mind as well as individual minds) enriches the material World 1, and in turn enriches World 2.

I have already referred to one possible metaphor for the relation between a universal mind and individual minds, namely that of a mainframe computer and terminals. Another metaphor, closer to that used in relation to similar ideas by Eastern religions, is that of a river of consciousness, with each individual being a branch stream, which begins at or after conception and rejoins the river at or after death. During life, each stream may alter, even divide (as in split-brain cases) or even (theoretically) join with another stream. Each person's concern for his own life is a branch stream's concern for its own future. It is natural and it is rationally justified; but should not be overstressed in view of the common origin and common destiny of all streams. Such a metaphor is inadequate in many respects. For example, it does not express the uniqueness and complexity of each individual brain–mind, or how the consciousness of each 'branch stream' begins in an inchoate way and (for human beings) develops into the full consciousness of a person. Further, the metaphor points against a continuing role for the 'river' during the life of the 'branch stream', whereas it may well be that the 'branch' is an expression of the 'river' throughout its life, and indeed that the 'river' has the consciousness of all its 'branches'. However, it perhaps correctly suggests that each 'branch' would not have access to the consciousness of other 'branches' or, during the lifetime of the 'branch', of the 'river' itself.

I have mentioned that the approach has perhaps some affinity with some Eastern religions. Perhaps also it has some affinity with Jung's idea of the collective unconscious. It is true that Jung asserts that 'a "universal consciousness" is a contradiction in terms, since exclusion, selection, and discrimination are the root and essence of everything that lays claim to the name "consciousness" ' (1983: 224). However, Jung's view of the psyche is that it includes not only consciousness, but also 'the illimitable field of unconscious occurrences as well' (p. 213). The latter include 'contents' which fall below the threshold of consciousness, and disagreeable contents which have been repressed (p. 214). These contents are presumably contents of something: they cannot be free-floating experiences, one would think, but must presumably be associated with some entity of which they *are* contents; just as for Jung consciousness is 'the relation between the ego and the psychic contents' (p. 212). In other words, Jung seems to limit consciousness to the ego and its contents, and to deal with the unconscious as quasiconscious contents of some other psychic entity or entities. His collective unconscious then might not be so different from my postulated universal mind; and such a mind might be conscious, if the application of that term is not restricted to the ego and its contents.

19.4. God

Let us accept the main thrust of this book, that certain conscious entities can make decisions which are not random but are made for non-conclusive reasons. Let us also accept that the passage of time is not an illusion, so that later events are dependent on earlier events in a way which earlier events are not dependent on later events. Let us now suppose (perhaps contrary to the thrust of the previous section) that such conscious entities are all matter-dependent, and so can exist only in association with the occurrence of appropriate (quantum) physical processes.

Then, it would seem, there must have been a period of some millions of years, from the Big Bang to the first emergence of conscious organisms in the universe, when only physical events occurred (that is, no mental events occurred) and all events were determined solely by deterministic laws and chance, in accordance with the quantum theory. With or following the emergence of conscious entities, however, there also must have emerged for the first time a new influence on outcomes, namely the capacity of conscious entities to choose between alternatives previously subject to pure chance. In time, this capacity evolved to the rationality of human beings.

This scenario seems to me highly implausible. It postulates that consciousness, choice, and reason, which themselves contribute to the determination of outcomes, emerged out of a pre-existing purely physical world in which all outcomes followed according to laws prescribing a combination of deterministic development and chance.

It has been asked, and doubted, if physical laws of nature can exist unless embodied in or instantiated by the physical systems which obey them. Whether or not they can, at least they do not need such physical systems in order, within the limits of language (including mathematics), to be formulated or expressed. However, the 'laws of nature', such as they are, concerning determination of outcomes by choice and reason, cannot be so formulated and expressed; and, so it would seem, could not in any sense be said to have existed prior to the emergence of conscious entities. Is it reasonable to think that without there existing any such 'laws', the physical, the deterministic, and the random suddenly gave rise to the conscious, the choosing, and (subsequently) the rational?

One reaction to this might be to say that it shows how unlikely the thesis of this book is, and in particular how specious my argument from evolution is. However, my argument from evolution merely starts with the fact of consciousness, and contends that its selection by evolution suggests it is advantageous and therefore efficacious: it does not say, or need to say, that evolution explains how consciousness emerged. And, for myself, the arguments of Part II seem strong enough to stand up, despite this apparent problem of emergence.

What I think the implausibility of the scenario suggests is the falsity of the supposition that conscious entities are all matter-dependent or even matter-associated; that they can exist and rational decisions can be made only in association with the occurrence of appropriate (quantum) physical processes. It is more reasonable to believe that the mental and the rational has not emerged from the physical, but somehow has existed at least as long as the physical has existed. Our present understanding of the physical is that it commenced with the Big Bang; and from our understanding of what physical conditions were like then and for some time after, it seems clear that there were then no physical structures appropriate to support any conscious entity or entities. The plausible conclusion is that any conscious entities then existing were not matter-dependent, as we are; and if we keep postulated entities to a minimum, we arrive at one conscious entity, not matter-dependent, existing at the time of the Big Bang.

This conscious entity, which may be identified with God, may plausibly have used rationality to devise physical laws of nature, just as human beings have used their lesser rationality to discover them (or at least, devise laws which with increasing likelihood increasingly approximate to them). It seems more likely that a rational being devised physical laws than that quantitative physical laws operating mechanistically on physical states gave rise to a non-mechanistic rationality which transcended the physical. There is still the 'who created God?' question. However, I feel more comfortable with the idea of a rational being without a beginning than with the idea of a physical world (with or without a beginning) which at some stage is without consciousness and rationality, but which later gives rise to consciousness and rationality: a rational being could have devised physical laws of nature, but physical laws of nature could not have devised rational beings (and, as I have said, seem unlikely to have given rise to rational beings by chance).

That is my basic argument for the existence of God. It is reinforced, I think, by other considerations:

1. The primacy and importance of consciousness. Without it, nothing might as well exist.

2. The residue. What I have called the residue in relation to the making of conscious decisions and the explanation of personal identity or continuity, and have associated with an idea of a universal consciousness (which may be, or be associated with, God) points to a transcendental consciousness.

3. Human qualities. Human beings have qualities with seemingly transcendental significance: creative, intellectual, artistic, moral. These go beyond what seems necessary for survival and reproduction, and also seem suggestive of a wider spiritual world.

4. The moral world. If it is the case that certain actions are right or wrong, some transcendental viewpoint is suggested. Of course, a simple approach falls foul of the question 'Is it right because God commands it, or does God command it because it is right?' Then, if the former, why does a command make it right? If the latter, God's command is superfluous. However, I think the question is one which requires Bohr's complementarity answer ('both and neither'), until we can understand the problem and express it more adequately.

5. Aesthetics. The beauty of the natural world, and of some human creations and qualities, again point to a wider spiritual world.

6. Need and benefit. Without religious belief, life can seem empty. Acceptance of religious belief can elevate and inspire (although if the beliefs are of certain kinds, and especially if they are intolerant and dogmatic, acceptance of them can produce disasters). Perhaps human beings need a role model of an ideal, powerful, rational, and caring personality. Simply to conceive of such a role model, and to seek to emulate it and maybe draw strength from it, seems to produce enhanced performance. It might be said that human beings for whom this is true are not adult and autonomous; although such a contention may itself manifest arrogance and lack of proper aspiration.

7. Cosmic coincidences. The laws of nature are such as to make life possible, but in many areas any slight variation of them would make life impossible. There are many who believe that, even given the laws as they are, the likelihood of life emerging is vanishingly small. The weight of this argument should not be overstated, because as Stephen Jay Gould tells us:

Any complex historical outcome—intelligent life on earth, for example—represents a summation of improbabilities and thereby becomes absurdly unlikely. But something has to happen, even if any particular 'something' must stun us by its improbability. (Gould 1985: 395)

There are powerful arguments *against* God's existence, in particular, God's obscurity and the problem of evil. Both are based on the assumption that God, if God existed, would be good. On my approach, this is a reasonable assumption. My principal argument is for the existence of a highly rational being at the time of the Big Bang. High rationality, on my approach, would involve (at least) approximate knowledge of what is good and right, and recognition of the weakness of reasons for not choosing them. My subsidiary arguments (4) to (6) point in the same direction.

If God is good, then, why is God so obscure? Why does God not manifest Itself, and indeed make it easier to know true moral values and the like? And why is there so much evil—suffering, wrongdoing, destruction of nature—in the world?

The best answer that can be given to these questions is to the effect that our insight is limited, and that perhaps things have to be that way: either because God's power is limited, or because obscurity and evil are necessary for some greater good, or both. To trivialize the problem, but not, I hope, too much, a puzzle is no fun if you know the answer, and a good story needs a villain (or at least, negative aspects within at least some of the characters). So on balance, to me, the arguments *against* do not outweigh the arguments *for*.

I must say, however, that arguments of this type seem to me convincing against some conceptions of God: for example, a conception of God as a good, all-powerful, and all-knowing Being, who created the world and human beings, and who will one day select one group of human beings for eternal bliss and another group for eternal misery. It seems to me inconceivable that a benevolent God would create human beings knowing that some (indeed, perhaps some known individuals) of them would suffer eternal misery. The supposed 'justice' of such an outcome is no answer. For one thing, even if one were to suppose (as is obviously not the case) that all persons have capacities and opportunities giving them all a fair chance of choosing good rather than evil, human beings fall into a continuous spectrum of merit from the very good to the very evil, making division into 'sheep' and 'goats' arbitrary and unjust (at least in relation to those near whatever dividing line is chosen). But, in any event, the creation of conscious beings knowing they will suffer eternal misery seems so abhorrent as to be impossible for a rational God.

A further point on the problem of evil: it is perhaps interesting to note the relevance of God's relation to time. If God is outside time, as it were, God can see all (from the beginning of time, if there is one, to the end, if there is one), including Its own interventions (if any) in the world in which time passes. There is no inconsistency with free will, but there may be some assurance that if God is benevolent all will be for the best. On the other hand, if God is within time, even God could not know the future, and in particular (even if otherwise all-knowing) could not know what choices human beings will make. Things might not be for the best, because human beings might make unexpected choices. (Indeed, on this view, how could *heaven* be possible? Saints in heaven, if they have free will, could still choose evil.)

Lastly on God, and evil, I return to my subsidiary argument (6). Can a religion be uplifting and inspirational without also being dogmatic? All the great religions appear to have a belief content which is inconsistent with that of other religions. And it is difficult to see how one can obtain the uplift and inspiration of a religion, without assenting substantially to its belief content.

The answer, if there is one, may be as follows. Religious truth is so far beyond our language and our ideas that it cannot be expressed by us except as allegories. Such truth may be allegorized, and thus in a sense approximated, in different ways, which are mutually inconsistent, but which are all approximations to the unexpressable truth. The best one can do is to choose the allegory that seems best to suggest the unexpressable truth, and adhere to that. Doing so, then, does not involve rejection of the others, even if they are inconsistent.

Thus, the Christian religion teaches that individual selves or souls are created by a loving God, while Zen Buddhism teaches that there is no individual self and no God. Indeed, one finds paradoxes within the doctrines of one religion: for example, the teaching in various religions that it is by losing one's self that one gets closest to one's true self.

In so far as one religion, for example Christianity, has claimed to be the one true religion, it seems contrary to the above. Such a religion may have great merits and insights: for example, as suggesting a God which cares sufficiently about evil and suffering to choose to be subjected Itself to terrible evil and suffering; and as placing care for others above compliance with legalistic rules. But can it be appropriate for any religion to claim unique status?

19.5. The Purpose of Life

It will be apparent from what I have said that I do not look forward to a straightforward individual personal survival of my death; though I do see a possibility of a wider consciousness which somehow includes and expresses itself in me (and all other persons). This wider consciousness may itself be God, or may in some way approach or be related to God.

Does this help at all in determining if there is a purpose of life, and if so what? The expression 'the purpose of life', and the related question 'why are we here?', raise questions of language. The word 'purpose' usually refers to the purpose of a conscious entity. Related questions could be seeking an explanation by way of cause and effect (so that some scientific account of cosmic evolution and the evolution of life could answer it) or for an explanation by reference to a purpose of a conscious Creator.

None of this seems satisfactory. We do not think that whatever purposes or objectives we as human beings happen to have constitute 'the purpose of life', or explain why we are here. We may consider that a scientific cause-and-effect account of the evolution of human beings is valid, but we do, I think, look for something more when we ask 'Why are we here?' The purpose of a conscious Creator similarly seems an inadequate answer. This has been explored in some detail in Nozick (1981: 585–94). For example, why should the fact that God had a purpose in creating us make that *our* purpose? And if we need to refer to a superior being for our purpose in life, why does God not need to refer to a further superior being for His, Her, or Its purpose?

What we are looking for, I think, is a purpose that we should try to recognize and pursue, which our lives if correctly lived will fulfil in fact, and which is right and good. It may also be God's purpose for us. I think that the notion of a purpose of life makes more sense in relation to a God, or some wider consciousness, than it otherwise would. The point is similar to that in relation to morality. If the only conscious entities are those of the animal (including human) world, then there could, it seems, be no purpose of life apart from the actual purposes which individuals select for themselves.

The answer to Nozick's questions can only be similar to that in relation to the similar questions concerning the right and the good, relying on Bohr's complementarity principle. Our purpose in life is so, because it is God's purpose; and it is God's purpose because it is right, and the true purpose in life: the full truth cannot be comprehended by our ideas and our language.

If there is a purpose of life, I would suggest that it has to do with the flourishing of conscious entities, especially human beings (and superhuman entities, if any, such as a universal consciousness and/or God); the preservation and enrichment of the natural world (indeed, all worlds); and the promotion of beauty, goodness, happiness. These may sound like 'motherhood' values, but they are, I think, not devoid of content, or even of controversy. Human flourishing is placed at, or almost at, the top of values to be promoted: as indicated earlier, each person may be considered of immeasurable value, not only as a mortal, but unique, complex, rational, feeling being, with vast capacity for good (and evil); but also as a manifestation, in a uniquely valuable form, of a universal subjective.

I have not included among the purposes of life the worship of God: as with the idea of judgement, the idea of God creating human beings for the purpose of their worshipping God seems unsatisfactory. We should appropriately value all conscious entities, and in the case of God this may mean worship. However, our purpose (and indeed probably God's), if any, must be more like the flourishing of all consciousness and the enrichment of worlds.

If something like this is the purpose of life, then that will be a matter to be taken into account in deciding moral questions. The flourishing of human beings would involve such things as lack of suffering, health, happiness, knowledge and understanding, virtue, good personal relationships, fulfilment of potential; and also (whether as means or end) peace and justice. The enhancement of worlds would involve both preservation of what is valuable, and creation of further valuable things.

None of this directly provides answers to traditional moral problems (consequences against principle, interests of self against interests of others), or the particularly difficult moral problems of the present time (conservation against utilization of natural resources for genuine needs, abortion, genetic engineering, etc.). Some general approaches are suggested, however.

So far as contemporary problems are concerned, this book (if it is on the right track) emphasizes how little we really know, and how far short of a full account of human beings would be even (say) a complete mapping of human DNA, or a complete unravelling of the neuronal circuitry of the brain. The book is therefore against action which could be justified only in the event of there being virtually complete knowledge, such as the application of genetic engineering to human germ cells (see Suzuki and Knudtson 1989). Thus, while acknowledging the force of philosopher Jonathan Glover's contention (in Glover 1984: 56) that opposition to changing human nature by genetic engineering is hardly justified by the history of the twentieth century, I incline to the view that even his careful discussion of the problem greatly underplays the risks.

In general terms, the book suggests that in dealing with human problems a proper balance should be sought between the 'scientific' approach of manipulating matter, and the 'humanistic' approach of appealing to the mind.

In relation to all the questions of this chapter, and indeed the two previous ones, however, I am inclined to think that our concepts and language are inadequate, and that seemingly contradictory answers may each have an element of truth: Bohr's complementarity again.

As appears earlier, I find difficulty in accepting individual immortal souls, and eternal bliss or damnation presided over by a distinct omnipotent God; yet I want to accept the enchantment or holiness of nature, the immeasurable worth of each person, a wider consciousness, and the great importance of decisions made by persons.

I recognize the mutual incompatibility of religions, and suggest that each can only be an allegory of a truth unexpressable by our language. I suggest that a commitment to values, and to beliefs, is good, and (for some people at least) necessary for full flourishing; but this must not involve rejection or intolerance of other values or beliefs—unless, of course, these values or beliefs can be seen to be not merely incomplete, but positively wrong and/or harmful.

So again there seems truth in both of mutually incompatible views, namely:

1. those requiring an open mind—scepticism, an acceptance only of rationally well-supported beliefs, the rejection of any true 'way'; and

2. those requiring a commitment to more speculative beliefs and values.

As for me, I find myself in the former position, but would like to move to the latter, carefully; and to find a world-view to which I can commit myself.

REFERENCES

ALEKSANDER, I., and BURNETT, P. (1984), *Reinventing Man* (Penguin, Harmondsworth).

—— —— (1987), *Thinking Machines: The Search for Artificial Intelligence* (Oxford University Press, Oxford).

ANDERSON, A. R. (ed.) (1964), *Minds and Machines* (Prentice-Hall, Englewood Cliffs, NJ).

ANSCOMBE, G. E. M. (1957), *Intention* (Blackwell, Oxford).

—— (1981), *Metaphysics and the Philosophy of Mind* (Blackwell, Oxford).

ARMSTRONG, D. M. (1968), *A Materialist Theory of Mind* (Routledge & Kegan Paul, London).

—— (1980), *The Nature of Mind and Other Essays* (University of Queensland Press, St Lucia).

—— and MALCOLM, N. (1984), *Consciousness and Causality* (Blackwell, Oxford).

BARLOW, H. B. (1985), 'Perception: What Quantitative Laws Govern the Acquisition of Knowledge from the Senses?', in Coen (1985).

BARRETT, W. (1987), *Death of the Soul* (Oxford University Press, Oxford).

BARROW, J. D., and SILK, J. (1984), *The Left Hand of Creation* (Heinemann, London).

—— and TIPLER, F. J. (1988), *The Anthropic Cosmological Principle* (Oxford University Press, Oxford).

BATESON, G. (1980), *Mind and Nature* (Fontana/Collins, Glasgow).

BELL, J. S. (1988a), 'On the EPR Paradox', in Bell (1988b).

—— (1988b), *Speakable and Unspeakable in Quantum Mechanics* (Cambridge University Press, Cambridge).

BERGLAND, R. (1985), *The Fabric of Mind* (Penguin, Ringwood, Victoria).

BLAKEMORE, C. (1977), *Mechanics of the Mind* (Cambridge University Press, Cambridge).

—— (1985), 'The Nature of Explanation in the Study of the Brain', in Coen (1985).

—— (1988), *The Mind Machine* (BBC, London).

—— and GREENFIELD, S. (eds.) (1987), *Mindwaves: Thoughts on Intelligence, Identity and Consciousness* (Blackwell, Oxford).

BODEN, M. A. (1972), *Purposive Explanation in Psychology* (Harvard University Press, Cambridge, Mass.).

—— (1977), *Artificial Intelligence and Natural Man* (Harvester Press, Hassocks, Sussex).

—— (1981), *Minds and Mechanisms* (Harvester Press, Hassocks, Sussex).

BOHM, D. (1951), *Quantum Theory* (Prentice-Hall, Englewood Cliffs, NJ).

—— (1980), *Wholeness and the Implicate Order* (Routledge & Kegan Paul, London).

—— (1984), *Causality and Chance in Modern Physics* (Routledge & Kegan Paul, London).

—— and PEAT, F. D. (1989), *Science, Order and Creativity* (Routledge, London).

BOHR, N. (1935), 'Quantum Mechanics and Physical Reality', *Nature*, 136: 65.

—— (1958), *Atomic Physics and Human Knowledge* (Wiley, New York).

BOHR, N. (1961), *Atomic Theory and the Description of Nature* (Cambridge University Press, Cambridge).

BOLTER, J. D. (1986), *Turing's Man* (Penguin, Harmondsworth).

BOND, E. J. (1983), *Reason and Value* (Cambridge University Press, Cambridge).

BORN, M. (1951), *The Restless Universe* (Dover, New York).

BOYLE, J. M., GRISEZ, G., and TOLLEFSEN, O. (1976), *Free Choice: A Self-Referential Argument* (University of Notre Dame Press, Notre Dame, Ind.).

BRONOWSKI, J. (1977), *A Sense of the Future* (MIT Press, Cambridge, Mass.).

BROWN, H. (1986), *The Wisdom of Science* (Cambridge University Press, Cambridge).

BROWN, H. I. (1977), *Perception, Theory and Commitment* (University of Chicago Press, Chicago, Ill.).

BRUNER, J. (1983), *In Search of Mind* (Harper & Row, New York).

BUSER, P. A., and ROUGEL-BUSER, A. (eds.) (1978), *Cerebral Correlates of Conscious Experience* (North-Holland, Amsterdam).

CAMPBELL, J. (1984), *Grammatical Man* (Penguin, Harmondsworth).

CAPRA, F. (1983), *The Turning Point* (Fontana, London).

CARTWRIGHT, N. (1983), *How the Laws of Physics Lie* (Oxford University Press, Oxford).

CHANGEUX, J. -P. (1986), *Neuronal Man* (Oxford University Press, Oxford).

CHOURAQUI, E. (1984), 'Computational Models of Reasoning', in Torrance (1984).

CHURCHLAND, P. M. (1984), *Matter and Consciousness* (MIT Press/Bradford, Cambridge, Mass.).

CHURCHLAND, P. S. (1986), *Neurophilosophy* (MIT Press, Cambridge, Mass.).

COEN, C. W. (ed.) (1985), *Functions of the Brain* (Oxford University Press, Oxford).

COTTERILL, R. (1989), *No Ghost in the Machine* (Heinemann, London).

COVENEY, P. V. (1988), 'The Second Law of Thermodynamics: Entropy, Irreversibility and Dynamics', *Nature*, 333: 409–15.

CRAIK, K. (1943), The Nature of Explanation (Cambridge University Press, Cambridge).

CROPPER, W. H. (1970), *The Quantum Physicists* (Oxford University Press, Oxford).

DANERI, A., LOINGER, A., and PROSPERI, G. M. (1983), 'Measurement and Ergodicity Conditions', in Wheeler and Zurek (1983).

DAVIDSON, D. (1976), 'Psychology as Philosophy', in Glover (1976).

—— (1979), 'Mental Events', in Honderich and Burnyeat (1979).

—— (1981), 'The Material Mind', in Haugeland (1981).

DAVIES, P. C. W. (1982*a*), *The Accidental Universe* (Cambridge University Press, Cambridge).

—— (1982*b*), *Other Worlds* (Sphere, London).

—— (1983), *God and the New Physics* (Dent, London).

—— (1984), *Quantum Mechanics* (Routledge & Kegan Paul, London).

—— (1985), *Superforce* (Unwin, London).

—— (1987), *The Cosmic Blueprint* (Heinemann, London).

—— (1989), Introduction to Heisenberg (1989).

—— and BROWN, J. R. (1986), *The Ghost in the Atom* (Cambridge University Press, Cambridge).

DAVIS, P. J., and HERSH, R. (1983), *The Mathematical Experience* (Penguin, Harmondsworth).

DAWKINS, M. S. (1987), 'Minding and Mattering', in Blakemore and Greenfield (1987).

DAWKINS, R. (1976), *The Selfish Gene* (Oxford University Press, Oxford).
—— (1988), *The Blind Watchmaker* (Penguin, Harmondsworth).
DELBRÜCK, M. (1978), 'Mind from Matter??', in Heidcamp (1978).
—— (1986), *Mind from Matter? An Essay on Evolutionary Epistemology* (Blackwell Scientific Publications, Palo Alto, Calif.).
DENNETT, D. (1978), *Brainstorms* (Harvester Press, Brighton).
—— (1984), *Elbow Room* (Oxford University Press, Oxford).
D'ESPAGNAT, B. (1976), *Conceptual Foundations of Quantum Mechanics*, 2nd edn. (Benjamin, Reading, Mass.).
—— (1983), *In Search of Reality* (Springer-Verlag, New York).
—— (1989), *Reality and the Physicist* (Cambridge University Press, Cambridge).
DEUTSCH, D. (1985), 'Quantum Theory, the Church–Turing Principle and the Universal Quantum Computer', *Proceedings of the Royal Society (London)*, A400: 97–117.
DEWITT, B., and GRAHAM, N. (eds.) (1973), *The Many-Worlds Interpretation of Quantum Mechanics* (Princeton University Press, Princeton, NJ).
DIRAC, P. A. M. (1958), *The Principles of Quantum Mechanics*, 4th edn. (Oxford University Press, Oxford).
DRETSKE, F. I. (1981), *Knowledge and the Flow of Information* (Blackwell, Oxford).
DREYFUS, H. (1979), *What Computers Can't Do*, rev. edn. (Harper & Row, New York).
DUBOS, R. (1978), 'Biological Memory, Creative Associations, and the Living Earth', in Heidcamp (1978).
ECCLES, J. C. (ed.) (1966), *Brain and Conscious Experience* (Springer-Verlag, New York).
—— (1984), *The Human Mystery* (Routledge & Kegan Paul, London).
—— (1990) 'A Unitary Hypothesis of Mind–Brain Interaction in the Cerebral Cortex', *Proceedings of the Royal Society (London)*, B240: 433–51.
EDDINGTON, A. (1929), *The Nature of the Physical World* (Dent, London).
EIGEN, M., and WINKLER, R. (1983), *Laws of the Game* (Penguin, Harmondsworth).
EINSTEIN, A., POLDOLSKY, B., and ROSEN, N. (1983), 'Can Quantum-Mechanical Description of Physical Reality Be Considered Complete?', in Wheeler and Zurek (1983).
EVANS, C. R. (1980), *The Mighty Micro* (Coronet, Sevenoaks, Kent).
FERRY, G. (ed.) (1984), *The Understanding of Animals* (Blackwell, Oxford).
FEYNMAN, R. P., LEIGHTON, R. B., SANDS, M. (1963), *The Feynman Lectures in Physics*, i and iii (Addison-Wesley, Reading, Mass.).
FINE, A. (1986), *The Shaky Game* (University of Chicago Press, Chicago, Ill.).
FINNIS, J. M. (1983), *The Fundamentals of Ethics* (Oxford University Press, Oxford).
FLEW, A., and VESEY, G. N. A. (1987), *Agency and Necessity* (Blackwell, Oxford).
FLOOD, R., and LOCKWOOD, M. (eds.) (1986), *The Nature of Time* (Blackwell, Oxford).
FODOR, J. (1975), *The Language of Thought* (MIT Press, Cambridge, Mass.).
FOLSE, H. J. (1985), *The Philosophy of Niels Bohr* (North-Holland, Amsterdam).
FRENCH, P. A. (1985), 'Fishing the Red Herrings out of the Sea of Moral Responsibility', in LePore and McLaughlin (1985).
FRISBY, J. P. (1979), *Seeing: Illusion, Brain and Mind* (Oxford University Press, Oxford).

GARDNER, H. (1987), *The Mind's New Science* (Basic Books, New York).

GARDNER, M. (1984), *Order and Surprise* (Oxford University Press, Oxford).

GHIRARDI, G. C., RIMINI, A., and WEBER, T. (1986), 'Unified Dynamics for Microscopic and Macroscopic Systems', *Physical Review*, D34: 470.

GIBBINS, P. (1987), *Particles and Paradoxes* (Cambridge University Press, Cambridge).

GILLESPIE, D. T. (1970), *A Quantum Mechanics Primer* (Intext Educational Publishers, New York).

GILLING, D., and BRIGHTWELL, R. (1982), *The Human Brain* (Orbis Publishing, London).

GLEICK, J. (1988), *Chaos* (Sphere, London).

GLOVER, J. (ed.) (1976), *The Philosophy of Mind* (Oxford University Press, Oxford).

—— (1984), *What Sort of People Should there Be?* (Penguin, Harmondsworth).

—— (1988), *I: The Philosophy and Psychology of Personal Identity* (Allen Lane, London).

GOMES, A. O. (1978), 'The Brain–Consciousness Problem in Contemporary Scientific Research', in Buser and Rougel-Buser (1978).

GOODMAN, N. (1965), *Fact, Fiction and Forecast* (Bobbs-Merrill, New York).

—— (1970), 'Seven Strictures on Similarity', in L. Foster and J. W. Swanson (eds.), *Experience and Theory* (University of Massachusetts Press, Amherst, Mass.).

—— (1978), *Ways of Worldmaking* (Bobbs-Merrill, New York).

GOULD, S. J. (1985), *The Flamingo's Smile* (Norton, New York).

GRAHAM, N. (1973), 'The Measurement of Relative Frequency', in DeWitt and Graham (1973).

GRAY, J. (1987), 'The Mind–Brain Identity as a Scientific Hypothesis: A Second Look', in Blakemore and Greenfield (1987).

GREGORY, R. L. (1984), *Mind in Science* (Penguin, Harmondsworth).

—— (ed.) (1987), *The Oxford Companion to the Mind* (Oxford University Press, Oxford).

GRIBBIN, J. (1985), *In Search of Schrödinger's Cat* (Corgi, London).

HACKING, I. (ed.) (1981), *Scientific Revolutions* (Oxford University Press, Oxford).

HARTH, E. (1985), *Windows on the Mind* (Penguin, Harmondsworth).

HAUGELAND, J. (ed.) (1981), *Mind Design: Philosophy, Psychology, and Artificial Intelligence* (MIT Press, Cambridge, Mass.).

—— (1985), *Artificial Intelligence: The Very Idea* (MIT Press, Cambridge, Mass.).

HAWKING, S. (1988), *A Brief History of Time* (Bantam, London).

HEARNE, V. (1987), 'The Cognitive Dog', *New Scientist*, 12 Mar., pp. 38–40.

HEIDCAMP, W. H. (ed.) (1978), *The Nature of Life* (University Park Press, Baltimore, Md.).

HEISENBERG, W. (1930), *The Physical Principles of the Quantum Theory* (University of Chicago Press, Chicago, Ill.).

—— (1989), *Physics and Philosophy* (Penguin, Harmondsworth).

HEMPEL, C. G. (1965), *Aspects of Scientific Investigation* (Macmillan, New York).

HERBERT, N. (1985), *Quantum Reality* (Rider, London).

—— (1986), 'How to Be in Two Places at the One Time', *New Scientist*, 21 Aug., pp. 41–4.

HEY, A. J. G., and WALTERS, P. (1987), *The Quantum Universe* (Cambridge University Press, Cambridge).

HILEY, B. (1983), 'Quantum Mechanics Passes the Test', *New Scientist*, 6 Jan., pp. 17–19.

HODGSON, D. H. (1967), *Consequences of Utilitarianism* (Oxford University Press, Oxford).

HOFFMAN, B. (1963), *The Strange Story of the Quantum* (Penguin, Harmondsworth).

HOFSTADTER, D. R. (1980), *Gödel, Escher, Bach: An Eternal Golden Braid* (Penguin, Harmondsworth).

—— (1986), *Metamagical Themas* (Penguin, Harmondsworth).

—— and DENNETT, D. C. (1981), *The Mind's I: Fantasies and Reflections on Self and Soul* (Harvester Press, Brighton).

HOLLAND, J., HOLYOAK, K. J., NISBETT, R. E., and THAGARD, P. (1986), *Induction: Processes of Inference, Learning, and Discovery* (MIT Press, Cambridge, Mass.).

HONDERICH, T. (1987), 'Mind, Brain and Self-Conscious Mind', in Blakemore and Greenfield (1987).

—— (1988), *A Theory of Determinism* (Oxford University Press, Oxford).

—— and BURNYEAT, M. (eds.) (1979), *Philosophy as it Is* (Penguin, Harmondsworth).

HOOK, S. (ed.) (1961), *Dimensions of Mind* (Collier, New York).

HOPCROFT, J. E. (1984), 'Turing Machines', *Scientific American*, May, pp. 70–80.

HOSPERS, J. (1967), *An Introduction to Philosophical Analysis*, 2nd edn. (Routledge & Kegan Paul, London).

HUGHES, R. I. G. (1981), 'Quantum Logic', *Scientific American*, Oct., pp. 146–57.

HUME, D. (1962), *On Human Nature and Understanding* (Collier, New York).

—— (1965), *A Treatise of Human Nature* (Oxford University Press, Oxford).

HUMPHREY, N. (1983), *Consciousness Regained* (Oxford University Press, Oxford).

—— (1986), *The Inner Eye* (Faber and Faber, London).

HUNT, M. (1984), *The Universe Within* (Corgi, London).

JACKENDOFF, R. (1987), *Consciousness and the Computational Mind* (MIT Press, Cambridge, Mass.).

JACKSON, F. (1982), 'Epiphenomenal Qualia', *Philosophical Quarterly*, 32: 127–36.

JAMMER, M. (1974), *The Philosophy of Quantum Mechanics* (Wiley, New York).

JOHNSON-LAIRD, P. N. (1987), 'How could Consciousness Arise from the Computations of the Brain?', in Blakemore and Greenfield (1987).

—— (1988), *The Computer and the Mind* (Fontana, London).

JONES, R. S. (1983), *Physics as Metaphor* (Sphere, London).

JUNG, C. G. (1983), 'Conscious, Unconscious and Individuation', in Storr (1983).

KAHNEMAN, D., SLOVIC, P., and TVERSKY, A. (eds.) (1982), *Judgement under Uncertainty: Heuristics and Biases* (Cambridge University Press, Cambridge).

KANE, R. (1985), *Free Will and Values* (State University of New York Press, Albany, NY).

KEANE, I. (1988), *Analogical Problem Solving* (Ellis Horwood, Chichester).

KIM, J. (1985), 'Psychophysical Laws', in LePore and McLaughlin (1985).

KOESTLER, A. (1975), *The Ghost in the Machine* (Picador, London).

KÖHLER, W. (1961), 'The Mind–Body Problem', in Hook (1961).

KRIPS, H. (1987), *The Metaphysics of Quantum Theory* (Oxford University Press, Oxford).

KUHN, T. S. (1970), *The Structure of Scientific Revolutions* (University of Chicago Press, Chicago, Ill.).

LANDSHOFF, P., and METHERELL, A. (1979), *Simple Quantum Physics* (Cambridge University Press, Cambridge).

LAYZER, D. (1990), *Cosmogenesis* (Oxford University Press, New York).

LEGGETT, A. J. (1987), *The Problems of Physics* (Oxford University Press, Oxford).

LEPORE, E., and MCLAUGHLIN, B. P. (eds.) (1985), *Actions and Events: Perspectives on the Philosophy of Donald Davidson* (Blackwell, Oxford).

LESHAN, L., and MARGENAU, H. (1982), *Einstein's Space and Van Gogh's Sky* (Macmillan, New York).

LEVIN, M. E. (1979), *Metaphysics and the Mind–Body Problem* (Oxford University Press, Oxford).

LIBET, B. (1966), 'Brain Stimulation and Conscious Experience', in Eccles (1966).

—— (1978), 'Neuronal vs. Subjective Timing for a Conscious Sensory Experience', in Buser and Rougel-Buser (1978).

—— WRIGHT, E. W., and FEINSTEIN, B. (1979), 'Subjective Referral of the Timing for a Conscious Sensory Experience', *Brain*, 102: 193–224.

LOCKWOOD, M. (1989), *Mind, Brain and the Quantum* (Blackwell, Oxford).

LONDON, F., and BAUER, E. (1983), 'The Theory of Observation in Quantum Mechanics', trans., in Wheeler and Zurek (1983).

LUCAS, J. R. (1964), 'Minds, Machines and Gödel', in Anderson (1964).

—— (1970), *The Freedom of the Will* (Oxford University Press, Oxford).

LURIA, A. R. (1973), *The Working Brain*, trans. B. Haigh (Penguin, Harmondsworth).

LYCAN, W. G. (1987), *Consciousness* (MIT Press, Cambridge, Mass.).

MCCUSKER, B. (1983), *The Quest for Quarks* (Cambridge University Press, Cambridge).

MCGINN, C. (1982), *The Character of Mind* (Oxford University Press, Oxford).

—— (1987), 'Could a Machine Be Conscious?', in Blakemore and Greenfield (1987).

MACKIE, J. L. (1968), 'The Paradox of Confirmation', in Nidditch (1968).

MCTAGGART, J. M. E. (1908), 'The Unreality of Time', *Mind*, 42: 457–74.

MALCOLM, N. (1982), 'The Conceivability of Mechanism', in Watson (1982).

MARR, D. (1982), *Vision* (Freeman, San Francisco, Calif.).

MARTIN, J. L. (1981), *Basic Quantum Mechanics* (Oxford University Press, Oxford).

MAULDIN, J. H. (1986), *Particles in Nature* (Tab Books, Blue Ridge Summit, Pa.).

MEDAWAR, P. (1986), *The Limits of Science* (Oxford University Press, Oxford).

MERMIN, N. D. (1985), 'Is the Moon there when Nobody Looks?' *Physics Today*, Apr., pp. 38–47.

MERZBACHER, E. (1970), *Quantum Mechanics*, 2nd edn. (Wiley, New York).

MICHIE, D., and JOHNSTON, R. (1985), *The Creative Computer* (Penguin, Harmondsworth).

MINSKY, M. (1987), *The Society of Mind* (Heinemann, London).

MISRA, B., PRIGOGINE, I., and COURBAGE, M. (1979), 'Lyapounov Variable: Entropy and Measurement in Quantum Mechanics', *Proceedings of the National Academy of Science, USA* 76: 4768–72.

MONOD, J. (1977), *Chance and Necessity* (Collins/Fount, Glasgow).

MORAVEC, H. (1988), *Mind Children* (Harvard University Press, Cambridge, Mass.).

NAGEL, T. (1974), 'What Is it Like to Be a Bat?', *Philosophical Review*, 83: 435–50.

—— (1976), 'Brain Bisection and the Unity of Consciousness', in Glover (1976).

—— (1986), *The View from Nowhere* (Oxford University Press, New York).

NEGOITA, C. V. (1985), *Expert Systems and Fuzzy Systems* (Benjamin/Cummings, Menlo Park, Calif.).

NEWTON-SMITH, W. H. (1981), *The Rationality of Science* (Routledge & Kegan Paul, Boston, Mass.).

NIDDITCH, E. H. (ed.) (1968), *The Philosophy of Science* (Oxford University Press, Oxford).

NOZICK, R. (1981), *Philosophical Explanations* (Oxford University Press, Oxford).

OATLEY, K. (1989), 'The Importance of Being Emotional', *New Scientist*, 19 Aug., pp. 19–22.

O'HEAR, A. (1985), *What Philosophy Is* (Penguin, Harmondsworth).

ORNSTEIN, R. (1986*a*), *Multimind* (Macmillan, London).

—— (1986*b*), *The Psychology of Consciousness*, 2nd rev. edn. (Penguin, New York).

PAGELS, H. R. (1983), *The Cosmic Code* (Michael Joseph, London).

PAIS, A. (1986), *Inward Bound* (Oxford University Press, Oxford).

PARFIT, D. (1976), 'Personal Identity', in Glover (1976).

—— (1984), *Reasons and Persons* (Oxford University Press, Oxford).

PEAT, F. D. (1987), *Synchronicity* (Bantam, New York).

PENROSE, R. (1986), 'Gravity and State Vector Reduction', in Penrose and Isham (1986).

—— (1987), 'Minds, Machines, and Mathematics', in Blakemore and Greenfield (1987).

—— (1989), *The Emperor's New Mind* (Oxford University Press, Oxford).

—— and ISHAM, C. J. (eds.) (1986), *Quantum Concepts in Space and Time* (Oxford University Press, Oxford).

PIRSIG, R. M. (1974), *Zen and the Art of Motorcycle Maintenance* (Corgi, London).

POLANYI, M. (1973), *Personal Knowledge* (Routledge & Kegan Paul, London).

POLKINGHORNE, J. C. (1984), *The Quantum World* (Longman, Harlow, Essex).

POLYA, G. (1954), *Mathematics and Plausible Reasoning*, i and ii (Princeton University Press, Princeton, NJ).

POPPER, K. R. (1959), *The Logic of Scientific Discovery* (Hutchinson, London).

—— (1982), *Quantum Theory and the Schism in Physics* (Hutchinson, London).

—— and ECCLES, J. C. (1977), *The Self and its Brain* (Springer-Verlag, Berlin).

POUNDSTONE, W. (1987), *The Recursive Universe* (Oxford University Press, Oxford).

PRIGOGINE, I., and STENGERS, I. (1984), *Order out of Chaos* (Bantam, New York).

PUTNAM, H. (1975*a*), *Mind, Language and Reality: Philosophical Papers*, ii (Cambridge University Press, Cambridge).

—— (1975*b*), 'Minds and Machines', in Putnam (1975*a*).

—— (1979*a*), 'Discussion: Comments on Comments on Comments: A Reply to Margenau and Wigner', in Putnam (1979*c*).

—— (1979*b*), 'The Logic of Quantum Mechanics', in Putnam (1979*c*).

—— (1979*c*), *Mathematics, Matter and Method: Philosophical Papers*, i, 2nd edn. (Cambridge University Press, Cambridge).

—— (1979*d*), 'A Philosopher Looks at Quantum Mechanics', in Putnam (1979*c*).

—— (1979*e*), 'Time and Physical Geometry', in Putnam (1979*c*).

—— (1981), *Reason, Truth and History* (Cambridge University Press, Cambridge).

PUTNAM, H. (1983*a*), 'Quantum Mechanics and the Observer', in Putnam (1983*b*).
—— (1983*b*), *Realism and Reason: Philosophical Papers*, iii (Cambridge University Press, Cambridge).
QUINE, W. V. O. (1960), *Word and Object* (MIT Press, Cambridge, Mass.).
RAE, A. I. M. (1986), *Quantum Physics: Illusion or Reality?* (Cambridge University Press, Cambridge).
RAWLS, J. (1971), *A Theory of Justice* (Harvard University Press, Cambridge, Mass.).
REDHEAD, M. (1987), *Incompleteness, Nonlocality and Realism* (Oxford University Press, Oxford).
RESTAK, R. M. (1983), 'Is Free Will a Fraud?', *Science Digest*, 91 (Oct.): 52–5.
RIDLEY, B. K. (1976), *Time, Space and Things* (Penguin, Harmondsworth).
ROLLIN, B. E. (1989), *The Unheeded Cry* (Oxford University Press, Oxford).
ROSE, S. (1976), *The Conscious Brain*, rev. edn. (Penguin, Harmondsworth).
—— and APPIGNANESI, L. (eds.) (1986), *Science and Beyond* (Blackwell, Oxford).
ROTH, L. M., and INOMATA, A. (eds.) (1986), *Fundamental Questions in Quantum Mechanics* (Gordon and Breach, New York).
RUCKER, R. (1984), *Infinity and the Mind* (Paladin, London).
RUTHERFORD, E. (1938), 'The Development of the Atomic Structure', in J. Needham, and W. Pagels (eds.), *Background of Modern Science* (Cambridge University Press, Cambridge).
RYLE, G. (1949), *The Concept of Mind* (Hutchinson, London).
SACKS, O. (1986), *The Man who Mistook his Wife for a Hat* (Picador, London).
SCHIFF, L. I. (1968), *Quantum Mechanics*, 3rd edn. (McGraw-Hill, Auckland).
SCHLEGEL, R. (1980), *Superposition and Interaction* (University of Chicago Press, Chicago, Ill.).
SCHNAPF, J. L., and BAYLOR, D. A. (1987), 'How Photoreceptor Cells Respond to Light', *Scientific American*, Apr., pp. 32–9.
SCHRÖDINGER, E. (1967), *What is Life? and Mind and Matter* (Cambridge University Press, Cambridge).
—— (1983), 'The Present Situation in Quantum Mechanics', trans. J. D. Trimmer, in Wheeler and Zurek (1983).
SCHUMACHER, J. A. (1986), 'The Quantum Mechanics of Vision', in Penrose and Isham (1986).
SEARLE, J. R. (1980), 'Minds, Brains and Programs', in *The Behavioural and Brain Sciences*, iii (Cambridge University Press, Cambridge).
—— (1984), *Minds, Brains and Science* (BBC, London).
SEARS, F. W., ZEMANSKY, M. W., and YOUNG, H. D. (1982), *University Physics*, 6th edn. (Addison-Wesley, Reading, Mass.).
SHALLIS, M. (1983), *On Time* (Penguin, Harmondsworth).
SHELDRAKE, R. (1983), *A New Science of Life* (Paladin, London).
SHERRINGTON, C. S. (1951), *Man on his Nature*, 2nd edn. (Cambridge University Press, Cambridge).
SHIMONY, A. (1988), 'The Reality of the Quantum World', *Scientific American*, Jan., pp. 36–43.
SHOEMAKER, S. (1984), *Identity, Cause and Mind* (Cambridge University Press, Cambridge).
—— and SWINBURNE, R. (1984), *Personal Identity* (Blackwell, Oxford).

SKYRMS, B. (1982), 'Counterfactual Definiteness and Local Causation', *Philosophy of Science*, 49: 43–50.

SLOMAN, A. (1978), *The Computer Revolution in Philosophy* (Harvester Press, Hassocks, Sussex).

—— (1984), 'The Structure of the Space of Possible Minds', in Torrance (1984).

SMOLIN, L. (1985), 'What is Quantum Mechanics Really About?', *New Scientist*, 24 Oct., pp. 40–3.

SNAPE, D. (1989), *Meet the First 30 Elements* (Science Teachers' Association of Victoria, Parkville, Victoria).

SPERRY, R. W. (1966), 'Mind, Brain and Humanist Values', *Bulletin of Atomic Science*, 22: 2–6.

—— (1983), *Science and Moral Priority* (Blackwell, Oxford).

SPILLER, T., and CLARK, T. (1986), 'SQUIDS: Macroscopic Quantum Objects', *New Scientist*, 4 Dec., pp. 36–40.

SPRIGGE, T. L. S. (1984), *Theories of Existence* (Penguin, Harmondsworth).

SPRINGER, S. P., and DEUTSCH, G. (1989), *Left Brain, Right Brain*, 3rd edn. (Freeman, New York).

SQUIRES, E. (1986), *The Mystery of the Quantum World* (Adam Hilger, Bristol).

STABLEFORD, B. M. (1984), *Future Man* (Crown Publishers, New York).

STAPP, H. P. (1985), 'Consciousness and Values in the Quantum Universe', *Foundations of Physics*, 15: 35–47.

STORR, A. (ed.) (1983), *Jung: Selected Writings* (Fontana, London).

STRAWSON, P. (1982), 'Freedom and Resentment', in Watson (1982).

SUDBERY, A. (1985), 'Popper's Variant of the EPR Experiment does not Test the Copenhagen Interpretation', *Philosophy of Science*, 52: 470–6.

—— (1986), *Quantum Mechanics and the Particles of Nature* (Cambridge University Press, Cambridge).

SUZUKI, D. T., and KNUDTSON, P. (1989), *Genethics* (Allen and Unwin, North Sydney).

SWINBURNE, R. (1986), *The Evolution of the Soul* (Oxford University Press, Oxford).

TAYLOR, C. (1982), 'Responsibility for Self', in Watson (1982).

—— (1985), *Human Agency and Language* (Cambridge University Press, Cambridge).

TERRACE, H. (1984), 'And Now—the Thinking Pigeon', in Ferry (1984).

TORRANCE, S. (ed.) (1984), *The Mind and the Machine* (Ellis Horwood, Chichester).

TOULMIN, S. (1972), *Human Understanding* (Princeton University Press, Princeton, NJ).

TRUSTED, J. (1984), *Free Will and Responsibility* (Oxford University Press, Oxford).

TURING, A. M. (1937), 'On Computable Numbers, with an Application to the *Entscheidungsproblem*', *Proceedings of the London Mathematical Society*, 42: 230–65; 43: 544–6.

—— (1950), 'Computing Machinery and Intelligence', *Mind*, 59: 433–60.

VON NEUMANN, J. (1955), *Mathematical Foundations of Quantum Mechanics* (Princeton University Press, Princeton, NJ).

—— (1958), *The Computer and the Brain* (Yale University Press, New Haven, Conn.).

WALL, P. D. (1985), 'Pain and No Pain', in Coen (1985).

WATSON, G. (ed.) (1982), *Free Will* (Oxford University Press, Oxford).

WATSON, W. H. (1967), *Understanding Physics Today* (Cambridge University Press, Cambridge).

WEBER, R. (1986), *Dialogues with Scientists and Sages* (Routledge & Kegan Paul, London).

WEINBERG, S. (1978), *The First Three Minutes* (Fontana, London).

WEIZENBAUM, J. (1984), *Computer Power and Human Reason* (Penguin, Harmondsworth).

WEYL, H. (1949), *Philosophy of Mathematics and Natural Science* (Princeton University Press, Princeton, NJ).

WHEELER, J. A., and ZUREK, W. H. (eds.) (1983), *Quantum Theory and Measurement* (Princeton University Press, Princeton, NJ).

WHITROW, G. J. (1980), *The Natural Philosophy of Time*, 2nd edn. (Oxford University Press, Oxford).

WIGNER, E. P. (1961), 'Remarks on the Mind–Body Question', in Wheeler and Zurek (1983).

WILBER, K. (1983), *Eye to Eye* (Anchor Books, Doubleday, New York).

WILLIAMS, B. (1976), 'The Self and the Future', in Glover (1976).

WINOGRAD, T., and FLORES, F. (1986), *Understanding Computers and Cognition: A New Foundation for Design* (Ablex, Norwood, NJ).

WITTGENSTEIN, L. (1974), *Philosophical Investigations*, 3rd edn. (Blackwell, Oxford).

WOLF, F. A. (1981), *Taking the Quantum Leap* (Harper & Row, San Francisco, Calif.).

—— (1984), *Mind and the New Physics* (Heinemann, London).

WOOLLEY, G. (1988), 'Must a Molecule Have Shape?', *New Scientist*, 22 Oct., pp. 53–7.

YOUNG, J. Z. (1985), 'What's in a Brain?', in Coen (1985).

—— (1988), *Philosophy and the Brain* (Oxford University Press, Oxford).

ZADEH, L. A. (1977), 'Theory of Fuzzy Sets', in J. Belzer, A. G. Holzmann, and A. Kent (eds.), *Encyclopedia of Computer Science and Technology*, viii (Dekker, New York).

ZOHAR, D. (1990), *The Quantum Self* (Bloomsbury, London).

ZUKAV, W. H. (1979), *The Dancing Wu Li Masters* (Fontana, London).

NAME INDEX

SUBJECT INDEX